WILLIA

D1160878

John Carey is Emeritus Merton Professor of English Literature at Oxford University, a Fellow of the British Academy and Chief Book Reviewer for *The Sunday Times*. His books include studies of Donne, Milton, Thackeray and Dickens, *The Intellectuals and the Masses* and *What Good Are the Arts?*

Praise for *William Golding*:

'Golding deserves rediscovery, and if he gets it, then this biography – sympathetic without being idolatrous, detailed without becoming boring, learned, witty, insightful and humane, a model of its kind – will be in large measure responsible.' Robert Harris, *Sunday Times*

'Excellent ... Golding has been fortunate in his biographer.' Frank Kermode, *London Review of Books*

'Funny, generous, humane and unsparing, Carey has a sharpness of eye and shapeliness of phrase that perfectly match his subject ... As a result we can now do to Golding what his writing habitually did to the world. We can look at him with fresh eyes.' Robert Douglas-Fairhurst, *Daily Telegraph*

'Ground-breaking ... a model of tact, delicacy, sensitivity, light humour and diligence.' Jerome Boyd Maunsell, *Evening Standard*

'Masterly.' Matthew D'Ancona

'The unobtrusive elegance of Carey's prose is a continual source of pleasure ... This book is rare among biographies of twentieth-century novelists in doing an effective job of joining the life dots to the art dots.' Leo Robson, *New Statesman*

'Admirable and continuously interesting.' Allan Massie, *Times Literary Supplement*

'Partisan, tough-minded, and taking the usual unsparing Carey line against anyone unwise enough to get in his way ... Carey is excellent on what gives the novels their distinctive patina, that odd mix of symbolism, derring-do, and elemental human hurt.' D. J. Taylor, *Independent*

'Carey's achievement in this exemplary study is to reveal the complexity of Golding's life and work.' Michael Arditti, *Daily Mail*

'Fascinating . . . Carey uses the access he has to Golding's personal letters, book drafts and journals to illuminate the author's writing process and untangle his thoughts.' Harry McGrath, *Sunday Herald*

'Does exactly what a literary biography should do and sends you back to the novels. They turn out to be just as good as we always thought.' Philip Hensher, *Spectator*

'Carey is a superb explanatory critic. He devotes a good half of his many pages to literary exegesis . . . They throw open a door on some of the most challenging, yet rewarding, fictions we have.' John Sutherland, *The Times*

'Fascinating . . . brilliant.' Raleigh Trevelyan, *Literary Review*

'Superlatively readable . . . sympathetic and beautifully written . . . a wonderful piece of work.' Kevin Power, *Sunday Business Post*

'Full of startling revelations.' *Tatler*

'Masterly . . . fascinating. Carey writes with refreshing clarity and Golding's peculiar life story is told with an attractive energy and relish.' Alexander Waugh, *Standpoint*

'Carey's is the first biography of this key author of the twentieth century and it is hard to see it being bettered.' Harry Mead, *Northern Echo*

'Superb . . . absorbing.' Richard Harries, *Church Times*

by the same author

THE VIOLENT EFFIGY: A STUDY OF DICKENS' IMAGINATION
THACKERAY: PRODIGAL GENIUS
JOHN DONNE: LIFE, MIND AND ART
ORIGINAL COPY: SELECTED REVIEWS AND JOURNALISM, 1969–1986
THE INTELLECTUALS AND THE MASSES: PRIDE AND PREJUDICE AMONG
THE LITERARY INTELLIGENTSIA, 1890–1939
PURE PLEASURE: A GUIDE TO THE TWENTIETH CENTURY'S MOST ENJOYABLE BOOKS
WHAT GOOD ARE THE ARTS?

as editor

WILLIAM GOLDING: THE MAN AND HIS BOOKS
THE FABER BOOK OF REPORTAGE
THE FABER BOOK OF SCIENCE
THE FABER BOOK OF UTOPIAS

WILLIAM GOLDING

The Man Who Wrote
Lord of the Flies

A LIFE

JOHN CAREY

faber and faber

First published in 2009
by Faber and Faber Limited
Bloomsbury House
74–77 Great Russell Street
London WC1B 3DA
Book design by Ron Costley
This paperback edition first published in 2010

Typeset in Janson MT by RefineCatch Limited, Bungay, Suffolk
Printed in England by CPI Bookmarque, Croydon

A CIP record for this book
is available from the British Library

ISBN 978-0-571-23164-5

2 4 6 8 10 9 7 5 3 1

Contents

Illustrations

Paul Joyce's portrait study of WG in 1977: 'a cross between Captain Hornblower and Saint Augustine' (Michael Ayrton).

Thomas Curnoe, WG's maternal grandfather.

Mary Elizabeth Curnoe, WG's maternal grandmother.

WG's mother Mildred with WG aged 2, Polly and Jo Golding, his paternal grandparents, and brother Jose in Savernake Forest.

WG's father Alec at 22, 'a lonely, embittered, alienated young intellectual'.

WG's mother Mildred on her wedding day in 1906; a 'leggy, gaunt, intelligent girl, high-spirited and witty'.

29 The Green, Marlborough: a 'map', WG said, of his 'personal mythology', which came back to him in dreams and nightmares.

Alec Golding reading to his sons Jose and 'a fair-haired, blue-eyed, sturdy little rascal called Billy' (WG), c.1914–15.

Jose and WG in Marlborough Grammar School blazer, c.1923.

WG playing the piano at 29 The Green; 'its yellow ivory keys were for ever embedded in his memory'.

Ordinary Seaman Golding with Ann and their first child David, January 1941.

WG deep in thought at the weapons research establishment MD1, 'Mr Churchill's toyshop', 1942.

An LCT(R) in action. WG captained one on D-Day and at Walcheren.

WG in uniform as a Lieutenant RNVR, with Ann, October 1944, just before the Battle of Walcheren.

Lieutenant Golding RNVR, senior officer of the Bishop Wordsworth's School Sea Cadets, with an unidentified Royal Navy Captain and the headmaster, Dr Frederick Happold.

WG in an amateur production of *A Winter's Tale*; 'simply explosive. Though in a minor part he dominated the whole show'.

WG and Ann on holiday in the early 1950s.

WG, nicknamed 'Scruff', at the teacher's desk in a classroom in Bishop Wordsworth's School, c.1960.

WG with son David in the garden of 29 The Green, 1945.

WG with daughter Judy near Lamorna Cove, Cornwall, summer 1953.

Charles Monteith at All Souls, early 1950s.

WG's submission letter for *Lord of the Flies*, annotated with Fabers' reader's comments.

Front cover of the original edition of *Lord of the Flies*.

Photo for *Vogue*, 1954.

Seahorse, with WG aboard, being hoisted onto a lorry for repairs, 1947/8.

Ann and Judy trimming WG's hair beard and hair, aboard *Wild Rose*, c.1959.

WG at the helm of *Wild Rose* with Pauline Lewis, David and Ann.

WG on the foredeck of *Wild Rose*, c.1957.

Tenace, a Dutch racing hoogaart. For WG she had 'the clumsy beauty of a double bass'.

WG at Hollins College, Virginia, 1961–2. America brought him 'fame, wealth and the adulation of the young'.

Aboard the river steamer *Maxim Gorky* on the Goldings' 1963 Russian trip.

The Cannes Film Festival 1963: James Aubrey (Ralph) and Hugh Edwards (Piggy) with WG.

At the Booker dinner 1980 when *Rites of Passage* won.

Front covers of the original editions of *Pincher Martin* and *Free Fall*.

WG with Melvyn Bragg on the Dorset coast during filming of the South Bank Show, 1980.

With Charles Monteith at the Royal Society of Literature, celebrating WG's installation as a Companion of Literature, 1983.

In Stockholm for the Nobel Prize, 1983: WG with Charles Monteith, Ann, HM Queen Silvia, HM King Carl XVI Gustav of Sweden.

WG and Ann with crew members aboard the *Hani*, Egypt 1984.

WG in his water garden at Ebble Thatch.

Cobber, with WG up.

WG (on right) with his friend Heinrich Straumann walking in the garden at Tullimaar, the Goldings' Cornish house, c.1988.

A Note on Sources

The story this book tells has not been told before. William Golding was a shy, private man, scornful of publicity, and of those who sought it, and strongly averse to the idea of a biography being written in his lifetime. None was, and the sources on which this first biography draws have remained largely unread and untouched since his death.

The Golding archive, which is still in the keeping of his family, and has not previously been made accessible to anyone outside it, is remarkably – and sometimes bewilderingly – rich. It far exceeds in bulk all his published works, and it comprises unpublished novels, both complete and fragmentary, early drafts of published novels, numerous projects and plans, two autobiographical works, one of them concentrating on his relationships with women, and a 5,000-page journal which he kept every day for twenty-two years.

Besides being an intimate account of his private life, and a treasure-house of memories of his childhood and youth, the journal is a behind-the-scenes revelation of the writer's craft, reporting each day on the progress of whatever novel he is at work on, tracing its origins, trying out alternative plot-lines, and criticizing, often violently, what he has written so far. Further, he began the journal as a dream diary, and though his waking life gradually came to dominate, he continued to record dreams almost to the end, together with his interpretations and identification of the incidents they recalled. As an author's systematic exploration of his unconscious and examination of his conscious life, Golding's journal is, I think, unique.

My other main source is the correspondence between Golding and his editor at Faber and Faber, Charles Monteith. It was Monteith who rescued Golding from obscurity. When they first met, Golding was a provincial schoolmaster, forty-two years old, who had written several novels, and sent them to every publisher he could think of, without success. The most recent of the rejects had come into Monteith's hands, and he worked with Golding to make it publishable, though no one else, either at Faber and Faber or elsewhere, thought that it was. It became a modern classic, *Lord of the Flies*, which has sold, to date, twenty million copies in the UK alone, and has been translated into over thirty languages.

Monteith remained Golding's editor, friend, consultant and champion for forty years. Together they developed a spectacularly successful working relationship, the record of which is preserved in hundreds of letters in the Faber and Faber archive. These have remained uninspected until now, and they provide an account of Golding's development as a writer, his plans, ambitions and fears, his thoughts about his written and unwritten books, his struggles with indecision and despair, and his anxieties as a husband and father and how they affected his work.

A minor problem in quoting from Golding's manuscripts is his spelling, which was sometimes erratic. It might seem better to correct it, or to draw attention to misspellings so that they are not taken for misprints. However, he anticipated both these alternatives with disfavour. 'It's a moody-making thought', he remarked in his journal on 1 March 1982, 'that some bugger will either silently (unobtrusively) correct my spelling, or even worse, interrupt the text with brackets and sic in italics. But my bad grammar and bad spelling was me.' Out of respect for his disquiet I have left any misspellings uncorrected and unsignalled.

I

Beginning

His earliest memory was of a colour, 'red mostly, but everywhere, and a sense of wind blowing, buffeting, and there was much light'. Together with this was an awareness, an 'unadulterated sense of self', which 'saw as you might with the lens of your eyes removed'. Whether this was actually a memory of his own birth, he is not sure. If so, it was remarkably trouble-free compared to his mother's experience of the same event. As soon as she had given birth to William Gerald Golding on 19 September 1911 she said to his father, 'That'll be all.'

In his next memory he is eighteen months old, maybe less. He is in a cot with a railing round. It has been pulled next to his parents' brass-framed double bed because he is sick with some childish ailment, and feels a little feverish. It is evening. Thick curtains hang over the window, attached by large rings to a bamboo pole. A gas jet on the wall gives a dim light. He is alone in the room. Suddenly something appears above the right-hand end of the curtain pole. It is like a small cockerel, and its colour is an indistinct and indescribable white. It struts along the pole, its head moving backwards and forwards. It knows he is in the cot, and it radiates 'utter friendliness' towards him. He feels happy and unafraid. Just near the mid-point of the pole it vanishes and the friendliness goes with it.

He hopes for it to return, but it does not. When his parents come to bed he tries to tell them about it, using the few words he knows. 'Thing', he says, or rather 'Fing', and 'Come back?' His father laughs, and assures him kindly that the thing won't come back, he's been dreaming. But he knows it was not a dream. Seeing it was not like dreaming, nor like waking. Its friendliness was 'like a whole atmosphere of natural love'. It seemed to come from 'the centre of all rightness'.

Struggling to tell his parents about it brings him for the first time up against 'the brute impossibility of communicating'. When he grew up he came to wonder quite what he had seen: 'Was it an exercise of clairvoyance before growing up into a rationalist world stifled it?' But he remembered it as one of the most powerful experiences of his life, a glimpse of 'the spiritual, the miraculous' that he hoarded in his memory as a refuge from 'the bloody cold daylight I've spent my life in, except when drunk'.

His first certainly dateable memory was his second birthday. He had been given a pair of white kid boots, and felt proud as he looked down and saw them projecting beyond the lace of his pinafore. The pride seems odd to him in retrospect, because it sorts ill with his lifelong antipathy to being tidy or smart or even clean. As an adult, he reflects, he washes or bathes only when the dirt starts to make him feel uncomfortable. But at two he was still, he thinks, 'half male and half female', so he took pride in adornment. He remembers, at about the same time, being pushed down the pavement at Marlborough, where they lived, by his nursemaid Lily. He is in a pushchair, not a pram, and dressed in a white silk frock. He is happy and excited because Lily has given him one of her hair-grips, a ring of tortoiseshell with a simple brass-wire clip across it, to pin back his shoulder-length blond curls. It makes him feel 'one of the right sort of people', that is, females. He thinks of girls as superior, beautiful beings, and understands their delight in being smooth, round, decorative and pretty. The hair-grip goes some way towards satisfying his deep desire to be one of them.

The little boy who saw the white cockerel, and the little boy wearing Lily's hair-grip, both remained part of William Golding. The spiritual and the miraculous, and their collision with science and rationality, were at the centre of his creative life. That was the white cockerel's legacy. The hair-grip boy came to see that what is admired as manliness is often synonymous with destruction and stupidity, and he developed a sympathy with men whose sexual natures took them across conventional gender boundaries.

2

Grandparents

His mother's family, the Curnoes, were Cornish, and lived in Newquay. His mother Mildred claimed that her aquiline nose derived from Phoenician voyagers, who, centuries before, had made the hazardous journey to Cornwall in search of tin. Perhaps the Curnoe menfolk got their taste for travel from the Phoenicians too. Golding's grandfather Thomas Curnoe and his two sons Tom and William, his mother's brothers, spent much of their lives abroad. Grandfather Curnoe went off to seek his fortune in the Californian gold rush and later took his skills as a mining engineer to Australia and South Africa. His copy of Mark Twain's *Roughing It* was passed down in the family, with his American address on the title page, 'Bodie, Mono County, Cal.'. Today Bodie is a tourist attraction, one of the best-preserved ghost-towns in the Wild West. But back in the 1880s it was booming. One outraged preacher described it as 'a sea of sin, lashed by the tempest of lust and passion'. In Golding's imagination, some of its wildness seems to have rubbed off onto his grandfather. On his Australian trip in 1974 he visited the deserted mining complex of Old Ballarat, another site of his grandfather's labours, and found himself wondering if the old man had left unknown Curnoe progeny there and in America. He inherited a naval cutlass from his mother's side of the family, with channels for the blood to run down, and perhaps this added to his boyhood impression of old Curnoe's wildness.

He thought of his grandfather as an adventurer who missed his chance. At the start of the nineteenth century Newquay had been almost non-existent, just a handful of fishing boats drawn up on the sand, and a house for the lookout. Then came the industrial revolution and the demand for coal. A harbour was built and a rail tunnel bored through the cliff to transport coal for the donkey engines. Grandfather Curnoe reckoned that this was the Newquay of the future, and invested the profit from his various gold-rushes in the mines, where it sank without trace. 'It came in minin, and 'tis goin' in minin,' he observed correctly. What Newquay actually became from the 1890s on was a tourist resort, and if only he had stayed at home and built a hotel he could, Golding estimated, have made a fortune.

It was said that Grandfather Curnoe worked abroad so much because he and his wife would have murdered each other if he had not. She was Mary Elizabeth (née Husband) and they had married in 1869. While he was off in the gold-fields she was reduced to taking in lodgers in her house in Newquay. Golding never saw his grandfather, and thinks he may eventually have just 'vanished', finding poverty-stricken Cornwall, a bitter wife and four children too much to bear. (In fact he died in Newquay in July 1904, seven years before Golding's birth.) Of his grandmother, on the other hand, he had clear memories. She was 'fierce, mean and dangerous', taller than his mother, and always clad in black from head to foot. Her face was brown, like a peasant's. Though his mother called her 'Ma', there seemed nothing maternal about her to little Golding. He remembers a terrible occasion when they were staying at his grandmother's, and his mother gave him a bath in the big bathroom. It was tremendous fun. She would soap his bottom and sit him at the top of the bath's sloping end. Then he would slide down and hit the warm water with a mighty splash. Suddenly their joy was cut through 'as with a sword'. A black creature flung open the bathroom door and stood there 'uttering bloody knives'. There was a 'whirling fury' and a slammed door, and his mother was left in tears gathering up the fragments of a broken mirror.

On a later visit – it was his third birthday – he saw, just once, his great-grandmother, a tiny creature 'in a black bombazine and lace cap and cape', slumped in a kitchen chair. He tried to speak to her, but could not make her understand. Instead she sang, over and over again, a single phrase: 'Down to the river in the time of the day'. She had been born, he records, before 1830, 'while the air was still echoing from the Battle of Waterloo'. (This was almost true: she was Mary Anne Husband (née Teague), born in 1824, and she died on 7 October 1914, a month after her great-grandson saw her).

He came to suspect that the menfolk of the Curnoe family had been addicted to drink, as well as to adventure. There was a strange, perhaps partly imagined, episode when he was playing with his brother Jose in the Curnoe house at Newquay, and came (he says) upon a room piled high with crates of empty whisky bottles and full soda siphons, which the two boys sprayed at each other. The womenfolk, including his mother, had, he thought, made their lives into a respectable fortress that 'drink and the devil' could not touch. Looking at photographs of three generations of Curnoe women he saw the same intransigence in each – hair tugged back and faces grimly set, daring the lens 'to pry below the protected surface'.

His paternal grandparents feature much less prominently in Golding's reminiscences than the Curnoes. Grandfather Jo Golding was a Bristol bootmaker, who 'cobbled all his life', his grandson recalled, but 'hadn't a penny' to bless himself with. As a boy Golding liked him, but he came to be a little ashamed of this side of the family, and condemned himself as a 'pure and perfect snob' for being ashamed. Jo's father Abraham had been a bootmaker too. Jo married Polly (or, more formally, Mary Anne Brain), described on their wedding certificate as a 'tailoress', on 3 March 1876, the very day Jo became twenty-one. Polly was twenty. They set up house in Kingswood, Bristol, and Alec, Golding's father, was born nine months later on 14 December 1876. He was the eldest of their three sons. The other two were named, imaginatively, George Walter Raleigh and Frederick Joseph Othello. Jo died in 1936, but Polly lived on until after the Second World War. There is a Golding family photograph of her with son, grandson, and great-grandchildren, taken in the summer of 1945. Alec remembered his parents as kindly and gentle. Golding's cousin Eileen described Jo as placid and approachable, while Polly inspired her sons to better things. But Abraham, Alec's grandfather, had been, Eileen thought, both religious and a drunkard, given to violently bullying his wife and children, and she believed that Alec's teetotalism and religious scepticism might both be traceable to this experience, whether at first or second hand.

Watching the TV comedy programme *Till Death Us Do Part* in the 1970s, in which Warren Mitchell played the raucously prejudiced, working-class Alf Garnett, reminded Golding of his 'proletarian' connections. He remembered the backstreets of Kingswood as being 'faintly sordid', and smelling of dirt and urine.

3

Parents

Alec, Golding's father, influenced him more strongly than any other human being, and fortunately we know a good deal about him because his journal, which he kept regularly from 1899 to 1905, and then more infrequently until 1918, survives. It covers 398 pages of a handsome Log Book, bound in black boards with maroon morocco spine and corners, and a hinged flap with a metal lock that clamps the back cover to the front. Alec says he always kept it locked. It portrays a lonely, embittered, alienated young intellectual who passes through suicidal depression until he finds, in love and marriage, something like happiness. It is also revealing about conditions in the new 'Board schools' set up under the Education Acts of the 1870s.

The preface to the journal, dated 27 December 1898, outlines Alec's previous life and current opinions. He went to Kingswood Wesleyan School at five and did well, eventually becoming a pupil teacher, a decision he has never ceased to regret, 'for if I hate anything in this world it is teaching youngsters – on such an insignificant salary too'. In 1895, when he was eighteen, he got his first job, at Crew's Hole School, then moved to Avon Vale School, and passed his London matriculation, first class, in January 1898. At the time of starting the journal he was at the New Higher Grade School, Fairfield Road, on £85 a year.

Under the heading 'My Ideas on Certain Important Questions' he lists his beliefs. He holds to 'the vortex theory of atoms', and believes that the Supreme Power is energy, as in gravitation and magnetism. Though he attends the local Moravian Church (a Protestant denomination dating back to Jan Hus and his followers in fifteenth-century Bohemia), he believes that Jesus Christ was simply a perfect man, and dismisses much of what the Gospels record as untrue, because they make Jesus say 'ridiculous things', such as 'He that believeth not shall be damned'. Darwin's theory of evolution is, in his view 'one of the most sublime conceptions of the human mind', and puts its formulator 'far and away above any scientist the world has yet known'. Acquaintances call him 'Atheist, Sceptic, Fool and Lunatic' because of these beliefs.

He considers modern society 'a perfect fraud' and hates class distinction. Social rank, and ownership of property, should, he holds, be based on a person's morality and intelligence, not birth. He believes in the equality of men and women, though he does not like 'cigarette-smoking, cudgel-swinging, manly-mouthed, public-speaking, bloomer-wearing' modern women. He shuns his female colleagues because of their 'frivolity' and they look on him as a 'freak'. Most of his pastimes are solitary (though he is keen on cricket for a while), and they all take second place to cramming for the exams that will lead eventually to an external London degree. He is bookish. Hugo's *Les Misérables* and Kingsley's *Alton Locke* and *Yeast* are among his favourites, and he admires Marie Corelli's *The Sorrows of Satan*, though when he reads her *Mighty Atom*, and finds that she believes an atom to be a 'curly, twisty thing', visible under a microscope, his admiration wanes. He starts writing 'a purely imaginative yarn' himself, but seems not to have persisted, and on another occasion he composes some verses, though he is disinclined to be 'added to the list of jingling, long-haired, dreaming rhymesters'. His Latin is advanced enough for him to struggle through some of Horace's *Odes* (his copy of *Odes* Book IV, edited by T. E. Page, 1898, and inscribed 'Alec A. Golding 4.9.99' is still among the books in his son's library), but he finds it 'deuced hard work'. He plays the violin and buys a second-hand harp; he paints in watercolour and oils, and he is an enthusiastic photographer. On the scientific side, he has a microscope, sends off to a firm in Birmingham for specimen slides, and keeps an aquarium. Cycling is a pleasure, but as his colleagues consider him 'miserable, ascetic and eccentric' he generally rides alone. For the same reason finding a companion to accompany him on his summer holiday is difficult. However, he has a week in Cornwall in August 1899 and is enraptured by the landscape and the sea.

He is extremely fastidious, and any hint of sexual immorality offends him. Kingswood is 'a little hell'. Its staple industry, the boot trade, has attracted 'scum' from Northampton, Leicester and Leeds. Vile language is heard on every street, even from children. Couples engage in 'obscene jests', and worse. There are many brothels – one at least in Soundwell Road where he lives. A lifelong teetotaller, he watches disdainfully, from his study window, the 'raucous and immoral' crowd that spills out from the pub opposite at closing time. Cornwall is little better. He is disgusted to see trippers copulating on the beach and in the fields. One girl, he reports, commits a 'bestial outrage on common decency' by perching ingeniously on a railing, and holding up an umbrella to keep the rain off, while her young man engages with her from behind.

Understandably, given this sensibility, he finds the rough Board-school children he teaches hard to deal with, especially as the normal class size is seventy or above. In November 1899 the chairman of the School Management Committee calls him in and tells him he is a 'failure', and a hopeless disciplinarian. In his 'mental agony' he con-templates suicide, and fears he may go mad. On his doctor's advice he takes two months off; he also applies for various alternative teaching posts, but is at a disadvantage since he has not attended either uni-versity or a teachers' training college. Things look up briefly when he gets a job at a school in Falmouth, but after one term he is displaced by a college-trained teacher. Back home he takes a post at Crew's Hole School, where he first taught. He never liked it, and now it is worse than before. The children are 'awful to cope with', and an 'undisciplined rabble' throw stones at him in the street, shouting 'Bloody old Golding'. The headmaster advises him to resign, and he feels he 'could cry with misery and hopelessness'.

His salvation came in November 1900 when he applied successfully for a teaching post in Newquay and took lodgings with a Mrs Curnoe. The Cornish scenery delighted him afresh, and he was soon repro-ducing it in watercolours and photographs. He found his landlady's daughter Mildred a 'sensible' young person, 'without conceit or aggressive forwardness', and when he played the violin of an evening she accompanied him on the piano. All the same, he felt awkward in her company, and wished she were a 'fellow' not a girl. At school, things do not go well at first. He is, once again, stoned and hooted at by the boys, and is puzzled by his unpopularity. His Darwinism tells against him, because he identifies himself, in his failure, as one of the unfit. Out on a walk he finds a baby rabbit which seems unable to move. He strokes it and puts it in a sunny spot, but next day finds it dead, and feels kinship with it because, like him, it is has failed in the universal fight for survival – 'poor little beggar'.

Despite this melancholy reflection, something has clearly changed for the better. Back home in Bristol for the Easter holiday in 1901 he goes to see D'Oyly Carte's productions of *The Mikado, The Gondoliers, Iolanthe* and *Patience*, and has 'never laughed so heartily'. He also enjoys Jerome K. Jerome's *Three Men in a Boat* – a 'healthy' contrast, he opines, to 'horrible' *Jane Eyre*, which is a 'forerunner of the sex novel abomination'. He and Miss Curnoe now go on walks together. He finds her 'intelligent company', unlike so many of her sex, and they discuss 'geology, tidal action, wave motion, plant life, animal life'. As the weeks pass, their conversations become less academic, and he no longer wishes she were a fellow. But he feels it would be dishonourable to propose marriage since he does not earn enough to keep her. Besides, she might turn him down. She keeps saying she wishes she could marry someone with money. This drives him frantic, as it was perhaps intended to, and he is soon so in love he cannot concentrate on anything else.

At last, in January 1903, she consents to marry him and he puts a ring – rubies and brilliants – on her finger. The struggle now is to find a job that pays more than Newquay. He takes a post in London at Addison Garden School, Shepherd's Bush, but hates it, and it pays only £95 a year. Mildred sends him advertisements and he applies, unsuccessfully, for a dozen jobs in the course of three months. She seems 'upset and irritable' all summer, but then rather shocks him by kissing him as his train leaves at the end of the holidays. It is a momentary aberration. Usually 'Dear M is against any "public" kissing'. In September 1904 he gets a job at a school in Swindon at £100 a year, but 'Dearest Mildred' is showing signs of impatience. She takes it into her head that she will be a 'pianiste' in a touring company, or, alternatively a 'useful help' with a family in Willesden. The 'diabolical' dangers attendant on either course horrify Alec, and he is taken aback when

Mildred tells him that she would prefer to get a 'situation' rather than marry, because she would be independent, whereas marriage is nothing but 'service without independence'.

However, their bumpy engagement survived. In September 1905 he took a post in Wiltshire, at Marlborough Grammar School, teaching Physics, Chemistry, Drawing and Botany for £125 a year, and on 3 January 1906 he and Mildred were married in Truro cathedral. He was thirty, she thirty-six. They rented a house at 8 Alexandra Terrace, Marlborough, and furnished it for £59 from Wolfe and Hollander, paying £3 a month on the instalment plan. They only just made ends meet, and though Mildred proved a 'splendid manager' they were down to their last pennies by the time his January pay cheque arrived. In July the school governors, perhaps hearing that Mildred was pregnant, granted him a rise of £5 a year, but he refused it, considering it 'beggarly' compared with the work he had done. They spent the summer in Newquay with Mildred's family, and she stayed there when he returned to school. On 7 October a telegram told him that Mildred had been safely delivered of a boy at 11 p.m. the previous night. They called him Joseph Thomas Curnoe Golding, but in the family he was always Jose (with a short 'o' to rhyme with 'dose') or José (his father and brother always used this form in their writing; it is not clear why).

Marriage and fatherhood transformed Alec, giving him new confidence. Nothing seems to be left of the young man who said he hated teaching youngsters. He is replaced by an inspiring schoolmaster who, everyone agreed, had an effortless rapport with children. It must have helped that Marlborough Grammar School was very small. The original Elizabethan grammar school had closed down in 1899 and its ancient buildings were demolished. The new school opened on 6 October 1905, so Alec was one of the first staff members. It was co-educational and had, at first just eighty pupils. Schools he had taught in previously, and hated, had that many in a single class. He stayed at Marlborough for the rest of his working life, and generations of pupils testified to his exceptional gifts. He was loved as well as admired. According to one ex-pupil he looked like a Cornish pixie – short, slight, with a round cherubic face, a gleaming bald pate ringed with white hair, and a snub nose with gold-rimmed spectacles perched on it. The school had no money to spare for scientific equipment, so he made it himself. To illustrate the generation of electricity he converted a treadle sewing machine into a dynamo, with a giant horse-shoe magnet and a pair of hand-wound coils the size of jam jars. When vigorously pedalled the whole apparatus shuddered and its flash-lamp bulb flickered triumphantly. He also constructed a water turbine using seventy or eighty teaspoons fixed by their handles in a wooden axle. Jets of water were played on the spoons and the turbine revolved at high speed, drenching the operator. His greatest feat was building a wireless set out of scrap materials such as kitchen paper, cigarette-packet foil, and bits of brass sheet. Since the school could not afford science textbooks, he wrote and printed those himself too. Copies of each page were made on a jelly hectograph – an early duplicator consisting of a gelatine pad to which texts or diagrams were trans-ferred using aniline dyes. Then Alec would sew the pages into Manila covers. His political views also proved enlightening to his pupils. 'It was', one of them recalled, 'through reading his copies of the *Labour Monthly* and through talking to him that I made my first acquaintance with Socialism – no easy thing in the East Wilts of the early twenties.'

His atheism seems to have caused him some inner turmoil. At least one pupil suspected that he suffered 'agonizing conflicts between reason and emotion'. On two occasions when he had to deputize for the head-master at morning assembly, he collapsed and had to be helped from the hall. He managed to get through the opening hymn, but broke down completely when it came to the prayers and the scriptural reading. Atheism did not, however, inhibit his fondness for biblical quotations, which he used in almost any situation. 'Go to the ant, thou sluggard' was a favourite for reprimanding inattention in class.

He took his external London degree in 1910, in Botany, Zoology and Animal Physiology, and *An Introduction to General Geography* by Alec A. Golding BSc was published by Cambridge University Press in 1915. It is an extraordinary volume, covering in 222 pages the place of the earth in the solar system, the causes of day and night, seasons and climates, the distribution of plants and animals, oceanography, geol-ogy, minerals, population density, races, religions and governments. He also kept up his painting – a large oil and several watercolours, one of them of Trevemper Mill near Newquay, are still in the family's possession. But in career terms he was utterly unambitious, and quite content to remain as deputy head. As a socialist he had little time for the pomp and circumstance of authority, and on school prize days he pointedly declined to assemble with local dignitaries and the school governors on the platform. His only concession to the grandeur of the occasion was to take a bottle of Indian ink and carefully paint out the chemical stains and bleach marks on his academic gown. In conservative Wiltshire his socialism, atheism and pacifism would probably have debarred advancement in his profession, even if he had wanted it.

Music was always important to him. He played the viola, cello, piano and flute, as well as the violin. To illustrate the vibration of columns of air to his science class he would cut a dozen lengths of bamboo, and turn them into flutes by boring finger-holes and stopping the ends with corks. Then he would distribute them to the class, and teach them to play simple tunes. A highlight of the school year were the pre-Christmas parties at which sandwiches, jellies, cakes and powdered lemonade were consumed, and valetas, military two-steps, and occasional waltzes and polkas danced, with Alec accompanying on piano or violin.

These fond memories show how he seemed to his devoted pupils. No comparable account of his wife Mildred survives, but in the mid-1960s Golding wrote an analysis of her character which includes things he had been told about her early life. She was, he says, a 'leggy, gaunt, intelligent girl, high spirited and witty', who shunned the rowdy Curnoe menfolk and longed for respectability. Like her husband, she was a lifelong teetotaller. A secret that came to light only after her death was that she was born in a pub. When Alec arrived on the scene, he fell in love, 'and so, perhaps, did she'. She was very aware of being six years older, which made the marriage 'a bit ridiculous' by the standards of the time. However, marriage was an escape route from home, so she accepted him, but with, Golding believes, 'a sense of shame'. The earliest photograph he has of her shows her in a white dress of about 1895, with fringes and bobbles. She holds her head a little defiantly, smiling up to the left with a look of humorous self-awareness, as if to say 'What nonsense it all is!' The line of curls carefully arranged along her high forehead only serves to accentuate that, whatever else, she is not 'softly feminine'.

She shared her husband's advanced views. Golding's essay 'The Ladder and the Tree' recounts that they would stand together 'proudly and indignantly' on the steps of Marlborough town hall, 'under the suffragette banner', heedless of the occasional overripe tomato lobbed in their direction. Family tradition has it that Mildred was, strictly, a suffragist not a suffragette, in that she campaigned for the woman's vote but opposed violent means. Like Alec she was a socialist and an agnostic, or perhaps atheist. Towards the end of her life she is reported as saying wistfully, 'I'd really like to believe in Christianity – it must be nice.' Like Alec, too, she was a musician. She played the viola, 'with concentrated detestation of that fiddling instrument', but loved the piano, and would sit erect as she played, 'dancing almost', and swaying her head in time with the music. They had musical evenings when neighbouring families would come and bring their instruments, and little Golding, in bed upstairs, would hear music, talk and laughter floating up, and the sound of the maid's feet (they kept a maid as well as a cook-housekeeper) hurrying along the hall with coffee. Masters and mistresses from school, and sometimes pupils, came to tea.

But his parents gradually withdrew from social life. He suspects it had something to do with Alec's not becoming a headmaster. His mother sensed that her husband was 'defeated', and felt ashamed. She still retained her lively interest in people, but it was carried on surreptitiously. He remembers her peeping at passers-by from behind curtains. All the same, they did not withdraw completely. They were mainstays of the orchestra at the Marlborough Operatic Society's annual productions, 'playing busily in front of the stage' while the local talent performed *The Dutch Girl* or *Merrie England*.

4

The House

In 1911 Alec and Mildred became tenants of 29 The Green, Marlborough. The Green is a grassy square, sloping towards the south, with the Swindon road running through it. Most of the houses have Georgian fronts, but, as Golding later described it, No. 29 was 'three slumped storeys' of lath and plaster, with a 'crazily gabled porch'.

This was the house in which he grew up, and it came back to him in dreams and nightmares all his life. It was a map of his 'personal mythology', he said, as much as a place to live in. He remembered it as low, dark and dirty. Parts of it, he believed, went back to the fourteenth century at least, though the list of recorded tenants dated only from the eighteenth. It had three wells (filled in) and two cellars. There was a small back garden with a lawn, flowers and a few trees, and as a child he was haunted by the idea that the garden had been part of the medieval burial ground of St Mary's church, which overshadowed the house. His brother told him, years later, that his father had dug up human bones there. It was a place of 'numinous dread'. In dreams he saw coffins poking through the lawn, or suspended in the earth beneath it as if in water. He felt that the darkness of the graveyard flooded through into the cellars of the house, which were eerie, ancient places, with walls of dripping flint and disused fireplaces and cupboards. A recurrent nightmare was of being in the cellar with a hideous crone advancing on him, and not being able to run away. In his journal in the 1970s he drew a plan of the cellars, labelling what he remembered as the 'dark parts', and his daughter Judy, coming upon it, instantly recognized them as the parts that had terrified her too when she went down into the cellars as a child. She remembers also a pair of stag's antlers hanging on the wall, 'very white and clean but not very friendly'. The feeling of 'grue', or 'unsafeness', that 29 The Green inspired could still overcome him as an adult. He described it as sensing a horror he knew he could not face. He would have liked, he said, to have lifted the house away from the church and churchyard and its haunted cellars, and flown it to a site far away where there was perpetual sunlight, 'one of the poles of the moon, perhaps, until the ghosts and demons were all blown away by the solar wind'.

When he was a child his mother compounded his supernatural terrors by telling him ghost stories. He came to think, in retrospect, that perhaps she intended it as a kind of inoculation against irrational superstition. She may have thought she was telling him stories she had heard in her childhood as an illustration of the 'absurdities people believed in the old days'. However, being Cornish, and 'superstitious like all Celts', she half-believed them herself, so the effect was by no means reassuring. His father, a truly rational man, did not believe them at all. How, he would ask, could anyone see a ghost if it is immaterial and therefore cannot reflect light? Little Golding found this objection totally convincing during daylight hours, but somehow it lost its cogency when night fell and his mother started telling her stories. One that stuck in his mind all his life was about a girl who committed suicide back in Cornwall in 'the old days', when suicides had to be buried at night in ground near the churchyard, not the churchyard itself. After her relatives had buried her they turned away and looked across the valley and saw lights moving in the farmhouse. 'She got back before they did,' his mother explained, and her small son was petrified: 'I felt myself freeze'. Whatever her intentions, it seems likely that there was a symbiosis between his mother's stories and 29 The Green. The dark old house made them more frightening, and they gave shape to its unseen horrors.

The house was linked in his imagination with physical repulsion as well as with the supernatural. There was an open drain by the back door, and the 'milkiness' of the water running down it came back to him in dreams mixed up with thoughts of his mother and infant sexuality. He came 'increasingly to detest the physical being of that house'. When he eventually left, it was 'like being let out of prison'. But the terror never quite went away. When he was eighty he had a fearful dream of a large red creature, something between a cockroach and a crab, scuttling around in the combined bathroom and lavatory at 29 The Green. He felt frozen with horror and disgust, and when his wife shook him awake his throat and mouth were 'wooden' with screaming.

The geography of 29 The Green shaped Golding in another way. Beyond The Green and at the other end of the High Street stood Marlborough College, one of the great public schools of England. The sight of its privileged young gentlemen filled him, as a boy, with 'hatred and envy'. At the time he felt guilty about such feelings, but later he came to consider them entirely reasonable. For Marlborough was a beacon of social injustice, and it thrust itself upon his attention every day. The social gap that lay between it and his family was 'as real as a wound'. The college masters, like the boys, radiated exclusiveness. 'In the Marlborough of my youth "College Masters" were a class as definable, as apart, as superior as army officers might be in Aldershot.' One, whom he got to know slightly, continued to patronize him, he felt, even when he had made his name as an author. Marlborough College featured in his adult dreams as a stronghold of upper-class graciousness that made him feel dirty and ashamed. The dreams brought it home to him that his ambition to succeed as a writer was linked to a childish wish to avenge himself on Marlborough College. 'The *truth* is my deepest unconscious desire would be to *show* Marlborough, and then piddle on them.' The sense of social inadequacy that dogged him all his life took root here. He always felt intimidated, he said, by 'top-drawer Englishmen', and traced it to his boyhood – 'it's Marlborough College all over again'.

5

Childhood

The other house that helped to form him was Karenza (Cornish for 'love'), Grandmother Curnoe's home in Newquay where his mother and father had met. Many family holidays were spent there, and it was at Karenza that he was born. The birth was not followed by any baptismal or other rites, presumably because they would have offended Alec's atheism.

Golding says more than once that until the age of six he was so 'blindingly aware' of his own ego and emotions that he was quite unconscious of the outside world. But in fact he retained some vivid memories of that early time, and several relate to Karenza. He remembers the kitchen, which had a wall clock, a 'large and complex' stove for cooking and heating water, and a big table of white, scrubbed wood. It was here that he had the disconcerting third-birthday encounter with his great-grandmother. That morning he had been handed a brown paper parcel, a present from his father who was back home in Marlborough. His mother asked him if he could guess what it was, and told him it was something big. He guessed a Zeppelin, since that was the biggest thing he could think of. But it was not a Zeppelin. When he unwrapped it he found a curved piece of wood with a string stretched between its ends. There was also a wooden rod with a rubber sucker on the end. He spent the rest of the morning shooting at a target on the kitchen door. It was the start of what he later described as a 'fascination' with bows and arrows, spears, and 'guns (naval) of all sizes'.

The grandeur of the drawing room at Karenza also stuck in his mind. There was an eight-day clock with brass balls that swung round first one way and then the other, and a potted palm, and coloured glass panels here and there, and a bow window with cushions on its window-seat. This gave him his first view of naval warfare. It was 1916, and

German U-boats were patrolling the north Cornish coast, sinking the little steamers that carried coal from Wales. Jose, being five years older, was allowed to go down to the quayside to watch casualties and survivors brought ashore. Golding was considered too young for this, but one day he was watching with his mother and grandmother from the bow window when three British motor torpedo boats appeared round Trevose Head and dropped depth charges off Newquay harbour mouth. Vast columns of spray shot up, and then an oil slick spread across the surface with black bobbles and specks floating in it. He came to suspect that this whole incident was a dream or vision, because his parents swore he never saw it, and could not have done. Yet he retained a deep inner conviction that he saw it, and perhaps he did. His daughter Judy's researches have found that on 10 March 1918 several vessels were searching for a U-boat off Trevose Head, and when the Spanish steamer *Cristina* was torpedoed some of them dropped depth charges. Oil and bubbles came to the surface, and on 25 March a diver found the wreck of a submarine lying in twenty-four fathoms with its conning tower practically blown off. It is true that this was two years later than the incident Golding recalled, but he was often vague about dates. It is also true that the 1918 event must have had many witnesses and been widely talked about in Newquay, so an imaginative child might come to think he had actually witnessed it. Either way, Golding's doubt, later in life, about whether he saw it or not is an acknowledgement of his tendency to confuse the imaginary and the real.

The 1914–18 war touched the Goldings less than it did many families. Alec was thirty-eight when it started, and his short sight made it unlikely he would be accepted for military service. Nevertheless, in 1916 he asked the school governors to release him, and attended a medical board at Devizes. He was pronounced fit only for field service at home, and the medical officer told him that the school board would not have let him go anyway. He took over an allotment in 1915 – its previous tenant had been killed in the war – and began growing food for the family on a serious scale. In 1916 he planted fifty-two rows of potatoes, as well as cabbages, parsnips, swedes, carrots and 200 leeks. There were also pullets, whose poor rate of egg production caused him concern. He watched his sons' development with satisfaction. At nine Jose was, he reported, impossible to keep from books. He had read *Ivanhoe, The Talisman, Westward Ho!,* and *Robinson Crusoe,* all unabridged. In September 1916 he started at Marlborough Grammar School and finished his first year at the top of Form I, doing so well that he skipped a form and began September 1917 in Form III. The second son, 'a fair-haired, blue-eyed sturdy little rascal called Billy', was 'most loving and demonstrative and very intelligent'. Billy was 'the artistic and musical boy. He can use his fingers, Jose cannot.' In the hard winter of 1917–18, when the thermometer showed fourteen degrees of frost, Alec took both boys sliding on Leg of Mutton pond. Another pleasure was having Hawthorne's *Tanglewood Tales* and Kingsley's *Heroes* read to them. Jose preferred the old Roman stories, 'but Billy prefers the Greek'.

Newquay, though, was Alec's ideal, not Marlborough. For Golding too it remained a magic place: not the town itself, which he thought 'cheap and nasty', the ugliest seaside town he had ever seen, nor even the ice-cream, though he always deemed that matchless ('the genuine Cornish Italian article'), but the beaches and their huge Atlantic waves. As a boy he swam in all weathers, even when it was raining. He never learnt the crawl, but relied on his 'vigorous breast-stroke' to cope with any surf the north Cornish coast could throw at him. His mother told him of the great storms of her childhood, when gobbets of yellow foam would stick to Karenza's window panes, though it was over a quarter of a mile inland. Another very early Newquay memory was of walking with his father along the little sandy beach inside the harbour. They came to a high step and his father lifted him over it. He remembers it because his father touched him, and he touched him again when he lowered him into a small pool among the rocks on Fistral beach. No such thing, he declares, happened before or again. 'That is all the touching I remember. We were not a touching family.'

Nor does he recall any physical contact with his mother. 'We did not touch each other. Our physical divorce was complete.' As a baby he had been bottle fed by his nurse Lily. Many years later, when his mother lay dying, and he was visiting her, she said she had been a bad mother to him. He thinks she meant there had been 'too little cuddling, too much bottle via Lily, too little bosom and rest'. It may be, though, that his dying mother had other things on her mind. In Golding's published pieces, such as 'Billy the Kid', she is presented as sweet and caring – adoring, even. She would declare in moments of lyricism that he had 'eyes like cornflowers and hair like a field of ripe corn'. But in fact she was violent. He recalls three occasions when she threw things at him. Once, when he was little, and had been having nightmares, he lay in bed in the dark whimpering for a light. His mother was in the next room, and suddenly a candle, a brass box of matches, and a brass candlestick struck the wall by his bed. Matches flew everywhere. There was no further word from his mother, and he cowered beneath the bed-clothes till dawn. On another occasion she threw a pair of trousers at him, perhaps forgetting there was a heavy seaman's knife in the pocket. They flew past his ear and struck a mirror behind him, showering him with glass. The third time he was an adolescent and having some sort of argument with her, and a metal pot full of hot tea just missed his head and crashed into the grate. In one of Golding's adult dreams about his mother she appeared as the Principle of All Evil warring against God – an extreme transformation, perhaps, but understandable.

Why she felt such fury is not clear. Maybe she just found him difficult. He recalls that, at age three or four, he had a fear of being 'controlled', and begged not to be put into 'leading reins', a sort of safety harness that toddlers often wore at the time. When, at the age of seven, he went to his first school (it was run by a Miss Hillier on the south side of Marlborough High Street, and they learnt the kings of England with their dates and 'a little bad French') he was at first violent and disruptive, or so he recounts in 'Billy the Kid'. He 'enjoyed hurting people' and his one aim was to fight and triumph over other boys during the break. Understandably he found himself isolated and unpopular, and went home in tears. Negotiations between his mother and Miss Hillier followed, and on his return he found the other children polite and friendly, having been lectured by Miss Hillier on the importance of forgiveness. 'Billy the Kid' is a self-indulgent piece – a famous author jovially unwinding and presenting himself as a loveable harum-scarum – and it would be foolish to treat it as strictly factual. All the same it may reflect early difficulties at school that involved his mother and tried her patience, and this may have added to a general exasperation that sparked her outbursts of violence. She made no secret of the fact that she had wanted a daughter, and perhaps she blamed him for not being one.

But it may be that her anger was more general, arising from frustration with her housewifely role. He suspected she yearned for a life of 'fashion and society', and fantasized about it. She would wander from room to room, with fixed eyes, deep in some interior story, occasionally muttering or talking out loud. Her dreams, she once told him, were of 'hobnobbing with royalty'. Dissatisfaction soured her. She had a vicious tongue, and could fire off devastating phrases. Once, when he was ten or eleven, she took him to see a production of Barrie's *Mary Rose* put on by the local Boy Scouts. The title role was played by a 'very pretty boy' called Geoff Duck, and young Golding 'fell in love with him, her, or it, on the spot'. Later, at a party, he stayed close to his heartthrob, who responded with camp affectation. His mother noticed, and ticked him off for 'following young Duck around like a dog'. It was, he says, 'like an explosion in my world', and made something that was natural seem wicked and disgusting. This incident may connect with another at about the same time, when they were staying with relatives in Newport, Monmouthshire, and he found himself in a bedroom with two pretty, excited young girls who were getting ready to go to a dance. He was too little to be treated as a male, so they laughed and joked with him as they put on their make-up, and one, turning suddenly with a powder-puff in her hand, said, 'Would you like some?' He jumped back and said 'No'. But in truth he would indeed have liked some, and felt ashamed for wanting it, and wanting to be female like them.

His parents were on their guard against any hint of sex. This 'Victorian attitude' seemed, to Golding, particularly absurd in his father, since he was a biologist. Reproduction, in Alec's biology, went as far as bees and pollen, and no further. It was never admitted that any creature had sex organs. The aim seems to have been to preserve his offspring's childish innocence. Golding remembers, when he was little more than a baby, asking his father if there really were fairies inside flowers, and Alec, after a struggle, replied 'Yes'. On occasions when girls were present, a close watch was kept. Prior to one of the school socials his parents organized dancing classes at 29 The Green, open to all pupils from his father's set, though only girls came. Golding thinks he was four or five at the time, but

Alec's journal tells us it was in February 1918, when he was six. He recalls the gas-lit drawing room, the Japanese prints over the mantelpiece with painted female faces (he later found out they were advertisements for prostitutes, though his parents never suspected), and the laughing, chattering, breathless girls. A pretty dark one called Edna won his heart. It was pure love, without desire – just delight in the existence of another person. If asked what he would like to be at fifteen, he would have said he would like to be like Edna. Mischievously he smuggled a whistle into the class and blew it to cause a disturbance. Everyone thought it a great joke, or pretended to, and the lovely Edna came over to where he was sitting on the sofa, talked smilingly to him, and took the whistle away. Encouraged, he fetched another whistle, then a comb-and-paper. Each time Edna came and talked him round amid general hilarity. The line of confiscated items stretched along the mantelpiece, and he was blissfully happy. The next week, though, there was no Edna. But he noticed a new girl among the dancers with a sullen, crumpled face. Then he realized she was Edna. She did not so much as look his way, and he guessed that his father had cautioned her to ignore him, to stop him showing off.

Something similar, he believed, happened with his next love – a little Belgian refugee girl whom he partnered in games and dances at children's parties in Marlborough town hall when he was six or so. She too 'vanished' and he suspected his parents were responsible. Being protected in this way made him inhibited, or so he imagines. At Miss Hillier's school there was a girl called Barbara he especially admired. She had masses of dark curls and was a leader in school society. Once, at a party, they were playing postman's knock and she called him outside. He followed her out and stood dumb with wonder at her beauty. 'Come on, then,' she laughed, but all he dared to do was plant a 'chaste salute' on her cheek. The improbable scene in 'Billy the Kid' where Billy Golding, after being forgiven, is 'hugged and mouthed and mauled' by all the girls in the school during a game of postman's knock reads like a fictional compensation for this real-life humiliation.

It was also impossible to discuss with his father and mother his irrational terrors of the graveyard and the cellars. Alec was imaginative, if sometimes over-ingenious, in scientific matters. He once put a speck of cyanide on his tongue to see what it tasted like. On another occasion he tried unsuccessfully to make a garden roller by filling a large cylinder with pink concrete. But his imagination did not stretch to the supernatural. Both parents made 'mild fun' of their small son's fear of the unknown. One winter afternoon when he was three or four they took him for a walk, as they did every Sunday, in Savernake Forest. This lay about a mile to the south of their Marlborough house, and with its beech trees and bracken fronds it became, Golding said, a 'settled part' of his being. It provided much of the landscape of *The Inheritors*. On this afternoon he was lagging behind and whining to be carried, and his parents, who were about fifty yards ahead, hid behind a tree for a joke. It was growing dark, and he saw, staring at him over the bracken to his left, a stag's head, with antlers. He screamed and ran. His parents, coming out of hiding, laughed, and would not believe he had seen a stag. But he knew he had, and that it was not an ordinary kind of seeing. Like the white creature on the curtain pole, the stag was from another world, though unlike that creature it had radiated 'stillness and terrible indifference'.

His father seems to have tried to cure his small son of his super-natural fancies. Once when they were at Newquay he took him to the graveyard out beyond the Tregunnel road and, pointing to an undug plot by the side of the path, explained to the child that that was where his father and mother would lie when they were dead. Golding remembers being utterly bewildered and, though Alec's intentions were no doubt sound and rational, it does not seem a promising method of banishing a child's fear of death. It was this fear that first aroused his fascination with ancient Egypt, as he explains in his essay 'Egypt from My Inside'. Through their tombs and grave-goods and mummies the ancient Egyptians, it seemed to him, brought life and death together. At seven he determined to write a play about them, but then realized he did not know their language, so he set about learning hieroglyphics. When he was with his mother in London he nagged her to take him to the British Museum's Egyptian collection, and Flinders Petrie, the great excavator of Egyptian sites, became his hero.

On visits to his father's parents in Bristol he got to know the Egyptian department at the Bristol City Museum, and he made lists, annotations and drawings of figures, vases, amulets and beads. His absorption led to a strange waking dream in which a museum curator, impressed by his knowledge of Egyptology, invited him to help unwrap a mummy. He was, he thinks, about ten at the time, and the curator took him to a screened-off section of the geology department, where a mummy lay on a trestle table. His job was to take the bandages as the curator unwrapped them, roll them up, and put them on a side table. His memory of the event is extremely sharp and detailed. Blue faience amulets came to light, hidden among the bandages, and when the mummy was finally unwrapped he laid his hand on the thick, leathery skin that covered its bones. It became, he says, 'the event of my life'. Yet it did not happen. There was no mummy and no bandages. When he went back to the museum next day he found that the screened-off corner of the geology room was a storage-space for maps.

Out of his knowledge of ancient Egypt he concocted an 'imagining' which he would use at night when, as often, he was frightened and could not sleep. He would make believe that he was a pharaoh lying on a large four-poster bed. It was out of doors, and the desert stretched red and flat to the horizon. His bodyguard of picked troops surrounded him, standing shoulder to shoulder and facing outwards. Each had a drawn sword with a red streak down the middle, reminiscent of Grandfather Curnoe's naval cutlass. Their trusty presence allowed him to go to sleep safely, despite the graves in St Mary's churchyard and the unthinkable horrors in the cellars of 29 The Green, only yards below his bed.

Another of Alec's shortcomings, apart from unease about sexuality and failure to believe in God, was pedagogic zeal. In 'The Ladder and the Tree' this is presented favourably: Alec teaches his small son to overcome his aversion to Latin, and earns his gratitude. But to judge from his son's unpublished writings Alec's unquenchable desire to instruct was in reality far from welcome. The reason, Golding complains, that he has never been able to understand anything properly, not even an ordinary calendar with its leap years and oddly named months, is that Alec insisted on trying to teach him before he was ready. He had it dinned into him that to learn something, no matter what, was one's first duty in life, and he half-believed it. It was to placate Alec that he pretended to be interested in science as a career. Perhaps Alec's relentless insistence on knowing things goes some way to explaining his son's lifelong distaste for research, and preference for trusting his imagination on matters such as medieval building techniques or eighteenth-century ships. Equally it may lie behind his liking for abstruse facts. He joked about his tendency to buy teach-yourself books on anything from Tibetan to the morphology of modern Swahili, and abandon them after a few pages.

In his son's recollections, Alec's earnest rationality made life at 29 The Green rather joyless. Jose and he were encouraged to be 'stiffly indifferent' to such occasions as Christmas and birthdays, and they were not celebrated at all once they had grown up. They had 'almost no toys' – none, in fact, except for two rather elaborate model yachts that Alec made. The rudders were constructed with particular ingenuity but, Golding unkindly records, had no effect on the direction the boats took. Since Jose was nearly five years older he was a remote and rather frightening figure. In an alarming adult dream Golding watched him dissecting a baby in the dining room of 29 The Green, and he felt this reflected his early relations with his bigger, more powerful sibling. Nothing so dramatic happened in real life, but their few attempts to play together were not successful. Once, in the garden of 29 The Green, Golding, aged about three, clung to the end of a long pole, normally used to prop the clothes line, while Jose swung him round faster and faster until his head came into contact with the wall and he lost consciousness. When he came round Jose adjured him not to tell their parents, but he did, and was disappointed that they treated it as a minor matter. After that, Jose did not trust him. The following summer Jose rigged up a tent on the lawn using walking sticks and rugs, and the brothers planned to spend the night there. When it grew dark, however, they both crept indoors and were ridiculed by their mother for being afraid of the gravestones. Their only other recorded game was a three-man version of cricket on Marlborough Common. A friend was bowling, Jose was keeping wicket, and Golding, at the crease, took a tremendous swipe at the ball and hit Jose across the side of the head. He ran home clutching his ear, followed by his whimpering and terrified younger brother, who was so appalled by what he had done (though Jose was not, in fact, badly hurt) that he crawled under the dining-room table and hid.

His parents, being intellectuals, were habitually critical of anyone in authority, and as a child he found this irksome. There was an occasion during the First World War, in 1917 or 18, when they were, as usual, denigrating the Allied generals and the British government with left-wing gusto and, exasperated, he demanded why they were always running other people down. Alec replied mildly that they were not. But it is to this incident that Golding traces his retirement into the escapist world of books. Jose and his father had given him *The Wonder Book of Ships for Boys and Girls* for his sixth birthday (despite the embargo on birthday celebrations), and the copy they gave survives. Published by Ward, Lock and Co., it is the sixth edition, 'with Twelve Coloured Plates and 320 Illustrations', and was evidently aimed at a wartime readership, containing sections on Life in the Royal Navy, Types and Classes of Warships, Submarines, Naval Guns, Building a Battleship and related topics. It is inscribed 'To Billy from Jose & Daddy. Sep:19th 1917'. He also read *The Boy's Own Paper*, and borrowed Jose's 1910 edition of Arthur Mee's *Children's Encyclopaedia*. But at the time, as he recalls, there were relatively few books written specially for children, so he made do with what he could get from the 'semi-adult world'. At ten he read Victor Hugo's *The Toilers of the Sea* in a Woolworth's sixpenny edition (this, too, is still among his books). Other authors he sampled were Jules Verne, P. C. Wren (*Beau Geste*), Mark Twain, Robert Louis Stevenson, Rider Haggard (*She, Cleopatra* and *King Solomon's Mines*), Alexandre Dumas and Conan Doyle. A book that, according to his brother, he read again and again when small was *Nat the Naturalist, or A Boy's Adventures in the Eastern Seas* by the prolific author of boys' adventure stories George Manville Fenn, originally published by Blackie in 1882 and given to him by his parents on his seventh birthday. It is about a teenager who goes on an expedition with his famous naturalist uncle, hunting for biological specimens among the islands of the Malay archipelago. To a modern reader it is an unappealing book. The pair spend their time shooting large quantities of exotic birds and collecting their skins. They also shoot some 'treacherous savages' on New Guinea, and they are loyally attended by an untreacherous savage whom they dub 'Master Ebony'. In his own accounts of his childhood Golding never mentions this book, perhaps feeling some disquiet about its old-world assumptions. On the other hand, in the 1980s he read it to his first grandson.

Music, like books, was an escape from the everyday world, though it remained more under his parents' direction. He started with the cello, which he played like a double bass because he was too small to play it sitting down. The sounds he made were excruciating, but he realized at once that music was 'unfactual, sensible and right'. He always associated cello music with his early unfocused feelings of sadness. One autumn evening when he was six his mother took her rather melancholy little son to see a Miss Salisbury who lived opposite the end of Silverless Street. He was carrying a quarter-sized violin, which Miss Salisbury was to teach him to play. For the next twelve years he saw her twice a week, holidays excepted, and she became the model for Miss Dawlish in *The Pyramid*. His memories of her were not favourable. She wore the uniform of a 'New Woman' – blouse, tie, no-nonsense suit, sensible shoes – and she smoked cigarettes and also a pipe. Her face was yellowish, like parchment, and, it seemed to his childish gaze, 'full of shallow, empty holes'. After a year he went with her to Swindon to take his Grade One exam, and made such a mess of the Bach test piece that he burst into tears, though the kind young examiner passed him. After that his parents decided he was too highly strung for any more music exams.

He thinks, without being sure, that he was taken to hear Paderewski play when he was eleven or twelve. But such outings were rare, partly because his parents were poor, and partly because, he believes, they associated anything theatrical with sex and felt uneasy about it. His mother took him to *Chu Chin Chow* when he was very small, and he was impressed by the moonlight scene. With his father he saw Harriett Jay's comedy *When Knights Were Bold*, which made him laugh till he fell off his seat, and also a play, title unknown, about two astronauts who go to Mars in an aeroplane and find that Martians sing and dance in spangles. He was enraptured and, recalling it later in life, seems to have harboured a grudge against his parents for cutting him off from the stage and the career it might have offered him.

The cinema, too, was an 'unspeakable pleasure'. His parents rather disapproved, but he went to Saturday matinees in both Marlborough and Newquay to watch flickering, silent cowboys and Indians, explorers, naval battles, and murder mysteries set in derelict houses that gave him nightmares. At Marlborough there were two rows of plush seats at the back and rows of kitchen chairs nearer the screen. He always sat alone in the middle seat of the front plush row, partly because his parents disliked his mixing with other children, and partly because he did not want to. The technical shortcomings of early film had, he believed, a marked effect on his youthful sexual attitudes. Female stars like Mary Pickford and Lillian Gish appeared with chalk-white faces, heavily made-up black eyes and mouths like blobs of liquorice, so he internalized a standard of beauty completely unlike real women. Also, as the cine camera made normal-shaped women look dumpy, stars had to be fragile, leggy creatures, and the ethos of early film dictated that they should in addition be timid and useless in emergencies. This was an era in which males came to the rescue of helpless femininity, and before kissing a woman even a villain took his hat off.

All in all, Golding's childhood as he describes it in his unpublished journals and memoirs could not be called happy. He was over-sensitive, timid, fearful, lonely, and imaginative to the point of hallucination. He was alienated from his parents and his brother and had no friends. So it is worth adding that, looking back, he took a sunnier view. In the first of his Ewing Lectures, delivered at the University of California in Los Angeles in 1961, he observed that the best writers are supposed to have had unhappy childhoods, but his was, by and large, 'very happy'. One of his earliest memories, he says, was coming upon his father, standing in the garden, on the wet lawn, after dark, looking up at the stars. He heard him murmuring to himself 'I wonder', and he asked him, 'What do you wonder?' 'I just wonder, it's all I can do,' his father replied, 'I shall go on wondering for the rest of my life.' His mother appeared carrying two overcoats, which she made them put on in case they caught a chill, and the two adults seemed to him 'very wise and august'. The incident gave him an image, he says, of 'what man ought to be' – a watcher and a wonderer.

6

Growing Up

Golding went to Marlborough Grammar School in September 1921 when he was just ten. He remembers how the building struck him on his first acquaintance with it. It had separate entrances for boys and girls, firmly marked over their respective doors, and 'a certain thickness of atmosphere' inside, particularly on wet days, which was, he thinks, identifiable as 'unwashed boy', and probably unwashed girl as well. The school had grown since his father started there in 1905, when it had only eighty pupils, but it was still very small. Even as late as 1938 it had only 300, so there were probably not many more than 200 when Golding entered the first form.

His brother Jose was already a star pupil, as Alec's journal testifies, and that, plus the fact that his father was a teacher, must have been felt as a pressure. He seems to have held his own, however. True, Latin mystified him at first, and he simply refused to try to get his mind round it. But after the fraught and tearful episode with his patient father that he recounts in 'The Ladder and the Tree', even Latin became possible. Out of school he kept up his music lessons with Miss Salisbury, though at the age of twelve he changed from the violin to the piano. He had been strumming on the piano at home since he was seven, and its yellow ivory keys were for ever embedded in his memory.

He was naturally left-handed, but was made to write with his right hand at school, and in later life he came to regard this as damaging. It had prevented him reaching professional standard as a pianist, he suspected, and had even (it is not clear how) made learning French more difficult. He had tried to achieve parity between his hands, drawing with his left, writing with his right; bowling left-handed, batting right-handed. This might mean, he thought, that he was making use of both sides of his brain, though 'confusedly', or perhaps that the right and left lobes of his brain were 'reversed'. Either way it could explain, he reckoned, why his outlook was 'different from that of the majority of people', and might also be one source of his 'basic and lifelong' feelings of 'inadequacy'.

It does not seem, though, to have affected his athletic performance. One advantage of a very small school was that, in sport, everyone had a chance to play everything, and he did. He had exceptional ball sense and was renowned for his slip-catching. He was also an outstanding sprinter, and competed at county level. In 1924, and again in 1925, he came second in the Senior (under sixteens) 100 yards at the AAA County Meeting at Trowbridge. In later years he told a rather surprised schoolmaster colleague that he had run the 100 yards in 10.8 seconds. Even as a child, he recalls, he was stocky, and never had an athletic physique. But his appearance was deceptive.

As a pupil at Marlborough he was able to observe his father's genius as a teacher at first hand. For Alec teaching was a performance. He talked and gestured so intensely that it was like watching an actor. To illustrate the relative nature of sense impressions, for example, he would 'hang' three imaginary bowls of water in the air before the class and pretend to be dipping his hands in them. The bowls, he explained, contained hot, medium and cold water. He put his left hand in the hot and his right in the cold. Then he dipped them both in the medium, and – lo! – his right hand felt it was hot and his left felt it was cold. It was spell-binding, but also, for a son who would himself become a teacher, intimidating, as Golding's reminiscence suggests: 'It was marvellous teaching, and I don't know that we – I – ever recovered from it.'

The equipment Alec had at his disposal was not much more advanced, his son reflects, than Galileo's, and he repeated Galileo's experiments, rolling an iron ball down a sloping plank, and exhausting the air from a glass tube to show that a feather and a penny dropped at the same speed. With a length of smoked glass, a tuning fork and the school stop watch, he measured the number of vibrations per second that produce middle C, and he rigged up a series of electrical relays that fired a copper bullet, as if from a gun. He drew human analogies, to make science more palatable. The so-called 'noble gases', he explained, were the ones that would not have anything to do with the other elements, while the non-noble gases grabbed whatever was around. Coal gas, for example, would combine even with the haemoglobin in human blood, which was why people put their heads in gas ovens to commit suicide.

This lesson stuck in Golding's mind for a particular reason. As soon as Alec mentioned gas ovens and suicide a hush descended on the class. Alec did not know why, and perhaps did not notice. But his son knew. A boy called Jack Amey, a friend of his, was sitting next to him. He was the son of the manager of the International Stores in the High Street, and only the night before Mrs Amey had put her head in a gas oven and killed herself. When the class was over and the other boys trooped out into the playground, he stayed behind and told his father about Mrs Amey. Alec gasped, and said urgently, 'Don't tell Mam.' It was 'the first dent I ever remarked in that friendly, caring, and all-too-omniscient figure'.

Alec was far and away the best teacher in the school. Golding's 'most fully disliked' teacher was Miss Pierce (nicknamed 'Granny'), a puritanical spinster who, he alleges, wanted any boy and girl seen together to be expelled. As a matter of fact Miss Pierce may have had a point, for the standards of sexual behaviour set by some other staff members left much to be desired. Golding relates an incident he witnessed in the summer of 1926, when he was fifteen. A school party were on a day's excursion, and accompanying them on the coach were Mr Sidney Pontefract, the headmaster, and the games master Mr Bill Clayton. Both were respected figures in the community; Captain Bill Clayton was a Great War veteran and had won an MC. On the way out they stopped at a pub, and the two masters disappeared inside. They stayed there for an hour, while the boys and girls sat in the coach and waited. Then Bill and Sidney returned and lurched down the gangway of the coach, stopping by a particularly attractive girl called Grace, who stood up tactfully. 'A fine child,' said Bill, patting her bottom. 'A very fine child,' Sidney agreed, taking her by the shoulders and pressing himself against her breasts. Grace giggled and blushed, not knowing what to do, and the two men dropped into their seats as the coach moved off.

Miss Pierce's − and Alec's − hypersensitivity to sexual impropriety seems, in this atmosphere, justifiable, and as he moved up through the school Golding learnt more about Bill and Sidney. Clayton, it transpired, regularly beat his wife, and Pontefract's wife Gertrude was the mistress of Mr Hickson, the headmaster of the boys' elementary school. Gertrude and Mr Hickson ran the Boy Scout troop, and while they were away camping in the New Forest Sidney would slowly drink himself into a stupor. Taking the key of the pavilion back to his house after cricket practice, Golding once saw him in this state. It was because of Gertrude's and Mr Hickson's conduct that Alec and his mother would not let him join the Boy Scouts. They wished to preserve him from moral contamination.

In 1924 Jose went up to Brasenose College, Oxford, to read history. His rapid ascent through the school, missing out Form II as his father boasted, may not have been an advantage in the long run. He found the Oxford syllabus tough going, particularly as he was competing with well-taught public-school boys, and he took an extra year to complete what was usually a three-year course. More disturbing to his parents, however, were his politics. On 3 May 1926, when he was in the Trinity Term of his second year, the Trades Union Congress called a General Strike in the United Kingdom, in protest at the pay and conditions of coal miners. Alec, listening to the news on his home-made wireless set, heard that Oxford and Cambridge undergraduates were being recruited to shift food from the docks. Anxious that his son, whom he assumed was a staunch socialist like himself, might be pressured to participate, he sent a telegram: 'Forbid you to take part in strike breaking'. Back came a telegram from the Principal of Brasenose: 'Your son left for the docks this morning with the rest of the college'. Alec was aghast that his son should betray the workers' cause, and wrote Jose a savage letter, only to receive an equally angry one in return. The atmosphere in the family when Jose came home for the vacation was 'sulphurous'. Alec felt that he had begotten a class traitor, while it seemed to Jose that his independence and his political beliefs were under threat. His younger brother 'enjoyed being indignant' along with his parents, but in fact he was not interested enough in politics to care either way.

Though his academic performance at Marlborough Grammar School did not match his brother's, William won at least one prize – a copy of Charles Maginnis's *Pen Drawing: An Illustrated Treatise* with a bookplate 'Prize Awarded to Wm G. Golding, Form III, for Drawing', signed 'S. Pontefract. Head Master'. In September 1927 he graduated to the VIth form, and his father marked the occasion by giving him a human skull, by which, he thinks, Alec meant to symbolize his arrival 'at some sort of intellectual frontier'. Its lower jaw was connected to the upper by springs, so that it could be made to gape or laugh, though normally it just grinned. He brought it home from school, resolving to sleep with it by his bed, but as darkness drew on he thought better of it. His mother, who considered the whole business disgusting, jeered at him for his cowardice, much to his fury.

A diary he kept from 1 January to 18 March 1928 survives, and gives us a glimpse of the daily life of Golding the VIth-former. He has two close friends, Cyril Aylen and Peter Gough, who come round in the Christmas holidays to play cards, draughts, table-football and chess and listen to the wireless. The three of them also enact mock trials, taking it in turn to be judge, prisoner and counsel. More athletic than the other two, Golding comes across almost as a parody of a keen, games-playing British schoolboy of the *Boy's Own Paper* era. When Mr Clayton (he of the school bus incident) cancels football practice because the ground is waterlogged, young Golding is robustly scornful ('You wet!! You wet!!!'). He plays for the school team, and defends them stoutly when they lose 7–0 in a cup-tie in Swindon – 'The score does not represent the play'. He almost loses a tooth boxing with Jose, who is on vacation from Oxford, and goes with him to see Swindon play Clapton Orient, where the home supporters' barracking offends his code of fair play ('I thought a footer crowd was supposed to be sporting'). Cricket practice starts on 22 February and he gives it his serious attention, learning to throw with his right hand so that fielding will not strain his bowling arm. At the end of term he is chosen school cricket captain.

Relations with his father are good. When he catches mumps ('this absurdly plebeian illness') it is his father, not his mother, who nurses him. Their musical interests also bring them together ('Dad has written the air for a string quartette and I am harmonizing it'). For a school production of *Twelfth Night* they assemble four violins, a cellist and a pianist. The violinists are himself, his father and two girls, whose names he gives as Dora Enser and Flora Spencer. In fact he has got their names mixed up. They were Dora Spencer and Flora Enser. His mistake suggests that at this stage he had little interest in Dora, though she was soon to play a considerable part in his story, as we shall see. They perform Rossini's William Tell Overture, the first movement of the Haydn's London Symphony and Pleyel's first Sonatina. It seems to go well, though he complains that 'the refreshments were microscopic'. His father and mother rehearse for the Operatic Society's production of *Florodora*, the great Broadway hit of 1900, which he loftily dismisses as 'a beastly modern musical comedy'. (He could not know, though he may have discovered later when he read his father's journal, that in 1903 Alec had taken his mother to see *Florodora* at the Princes Theatre Bristol.)

His twice-weekly piano lessons with Miss Salisbury start again after the Christmas break, and she gives him a new Beethoven Sonata, No. 20, to learn. He refers to her by her nickname, 'Dapper', and from what he writes about her later he seems to have become increasingly critical of her at about this time. She had been at the Royal College of Music with Dame Ethel Smyth, and had an ARCM and FRCO. But in young Golding's view she was 'entirely without talent'. A joyless mechanical accuracy was her limit as a musician. As a violin teacher she had been poor – unable to play the instrument herself, or even tell when she was out of tune – and her piano teaching was unadventurous. Reading between the lines we can sense the tension between an assiduous teacher, firm about getting the notes right, and a rather arrogant adolescent who spent hours every week listening to concert virtuosi on the wireless, and whose dashing attempts to emulate them were coldly received. He had no doubt that his taste was superior to hers, and when she lent him an oratorio she had published in her youth he pronounced it (though not, one hopes, to her face) 'slush'. In justice to Miss Salisbury he admits that when he eventually plucked up courage to tell her he would like to take a piano exam, her you-can't-fake-the-fingering approach paid off, and he got high marks. As he recalls it, his rendering of Beethoven's 'Pathétique' Sonata nearly blew the examiner out of the room. It was jealousy of his friend Peter Gough that had driven him to acquire some serious musical qualifications. Peter had come to 29 The Green one day and played several works including Mendelssohn's

Andante and Rondo capriccioso in E major, Op. 14. Golding's parents came in and listened and said how good Peter was – 'far better than you', they added indignantly, as if he had let the side down. He was 'furious', and settled down to learn the piano properly.

His critical faculties, rigorous in musical matters, seem to have relaxed in the cinema. The VIth-form diary records his going to see *Michael Strogoff*, an adaptation of a Jules Verne story about a tsarist courier who is sentenced to be blinded by a Tatar warlord, but escapes and fights a spectacular duel with his hated foe ('a very good film'); *The Flag Lieutenant*, a 1926 remake of a 1919 stiff-upper-lip war drama ('an extraordinarily good film'); and *The Black Pirate*, an early Technicolor feature, only the third ever made, which includes a famous scene where Douglas Fairbanks, as the pirate, sticks his dagger in a mainsail and rides it all the way down, cutting the sail in half.

The books he reads include T. E. Lawrence's *Revolt in the Desert* ('a very good book'), E. F. Benson's *Colin II* ('a suggestive book concerning modern Devil Worship'), and two of Edgar Wallace's African novels, *Bosambo of the River* and *The People of the River* ('both cleverly written'). But the popular novelist and playwright Ian Hay emerges as his favourite author, and he polishes off two of his books, *Half a Sovereign* and *Paid With Thanks* in a single day. Neither Ian Hay nor Edgar Wallace feature in the adult Golding's recollections of his teenage reading, which tended to be more august.

The diary reports with some satisfaction on his school work. His French is 'progressing astonishingly well', and he starts a 'more or less systematic study of biology'. His father's efforts to reconcile him to Latin have evidently paid off: 'I got full marks for Virgil'. In his 1961 Ewing Lecture, Golding said that he first began to learn Greek when his father pointed out that the footnotes in Edward S. Creasy's *Ten Decisive Battles of the World* (which begins with the Battle of Marathon) were left in Greek, and that this was the start of his 'passionate affair with that miracle of languages'. It sounds like a boyhood memory, but in the 1926 diary he records that he has progressed no further than learning the Greek alphabet, and he jokily transcribes some English words ('The fact that I am very pleased with myself') in Greek characters.

He devotes considerable thought to writing poetry, and copies out his 'latest effort' on 2 January:

> Mid full fair flowers a silver shimmering pool
> Shone like a stone set in an ornament
> Yet having that that's lacking in a jewel
> For all the soft swayed flowers gave full a scent.

The shortcomings of this were evidently pointed out by someone – perhaps Jose, perhaps his father – for he complains of the 'unkind' criticism it has received, and feels that he has 'suffered too severe a reverse to write any more poetry yet awhile'. However, within a few days he is at it again, composing 'a poem which should turn out rather well', though he is 'hung up for a word with a heavy-sounding vowel to complete it'. After 'two days of hard thinking and much book research' he hits on the very thing, and transcribes the result:

> The sombre light from some red-glowing moon
> Droops like a crimson cloak with far-flung folds
> Lulling a land most sunk in drowsy gloom
> And clothing it in red and sable robes.

The admiration for Tennyson evident here makes him unwilling to engage in the hurly-burly of class discussion on the poet: 'Pont is going to do the Lotos Eaters next week. He will ruin them for me.' Like the sensitivity to criticism, this wish for aesthetic privacy characterized the adult Golding as well as the adolescent. When musical friends complained that he did not go to their concerts, he explained that he found it 'disturbing' to listen to music surrounded by other people.

Unpromising though young Golding's poetic efforts clearly are, there can be no doubt of their deep importance to him. From now on he would think of himself as a poet. It was that, he felt, which set him apart from the rest of the world, as well as from his own family, especially his brother, who outshone him academically. 'Letter from Jose, with the usual prosaic, unemotional phraseology', he notes slightingly in his diary. Perhaps Jose gave him Quiller Couch's *Oxford Book of English Verse* for his eighteenth birthday hoping the models it provided would improve his brother's compositions.

The other striking thing about the schoolboy diary is the absence of any interest in the opposite sex. As we shall see, this is misleading. What inspired the unpromising poems was pure, boyish love. But no whisper of it gets into the diary. It seems to belong to that stage, just before puberty, when boys go through a curiously old-fogeyish phase, becoming miniature middle-aged bachelors, and often developing quite abstruse scholarly interests. 'There is only one thing I pray I have got, and that is the mind of an antiquarian,' he avows after listening to a talk about Southwark cathedral on the wireless. No doubt boys in 1926 developed sexually later than they do now, but Golding, in retrospect, realized that he had been unusually slow to catch on to the facts of life even by contemporary standards. It was impossible to discuss such matters with his parents, and the boys at school excluded him from their sex talk because he was a master's son. So he grew up ignorant and inhibited.

The unpublished memoir *Men, Women & Now*, which he wrote partly for his wife Ann and partly for himself in the mid-1960s, describes his sexual awakening and the events that followed in considerable detail. He had a vague idea that men and women were made differently, but did not know how, and he recalls examining nude female statues – or the few that came his way – in hope of enlightenment, only to find that they were disappointingly smoothed off between the legs. Discovery of his own physical development came in a 'particularly ridiculous way'. He was climbing a flagpole on Marlborough Common, merely as a boyish prank, and the friction, he found, induced an agreeable sensation. So he continued to climb, and at the top achieved a climax. He returned to earth, exhausted but wiser. At this point, though, he imagined that what he had experienced was unique to him, rather than common to males. For the rest of the summer he climbed the flagpole frequently, because it did not occur to him that there could be any other way of procuring the same satisfaction. Only with the coming of winter was he forced to ponder that sex might not be essentially linked with flagpoles, and his experimental interest switched to the stout wooden door of his parents' bedroom. If he opened it, and climbed up until his legs were hooked over the doorknobs on either side, while his hands clasped the top, he could, he discovered, haul himself up and down against the door's edge and achieve the desired result. His parents, downstairs listening to the wireless, imagined that he was engaged in body-building exercises – as, indeed, he was. His biceps became exceptionally well developed.

No doubt some allowance must be made for comic exaggeration in all this. On the other hand, Golding's professed aim was to write a factual account to help him explain – to Ann and to himself – why he found it hard to create women characters. Eventually, as he recounts it, he realized that everything the door and the flagpole had given him could be attained by a simpler means in his own bedroom. Alec, he suspects, may have guessed what was going on. 'Did my father consult gravely and angrily with someone,' he later wondered, 'with our family doctor, perhaps?' At all events, his 'peculiarly dreadful relationship' with his father seems to have begun at this time. The fantasies that accompanied his lonely sexual pleasure were of ideal women, 'exquisite, docile' creatures, with the features of film stars or models in advertisements. Meanwhile the real girls he saw around him in the classroom – 'bulging, greasy, giggling or too solemn' – inspired disgust and hostility. He imagined that, between their legs, they were 'cleft from front to back, a long disgusting cleft', for otherwise how could something as large as a baby get out? At the same time he resented the 'shameful attraction' that they – or some of them – exerted. 'What did they mean by daring to exist?' In this way he changed from the little boy who admired girls and wanted to be like them, to an 'adolescent, cynically and brutally prepared to exploit any girl he could get hold of for his own selfish and immediate pleasure'.

There were two girls who particularly disturbed him. One was Mollie Evans. He sat behind her in class and was troubled by the beauty of her neck. Her other attractions included long-lashed, grey eyes, delicate arms and breasts, and an eighteen-inch waist. She was shy, mild and pious, and not much given to thought, or so he believed. Rather, she had 'a lot of the feminine capacity to enjoy mere existence, sitting in her pretty skin'. Her parents were the local shopkeepers in Great Bedwyn, near Marlborough, and there was madness in the family. She had an uncle who had killed his wife and himself. Her father was under the illusion that marital relations had given him a disease that caused spots on his hands. Young Golding's feelings about Mollie were confused. He knew her as someone he would not like to hurt. But he also knew her as a 'female thing' he wanted to punish and dominate. In time he was to make her suffer, and looking back years later he suspected that that suffering had been the most profound emotion of her life. 'I wish it were not so.'

The other girl who attracted him at school aroused simpler feelings. She was the Dora Spencer we have already met as a violinist. Unlike Mollie, Dora had no 'Dantesque, Platonic aura'. She was just very sexy. Her father was an ex-army man employed by the local council, and she would frequently walk, in what seemed to Golding a peculiarly sugges- tive manner, past 29 The Green on her way to and from her parents' bungalow on the Swindon road. Golding, 'thundering imperfect Chopin, Liszt, or Beethoven' on the piano in the drawing room, and his brother Jose at one of the upstairs windows, would observe her passage. Dora read books, and aspired to be cultured. She was also a Roman Catholic, and 'had a sense of sin'. Golding attracted her because he was thought to be 'different, austere, artistic, intellectual'.

This was a persona he had carefully developed. Puberty had brought self-consciousness, and he had found walking down Marlborough High Street to the bookshop a 'desperate trial', because the lads of the town and the stable-boys lounging against the shop-fronts would snigger as he passed, though they never laughed at the other grammar-school students. It filled him with 'furious shame', so he pretended to be abstracted and absorbed. He would sit on the edge of the pavement reading Edith Sitwell's *Bucolic Comedies*, and ignoring his tormentors, and after a time he became genuinely unaware of them. Dora, he thinks, may have sympathized with his 'contemptuous, burning withdrawal'. Besides, he was five years older, so she was naturally rather in awe, and it was generally known that Mr Pontefract had opined that young Golding would 'go far'.

7

Oxford

His relations with Mollie and Dora were still at this preliminary stage when he went up to Brasenose College, Oxford, in the autumn term of 1930, shortly after his nineteenth birthday. He had been looking forward to it. When Jose went back to Oxford for Hilary Term 1928, the VIth-form diary comments 'Lucky beggar! If all goes well I shall follow him in 3 years'. By the time he did follow him Jose had graduated and was teaching at a school in Grantham (where he was to remain for the rest of his working life). Neither of the Golding boys went to Oxford on a scholarship, so Alec had to pay all their fees and expenses out of his meagre salary. Feeling the pinch, he and Mildred decided that they would have to dispense with their cook-housekeeper, and make do with a maid-of-all-work. It is an indication of the watchful eye of snobbery at the time that the school governors let it be known they disapproved of a grammar-school master lowering his social standing in this way.

The prospect of doing the cooking herself cannot have cheered Mildred, especially as the economic constraints were so tight. Their Sunday joint, Golding recalls, was usually made to last till Thursday, and on one occasion a sirloin of beef had so obviously gone off that the family refused to eat it, while Mildred insisted it was impossible to throw it away. In the end she consigned it to the dustbin, but indignantly, as if it was their fault. All this may help to explain why she greeted her son's elation at the prospect of the freedom and stylishness of Oxford with one of her poisonous barbs – 'Don't think you're going up there, *swaying about.*' Deflated and blushing, he walked away.

His Oxford application form survives, recording that he has passed the Oxford School Certificate in 1928 with credits in English, Science, Latin, French and Scripture, and that his course of study at Brasenose will be Botany. Founded in 1509, Brasenose (abbreviated BNC) occupies a rather cramped site in the centre of Oxford, and lacks a college garden, but it overlooks one of Oxford's – indeed, Europe's – most beautiful locations, Radcliffe Square, which has James Gibbs's circular, domed library, the Radcliffe Camera, at its centre, and is flanked by St Mary's church with its elegant fourteenth-century spire, All Souls College, with Hawksmoor's twin towers, and, on the north, the awesome limestone cliff of the Bodleian, one of the great libraries of the world. By present-day standards, Brasenose in 1930 was tiny. It had five fellows, five lecturers and 175 undergraduates. Its Principal was Charles Henry Sampson (who had sent the telegram about Jose and the General Strike).

Its setting and companionable size would have made it heaven-on-earth for many students. For Golding it was the opposite. The true story of his Oxford years would make 'unbearable reading', he said. He could 'never pretend he was happy'. The reasons are not far to seek. Oxford in those days was a predominantly public-school institution. Only one undergraduate in twenty, Golding recalled, was a grammar-school boy, so 'I suppose we felt a little uncomfortable'. At BNC the proportion was smaller. Of the seventy-one undergraduates who entered the college with Golding in Michaelmas Term 1930, he was the only one from a grammar school, and fifty-three of them had been to leading English public schools. Their relative wealth, and the friend-ships they had already forged at school, inevitably set them apart. But in addition to this, Brasenose was renowned for its sporting prowess, especially in rowing and rugby. It was the kind of college to which the public schools sent their brawnier and less cerebral products. Golding, though a talented athlete by Marlborough Grammar School standards, made no impression at Brasenose. The twice-yearly college periodical, *The Brazen Nose*, has sections for sporting clubs (Rowing, Football, Rugby, Tennis, Cricket, Athletics) but his name appears in none of these, nor anywhere else except the 1934 class-list when he got his degree.

Looking back, he saw his time at Brasenose as a 'disaster'. But he did not blame his parents. They were simply ignorant. Rather, it was Sampson's fault. He should have advised them to send their sons to London University. In Oxford's atmosphere of narcissism and camp affectation he, a 'callow youth from grammar school', felt lost. He had 'nothing to offer the dons in the way of youth, beauty, wit, brains'. He scorned the foppish 'varsity' slang ('Pragger Wagger and Mamagger's Mammugger') and despised Brasenose's ignorant, 'games-crazy hearties'. Oxford was an 'obscene place'. At first, it seems, he tried to make himself interesting by inventing an alternative identity. A fellow student recorded of Golding in his diary: 'He enjoys lying but only if he is clever enough not to be found out i.e. he does not like lying but he does like success in lying. In his first year, Hamish tells me, he claimed to hail from Russia and got away with it.' To make matters worse, he was not interested in his subject. He had agreed to study science only to placate his father. Music, he realized, would have been the right subject for him, but at the time Oxford had no undergraduate music course.

So he found other things to do, and treated the university as 'a kind of bed and breakfast'. Oxford, for him, was 'bookshops and cinemas' plus 'repertory theatres and concerts'. The bookshops were wonderful – 'books, books, books everywhere, back rooms, ladders, built out shelves'. He was poor, so he ran up debts, and sometimes, he hints, stole. Writing in his journal in 1978, he tells of being in an Oxford bookshop only the previous day and finding himself tempted to steal a volume of Martial's *Epigrams*. Rather to his surprise, he says, he resisted, 'from a genuine distaste for stealing' – and adds, 'It would not always have been so.' He hired a piano ('quite likely', he thinks, he 'never paid for it'), and kept it in his top-floor room. As for concerts, he recalls hearing Artur Schnabel play Beethoven's *Diabelli Variations* in Oxford town hall (and stopping, and starting all over again, because a lavatory was heard flushing somewhere in the building), and the great harpsichordist Wanda Landowska coming to play at the Oxford Music Club. The morning after her concert he and some other enthusiasts found their way to her practice room and timidly asked her to play C. P. E. Bach's *Solfeggietto* and Louis-Claude Daquin's *Le CouCou*. She happily obliged.

Another brush with greatness in his first year at Oxford, recalled humorously years later, happened when he was looking over a bridge by Magdalen Deer Park and a 'tiny mustached and hatted figure' came and stood by his side. He recognized him as Albert Einstein, who had come to Oxford as a temporary refuge from Nazi Germany. Young Golding had no German, so could not communicate, but he beamed at

Einstein in an attempt to convey 'the affection and respect that the English felt for him'. They stood together for about five minutes, then Einstein pointed to a trout 'wavering in midstream' and said '*Fisch*'. 'Desperately', Golding recounts, 'I sought for some sign by which I might convey that I, too, revered pure reason. I nodded vehemently. In a brilliant flash I used up half of my German vocabulary. "*Fisch. Ja Ja.*"' Then Einstein drifted away.

A favourite Oxford occupation was taking hot baths: 'Probably the baths at BNC saved my sanity. It was something to do.' For a boy brought up in the primitive conditions of 29 The Green, which he likens, in his schoolboy diary, to a 'refrigerator', limitless hot baths were a luxury. In a dream many years later he links them with class distinction. A socially superior undergraduate tells him there is a vast bath of hot water in a part of the college he has never visited: 'I was not one of the elite for whom the bath was intended.'

Another activity at Oxford was learning to fly. Little is known about this, but it is clear it happened. The index card recording his interview with the University Appointments Committee on 22 February 1934 lists under the heading 'Experience' the two words 'Private flying', or possibly 'Practice flying', which are then crossed out. In his journal in 1974 Golding recalls 'the old Avro Avian in which I used to fly', adding that it could be 'cranked up to ninety in level flight and cruised at sixty-five'. An earlier journal entry of 20 September 1972 records a dream he has just had in which he has landed an Avro Avian on the wrong airfield and 'enemies', one of whom is his father, try to stop him taking off again. His comment on the dream is that Alec '*did* stop me flying'. Oxford University Air Squadron, founded in 1925, had Avro Avians, and undergraduates could learn to fly with them. However, if Golding had joined the Air Squadron it would surely have merited mention on his Appointments Committee card, so it seems likelier that he learnt with a private club. The Avro Avian was the commonest trainer at the time. A twenty-eight-foot wingspan two-seater biplane, it was powered by a 100 hp Armstrong Siddeley Genet Major engine and could cruise at 85 mph with a maximum speed of 100 mph, so perhaps the one Golding flew was in need of an overhaul. Why Alec put a stop to the flying lessons is not known, but the likeliest explanation is expense.

In this directionless stage of his life, Golding became, he says, a scientific rationalist like his father, though without Alec's moral sense. 'Moodily, bitterly, and in the end, I suppose, almost indifferently', he deduced that good and evil were relative, and that if he cared he could say (like Satan in Milton's *Paradise Lost*) 'Evil be thou my good'. Reading a life of Beethoven, and learning how the composer had dealt with his publishers, helped to make him 'financially dishonest in the matter of bills and borrowing'. He took to laughing at 'all religion, all mysticism, all possibility of spiritual experience'. In his first year at Oxford he was holding forth in this way when another undergraduate – he recalls his name as Copplestone-Boughey – asked him if he believed in hypnotism. He said he did not, but was willing to give it a try. 'I was eager for any experience that would release me from an increasingly grey daylight and from the labs where the frogs twitched and the rabbits' guts swelled in the hot summer humidity.' Some time later he regained consciousness, to find his companion 'white and shaken'. Apparently it had taken a long time to get him out of his trance, and the words he had spoken while hypnotized were 'like a chapter of the Old Testament'. After this 'ludicrous incident' they avoided each other. Recording it years later, he thought it might not have been 'straight hypnotism', but that he might have become, while unconscious, a 'medium', which would mean it could be evidence – like the white cockerel and the spectral stag – of a reality beyond the rational.

His chosen reading, in his rationalist phase, was Voltaire's *Dictionnaire Philosophique*. Published in 1764, and arranged in an alphabetical format, this was a relentlessly sceptical and wryly humorous rejection of all forms of superstition and fanaticism. Voltaire identifies religions, and particularly Christianity, as the great source of misery in the world, and dismisses metaphysics as ignorance. Reading it, Golding says, kept him 'feeling cheerful'. He seems, at the same time, to have hardened himself emotionally. Concurrently with his going up to Oxford his friend Peter Gough had started at London University, but soon fell ill with pernicious anaemia. This condition, the result of a B12 vitamin deficiency, can now be diagnosed and treated very easily, but in 1930 it often proved fatal, and Peter died. Miss Salisbury believed young Golding would be heartbroken at the loss of his friend, and, even though she knew he was an atheist, she arranged for the vicar to come to one of their music lessons during the vacation and give him comfort. This was, he recalls, a 'terrible embarrassment', and also needless, for in fact he had regarded Peter's death with 'merciless objectivity'. A disillusioned realism also marked his political stance. On vacation from Oxford he went to a League of Nations meeting in Marlborough town hall and asked, in question time, if, in the face of aggression, the League would use force. The reply was no. which convinced him that the League would be of 'minimal' use.

In the Easter vacation of his first year at Oxford he met Dora again. He later suspected that she engineered the meeting with the help of a mutual friend, because she was intrigued by what she saw as his sophistication. It happened in Marlborough High Street, and Dora, not yet sixteen, wore a white silk blouse and gym slip. It was a warm evening and the two of them walked up to the Common, he pretending 'lofty indifference', when all he really desired was to get his hands on her, while she tried to make interesting conversation. He felt sure that 'she wanted heavy sex and at the same time was frightened of it'. This information was, he claims, 'visibly written on her' – on her smooth skin, her shiny hair, and her 'pert, ripe, desirable' mouth. They sat on a bench near a clump of trees. Dora, it soon transpired, had nothing on under the gym slip except the blouse and a pair of white silk knickers. She was willing to be kissed and hugged, but took fright when he tried to touch her breasts. Soon they were 'wrestling like enemies'. At fifteen she was under the legal age of consent, 'a point which did not occur to me as I tried unhandily to rape her'. She clamped her knees together and began to snivel. Exasperated, and angry that he had 'made such a bad hand at rape', he shook her and shouted, 'Hold your row, you silly little bitch, I'm not going to hurt you.' At that she began to howl, and her nose ran. He hated her and felt sorry for her at the same time, so he blew her nose and patted her, and they sat silently for a while, then walked back to the edge of the Common where they parted without a word.

Back in Oxford, he had few friends. He recalls reading through the complete run of *Punch* in the Junior Common Room – a pastime that, surely, only the loneliest would resort to. But he was not quite solitary. There were three other students he was on familiar terms with – Charles Allen, J. A. C. Pearce and Adam Bittleston. Allen boasted that a knowledge of French and Latin had enabled him to read Dante, which depressed Golding because, though he had struggled through Antonio Fogazzaro's *Il Santo* (a novel banned by the Catholic Church because of its author's attempt to reconcile Darwinism and Christianity), he could not translate Dante. So, cowed by Allen's superiority, he abandoned his study of Italian – an illustration, he later thought, of his 'inferiority complex, or weak will'. However, Allen was also the first classicist he had met, and talking to him about literature made him yearn to be a classicist too, though he quailed at the prospect of spending six years learning Greek irregular verbs. A copy of Homer's *Iliad* edited by Arthur Platt (Cambridge University Press, 1894), and firmly marked as the property of C. G. Allen, 1 Jubilee Road, St George, Bristol, is still in the Golding archive – a testimony to Allen's success in arousing his friend's interest in Greek.

Pearce was an aesthete, a rare species in BNC. He had relatives in Florence, had met people like Henry Moore and Benjamin Britten, and did not do much work at Oxford – all of which Golding may have found appealing. He had studied Latin and Greek at Charterhouse, and introduced Golding to a lyric by Alcman in the *Oxford Book of Greek Verse*, which meant little to him at the time as he still knew only the Greek alphabet, but which he later came to admire greatly. Together they experimented with Persian script, which led to their meeting a Persian 'with an immoral passion for an angora cat' (a memory that is left tantalizingly undeveloped). They also went on a holiday to the Scilly Isles together with Jose, taking a boat from Penzance, and found them 'remote and idyllic', Pearce recalls. They spent two nights drinking under the moonlight, and slept on the shore in a boat at St Mary's, until someone came and urinated against the side, then they wandered up into the town and slept in a deserted stable yard in a cart, which turned out, when daylight came, to be a hearse. Pearce thought that Golding was 'something of a misfit' at BNC, as he was himself, and he remembered him playing the Moonlight Sonata 'very beautifully' on his hired piano in the attics.

Adam Bittleston meant more to him than the other two, and remained a friend for life. Unlike Golding he came from a privileged background. His father was Major Kenneth George Bittleston of the Royal Horse Artillery; his mother, Alice, was niece of the second Viscount Halifax. He was physically singular, six foot five inches tall, and deeply religious. Though he was a couple of months younger, he had come up to Brasenose a year before Golding and was already a committed follower of Rudolf Steiner, the founder of a belief system known as anthroposophy. Steiner (1861–1925) was an enormously prolific Austrian-born scholar, educator and occultist, who carried out 'spiritual research' under the aegis, at first, of Madame Blavatsky's Theosophical Society. He aimed to apply his training in mathematics and science to the experiences of the spiritual world he had had since childhood, so as to subject them to rigorous verification. There is no necessary division, he taught, between faith and knowledge: the educated spirit can be as dependable in its perceptions as the scientific brain. Truth is both an objective discovery and 'a free creation of the human spirit'. Anyone can acquire knowledge of the spiritual world through self-discipline and meditative training, and become morally enlightened.

On a larger scale, he believed in a vast scheme of cosmic evolution, guided by spiritual hierarchies. Christ, he taught, is central to all religions, though he goes under different names, and all religions are, for their time and place, equally true. The 'Christ-being' is not just the Christian redeemer but the pivot of earth's evolutionary processes and human history, and is manifest in all cultures. A movement for the renewal of Christianity called 'The Christian Community' was set up in the 1920s under Steiner's influence, and his ideas have had a lasting impact on many areas of life, including education, alternative medicine, organic agriculture, art and architecture.

Sceptics have derided his supposed power of super-sensible perception, and have pointed out that his view of cosmic history is at odds with the discoveries of modern physics and astronomy. But it is easy to see why Steinerism, as expounded by the enthusiastic Bittleston, interested Golding. It was light years away from the *Dictionnaire Philosophique*, but it seemed to offer a reconciliation of his father's scientific rationalism and his own spiritual experiences, dating back to the white cockerel and the Savernake stag. Eventually he was to reject anthroposophy and find its adherents comic, whereas Bittleston spent his life as a serving minister in the Christian Community. Yet Bittleston's Steineresque ideas left a permanent trace on Golding's beliefs. For his part, Bittleston admired Golding's poems and sent them to an editor at Macmillan, who agreed to publish them in the Macmillan's Contemporary Poets series.

In his journal Golding says that at the end of his fifth term, that is, round about Easter 1932, he was sent down from Oxford. That seems to be an exaggeration. For an undergraduate to be sent down a decision of the college Governing Body would be necessary, and none is minuted in Golding's case. On the other hand, the fact that he missed what should have been his sixth term is borne out by the Brasenose Tutorial List for Michaelmas Term 1932, which shows that he has kept five terms, not six like the other students in his year. Possibly his tutor suggested to him at the end of his fifth term that there was no point in his continuing, since he had not been working. After five terms he had still not completed the preliminary exam in Natural Science. He had taken the Physics part after his second term, the Zoology part after his third, and the Botany part after his fourth. That left Chemistry, which he could have taken after his fifth, but did not. His tutor, Thomas (later Sir Thomas) Weston Johns Taylor (1895–1953) was cultivated and, from all accounts, friendly – a chemist, field naturalist, watercolourist, amateur musician and voracious reader. There is no reason to suppose he disliked Golding. More likely he saw that this clever young man was not interested in his course, and wanted to save him from wasting any more of his time.

There is, however, another version of why he left Oxford after his fifth term. Years later he told his daughter Judy that he had stopped running in the middle of an inter-collegiate relay race – he just got fed up with it – and as a result the Dean 'tore a strip off him' and 'told him he'd played the piano over his (the Dean's) head every night, and would he please not come up again for the next term'. In fact BNC did not have a Dean in Golding's time, but the disciplinary functions normally carried out by the Dean were part of the Vice-Principal's role, and the Vice-Principal was William T. S. Stallybrass, who did indeed have a room directly under Golding's on Staircase 4 in the Old Quadrangle. Stallybrass, later Principal of BNC, was an old-style Oxford don, famous for his dinners 'embellished with gleaming silver from three huge chests and the best of wines'. His favourite saying was

'It's a good thing to keep the old traditions, especially the bad ones.' It is quite possible that he would have lost his temper with a lowly and insignificant student such as Golding, and to Golding Stallybrass must have seemed like some incontrovertible component of the English constitution (though in fact he had been born William Sonnenschein: the family prudently changed its name in 1917). Whatever actually occurred, by the end of his fifth term BNC evidently seemed even less welcoming than it had before.

Golding did not tell his parents what had happened, but went down to Cornwall and got as far as St Ives. There in the gents lavatory in a pub he found a fair-haired girl who was seemingly being molested by three sailors, and was laughing and trying, not very hard, to escape. Quixotically, he rescued her – realizing only later that she must have gone in there quite willingly. Her name was Sheila Garnett, and she was pretty, childlike, promiscuous, and 'as uncomplicated as spring water'. Her parents ran an old people's home in Penzance, though at the time of Golding's arrival there was only one elderly lady in residence, whom Mrs Garnett referred to cheerfully as 'the terminal'. This left spare beds, and Golding, as lodger, was allocated one of them. Each night Sheila joined him in it. He spent much of the day in a hired sailing dinghy (presumably he had learnt to sail during summer holidays at Newquay), but they bathed and went to cinemas, dances and pubs as well. Once they set out to walk from Penzance to Land's End, taking with them a bottle of cherry brandy, and kept going until they fell, laughing, into the hedge and slept it off, waking with 'simultaneous headaches'. He could never recall how they got back. She did not, he thinks, derive much pleasure from sex, but she realized other people enjoyed it and liked making them happy. All she disliked in him were his 'frequent tragic and drunken sorrows'.

The idyll ended when his mother in far away Marlborough somehow got wind of the affair, and his parents stopped his allowance. So he went home, and there were earnest discussions about his future. These were witnessed by a new member of the household, Eileen Haydn Davies. She was Golding's twelve-year-old cousin, the daughter of Mildred's younger sister Estée and her husband Edgar Haydn Davies. Estée had died two years before, so Eileen was spending the summer with her aunt and uncle. When her father Edgar died the following year, Alec and Mildred adopted her. She had vivid memories of the summer of 1932. There were 'ructions, with people closeted in various rooms'. Golding wanted to go back to Oxford and read English Literature. Alec was against this. For one thing it would mean taking an extra year. On the other hand the alternatives were to give up Oxford altogether, or waste his final year reading a subject he disliked. In the end Alec came round, and helped his son cover the whole of the first year of the English course, which he had missed, during that summer vacation. Among other things, he heroically copied out a translation of the Anglo-Saxon epic *Beowulf*.

In August Golding went up to Oxford to see his tutor and it was agreed that he should take the final part of his science preliminary examination in October, and then change to English. A few days later he received an abrupt letter from the bursar of BNC, demanding the payment of £73 4s 1d battels (that is, bills he had run up in college) before he could be allowed to return. Seemingly he wrote to the Principal asking to be allowed some delay in payment, for there is a letter in the Brasenose archive from C. H. Sampson (who was on holiday in Yorkshire) to the bursar, enclosing a draft of a letter to be sent to Golding. It is scarcely a model of pastoral care:

Dear Golding,
As at present advised I can only support the Bursar's request that you should discharge your debt to the College before undertaking further liabilities.
Yours sincerely,

No doubt Alec obliged, as usual, for on 5 September Golding sent the Bursar a cheque to cover his battels and another for the entrance fee for the Chemistry prelim – which he duly passed the following month.

Meanwhile he contrived to see Sheila one last time, despite his parents' vigilance. On the visit to Oxford to see his tutor, he bought some books on credit from Thornton's bookshop, walked across the Broad, and sold them to Blackwell's. With the funds liberated by this transaction he travelled down to London, met up with Sheila, and took her out to dinner. She was in high spirits. Another lover had succeeded to Golding's bed, and she had been to a dance with three nice gentlemen in a motor car, and pleasured them all on a grass verge between St Ives and Penzance. This was, he surmised, a way of telling him as kindly as possible that what they had had together was over. They had a last drink in a pub near Charing Cross, then he put her in a taxi and never saw her or heard from her again.

Reading English Literature at Oxford must have seemed a little flat after Sheila. The syllabus was unreformed. Almost all nineteenth- and all twentieth-century literature was excluded, as unworthy of academic study. Large doses of Anglo-Saxon and Middle English – much of it of purely philological interest, if that – were administered. Golding's Anglo-Saxon tutor C. L. Wrenn was still a byword for tedium in 1950s Oxford. H. F. B. Brett-Smith, a Fellow of Hertford College, who took him for the 'modern' (that is, sixteenth- to eighteenth-century) part of the course, was a specialist in early drama and may have been more interesting. A good-humoured letter, upbraiding Golding for losing the testimonials he had supplied, sending copies, and thanking him for a copy of his published *Poems*, survives from January 1935. But, like so much at Oxford, Brett-Smith induced uncomfortable class feelings in Golding. Dreaming about him only two years before his own death, he noticed that all the other undergraduates present were in dinner jackets, while he himself was in a lounge suit. Brasenose was not, to judge from its degree results, the most lively place for studying English. In 1930, the year Golding went up, there was only one Brasenose candidate in English Schools and he got a fourth, the lowest possible class. There were no Brasenose candidates in English the following year, and in 1932 there were four, of whom three got thirds and one a second. The inadequacy of the Oxford syllabus, and the quality of the Brasenose teaching, left surprising gaps in Golding's reading. Many years were to pass before he read Wordsworth's *The Prelude* or any of Pope's poetry, and he never got round to reading any Thomas Hardy. French literature seems to have engaged him more, perhaps because he did not have to study it with Wrenn and Brett-Smith. He read old French romances at Oxford, the *Chanson de Roland*, *Tristan et Iseut* and *Aucassin et Nicolette*, and while he was in Penzance with Sheila he bought an 1834 *Collected Works* of Molière. At one point, it seems, tutorials with Wrenn became so boring that he simply could not face them. There is a draft letter, in pencil, in the archive, probably written after Christmas 1933:

Dear Mr Wrenn,
Thank you for your letter. I hope your Christmas has been a pleasant one. At the end of last term – the last week in fact, I was so unutterably weary of work – having had more than enough to do and having done all of it – that I deliberately cut lectures and tutorials from sheer lack of the will-power necessary to attend them. You will recognise that this is not an excuse but a confession. However I wish sincerely to apologise to you not for a contravention of university law but for my lapse from good manners which you must regard and rightly as an insult. Please accept my apologies for this which are offered not as an excuse or extenuation but in all sincerity. I am no longer of an age to be stood in the corner for not having learnt my lessons and what I lost by not attending one of your tutorials is only to apparent to me.

Whether this letter was ever sent is unknown.

It was in the summer of 1933, halfway through his English course, that he took up with Dora again. There had been three or four 'unsatisfactory' meetings since their wrestling match on the Common, but now she was eighteen and more experienced. They went together to Rabley Woods and she leant against a tree, laughing, while he undid his flies. Her response was unromantic but, in its way, appreciative: 'Should I have all that rammed up my guts?' 'Yes,' he replied, hoarsely, but Dora explained she was having a period so he would have to wait, 'It'll be OK tomorrow.' As they were walking up to the woods the next day she told him casually that Bill Clayton, the games master, had said he would like to whip her, 'He said I'd like it.' 'Did you let him?' Golding asked. 'My God, no! Of course not!' she replied.

Their copulation that day seemed 'cold and abstract', but other days that summer were better. They made love among the ferns and spotted orchids and the huge shadows of trees, and he felt boyish and inadequate as he watched her reaching her lonely ecstasy, turning away her head, 'eyes shut, forehead lined, a kind of anguish, concentrated on reaching through her slow rhythms, a far, deep spot, dark and wicked'. He also played a lot of tennis and cricket and was 'terribly healthy'. One evening when he met her up by the woods she seemed unusually sullen and withdrawn. Alarmed, he asked if she was pregnant, but she snapped back that she wasn't, 'A fat lot you'd care. Or anyone.' She flung herself down on her side in some gorse, and he lay beside her pestering. Her dress was up round her waist and she rolled away from him onto her stomach. Laughing, he grabbed her knickers and jerked them down, and found himself gazing at 'a girl's white bum, round as a penny in all its endearing ridiculousness, and whipped, not two hours since, to ribbons'. In an instant she had tugged her knickers up and was staring at him, defensive, appalled and ashamed.

After that they did not meet for a while. It occurred to him that he had a kind of hold over her, or she might think he had – might think he would 'shoot his mouth off' about what she and Bill Clayton had got up to. Perhaps for this reason she became 'sullenly and bitterly malleable', and they recommenced their open-air sex sessions. One evening they were lying on a hill overlooking Marlborough. Far away in the valley they could see the green patch of the school playing field, with white specks moving about on the tennis courts and cricket ground, and the tiny black figure of Golding's father supervising the proceedings. Even though he knew he must be indistinguishable at such a distance, he felt embarrassed, and tried to hustle Dora into the wood. But she refused, insisting that it must be 'here or nowhere'. So they made love where they were, and looking back guiltily under his arm he imagined that the tiny black figure was shading its eyes and looking in his direction. When he got home his father had not yet returned, so he went into the drawing room and played the piano. Five minutes later he heard his father come in through the front door, pause in the hall and go upstairs. He crept to the drawing-room door and peeped out, and there, swinging on the hat-stand were his father's 'ancient but still serviceable binoculars'.

It was Dora's revenge. He worked out later that she must have gone to his father for help or advice about something – the unwelcome attentions of men, perhaps – and he had boasted about his two exemplary sons, and she had scornfully advised him to take his binoculars to the playing field on two particular days – two, because the week before, it turned out, she had played the same trick on his brother Jose, who was also having an affair with her during his summer holiday from his teaching job in Grantham. A week or two later his father 'affecting a gross and jovial masculinity which sat very ill upon him', cautioned him about taking care not to 'get a girl into trouble'. Meanwhile Dora had disappeared, and it transpired that she had got a job in London.

They did not meet again for more than a year. But in late autumn 1934 he was back in Marlborough when the Mop Fair was on. This was an annual carnival, when people flocked in from the surrounding villages. For a quarter of a mile the High Street was closed to traffic and lined with shooting galleries, roundabouts, coconut shies and sideshows; crowds churned and lights flared. It had always enchanted him as a child, but in his mature intellectual remoteness he found it raucous and trivial, and was leaving when Dora came up to him, smiling. By this time he had got Mollie Evans back, 'or was in process of getting her'. He does not say how he had previously lost her, but the thought of her made him even more unwilling to be with Dora. However, she grabbed him by the wrist and insisted on accompanying him. She suggested they went for a drive in his father's car – an 'ancient fabric-hooded Morris'. They found, though, that it was boxed in by other cars, so they went to the Roebuck for a drink instead. On the way Dora, who, he noted, was considerably more sophisticated after her year in London, told him she had just come back from a trip to Germany 'with the boss on business'. This made him feel jealous and provincial, so when she asked 'How's your poetry?' he told her that it was going to be published. Up to now he had kept this 'proud' and 'vital' secret from everyone except his family. 'It was something to put against my social inadequacy' and 'the heavy weight of Marlborough College'. But Dora was unimpressed. All the boys who write poetry say they are going to be published, she retorted, but they never are. Yes, he insisted, his voice cracking with passion, 'Macmillan's Contemporary Poets. I'm a contemporary poet.' 'I should like a copy,' she said.

When they got to the Roebuck she asked for a whisky and while they were drinking she told him how good her boss was in bed: 'better than you'. He replied, accurately, that they had never been to bed, and she parroted him mockingly 'Never been to bed. Cheers!' At this point, through a stroke of ill luck that Freud would have had no difficulty in explaining, he made a bad mistake. Smiling, he lifted his glass and said 'Bottoms up!' Dora looked shocked, and seemed abstracted for a few moments, and then she enunciated in a loud, slurred voice, 'It all began when you raped me.' Several of the drinkers in the Roebuck that evening knew both of them, and their families, and an awestruck silence fell. 'I didn't,' Golding heard himself croak. 'Up by Rabley Woods,' she continued, 'I didn't want to, I wasn't more than fifteen at the time.' There was a clatter of glasses being replaced on the bar as customers left. It was, he felt, 'the logical, vicious end of a relationship that had begun in vice and prospered viciously'. Outside, she seemed to want to make it up, calling him 'Billy', and asking him to walk her home. 'You can go to hell,' he said.

He saw her only once more. It was years later, during the war. He was on leave from the navy, and with his wife and little son on Marlborough Common. A hundred yards away was another woman with a little boy. 'Isn't that your old girlfriend?' his wife asked. The other woman sat up and waved. It was Dora. 'If I had been different from what I am I might have walked over and said simply "Forgive me for what I was, as I forgive you for what you were."' But he was angry, and felt defensive on behalf of his wife and son, so he turned his back. He heard later that she had divorced and remarried, and gone with her new husband to an American campus.

It is perhaps worth asking why Golding remembered Dora with such hatred. The account in *Men, Women & Now* is not just condemnatory, it defames her to a degree that goes beyond anything he could actually have known. He insists that she was 'depraved by nature'. He imagines her, at the age of thirteen, 'beginning to burn' and 'fingering herself', as she lay in bed listening, through the 'matchboarding wall' to the 'steady crack, crack, crack' of Clayton beating his wife in the next-door bungalow, and the woman's 'shrieks of terror or delight or both'. At fourteen, he imagines, she was already as 'sexy as an ape'. A possible explanation for this need to fashion her into something monstrous is that he cannot forgive her for arousing his own sadism. In *Men, Women & Now* the sight of her whipped bottom is described with lingering precision. He finds it 'loathsomely exciting', and cannot get it out of his mind. Such sights 'burn themselves into the eye and may be examined

ever after, in minute detail. They fade only, I should think, with death.'
He was aware of, and repelled by, the cruelty in himself, and was given
to saying that, had he been born in Hitler's Germany, he would have
been a Nazi. Dora seems to have played her part in this self-knowledge.

Following the Dora story has taken us a little ahead of ourselves. The
unfortunate affair at the Roebuck happened in October 1934, four
months after Golding went down from Oxford. His father's surprised
scrutiny of his two sons and his ex-pupil Dora Spencer through
binoculars had been in the summer vacation of 1933, before Golding's
final year. In the interim he had clearly begun wondering what he would
do when he went down, and he arranged to have an interview with
Oxford University's Appointments Committee, which advised undergraduates about careers. The interview took place on 22 February 1934
and the index card on which his two interviewers jotted down their
impressions survives in the University archives. 'A stout fellow – fat
faced – Not quite', the first writes, 'He's cheerful and probably
ath[letic] – I don't think he has much chance of [a job in] administra-
tion'. 'Not quite', in this context, is Appointments Committee parlance
for 'Not quite a gentleman'. This is borne out by the index card for
Golding's later interview with the same committee in 1937, when he was
back in Oxford doing a Diploma in Education, which states baldly 'Not
quite a gent'. The other interviewer on 22 February 1934 wrote: 'a bit
stout – strong physique – fair hair – On the whole unimpressive and fit
only for day schools', meaning, not fit to be a public-school master.
'N.T.S. with slight accent only. May come on'. 'N.T.S.' was middle-class
slang for 'Not Top Shelf'. This second interviewer saw Golding again
on 18 May and seemed to think two and a half months had improved him
a little: 'A bit dull and heavy – but a nice enough fellow. Attracted by the
Egyptian Educ[ation] service & might apply. A decent sincere man with
a bit of free lance spirit about him'. Readers acquainted with Robert
Graves's achingly funny account of his own experience with the
Egyptian Education service in *Goodbye to All That* may think it fortunate
for Golding that he did not pursue this option. At the bottom of the
card are the interviewers' summaries of reports from Brasenose. The
Vice-Principal, Stallybrass, rates him: 'Not very attractive, but responsible and a good pianist'. Taylor, his tutor, shows more interest: 'No bent

for science – keen on literature and artistic affairs – might get a first in English', and Brett-Smith's favourable report is summarized as 'Worked well and read widely. Recommends'.

He got a second, not the first Taylor thought possible. Of his three friends Charles Allen got a first, Jack Pearce a third, and Adam Bittleston a fourth. In those days all candidates in a Final Honour School had to attend a viva voce examination – that is, they were seated alone before the assembled board of examiners, clad in their academic robes, in an echoing room in the Examination Schools, and formally interrogated about the answers they had given in their written papers. If, as Taylor suggests, Golding was close to a first class, the viva would have been decisive, and in such cases might last up to an hour. Public-school polish and social poise were, of course, advantages in vivas, and Golding, who was far too intelligent not to have known what his Appointments Committee interviewers were thinking about him, would no doubt have felt the same 'social inadequacy' (as he phrased it in the context of Dora and his poetic ambitions), when paraded before a bunch of Oxford dons. This could hardly have improved his performance at the viva, and the feeling that he had not done himself justice lingered. At the age of seventy-two, lying in bed and trying to get to sleep, he found himself composing 'the speech I should have made before my assembled inquisitors at my viva'.

A few years before this, when he was in his mid-sixties, he went to a dinner in Merton College, and was awed by its magnificence compared with Brasenose. He was shown round the medieval library – the oldest in Britain – and the enormous chapel with (as he rather exaggeratedly reports) 'acres of thirteenth-century glass'. It made him realize what a small place Brasenose was. You could, he reflects, fit most of Brasenose into Merton's ante-chapel, and it seems to occur to him that he could have been happier as an undergraduate at Merton. He was probably wrong. As the Appointments Committee cards bear out, he would have been regarded as an inferior anywhere in Oxford. It was a hurtful but valuable experience. His son-in-law Terrell Carver has remarked that Golding was 'interested in humiliation'. It is an interest that runs right through his novels from first to last. What he suffered at Oxford was turned to creative account.

8

Drifting

Golding's interviews with the Appointments Committee did little to clarify his thinking about what he should do after Oxford. He thought of himself as a poet, but could that really provide him with a livelihood? During his years at university he had planned a whole series of major poetic works, but somehow none of them got written. They stayed in his mind as frustrated ambitions or discarded fragments. We know about them only because ten years later, in the run-up to D-Day, when he was aboard his rocket ship and awaiting orders to sail, he wrote in a newly bought notebook, in which he had meant to keep the ship's petty-cash account, the inner history of himself as a poet.

He says that he started writing poetry 'at the age of about seventeen', when he fell 'hideously, beautifully and catastrophically' in love. She was just fifteen, and a fellow pupil at Marlborough Grammar School. At night he would lie in bed desperately trying to forget her. One day a line from the *Golden Treasury* came into his head, so he looked up the sonnet it came from, and burst into tears at its beauty. From that day on it seemed to him that to be a poet would be 'the most glorious thing in the world'. However, the difficulty of finding rhyme-words twisted the sense of what he wrote. Though he was aching with love, he would end up writing 'four lines about an asphodel'.

Clearly the girl he fell in love with was Mollie Evans, whose beautiful neck had disturbed him when he sat behind her in class. Clearly, too, the poems in his VIth-form diary fall into the 'four lines about an asphodel' category. Neither the poems, nor the diary's record of football practice and games of draughts with his male chums, give any inkling that the teenager who penned them was secretly and desperately in love. He could not put the 'queer jealousy and excitement' that Mollie caused him into words, so he was left with an ardent desire to write, but no subject. At Oxford he wrote about Greek mythology, because Keats, whom he admired, had done so. He lived 'a monk-like life in digs', and churned out 'prurient, sentimental muck' about 'the moon and Endymion'. He confesses that he was happy when his schoolfriend Peter Gough died, thinking it would empower him to write a great mythological elegy like Milton's *Lycidas* or Shelley's *Adonais*. But he found, when he tried, that he was incapable of emotion, because his intellect insisted on analysing it, and that destroyed the emotion. He started a tragedy on the theme of Daedalus – the mythological inventor whose son Icarus flies too near the sun with his father's waxen wings, and falls to his death – and managed to write some lines about water-meadows that he felt were quite good. Unfortunately there was no room for water-meadows in the tragedy, since it took place in a cave, and the description of Daedalus's laboratory with its blue lights and retorts was, he feared, too obviously reminiscent of matriculation science. So he ditched it.

His next idea was a narrative poem in four books about Pandora, but he got no further than a description of a male character 'snoozing gently in what was very like the garden of 29 The Green, Marlborough'. After that he decided to write a symphonic poem, vaguely connected, he felt, with Robert Bridges's *Testament of Beauty*. 'The sheer joy of the whole conception' buoyed him up, and he saw it 'luminous' and 'complete' in his mind's eye. But not a word was ever written. So it goes on – a comic catalogue of failure that is also, at some level, a lament for wasted talent. 'Masterpiece after masterpiece' was conceived, 'beautiful and evanescent as ranges of clouds'. They kept him up all night, and 'sometimes I very nearly put pen to paper'. One 'major work' was a fantastic ballet called *The Chimney Falls*, 'a curious blend of mysticism and socialism', about a Mrs Bunce and her son Alfie, who live in the shadow of an enormous factory chimney. Another was a six-volume novel of which he wrote only the first sentence: 'Proverbs are the refuge of the inarticulate.' The notebook in which he records all this is a strange document, facetious and cynical, but also desperate, even hysterical. He thought it probable that he had only a month or two to live, if that, and that he would die with nothing achieved. Though he jokes about his unfinished 'masterpieces', it is not funny.

'Strewn along the short path that I have come', he concludes, 'are the tatters of great conceptions. I might date my life not by the outward signs, the common incidents, but by these fierce disappointments.'

However, he had managed, while at Oxford, to finish some short poems. His friend Adam Bittleston persuaded Macmillan to publish them, and *Poems* by W. G. Golding appeared in the autumn of 1934. Though they came out in the series called Macmillan's Contemporary Poets, they were markedly uncontemporary. T. S. Eliot's *Prufrock and Other Observations* had appeared in 1917; W. H. Auden's first book, *Poems*, in 1930. These two poets changed English poetry, but not in a direction that Golding wanted to follow. Riffling through the slim volumes in Marlborough bookshops he found modern poets being 'cryptic', and he decided there was no point in publishing 'obfuscated verses that only a coterie can understand'. As a result, the thirty lyrics he includes in *Poems* might have been composed in the 1890s. They use archaic diction ('thee', 'thou', 'withouten', 'nay', 'my lady'), and there are echoes of Tennyson, Ernest Dowson and Edward FitzGerald's *Rubaiyat of Omar Khayyam*. What there is not is any trace of William Golding. The gulf between the frustrated, cynical undergraduate and the writer of *Poems* is wide. It is illustrated by the poem 'Summer', which bears the sub-title 'For Sheila', indicating that it was written for the cheerful, promiscuous young woman who shared his bed in her parents' old-folks' home in the summer of 1932.

> At noon the drowsy sun-winds brush
> A shadow from the swarted corn.
> At noon the linnet and the thrush
> Sing dirges for the light of morn.
> And Oh! I think our world is dead
> So much is fallen, so much fled.
>
> At eve the larks leap in the sky
> And sing between the cloudy bars,
> At dusk the nightingale awakes,
> And pines upon the restless stars—
> And I could lie and close my eyes,
> And cry for you as a child cries.

That is perfectly respectable Georgian poetry, but it could have been written by almost anyone. All the realities of his affair with Sheila – rescuing her from a gents lavatory, their drunken escapade with the cherry brandy – are erased, because Golding, in 1934, does not believe poetry ought to mention such things.

He showed this poem to Sheila when they met in London, after he had raised money on the books that he had got on credit from Thornton's, and he thought that was why she told him that evening about her affairs with other men. It was to warn him not to depend on her. Remembering the occasion thirty years later, he quotes the poem's last two lines, and comments, 'It wasn't true, of course – except in the minimal sense that I yearned even for her minimal security; and she knew it wasn't true.' We should not miss the 'except' there. Behind the vague sorrows of *Poems* lay something real – the insecurity of a twenty-three-year-old who was facing the terrifying prospect of earning his own living, and could see no place for himself in the world. He felt he had abilities that set him apart, but Oxford had told him only that he was socially and academically inferior.

He had to wait some weeks before *Poems* received its first and only review. In the *Times Literary Supplement* of 7 February 1935, under the heading 'Some Modern Poets', it was briefly noticed along with five other collections. The anonymous reviewer compared Golding unfavourably with Miss Yvonne Ffrench, whose collection *Amazons* was his favourite. For a young man who had set such store by his poetic gifts, this must have been a bitter anticlimax, and it put paid to his chances of a poetic career. In May 1937 he offered to send Macmillan a second batch of poems ('of about twice the size, and, I hope, of at least twice the quality of the first volume'), but they were 'no longer interested'.

So what should he do? One possibility was that he might become a professional actor, and in his first years in London after coming down from Oxford he tried to gain some theatrical experience. Little is known about this. No playbills or programmes survive. When I asked him about it in an interview in 1984 he said that he had been given parts at the Little Theatre in Hampstead and the Citizens' Theatre in Bath, 'but it was very, very much fringe, and I was a sort of occasional hanger-on ... It was very, very trivial sort of spear-carrying.' He told

John Mortimer that he had acted in plays by Noël Coward, and played Danny, the central character in Emlyn Williams's *Night Must Fall* – a psychopath who keeps a head in a hatbox. What was he like as an actor? I have met only two people who saw him on stage. Both saw him in amateur productions, not the professional theatre, and one was too young at the time to remember whether he played Prospero or Caliban. The other was more discerning. This was Terence Barnes, senior English master at Bishop Wordsworth's School, Salisbury, and Golding's colleague for many years. He remembered him writing and acting in an adaptation of Chaucer's *Pardoner's Tale* which was produced twice, once at the school and once at Longford Castle. Golding played the narrator, and 'when you saw him on stage you were aware of an almost hysterical release of energy'. The other time he saw him was as the Clown in *The Winter's Tale* – an open-air production with the local Phoenix Players. 'I shall never forget Bill's first entrance: it was simply explosive. Though in a minor part, he dominated the whole show.' He used his acting skills in everyday life, or so it seemed to his brother-in-law Richard Brookfield. He found Golding 'a very multi-faceted person'. He 'didn't want to reveal himself too much. That's why he developed so many facets.' It was impossible to be sure what his central core was. Even when he played cricket he 'exhibited a sense of style like a professional cricketer at the crease'. His life was acting. But his experience of the stage showed he could not make acting his life.

Then there was the possibility that he might earn his living as a pianist. Quite late in life, in his journal, he reflects that he would have sold his soul to Mephistopheles to have been a concert pianist. But he also recounts there the series of events that made him realize it was impossible. He had moved to London in 1935, presumably because that was the likeliest place to find work as an actor, and, thanks to Adam Bittleston, had been given a room in the headquarters of the Christian Community at 1001 Finchley Road, which functioned as a rudimentary guest-house. Several times a week there was a service in the chapel (actually the converted front room), and he would play the piano on these occasions. The high priest of the Community was Alfred Heidenreich (whose book *Growing Point* tells the story of the

Community's foundation) and he nurtured the hope that young Golding's piano playing might be good enough to make him a financial asset to the struggling band of anthroposophists in his care. 'I want you to play something longer today', he told his young protégé one morning. 'Someone is coming and I want him to hear you. Do your best.' At the appointed hour an elegant, willowy young man arrived and seated himself in the congregation. Golding recognized him instantly. He was called Ian Aulay, and less than a year earlier their paths had crossed in singularly unhappy circumstances. Aulay had been giving a recital at the Wigmore Hall, which Golding attended. Arriving at the hall he had made his way to the inner door, where he found two people, the manager of the hall in a dinner jacket and a young man in full evening dress who was bemoaning to the manager the fact that no one recognized him. Without thinking, Golding handed his ticket to this young man to be torn in half. Of course, it was Aulay, and as he made his way to his seat he heard the affronted instrumentalist saying in 'tragic and exasperated tones' to the manager 'You see?' The hall was four-fifths empty, and the recital was competent, but no better than hundreds of young pianists could have done.

It occurred to Golding that his faux pas over the ticket must have helped to bring home to poor Aulay that 'the bright lights of the concert world were not for him'. Now here he was, sitting in the congregation, and waiting for Golding to play Beethoven's Opus 110. It was evident Aulay had recognized him – 'I saw him catch sight of me at the piano, and waver' – and, with the memory of Aulay's undistinguished but competent playing in his ears, he performed 'disastrously', and 'knew myself for the rank bad amateur I was'. Aulay left quickly after the service, but what he said to Heidenreich before he went plainly exploded any hopes of a profitable musical career for the Community's young accompanist.

In the autumn of 1935 he left the Christian Community house in Finchley Road and took up his first teaching post at Michael Hall, a co-educational Steiner school in Streatham, Surrey. Since he had no teaching qualifications, it was presumably Bittleston's influence that got him the job. But his reputation as a virtuoso pianist probably helped, and evidently survived Ian Aulay's thumbs-down. Writing later about how great pianists like Rubinstein get away with making 'splurging impressive noises', though they do not actually play the right notes, he recalls doing the same thing himself at a concert at Michael Hall, where he played Carl Tausig's arrangement of the D minor toccata and fugue 'to the admiration of the groundlings and the fury of the music mistress'.

Michael Hall had been founded in 1935 by a group of ladies who were interested in Steiner's ideas. One of them, Daphne Olivier, had gone to a lecture Steiner gave in Torquay, and consulted him afterwards about setting up a school. He said she would need a man's help, so she got her husband Cecil Harwood involved. He was an anthroposophist and had been on the fringe of the Inklings, the group of Christian fantasists, including J. R. R. Tolkien and C. S. Lewis, who used to meet at the Eagle and Child pub in Oxford for beer and manly chat. The school occupied two big Victorian houses with gardens and tennis courts at the back. A middle section had been built between them to provide a school hall with a chemistry lab above it which housed the school piano, on which Golding played. Funding seems to have come from wealthy, high-minded local families. Harwood was in effect the headmaster, though officially all the teachers were free spirits and a company of equals. Within the school there were no exams, grades or placings. It was idealistically non-competitive, though pupils sat the usual public examinations. There were about 200 boys and girls, with boarders as well as day-pupils. One boy who was there during Golding's time remembers him having 'enormous enthusiasm and lots of fire'. He was short tempered and had difficulty keeping order, so he hit on a winning formula. The lessons were forty minutes long, and if the pupils tried really hard in the first half he would tell them a story in the second half. He could create stories with no apparent effort, 'terrifying tales of magicians and sorcerers' with 'vivid language', though they were sometimes hard to follow.

One of his duties, as he recalls in an unpublished section of *Scenes From A Life*, was to accompany various musicians who came to give free concerts, and this led to several episodes that made him feel low and incompetent. A horn player expected him to sight-read a piano version of the Strauss Horn Concerto, and a violinist who played at

Glyndebourne was disparaging when she found he could not manage the final allegro of a Bach harpsichord and violin sonata. 'I shall never play with you again,' she declared icily. Worse was a concert with a cellist during which, when he flipped over the page of his score, the whole thing disintegrated, sending a cascade of sheets in all directions. One disappeared into the bowels of the grand piano and he was obliged to leave his seat and scrabble for it. The bewildered artist stopped playing her cadenza and, in the shocked silence, was heard inquiring plaintively, 'What has happened? What has happened?'

Golding embroiders these episodes to reinforce his impression of Michael Hall as a farcical place. His opinion of Steinerites plummeted as he learnt more about them and their beliefs. He gives an irreverent account of a typical service in the Finchley Road chapel. The congregation would consist of a few old ladies, and High Priest Heidenreich would make his entrance 'wearing pastel robes and a rather Japaneseish hat'. A server, also in pastel robes, followed. Heidenreich would stand with his back to the altar, his left arm stretched sideways and his right pointing upwards, like a 'lightning conductor for whatever it was that had to shin down him'. Addressing the server, he would pronounce the words 'Christ – in – you', with an impressiveness that was almost threatening, and, maintaining his celestial point-duty pose, would proceed to look meaningfully at each member of the congregation in turn, while 'giving a series of little bobs with his head like a woodpecker'. Golding was always the last to be bobbed at, and he felt more and more, as time went on, that Heidenreich despaired of him – as indeed he had reason to do, for Golding was finding the 'outrageous complications' and the 'calm assertions of universal knowledge' that Steinerism entailed increasingly difficult to swallow.

The general level of education among the teachers at Michael Hall was, he judged, 'abysmal', but they resented any suggestion that they did not have sole access to truth. He recalled how, at a weekly staff meeting, Harwood had recommended one of C. S. Lewis's early books, remarking that it was wonderful to read something by a man who was not an anthroposophist, yet wrote things with which all anthroposophists could agree. There was an appalled silence. Every face registered outrage, indignation and fear. For Harwood's careless comment had threatened 'their reason for existing, their unique grasp of a million universal truths'. While Golding was still living in 1001 Finchley Road, Bittleston, who was ordained a priest in the Christian Community in 1935, had commissioned him to write a verse-drama along Steineresque lines, and it was produced and performed by members of the Community. Entitled *A Play of Persephone* it is a version of the classical Persephone legend. Its message is that 'human life is sick' because Demeter's 'ways of wisdom' have been abandoned. A 'Sun-Hero' comes on at the end to redeem the world from selfishness, warfare and other ills. From a literary angle the main influence is Milton's *Comus*, and the Golding archive contains an edition of Milton's earlier poems, including *Comus*, which is stamped on the title page 'The New School, 40 Leigham Court Road, Streatham, SW 16'. The New School was what Michael Hall was originally called, so it seems likely this is the copy Golding used when writing his play and for some reason failed to return to the school library.

The 'terrifying tales of magicians and sorcerers' he quietened his unruly pupils with would have been more worth having, but have not survived. Perhaps, though, we can get an idea of what they were like from a story he made up around this time while on a walking holiday in Wales. Forty years later he was still trying to work it into a publishable form, though he never did. He called it *The Mountain Ash*, and it is about a shepherd boy whose tribe lives on a plain between the sea and the mountains. He drives his flock to the highest pasture, from which the plain looks so small that he can cover it with his hand. So he takes a flint as his orb and a bulrush as his sceptre and a twist of creeper as his crown, and goes down to his tribe and tells them he is their king. They build a hall for him and he sits in state. But the climate changes. The summers grow shorter; ice encroaches. The tribe decide to cross the mountains to reach a warmer land, and they invite the king to come too, but he angrily refuses. So he remains in his hall alone, year after year, waited on by a tribe of shadows, while his beard and hair grow long and the hall fills with cobwebs. One day, with a noise like thunder, a glacier breaks into the hall, and where the door had been 'sparkled a blue and white cliff of ice'. So at last he decides to follow the tribe across the mountain. But it is too late. Near the top, exhausted, he clings to the rock, his fingers and toes thrust into crevices. The snow falls, and his limbs grow warped and rough. After many years the ice age passes. The ice cliff falls into the sea and floats away. Spring comes. Where the king hung is now a mountain ash, its roots in the rock crevices. It bears red berries in autumn, and one day a bird on its way to the warm south stops to feed in its branches.

We do not know who Golding made this story up for. Perhaps just for himself. But if it was for someone else it was probably Mollie Evans, who was the most important woman in his life throughout the 1930s. During and after his Oxford years their relationship grew closer, and it seems that he felt guilty about being away from her so much. He dreamed years later that he was being angrily interrogated by his brother Jose about leaving Mollie and going off to live in London. According to his young cousin Eileen, who was living at 29 The Green, and was a schoolfriend of Mollie's, on the occasions when he was back in Marlborough he would see her mostly at her parents' home in Great Bedwyn. He told his daughter Judy that he had once walked all night through Savernake Forest, arriving at Mollie's parents' cottage in the morning. She had leant wanly out of an upstairs window while her parents talked to him and, though he did not understand it at the time, he realized later that she must have been having her period. That was probably of more than theoretical interest to him. Another of his bad dreams, years afterwards, was that Mollie was going to have a baby and he would have to marry her. Writing about her in *Men, Women & Now* he says that she was sexually frigid, but evidently this did not prevent a physical relationship developing. At some point in the 1930s they became formally engaged, and he gave her a ring. Eileen thinks this was the result of pressure from Mollie's parents. There was a subtle class difference between the Goldings and the Evanses. The Evanses, who kept the bakery at Great Bedwyn, probably had more money, and they had a car before Alec got one. But, as shopkeepers, they were a notch or two below the Goldings on the minutely calibrated scale of class that operated at the time. This did not affect the Goldings' view of Mollie. They liked her and wanted their son to marry her. But perhaps it made the Evanses wary about Mollie being taken advantage of without a formal engagement.

Being engaged seems to have renewed Golding's concern about how he would earn his living. He felt happy when making up stories. On his Welsh walking holiday *The Mountain Ash* was 'the kind of thing that kept me a few inches above the ground as I cantered along, looking inward'. Could he, perhaps, become a novelist? On 1 July 1936 he sent a letter to Macmillan from Michael Hall:

Dear Sir,

About eighteen months ago you published a first volume of my verses. I have now nearly finished a novel, and wish to know;

    a) whether I can use any of these verses in it – since I suppose you hold the copyright

    b) whether you publish novels – since I propose to submit it for your consideration, when finished.

Yours sincerely,

W. G. Golding

It seems likely the novel he refers to is *The Mountain Ash*, for his journals, though full of reminiscence, mention no other fictional work from this period. The approach to Macmillan evidently came to nothing, but he did not give up his literary ambitions. In the summer of 1937 Harwood's wife Daphne Olivier wrote, on Golding's behalf, to the novelist David Garnett, asking how one might make a living by writing. David 'Bunny' Garnett had come to prominence with the fantasy-novel *Lady Into Fox* (1922). As a member of the Bloomsbury Group he was the kind of literary figure Golding came to hate, and in response to Daphne Olivier's inquiry he wrote her young protégé an offhand and flippant letter. Reviewing, he warned, was not a good job, though easy enough to get. All one had to do was walk into the *New Statesman* office, 'express youthful aspirations and smile at Raymond Mortimer'. Alternatively there was the new magazine *Night and Day* ('an imitation *New Yorker*') which needed a 'funny, angry' man to write for it. 'But the chance of your being a funny, angry man is slight, probably you are as milk and water as I am.' Golding evidently decided that a teaching qualification would be a surer bet, and in 1937 he went back to Brasenose to read for the Oxford Diploma in Education.

The Diploma was a one-year course with a term's teaching practice in the middle of it, and he did his teaching practice at Bishop Wordsworth's School, Salisbury. Whether he chose it or it was chosen for him is not known, but it was to be crucially important for his imaginative life. It had been founded in 1890 by John Wordsworth, Bishop of Salisbury (whose grandfather was the poet William Wordsworth's brother), and it had buildings in the cathedral close. 'My idea', Wordsworth explained, 'has been to found a school, open to parents of very modest incomes, in which boys could acquire some of the tone and spirit of one of the old public schools.' In 1927 Frederick Happold, from the staff of the Perse School in Cambridge, was appointed headmaster, and rapidly improved its status and reputation. Between 1931 and 1933 he raised money to extend its buildings and playing fields, and in 1936 he was elected to the Headmasters' Conference, making Bishop Wordsworth's nominally a public school. A Cambridge graduate with progressive ideas, he wanted to develop a meritocracy (he wrote a book called *Towards a New Aristocracy*), and he started a choral society, a school orchestra, a drama society called The Bishop's Players, and a body called the Company of Honour and Service, which was designed to train boys to be more socially aware. Melbourne University made him an honorary LLD for his educational work, and although he attracted jealousy and mockery from some of his staff, he was the first person to realize what an exceptional person William Golding was.

In that respect he differed from the staff of the Oxford University Appointments Committee. On 20 October 1937, at the start of his DipEd year, Golding was interviewed by a member of the committee, as he had been while an undergraduate, and the verdict, though less negative than before, still saw him as limited in his opportunities by his social class:

> Day school type. Mature. Wide experience. Qualifications wide and interesting. Not quite a gent but good enough for all day schools. Speaks up well. No accent. Took to school teaching as a pis aller from the dramatic line, but now likes it. Keen also on RAF and AEC. Quite a likeable, sensible man.

A note on the card reads '1938 B Mus (1st part) Piano viola violin cello'. The Oxford Bachelor of Music was a post-graduate degree which required candidates to sit two examinations and submit an original composition, but there is no evidence in the university archive that Golding was ever a candidate for it, and it seems possible he mentioned it to the Appointments Committee as something he was planning to do. One piece of evidence that happens to survive tells us that he was active musically during his teaching-practice term not only in the school but beyond. A 1938 programme for a Salisbury Musical and Orchestral Society Concert, conducted by Sir Adrian Boult, lists W. G. Golding among the cellists.

He passed the DipEd exams in June 1938 but he seems never to have submitted the 'Certificate of Efficiency' which was required for the award of the Diploma. This certificate was a statement by the head of the teaching-practice school that the candidate was 'efficient as a teacher and as a disciplinarian'. Perhaps Happold felt unable to supply it, despite his admiration for his young trainee teacher. He had had difficulty keeping order at Michael Hall, and Judy Carver believes that once after the war, when her father was teaching at Bishop Wordsworth's, there was a rumpus in his class and Happold came in and ticked the boys off, saying that they should respect Golding because he was highly thought of in the world outside. So disciplinary difficulties may have arisen during his teaching practice. At all events, it seems he did not, strictly, complete his DipEd, and there is no date of issue for the Diploma on his record card in the university archive.

In September 1938 he applied for, and got, a teaching job at Maidstone Grammar School for Boys, in Kent. His application was successful chiefly, Judy Carver thinks, because he had paper qualifications in music, allowing the school to say they had a qualified supervisor for their first-ever music candidate for the Higher Certificate of Education (the equivalent of today's A-level). In fact he did not have any university qualification in music, but the piano exams he had passed under Miss Salisbury's instruction were evidently considered sufficient. Maidstone Grammar School, founded in 1549, was several steps above Bishop Wordsworth's, socially and educationally. Michael Tillett, the music student Golding was hired to coach, remembers him as 'sociable, gregarious, active, energetic, often at the centre of a knot of interested schoolboys'. He was rather scruffy, and did not wear a gown like the other masters, just a sports jacket. He taught English and co-operated on a production of *Julius Caesar* in which Caesar's assassination was preceded by an initially soft but gradually increasing drum-roll to create an atmosphere of menace – then there was silence and the sound of Caesar's body falling backwards with a thump from the high point on the stage where he had been standing. As well as thinking up this stage-effect, Golding taught the boy who played Caesar how to fall backwards without hurting himself. A programme and cast list for the production in March 1939 survives, naming the producers as Mr J. C. B. Carter, the senior English master, and Mr W. G. Golding. A boy who was in the audience recalls that for him and his friends the highlight of the production was the moment Golding, who was taking applause at the end, turned round and applauded the cast, 'and we spotted a hole in his trousers with a little round patch of white'.

This should remind us, to digress for a moment, that Golding was not scruffy just from choice. He was hard up all through the 1930s, and had never been good at managing his finances. Most of the letters in his college file at Brasenose are reminders from the bursar that he has not paid his battels, together with demands that he should do so forthwith. Once or twice they are accompanied by replies from Golding, expressing surprise and disbelief at the sums involved. The college's letters become noticeably terser as time goes on, modulating from 'Dear Golding' to 'Dear Sir' and from 'Yours sincerely' to 'Yours faithfully', and omitting the 'Esq.' after his name. He was still in debt to the college to the tune of £22 18s 5d after completing his Diploma in Education in the summer of 1938, and on 8 November the bursar sent a brief demand for payment 'by return' to 5 St Thomas' Square, Salisbury, the digs he had taken during his teaching practice at Bishop Wordsworth's School. By the time this letter had been forwarded to him, a second demand was on its way, addressed to his Maidstone digs at 53 Hastings Road. Golding's reply, sent on 11 December, explains that the first letter was delayed and asks the bursar to 'consider the following facts':

> My father wished to keep me at Oxford during last year, while I was getting the Diploma of Education. He was ready, and as far as I know is still ready, to pay the amount owing; but I wished if I

could to pay for at least the last term myself. As however I have been teaching for only three months, and have about £9 to pay to Messrs. Truman and Knightley for finding me this post, I simply have not the money to pay you the full amount. I can of course ask my father to fulfil the over-generous promise that he made; but I feel personally, to put it frankly, that BNC can afford to wait longer for payment than he can.

I shall be glad therefore if you will allow me to pay off this debt in instalments.

If that is agreeable, would you be good enough to suggest some arrangement?

The bursar replied that he did not 'agree entirely' with the view that the college could afford to wait, but promised to see what might be done if Golding would advise him what instalments he could produce and when. There is nothing on the file to show whether he received any reply to this offer, but certainly no instalments were paid, and the bursar continued to pursue his quarry throughout the Second World War. In February 1941 he wrote to the headmaster of Maidstone Grammar School, only to be told that Golding was now in the Royal Navy on active service. Undeterred, he wrote to the headmaster of Bishop Wordsworth's in 1943, and received the same reply. By the end of that year the debt the college was labouring under had soared (presumably through the addition of interest) to £23 11s 9d Golding eventually paid up on 6 June 1957.

So much for the hole in his trousers in March 1939 and its financial context. Everyone's recollections of his time at Maidstone suggest that he was a popular, keen young schoolmaster who gave of his best both in and out of the classroom. Tillett remembers that in a school concert in 1938 he played the part of 'The Dude' in the sketch 'The 'Ole in the Road', in immaculate evening dress with a white silk scarf. In the 1938 Christmas concert, which was a sort of pantomime, he played Snow White, wearing long blond plaits, and was, according to his brother-in-law Richard Brookfield, an 'outstanding success', though 'rather coy' in the part. Subsequently his nickname in the school was Goldilocks.

But he was far from being treated as a joke. His status as a published poet attracted interest among the literary-minded – a copy of his 1934 *Poems* circulated around the VIth form – and, most importantly in a boys' school, he was good at games. In a cricket match between the School and Mr Kemp's XI on 21 June 1939 he took three wickets, including that of the School XI captain, bowling 'respectable leg-breaks', and scored 7, batting low in the order. A memory treasured by the novelist John Stroud was that when he was a pupil at Maidstone he 'bowled a nippy in-swinger into the midriff of his English teacher William Golding'. When autumn came he showed his prowess on the rugby field. By this time the war had started and travel to other schools was difficult, so a team of masters and boys played against local army units. On 14 October 1939 he played in the scrum against 336 Company Royal Engineers. The school won 11–6.

Michael Tillett, who later became director of music at Rugby, could not remember much about Golding as a music teacher, except that when he wrote an essay on the symphonies of Sibelius ('brilliant, I thought') Golding returned it with a mark of 13/20 and the comment 'Good'. But the new master did get together and direct a small choir which had three basses (Tillett was one), and at a Christmas carol concert they performed a Golding arrangement of 'Adam Lay Ybounden'. The setting for the phrase 'Four thousand winters' was long remembered by its bass performers, but the arrangement unfortunately contained some consecutive fifths, spotted by other staff because the composer wrote the music up on the blackboard, where it stayed until they had memorized it.

By the autumn of 1938 few people believed that war with Hitler's Germany could be avoided, and the young throughout Europe became increasingly politicized. Golding joined the Left Book Club, founded in 1936 by Victor Gollancz, which had 57,000 members by the outbreak of war, and 1,500 Left Discussion Groups scattered throughout the country. Another sign of his developing social conscience was that he started teaching evening classes at Maidstone jail, 'trying to keep the place alive, I suppose', as he later put it, though 'it was more or less the three Rs because most of the prisoners were illiterate'. Soon after taking up his appointment at Maidstone, he met a radiantly beautiful young woman at a Left Book Club meeting in London and, so family tradition has it, they walked away from the meeting talking animatedly in French. Her name was Ann Brookfield and, it turned out, she lived in Maidstone.

In social terms she was a cut above Golding (and, of course, Mollie), which may have made her more desirable. She had 'fancy boyfriends with cars'. A photograph taken in 1935 shows her on a boat on the Rhine, surrounded by four admiring German soldiers. The Brookfield family owned a high-class grocery shop, Ibberson and Wood, in Lower Stone Street, Maidstone, and were well known in the town. Earlier in 1938 they had suffered two tragic blows. Ann's father had died of cancer, and her brother Norman had been killed in Spain. He had been a very bright boy, but would not go to university because he thought it unfair when the poor could not afford to. Instead he passed Higher Certificate Spanish in a single year, joined the Communist Party, and went to Spain with the International Brigade. He died in the Battle of the Ebro, and his body was never found.

Ann, born in September 1912, was a year younger than Golding. At Maidstone Grammar School for Girls she had been good at everything, especially maths. By the time she was seven she was in a class for nine-year-olds, so she was made to repeat two years, and this killed her desire to learn. She did not complete her matriculation or get a county scholarship, but left school and went to Reeds paper mill as an analytical chemist. She took evening classes in chemistry, which her daughter thinks may have been run by London University. Sports mad, she organized hockey teams at Reeds, and played hockey for Kent. She loved cricket too. Her brother Richard remembers that in politics she was fiercely leftist. He was shocked by her emphatic opposition to private charity. It was the state's responsibility to look after people, she said, and private charity just shored up the status quo. Her intransigence upset her mother, but Golding seemed to accept it quite meekly – though Richard suspected he did not really go along with it. Ann struck her brother as very ambitious: 'she'd have liked a theatrical career if she'd had the talent and training'. After the war, in Salisbury, she shone in Studio Theatre productions, among them Aldous Huxley's *The Gioconda Smile*. She was a rebel, and a trail-blazer for her younger siblings. When her parents issued an ultimatum about coming home late she confronted them and they had to back down. Altogether she was a 'competent and formidable person'.

There were ten Brookfield children in all and most of them, like Ann and Norman, were on the left in politics. The family was renowned for its Communist Party sympathies. It was said that they had once stood outside the headquarters of the local Conservatives singing 'The Red Flag'. Ann's younger sisters, Joan, Nancy and Betty, all married staunchly left-wing husbands. Golding later wrote that no one in his and Ann's generation could fail to be influenced by Marxism. Further, the imminence of a European war, and the high probability they would not survive it, gave them all a sort of desperate freedom from care. Their generation had 'no discernible future', so what they did outside of politics 'did not seem to matter'.

In this mood he took two momentous steps. 'I ditched the girl I was going to marry and married Ann instead.' This terse summary of what happened comes from an unpublished manuscript that he wrote, probably between October 1968 and January 1969. It occupies only a few pages in a notebook, and has no title (its opening words are 'It was 1940'), and its tone, as the above quotation suggests, is brutally self-accusing. The way he had treated Mollie weighed on his conscience. Forty years later he was still haunted by guilty dreams. In one, he finds her naked corpse at 29 The Green and tries to bind her wrists together so that he can drag her out and bury her in the garden. But they are stiff with rigor mortis.

How Mollie felt we can only guess. Eileen records that she was 'terribly hurt'. She never married, and there was a poignant incident some eight years later when Eileen, now grown up, and something of a second mother to the two young Golding children, David and Judy, had taken them to Smith's in Marlborough High Street to change some library books. When they got there, Mollie was just coming out. It must, Eileen felt, have been heart-rending for her, because they were lovely children to look at, Judy with golden hair, David with a 'sort of joyous, fresh, "Isn't the world thrilling?" look'. Eileen had each of them by the hand, and she and Mollie said hello. Then Mollie said 'Are these Bill's children?' and Eileen said they were. In *Free Fall* Mollie becomes Beatrice, who goes mad after being deserted by

Sammy Mountjoy. Whether the real Mollie suffered some kind of breakdown, Eileen did not know. But in *Men, Women & Now* Golding went out of his way to point to madness in Mollie's family, which may suggest that her mind did give way for a time.

His parents were mortified when he threw her over, and refused to come to his wedding. Mollie had been a pupil of Alec's, so he felt protective. He remembered her as a bright girl, good at languages, not the pretty, unthinking creature Golding describes in *Men, Women & Now*. Ann and Golding escaped briefly from the upset in the summer of 1939 and went to France for a holiday. It seems he had been to France once before, possibly in the summer of 1930 when he left school. He reminisced about travelling south on an overnight train, sitting up on an old-style wooden seat, and meeting communists in the Savoy mountains. On the 1939 trip he and Ann visited Chartres cathedral, which, Ann told her daughter, was 'good for hangovers' because of the dim light. They had little money to spare and stayed in the cheapest hotels – the kind, Golding recalled, that the Germans call *Stunden Zimmer*, rooms by the hour. Ann had an engagement ring, but not one he had given her. Like him, she was already engaged when they met. Her fiancé was in Malaya and returned to England only after she had married, and after Golding had gone off to join the navy. What must have been a rather awkward meeting between her and her ex-fiancé took place in the drawing room at 29 The Green, where she was staying with the Golding parents, and she handed back his ring. But she had it on her French holiday, whereas Golding had told Mollie to keep hers – a detail reversed in one of his guilty dreams about her, where she gives him back a ring – 'It is huge, silver. The top opens to reveal three artificial roses of precious metals.' This dream came fifty years after he had left her.

Ann and he were married in Maidstone register office on 30 September 1939, four weeks after the declaration of war and five months after they had first met. He was so hard up that Ann had to pay half the cost of her wedding ring. When they joked about it in later life he would invariably say, 'Gosh! Did I really pay half?' Poverty and insecurity were not funny at the time, and this was brought home by two events that happened in quick succession. Ann fell pregnant and Golding lost his job. The pregnancy was unplanned. 'I did not consciously set out to beget a child,' he records in his self-accusing manuscript, 'but to fuck an extremely pretty girl who liked it' (as opposed, the implication is, to 'frigid' Mollie who did not). They had not bothered with birth control, 'I partly from carelessness and partly because I believed from previous encounters that I was sterile.' Why he was sacked from Maidstone Grammar School is less clear, but he says that it was for 'an unacademic combination of drink, women and politics'. How far back his drink problem went is uncertain, but this seems to be the first time it caused real trouble, and others beside the school staff noticed it. Ann's mother took against her future son-in-law because he drank.

Freddie Happold came to the rescue by inviting him to come back and take up a teaching post at Bishop Wordsworth's School, and he started there in April 1940. John Browning, then a senior boy and later a master at the school, told me that Golding 'made no impact at all; he was totally insignificant'. Others, lower down the school, remember his working on *Julius Caesar* with them, especially the mob scenes and the murder of Caesar. John Hughes, who was fourteen at the time, recalls 'this somewhat dishevelled new man' arriving, and telling the class to imagine they were a riotous mob. He sent them to the back of the hall, by the wall-bars, and told them to rush towards him yelling and scream-ing as hard as they could. After their first attempt he told them they were hopeless nincompoops and ninnies, with no notion of the kind of tension and aggression a bloodthirsty mob would have. Their second attempt was not much better, he said. He showed them appropriate facial expressions for someone in a murderous frame of mind, and told them to imagine they were going to kill someone with a dagger. 'How would you do it?' They held up the dagger in the classic, over-arm pose, but he showed them that you must thrust the dagger up into the belly and rip it open. 'This', Hughes thought, 'was very impressive.' Another old pupil remembers that Golding brought his dramatic expertise to bear upon a production of *Oedipus Rex* in December 1940, before leaving to join the navy.

At this time too, if not earlier, during his teaching-practice term, he came to know two of the other masters who were to be lifelong friends. One was John Milne, the other Tony Brown. Milne was a flautist and a pianist, and had been something of a musical star when he was up at Oxford. He joined the navy at the same time as Golding, but Brown, who had had polio as a child, and walked with a slight limp, was unfit for military service and stayed on at the school during the war. Five years older than Golding, he was an outstanding pianist and organist and, his daughter Sally remembers, 'quite a good bassoonist as well'. His and Milne's musical gifts aroused Golding's profound admiration as well as his sense of inferiority. Brown, who had recently married, had a flat in Salisbury at 27A The Canal, but the Goldings rented a cottage called Little Thatch in the village of Bowerchalke, nine miles from Salisbury, to which, after various vicissitudes, they were to return after the war.

Their child was expected at the end of August, but when the birth was a fortnight overdue it was decided that labour should be induced. It was a long and difficult delivery, but on 9 September 1940 Ann bore a son. He was, Golding recalls, 'small and weak and she had to feed him every three hours'. Then, a few days after the birth, the doctor told her that her son had *talipes equinovarus*, the medical name for club foot. In the untitled manuscript Golding is intent on recording his feelings towards his son right from the start, with absolute honesty, in order to trace the origins of the difficulties between them. When Ann told him what the doctor had said, he writes:

> My first reaction was one of terror and great pity for Ann. This feeling was subsumed in the feeling that we, or if you like I, had joined the twilight ranks of those afflicted people I had tended to avoid, those with factual but uncommunicable tragedies of madness or deformity.

They decided to give their son just one name, David – unusual at the time when most children in their social class had two or three. They told themselves that they did this because they were no-nonsense people, unconcerned about family and inheritance. But Golding wonders how far it also expressed his 'desire to inflict a deprivation on the baby that I resented'. The resentment was 'inextricably mixed into my natural love and pride'; nevertheless it was there:

Just as a child who looks forward to a present, then finds it inadequate, will resent the giver, so I resented the sudden decline from prospect of a healthy athletic son to prospect of a cripple.

To look ahead for a moment, David did not become a cripple, as the manuscript goes on to explain. Thanks to the expertise of the doctors and Ann's resolution to do all she could for her son and her husband, the condition was cured. But it took years of difficult wartime journeys and long waits in dirty, crowded clinics. At first David had to have both feet splinted together, then he wore special orthopaedic boots. Ann, left behind in Bowerchalke when her husband joined up, felt isolated. She was miles from her own family in Maidstone, it was wartime, and there wasn't even a telephone.

She moved into the Old Vicarage with John Milne's wife, and Little Thatch was sub-let to a Colonel and Mrs Walker (who renamed it Ebble Thatch because the River Ebble ran past the bottom of the garden). When Ann wanted to move back, Mrs Walker pleaded that they should be allowed to stay, as she had not been able to have children and was now pregnant and was forbidden to move. Ann gave way, and Golding later indignantly complained that the Walkers proceeded to buy Ebble Thatch 'behind our backs', while 'we were homeless'. In fact it seems that the owner of the cottage, before negotiating with the Walkers, gave the Goldings the chance to buy it, but they had 'no capital at all and precious little income', so could not. Golding's unreasonable fury is an indication of how much his years of poverty rankled, rather than an indictment of the Walkers.

Excluded from the cottage, Ann and her little boy went to live at 29 The Green with Golding's parents, whose natural goodness and generosity were aroused by their grandson's misfortune. Getting to know Ann helped to reconcile them to their son's marriage, though they were not persuaded that his leaving Mollie had been the right course until much later. Eileen, who became the Goldings' adopted daughter, takes the credit for this. She eventually convinced them that Mollie would have been quite wrong for Golding. She was 'very sweet and very nice but a bit of a doormat', and if he had married her, she told them, he would never have written the novels. By contrast, Ann's toughness and determination were to help her cope with being Golding's wife, and they also saw her through the ordeal of curing David's disability. Tony Brown's son Tim told me of an incident that illustrates this, and that seemed strange and even cruel to him at the time. David was briefly a pupil at Salisbury Cathedral School, which Tim attended, and he remembers sitting in the cricket pavilion with Ann and his own mother watching David running in a race, 'although he had what I thought of at the time as a club foot, or a gammy foot of some sort'. Ann was urging him on and shouting 'Don't look back!' When the Browns discussed it at home they thought it odd that David, being lame, should run in a race at all. But that he did so is an index of Ann's resolve that her son should be healthy and normal.

9

The War

The Second World War changed the lives of everyone who lived through it. In *Men, Women & Now* Golding records that, for him, it brought about 'a sort of religious convulsion which is not uncommon among people of a passionate and morbid habit'. It gave him, for the first time, 'a kind of framework of principles which I still hold mainly, even when I am untrue to them', and it made him see the 'viciousness' and 'cruelty', not so much of the Nazis, as of his own youth. 'I have always understood the Nazis because I am of that sort by nature.' He adds that it was 'partly out of that sad self-knowledge' that he wrote *Lord of the Flies*.

He learnt other things about himself during the war, among them that he could think clearly and act courageously even when terrified. On the day war broke out, his brother-in-law Richard Brookfield recalls, the air-raid sirens sounded in Maidstone directly after Prime Minister Chamberlain's broadcast. There was a brief panic, but Golding quietened everyone down. 'Let's be calm about this', he advised, 'Let's play something'. So, at 11 o'clock on a Sunday morning, they sat down and played bridge. Later in the war he found out 'what a breath-shortening, heart-thumping situation it is to go into battle from cold'. But he could control his fear, he found, by assuming a fixed grin – an extension of his acting skills. The men who served under him misinterpreted this. 'Look at him, he's had blood for breakfast,' they would say. But in fact it was a sign of terror. Being frank about his fear was part of his determination to view himself objectively. He told Tim Brown how scared he had been during training, even when they were just using thunder-flashes, let alone live ammunition.

He joined the navy as ordinary seaman D/JX240266 on 18 December 1940, reporting for duty to HMS *Raleigh*, a shore establishment on the outskirts of Torpoint in Cornwall. Six weeks later, he was posted to HMS *Drake*, alias the Royal Naval barracks at Devonport, Plymouth, to complete his basic training, and within two months he found himself travelling north to the British naval base at Scapa Flow in the Orkneys, to take part in one of the most dramatic episodes of the war at sea, the hunt for the *Bismarck*. This legendary German battleship had been designed to prey on the Atlantic convoys, and she set sail, accompanied by the heavy cruiser *Prinz Eugen*, on 18 May 1941. She was spotted in a Norwegian fjord by a Spitfire reconnaissance plane, and Royal Navy warships were instantly alerted to watch the various routes she might take into the Atlantic, while the Home Fleet sailed from Scapa Flow to intercept her. This consisted of the battleships *King George V* and *Repulse*, the aircraft carrier *Victorious*, seven destroyers, and the cruisers *Aurora*, *Hermione*, *Kenya* and *Galatea*, in the last of which Ordinary Seaman Golding was a rather unwilling crewman.

His chief feelings, he remembers, were misery, humiliation and fear. As an ordinary seaman he was 'the lowest form of life among more than six hundred men'. Moreover, he was twenty-nine years old, whereas most ordinary seamen were boys. He felt debased and wretched, missing his wife, child and home. His sadness prompted a strange moment of Proustian recall. It was nearly midnight; they were off the coast of Iceland, sailing through the glimmering blue of the polar night, and he was on lookout on *Galatea*'s port side. Behind him was the bridge, and he could hear the strange clicks and whistles of the ship's asdic and radar. Suddenly the clock at 29 The Green, Marlborough, struck one. It was unmistakable. He knew it instantly. He could almost see it. It was an old wall clock – his father had thrown the case away and hung the face and pendulum beside the drawing-room door. Whatever it was in the ship's electronics that had made the noise, it was exactly the same as the clock's noise 2,000 miles away. 'I swear if the trace of that note and the note of my father's clock were frozen as a display on a cathode tube they would be identical.' Memory of home overwhelmed him, and 'my heart was squeezed small as a nut with abject misery'.

Meanwhile the *Bismarck* was heading for the Denmark Strait, the gateway to the Atlantic, between Iceland and Greenland, where she was spotted on 23 May by the cruisers *Suffolk* and *Norfolk*. In response to their signals a battle group consisting of the new battleship HMS *Prince of Wales* and the battlecruiser HMS *Hood* made full speed to the Denmark Strait, and came within range of the *Bismarck* and *Prinz Eugen* early on the morning of 24 May. The *Hood* opened fire at 0552 hours at a range of 12.5 miles and the German ships returned fire at a range of 11 miles. Within two minutes the *Hood* was on fire, and at 0600 hours a shell penetrated her ammunition magazine and she blew up. More than 1,400 men were lost. There were three survivors. The *Prince of Wales* broke off the engagement and the *Bismarck*, shadowed by the *Suffolk* and *Norfolk*, headed south, though at a reduced speed, as she had sustained some damage in the battle.

News of the *Hood*'s loss brought widespread grief and consternation, and Churchill commanded that every available naval unit must be committed to hunting down the German raider. When the *Hood* sank, the battle fleet of which *Galatea* was a part was still about 330 miles away to the south-east. At 1440 hours on the 24th Admiral Tovey, the fleet commander, sent the aircraft carrier *Victorious* and the cruiser squadron, including *Galatea*, on ahead, to a position from which the carrier's torpedo bombers – they were nine Swordfish biplanes of 802 Squadron – could attack. Despite very bad weather the attack went in just after midnight on the 25th, but made only one hit and caused little damage. Worse, at 0400 hours the *Suffolk* and *Norfolk* reported that they had lost contact with their quarry. The *Bismarck* had shaken off her pursuers.

Admiral Tovey, still 100 miles away with the main fleet, ordered the *Victorious* and the cruiser squadron to start a sea and air search, and that is how Ordinary Seaman Golding came to find himself, at 0300 hours on the morning of 26 May, on lookout on *Galatea*'s port bow, sweeping the horizon with binoculars, an experience that produced one of his most vivid pieces of war writing – a single sheet of typescript, of uncertain date.

We were hunting and being hunted through a seascape of colours
I had never seen before – every shade of blue and white and green,
ice, green and white and blue, scattered over the sea that was flat as
stretched shot silk. It was the long summer – daylight all the time

and yet strange, with the kind of remoteness that comes from viewing with eyes accustomed by now to lack of sleep and a mind so habituated to danger that it ceased to be anything but a continual, only semiconscious worry like a too heavy bill that will have to be paid.

As he watched the long ice wall against which the enemy was expected to appear, he had a sense of the 'preposterousness' of their quest – hunting a huge battleship in their 'floating eggshell of a cruiser'. It seemed unreal. Then suddenly he saw leap into the air, far off, at an angle of 25 degrees from the bow on the port side, the column of water that told him a naval shell had hit the water.

I pulled myself together, and in a crisp voice worthy of *In Which We Serve*, made my announcement.

'Bearing Red 025, sir, shellfire, distant.'

Then there was a commotion. Bells rang, orders were shouted, the gun barrels of our two forrard turrets moved individually and restlessly like the fingers of a pianist about to play, then settled together on Red 025. There was a long pause.

Nothing much happened. Long before the captain approached me I knew what I had done. But he *did* approach me at last, after the ship had been stood down from action stations. I felt his arm on my shoulder and a friendly pat. He murmured.

'I don't suppose you'd ever seen a whale spouting before.'

It wasn't long after that that we passed it, him or her, rolling along in the sea, now and then blowing up a high jet of spray, at home, casual, enormous, like a reef.

As for the *Bismarck*, she was spotted later on 26 May by an RAF Catalina from 209 Squadron which had flown across the Atlantic from Northern Ireland. The aircraft carrier *Ark Royal*, the battlecruiser *Renown* and the cruiser *Sheffield* were diverted to intercept her, and at 2100 hours on 26 May a torpedo from one of *Ark Royal*'s Swordfish disabled her steering gear, so that she could only steam in a wide circle in the direction of the approaching battleships *George V* and *Rodney* (which had joined Admiral Tovey after the *Repulse* had run short of fuel and been sent back to Newfoundland). They opened fire on the crippled ship at a little before 0900 hours on 27 May, and at 1039 the *Bismarck* sank. The heavy cruiser *Devonshire* and the destroyer *Maori* picked up 110 survivors, but 2,100 men were lost.

Another direction in which Golding's education was extended on board *Galatea* was the sexual. On the lower deck he observed a thriving homosexual underworld, and gained knowledge of its routines and vocabulary. He learnt that the slang for buggery was 'having a bit of a grommet', and that the usual fee was ten shillings. Recording this in his journal later he added the scholarly gloss that there was a Spanish and Portuguese word *grumete*, meaning a ship's boy, which became 'grommet' in Elizabethan English, and that the word also denoted a circle or loop of rope that was shaped like a sphincter. A scene he remembered for many years took place when *Galatea* had been at sea for about three weeks. A 'pretty boy', with a white, twisted face, sat at the mess table and spat into his sleeve, as if in disgust, and a leading seaman, watching him carefully, said 'I know what you've been doing' – in a voice that 'had contempt in it like a torpedo'. The boy's eyes filled with tears, and he looked imploringly at the leading seaman, but the man only murmured, 'with a mixture of lust and venom', 'You lovely slut!' Such memories may have come back to Golding when, forty years later, he set out to write about the below-decks adventures of the Reverend Colley.

He left *Galatea* in July 1941 and was sent to the Royal Naval base at Liverpool, HMS *Eaglet*, where, for a short time, he had the relatively humdrum duty of guarding Gladstone Dock. It was a fortunate move. Very soon after his spell of service on *Galatea* ended, she joined the Mediterranean fleet, based in Malta, and on 14 December 1941 she was torpedoed and sunk off Alexandria by the German submarine *U-557*. Twenty-two officers and 441 ratings died, many of them known to Golding. They included her commanding officer Captain E. W. B. Sim, who had been kind about the whale. A memory of his brief guardianship of Liverpool docks was that there was an American ship alongside (after the fall of France, Liverpool and the Clyde had become the principal import docks), and one of the sailors called down, 'Hey, Limey, can you catch?' He said he could, and the sailor proceeded to throw down a number of oranges, one by one. In wartime oranges were, of course, 'fantastic luxuries', and he saved them carefully to take home to David.

But he was soon at sea again, this time aboard HMS *Wolverine* (D78), a destroyer engaged, during the months he was with her, in escorting the Atlantic convoys on which German U-boats were preying with devastating effect. The naval historian Jock Gardner thinks he probably joined her as a potential candidate for a commission, to be instructed in the duties of an officer of the watch. She was a rather elderly craft, built soon after the First World War, and for Golding she spelt danger and discomfort. During one storm south-west of Ireland, he recalls, they were hove to for twenty-four hours. Conditions below deck were 'cramped, crowded and unavoidably liable to infestations'. For long periods he was never dry. After one spell at sea he noticed a ring of red marks round his waist and consulted the doctor, who, evidently suspecting body lice, ordered immediate counter-measures. All his gear was baked, and he had to scrub himself with disinfectant in a cold bath. He was sensitive, as usual, to the 'humiliation', but it might, he reflected, have been worse – he might have been scrubbed rather than allowed to scrub himself – and he thought gratefully that the authorities were taking care 'to make the whole episode as little as possible injurious to my *amour propre*'.

There were brighter moments. The rating who usually shared a watch with him on the *Wolverine* confided that his favourite fantasy was having sexual intercourse with a female member of the Salvation Army in full uniform – a memory Golding filed away with his other new insights. Another thing to set against the constant dread of U-boat attacks was the relief of reaching safety. He recalls, with gratitude, what it was like, after three weeks on convoy duty, to come in sight of the lighthouses that told him they were almost home. He lists them with lingering pleasure – Inishtrahull, in County Donegal, the northernmost point of Ireland, Trevose, Godrevy, Longships, 'coming up one after another, faithfully to time, as the flotilla butted a head sea along the narrow swept [that is, mineswept] channel'. Last came the Nab, a 92 foot metal cylinder perched at an angle near the Nab rock a few miles south-east of Bembridge, 'glaring awfully with its twin lights out of an armoured head, like some marine Ned Kelly'. The lights, dependable and welcoming, offered 'in all that welter, and with all our amateurish, half-learned navigation, the sense of something *friendly*'.

Towards the end of October 1941 he left *Wolverine* and was transferred to the Royal Naval barracks at Portsmouth for a training course. He was there only a month, but that was enough to give him an idea of what the civilian population of the city had been suffering from air raids. Portsmouth was the target for sixty-seven major raids, and one of them, a couple of months before Golding arrived, was the worst on any city apart from London in the whole of the Battle of Britain. There are many accounts of the terror these attacks caused – the deafening, almost continuous explosions, the fear of imminent death, the stifling smoke and fires and falling buildings, the impossibility of escape. Golding told an interviewer, years later, how, during a raid on the barracks, he had been alone in a slit trench with a thin concrete roof and a wooden seat on one side. There was a machine gun going off outside, and he envied the gunners because at least they had something to do. Afterwards he found that the gunners had survived, but twenty yards away a petty officer had been trying to calm a group of unruly seamen who had joined the service that day. 'To show them they shouldn't worry he'd stood up, said, "Look, you can even stand up in an air raid", and instantly been blown in two.' That night they went to sleep in their hammocks with a 500lb delayed-action bomb under the floor a few yards away. He remembered wondering, in an 'experimental, pulse-taking way', as he cowered in the trench, what he would give to be allowed to get away to safety – exactly who, among all the people he knew, he would offer up to save himself. He found that he was so frightened he was prepared to sacrifice almost everyone – except Ann and David. So, though love might not always be stronger than fear, he concluded, 'some love was stronger than some fear'.

He made up his mind to apply formally for a commission – his application form is dated 8 November 1941 – and four days later he was transferred to HMS *King Alfred* in Hove, actually the recently completed Hove Marina, which the RNVR had opportunely requisitioned, along with Lancing College, as its officer-training centre. He applied under the Commission and Warrant Scheme, which was open to serving ratings with a minimum of three months' sea experience who were assessed as having officer potential by their commanding officers. After a twelve-week course, successful cadets passed out as sub-lieutenants, their badge of rank a single wavy gold stripe on the jacket cuff (which accounted for the RNVR's nickname 'the wavy navy'; Royal Navy gold stripes were straight). On 19 February 1942 Temporary Sub-Lieutenant Golding got his wavy stripe, and three months later he was promoted to temporary lieutenant.

His first posting as an officer was off-beat and almost fatal. In September 1939, Churchill appointed Professor Frederick Lindemann as his scientific adviser, with the job of developing special mines for use against shipping on the Rhine. This was the germ of what became MD1, an establishment for devising new weapons, contemptuously known as 'Mr Churchill's toyshop'. In fact it proved remarkably successful and eventually designed weapons for all three services. It had various early homes but had happily settled by the end of 1940 at The Firs, Whitchurch, near Aylesbury in Buckinghamshire. It was an army establishment, commanded by Major General Sir Millis Jefferis KBE MC, but soon after the move to Whitchurch Commander Goodeve of the Royal Navy approached Jefferis, asking if he could set up a special weapons establishment for the navy on the same site. Jefferis agreed, and a group of officers and ratings arrived, headed by Lieutenant Brinsmead RNVR. Among them was Golding.

How he came to be there is a mystery, but the likeliest explanation is that Lindemann, who had been a science professor at Oxford, encountered him during his first two undergraduate years while he was still reading for the Natural Science Prelim, and was impressed enough to remember him. The MD1 naval contingent did some important work, developing an anti-submarine weapon called the Hedgehog which went into service late in the war and was credited with thirty-seven submarine killings. By this time, however, Golding had long ceased to apply his inventiveness to naval weaponry. What happened was later described by Colonel R. Stuart Macrae, historian of MD1 and also its second-in-command. He found, he recounts, that some naval officers were 'a little carefree' when dealing with explosives. In particular 'a Lieutenant Golding' was said to be walking about the place carrying not only a supply of electric detonators but also a dry battery in his pocket. (Macrae, writing in 1971, clearly had no idea that Lieutenant Golding had, since the war, acquired some celebrity as a novelist.) He 'had him hauled in right away' and asked him if this rumour was true. He admitted 'with a disarming smile' that it was, but assured Macrae that there was nothing to worry about, because he kept the detonators in one trouser pocket and the battery in another.

I explained patiently that if he went on like this he would, sooner or later, in a moment of mental aberration, contrive to get both detonators and battery in the same pocket. As I did not want to have any eunuchs about the place, he would cease this practice at once. He retired hurt, but he was more hurt a few weeks later. For he slipped back into his old ways and the inevitable happened. He was extremely lucky because, although he was quite badly burnt, his love life was not affected – not for long, anyway.

David Angier, son of the assistant director of MD1 Norman Angier, was only nine at the time, but he has clear recollections of Golding's sojourn at the weapons establishment and its explosive finale. The Goldings rented one of a row of cottages in Horseshoe Crescent, Beaconsfield, and became friends with the Angiers. 'What I remember him for most, of course, is his piano playing, particularly his playing of Liszt which father said was more Hungarian than Liszt ever imagined.' The Angiers had a grand piano, which had come out of the Decca recording studios where Norman worked before the war, 'so Bill Golding was able to perform'. Ann's looks impressed young David even more. He remembers taking a bottle of milk round to Horseshoe Crescent – he thinks Ann phoned for it – and the vision of beauty that opened the door has stuck in his mind ever since. Golding was 'quite a lot of fun, and quite a rumbustious character. He treated children as equals, and so did all the other scientists.'

Beaconsfield in the 1940s was deep in the country. You didn't see cars very often. Parties of cyclists used to come through at the weekends. There were no bombs except for three stray ones that dropped in a field one Saturday night – the whole population trooped out on the Sunday morning to look at the holes. So it was a safe rural retreat, and if it had not been for the detonator incident Golding and his family might have stayed there till the end of the war. Norman Angier and Golding got on well – Norman drove to Whitchurch each day and gave Golding a lift. But after the accident David can remember 'some fairly derogatory comments' about how stupid it was of Golding to take risks with a detonator. It had been drummed into him and his brother that what looked like 'a simple little aluminium tube was really a lethal piece of metal', and he thinks Golding 'was probably lucky to keep his leg'. He also thinks that the affair was hushed up because Golding should not have been allowed to carry detonators around. 'There must have been a lot of people keeping very quiet about it.'

Thirty years later Golding had a strange dream in which he and General Sir Millis Jefferis are walking together to some 'official place', and he takes the opportunity to tell the general, 'with some emotion', how much the army, the country and the world owe him. The general replies 'briefly, and in a manly way', that Golding did very well in the war. 'I take this as the equivalent of a decoration. I am moved. I bend and kiss his right, whitish, washleather glove.' Perhaps this was some kind of dream-compensation for an incident of which he felt ashamed. The immediate aftermath of his carelessness must have been painful and distressing. The accident happened on 30 November 1942, and his naval record states that he was admitted to the Royal Buckinghamshire Hospital, Aylesbury, on that day – eight months after he had joined MD1 – with a 'Bomb Injury' to his right thigh. He was there for six weeks, then 'discharged to home address' on 16 January 1943, only to be admitted to the Royal Naval Hospital, Chatham, five days later, remaining there until 22 January.

By 13 February 1943 he had recovered and was 'found fit for General Service', and a week later he was posted to Port Edgar, Fife, the home of the navy's minesweeping operations, for a minesweeping course. In March he moved on, for more training with mines, to HMS *Claverhouse II*, the RNVR base at Leith, near Edinburgh, formerly the Granton Hotel. These postings indicated a new direction in his naval career that was to take him across the Atlantic. America had joined the war after the Japanese attack on the American naval base at Pearl Harbor on 7 December 1941, and under the Lend-Lease Programme the United States agreed to supply Britain with minesweepers built in various

American yards. They were called British Yard Minesweepers (BYMS), and 150 of them were transferred to the Royal Navy under Lend-Lease, crews being sent out from Britain to bring them back across the Atlantic – not an enviable task, as they were small boats, about 100 feet in length, with wooden hulls to minimize their vulnerability to magnetic mines, and a shallow draught so that they could operate close to the shore.

Golding sailed out on the *Queen Elizabeth*, sharing a first-class cabin with eleven other young officers. By luck, one of them had read Greats (Greek and Latin Literature, Philosophy and Ancient History) at Oxford, and as Golding had a copy of the *Oxford Book of Greek Verse* with him, and was beginning to teach himself Greek, the two of them spent much of the week-long voyage reading Homer together. During one session they were interrupted, much to Golding's irritation, by a Royal Navy captain, who seemed to think it paradoxical that two young men engaged in one war should be reading about another.

Learning Greek was of profound importance to Golding's thought and writing. Greek literature became a passion, and it testifies to his powers of application that he could concentrate on acquiring this complex and abstruse language in the nervous hours of waiting that wartime naval service entailed. In his unpublished novel *Short Measure* a schoolboy, who has unthinkingly opted to learn Greek, takes one look at the 'trellis works of declensions, page after page, covered with lace-like paradigms, rules, exceptions, irregulars' in a Greek grammar, and gives it up for ever. Perhaps that reflects Golding's own first impressions. Tim Brown remembers him saying that he also taught himself chess, another lifelong obsession, during 'the boring times in the navy', using a book 'by an American called Mason'. This must be the celebrated Irish-American chess champion James Mason (1849–1905), whose *The Art of Chess* (1905) was a best-seller, and went through many editions.

The enormous size of the *Queen Elizabeth*'s saloon impressed Golding, as did the prodigious slowness of her roll – a contrast with the *Galatea* or the *Wolverine*. He would watch the people at the other end of the room, fifty yards away, tilt very slowly to the left, and then very slowly to the right, and it seemed to take many minutes. When they arrived in New York they were ferried to the Barbizon Plaza Hotel, now Trump Parc, famous when it was built in 1930 for its flamboyant top, constructed of glass tiles that lit up, though in wartime this effect was probably muted. The whole building had been taken over by the Admiralty and adapted to house junior officers. No women were allowed, except in the basement bar where half a dozen, whom Golding presumed to be prostitutes, sat sipping from glasses of something, perhaps water. Beer was ten cents a glass, and a lot of it was drunk. The British officers were taken out to the Atlantic coast for a navigation course, which was identical to a course Golding had already done in England, and after that they were left to kick their heels while their minesweepers were being built. Writing about it later in *Scenes From A Life*, Golding estimated he was there for five months, though actually it was less than three, which is an index of his boredom.

He took to going off by himself on 'cultural expeditions', one of which was to Coney Island, the amusement park to the south of Brooklyn. It was much further away than it looked on the map – clearly, he says, his navigation course had not done him much good – and he arrived after dark to find it almost deserted and dimly lit, because of wartime regulations. German U-boats were operating off America's eastern seaboard, so a partial blackout was in force. He could make out carousels and big dippers and giant racers in the gloom, and sideshows with little twinkling lights. He passed one which had a metallic voice shouting 'Atrocity! Atrocity! Atrocity!' and saw, over its entrance, a vast reproduction of the Victorian painting of the execution of Lady Jane Grey by Paul Delaroche (now in the National Gallery), which he remembered seeing as a boy in Arthur Mee's *Children's Encyclopaedia*. Underneath was a caption that read LATEST NAZI ATROCITY. He felt amused at first, thinking how it showed the ignorance and self-centredness of Americans, or at any rate the ones Coney Island was designed for. Then he felt a wave of nostalgia, as he remembered reading on the old rug by the living-room fire at home. As he thought of the poor young girl, only sixteen, kneeling, blindfolded, and fumbling for the block – 'Where is it? Where is it? I cannot find it' – horror overcame him, for it was, of course, an atrocity – 'one in the long nightmare which is the bedrock of being human'.

So he felt 'even glummer than before, if that were possible', and to cheer himself up took a ride on the Giant Racer. This was a mistake.

He was the only person aboard the fifty-yard-long contraption as it sped through loops and dives and jarring swerves, and he felt a fool. The machinery let out a cacophony of shrieks, which it seemed to him was like an invisible audience of girls 'convulsed with jeering contempt' at the spectacle of him, dressed up as a naval officer, on a children's fairground machine. It was yet another humiliation, though this time only an imagined one, and he climbed out of the Racer with his legs shaking. That was the last time he ventured out of Manhattan. At last at the beginning of June 1943 he went aboard BYMS191 as first lieutenant (that is, second-in-command), and sailed across the Atlantic and through the Mediterranean to Port Said.

He stayed at the Royal Naval base at Alexandria for about three months, probably engaged in minesweeping duties in the eastern Mediterranean. Then, at the beginning of October 1943, he returned to Portsmouth, where he received orders to report to Combined Operations Headquarters at 1A Richmond Terrace, London. Talk of the Allied invasion of Nazi-occupied Europe had been in the air for some time, but perhaps this was the first inkling Golding had that he might be a part of that momentous operation. He was sent up to Troon, in Scotland, on 10 November, to be trained in the handling of landing craft, on the stretch of water between Oban, on Scotland's west coast, and Lamlash on the Isle of Arran in the Clyde estuary. A fortnight later he was admitted to the Royal Naval Hospital at Haslar, near Gosport in Hampshire, with what seems to have been an attack of jaundice. Presumably he was on leave when he fell ill, otherwise he would have been hospitalized in Scotland. At all events, he was discharged in a couple of weeks and went back to learning about landing craft.

They came in various guises. Golding referred to the whole species as 'dangerous steel boxes', which was an apt description. The basic model, the British Mark IV LCT (Landing Craft Tank), was 196 feet long and 36 feet wide, with a flat bottom and a ramp at the front that could be let down. It was powered by two 500-hp diesel engines, had a maximum speed of 9 knots, and was equipped with radar – the British 970 model – as well as a navigation aid called the QH, and a gyro compass. As its name indicates, it was designed to carry up to a dozen tanks as well as infantry, but an LCT could be adapted by constructing an extra deck over the tank space, and mounting guns on it, which would make it a gunship for giving fire support to troops going ashore, called an LCT(G), or it could have anti-aircraft ('flak') guns mounted on it, which would make it an LCT(F). There were various other permutations. Golding, however, soon discovered that he was to be put in command of a new type of LCT, called an LCT(R), which stood for Landing Craft Tank (Rocket).

They were the brainwave of a Colonel Langley, and had been used experimentally at the Sicily landings in July 1943. Essentially they were an answer to the question of how to drop the maximum number of high-explosive shells on the enemy without going to the time and trouble of building artillery guns and manning them with gun crews. In an LCT(R) the extra deck over the tank space was covered with (depending on the model) either 936 or 1,008 5-inch rocket projectors, designed to be fired in salvos of either thirty-nine or forty-two rockets, in quick succession, by a system of electrical triggers operated by the captain from the wheelhouse on the bridge, while the rest of the crew sheltered below decks. The normal crew for a rocket ship was two officers and fifteen men.

The intense heat and the flame and smoke that engulfed the whole ship when the rockets were fired were a worry for the designers. One of those responsible for finding out how to protect the crew was Professor James Lovelock, later a friend of Golding's. He spent a lot of time in the Channel aboard prototype rocket ships, observing test firing, and his description of them brings out the almost gimcrack simplicity of the whole design. The projectors were just tubes, he explains, filled with sticks of cordite, which 'went off like an ordinary firework rocket', burning for about three seconds, and throwing their projectiles hundreds of feet into the air. They made a 'fearful noise', scorched all the paint off the deck, and seemed likely to incinerate the crew. 'The other danger, when they fired the lot, was that the downward pressure of the gas would split the ship in half. They were very afraid that was going to happen. Because it was all put together without any proper engineering constraints, under wartime conditions.'

For those on whom the projectiles fell rocket ships were, of course, even more terrifying than they were for those aboard them. Each rocket carried a 7lb high-explosive head, and successive salvos were fired as the ship moved forward, laying a blanket of explosions up the beach. The width of the blanket was 700 yards, and could not be controlled, but the depth for a complete broadside of twenty-four salvos could be varied from 300 to 1,000 yards, depending on the ship's forward movement during firing. Aiming was very primitive. The projectors were arranged in stands of six, fixed at an angle of 45 degrees to the deck, and they had a range of about 3,500 yards. The rocket-ship's commander had to point the ship's bow accurately at the target, judge the distance from the beach either by radar or by visual reckoning, and fire his salvos at predetermined intervals to gain the desired depth of blanket. This manoeuvre called for pinpoint navigation, and since LCTs were notoriously difficult to steer, owing to their flat bottoms and undersized rudders, hitting its target was not something a rocket ship could guarantee. Set against this disadvantage was its prodigious firepower. A single rocket ship was said to be equivalent to 80 light cruisers or 200 destroyers.

At Troon in November 1943 Golding had taken command of one of these perilous new craft, LCT(R)359, and began to learn to direct it in battle. When he came back from sick leave in January 1944 he was put in command of his second ship, LCT(R)439. Then, on 6 February, he was transferred to HMS *Turtle*, a hutted camp on the outskirts of Poole in Dorset, which housed the Combined Operations Training Establishment and the Royal Naval Assault Gunnery School, and was the base for training personnel for the Normandy landings. Weeks of intensive preparation followed, with innumerable practice landings along the south coast and firing practice at Studland Bay near Poole. Golding was sent briefly towards the end of February to the Admiralty Compass observatory at Slough for a gyroscopic navigation course, and on his return he took command of his third rocket ship, LCT(R)460.

Despite the tension and the waiting it seems that this was one of Golding's happiest times. Sailing alone in a dinghy round the inlets of the south coast gave him leisure to think and see. He found a new capacity in himself for wonder, marvelling at 'the delicate beauty of land and sea and sky'. He came to know unfrequented beaches that had on them 'the brightness one remembers from childhood'. They were like 'new moons of white sand', or like 'the base of a fingernail'.

Everything seemed miraculous – the Solent, dazzling blue like the wings of a butterfly; the miles of still water, 'lovely as a misted sapphire'. In this mood he came to realize how much of his life had been spent buried in books, and missing the immediacy of real things. Now he felt that he was chipping the 'literary enamel' off the world, and seeing it for itself. 'These were precious discoveries.'

Another pleasure, unlike anything he had felt before, or was to feel again, was a sense of comradeship with his brother officers. They would race their sailing dinghies, strictly against the commanding officer's standing orders, past Furzey Island to a point called Pottery Pier, which they used as a racing mark. Of course the training had its tedious side too. Again and again he took his rocket ship in and out of the Beaulieu river, and on several occasions ran it aground at the entrance. He came to know every sea-mark and hazard of the coast – the place inside the entrance to Poole harbour where the ungainly rocket ships would start to perform 'impromptu war dances, caught between wind and tide, swinging about, menacing everything in sight'; the strange isolated pinnacle on the cliffs called Old Harry, perched above the beach that his support squadron would regularly blast with high explosive. 'Range on Old Harry' he would shout down to his radar operator, running his ship in past the buoys to fire off the rockets 'in the teeth of the combers smoking in towards the bar'. Meanwhile, inland, the ceaseless sound of automatic riveters in the docks, and the 'random blue flashes' of the welding machines, were a reminder of the great battle that awaited them all.

The notebook in which he recorded his thoughts while waiting for D-Day had been bought to keep the ship's accounts in. But he could not bear to defile its pure white pages with columns of figures. 'Aussie', his first lieutenant, he decided, would have to look after the accounts, aided by 'Mr Midshipman Fisher, who is my second officer'. Instead he entered in the notebook his long account of falling desperately in love as a teenager, and starting to write poetry, and of all the 'masterpieces' he never managed to finish or, often, even start. The flippancy seems designed to keep nervousness at bay, as, perhaps was his attempt to distance himself by observing the men, ships and weaponry that surrounded him as if they were some alien life form.

The whole combined operations service is fantastic. See us all creeping through the mists of dawn towards the shore, and you are reminded of the grotesque specializations of pond life. Each of us is no earthly use saving only for its specific job, and that job we can do with a sort of insect automatism. This craft on our starboard hand, for example, can do nothing but make smoke – smoke is his beginning and his end, he thinks and dreams thick impenetrable smoke. That beetle-like procession, over there to port, would be helpless if anything larger than a dinghy attacked it; but once it touches the beach, it erupts a stream of savage, mauling tanks, before which infantry must die, or run. There are many other even queerer specializations; and I perhaps am the most spectacular. But alas, the pleasure of writing about myself is denied me – for I am Most Secret.

Dating the successive entries in the notebook precisely is not usually possible. But the one that follows immediately after this tells us that it is two days later, and the exercise has finished. It had been tense, what with 'getting my craft to the right place at the right time', and avoiding those who were getting theirs to the wrong place and having 'nervous hysteria' about it. In the aftermath, he and his crew diverted themselves by building a makeshift dinghy. He bribed someone to fit it with a keel, and the coxswain, the mechanic and four of the crew fixed up its mast, which was really just the shaft of a boathook. He imagined sailing off into the dawn in this ingenious cockle-shell, and crawling over 'unvisited saltings' with a gun, to provide the crew with roast duck. His friendly and informal relations with those under his command are not what we might have expected from so shy and solitary a man.

Though D-Day was close, exactly when they would set sail was still unknown, and the entry after the one about building the dinghy announces a reprieve.

And yet more good news! The buzz has reached me that we are here for three more days, so that I shall get Ann to run down for two of them, and spend nearly all my time ashore. I was here once before, ten years ago, and it is a good place.

Then a line is drawn across the page, followed by the last entry that he made in his notebook before D-Day.

> Yes it was a good place: so good a place, so happy a thirty hours that I must not think about them lest the walls of my cabin crush me, and hurt.

The happy thirty hours must have been before 28 May, for on that day strict security measures came into force. All outgoing mail from the ships was impounded and there was no more going ashore, or even using telephones. On 31 May the commander-in-chief of the Allied Expeditionary Force issued a special order of the day, telling those under his command that it was their 'privilege to take part in the greatest amphibious operation in history'. D-Day had been fixed for 5 June, but the weather forecast on Sunday morning, 4 June, was so bad that Eisenhower decided to delay the landings for twenty-four hours. Early on 5 June the first assault forces from Spithead and the Solent set sail, making their way eastwards along the coast and then turning south to pass through 'the Spout' – a corridor of ten channels through the long snake of the minefield that stretched from Boulogne almost to Cherbourg. British minesweepers had cleared and marked these channels by the evening of 5 June, and during the night the assault convoys from various bases on the south coast followed them through. By 0500 hours they were in position off the French coast.

There are many accounts by those who took part of the awesome sight the invasion fleet presented at daybreak. There were nearly 7,000 vessels, including 1,213 warships and 4,125 landing craft, and the fleet was protected by 2,000 planes. During the night three airborne divisions had been dropped to prepare and secure the eastern and western extremities of the future bridgehead, and from midnight to 0500 1,056 British heavy bombers dropped 6,000 tons of high explosive on the German defences. Liberators and Fortresses of the American air force took over at 0500 and dropped a further 4,000 tons. When dawn broke grey, cold and rainy at 0558, Allied warships opened fire on the German coastal batteries along the whole fifty-mile front. It was the heaviest rain of shells ever poured on land targets from the sea.

Almost unbelievably, the Germans were taken completely by surprise. This was due partly to Allied air superiority that kept the Luftwaffe grounded, and destroyed enemy radar installations, and partly to a massive deception operation that had led the Nazis to expect landings in the Pas-de-Calais and Belgium. So, for the naval force, the fierce resistance the commander-in-chief had warned of did not materialize. As Captain S. W. Roskill records in the official history of *The War at Sea*, 'the enemy's response to the approach of the assault waves was almost negligible. No air attacks took place, and the coastal batteries, though they fired a few shells at the transports, did no damage.' The coastline had been divided into five beaches, each to be attacked by an Allied division of 150,000 men. On the west were Utah and Omaha, comprising the American sector; then, reading from west to east, came Gold, Juno and Sword, the British and Commonwealth sector. The naval firepower supporting the landings was provided by virtually every type of armed vessel afloat, from battleships down, and included thirty-six of the new rocket ships, fourteen allocated to the western sector and twenty-two to the eastern. Golding's LCT(R)460 belonged to the latter group, and his target was the central beach, Gold. This was five miles wide, stretching from Longues-sur-Mer in the west to St-Aubin-sur-Mer in the east and including Arromanches-les-Bains, the eventual site of the artificial Mulberry Harbour. The British 50th Infantry Division was to go ashore on this beach, with the 47th Royal Marine Commandos, and the 8th Armoured Brigade. H-hour was 0725, and the rocket ships were to fire off their salvos in the quarter-hour before the infantry landing.

Almost everything Golding wrote about his war experiences is still unpublished. But in November 1961 an essay called 'The English Channel' appeared in *Holiday* magazine (later reprinted in his collection *The Hot Gates*), which includes some paragraphs on D-Day. Compared with the account he wrote at the time in his newly purchased notebook, they are quite light-hearted. The essay starts with Golding looking down at the Channel from an airliner, the first time he has ever done so, and remembering, as they fly over the Isle of Wight, what it was like to be part of the invasion fleet fifteen years before. 'I saw seven (or was it eleven?) thousand ships at anchor. They filled thirty miles of anchorage.' From the air, he imagines, they would have appeared as separate ships. 'But down there you couldn't see water – just gray paint and a wooded hill or two.' When they set sail, he recalls, he left his first lieutenant in charge and 'turned in, to be fresh for D-Day', but, returning to the bridge at 0200 hours, he found that they had fallen behind the convoy and were lost. His first lieutenant had not liked to go any faster because it was so dark.

Indeed the Channel was big that night, oceanic, and covered with a swarm of red stars from the planes and gliders moving south. I found that we were miles west of our position. So we turned southeast and steamed at full speed all night over jet black waves that were showered with sparks of phosphorescence and possibly loaded with mines.

I stood there all night catching up and felt history in my hands as hard and heavy as a brick. I was frightened – not immediately of the mines that we might set off at any moment, nor of the batteries ashore, nor the thousands of enemy aircraft we had been promised. I was frightened, of all things, of being late and jeered at. I find him funny now, that young man with the naval profile and the greening badge on his cap.

When morning came he was in sight of the French coast and saw 'a forest of black trees hundreds of feet high', which were the rockets being fired by the rocket ships off Sword beach, to their left. He watched an Allied plane flying near the first salvo.

There was the fatal geometry of his curve and the trajectory of the rockets; he touched one just as it was turning to come down. There was a bright smile of flame, the flash of a grin five thousand feet up. Then the two sides of the smile dropped away, fell, slid slowly and sadly down the sky as if it wasn't such a joke after all.

That is all 'The English Channel' has to say about D-Day. The essay turns to other subjects.

But we know that the landing on Gold beach went well, and the supporting naval fire from four cruisers, thirteen destroyers and the gun- and rocket-carrying LCTs was accurate and effective. By contrast with the terrible carnage the Americans suffered on Omaha beach, the leading units of the 50th Division got ashore with relatively light casualties. Nearly fifty years later, on 31 August 1991, Golding was on his way back from a holiday in France with Ann and their son David, and they passed through Arromanches. David recalls that his father was distressed because he recognized the distinctive outline of two houses on the seafront and thought that they must have been hit by his rockets. 'He didn't know if he'd killed any civilians.' (In the 1960s, lunching at the Savile Club, Golding told the historian M. R. D Foot that, having fired his rockets, he realized to his dismay that he was bombarding the Grand Hotel at Cabourg, the model for Proust's Grand Hotel at Balbec. This, however, was a flight of fancy. Cabourg lies miles to the east of Gold Beach.) He also told David that he had indeed crossed a minefield to catch up with the D-Day invasion fleet when his Australian sub-lieutenant lost contact with it. Mines would be tethered at varying depths, so the shallow-drafted landing craft would pass safely over a large proportion of them, and the density of mines might well be no more than three or four per square mile. All the same, LCT(R)460 had amazing luck.

With their immediate task completed, the support landing craft moved over to the east of the invasion beaches and anchored there in close formation to defend the invaders' exposed flank from possible air or sea attack. About seventy vessels in all, they were formed, on 8 June, into the Support Squadron Eastern Flank (SSEF) under Commander K. A. Sellar. But there was not much for them to do, and Golding was among the many officers and men who enjoyed a spell of shore leave. As the summer drew on, however, it became clear that another test was in store for some of them. The Battle of Walcheren is not among the most famous engagements of the Second World War, but it was one of the most heroic. It was also strategically vital. After the breakout from Normandy, the Allied advance through France and up into Belgium was swift, but it stretched supply lines alarmingly. Each of the four advancing armies needed a million gallons of petrol a day, apart from other supplies, and everything had to be brought up from Cherbourg and the Normandy beaches. Eisenhower realized that the invasion would stall unless a new supply route could be opened up, and on 4 September 1944 the British 11th Armoured Division took the key Belgian port of

Antwerp with its dock installations still intact. However, the seaward approach to Antwerp lies along the Scheldt estuary, which snakes away westwards for thirty miles, its northern shore formed by the peninsula of South Beveland and the island of Walcheren, and its southern shore a terrain of dykes and polders stretching towards Zeebrugge. All this territory was held by the Germans, and until they could be dislodged Antwerp was useless to the Allies.

Both sides were aware that the reconquest of Europe hung in the balance. On 4 September Hitler gave 'fortress status' to Walcheren and South Beveland, which meant that they must be defended to the last man and the last round. However, in a terrible and costly two-month campaign, the 3rd Canadian Infantry Division cleared the south shore of the estuary, and the 2nd Canadian Division, assisted by the British 79th Armoured and 52nd (Lowland) Divisions, took South Beveland. That left Walcheren, a flat, diamond-shaped island ten miles across, and mostly flooded, since the dykes had been deliberately breached by the RAF. It was garrisoned by the 70th Division of the German XVth Army under General Gustav-Adolf von Zangen, and formidably defended by sixteen major coastal batteries in huge concrete emplacements.

The Allies planned a three-pronged assault, dubbed Operation Infatuate. The Canadian 2nd Division would attack from the east across the causeway from South Beveland; No. 4 Commando and 155th Brigade would make an amphibious landing at Flushing, on the island's southern tip; and, from the west, RM Commando's 4th Special Service Brigade would go ashore near the town of Westkapelle, supported by Royal Naval units. The naval presence would consist of three battleships, HMS *Warspite*, HMS *Roberts* and HMS *Erebus*, to give long-range support with their 15-inch guns, and a frigate, HMS *Kingsmill* with the naval force commander aboard. In addition there would be a selection of twenty-seven support craft from the SSEF to provide short-range fire-cover, including four LCT(F)s, eight LCT(G)s and five LCT(R)s, one of which, LCT(R)331, would be commanded by Lieutenant W. G. Golding.

It must have been clear from the start to all those participating that this collection of adapted landing craft was wholly inadequate to take on the German coastal batteries. Essentially its role was to attract the enemy firepower so that the commandos could get ashore unscathed.

In that respect it had some not very remote similarities to a suicide mission. On 17 September Golding was sent to Troon for yet another navigation course, and the next day he took command of LCT(R)331. His daughter Judy has two photographs taken in the garden of 29 The Green, one of her parents with Golding in full uniform, including hat and greatcoat, and her mother in a fur coat. The other, obviously taken at the same time, is of her father with David on his knee. From internal evidence (the time of year, the clothes, the expression) she thinks it very likely they were taken the day he left to take part in the Walcheren operation. He looks 'very solemn, as if he didn't expect to come back'. It was perhaps because he thought he faced extinction that he took another step towards a kind of immortality, more substantial than a couple of photographs. Judy was told by her mother that she was conceived shortly before her father left for the battle.

The naval force set sail from Ostend during the night of 31 October and came in sight of the Walcheren shoreline as dawn broke on 1 November. At 0800 the squadron commander got the news that fog in the south of England had prevented any planes taking off, so there would be no air support and no spotter planes to direct the fire of the battleships. This was a disastrous development. In reconstructing the events that followed, several sources can be drawn on. Golding's official report of the battle, written on 10 November, survives. In addition there is a more outspoken account in a paragraph added in the notebook where he had previously recorded his thoughts prior to D-Day. It begins: 'This is the true story of the assault on Walcheren, as I saw it.' After the war he sometimes discussed his naval experiences with his son and daughter, and further details about Walcheren can be gleaned from their memory of these conversations. In January 1962 he published an essay called 'Through the Dutch Waterways' in *Holiday* magazine (later reprinted in *A Moving Target*), which tells of a family holiday in Holland in 1960, during which he revisited Walcheren. The printed version of this essay does not mention the battle. But there is a manuscript draft that recalls it at some length.

His official report records that the first enemy shell landed off his port side at 0800 hours and from then to 1245 LCT(R)331 was under continual shell fire. As he came up out of his cabin at 0800 he could see

Walcheren and the Westkapelle lighthouse about eight miles off, but nothing could be identified on the radar, partly because of interference. Together with two of the other rocket ships, LCT(R)378 and LCT(R)457, he was on the northern edge of the force, and he could see the line of assault craft stretching astern to starboard. At 0900 came a moment of decision. The radar indicated that he was in position to start his final run-in and fire his salvos. But it was clear to him, from visually reckoning the distance to the coast, that this was 'grossly inaccurate', and he was still much too far out. The other two rocket ships, one of which, 457, was commanded by the flotilla officer, 'apparently preferred to take this range at its face value' and hung back. But he decided that his right course was to ignore the radar range and proceed inshore. So he did. At 0930 he was able to identify Westkapelle lighthouse on the radar, and found that the range was still 8,800 yards, as against the usual rocket-ship range of about 3,500 yards. At 0945 he 'came suddenly under a barrage of very heavy fire', but held his course. There was something 'amusing – though slightly uncomplimentary', his report observes, about the alacrity with which the other landing craft, seeing him coming, cleared a passage to let him through – a tribute to the fearsome firepower of the rocket ships. He fired his first salvo at a range of 4,300 yards and ceased firing at 4,000 yards. He then turned to starboard and proceeded out to sea. Once the smoke had cleared he could see that the shoot had been entirely successful. Westkapelle was covered in bursting rockets, and quite suddenly there was an 'immense explosion' in the middle of them, after which 'Westkapelle began to burn steadily'.

For some reason, his report adds, LCT(R)331 had not been fitted with a fireproof hut on its bridge, to shield the captain, who had to fire the rockets electronically while the crew sheltered below deck. 'Previous to firing, I had been in some doubt about the wisdom of this arrangement. I am now of the opinion that the discomfort of firing in the open is counterbalanced by the gain in freedom of movement. The heat and blast is not unendurable, though breathing is inadvisable and beards should not be worn.' This moment of humour is followed by something more serious. Though the report avoids any comment on the activities of the other two rocket ships in his northern sector, beyond his initial observation that they seemed to take the radar reading at face value and hung back, he says that he wishes to draw particular attention to the confusion that may occur between the shoreline and inshore craft, as they show up on a radar scan. In his opinion the radar scan of the shoreline should never be used for ranging, 'without other and independent means of checking'. What had in fact happened in the early stages of the attack, as these guarded words refrain from stating, was that the two other rocket ships, LCT(R)378, and LCT(R)457 captained by the flotilla officer, had misread the radar scan, taking inshore craft as the shoreline, and opened fire when too far out, so that their entire barrage fell among the LCTs approaching the coast, causing thirty casualties, though fortunately none of them was fatal.

As against the sang-froid and discretion of the official report, the account of the morning that he added at the end of his pre-D-Day notebook is direct both about the other LCT(R)s and about his own feelings:

The F.O. [flotilla officer] was hanging back, with 378, and I couldn't understand this. The first shell made my heart beat quickly and I tried to stop my teeth chattering, because now I knew it wasn't going to be an easy assault. We'd had an argument, silly as it sounds, as to what time H hour was. The orders said 945, but I seemed to remember the briefing as 10.20 – and the radar was showing us nothing. Most of the other assault craft were firing now. If the F.O. thought that 0945 was H hour, then his actions were peculiar. He was hanging about miles too far off the beach, and 378 was keeping with him. The radar began to show up assault craft, and West Kapelle, and finally I decided to cut loose and run in. Odd shells were dropping here and there. I was feeling unhappy, but fairly fatalistic. I was worried about the obvious ballsup that the rockets were making. It was a chilly morning, but fairly clear.

The notebook ends there, but the official report tells us how Golding spent the rest of his day, after firing his rockets and heading out to sea. At 1045 he and the two other north-sector rocket ships were ordered to sail up and attack the coastal batteries near the town of Domburg, about four miles north of Westkapelle. He found it difficult to keep up with the other two, so steered a course a little nearer the shore. He sighted a buoy ahead and steered to the starboard of this because he reckoned that the enemy guns would have an exact range on it. The flotilla officer's ship, LCR(R)457, which was in the lead, did not take this precaution, however, and 'vanished in a salvo of shell bursts' as it sailed past the buoy. Nevertheless all three ships managed to fire off their rockets and put out to sea.

'During the whole of the time in which we were within range', the official report observes in its summary of the day's action, 'the enemy made persistent attempts to hit us but without succeeding. We were very lucky.' The final sentences pay tribute to those less lucky. 'I cannot conclude without saying how much I and my ship's company admired the sustained fighting of the inshore craft. They were an inspiring sight.' A horrifying sight, too. Golding told David in one of their post-war conversations that 'six big yachts were converted with guns and machine guns and a young crew to draw the fire of the Germans'. They were, he said, men he knew well, and 'they all got killed'. What this refers to is a special group of small craft that formed part of the naval force and were ordered to close right into the shore shortly before H-hour. Two of them, LCG(M)s 101 and 102, were, according to historian Gerald Rawling, entirely new types of support craft being tried out in their first operational role. Smaller than a normal landing craft, they carried two 17-pounder guns and were designed to run right into the beach and engage targets. They were escorted by six LCSs, small, fast boats with one 6-pounder gun and machine guns. Attacking coastal batteries with these armaments called for desperate heroism. LCG(M)102 was soon a blazing hulk on the beach; there were no survivors. LCG(M)101 got away from the beach but then sank; two of her crew were killed and four wounded. The three LCSs in the south sector were all hit and blown up; only one man survived. The three LCSs on the north escaped, though one was set on fire by a direct hit, and had to be towed out of danger. Of the twenty-seven craft that went into the attack, twenty were either sunk or severely damaged, and 372 men were either killed or wounded. However, their sacrifice enabled the commandos to get ashore with only light casualties, and by 8 November Walcheren was in Allied hands.

David's conversations with his father yield a few more details. The flotilla officer did indeed misread the radar signals, Golding confirmed, and thought the Allied landing craft were the coastline, whereas his own dead reckoning told him he was still far out. He waited, before firing his salvos, until the coastline really showed up on the radar screen, and achieved such accuracy that 'the rockets walked up the street in front of the marines'. There was a concrete tower on the coast at Westkapelle, and a fluke shot penetrated one of its slits, exploding the ammunition – 'flames stood up like two ears'. After the day's action he anchored off the south of the island and a storm blew up. An officer in another craft whose anchor was dragging signalled for help and even fired shells to attract Golding's attention, but there was nothing he could do.

Memories of Walcheren haunted him for the rest of his life. When he recalled the pleasure of dinghy-racing off the south coast during his months of pre-D-Day training, he also grieved:

> Even the men who shared it with me are gone. For some I saw blown up in a dreadful morning off Walcheren, and others still more dreadfully lost, mined and sinking in a north sea gale, and I unable to turn my ship towards them. These are memories that dim the sunlight.

Clearly these are the incidents he spoke to David about.

But another horrifying memory proved at first more difficult to locate. In his journal on Armistice Day 1974 he writes, 'I am sure my midshipman's mother still mourns him', and in an entry two years later he remembers 'my poor little midshipman hanging onto the side of the sinking ship and saying "My legs are gone."' It turns out that this memory was not of something he saw but something he was told. Judy learnt, from their conversations, that Midshipman Fisher, who served with him on D-Day, was, through his good offices, transferred before the Walcheren operation to the Flotilla Officer's ship LCT(R)457. This was the craft that 'vanished in a salvo of shell bursts' as the three rocket ships sailed up to Domburg, but managed to put out to sea after firing its rockets. However, the Admiralty records show that a few days later, on 5 November 1944, it hit a mine thirteen miles NNW of Ostend, while in convoy on its way home, and sank. Fisher, who by this time had been promoted to sub-lieutenant, was killed, but some survivors were picked up by another craft. Golding told Judy that he visited one of them in hospital – she thinks it was in Ostend and that the survivor was the flotilla officer. It must have been from this survivor that Golding learnt of Sub-Lieutenant Fisher's death, for which he was in a sense responsible, since he had arranged his transfer to LCT(R)457. In the same hospital he saw wounded civilians from Walcheren, whom he believed had been evacuated before the battle.

The manuscript draft of 'Through the Dutch Waterways' gives an impressionistic account of the day's action, starting with the sinister appearance of the coastal dyke as the Allied ships approached in the early morning, 'slate grey, and studded with eyes that opened redly, or blinked as though they resented being wakened so early from their sleep'. Soon shells were bursting around them in the water, 'grumblingly', leaving behind 'a filthy whirlpool of oil – fire shells which would have set us burning like a torch'. For six hours he was part of an assault that 'looked like a newspaper idea of a naval battle':

Ships mined, ships blowing up into a Christmas tree of exploding ammunition, ships burning, sinking – and smoke everywhere slashed by sudden spats of tracer over the shell fountains and the broken, drowning men.

After these memories, the 'Through the Dutch Waterways' draft passes on to an account of their 1960 family holiday. In the town of Veere they meet a Dutch judge, who insists on taking him up the tower at Middelburg for a view of the island. Looking out towards Westkapelle he sees it has been rebuilt, and admits to the judge that he helped to destroy it.

Twelve hundred five-and-a-half inch rockets, fired in seventy-two seconds. When we came out of the smoke of discharge, there was half a mile of smoke, flames billowing up inside the dyke, and the church was on fire.

The judge asks what he feels, seeing it now, and he replies, 'Strangely little.'

Reports and rumours of the slaughter at Walcheren reached home before the survivors. Ann 'heard on the news how tough it had been', and David remembers – he was four at the time – her screaming when his father walked into the house. She had thought he was dead. That was really the end of Golding's war. On 10 June 1945 he relinquished his command of LCT(R)460 and was transferred to a pool of officers awaiting a new ship. He later told David that he was offered a command in the Far East. No one knew at the time that the war against Japan would end at Hiroshima and Nagasaki, and in mid-1945 the navy was getting into gear to send a large-scale amphibious force to take part in the war in the Pacific. In the event it was not sent, and in any case Golding declined the offer of a command. On 10 August he attended a demob centre at Westcliff in Essex, and he was released from the armed forces four days later.

Teaching

In autumn 1945 Golding went back to his teaching job at Bishop Wordsworth's School in Salisbury, where he was to remain until 1961. He disliked teaching very much, not only because he wanted to be a writer, but also because, when he thought about it on any level deeper than the routine, he did not know what it was for. He wrote, towards the end of his life:

I never knew what education was about. Of course, I could have lectured on it every day of the week if asked, firing off the usual bromides like a vaguely healthy smell – but while I was really teaching children, I could never have told an eager enquirer what the practical point of my endeavours was supposed to be.

He was troubled by guilt about his incompetence as well as his lack of commitment. However, he was unqualified for any other job, and had a growing family to support. When he left the navy his son David was five, and in July 1945 Ann had given birth to their daughter Judy.

They were poor, and lived in what Golding called 'a lousy council flat' in Salisbury. That seems an embittered view. David has much brighter memories. In his recollection, 21 Bourne Avenue was a substantial Victorian vicarage on three floors. The Goldings had the middle one, and a Major and Mrs Mellis lived in the top flat. Major Mellis was a gardener and something to do with war graves. A Mrs Randall, followed by a family called Macdonald, lived on the ground floor. There was an 'enormous' garden for him and Judy to play in with trees and grass and a strawberry bed. He and his parents both had spacious bedrooms – Judy's was smaller – and his had a window over the garden. There was a sitting-cum-dining room, a kitchen, a bathroom with a stained-glass window and a separate lavatory with a 'Vacant/

Engaged' sign. In the desperate housing shortage after the war most people would have thought this acceptable, and Golding's adverse reaction reflects his dark mood, which went far beyond his personal circumstances. The desolation of post-war Europe induced pity and rage, expressed in a poem called 'Winter Night, 1945' that he wrote at this time.

> This prison of the dark is wild with tears,
> With agonies and tortured questioners,
> With voices of the murdered, the half-dead,
> Of lost and piteous children sick for bread.
>
> Sleep easy and sleep quiet, prosperous man,
> Only the innocent hold out their hands.
> Time killed your heart and you can hear
> Not so much noise as when tall grasses stir.

His dejection was apparent to those close to him. Richard Brookfield, his brother-in-law, found him changed after the war, less approachable, less outgoing, more critical. Ann's mother gave a graphic description of him coming home from work exhausted and flopping down – constantly out of tune with what he was doing, and regarding it as a waste of time. She felt sorry for Ann because he did not seem to make much of a contribution to the home. His relations with David were a further complication. Like many children of fathers returning from the war, David confesses that he felt his 'nose out of joint'. He had been the centre of his mother's attention, and suddenly she was 'very wrapped up' in this unfamiliar 'man in shiny clothes'. Golding told Frank Kermode that he could imagine, in retrospect, what it must have been like for his small son 'to have a bearded bully coming in and running the house'. But the resentment was not only on the boy's side. Looking back at his own behaviour, he recognized that there had been anger and cruelty in his treatment of David.

On one occasion when he was perhaps four years old, I got him to pillow fight me. I squatted down and banged at him and he tried to bang at me. He never hit me of course, only the pillow, but I hit him when I liked and enjoyed it. We stopped when he was on the verge of tears. I never let him hit me, never pretended to fall over. I presented and maintained an appearance of invulnerability. I have always remembered this with the bitterest self-condemnation: the more so since now I believe the whole scene was not only itself, but also symbolic of a relationship.

Another time Ann had put David down for his afternoon's rest – they were staying with Golding's parents – and he started to yell and try to get out. 'So finally I locked him in. He went on yelling, getting wilder and wilder.' Golding's mother intervened, warning 'You'll break the child's spirit!', so he unlocked the door, feeling relieved at this solution to the difficulty. He adds that he had other memories of David's childhood that were 'sunny enough'. There were games, walks, cycle rides, story-telling – 'all the usual father stuff'. Nevertheless, lingering feelings of guilt and antagonism in his attitude to his son may have been part of his general dissatisfaction with himself and his life when he returned to schoolteaching in 1945.

Inevitably the dissatisfaction was shared by his pupils. The room where he usually taught had a narrow aisle between the blackboard and the front desks that extended along the side by the door, forming an 'L'. Golding's regular practice was to enter the room, tell the class to continue with some task – reading *Northanger Abbey*, or doing the next exercise in O'Malley and Thompson's *English I* – and then walk back and forth along the 'L' for the rest of the lesson. Sometimes he would have a volume of Greek in his hand and read as he walked; sometimes he would laugh or talk to himself. 'The high-spot came', one boy recalled, 'after he left the room and we calculated the distance he had walked. Folk memory suggests that it was miles.' A variation was for him to set the class some task that involved them looking after themselves, and then sit at the master's desk writing in longhand in a school exercise book. The boys were aware that he was an unpublished novelist, but he never discussed his fiction with them. Occasionally, though, an English lesson would start with manuscript pages being distributed for the boys to count the words on each page. As far as they could gather from these piecemeal extracts, they were from 'adventure stories, a sort of cross between Alistair MacLean and Rudyard Kipling'.

(Of the unpublished novels, the one this sounds most like is *Circle Under the Sea*, which we shall come to.)

His nickname among the boys was 'Scruff', alluding to his unkempt beard and hair ('Einstein in the last week of his life,' as one wag described him), and to his baggy corduroy trousers and shapeless Harris tweed jacket. The gown he sometimes wore appeared to consist largely of holes held together with bits of once-black material turned green with age. His fingers and beard were stained yellow with nicotine. All this contrasted with the formal suits favoured by other masters, but particularly with the immaculate attire of Terence ('Gus') Barnes, head of the English department, comprising a khaki shirt, primrose-yellow tie, dazzlingly polished brown shoes and a King's College Cambridge blazer.

On only one day in the week did Scruff appear less scruffy. Together with John Milne he ran the School Combined Cadet Force, and was senior officer of the Sea Cadets, so on Wednesday, which was Sea Cadets day, he would arrive at school in a neatly pressed uniform, with his hair combed. One of his duties was to test Cadets for proficiency in Morse. 'Seated at his desk with his Morse buzzer', one recalls, 'he seemed the epitome of the grizzled sea-farer.' At weekends he used to take the Cadets down the Solent in their whaler. This was a slender boat, twenty-seven feet long, with two masts and three sails, which could hold about ten boys. It has stuck in the mind of more than one of them that their senior officer used to forget to bring adequate rations for himself – and for David, after he became a pupil at Bishop Wordsworth's – and so was obliged to 'cadge from the rest of us'. Other memories are of the Cadets having to sleep on a pebble beach, marked PRIVATE, one night when they were becalmed miles from base, and of Scruff thumbing a tow from a motor boat when they were caught far downstream late on a Sunday night. They all seem to have enjoyed it very much: 'The cold, the rain, the blistered hands from rowing, the seasickness and sheer terror in the gales, that was the life.'

The affection implicit in these anecdotes seems to have been quite widespread among the boys, even those who were exasperated by his neglect of their education. They seem to have intuited that he was essentially kind and gentle, despite occasional outbursts. At one noisy assembly, soon after his return from the navy, he climbed on the stage and thundered, 'If you don't all pipe down immediately, I will bring back every man-jack of you at half past four,' which quickly restored order on the quarter-deck. On the other hand, when a boy put a book on top of a classroom door that was slightly ajar, so that when Golding entered it fell on his head, he did not attempt to identify or punish the culprit, but gave them a mild lecture about not damaging books. There was a tendency among the boys, too, to excuse his failure of communication as merely a sign of his extreme shyness. Andrew Harvey, head boy at Bishop Wordsworth's in 1961–2, remembers his frequent gesture of drawing a hand down across his face and beard, as if lowering a screen. If social contact threatened, Golding's naval uniform could serve as a shield. He would wear it for the meetings between parents and teachers held in the school hall. The procedure at these gatherings was for parents to buttonhole any member of staff with whom they wanted to discuss their son's progress. Golding would appear in his smart uniform, 'like royalty entering a room', march slowly up the body of the hall and, if no one spoke to him, leave by a side door. 'I was fascinated by this,' a pupil recollects, 'and counted it fourteen times in one hour.'

The other members of staff seem, on the whole, to have taken a less charitable view of Golding's eccentricities than the boys. He was, one of them told me with asperity, 'neither a dedicated nor a gifted teacher'. This same colleague remembered going into rooms where Golding had been teaching, and finding piles of exercise books left there. 'If you leafed through them you would find that they all carried the same sort of request – "Please, sir, will you mark my last three pieces of work."' In breaks and at lunch hour, Golding would sit apart from the other masters, learning Greek or, later, 'scribbling' in notebooks. 'He used to get no end of leg-pulling, "How's the masterpiece coming on . . . ?" He took it all in good spirit.' Maybe he did, or maybe it rankled. His radio play *Break My Heart*, broadcast in 1966, is set in a school readily identifiable as Bishop Wordsworth's, and features a master called 'Jerry', who never speaks, but sits in a corner of the staff room trying to write novels. He is mocked by his colleagues for his literary ambition:

ROBINSON: Has Jerry had his coffee yet? Jerry!

BINDER: Let him be, Henry, my old ... He is happier so.

ROBINSON: I simply can't understand it. He sits there day after day, term after term, never saying a word, scribble, scribble, scribble ...

BINDER: Don't you know?

ROBINSON: Know what?

BINDER: Frustrated author. Tries to write novels.

ROBINSON: *No!*

BINDER: Fact, dear boy, and the man can't even spell. Pathetic, I call it.

This last shaft is well aimed, for the journal reveals that Golding's spelling was indeed shaky.

He was also mocked by the other teachers for what they regarded as his nautical posturing. He and John Milne would go sailing with the Cadets, and Milne was overheard asking, 'Well, Bill, have you been shipping it green in the Channel this week?' (naval jargon for having a wave come over the deck). 'We gave him no end of hell on this one,' an ex-colleague told me. They 'gave Bill hell', too, when Happold rather tactlessly praised him at a meeting of selected masters. 'Golding?' the headmaster remarked, 'Well, Golding is a *rara avis*, isn't he?' After that he had to endure colleagues inquiring, 'I say, anyone seen that *rara avis* round here?' The banter increased when Golding became successful. When news reached the staff room that their erstwhile colleague had won a Nobel Prize for literature it was spoken of almost with resentment, as if it were unjust that a 'very ordinary chap' should achieve such distinction. 'It was a complete astonishment to all those who knew him that he had in fact got this in him.' But a different reason for his unpopularity was that he was seen as standoffish. 'At the end of term we used to go to the King's Arms, seven or eight of us, and wives would join us at some indicated point in the afternoon. Bill never joined us at all ... Not outgoing.'

However, he was admired for his integrity, even by those who were otherwise unimpressed. 'Bill had his own morality,' I was told, 'his own code of ethics.' The stand he took over the Bentley case was especially remembered. On 28 January 1953, Derek Bentley, a nineteen-year-old who was illiterate and had a mental age of eleven, was hanged for the murder of a policeman, although the fatal shot was fired by his accomplice, Christopher Craig (who could not be hanged because he was under age), and Bentley was already under arrest when it was fired. 'Bill was absolutely incandescent. Not for very long but it was absolutely clear. He said, "In the old days they used to tie horses and pull people apart – this is the same." I said, "It isn't the same, Bill." "Same thinking," he said, "Same thinking."' A poem, 'Words for a Sensitive Juryman', seems to have been written with the Bentley case in mind.

> We've hanged a boy for the job he did
> Though he wasn't much bigger than anyone's kid.
> He was quick on the trigger and soft in the head
> But we've taught him a lesson and now he's dead.
>
> Out in the coalshed streetlights gleam
> Through a rent in the tin on a rope and a beam
> And down our passage the family clothes
> Are hanged by the nape in silent rows.
>
> So I daren't go and open the door lest in
> Should slither a sack with a twisted grin
> That jabbers of justice and jeers at truth
> And claims a neck or an eye or a tooth.

It is worth adding that Golding's view eventually prevailed. Bentley was granted a posthumous royal pardon in 1998.

A trainee-teacher, Donald Culver, who spent his practice term at Bishop Wordsworth's in the first three months of 1955, has contributed an observant account of how Golding struck an outsider. He remained, Culver noticed, detached from 'the banter, the jokes, the internal politics'. His appearances in the staff room were limited to collecting his morning tea and sitting, 'in an uncommunicative but not unfriendly way, chain-smoking Woodbines while reading Homer – in Greek'. If he conversed it would be in a 'quiet, gentle, almost other-worldly tone'. There was a little anteroom which seemed to be off limits to others, where he would clatter away on an elderly typewriter whenever he had a free period. He spoke to Culver only once, confiding to him that New

York skyscrapers had two types of lift (or 'elevator'), express ones that stopped at every tenth floor and slow ones that stopped at every floor. In Manhattan during the war he had learnt that the quickest way to get to, say, the thirty-eighth floor was to take the express to the fortieth and then the slow lift down to the thirty-eighth. 'He commended this piece of wisdom to me', Culver recalls, 'as though he had passed on the Secret of Life.' It crossed his mind that Golding was enjoying some sort of joke at his expense, and he came to suspect 'some of his characteristics of contrivance'. Granted, he was no ordinary man, 'but did he also cultivate an image?' This was the same suspicion of play-acting that had occurred to Richard Brookfield before the war.

Break My Heart depicts the other members of the school staff as lazy and disaffected, uninterested in the boys and sick of teaching, which one of them describes as 'dreary and degrading'. Maybe Golding presented them like this just for the purposes of his plot, or perhaps it was a way of registering that, inefficient as he had been as a teacher, he was no worse than the others. At all events there is in fact plenty of evidence to show that the other staff members were, by contrast with him, much admired for their teaching, not least those in the English department. The head of English, Terence Barnes, had read English at Cambridge and attended the lectures of F. R. Leavis, the most famous English literary critic of the mid-twentieth century, who, through his disciples, re-invented the study of English literature, transforming it from a *belles-lettristic* pastime to the central discipline in any culture – a discipline that refined the sensibility and honed critical skills so as to fashion a defence against what Leavis saw as the ever-encroaching vulgarity and mindlessness of the mass media. Barnes was not just a follower but a friend of this choleric celebrity. He stayed with the Leavises in the vacations, and contributed to the Leavisite journal *Scrutiny*. Two of his articles had the rare distinction of being reprinted by Leavis in his *A Selection from Scrutiny* (1968). Golding's antiquarian studies under C. L. Wrenn at Oxford and his absorption in the literature of ancient Greece were poor equipment for competing with the magnetism of the Leavisite mission, as embodied in Barnes, or challenging its intimidating certainty about which authors were, and which were not, life-enhancing. The contrast was not lost on the boys. Andrew Harvey remembers Barnes as a 'wonderful teacher', who introduced them to poets such as Crabbe, of whom they had never heard before, whereas Golding was quite simply 'the wrong person to be a schoolteacher'.

There is one intriguing scrap of evidence which suggests that Golding made some attempt to lessen the gap between Barnes's knowledge of contemporary literature and his own. Among the books still in his library is a copy of Stuart Gilbert's *James Joyce's Ulysses: A Study* (Faber and Faber, 1930) which is inscribed on the flyleaf, in black ink, 'F. R. Leavis, March 1931'. Beneath this is the pencilled inscription 'T. R. Barnes'. It is unthinkable that Barnes would have purloined a book from his hero's house, and the only alternative explanation is that Leavis gave his copy of Gilbert's study – one of the earliest and best introductions to *Ulysses* – to his disciple. Presumably it came to be among Golding's books because he borrowed it from Barnes in hopes of coming to terms with Joyce's baffling masterpiece.

Barnes was a formidable competitor on other counts. He had done a diploma in French at Cambridge, as well as the English Tripos, and he was famous for reading the whole of Proust's *A la Recherche du Temps Perdu* to his wife aloud in French, translating as he went along. Boys reported seeing him at it in the kitchen, book in hand. He was even said to do it in bed. Perhaps Golding's decision, late in life, to take French lessons testifies to a lingering sense of inferiority to his erstwhile colleague. For his part, Barnes, when I spoke to him in 1985, gave a measured appreciation of Golding's achievement, while acknowledging that they were 'never very great friends'. 'He certainly wanted to be, and perhaps was, deeply religious, and he read a vast amount of theology and philosophy. He did not like it at all when I occasionally teased him about this.' He acknowledged Golding's generosity. After the publication of *Lord of the Flies* he started to do book-reviewing, and would turn up in class with an armful of new novels and hand them round to the boys – 'Tell me what you think about that.' They were very eager, but one master, a strict Baptist, 'found that a novel Bill had distributed had some unsavoury scenes in it – explicit sex, or something – and complained to the headmaster. Bill was furious.' Like many of those who knew Golding well, Barnes found him 'a knockout as a comic raconteur – much funnier than his books'. The two of them would play chess in the staff room, and Golding was 'first class'. You were lucky to get a draw out of him in a whole term, 'and by God he likes to win; if he loses he worries about it for hours'. Even in hockey, which no one else took seriously, 'he would play like a demon rather than lose'. The concentration that went into staff-room chess games tallies with boys' memories. '"Scruff" and "Guss" could be descried through the smoke in the staff room', one recalls, 'playing chess during break.' Once when they were deep in a game a boy appeared for a lunchtime oboe lesson. 'Go to the music room,' Golding told him, 'put it together and blow. I'll soon be along.' He did not play chess with the boys, though at a time when there was a chess craze in the school, and everyone was carrying a pocket chess set, he challenged fifteen of them to simultaneous games. They laid out their sets in a classroom next to the chapel, and Golding walked round making his moves. The boy who remembers this had already lost his queen when time ran out and the games had to be concluded. 'We were certainly impressed with Mr Golding's chess skills.'

The other member of the English staff with whom he was unfavourably compared by pupils was Derek Warner, an elegant Cambridge graduate who ran the Studio Theatre in Salisbury and produced school plays. Andrew Harvey had parts in several of them, including Edgar in Warner's *King Lear* (which was favourably commented on by Marius Goring, a friend of Happold). Harvey remembers Warner as 'slightly foppish' and charismatic. He smoked a cigarette in the playground, which was considered rather dashing, and always stubbed it out on the same drainpipe (legend has it that a practical joker once put a small charge of gunpowder on this exact spot). Warner's arrival was evidently perceived as a threat by Golding, for though he could not hope to compete with Barnes on an academic level, he alone had real-life experience as an actor, so could rule the roost where drama was concerned – or so it seemed until Warner came along. More than twenty years later Golding was still having bad dreams about the shock he sustained. In January 1972 he dreamed of 'the competitiveness between Derek [Warner] and myself when he first came to Bishop's School and more or less took over the drama, as I suppose I once tried, at least, to take it from Terence [Barnes]'. A few months later he dreams that he is once more back at Bishop Wordsworth's, and

Happold, the headmaster, announces that he is making Derek Warner head of English. Golding, in the dream, retorts that he is not coming back unless he is made head, and rushes out furiously 'crying with rage and humiliation'. He wakes up feeling 'worthless and miserable'.

Other aspects of his unhappy years at Bishop Wordsworth's continued to trouble his dreams until late in life, and the thread that runs through them all is awareness of his own incompetence. He dreams that he is in a classroom full of parents, where 'the issue of my being a good enough teacher' is under discussion; or that Happold is interrogating two boys from his class, and is, he fears, bound to detect his 'extreme lack of diligence'; or that other staff members have noticed his 'extraordinary slackness'; or that he has not filled in his register for years; or that the head is coming to see what work he has done with a certain class, and he is aware that though it is halfway through the term he has done none at all – has, indeed, never been into the class in question, as a result of his taking down the timetable wrongly. His anxiety extends to his responsibilities with the Sea Cadets: he dreams the whaler has sunk and the Cadets are rowing under water.

The member of staff he was closest to was Tony Brown. They remained friends for life, and the two families got to know each other well. When they first met, the Browns were living in a 'grotty' flat in the middle of Salisbury, over a hairdresser's and a garage. They stayed there until 1951, when Tony was appointed head of music at Canford School, about twenty-five miles away, and took his family to live in staff accommodation there. But the Goldings would still drive over once or twice a week, especially on Sundays. The two men would retire to the music room for chess and philosophical talk, while their wives chatted in the kitchen. In 1968 the Browns moved to a cottage called Misselfore in Bowerchalke near Salisbury, where the Goldings were living, so contacts between the two families became even more frequent.

Tony, five years older than Golding, was a brilliantly gifted pianist and organist, and his wife Fiona (they married in 1938) played violin with the Bournemouth Symphony Orchestra. All the children became professional musicians. Iona, the eldest, born in 1941, was a word-famous violinist and conductor, who joined the Academy of St Martin in the Fields when it was first established. Tim, born 1943, became principal

French horn with the BBC Symphony Orchestra; Ian, born 1945, is a freelance accompanist, plays with the Nash Ensemble, and directs his own orchestra, the Henley Symphony; and Sally, born 1946, played viola with the Bournemouth Symphony.

While Tony was teaching at Bishop Wordsworth's he also taught piano to choristers at the Cathedral School (among them the future organist and composer Bernard Rose). Readers of *Lord of the Flies* often assume, incorrectly, that Golding taught choristers. In fact he had no professional connection at all with the choir school, but it is just possible that some chat about chorister behaviour was passed on in his conversations with Tony. Tony's son Tim, a chorister himself, sat in on their talks when he was deemed old enough, and remembers some of the religious and philosophical issues they covered. Tony came across as a convinced non-Christian, and Golding, asked if he was a Christian, replied, 'No, but I like to think of myself as a religious person.' He named Sir James Frazer's study of mythology and comparative religion, *The Golden Bough*, together with Homer's epics, as books that had influenced him, was sceptical of J. W. Dunne's *An Experiment With Time* (which theorizes that all time is eternally present), and shared Tony's interest in Jung's last psychological work *Man and His Symbols* (published in 1964). They also discussed science, and Golding gave Tony a book about the astronomer Edwin Hubble, who was the first to prove that galaxies exist beyond the Milky Way. They both admired Bertrand Russell, and Tony was much taken with *Freedom in the Modern World* by the Christian, communitarian moral philosopher John Macmurray.

Another of Tony's enthusiasms was the German American social psychologist Erich Fromm, among whose ideas was a reinterpretation of the Fall story and Adam and Eve's exile from the Garden of Eden. For Fromm, Adam and Eve were right to seek knowledge of good and evil. Human beings should have the courage to take independent moral action and use their reason to establish moral values, rather than adhering to authoritarian dictates. Tony had read Fromm's *Fear of Freedom* (1941), *The Sane Society* (1955) and the international best-seller *The Art of Loving* (1956), and, Tim is certain, discussed them at length with Golding who was to become, or perhaps was already, deeply interested in the idea of the Fall. Tim's own conversations with Golding elicited that he admired Aldous Huxley and Evelyn Waugh, and had a mental image of Homer 'sitting in the shade of a beached boat (or protected from the rain) telling stories' – which, he added, was what he wanted of himself, 'to be a story-teller'.

Virtually every time they met, Golding and Tony would play chess, and Golding usually won. The wish to defeat an opponent so often defeated before seems strange, and it is clear that the nature of his relationship with Tony intrigued the Brown family, including Tony, whose suspicion was that his friend might be a repressed homosexual. Golding took the chess games very seriously. Tim remembers the 'little books' in which he would note down each move as they went along. One of these survives, a hardcover, feint-lined W. H. Smith & Son A6 notebook, recording twenty-four games of which Golding won fifteen and Tony six, with three draws. Tim himself played Golding a few times and won once – it was soon after *The Spire* was published, and Golding gave him a copy which had a drawing of a chess king with a French horn wrapped round it, inscribed 'To the Master' ('of the French horn, that is', he joked, when he handed it over). Tim's sister Sally had been taught chess by Tony when she was four, and later belonged to the Bournemouth Symphony Orchestra's Chess Club. She remembers the different styles of gamesmanship adopted by Golding and her father. 'Tony would make under-breath comments as he played, "Beastly man", and so on. Bill stayed silent, or laughed.' She was in awe of him, especially of his beard. When she first played him at the age of ten, and lost, he advised, 'You have to learn to play the board, not the beard.' Like Tim, she beat him only once. Both Tim and Iona Brown looked on Golding as a 'second father'. Iona was eager to defend him against the charge of cynicism. He was, she insisted, no cynic, but had 'deep passion', as well as extraordinary modesty. He was 'on a different level of feeling from others'. Sally Brown recalls that Iona, like her father, thought Golding was homosexual. Iona felt it explained Golding's attachment to Tony, plus the fact that 'Bill clung to Tony because he was the consummate musician Bill wanted to be'.

Golding would often go round to the Browns' flat for music-making sessions, playing oboe or cello or piano (the cello, a makeshift instrument, was dubbed 'the orange box' or 'Taté & Lylé'). He also sang to

Tony's piano accompaniment. On one occasion they were joined by the conductor Maurice Handford, an old boy of the school, for a performance of Benjamin Britten's *Serenade for Tenor, Horn and Strings*, with Golding's 'fine tenor voice' accompanied by Handford on the horn and Tony Brown playing the piano version of the orchestral score. Music seems to have relaxed Golding in his dealings with colleagues and pupils. He and John Milne would sit at two pianos, Terence Barnes recalls, and 'extemporize wildly on any tune from "Three Blind Mice" upwards'. He had taught himself the oboe well enough to play in the school orchestra and Derek Dawkins, a VIth former and leader of the orchestra, was an amused spectator of the elaborate warming-up procedure he would go through prior to playing, which entailed sucking the reeds to moisten them and making 'amazing kissing noises', which were patently directed at Fiona Brown, Tony's 'talented and glamorous' wife, seated among the violins.

Although many pupils found Golding neglectful, it must be stressed that many did not. For some he was a true educator who provoked them into thought instead of trying to cram them with facts. Both in English and Religious Knowledge he would question boys about their own insights and perceptions. In philosophical or political discussions he would use role-play, getting pupils to defend particular standpoints, such as communism. He would also deliberately provoke. In a 1945 discussion of the wartime miners' strike with the Science VIth, the boys were 'all king and country', and thought it terrible for the miners to have gone on strike during the war. But Golding interposed drily, 'What better time to strike?' John Jacobson, a boy in the class, never forgot it. These once-a-week 'English Cultural' lessons with the Science VIth seem to have been some of his most inventive. He taught them to write blank verse, introduced them to Meditation and the Philosophy of Science, told them about Greek tragedy, and read Sophocles in translation. Jacobson remembers him reading *Don Quixote*. The favourite authors he introduced them to included, rather surprisingly, Addison and Steele. His reading of the last chapters of Captain Scott's diaries 'made a huge impact', and when he read poetry, Derek Dawkins felt, 'all the angels in heaven stopped to listen'. Poems he read stayed in boys' minds all their lives, along with the sound of his voice. Alan Harwood, who was taught English by Golding in the lowest form, found this happened with Edward Thomas's 'Adlestrop'. When *Lord of the Flies* was published in 1954, he read them extracts from that, and when, in the same year, Ernest Hemingway won the Nobel Prize for Literature, Golding was exultant and read them *The Old Man and the Sea*, 'an unforgettable experience'.

For some boys it was what he said about religion that had the deepest effect, and given his statement to Tony Brown that he was not a Christian his comments can seem surprising. Once he asked a boy what made the Bible different from other books and, when no answer was forthcoming, roared, 'It's the only one that's the word of God!' He would fire questions at them like, 'How many of you say your prayers at night?' and, to those who said they didn't, 'Why not?' He got them thinking about ethical matters by recommending that, at the end of each day, they should make a practice of reviewing the good and not so good things they had done. They got the impression that he was a 'devout Christian', and that he taught them about the other main religions only because he was obliged to. The Christian heaven, he said, which meant sitting contemplating God's creation, was better than the Islamic paradise, because surely having all those houris and every known luxury would get boring after the first hundred thousand years. In one RE lesson he came into the room, took a piece of chalk and, starting at the door frame, drew a line round the walls of the classroom at shoulder height. He put an X about six feet from the door, and another X at the end of the line on the fourth wall. The line, he explained, represented their spiritual life. The first X was the moment of conversion when a person consciously acknowledged his faith in Jesus Christ. The second X marked the moment of illumination, the ultimate stage in spiritual development when a person achieved a knowledge of God's presence and eternal union with him. 'Needless to say he offered us no certainty that many of us would reach this stage in our lifetimes.' The boy who recorded this later became a Church of England minister. He detected in Golding a 'living spirituality' that could communicate itself to others – even a young rugger-playing 'peasant' like himself.

Dramatic and gripping though such exhibitions were, they were not particularly useful in covering the RE syllabus. After a form had 'slogged through' the wording of one of the creeds for six weeks, Golding came in and said he was sorry but it was the wrong one. Though put out, they admired him for owning up. His bids for profundity could misfire. A member of the Science VIth recalls a discussion of religious experience which included an excursus on Golding's use of introspection to locate his own position in the scheme of things. Clearly this was a topic of such significance to him that it brought out an unusual degree of commitment and frankness, as well as considerable drama and suspense. There was much painful tunnelling through the Golding psyche as they approached, step by step, the moment of revelation. He seemed at one point to hesitate, leaning towards the blackboard, chalk in hand, and evidently wondering whether to bare his soul before such an audience. Then, deciding it was too late to draw back, he continued: 'When you have completely penetrated past the trappings of your personality, you are left with ... A presence? A feeling? I can only describe it as a shape like this' – and he drew on the blackboard something rather like a pear lying on its side. The class erupted in silent hysteria, and Golding was evidently both embarrassed and angry. Robert Naish, who recorded this anecdote, saw how intensely he wished that he had kept his own counsel. When, in later years, he read of Golding's openly confessed gratitude that he had been able to give up schoolteaching, he felt he could sympathize.

All the same, schoolteaching provided him with insights that were valuable for his future work, most obviously for *Lord of the Flies*. It occurred to more than one boy that Golding stirred up antagonism between them in order to observe their reactions. As master in charge of a trip to Figsbury Rings, the huge earthwork, probably Neolithic, to the north-east of Salisbury, he gave permission for the boys to form into two groups, one to attack the enclosure and the other to defend it. In class discussions he encouraged them to adopt extreme and opposed political positions. When delivering the second Ewing Lecture at the University of California at Los Angeles in 1961, he confessed that he had learnt to understand the nature of small boys with 'awful precision' because he had introduced 'a certain measure of experimental science' into his teaching of them. He had decided to see what would happen if they were given more liberty, and if the restraining pressure of adult life were removed. 'Well, I gave them more liberty, and I gave them more liberty, and more, and more, and more – I drew further away. My eyes came out like organ stops as I watched what was happening.' He does not say precisely what *was* happening, but he hints that there was eventually a danger of someone being killed. 'Give me liberty, or give me death – well it was a point where these were no longer simple alternatives.' Though more extreme than anything in the boys' recollections that have survived, this tallies with their sense that they were being manipulated and observed.

It seems that individual pupils at Bishop Wordsworth's did not provide models for the boys in *Lord of the Flies*. But Golding told them 'you might recognize bits of yourself', and they did. They were sure that Ralph was partly based on one of their number – 'tall, good leadership material outwardly but with few ideas', and they thought that Piggy was perhaps based on a boy who was excused games for medical reasons and was the butt of everyone's jokes, 'but who took everything that was thrown at him'. There was a pair of identical twins who perhaps suggested Sam 'n' Eric, and one boy who described himself as 'a loner' and suffered from epileptic fits believed there was something of him in Simon. This claim was contested, however, by another ex-pupil whose school nickname was Simon and who considered himself the model, while yet another concluded that 'try as we might we could identify no one in the story'.

In *Men, Women & Now* Golding tells of a different kind of observation that his time as a schoolteacher allowed, relating to his theories about sexuality. He remembers producing *Murder in the Cathedral* at Bishop Wordsworth's in 1959. As in all the school plays, the female parts were taken by boys, and he chose four boys to be the Women of Canterbury. He taught them 'the basic movements of a woman's body', dressed them up, played the piano for them to dance, and told them, 'I want you to enjoy being girls.' The result, he says, was 'the breaking up of all the dams and barriers'. The boys were 'so happy' – as if they were realizing an ambition they had had for years, as, indeed, he believed they were. It was as if they could not believe their luck. For what an adolescent boy has to bury deep out of sight, and think of as a private shame, was here given 'adult sanction and a social aim'. It was treated as 'what it is, that is, something natural'. Every little girl wants to be the fairy on the Christmas tree, and 'tell it not in Gath, but so does every little boy'. In our society children are sexed as a vet sexes kittens by examining their 'rudimentary sexual organs', but other realities are ignored. He goes on to regret, in *Men, Women & Now*, that he never realized, as a child, how common these feelings were in boys, so was left believing them peculiar to himself.

As important as anything he learnt from the boys was the sense of place he developed in his time at Bishop Wordsworth's, the knowledge of Salisbury, especially its cathedral and close, and of Stonehenge and other prehistoric sites in the surrounding countryside, which fed his imaginings about the remote past. He would take visitors on tours of the cathedral, pointing out curiosities such as the tomb in the south nave aisle, the occupant of which, so legend had it, had died of arsenic poisoning, and when it was opened in the nineteenth century it was found that a rat had got in among the bones and died, poisoned by the arsenic that was still there. He would point out, too, that the cathedral's spire is slightly impacted on one side. He told his publisher Charles Monteith that he had been in every house in Salisbury Close, and that they were like 'a compendium of English domestic architecture' – 'you could write a fair-sized book on the plumbing' alone. One house had a room where Handel gave his first concert in England, and there was another room decorated in Gothic Revival style for a visit by the Prince Regent, who never arrived. Golding's friends Wayland and Liz Kennet remember that on walks on the Wiltshire Downs and Golden Ball Hill, near Avebury, he would show the children how to identify bits of pottery. They still have a jam jar full of shards he collected. For fifteen years he ran the Bishop Wordsworth's School archaeological society, 'taking part in odd digs around the place', and pupils would bring him 'spearheads and things like that'. When archaeologist and author Ian Blake was excavating an Iron Age site at Pimperne Down, Dorset, in 1960, Golding visited the dig and showed great interest in what they were unearthing. At Stonehenge, he told Stephen Medcalf, he had noticed the carving of a Mycenaean dagger on one of the stones long before it became the subject of common observation and controversy. Add to this that every day of his working life for sixteen years he saw the cathedral spire from his classroom window, and saw it in process of construction, or rather reconstruction, for in the 1950s the top thirty feet of the spire were taken off and rebuilt. The father of one pupil, Mark Merrill, who played bassoon in the orchestra with Golding, knew the clerk of works and was allowed up the spire while repairs were in progress. Another pupil remembers how, day-dreaming in lessons, he would watch the little railway going up and down the spire taking blocks of stone for the repairs.

II

Unpublished Novelist

In his breaks and lunch hours and holidays while he was teaching at Bishop Wordsworth's School, Golding wrote three books and sent them out hopefully to publishers, all of whom sent them back. When he started and finished each one is hard to say. But they were all written before 1953, when *Lord of the Flies* was accepted by Faber and Faber, and the earliest of them was almost certainly completed in 1948. It is an account of the Golding family's boating holiday the previous summer, and he called it *Seahorse*. Being non-fiction, it is the most informative from a biographical angle, and it reveals his resentment of wealthy people, and the bohemian, nonconformist postures he adopted to help him cope with this feeling.

It starts with his memories of the joy he got from sailing round the bays and inlets of the south coast during his months of training for D-Day, and his desire to share these pleasures with his family. But when he looks up the prices of yachts and dinghies it becomes gallingly clear that the Goldings are 'away down below the level of people who can afford to sail'. Undaunted, he proposes buying an old hull and converting it into a kind of floating tent, so that they can have a camping holiday on the water. David, aged nearly seven, is enthusiastic, Ann is game, and Judy, aged two, is too young to be consulted, so he pays £42 10s for a decommissioned lifeboat, moored on the River Itchen. She has nine inches of rainwater in her bilge and no fittings, not even a coat of paint. She is, in fact, very evidently just an old lifeboat, with loops of rope still hanging along her sides for the shipwrecked to clutch at. In surviving photographs she resembles the little paper cutouts pinned on donors on Lifeboat Day, though less neat.

Golding drew up plans for cabins and bunks, only to find that wartime regulations made it impossible to get wood. So he rigged a tarpaulin over the middle of the boat, to serve as living quarters, and borrowed a mast and sails from the Cadet Corps whaler. A rudder was constructed out of the wooden partition in their coal shed. Ann had been scraping and saving tinned food for months (rationing of some foodstuffs was even harsher than it had been in the war), and they managed to get hold of some ex-army blankets, tin plates, buckets and bowls, and a lavatory seat from a house that was being rebuilt. At last on Monday, 11 August they loaded it all into helpful Tony Brown's car and he drove them to Southampton. When they saw the boat Judy burst into tears, David rushed about in wild excitement, and Ann was numb with shock. They had lunch at a British Restaurant, then Tony drove away 'with a sad and thoughtful face'.

Back aboard, they waited for the tide to lift them off the mud, then hoisted sail and headed downstream. Some of the disadvantages of *Seahorse* (as they decided to call her) soon became apparent. Her sails were not big enough, so progress was slow – sometimes imperceptible. The rudder was too small, which made steering difficult. However, the sun shone, and continued to do so through the whole scorching summer.

At first the discomforts of a sailing holiday outweighed the pleasures. The Primus was recalcitrant, the tea tasted of paraffin, Judy yelled much of the time, and getting ashore meant wading through 'stinking and deadly' mud. They ran aground, and sat and fried for an endless afternoon, waiting for the tide to turn. Ann suggested that perhaps they should stick it for two more days and then go home. But gradually things improved. The wind picked up, and as they reached more open water they started to feel the freedom of sail, landing when they liked on beaches for the children to play. At Lepe they went ashore and a friendly young man gave Ann and David a lift into Exbury to do some shopping. Golding stayed on the beach and played with Judy 'the Solent quivering below me, flecked with random sails'. In Exbury Ann sent a picture postcard to her parents-in-law – one of five from this holiday that survive – dated 17 August: 'Isn't it hot! Our boat is a centre of interest ... Interested faces peer over the side just as one is about to pot or change Judy.' She and David brought back a basket of huge blackberries, so there were stewed blackberries and custard for tea.

Golding's account of their progress is interspersed with self-examination. He repeatedly loses his temper with David, knowing it is unfair, but unable to stop. He tends, he notices, to go up 'a winding stair of temper' till he finds himself 'isolated at a great height for no apparent reason'. After one flare-up he reads his son the story of Odysseus and Nausicaa to compensate. He also castigates his own lack of willpower. He has always found 'honest work nearly impossible to do'. If he contracts a vice – smoking, say – he becomes a slave to it, and will smoke up to sixty a day. What arouses these reflections is the subject of sea-bathing, which he dislikes, and would not, he says, have the willpower to do at all if the 'moral compulsion' of his 'water-minded family' had not driven him to it as a child. He recalls how, on his undergraduate holiday with his brother in the Scilly Isles, Jose blithely dived into the sea while he sat shivering with terror above the black water, where 'brown slimy strapweed swayed and quivered'. But now, on the *Seahorse* holiday, he bathes, and urges his children to brave the water, passing on the 'moral compulsion'.

From Lepe they decide to sail across to the Isle of Wight, which proves alarming. There is not enough wind, and the current threatens to sweep them out to sea. He snarls at David and loses his temper with Ann, who remains 'cold and dignified'. Judy, sensing the tension, yells. Forced to take to the oars, he and Ann row till their arms are 'limp as seaweed', and manage to reach Colwell Bay. There friendly holiday-makers in canoes and kayaks cluster round, and they feel that 'at any moment with blowing of conches and beating of drums, the chief would appear and rub noses'. After a happy afternoon on the beach they turn in early, only to be woken about eleven by young people from the nearby Butlin's holiday camp who have come down to the beach for 'songs and whoopee'. Early next morning the campers are at it again, doing physical jerks on the beach while a loudspeaker clangs out 'jolly music'. Watching, the Goldings feel snobbish, and are ashamed of it.

A nastier experience of class distinction awaits them, for they decide to drop down the coast to Totland Bay and Freshwater. With the tide against them, they have to toil at the oars again and they realize, as they pass some smart motor cruisers, that they are being scanned through binoculars by their amused owners. Ann goes 'puce' and Golding snarls the rudest things he can think of, while uneasily aware that their 'circus rig-out' must indeed look ridiculous. There is enough of the Marxist in him, he reflects, to regard super-tax payers as the enemy, and both he and Ann take against Freshwater. The local accent is 'at least a semitone nearer the roof of the mouth' than at Colwell Bay, and they are over-charged for a poor tea in a 'flash' café. They christen it 'Bilgewater' and hurry back to Colwell Bay where, at supper, they discover the delights of powdered mashed potato ('miraculous'). Ann's postcard home from the Isle of Wight makes light of their upset: 'We talk in loud voices about our yacht (while well away from Seahorse) and skulk aboard unseen – or so we hope.'

The English class system had survived the war, but many men and women returning from the forces had acquired education and experi-ence which made them antagonistic to it. As young impoverished intel-lectuals, the Goldings shared this resistance. The beard Golding grew during their trip – 'ginger, and about half an inch long' – was itself a social statement. Beards became common among the disaffected young in the 1960s, but were very unusual in 1947. He had grown a beard in the navy, but shaved it off when demobbed. The Bishop Wordsworth's School photograph of 1946–7, taken at the end of the summer term, shows him beardless. Now, on his boating holiday, he lets it grow again. This marks him as an outsider, but since his beard was a reversion to his seafaring days it could also be seen as a claim to status. His transition from schoolmaster to naval officer in the war represented a social elevation. Having captained a warship – even a lowly LCT(R) – he had no need to feel inferior to the jeering yacht owners. Back at school the beard's dual role became apparent, since it was both an element of his unconventional 'Scruff' persona and, on Wednesdays, part of his immaculate naval officer's get-up.

It was not just the beard that he grew on the *Seahorse* trip that signalled his rejection of conventional values. He wore an 'amazingly dirty' pair of old flannel trousers cut down into shorts 'in a careless sort of fashion', and he and Ann allowed Judy to run around on beaches naked, which would certainly have offended the strait-laced in the 1940s. In addition to these assertions of bohemianism, Ann's beauty could be seen, at any rate by Golding, as a social leveller. He describes an incident when *Seahorse* was overtaken by a 'magnificent yacht' in the Solent, and the elderly owner shouted jocularly, 'That's a nice engine you've got there.' 'I'd change any time,' Golding joked back, whereupon the young man at the yacht's wheel, glancing meaningfully, so it seemed to Golding, 'from the lady at his side to our radiant Ann', called out 'So would I.' So much for mere money and what it can buy. Nevertheless they are constantly reminded of their poverty. Going ashore one evening they buy three handfuls of chips and three pieces of fish, and only when it is all packed up are they told it will cost them six shillings. 'I couldn't even enjoy it for thinking of the price.' Soon they have to phone Tony Brown and ask him to send them five pounds.

Sailing back to the mainland they land up at Keyhaven, and immediately realize it is a mistake. It is 'highfalutin', and large notices posted by the Watch Committee warn them they are not welcome. Nevertheless they decide to risk it. Ashore they feel 'anti-social in a Viking sense' compared with the clean, well-dressed locals. Ann's postcard home is defiantly upbeat ('We came here yesterday after a lovely run across'), but when they leave the harbour next morning wind and tide make *Seahorse* unsteerable, and with 'terrible inevitability' she bumps destructively along 'a row of expensive sailing dinghies polished like pianos'. Luckily the owners are nowhere to be seen, but Ann is 'white and shaken and humiliated', and Golding feels 'a public fool'. Then, to add 'yet another episode to our farcical performance', they run aground under the eyes of Keyhaven and its 'supercilious Watch Committee'. When they finally get off they have to sail past a line of luxury cruisers and the crews come out 'in their holiday attire', and laugh at them.

This was their worst day, and their worst night followed, for they decide to make for Christchurch on the Dorset coast and darkness overtakes them. The sea roughens, they both collect bruises, and Ann wrenches her shoulder. They have no idea where Christchurch harbour is, and it seems they may have to beat backwards and forwards in the bay all night. Fear assails them, and guilt, as they think of the danger they have put their sleeping children in. Taking a bearing on the shore lights, Golding realizes they are being driven southwards into the English Channel, and almost panics. Then the sky clears and the stars, 'like a cloud of silver bees in the rigging', show him that the wind has shifted and they are going north. How strange, he thinks, in the days of radar to be sailing by the stars 'like any ancient Greek'. They see the shapes of trees ahead, and the wind pushes them through the harbour entrance. He dumps the anchor overboard 'in a chrysanthemum of phosphorescence', and they sit with their feet in four inches of water at 1.30 a.m. on a Sunday morning and 'giggle weakly at each other'.

When they wake they see swans 'sleeping like white petals on the water', and the tower of Christchurch Priory two miles off. It looks idyllic, and proves so. Ann's picture postcard home, sent later that Sunday, admits that they have fallen in love with the place, 'hundreds of swans, the sun, the Priory', and its bland opening sentence – 'Arrived here Saturday evening' – wisely omits any mention of the night's terrors. The days that follow are the happiest of the holiday. One afternoon they climb Hengistbury Head, finding acres of heathery ling at the top, and look out over 'what surely must be the loveliest view in England'. They make friends with another couple called the Dunlops – the husband ex-RNVR like Golding – who have a converted Dutch barge just along the beach from *Seahorse*. David learns to swim with an old lifebelt, looking 'frog-like and most appealing in his tiny red bathing costume'. On a solitary walk, Golding comes to the conclusion that he is incapable of logical thought – does not, indeed, really think at all. What he does is 'dream in pictures'. When he gets back, Ann has found a mussel with a little pearl in it. This sets him wondering about ancient beliefs – that a pearl is a drop of dew that falls into a shell when it opens to heaven; that swans sing before they die. Such stories, he surmises, come from the 'creative unconscious', as do dreams, art, poetry, music and the scriptures of the world's religions. Walking around Christchurch he muses about geology, and how we tend to assume shorelines, sandbanks and beaches are permanent, whereas they change all the time. He would like to have charts at twenty-year intervals going back a thousand years, so that he could see an estuary grow 'as you can watch a flower bud, unfold and fall, in a minute or two of film'.

Their holiday almost over, they sail along the coast to Poole, which brings back memories of the assault-craft training before D-Day, and how through those months he was constantly 'hag-ridden by various phobias'. Still hag-ridden, he lies awake that night wondering if he ought to have put his family in such danger, 'practically sobbing with grief' as he imagines *Seahorse* a splintered wreck and their pale bodies washing about in Studland Bay. Next day they go into Bournemouth to shop and feel repelled by the crush of money and people. From this holiday on, they vow, they are committed to the 'tramping life' and will cheerfully side with the 'ragged and carefree'. Ann's last picture postcard, sent from Poole, says that they hate the thought of returning to ordinary life, and that it 'will be interesting to see what colour we all turn after a bath'. The navy help them to get *Seahorse* out of the water. They call in at HMS *Turtle*, the RNVR shore establishment, where the duty officer recognizes and welcomes Golding. Soon a tow-rope has been looped around *Seahorse* and a lorry pulls her up onto the quayside, where she sits, with water dribbling out of her bilges, looking ungainly and pathetic.

The book ends with their homecoming. But they spent their next summer holiday in *Seahorse* too, by which time she was more comfortable and seaworthy. Golding had her transported to the garden of 21 Bourne Avenue, where he worked on her in his spare time, constructing decking and caulking her hull. His son can still remember the smell of pitch. The Salisbury city engineer, a Mr Rackham, objected to the presence of a 'yacht' in the garden, and complained that the Goldings had bent the railings getting it in. However, Golding's amateur shipbuilding evidently proved worthwhile. Ann's picture postcard to her parents-in-law the next summer, sent from Lepe on 27 August 1948, reports that *Seahorse* 'is sailing much better than last year', and that the children are enjoying the sand and water. Seemingly Golding wrote a narrative of this second holiday also, but perhaps he was dissatisfied with it, for on 10 December 1979 he noted in his journal that 'the manuscript of Seahorse part two has never even been typed', and it seems now to have disappeared. *Seahorse* disappeared too. She was moored on the west side of Southampton Water near the Test estuary, but when Golding and his son went to fit her up at the start of the 1949 season she had vanished. Perhaps she had slipped her moorings, or been stolen. David still remembers his father's silence when they came to the place where she should have been.

They could not afford another boat, so that was the end of their seafaring for a while. But on a later holiday, in 1951 or 52, they hired a fourteen-foot dinghy, the *Aphrodite*, while they were staying in the

Cornish fishing village of Mousehole, and sailed her to Land's End. It precipitated another of those crises that tended to occur when they went sailing, for when they tried to get back they found they had miscalculated the current, and were being carried westward. They 'rowed like hell', David recalls, with splintery wooden oars. But in the end a friendly fisherman, whose boat, unlike theirs, had an engine, towed them into the easterly stream and was rewarded with £1.

Did *Seahorse* deserve to be published? Yes and no. It is over-detailed, slow paced, and thick with nautical terminology. On the other hand, it might have found an appreciative readership among the kind of serious, thoughtful young people, with education but not much money, who provided an eager audience for the Third Programme (the forerunner of BBC Radio 3), which had started broadcasting in September 1946. An observant publisher would have seen the distinction of the writing and suggested some redrafting, but none did. His next book, *Circle Under the Sea*, draws on his nautical knowledge, as *Seahorse* does, but there is a scene early on where one character explains to another the technical terms of small-boat sailing. This is obviously inserted for the readers' benefit, so perhaps a publisher who rejected *Seahorse* had pointed out how difficult it was for landlubbers.

Golding later described *Circle Under the Sea* as 'Arthur Ransome for grownups', and it is much more of an adventure story than *Seahorse*. Ben Hamilton, its hero, is big, strong, peaceful and unambitious, and makes a modest living writing adventure stories for boys. He has agreed to take two friends, Geoffrey Amoy, a young schoolmaster and amateur archaeologist, and Geoffrey's sister Penelope, who is just down from Oxford, on a boating holiday aboard his thirty-four-foot ketch *Speedwell*. Geoffrey insists on being taken to the Scilly Isles, because he has a theory that the remains of a prehistoric civilization lie under the water offshore, with submerged megaliths of the Stonehenge type, and he intends to search for them. He has invented a device consisting of hollow steel tubes and a plunger for taking cores of earth from the sea bed, which will, he hopes, aid the search and make his name as an archaeologist. Unfortunately he has boasted about his theory to a rival scholar, John Bentley, who has teamed up with a dilettante archaeologist and millionaire, Sir Henry Miller, and they too arrive on the Scilly Isles aboard Sir Henry's luxurious motor yacht *Minotaur*, eager to find Geoffrey's underwater monuments before he does.

There is a sub-plot that concerns Michael Amoy, Geoffrey and Penelope's younger brother. Michael was a sub-lieutenant in the navy during the war, and served on a ship that Ben commanded. But he has gone to the bad, and has had a spell in prison. He is disconcerted to meet his brother and sister and Ben because he is in league with a gang of ruthless international smugglers, two of whom have come with him to the Scilly Isles and will, he feels sure, kill him if they think there is any chance he will rat on them. Everything comes right in the end. The dilettante Sir Henry tires of the underwater search, after Ben has fed Bentley with false information, and steams off to Egypt. Ben, Geoffrey and Penelope rescue Michael from his criminal associates and get him aboard *Speedwell*. They find that the gangsters are pursuing them in their fast cutter, but Ben skilfully steers among treacherous rocks and currents, and the smugglers, rashly trying to follow him, are wrecked and drowned. When the three friends return to their archaeological operations, Ben dives over the side to free a snagged anchor chain and discovers a prehistoric monolith, which turns out to be part of a great stone avenue. So Geoffrey's theory is validated and Ben generously lets him take the credit for the find. Finally Ben and Penelope, who have fallen for each other, are happily paired off.

From a biographical angle the fascinating thing about *Circle Under the Sea* is that Golding has sliced himself in half to make the two main characters. Big, peaceful Ben, with his 'slightly prominent tummy', his naval background and his sailing skills is the Golding who learnt to commune with nature on his lonely sailing expeditions along the south coast during the war, and *Speedwell*, a converted ex-navy cutter, 'practically home-made', with an 'absurdly small sail-area for her size', is *Seahorse*. Ben is sensitized to the rhythms of nature. He hears 'the breathing of forests', and watches tidal creatures, limpets and sea anemones, in their different world. He also has, like Golding, a capacity for supernatural experiences. He feels a kind of mystical union with his boat: 'clairvoyantly he was identified with the straining sails'. There is an episode where he goes ashore to fetch water, and finds a dark tarn among trees which seems inexplicably menacing. 'This was where, ages ago, something odd had happened to him. He shivered.' He tells himself that it is 'rot' and that he is imagining things, but cannot shake off the sense of evil. Among the trees he finds Michael, and fights him when he jeers at his love for Penelope. Later, after the fight, and after he has dived and found the monolith, his memory of the tarn, and of the gigantic monolith's appearance, covered in waving weed like a living thing, combine in what seems to be an allegorical dream about the spiritual meaning of his ordeal.

The Man of Authority took Ben by the right hand and drew him to the edge of the tarn. Ben saw his own arm was black with filth. The Man of Authority was queerly dressed and his movements were a sort of speech, like dancing. The waters of the tarn were a dead and awful black. Ben knew he must dive. The Man of Authority spoke a word that created something of itself and Ben threw himself into the water. At once he was in a green world, rushing through depths where there was no direction but down. Now he was standing in the open and a shock-headed giant was lumbering up the hill towards him.

The Man of Authority has not been mentioned before and is not again, and the passage is like nothing else in the book. We seem to have jumped forward to the Simon scenes in *Lord of the Flies*.

But if Ben is Golding, so is Geoffrey. He is the side of Golding that Golding observes, condemns, and knows he cannot alter. Geoffrey is a schoolmaster, and hates it. 'I'm a failure ... I'm a bad schoolmaster, an underpaid, starved dominie, an usher without hope of fame or position'. He is ashamed of being poor and thinks poverty indecent. Just as Golding filled every spare moment with writing, desperate to escape from a job he detested, so Geoffrey pins all his hopes on his researches into prehistory: 'I'm an archaeologist. That's my life – my real life'. The professional archaeologists, however, are no more encouraging to Geoffrey than the literary professionals were to Golding. They think him mad. He yearns for fame:

If I thought I should live out my life with no record, no one to say 'Geoffrey Hamilton did this', nothing to lift me out of the anonymous ruck – I should shoot myself.

Geoffrey's surname is Amoy; it is Ben's that is Hamilton. Golding's typing slip, confusing the two characters, suggests that at some level he was aware they were both him. Nevertheless his characterization of Geoffrey is unsparingly negative, exposing the man's essential shallowness. Even his ambition is not for knowledge as an end in itself but merely for public recognition. Towards the book's end, after the great discovery has been made, he basks in the anticipation that he may now get a title. 'Sir Geoffrey and Lady Amoy,' he intones, blowing a contented wreath of smoke from his cigarette.

Like Golding, Geoffrey has a drink problem. He tries to borrow money for liquor from Ben, who objects that life is expensive enough without 'rot-gut'. Undeterred, he rows ashore and gets helplessly drunk. On his return he rolls into Ben's bunk, and as Ben uncomplainingly pulls the blankets over him:

> Geoffrey opened his eyes for a moment and saw Ben. He spoke out of the bitterness of his essential self, that drunkenness had made honest.
>
> 'Go to hell,' he said and fell asleep.

Drink made Golding angry and abusive, even to those who were close to him, and friends often wondered why. Perhaps 'the bitterness of his essential self' is an attempt at self-understanding. Geoffrey's stagy amends next morning ('My dear Ben,' he said, 'I apologise. I abase myself. I am a worm. Tread on me') are still less appealing than his drunkenness. The post-binge shame and embarrassment that Golding expresses in his journals suggests that here too Geoffrey may be a self-portrait.

For Geoffrey, as for Golding, chess is an outlet for aggression. He boasts that he plays an 'inexorable' game – his sister describes it as 'brutal'. Gentle Ben, by contrast, does not take it seriously ('I always get the horses moves wrong. They can jump over can't they?') and Penelope easily checkmates him. She explains to Ben that Geoffrey does not like people the way Ben does – 'They are just shapes that move about' – and that this is because he is bitter: 'He's always wanted success and never got it'. It shocks Ben most of all to learn that Geoffrey's wife Muriel is expecting their first child, and that he has chosen to pursue his archaeological ambitions rather than be with her. Golding, too, was worried later in life that he had in some sense sacrificed his family in order to achieve success as a writer.

And yet, negative as Geoffrey's characterization is, there is a moment when the reader, and Ben, are forced to look beyond his faults. At night in the lamp-lit cabin Geoffrey is working at his archaeological calculations, utterly absorbed, and unaware that Ben is watching him. The light reflected from the white paper gives his face the look of 'one of those lean statues you come across poised in the carven recesses of a cathedral'. Then Geoffrey lifts his head, so that the light pours over his face, and his eyes gleam out of their deep hollows.

> Ben knew that Geoffrey did not see him, nor the bunk, nor the boat – his eyes were focussed on some impalpable creation of the mind. The bones of a skull were the visible foundation of that mask, awful in its asceticism and abstraction.

'What is the most interesting thing there is to talk about?' Golding once asked a couple of friends he was dining with, and when they made tentative suggestions he contradicted them, 'No: the most interesting thing to talk about is saints – miraculous, levitating saints.' That Geoffrey has the asceticism and dedication of a saint is suggested by the reference to the cathedral statue, and there is another image that puts the relationship between Geoffrey and Ben in a new perspective. For the mask of bone that Geoffrey's lamp-lit face resembles looks forward to the mask of bone that, it seems to Lok, the pale, hairless new men wear in *The Inheritors*. Once we have made the connection, we can see that gentle, innocent, unintellectual Ben is rather like a Neanderthal beside fierce, ruthless, clever *Homo sapiens* Geoffrey.

These moments of profundity and uncanniness may have harmed the book's chances of publication. They would have seemed out of place to a reader expecting a run-of-the-mill adventure story. Jonathan Cape, one of the publishers who rejected it (even though Golding, in submitting it, said that he was 'willing to cut it about as required'), thought it fell between two stools, being unsuitable either for juvenile or for adult readers.

The third unpublished book was called *Short Measure*, and it shifts the scene from Golding's boating holidays to his day job at Bishop Wordsworth's School. In the novel it is not called Bishop Wordsworth's but Stillbourne Grammar School, and Salisbury cathedral, adjacent to the school, becomes 'the Minster'. *Short Measure* has an anti-hero, Philip Stevenson, who is a new master, hired to teach English, Drama and some Music, and the novel starts on his first day at the school. Like Geoffrey in *Circle Under the Sea*, Philip is a hostile self-portrait. A bully, show-off and drunkard, scruffy and not over-clean, he served in the war (though the RAF not the navy), and he talks about the 'spiritual beauty' of flying in a way that looks forward to Johnny in *Free Fall* and back to Golding's Avro Avian flights at Oxford. Philip fancies himself as a drama director. We watch him rehearsing boys in *Hamlet*, and urging Laertes to be more aggressive, in a way that recalls Golding's *Julius Caesar* rehearsals at Bishop Wordsworth's. His mind is stuffed, like Golding's, with scraps of Shakespeare, he prides himself on being good at chess, he is a negligent teacher, and he writes poetry. His study is a mess. When the cupboard is opened a pile of music, a cello string, a copy of T. S. Eliot's poems, and a bottle of dark ale fall out. His class register has not been filled in for weeks, but it contains notes for a poem:

> ... in some dark wood
> There grows a tree that chills my blood.
> ... from that tree
> Four seasoned planks will coffin me.

Philip's colleague in the English department is Veronica Laney, an attractive young woman who had been given to understand, by the weak, vacillating headmaster, that she would be producing *Hamlet*. Her dispute with Philip over who should be in charge of drama at the school reflects Golding's fraught dispute with Derek Warner over the same issue, which he was still having bad dreams about twenty years later. The antagonism between Veronica and Philip is instant, but complicated, because she finds him both repulsive and sexually attractive, while he is infuriated by her female poise: 'I'll knock you off that high feminine horse of yours,' he thinks to himself, 'I'll make you writhe' (echoing what Golding, in *Men, Women & Now*, recalls feeling about girls at school, especially Mollie). 'Trembling with the desire to hurt and triumph', Philip deliberately humiliates Veronica in front of the boys, perversely ridiculing her modish enthusiasm for apron-stages and early music ('Nonsense. Elizabethan music was dreadful'). But he can be charming when it suits and persuades her to come away with him for a weekend. Once he has seduced her, he is remote and callous, deriding the idea that the sexual act is romantic ('You might as well be romantic about blowing your nose').

Having borrowed money from her he gets drunk and recites as much as he can remember of one of his poems, 'The Ballad of Black Peter and Sallow Jack'. Like the fragment found in his class register, it shows how far W. G. Golding had come as a poet since the 1934 *Poems*:

> The priest called Sallow Jack stood by
> A sooty wall that kept him dry,
> Gazing with righteous eyes upon
> A huddled dead drunk of the town.
>
> It was Black Peter. Night and day
> To him were equal, where he lay
> Like an old coat beside the road
> His stubbled cheek in gutter mud.
>
> Jack's eye was on the alley's end
> He had no wish to meet a friend.
> 'Peter arise!' said Sallow Jack ...

Unluckily for Veronica, a fellow guest at the hotel where she and Philip stay recognizes her. It reaches the ears of a school governor, so she loses her job. Philip, however, has not been recognized, and is terrified she will give him away. That she does not is a final confirmation of her personal worth as against his baseness and cowardice.

Philip can be read not just as Golding's depiction of his own worst traits, but as his idea of what he might have turned into if he had married Mollie. At one point Philip tells Veronica about how he fell 'hideously' in love with a girl in the same form at school, a 'pale hank of a thing' with an aura of purity, and it is very like Golding's account of falling in love with Mollie. Because she was 'prudish', Philip explains, and had a habit of saying 'Maybe' (like Beatrice in *Free Fall*), he longed to 'chain her' and 'break her'. So he married her, and they have a son. She is 'utterly dumb, devoted, good and dull', which is why he is a habitual womanizer and a difficult husband: 'I give her hell.'

Apart from Philip, the most interesting character in *Short Measure*, from a biographical viewpoint, is Robert Farquharson, who is Philip's unsuccessful rival for Veronica's favours, and teaches Greek, which the modern-minded, philistine headmaster is phasing out of the curriculum. Farquharson decides to write a pamphlet about the educational value of Greek, and his vain attempts to assemble any arguments that are remotely convincing show us Golding throwing a critical light on his own obsession. Greek literature, Farquharson thinks, teaches that men should be 'stately, generous and brave'; that honour should be 'as precious and as easily lost as chastity'; that life is a tragedy, but that the tragedy should be faced with dignity. 'He had no sense of humour', Golding interjects, 'to tell him that he was talking pretentious tripe.'

There is a brilliant confrontation between Farquharson and Philip – a Philip who, in his provocative contrariness and his clever use of minimum knowledge to maximum effect resembles Golding at his story-telling best. This scene is not presented directly but through Farquharson's bitter memories of it. When he mentioned Homer to Philip, he recalls, Philip, 'with an outrageous lack of respect for the decencies', retorted, 'He's better in Chapman' (that is, in the Elizabethan English translation). And when Farquharson began a laborious defence of the Greek language:

> Philip had remarked coldly that the Greeks had thrown out the only euphonious letter in their alphabet, to wit, the digamma, and substituted for it a trip or hiccup.
>
> 'And when,' Philip had said with pretended passion, 'someone produces an Iliad with the digammas put back, you scholars turn up your noses at it.'

This display of esoteric knowledge silences Farquharson, who is outraged to learn later, from another master, that Philip has no Greek, only a friend who knows some and a retentive memory. It is a scene that, with beautiful lightness and strength, pits two aspects of Golding against each other – his love of Greek and his urge to contradict received opinion – and questions them both.

Golding's friends the Browns appear in *Short Measure* as the Thornes. Tony is Guido Thorne, Fiona is Neila, and they have six children, all at the infant or toddler stage, rather than their real-life four. They are feckless and irresponsible; their flat is dirty, their children neglected. Guido, though a brilliant musician, is unable to cope with the real world. Tradesmen hammer at their door, in pursuit of unpaid debts, and Guido and Neila huddle fully clothed in bed, pretending not to be there. Neila flirts with Philip, but perceives that he is attracted to Guido as well as to her – 'Philip, dear, which of us would you like to sleep with?' (which seems to indicate that Golding was aware of the Browns' suspicions about his repressed homosexuality). Guido is eventually appointed director of music in a big public school – a reference to Tony Brown's appointment at Canford, which dates *Short Measure* in or after 1951.

Throughout the novel we follow the fortunes not only of Philip but also of a VIth former named with suitable near-anonymity Smith, A. R. Philip casts him as Gertrude in *Hamlet*, so they meet at rehearsals, but otherwise the novel's two plots – the doings of Philip and the doings of Smith, A. R. – make almost no contact with each other. That is, indeed, the point. For Smith, A. R. is neglected by everyone in the school. He passes among them virtually unnoticed, and is content to do so, aiming to get by with as little work and effort as possible. His life has collapsed and he has retreated into a sort of numb indifference. His mother has died and his drunken stepfather neglects him, but no one at the school has bothered to find out these facts, least of all the headmaster, who is preoccupied with petty administrative details.

But one master decides that Smith must be helped. This is 'nervous, fluttering' Mr Billet, an ineffective teacher, who thinks of himself as 'useless' – an opinion shared by boys and masters alike. He prays regularly in the Minster, though he is too modest to describe what he feels as 'religious belief'. One day, while he is at prayer, a phrase from the Bible, 'Feed my lambs' (Jesus's words to Peter in John 21.15–18) passes through his mind, accompanied by a strange glow of warmth, and at the same time Smith, A. R.'s blue eyes and blond hair seem to hang before his eyes. He feels that he has been entrusted by God to care for Smith, and he finds that he is trembling with gratitude.

Smith has come to his notice through a series of events that Mr Billet only partly understands. Though he has managed to avoid being on any master's timetable, Smith cannot avoid a routine interview, early in the term, with the headmaster about what career he intends to follow on leaving school. Nonplussed he says, on the spur of the moment, that he intends to enter the Church, though in reality nothing could be further from his mind. The headmaster shows no interest, apart from the administrative arrangements, and tells him he must start Greek with Mr Farquharson. With equally little interest, Farquharson sets him some preliminary exercises. By chance Mr Billet hears about what Smith has told the headmaster, and on his knees in the Minster he feels that his mission may be to 'help a future priest'.

Smith, meanwhile, has no intention of learning Greek, so he bribes the only other VIth former studying Greek to do his exercises for him. He raises the necessary money at first by selling the books his mother gave him. We see him relinquishing a copy of Grimms' Fairy Tales inscribed 'To Bertie with love from Mother. Xmas 1941'. Once these have gone, he needs a new source of revenue, and fortunately at this point Mr Billet, entrusted by God with the care of a future priest, puts him in charge of the school museum which contains a valuable coin collection. Smith starts selling the coins to a local dealer, but he is tormented by anxiety, realizing that his life is slipping into chaos, and that his thefts are sure to be discovered. The end comes quickly. The dealer he has sold the coins to sells them on to the local museum, and the curator is an old boy of the school who helped to look after the collection and recognizes them. From him, the headmaster learns what Smith has done.

Just before the truth comes out Billet is sitting in his classroom musing about Smith's soul, and also about his body – 'the thin body, the fair hair, the delicate head'. The emphasis is enough to suggest that his interest in Smith is physical as well as spiritual. Billet's mind strays to 'the Curé of Ars' and his 'miraculous knowledge of the confessing soul', and he concludes that 'to be a successful schoolmaster, you needed to be a saint'. The Curé he is thinking about was one of the saints Golding most admired, and this seems to be his first reference to him. He was St

Jean Baptiste Marie Vianney (1786–1859), a humble country priest of no great intellectual distinction who became the parish priest of Ars, a remote town near Lyons. Over the years his exemplary poverty and austerity, and the insight into the human soul he showed in the confessional, became famous, and by 1855 he was attracting 20,000 pilgrims a year. He was canonized in 1925. Billet, inspired by Vianney's example, confronts the headmaster in the novel's final scene, and insists that Smith should not be expelled but given another chance, a 'breathing space for Grace to work'. The headmaster calls him a fool. 'What do you want?' he sneers, 'An altar?' – and Billet, like one who recognizes a 'sublime truth', nods: 'We need an altar.' At that moment the phone rings. The headmaster answers it, listens, and turns pale. Smith, fleeing the approaching nemesis, has rushed through the school gates into the path of a lorry, and been killed.

The most distinguished of the three unpublished books, *Short Measure* gets its power not just from its gripping narrative and uncomfortably convincing characters but also from the originality of its design, which juxtaposes two interlocking plots. It seems just possible that Golding got the idea for this experimental structure from Joyce's *Ulysses*, or more probably, since *Ulysses* was still banned in Britain, from reading the synopsis of *Ulysses* in Stuart Gilbert's book, borrowed from Terence Barnes. In both novels a young man (Stephen Dedalus; Smith, A. R.) and an older man (Bloom; Philip) inhabit separate narratives that occasionally intersect.

But *Short Measure*'s rejection by publishers is not wholly surprising. To a cursory reader the two plots might seem just unconnected. Also, knowing something of Golding's biography, and recognizing Philip as a self-portrait, adds an interest that would escape an outsider. Jonathan Cape, though he declined to publish it, was impressed enough to ask to see more of Golding's work. He praised the handling of the Philip–Veronica relationship, and this encouraged Golding to write back offering to cut the novel down to just that plot – an indication of his eagerness to get published. But Cape thought revising *Short Measure* would be inadvisable.

This was the first novel in which Golding took fictional notice of the creatures who were seated at the desks around him as he walked up and down the classroom, apparently self-absorbed. In his study of Smith, A. R. the vulnerability and the impregnable, panic-stricken privacy of the adolescent boy are keenly observed. But the book's main emphasis is on the cruelty of young males. Veronica has the job of teaching English to the Remove, a class of educationally sub-normal boys, some of them barely literate. Bored and resentful, they devote their considerable ingenuity and cunning to making her life intolerable. Her vain attempt to interest them in Coleridge's *The Ancient Mariner* is one of the most realistic classroom scenes in English writing, comparable to D. H. Lawrence's account of Ursula Brangwen's initiation as a teaching assistant in *The Rainbow*.

The Remove's disruptive tactics are depicted in such detail that it seems possible they were drawn from life. One of Golding's pupils remembers that the only time he lost his temper in class was when they were reading a Shakespeare play, and two of the boys sniggered at some fancied sexual innuendo. There is a similar occurrence in Veronica's *Ancient Mariner* class when a group of boys pretend to be shocked by the word 'bloody' in Coleridge's line about the 'bloody sun at noon'. Golding describes what Veronica is forced to endure as 'legal and dreadful torture'. Perhaps he spoke from experience.

12

Breakthrough

The idea for the book that changed Golding's life, and was to enter the lives of millions of readers, came to him in the course of a conversation with Ann. Many years later he told an audience of students in India how it happened. They used to read to David and Judy at bedtime, and the books they read – *Treasure Island, Coral Island, The Swiss Family Robinson* – were often about islands. One winter evening they had been reading one of these books, had got the children to bed, and were sitting by the fire 'in a state of complete parental exhaustion', when, staring into the fire, and 'thinking of this and that', he had a brainwave: 'Wouldn't it be a good idea if I wrote a book about children on an island, children who behave in the way children really would behave?' Ann was enthusiastic, and told him to get on with it.

The books of his that were at that time 'revolving round the English publishing world', and regularly falling on his doormat with rejection letters, were really 'written by other people', he felt. But he saw straight away that the book about boys on an island would be '*my* book', and, once he had worked out the story, it 'came very easily'. It came first in 'two pictures'. One was of a little boy standing on his head in the sand, delighted to be at last on a real coral island, and the other was of the same little boy being hunted down like a pig by the savages the children had turned into. He saw that what he had to do was join the two pictures, and then the story 'started to flow naturally'.

His private memories of the book's composition, recorded in his journal, make it sound less easy. Writing it had been 'right on the edge of the impossible'. He had 'dredged around for conversation'. But though the dialogue proved difficult, the local colour was pure pleasure. 'One thing that none of the critics know is how far such enjoyment as I got from writing the book stemmed from being on a coral island. Hence the elaborate description of natural phenomena.'

Like his other books, it came into being during school hours. Malcolm Cooper, who was a pupil at Bishop Wordsworth's from 1948 to 1955, recalls that during the months when *Lord of the Flies* was being written, 'for RE lesson after RE lesson, in Room P, behind the stage of the school hall', Golding would come in, set them some work to get on with, and then devote himself single-mindedly to writing in an old Bishop Wordsworth's School rough book, out of sight below the table at which he sat. Another pupil, Alan Harwood, learnt later that boys in the class above his had bits of *Lord of the Flies* read aloud to them during its gestation period. According to Bishop Wordsworth's folklore, the final words of the novel were written, under cover of Golding's old green-stained gown, at a Founder's Day Service. Whatever the truth of this, Golding's journal tells us that he began writing the book in 1951 and finished in 1952.

The novel's original title, under which he sent it out to publishers, was not *Lord of the Flies* but *Strangers From Within*. It went first to Jonathan Cape, naturally enough, since Cape had taken the trouble to send back criticism of *Circle Under the Sea* and *Short Measure*, and had asked to see other work. In his covering letter he said he had taken to heart Cape's advice about writing either for juveniles or for grown-ups, and this book was for grown-ups. Its plan was, he thought, original, showing how a group of boys try to make 'a reasonable society for themselves', and how 'even if we start with a clean slate like these boys, our nature compels us to make a muck of it'. He posted this letter and the typescript to Cape on 1 January 1953. On 5 February Cape returned it, regretting that 'it does not seem to us that you have been wholly successful in working out an admittedly promising idea', and suggesting that he might try André Deutsch. So he did, and they rejected it on 17 February.

Next he tried Putnam & Co., sending it to their London office on 19 February. They took three months to make up their mind, and gave it the thumbs-down on 12 May. Out it went again the very next day to Chapman and Hall, who returned it on 11 June. Had Golding been so minded, he could by this time have worked out that it took a publisher, on average, forty-nine days to decide they did not want his book. From that angle the next rejection, by Hutchinson, was at least quicker than average. It went to them on 12 June and came back on the 24th. The thought evidently struck him at this point that a literary agent might be useful, and he sent his typescript, on the same day that it had arrived back from Hutchinson, to Curtis Brown, one of the best known British agents. Evidently they declined to try it out on any publishers at all, however, and returned it on 19 July. It was now nearly seven months since he had started circulating it, and his persistence is an index of his faith in the book and probably of Ann's too. Undeterred by Curtis Brown's pessimism, he tried The Bodley Head. It went to them on 24 July and was back on 20 August. Unusually, he let a month elapse before having another go, probably because he was on holiday with his family. But on 14 September he was home again and sent his by now rather tattered typescript to Faber and Faber.

The accompanying letter, written in an untidy scrawl, is scarcely alluring, and perhaps, if it was what he usually sent, it goes some way to explain publishers' reactions.

Dear Sir,
I send you the typescript of my novel
    'Strangers From Within'
which might be defined as an allegorical interpretation of a stock situation.
    I hope you will feel able to publish it.
Yours faithfully,
William Golding.

The professional reader employed by Faber and Faber to assess new works of fiction was a lady called Polly Perkins, about whom very little now seems to be remembered apart from her one big mistake. She read for a number of other publishers besides Fabers, and for a leading literary agent. Having read, or at any rate looked at, Golding's typescript, she recorded her verdict in green biro on the top left-hand corner of his letter:

Time: the Future. Absurd & uninteresting fantasy about the explosion of an atom bomb on the Colonies. A group of children

who land in jungle-country near New Guinea. Rubbish & dull.
Pointless.

This assessment is followed by an 'R' in a circle, signifying 'Reject'.

And that would have been that, if Charles Monteith had not intervened. Monteith was to become a legendary publisher, but in 1953 he
was just starting out. Born in 1921 into an Ulster Protestant family, he
had grown up in Belfast and been educated at the Royal Belfast
Academical Institution. He won a scholarship (called a demyship) to
Magdalen College Oxford, read English, and got a first-class honours
degree. In 1940 he joined the army and served with the Royal
Inniskilling Fusiliers in India, then in Burma, rising to the rank of
major before being severely wounded in the legs by a mortar bomb.
After the war he returned to Magdalen to read Law, got a first in that
too, and in 1948 won a Prize Fellowship at All Souls. This is one of
Oxford's most coveted distinctions, not least because, though Prize
Fellows often pursue careers in London, as Monteith did, they remain
Fellows of All Souls for life and retain rooms there. All Souls became
his second home; he regularly spent weekends there, and entertained
the authors he was publishing, Golding among them, to lunch or
dinner in the college.

He took the Bachelor of Civil Law degree in 1949, and was called to
the Bar of Gray's Inn. But he felt he was not aggressive enough as a
barrister, and having met Geoffrey Faber, the chairman of Faber and
Faber, at All Souls, where he, too, was a Fellow, Monteith joined the
firm in 1953. Later he became vice-chairman, and, in 1977, chairman.
But in 1953 he was a new boy, and in a dauntingly distinguished
environment. For Faber and Faber were unquestionably the leading
literary publishers in Britain. Originally Faber and Gwyer, the company became Faber and Faber in 1929, when Geoffrey Faber bought
out Lady Gwyer (there was no second Faber, but Geoffrey thought the
suggestion of a partnership sounded more impressive than a single
name). The eminence who shed light over the whole enterprise, and
ensured Faber and Faber's dominance of contemporary writing, was
T. S. Eliot, whom Geoffrey had signed on as Faber and Gwyer's literary adviser back in 1925. Eliot was still active in 1953, occupying a rather

cramped office – a garret with sloping ceilings that had originally been a maid's bedroom – in the big Victorian family house at 24 Russell Square which was the firm's headquarters. He regularly attended the Wednesday meetings of the Book Committee, and it was thanks to him that W. H. Auden, James Joyce, Stephen Spender, Ezra Pound, William Empson and Louis MacNeice became Faber authors. Fabers had also published Stuart Gilbert's guide to *Ulysses*, which Golding had borrowed from Terence Barnes.

Though their list was go-ahead, in other respects Faber and Faber were rather old-fashioned. There was no marketing department, and sales ledgers were completed daily by hand. Nor was there a publicity department: sending review copies to literary editors was considered the only publicity necessary. Appointments and promotions within the firm could be of a rather personal nature, and when considering Monteith's suitability, Geoffrey Faber seems to have sought the opinion of friends, one of whom, at least, was evidently intent on making mischief. In February John Sparrow, the Warden of All Souls, wrote ('in confidence') to say that in his view Monteith had 'flair but not taste', and that 'the coarseness of his fibre' would 'grate on' T. S. Eliot. He added that he had sat next to Eliot recently in All Souls, 'but did NOT say ANY-thing' to him about Monteith. This was untrue. Faber immediately sent Sparrow's malicious letter to Eliot, who replied that Sparrow had made his disapproval of Monteith 'very clear indeed'. However, having taken Monteith out to lunch, he had formed a very different opinion from Sparrow's. He disagreed wholly about Monteith's alleged coarseness, and, as for taste and flair, 'from the viewpoint of a firm's solvency', flair might well be 'a more valuable asset than taste'. Eliot's support was evidently decisive, and Monteith's appointment was confirmed in May. He was to bring to Faber and Faber a list of authors quite as distinguished as Eliot's, among them Samuel Beckett, John Osborne, Philip Larkin, Tom Stoppard, Christopher Hampton, Ted Hughes, Tom Gunn, Douglas Dunn, Seamus Heaney and Paul Muldoon. But Golding was his first catch – though when he picked the typescript of *Strangers From Within* out of the reject pile one Tuesday afternoon in late September 1953, he was, to begin with, by no means sure how much of a catch it was. It had a dog-eared, shop-soiled look. The first dozen or so sheets were yellowish at the edges, showing that they, at least, had been read a number of times. The rest were whiter. Though Monteith had been a publisher for less than a month, he could already spot a typescript that had been the rounds, and as he started to read he could see why. The first pages described a nuclear war, and contained no characters at all. Later, attention switched earthwards, where there was a hurriedly organized evacuation of schoolchildren. The planes in which they flew had detachable cabins, 'passenger tubes', which could float to earth beneath giant parachutes. Then the focus switched to a particular plane, to a fierce air battle over the Pacific, to the release of the passenger tube, to a tropical island and – at last – to some human beings, who were all boys.

As Monteith continued to read he found that he was increasingly gripped. The island was brilliantly real, and the boys were real boys. Having been 'a fat, spectacled boy at school' himself, he 'squirmed for Piggy' when Ralph betrayed the secret of Piggy's nickname, to the accompaniment of 'the appalling sycophantic laughter of the crowd'. After work in the office had ended for the day, he said he would take the manuscript home to read properly, and when he had finished it he found he could not put it out of his mind. He realized it had flaws. Some were superficial – commas studded the pages 'as thickly as currants in a fruit loaf', and Piggy's 'common' speech, represented by misspellings such as 'ass-marr' for 'asthma', was overdone. But two flaws were more serious. The first was structural: in addition to the description of atomic war at the start there were two other needless digressions – a description of an air battle above the island, from which the dead airman drifts down by parachute, and, near the end, a description of a naval battle between an enemy fleet and the fleet to which the 'trim cruiser' that rescues the boys belongs.

The second major flaw, more difficult to put right, was Simon, who was very evidently a Christ figure. At times he would retire to a secret place in the jungle where a voice spoke to him from the flowers; a vision assured him that Ralph would get home safely – an assurance he later passed on to Ralph; he also led some of the boys in Good Dances on the beach, and, alone and terrified, but not vanquished, confronted the pig's head, alias Lord of the Flies. For Monteith, Simon was not credible, and he was clear that any purely miraculous events in the narrative must be 'made ambivalent, eliminated, or "toned down" in such a way as to make Simon explicable in purely rational terms'.

The typescript that Monteith read has not survived. But Golding's original manuscript has. It covers 142 wide-lined pages of a green, hard-cover school exercise book and, like other Golding manuscripts, it is very closely written, packing as many words onto the page as possible and ignoring the ruled lines. There are red-biro notes about what Ann thinks at various points, and at the end is a pencilled note: '1600 2nd October 1952', which is presumably the time and date of completion. The first thing that strikes a reader of the manuscript is how much of the book is already there, intact and final. The major dialogues and conversations, and the great poetic scenes like Simon's body being swept out to sea, or the dead parachutist treading the treetops as he is blown down the mountain by the gale, are already in place, though they underwent some polishing prior to the printed version. Another thing that reading the manuscript shows is that the typescript Monteith read was not quite the same as the manuscript. In typing, Golding had made some additions. So of the three digressions Monteith complains about – the description of nuclear warfare and the air battle at the start, the air battle halfway through, and the naval battle at the end – the second and third are not in the manuscript at all, and the first is very brief. By the end of the second page of the manuscript Ralph is already exploring the island. So the digressions were second thoughts, added during typing, and not part of the original design.

Monteith's account of the supernatural treatment of Simon in the typescript, on the other hand, tallies quite closely with the manuscript. In the manuscript Simon has an intuition that there is a 'prohibition' against eating the fruit on the island.

A prohibition implies a person who prohibits. To a rational human being the person implied might seem to be Simon himself, but Simon was not entirely rational. In that molten moment Simon knew that there was a person in the forest who had forbidden him to eat of the fruit, and that knowledge was as if someone had squeezed his heart.

He knows that he is going to meet someone, and that no power on earth can stop him.

Then Simon met the person who had forbidden him to eat the fruit. The other person came out of the silence, swamped Simon, filled him, penetrated his limbs like bees the empty air. This person among the simultitudinous simplicity of his being – if being was the word – was merciful and veiled Simon's eyes and dulled the feelings of his body. Even so the implications of what he was allowed to know filled Simon with wild delight. He went bounding into the open space, dancing, and the butterflies danced round his head, and the other person danced with Simon, courteously, so for that time they were one: and Simon opened his treasure and was accepted even though he saw the poorness of the gift.

Simon wants to bring all the boys to meet the 'other person' and be 'healed, happy and without fear', so he hurries back to the lagoon and, 'filled with knowledge and mystery', begins to dance. The smaller boys watch, laugh, and then start dancing too, because 'they knew in their blood how important these strange gestures and the stately weaving were'. When Jack and Ralph come back from swimming they join the dance, but Jack soon gets tired of it. 'Let's race,' he says, and the others chase after him, with Simon shouting, 'No! Not like that.' Left behind, he realizes that he is 'alone in a curious inside way that was like a pain to match his other happiness'.

One effect of this episode is that when Simon later confronts the pig's head he has a supernatural status and a sense of mission that are lacking in the printed version. After 'hearing' the pig's head speak, he faints. But when he regains consciousness his mind turns, as it does not in the printed text, to the possibility of offering himself for martyrdom.

Supposing one could offer Simon to the beast as a bribe? So that the beast would let them all alone? Curiously Simon examined the idea, liked the promise of peace and innocence. Only some time later did he remember that he himself would not be sharing it. But the idea remained. Without understanding why he did so Simon turned and began to pick his way towards the mountain ... He would face the beast, make an offer. Then perhaps would come a time when the beast would leave the island.

This passage gives a moral logic to Simon's behaviour which it lacks in the printed version. As we shall see, Golding would later speak of Simon as a 'martyr'. But the willing offering of oneself that martyrdom requires does not happen in the book, where Simon's death is merely the result of a misunderstanding.

A third passage, or series of passages, that give Simon special status relate to his assuring Ralph that he will get back home. In the manuscript this is an afterthought. After the end of the last chapter Golding adds some passages to be inserted into various earlier chapters. In Chapter VII he adds Simon assuring Ralph, 'You'll get back to where you came from', and in Chapters XI and XII he inserts brief mentions of Ralph gaining strength from remembering what Simon told him: 'Simon said I'd be all right. Simon. He had light round him. When he told me.' Clearly it would be necessary to delete this supernatural illumination, together with Simon's encounter with the 'other person', in order to make him 'explicable in purely rational terms', as Monteith wished.

At the next Book Committee he reported that the book was odd and imperfect, but potentially very powerful, and that he would like to discuss it with the author. However, there was general doubt about this course – after all, Monteith was very junior – and it was decided that others should read the typescript first. On 15 October Monteith wrote to Golding, apologizing for keeping the typescript for 'rather a long time', and explaining that, though they were interested, they had not yet reached a decision. This was the most encouraging letter Golding had ever received from a publisher, and he wrote back on 20 October saying he was 'glad Messrs. Faber are interested', and that he hoped they would decide to publish.

Meanwhile at Fabers two editorial colleagues agreed with Monteith about the book, and Geoffrey Faber, having read it, was prepared, though with doubts, to support him. But the sales director, W. J. Crawley, whose judgement about whether a book would sell was regarded as infallible, kept it for a couple of weeks, then brought it to the Book Committee and, with a ruefully apologetic glance at Monteith, pronounced it unpublishable. A heated discussion followed, and it was decided, thanks chiefly to the chairman, who was unwilling to dampen a young editor's enthusiasm, that Monteith should meet the author and discuss changes, while emphasizing that Fabers were in no way committed to publishing it. So on 27 November Monteith wrote to Golding, who must surely by this time have been getting apprehensive, suggesting they meet in London for lunch or tea on 3, 7 or 10 December. Golding answered by return that he would come on the 3rd and be at Russell Square by 12 noon.

Monteith imagined that he would meet a young clergyman, given the theological substructure of the book. So his visitor's neatly trimmed beard, flannel trousers and tweed jacket surprised him – though when he learnt Golding was a schoolmaster he saw at once that only a schoolmaster could know, so intimately, how awful boys could be. What Golding thought is not recorded, but probably he found his host rather daunting. Monteith was a draper's son, but an Oxford education, an army commission and his brief career as a barrister had moved him up the social scale. He was tall and distinguished-looking, with a deep-toned, carefully cultivated patrician voice (as a barrister he had found his Irish brogue disadvantageous, and had eliminated it), and even his slight limp, a relic of his war wound, seemed to add grandeur to his presence. For Robert McCrum, a later recruit to Faber and Faber, Monteith was 'as grand as they come; a Bentley to my Ford Fiesta'. The most vivid impression of the imposing figure Golding met that day is given by John McGahern, another Monteith author, in his novel *That They May Face the Rising Sun*, where the character Robert Booth is a portrait of Monteith. McGahern describes Booth as 'a secretive, complicated man' – which fits Golding as well as Monteith. Both avoided intimate relationships, preferring a kind of jovial bonhomie, and it was at that level that their friendship, which meant a great deal to both of them, prospered.

At their first meeting Monteith was nervous, and felt Golding was too, though as they talked 'a cautious trust, and even liking' seemed to be established between them. He made his suggestions for revision and Golding promised to take his typescript back and consider them. He worked, it seemed to Monteith, amazingly fast. Within three days, on

6 December, he sent the emended version of the beginning, middle and end back to Monteith. His accompanying letter points out that he has done away with the separate Prologue, Interlude and Epilogue – the nuclear war, the air battle and the sea battle – and 'merged them into the body of the text'. The surviving manuscript does not have a separate Prologue, Interlude and Epilogue, which helps us to understand how Golding could eliminate them so quickly. He was, in effect, just returning to his earlier version. The first chapter now begins, he points out in his letter to Monteith, with Piggy and Ralph meeting, and the story of how they got there is allowed 'to come out in conversation'.

'Simon', Golding writes, 'is the next job, and a more difficult one. I suppose you agree that I must convey a theophany of some sort or else he won't be as big a figure as he ought.' 'Theophany' means the appearance, or showing forth, of a god, so the point Golding is making concerns the passages where Simon, in the original version, is in contact with the divine – the passages which Monteith (brought up as a Presbyterian but now an agnostic) had determined, after his first reading, must be omitted, so that Simon could be 'explicable in purely rational terms'. Golding's letter, while insisting that he must 'convey a theophany', agrees to 'cut down the elaborate description of it', and to 'try to get the same effect by reticence'. He has cut, he adds, a dream that Ralph had about his father and is making Piggy's speech ungrammatical but not misspelling it. 'Rereading the novel as a stranger to it,' he admits, 'I'm bound to agree with almost all your criticism and am full of enthusiasm and energy for the cleaning up process.' At their meeting, Monteith seems to have expressed doubts about the book's rather puzzling title, so at the end of his letter Golding – never at his best when inventing titles – tries again. 'What do you think of A Cry of Children as a title? It's got at least two levels which is more than the other one had.' In conclusion he thanks Monteith for 'a very pleasant meeting and lunch'.

The changes Golding had made were even better than Monteith had hoped for, since all he had suggested was a drastic shortening of the nuclear war passages, and Golding's more radical solution was to cut them out altogether. He noted much later, writing in his journal, that the structure Monteith had guided him towards was a classical one – that is, starting the action in the middle, *in medias res*. It was a technique used by the Greek dramatists, and recommended by Aristotle. In 1953 Golding had, it seems, been reading Greek drama, probably in preparation for his production of Euripides' *Alcestis* at the Studio Theatre in Salisbury in 1954. A second-hand Aeschylus, inscribed 'William Golding, Salisbury, Wilts, 1953' is still in his library, as is a 1953 reprint of Euripides' *Bacchae*, edited by E. R. Dodds. Perhaps this is why, as his journal records, he 'leapt on' Monteith's suggestion about how to start his novel, 'regarding it as an illumination'. On 14 December Monteith sent back the emended portions of the typescript with pencilled suggestions. 'You are perhaps still tending to over-emphasize,' he cautioned, 'to make points rather too directly', and though he thought the new title better he was not completely happy with it.

In a letter four days later Golding accepted Monteith's corrections in full, as well as his criticisms. 'I recognize my own anxious tendency to overstate and propose to guard against it.' He enclosed some redrafted 'Simon extracts', adding that he was off with his family to spend Christmas with his parents at 29 The Green. Monteith's reply, sent on 30 December, conveyed that he was not completely satisfied, but nevertheless it was generally encouraging. Golding had 'hit on the right approach to this most tricky of all the problems in the novel', and the 'tentative emendations' Monteith was pencilling into the typed extracts before returning them were just a '"toning down" of emphasis'. The danger to be guarded against now, he thought, was turning Simon into a prig, 'a self-righteous infant who insists on saying his prayers in the dorm while the naughty boys throw pillows at him'. It was enough, in the early stages, simply to indicate that Simon was 'in some ways odd, different, withdrawn, and therefore capable of the lonely, rarified courage of facing the pig's head and climbing the mountain top'. Though mildly stated, Monteith's position is here evidently different from Golding's wish for the novel to contain a 'theophany'. Being odd, different and withdrawn are not at all the same as having direct communication with the Deity. At the end of his letter Monteith concedes that 'the allegory, the theophany, is the imaginative foundation', but insists that 'like all foundations' it is 'there to be concealed and built on'.

Golding did not object. On 10 January 1954 he sent a complete draft, fitting together the various passages they had worked on. 'I've everywhere incorporated your suggestions,' he pointed out. But the strain, he now revealed, had made him ill. He could hardly bear to look at the novel, partly because of a nasty bout of tonsillitis, 'and about the highest temperature ever recorded', but mostly because of 'the effort of patching – so much more wearing than bashing straight ahead at a story'. He suggested a new title 'Nightmare Island', though feared it was too crude, and added, 'If you want to throw away any more Simon go ahead.' Monteith replied at once, expressing contrition at having 'badgered you so much about the novel'. But he had got what he wanted – almost. In a letter of 11 February 1954 he reported that he had done a bit more editorial work, toning down Simon and redrafting some sentences, and asking Golding to let him know if he wanted the typescript back to look at these. It seems he did not, and perhaps was less inclined to because the 11 February letter at last announced that Fabers were prepared to publish the novel. The terms they offered were an advance of £60, 10 per cent royalties on the first 2,000 copies sold, 12.5 per cent on the next 3,000, and 15 per cent after that. In fact at the Book Committee meeting Monteith had suggested a £50 advance, but Geoffrey Faber, in view of the author's patience, made it £60. On St Valentine's Day, 14 February, Golding declared himself 'delighted' with these terms.

The problem of the title remained. Monteith's 11 February letter passed on some suggestions – 'This Island's Mine', 'Beast in the Jungle', 'An Island of their Own', 'Fun and Games' and (apparently Monteith's favourite) 'The Isle Is Full of Noises' – from *The Tempest*. Golding came back with 'To End an Island'. But it was another editor at Fabers, Alan Pringle, who thought of 'Lord of the Flies'. Monteith liked it and passed it on to Golding on 25 February, adding, in the same letter, that Fabers' production and design department was adamant that the novel must have chapter headings. Golding's reply, sent on 28 February, was, like many of his early letters, in red biro ('pedagogic pink', as he called it). He accepted the new title and concurred over chapter headings – 'Go ahead if you think they're a Good Thing' – while admitting 'my instinct is slightly against them'. So Monteith drew up the list of chapter headings used in the published novel, which Golding accepted without demur.

The complete typescript which Golding had sent on 10 January survives, and is evidently the copy from which the printer set up type. It is double-spaced and bound in a loose-leaf notebook, and there are pencilled and red-biro deletions, alterations and additions throughout. There are also a few places where Golding has pasted a slip of paper, with a new version of some lines, over the original typescript. It seems that the red-biro annotations are Golding's and the pencilled ones Monteith's. The latter include the chapter headings and instructions for the printer, but they also show Monteith pursuing his policy of reducing Simon to 'rational' proportions. At one point he crosses out more than a page in which Ralph thinks Simon had an 'aura' round him and was 'charged with a particular significance', and he also deletes a later passage where Ralph thinks 'Simon had a not-light round him' (meaning, presumably, a light that was not a natural light). This process of demystifying Simon continued while the book was in proof. In the last chapter, Ralph's agitated thoughts as he flees appear in the typescript as:

> Don't scream.
> You'll get back.
> A not-light.
> Now he's seen you.

But 'A not-light' does not appear in the printed text or in page proof. Evidently Monteith's keen eye detected and eliminated this last trace of the supernatural Simon at the galley proof stage.

The book went into production on 1 March. Golding wrote to ask that the dedication 'To my Mother and Father' should have a page to itself at the front, and Monteith passed this on. On 25 April Golding was already impatiently expecting galley proofs, and Monteith replied that they would be ready on 10 May, meanwhile sending a copy of T. S. Eliot's new play *The Confidential Clerk* for him to read. By 20 May, immersed in the proofs, Monteith was worried that Ralph's long hair falling blindingly over his eyes in the desperate chase at the end – symbolizing the eclipse of reason and intelligence by irrationality, instinct and panic – was perhaps referred to too often. 'If you don't mind I think I'd like to delete *some* of the references to it,' he wrote. Golding replied by return, 'By all means cut Ralph's hair for him – I had some doubts of it myself.' So Monteith took out every second mention of it. As Golding read the proofs he evidently came to see how worthwhile all the 'patching' had been, and was grateful to Monteith for making him do it. 'I think you have done a very clever and helpful piece of work,' he wrote on 17 June. 'The novel is swift now, with a measure of subtlety and tautness. If it achieves any measure of success much will be due to your severe but healthy pruning.' Monteith thanked him for this 'very nice letter', and Golding, in reply, reasserted that he now felt 'very cheerful' about *Lord of the Flies*, 'and full of surprise that I could ever have written anything so interesting'.

Meanwhile Monteith tried to whip up some advance publicity, but without much success. A committee set up by the first Cheltenham Book Festival did not even shortlist it for their first-novel award, and it did not have any better luck with the Authors' Club's annual Silver Quill. It seemed as if the Book Society might give it some space in their monthly magazine, but on 20 July Monteith broke the news to Golding that they were not going to accord it an official recommendation after all. Golding replied that their recommendations were often no good, and maybe Fabers should overprint the cover 'Not Recommended by the Book Society'. He apologized for his frivolity, 'but I've just been sailing and am still feeling rather bluff and seamanlike'. There was better news on 6 August when Monteith wrote to say that *Lord of the Flies* would be the *John O'London's Weekly* book choice for September. But this hope proved delusive, for his next letter reported that *John O'London's* was to cease publication on 10 September, a week before its accolade was to be conferred. The magazine's untimely death was the more galling because the poet and critic Richard Church had written an enthusiastic review of *Lord of the Flies*, calling it 'a most significant novel, worthy of survival as a work of art'. It was the very first response from anyone that recognized the book's greatness, and would have been published along with the book-choice announcement. Golding wondered if it could be 'saved from the wreck', and Monteith got Church's permission to use it in advance publicity.

At last, on Friday, 17 September 1954, *Lord of the Flies* was published, one year and three days after Golding had sent it to Fabers. At Bishop

Wordsworth's School a zinc bath packed with ice and bottles of champagne appeared in the staff room, and there were convivial scenes.
One master, Walter Watson, a fitness fanatic renowned for standing on
his head on a mountain peak, stood on his head, when the rejoicing
was over, on the small peak of ice that remained in the bath. The novel
got its first review that same day, Pat Murphy in the *Daily Mail* finding
it 'most compelling' – 'I fell under the terrible spell of this book and so
will many others.' Next day was even better. John Connell in the
Evening News called it 'vivid and enthralling', *The Times* judged it 'most
absorbing and instructive', praising its 'vivid realism', and *Time and
Tide* hailed it as 'a work of universal significance' and its author as 'a
truly imaginative writer who is also a deep thinker'. On the 19th only
one of the Sundays bothered to give it a notice, but that was a winner.
The poet Stevie Smith, in the *Observer*, acclaimed 'this beautiful and
desperate book, something quite out of the ordinary'. By this time, one
hopes, Polly Perkins and the directors of several publishing firms were
beginning to feel rather poorly.

The praise continued in the following weeks, with not a single
dissenting voice. Walter Allen, a big gun of the critical world, told *New
Statesman* readers that Golding had produced something 'like a fragment
of nightmare', and that 'no one who writes as well as he does could go
wrong'. The celebrated novelist Francis Wyndham used the same
analogy in the *London Magazine*, praising the 'impression of increasing
nightmare' the book created, and Douglas Hewitt, another distinguished critic, found it 'completely convincing', 'very frightening' and
all-in-all 'magnificent' in the *Guardian*. 'A first novel of great promise,'
was John Metcalf's verdict in *The Spectator*, 'a remarkable, bitter piece of
writing', and, he added, accomplished 'without the use of a single jargon
phrase'. In *The Listener* George D. Painter, the great biographer of
Proust, agreed that Golding 'writes with style and authority', and John
Betjeman (an old boy of Golding's hated Marlborough College) found
the book 'readable and bloodcurdling' in the *Daily Telegraph*. Scotland
was similarly impressed: 'an astonishing achievement' (*Glasgow Herald*);
'a brave, disturbing book' (*The Scotsman*). In the *Church Times* Katherine
Farrer, a fellow novelist, called it 'poignant, credible and terrifying',
and *Vogue*'s Books for Christmas carried a recommendation by Siriol

Hugh Jones, identifying Golding's novel as 'an extraordinary feat' of imagination. Probably the tribute that pleased Faber and Faber most, though, came from E. M. Forster, who put *Lord of the Flies* ('Beautifully written, tragic and provocative') first among his books of the year in the *Observer*. Golding was 'tickled pink'. There was private praise from equally estimable sources. C. S. Lewis wrote to Monteith, ten days after publication, to say that he and his brother had both read the book and it was a 'brilliant success', and Mary Renault wrote to Golding out of the blue to say that during her time in South Africa she had glimpsed 'the nature of savagery', and that 'the way you have sounded the universal elements in this horror strikes me as masterly'.

Monteith congratulated his author on 'the wonderful reviews', and gave notice that Arthur Calder-Marshall would be reviewing *Lord of the Flies* on the BBC Home Service on 17 October. 'The Lord defend me from getting cocky', was Golding's reaction, adding that his wife and children had agreed to keep his ego under. He picked out Richard Church's praise for the book's 'economy of effort' which, he said, 'should be properly addressed to you and your pruning hook', adding, 'you know how conscious I am of your help'. The other good news in early October was that Ealing Studios, Pinewood, Columbia and MGM were all interested in the film rights. Pinewood pulled out before the end of the month, however, Sergei Nolbandov writing to Monteith to say that they thought problems of 'censorship and adverse public reaction' made a film version impossible. This was unfortunate because the British director Phil Leacock and the producer Michael Hankenson made an offer of £100 for a two-month option and £700 or £800 for the story, but only if Pinewood, the studio Leacock was under contract to, would take it. Golding accepted these terms enthusiastically, and inquired if there was, in addition, any chance of a percentage on the gross takings. However, on 5 November Hankenson rang Monteith to say that Pinewood would not reconsider, so the deal was off. He and Leacock were still keen, though, and arranged a meeting with Golding. He wrote to Monteith at the end of November to say they had got on well, but on 21 January 1955 he reported that hopes of filming had been finally dashed because the censors would grant only an X certificate.

He remained jubilant about the novel, though, exclaiming in the same letter, 'What a good book *Lord of the Flies* is. I've just re-read it and am quite convinced I never wrote it. It's much bigger than I am. Perhaps it was done in committee like the authorized version' (a reference to the 1611 English Bible, which was the work of six sub-committees). He felt, he said, 'moved and inadequate' when Monteith told him that T. S. Eliot had liked it. Apparently Eliot was told by a friend at the Garrick that Faber had published an unpleasant novel about small boys behaving unspeakably on a desert island. In mild alarm he took a copy home, read it, and told Monteith next day that he had found it not only a splendid novel but morally and theologically impeccable. There are reasons for believing that Golding's thoughts about Eliot were not, or were not to remain, quite as reverential as his letter to Monteith suggests. His journal records two occasions when they met, one a lunch party given by Monteith on 13 October 1955, and the other at a Faber party.

Eliot was fairly impressive in a Donnish sort of way, but not excessively so. Charles [Monteith] led Ann and me to see him as to a god. We sat fairly mum while he talked of umbrellas and rubber trees. Later he informed me that Simon in Lord of the Flies must be cut to the bone. 'We cannot portray a saint, Mr Ah. But for evil we need only look into our own hearts'. The silly old twit. As if I hadn't known that. Another time at a Faber cocktail party Frazer [G. S. Fraser] the Anthologist cannoned into my back so that I bowed forward and spilt champagne down Mr Eliot's trousers while he was saying 'No, no, no' to Arthur Koestler. Thus I not only worshipped at the god's shrine but poured a libation, not to say an anointment. He leapt back with an agility startling in one so mummified, striking out at his salt and pepper Edwardian trousers. I cannot say that we were intimate friends.

The flurry over film rights had evidently set Golding thinking about money, which he was much in need of. He wrote on 17 October 1954 to say he was 'dreadfully busy' because, 'what with school fees and the rest of it', he was having to supplement his teacher's salary by lecturing to 'bored army types' about music, and taking WEA classes on the seventeenth century and the modern novel, 'about which I know nothing'. He had, in fact, been on this treadmill for several years. An appreciative testimonial survives, dated 31 July 1946, and signed by W. J. Rees, the resident tutor for adult education in South Wiltshire, which attests that Golding has, during the past year, taught classes ranging from small village groups, including Women's Institutes, to large gatherings of military types, both men and ATS. School fees, mentioned in his October 1954 letter, were a worry because they had decided that David would have a better chance of doing well in his A-levels if he left Bishop Wordsworth's and boarded at Michael Hall, the Steiner school where Golding had taught in the 1930s, which had moved out of Streatham and relocated in Sussex. In the event David did not go there till 1958, having gained an A-level in Maths at Bishop Wordsworth's, and instead of boarding he stayed with one of the masters. Meanwhile Judy was put down for the Godolphin School in Salisbury, and started there as a day girl in September 1953, aged eight. The Goldings were poor, but they believed in spending money on education, so just how much profit there might be in authorship, and how far it would allow him to offload other work, were pressing questions. 'Am I going to make any money out of L of F?' he inquired. 'If so I will let the army and the RAF go and get down to it. Also I should like Fabers to cover the expenses!' Probably the last sentence was a joke, or half a joke. He added that literary agents, 'shady and otherwise', were pursuing him, asking about American rights. 'Is Fabers going to publish in America?' Evidently Curtis Brown, the agents who had summarily rejected *Strangers From Within*, were now eager to sign him up and, he tells Monteith, he has said he will let them have 'short stories and anything else apart from novels'.

On 21 October Monteith replied diplomatically to this rather discontented letter, beginning with an affable compliment ('frightfully good review in this morning's *Listener*'), and reporting that he was 'delighted' they were going to reprint *Lord of the Flies*. (The reprint was a modest 2,000 copies on an initial print-run of 3,000.) The matter of literary agents, he suggested, should be postponed for discussion next time Golding was in London. 'The theory is that agents exist to protect defenceless authors from the inhuman rapacity of publishers,' he explained. His own view, he said, was that it is indeed often very useful to have an agent, but it was a matter of deciding whether what the agent could do was worth the 10 per cent he would take. The question of an American edition was a ticklish one, and Monteith simply says that his colleague Peter du Sautoy is currently in the States trying to find a publisher.

In fact Fabers' files reveal a record of American rejections that rivals the English one – and this despite the fact that American publishers were sent early proof copies, so were able to read the novel in its final form, rather than the original, unrevised typescript that had been sent to English publishers. Between June 1954 and April 1955 *Lord of the Flies* was turned down by E. P. Dutton & Co. Inc. (afraid it 'might not get off the ground'), J. B. Lippincott Co., Harcourt, Brace, The Viking Press ('unlikely to sell well here'), Duell, Sloan and Pearce, Inc., Harper & Brothers, The Macmillan Company, Doubleday, Criterion Books ('don't think that this book has much chance commercially in this country') and Charles Scribner's Sons, Ltd. Alfred A. Knopf turned it down initially, then asked in February 1955 for another copy, so that Mrs Knopf could reconsider it, then turned it down again. Eventually on 12 April 1955 du Sautoy got a cable from T. R. Coward of Coward-McCann Inc., Madison Avenue: 'Like Golding offer 1000 advance against 10 Percent Royalty to ten thousand usual split reprint book clubs etc. Coward'. Faber and Faber cabled their acceptance on 14 April, and on the 18th du Sautoy passed on the good news to Golding, who was 'delighted'. 'I've always wanted to see the Grand Canyon,' he told Monteith, 'and who knows?' To du Sautoy he wrote, 'A thousand dollars sounds an enormous sum relatively.' Perhaps he meant relatively to Fabers' £60.

However, his gratitude to Monteith was too great for him to consider ratting – or even seeming to rat – on Faber and Faber. 'I should hate Fabers to feel I was incapable of playing as fair a game with them as they with me,' he wrote on 21 November 1954, a month after receiving Monteith's soothing letter. He was, he said, 'worried' about Curtis Brown, because he had offered them *Seahorse*, 'a dilatory, formless thing about sailing' that he had written 'about seven years ago', and was astonished that they had jumped at the idea, saying that publication could be very profitable. It had been turned down by 'a number of publishers' when he first wrote it, so he had regarded it as a dead loss and forgotten about it. 'What shall I do?' Should he, perhaps, let Curtis Brown see it and say that if it was any good they must send it to Fabers? Replying on 26 November, Monteith fell in with this suggestion, but cautioned that he should be 'pretty careful' about his second book, after the 'superb' reception of *Lord of the Flies*. This wise warning was heeded. Golding replied that he was, after all, unlikely to publish *Seahorse*. What he had intended was to break it up into articles, but it ought not to be published for years, 'until you succeed in making a name for me'. He knew it would be fatal to follow *Lord of the Flies* with 'a load of trash'. The only danger was the 'lure of quick money'.

What emerges from the correspondence is the good faith of both men, and also Monteith's skill at personal relations. Faber and Faber were to remain Golding's agent as well as his publisher for the rest of his life, an arrangement of great profit to them, and arguably to him too, and the achievement of this goal was entirely the result of Monteith's understanding, patience and literary judgement. He spotted Golding's potential when no one else did, and his faith in his extraordinary gifts did not waver. Though critically acclaimed, *Lord of the Flies* was not a runaway success in the bookshops. At the end of its first year it had sold 4,662 copies – a decent showing, but by no means a best-seller. But months before it was published, and months before the critics had pronounced on it, Monteith was confidently asking Golding for a second novel.

13

The Inheritors

It was on 21 June 1954 that Monteith wrote asking what the next novel would be, and he got a long, anxious letter in return. Golding explained that he had started a novel called *In Search of My Father* about a year back, and had written 130,000 words, leaving perhaps 30,000 to go. It was about the father–son relationship – how all sons 'mythologically' go off to find their fathers 'and end up by displacing him in the world, killing him in fact, and loving and pitying him at the same time for our mortality'. The book had become 'a picaresque, with adventures hair-raising and smutty'. But rewriting *Lord of the Flies* had intervened, and *In Search of My Father* had faltered. His manuscript was illegible, but he could type out a sample chapter if Monteith wanted. He also had an idea for a play called *Dionysius*, 'about the forces of nature which we have evoked'. Alternatively there was *Short Measure*, 'about a schoolboy who is killed by the preoccupation of the people who should be looking after him'. He had sent it to 'over twenty publishers', including Fabers, most of whom said it was good material and vivid, but badly integrated. Monteith, he added, could justifiably reply 'paddle your own canoe', but he would be grateful for advice because he had 'so little critical faculty' himself.

Thanking him for his 'very interesting letter', Monteith was eager to see the chapter of *In Search of My Father*. The other two suggestions obviously attracted him less. Plays were 'pretty hopeless publishing propositions', and if *Short Measure* had had so many rejections it might mean it was 'the unpublishable first novel which practically all success-ful writers have somewhere in their bottom drawer'. However, he should feel free to send them along too. Golding replied in red biro to say that 'exams and what not' had caught up with him and there would be some delay. But within three weeks he had sent *Short Measure*, proposing that perhaps it should be burnt, and a 'lump' of *In Search of My Father*, in which, he explained, the 'nasty customs' were derived from his 'classical and anthropological reading'. Monteith might 'detect some Zenophon here and there' (spelling proper names was never Golding's forte), 'the bits missing from the school editions'.

The play called *Dionysius* and the unfinished *In Search of My Father* (which Golding also refers to as 'Telegonus in Search of His Father') both survive in manuscript. They both fuse myth with science fiction in a way that brings home how closely connected the two forms were for Golding. In *Dionysius*, Pentheus, a negligent, dreamy farmer, despised by his quarrelsome family, returns from the fields one day and surprises them all by announcing that it is 'the greatest day in all our lives', that he has fought his way through to the truth 'from flash to flash of incandescent understanding', and that 'we shall be richer than the kings of the earth'. While they are still reeling in astonishment a beautiful, golden-haired young man walks in, smiling, and asks Pentheus what he wishes him to do. He tells him to light the lamp, which has gone out, and the flame instantly rekindles. It becomes clear that the young man is the god Dionysius, and is at Pentheus's command. 'I can have what I want,' Pentheus rejoices, 'power, respect, place of rule and comfort, knowledge and a purple path among men.' For Golding, recently successful after years of frustration, the story may have had some personal resonance, but it is not a very good play.

In Search of My Father, on the other hand, is magnificent. The hero is Telegonus, son of Calypso by Odysseus, and his mother sends him off to track down his father, whom he eventually kills. His adventures, often bizarre and horrific, are told in some of Golding's most spectacular prose. In the twenty-five-page section that he typed out for Monteith, Telegonus is captured in battle by the Chalybes, a cruel and sinister race famed for their metalwork. Though Golding found them, and some facts about them, in the pages of ancient history, they bring to mind the alien creatures met with in H. G. Wells's science fiction, such as the Selenites in *The First Men in the Moon* or the Morlocks in *The Time Machine*. They are small and vicious, practise horrible sexual tortures, and speak by inhaling rather than exhaling, which makes their language sound remote, so that 'the listener is deceived, thinking

another man has spoken further off'. Telegonus is a science-fiction
creature too. Being the son of a goddess, he is half immortal, and has
strange powers. He can outrun horses, for example. As narrator, he
recounts his adventures with searing clarity. Taken by the Chalybes to
their capital city, he is dragged before the king, who lives in a gloomy
cavern. Behind him in the darkness Telegonus can make out 'peculiar
objects like pale jars for wine or corn'. When the king leaves his cave,
these objects follow.

> The pallid, jar-like objects had emerged from the shadowy palace
> and were grouped behind him so that I could see that they were
> boys, naked and painted, and hideously fat. They were patterned
> in blue and red, some wore bangles of gold, or necklaces and they
> looked at me with eyes far more lifeless than the precious stones
> that lay on their white, padded breasts.

> These creatures are the king's favourites. They are kept in cages
> and stuffed with food, so that they suffocate in their own fat within a
> few years. To show his favour the king has them taken from their
> cages, pricks patterns in their skin with needles, and rubs in indelible
> dyes, which is a prelude to love-making. Among themselves their only
> pleasure is a soft, continual stroking of each other, that Telegonus,
> who is caged and fattened with them, finds abhorrent.

> There was a nightmarish quality about this society of harmless but
> repulsive monsters. They were like the fat and blind things that
> live under damp stones or rotting wood. Their very movements,
> the sluggish stroking of the damp fingers had the repetitive
> timorousness of feelers or palps. They were pitiable and loathsome
> like insects.

That Golding should have left this marvellous novel unfinished,
and that it should have languished unread for half a century, seems
somehow scandalous, and is a measure of the destructive power of his
self-criticism.

By 28 July 1954 Monteith had read the excerpt he had been sent and
was 'enormously interested'. It had given him bad dreams about 'pale,
tattooed fat boys', but he was eager to see the rest. *Short Measure*, on the

other hand, lacked 'imaginative fire', and was best abandoned. This may seem severe, but we must remember Monteith was looking for something striking and unusual enough to follow *Lord of the Flies*, and in that role *Short Measure* might look tame. What would not? This was a problem on Golding's mind too. On 10 September, a week before the publication of *Lord of the Flies*, he reported that he had written more of *In Search*, 'but it's going slowly'. Then came *Lord of the Flies'* publication day and the critical acclaim, and his confidence was shattered. He was scared stiff, he told Monteith in a letter of 17 October, by the favourable reviews. They seemed to put the novel he was writing 'right out of court'. By comparison it would seem just another historical epic – 'an inferior "Sinuhe the Egyptian" or "Long Ships"'. These were two best-sellers of recent years, Finnish author Mika Waltari's *Sinuhe the Egyptian*, published in an English translation in 1949, and the Swede Frans Gunnar Bengtsson's Viking adventure story, *The Long Ships*, based on the Norse sagas. By comparison with *In Search of My Father* they are just run-of-the-mill historical blockbusters, and Golding's failure of nerve was quite unwarranted. However, it was insuperable. 'After three breakdowns and a marked distaste', he reported, he had put *In Search*, 'two thirds written', on one side. But he had written 'nearly a quarter' of another idea, and was going on with it 'at a tremendous lick'. 'It's about H. Sapiens and H. Neanderthal', and its provisional title was *The Inheritors*. Monteith confessed he was 'a bit sorry' that *In Search* had been shelved. But he was looking forward to 'the new one', and on 27 October Golding wrote to say he was 'scribbling madly' at it, and it was 'half done'. He came to London in early November to be photographed for *Vogue* ('the most frightening experience I've had since D-day'), and on the 18th Monteith sent along another little confidence-booster – that *Lord of the Flies* was the November choice of the *Comité Littéraire Franco-Britannique*.

Golding wrote on the 21st to say he had completed *The Inheritors* 'about a week ago'. In fact we can date it more accurately, because at the end of his manuscript Golding inscribed, with military precision, 'First draft finished 1315 on the 11th November in 29 days'. The triumphant note suggests that he knew he had written something great. He always thought it his best book, and many critics would agree. His letter to

Monteith added, however, that it needed 'much reorganization'. A follow-up letter on the 31st said he would like Monteith to see it but it was impossible because his handwriting was illegible 'even to my wife'. That was an exaggeration, but it provided an excuse for doing a bit more work on it before subjecting it to Monteith's critical scrutiny. He would reorganize and type it over Christmas, he promised, 'Then I suppose I'll have to go back to "In Search of".' Wisely unpushy, Monteith replied that he would much rather wait for a legible version.

Golding's Christmas must have been the happiest he had had for a long time. But it was also busy. Fired by success and – at last – fame, he was irrepressible. 'I go on bashing out the Inheritors which you shall have as soon as I show it to anybody,' he assured Monteith. But in addition Eyre and Spottiswoode had asked him to collaborate on a fantasy book, and over Christmas he had written something that might do. It was the story of a sailor who manages to reach Rockall in mid-Atlantic after his ship goes down. 'Would you like to see it (if I can get round to typing it) before E & S do? It's called "The Rescue".' Being 20–25,000 words long it was 'too short to be called a novel and too long for a short story. Very trying.' Monteith wrote back promptly that, yes, he did want to see it before any other publisher had a look-in. He also passed on the news that Arthur Calder-Marshall, in a talk on the BBC European Service, had picked Golding as the most exciting new author of 1954, and he enclosed, as a late Christmas present, an anthology of science fiction. It was a sign of their growing friendship. They were still 'Dear Golding' and 'Dear Monteith' – first names did not trip off the pen so easily in 1954 – but the care and trust they both felt are evident from their letters. Thanking him, Golding acknowledges he is a science-fiction 'addict'. He started with Jules Verne as a boy, and admires Ray Bradbury's story 'There Will Come Soft Rains', C. S. Lewis's *Out of the Silent Planet* and James Blish's *A Case of Conscience* (which he must have read in the 1953 *If* magazine version, because the novel was not published until 1958). He enjoys being given books: 'Usually I have to borrow them or buy them from the tuppeny box outside second hand book shops.'

The Inheritors was 'coming on fast', he reported. 'I've learnt to compose at the typewriter which is a help', and he promised not to send *The Rescue* to Eyre and Spottiswoode. However, it was too short to be published alone, and 'I've nothing to go with it at the moment except a short story which Curtis Brown can't sell because it's about the Sacrament. It's the best thing I've written.' This short story was 'Miss Pulkinhorn'. Narrated by a cathedral organist, with a subtlety and obliqueness worthy of Joseph Conrad, it tells how Miss Pulkinhorn, a self-righteous bigot, resents (and envies for his selfless holiness) an old, derelict man who worships three times every day in the Chapel of the Sacrament, his eyes ecstatically fixed on the sanctuary lamp, which is lit only when the sacramental bread and wine are in the chapel. One day Miss Pulkinhorn, in order to show that the old man's ecstasies are mere superstition and nothing to do with the presence of the sacrament, lights the lamp, although the sacramental elements are not there. The old man comes and worships as usual, but when the verger arrives and blows out the lamp he realizes that he has been deceived (and, we assume, realizes that his ecstasies have been self-induced, not caused by the presence of the sacrament). The shock kills him. Miss Pulkinhorn, tormented by the guilty knowledge that the organist-narrator saw her light the lamp, soon dies too.

When he wrote this story is unclear, but it seems to have been in the same frantic four months before and after Christmas 1954 that gave birth to *The Inheritors* and *Pincher Martin*, as *The Rescue* was eventually retitled. As he could not get 'Miss Pulkinhorn' published as a story he turned it into a radio play, and it was broadcast on the BBC Third Programme, produced by David Thomson, with Hugh Burden as the old man, on 20 April 1960. *Encounter* published it as a short story the following August. Hinging on the reality, or otherwise, of religious experience, and on what happens when it is brought up against 'scientific', testing, its subject was of perennial interest to Golding, and it is no wonder he rated it so highly. Further, the old man, saintly, rapt, innocent, almost a lunatic, prefiguring Matty in *Darkness Visible*, and no doubt associated in Golding's mind with Viannay, the Curé of Ars, was a type of deep importance to him. Like *The Inheritors*, the story sets two opposed kinds of being against each other. So, for that matter, does virtually everything he wrote, as he acknowledged. Discussing with a friend the possible etymology of the name 'Arthur' from *artos*, a Celtic word meaning 'bear', he remarked how the light of the grail-quest undertaken by King Arthur and his knights is 'crossed at right angles' by something black, animal and inarticulate. 'That's what all my novels are about,' he added, 'only no one has seen it.'

Monteith quickly wrote to say he would like to read the sacrament story 'as a Golding fan rather than a publisher'. But it was, naturally, *The Inheritors* that he was chiefly interested in, and Golding sent what he described as the first 'legible draft' on 15 February 1955. He explained that his usual practice was to write two longhand drafts, then type a third and 'muck about with that'. But this time he had written 'a sketch', then typed 'a reorganized version which I hoped would bore a tunnel through the story'. He had not bothered, he said, about style, spelling or punctuation, but had driven on in 'a mad and uninspired rush' to get it into a shape where he could leave it for a bit and then go back to it. So what he was sending was just 'a roughly shaped bit of marble or gritstone or putty'. It was 'nowhere near final – hardly begun in fact', but if Monteith could bear to 'skip through' it, his objective criticism would be of 'enormous value'.

These disclaimers might seem overdone, but they reflect the nervousness Golding felt about his writing. Some of those who knew him best, among them the critic Stephen Medcalf, felt that the man they met and talked to was simply not the same as the man who wrote the novels. Medcalf went so far as to imagine that the novels were written by a 'daimon' or supernatural agent. Golding himself was half-prepared to countenance the idea. 'That is right,' he agreed, 'Sometimes I have felt it myself and been astonished at what it accomplishes'. But he also felt the daimon idea was 'too simple', even if there was 'something in it'. When writing in his journal he gave his 'real', everyday self curious comic nicknames ('Pewter' and 'Bolonius') to distinguish the ordinary Golding from Golding the novelist, who remained, it seems, outside his knowledge and control. He once said to me, speaking of his writing, 'You must understand, I can only just do it.' Perhaps all this is no more than a variant of the age-old idea that the writer is inspired by a 'muse'. Perhaps, too, such a notion was encouraged in Golding by the desire to believe that the phantom stag in Savernake Forest and the strange white bird on the curtain pole in his parents' bedroom were not just illusions. At all events, the suspicion that the creative act was, or was almost, and might become entirely, beyond his unaided powers, seems to have been an element in the exceptional apprehension, doubt, and serial redrafting that accompanied his creativity.

One reason for wanting to get the book out of the way was that they were having to move house – not far, just across the road, in fact, to Flat 2 St Mark's House, which was another big Victorian vicarage. This was because the house they were in was being derequisitioned. The new flat was not council owned, so he would have to pay 'loads of rent like a real rate-payer', and was consequently hard up. He knew that buyers had been found for the French and German rights to *Lord of the Flies*, and he ventured to ask whether he could have the advances on the foreign editions as soon as the contracts were signed. Monteith sent £100 by return – the advances, he explained, had not arrived yet, but this was an interim payment. Ten days later, on 26 February, he sent a long letter from All Souls which must have been just as welcome. He was delighted with *The Inheritors* and urged Golding to let him publish it as it stood, or with a little 'superficial editing' which he could undertake to do at the London end. He added, though, that the decision was Golding's, and if he wanted his book back for major remodelling, he would send it. The terms would be £120 advance, royalties of 12.5 per cent on the first 4,000 copies, and 15 per cent after that.

Monteith's delight had not been immediate. He recalled much later finding the heavy, foolscap envelope containing *The Inheritors* on his desk one morning, and taking it home with him after work.

That evening I started to read it and after two pages put it down, filled with intense and utter dismay. 'O God', I said to myself, 'first it was schoolboys, now it's cavemen. Bloody *cavemen*' ... But I took it up again and, apart from a hurried supper, didn't put it down until I'd finished it. It was another masterpiece. It was a masterpiece as original, as compelling, as powerful – perhaps even more original, and more powerful – than *Lord of the Flies*. And I realized to my surprise, after at least two re-readings, that I had no changes whatever to suggest. It was perfect as it stood.

Golding replied from his new flat on 28 February, to say that he was 'a bit startled to find The Inheritors is finished'. He had thought some alterations were needed. Perhaps, though, he could make changes in galley proof. As for the terms Fabers offered, they seemed 'very generous'. Monteith, with an eye to expense, decided that the alterations, if he wanted to make them, should be made in the typescript, and sent it back asking him to return it in ten days at most – then it could go straight into page proof and skip galleys. His letter crossed with an anxious one from Golding asking whether 'a palaeontologist, anthropologist, archaeologist, hard-headed scientist' should not read the manuscript before publication, 'I haven't done any research for the book at all – just brooded over what I know myself.' Monteith replied firmly that the book did not need an expert: 'If he had any suggestions to make they would be the wrong sort of suggestions.' This was shrewd. The interference of an expert at this stage would have been fatal, as we can tell from the comments made about the novel by the anthropologist, Dr Calvin Wells, a pioneer of palaeopathology, in a BBC World Service programme about Golding in 1966. *The Inheritors*, Wells objects, is 'completely inaccurate' in portraying Neanderthal man with hands hanging down to his knees, partly running on all fours, and having feet that can pick up objects as easily as a monkey. The description of Neanderthals as still living in a world dominated by smell is 'probably ten million years behind the times'. Golding might have replied that he was writing imaginative literature, but his belief in science was sufficient for him to have felt uneasy in dismissing objections like Wells's, and the result would probably have been the abandonment of the whole project.

When he returned the emended typescript to Monteith more anxious questions were scrawled on the back of his letter, together with the note 'Ignore these if you like'. Were the first chapters too slow? He had left the terrain confused, did it matter? Perhaps he had not included enough of the usual 'prehistoric impedimenta' such as pterodactyls and aurochs – 'Isn't the forest a bit 20th-century?' Were the names all right? 'The fall is a most important visual image. Is it clear enough?' He should not worry about any of these points, Monteith assured him, but 'leave everything as it is'.

On 16 March Golding sent along his epigraph for *The Inheritors* – a quotation from H. G. Wells's *Outline of History.*

We know very little of the appearance of the Neanderthal man, but this ... seems to suggest an extreme hairiness. An ugliness, or a repulsive strangeness in his appearance over and above his low forehead, his beetle brows, his ape neck, and his inferior stature ... Says Sir Harry Johnston, in a survey of the rise of modern man in his *Views and Reviews*: 'The dim racial remembrance of such gorilla-like monsters, with cunning brains, shambling gait, hairy bodies, strong teeth, and possibly cannibalistic tendencies, may be the germ of the ogre in folklore.'

Golding was feeling low when he sent that along. He had flu, and the house move had been hell. 'We still live in an atmosphere of bare boards and lino that won't fit.' All the same, Wells's guesswork prompted a laugh: 'I still find that quote as uproariously funny today as I did many years ago when I first read it.' His father was a keen Wellsian, and regarded the atheistic, science-worshipping *Outline of History* as pure truth, and that may have spiced Golding's defiant laughter.

In *Lord of the Flies* he had written *Coral Island* in reverse, upending R. M. Ballantyne's idealistic white-imperialist assumptions, and he had made the reversal explicit – 'Jolly good show. Like the Coral Island', booms the ignorant naval officer at the end. In *The Inheritors* he reverses Wells's progressivist prejudice and makes the Neanderthals innocent, unfallen creatures. They live on berries, roots, grubs and fungi, and do not kill or have any weapons. They eat meat only when they come upon the uneaten prey of some big-cat predator, and even then they think it is wrong, and apologize to the dead prey, explaining they were not the killers. They worship a mother-goddess Oa, out of whose belly all life comes, and to whom all return at death. Only women approach Oa's sanctuary. It is considered too terrifying for men. Men, on the other hand, usually do the thinking, which consists of seeing mental 'pictures' and conveying them to others by gesticulating and 'dancing out' meaning as much as by speech. The speech of the 'new people' (*Homo sapiens*), who suddenly appear in the Neanderthals' homeland, is unaccompanied by dance or gesture, and seems to them like strange 'jabbering'. Despite Golding's rejection of Wells, it is from Wells that he apparently got the idea for his Neanderthals' pictorial thinking, as Craig Raine has pointed out. In *A Short History of the World*, Wells wrote, 'Primitive man probably thought very much as a child thinks, that is to say, in a series of imaginative pictures.'

The story *The Inheritors* tells is of the destruction of the Neanderthals by the new people. The new people have spears and bows and arrows and dugout canoes to cross water, which seems unbelievable to the Neanderthals, and they are capable of logical thought. Pathetically, the Neanderthals regard them with awestruck admiration, unable to understand, at first, that they intend their extermination. At the start there are eight Neanderthals: an old woman and an old man called Mal, a couple, Fa and Lok, with a young girl-child, Liku, who carries a doll or fetish called the 'little Oa', and another couple, Nil and Ha, with a baby whom they call 'the new one'. Lok likes clowning and making people laugh, but he is not very bright. At the end he is left alone, the only one to survive, apart from the baby, whom the new people steal, because one of their women has lost her child and she takes the little Neanderthal as a substitute.

Golding's problem in the novel was to convey the Neanderthals' different way of apprehending the world. An instance of its triumphant resolution is Lok's first encounter with one of the new people, whom he sees on the other side of a river.

> The man turned sideways in the bushes and looked at Lok along his shoulder. A stick rose upright and there was a lump of bone in the middle. Lok peered at the stick and the lump of bone and the small eyes in the bone things over the face. Suddenly Lok understood that the man was holding the stick out to him but neither he nor Lok could reach across the river. He would have laughed if it were not for the echo of the screaming in his head. The stick began to grow shorter at both ends. Then it shot out to full length again.
>
> The dead tree by Lok's ear acquired a voice.
>
> 'Clop!'
>
> His ears twitched and he turned to the tree. By his face there had grown a twig, a twig that smelt of other, and of goose, and of the bitter berries that Lok's stomach told him he must not eat. The

twig had a white bone at the end. There were hooks in the bone and sticky brown stuff hung in the crooks. His nose examined this stuff and did not like it. He smelled along the shaft of the twig. The leaves on the twig were red feathers and reminded him of goose. He was lost in generalized astonishment and excitement.

This illustrates the book's emotional power as well as its sensory originality. For Lok, in his understanding, is a child. We feel concern for him as we would if he were a toddler, facing a killer and not knowing it, thinking, even, that the killer is being friendly and offering the stick he holds out as a present. Of course *Lord of the Flies* has its moments of pity. But the boys on the island seldom arouse the unmingled, helpless pity that we feel for a baby or an animal that is facing danger. Lok does.

Lok's puzzlement over the bow and arrow recalls little Golding's puzzlement when he was given a bow and arrow for his third birthday, and it exemplifies what theorists have called 'defamiliarization'. But a simpler term would be just 'seeing things differently', and for Golding seeing things differently extends further than just the visual. The turnaround technique he applies to *Coral Island* and Wells's *Outline* involves seeing ideas and theories differently and, as critics were quick to notice, *Lord of the Flies* and *The Inheritors* both end with a switch of viewpoint. The naval officer sees the savages hunting Ralph as 'a semicircle of little boys', and the new people see innocent, loving Lok as a 'devil'.

Both Golding's first manuscript draft and the typescript he sent to Monteith survive. The manuscript is written in red biro in a Bishop Wordsworth's School green hardcover exercise book. The dates on which he wrote each part are entered at the tops of the pages, the first 15 October and the last 11 November 1954. An alternative title, 'The People' is written at the top of the first page. The story is broadly the same in both versions, but several incidents that occur in the manuscript are omitted from the printed text, though written with the same, or even greater, tenderness and horror and poetic originality as the rest. No idea of the manuscript version's special quality can be given by arbitrary quotation. It cries out to be published as a novel in its own right. At the end Golding has written some notes or reminders to himself ('Addenda after finishing draft. Now able to think of the whole'). These relate to what seem to him the crucial moments in the book and the things he wants to emphasize in the rewrite. 'High point of book is picture of Lok in the clearing with the little Oa in his hand'. In both the first draft and the rewrite Lok fails to realize that his child Liku has been killed and eaten by the new people until, when all the others are dead, he digs up her skull and her doll. This is the culmination of the Neanderthals' tragedy that Golding's note refers to.

But most of the notes he wrote for the rewrite refer to the idea that the new people are not impelled by mere wickedness or cruelty but by some irresistible force – progress or destiny or natural selection. 'The new people must be forced by *circumstances and their own natures* to destroy the people'; 'They must come *from* somewhere (the sea?) and be going *to* somewhere'; 'Can I not get the approach of fate, the slow closing in?'; 'The central symbol is the waterfall, the time stream; the fall, the second law of thermodynamics. It must be vivid.' This ties in with what Golding told the critic Virginia Tiger – that he wrote the first draft as a rebuttal of the nineteenth-century doctrine of progress but, in the rewrite, stressed, on the contrary, the evolutionary life force which drives the new people upwards 'at a higher level of energy' than the Neanderthals possess. This is symbolized by their ability to travel up the river against the current. The waterfall is described at much greater length in the rewrite, to bring out its symbolic force, and Fa is swept to her death over it, whereas in the first draft she is killed by a spear thrown by one of the new people. Golding's reference to the second law of thermodynamics is clarified by something he wrote in an essay on Yeats, published in *Holiday* magazine in 1963, which Tiger quotes:

> The Satan of our cosmology is the Second Law of Thermodynamics
> which implies that everything is running down and will finally
> stop like an unwound clock. Life is in some sense a local
> contradiction of this law ... we should be cheered when life refuses
> to submit to a general levelling down of energy and simply winds
> itself up again.

Water passing over the fall, from a state of high to a state of low organization, is an illustration of the second law, but the new people, defying the current, and pushed on by 'a new intensity, new vision', are a local contradiction of it. It is almost as if the first version of *The Inheritors* were written by the religious Golding, who mourns the destruction of innocence, and the revised version by his Wellsian, rationalist, scientific father Alec, who pitied the victims of evolution, like the dying rabbit he found ('Poor little beggar'), but believed firmly in evolution nonetheless.

The surviving typescript of the novel is the one Golding sent to Monteith and Monteith returned for him to correct. Most of the corrections are in red biro, but some are Sellotaped in on separate typed slips, and a note to the printer about the positioning of one of these, in Monteith's hand, shows that this was the copy from which type was set up. The number of words on each typewritten page has been written, sometimes in pencil, sometimes in ink, at the top, each time in a different hand. This bears out the recollection of Golding's pupils that he used to distribute typed pages around the class and get them to count the words. It seems that they did not all realize what a great privilege it was.

Monteith sent *Inheritors* proofs out to the organizers of the *Daily Mail* and *Evening Standard* Book of the Month choice, and to the celebrated archaeologist Sir Mortimer Wheeler, who returned rather ponderous approval – 'an interesting experiment in the *crepuscule* of human intelligence'. But the really exciting news that he was able to share on 14 July was that the BBC were to broadcast a radio version of *Lord of the Flies*. It was to be by Giles Cooper, and Christopher Whelan had composed 'atmospheric music', using a boys' choir. It went out on Sunday, 28 August, with a repeat in November, and helped to spread Golding's fame far beyond the reading public, as well as to polarize opinion. Some papers, notably the *Sunday Times* and the *Observer*, were disdainful, but Ian Low in the *News Chronicle* thought that 'nothing on the Home or Light for the past fortnight has been half as good as the Third's *Lord of the Flies*'. The BBC's audience research department reported that the play had made a 'far greater impression' than the audience appreciation indices might suggest. Many listeners were both 'fascinated and utterly appalled', so had difficulty deciding what rating to give. While registering their 'intense dislike of this ghastly radio nightmare' they conceded that 'admiration and repulsion cancel each other out'. A minority, however, 'condemned the play wholeheartedly as pointlessly – because unrealistically – nasty'.

Golding missed the broadcast. He replied blithely to Monteith's letter of the 14th to say that on 28 August he would be afloat 'somewhere in the neighbourhood of the Scillies'. He had, he reported, finished and sent off the story for Eyre and Spottiswoode's fantasy volume (this was 'Envoy Extraordinary', later reprinted in *The Scorpion God*), and they seemed 'quite excited' about it. 'Now I haven't a ghost of a notion in my head for anything else.' As it happened he was not near the Scillies on 28 August after all. 'Owing to the sinister threat of the Inland Revenue' (warning him, presumably, of the tax payable on royalties and WEA earnings), he decided to economize. 'We ended by sailing a minute and battered dinghy on the south coast of Cornwall – day sailing of the humblest type.' But as wireless reception was bad in his remote hideaway he missed the *Lord of the Flies* broadcast anyway. The house he had taken was in Polruan, a small village opposite Fowey. His parents, his brother Jose and Jose's wife Theo were there as well as the Goldings. The dinghy, property of the Bishop Wordsworth's School Sea Cadets, came by train to Lostwithiel, and he and David picked it up and sailed it down the River Fowey to their house, which had a small quay. He had brought an advance copy of *The Inheritors* with him, and showed it to Judy, now aged ten, who thought the cover very good. But he told her not to read it.

It was published on 16 September 1955, with a first printing of just over 5,000 copies. Reading through the reviews reminds one that, despite the notice *Lord of the Flies* had attracted, Golding's reputation had not yet taken off. Publication of a new novel by him was not yet an event, and at a pinch a literary editor could ignore it. Only one of the Sundays reviewed *The Inheritors* the weekend after it came out, and a week later the *Sunday Times* gave it a mere two sentences in its 'Short Reports' column, where Phillip Day judged it 'A *tour de force*, but very long drawn out.' The reviews that did appear, though, were nearly all enthusiastic. The day after publication Douglas Hewitt in the *Guardian* reckoned that, though it was not always successful, when it worked it achieved a success 'that makes the successes of most contemporary novelists appear cheap and easy'. John Davenport in the *Observer*, on the 18th, called Golding 'the most purely original' novelist of the last decade – 'he does not merely dazzle, he stirs' – and on the 23rd the classical scholar Peter Green, later a close friend of Golding's, left *Daily Telegraph* readers in no doubt: 'a prose quite astounding in its poetic clarity ... the most astonishing and original *tour de force* I have seen since I first reviewed a novel. Mr Golding is a genius.' Isabel Quigley was equally positive in *The Spectator* on 30 September: 'the most original and imaginatively exciting novelist we have today ... enthralling ... a many-dimensional and astonishing book'. Plaudits continued spasmodically in the months that followed: 'compelling ... outstanding' (*Times Literary Supplement*); 'a great feat of sympathetic imagination' (G. S. Fraser, *Encounter*); 'a brilliant and audacious feat of imaginative writing' (Bruce Bain, *Tribune*); 'an extraordinary imaginative achievement' (Richard Rees, *Twentieth Century*); 'a splendid work of imagination ... His vision is true, sad and superbly conveyed' (Philip Oakes, *Truth*). There were tributes, too, from further afield. Australia's *Melbourne Age* found it a 'startling leap of imagination', and the novelist Olivia Manning, in the *Jerusalem Post*, thought it as 'remarkable' as *Lord of the Flies* – 'the tragedy of the dying species is brilliantly dealt with'.

The only really crass comments came from the two ends of the political spectrum. The British Marxist, ex-Roedean schoolgirl, and leading member of the Communist Party of Great Britain, Margot Heinemann, found it 'pretty tough work understanding' the book, and disapproved of what she took to be its message: 'why present the ascent of man as a tragedy at all?' The *Times* offered its thoughts in a brief paragraph buried in a general piece on new novels. The names of the characters, it noticed, were unlike those of *Times* readers – 'It is hard to make characters called Lok, Oa and Fa of any passionate interest' – and it concluded that it would have been wiser to keep Neanderthal man 'behind the bars of an outline of history', rather than encouraging him to 'run wild through luxurious forests of imaginative prose'.

The *Vogue* photograph that Golding had found it such an ordeal to pose for appeared at last in their October 1955 issue, with a short piece praising *The Inheritors'* 'literary virtuosity'. It had been taken the previous November, to go with a review of *Lord of the Flies*, but they had decided to produce a travel number instead – much to the indignation of the Golding children. The end result did not much impress the sitter: 'Don't bother to look at *Vogue*, please,' he advised Monteith. 'It makes me look as if I were seated in the police station trying ingratiatingly to explain away my possession of a packet of dirty postcards.' The same letter reveals some of the strain he felt in juggling his full-time teaching job with the growing demands of authorship. Monteith had asked him and Ann (who now had a part-time post teaching arithmetic at a local boys' school) to a lunch at L'Etoile in Charlotte Street to meet T. S. Eliot, before the Faber party on Thursday, 13 October. He accepted, after at first refusing, and explained the awkwardness they felt: 'You see, we both teach, and I have tried to effect a complete dichotomy between what is due to the school and what is due to the career of an author now blooming like a Christmas rose'. As for the reviews of *The Inheritors*, he could not 'imagine a much better write-up than Davenport's', and Isabel Quigley's in *The Spectator* was a 'smash-hit'. All the same, though critics had been 'most respectful' he was uneasy. 'I feel the touch of the Higher Criticism like a cold wind, and see myself spiralling up towards being a third programme novelist, universally admired, but unread. I shan't change, because I can't – but I'd like to know.' And in particular, he added, he would like to know how *The Inheritors* was selling. Since he was writing on 28 September and it had been published only on the 16th, this was a little premature. However, Monteith, having consulted Peter du Sautoy, was able to report on 3 October that it had sold 1,800 up to the end of September, and was 'selling strongly in the last week'. Golding was evidently not much cheered. Monteith had asked for a list of the 'chumps' who had turned down *Lord of the Flies*, and sending this along on 28 October he remarked sardonically that his earnings as a novelist so far had 'just about covered my outlay on postage' in previous years. On the contrary, Monteith replied, both published novels were 'selling very steadily', and *Inheritors* sales were approaching 3,000. Privately he communicated to Peter du Sautoy that Golding was 'obsessed by the idea that he's never going to make any money by writing. The answer to this seems to be that he has and is. Perhaps he has no idea at all about the average earnings of novelists.'

Another slight cause of friction was 'Envoy Extraordinary', the story written for the Eyre and Spottiswoode fantasy collection, which had been sent to Monteith by Curtis Brown. When he wrote his thank-you letter for the L'Etoile lunch and the 'galactic party' afterwards, Golding added that he hoped Monteith had managed to read it to the end. He certainly had, Monteith replied, and had sent it on to Eyre and Spottiswoode – 'lucky people! It is superbly good.' Evidently the party had established a new level of informality, because, for the first time, Monteith starts his letter 'Dear Bill' and ends 'Yours ever, Charles' – and from now on they are always 'Bill' and 'Charles' to each other. Perhaps Monteith slipped into a warmer tone because he sensed some hurt on Golding's part, and indeed Golding's next letter revealed that he had hoped Fabers would publish 'Envoy Extraordinary' and was 'very sad' they were not going to. This took Monteith completely by surprise, as he explained in an internal memo to du Sautoy. He wrote soothingly in reply, suggesting that Fabers might republish the story in a volume along with the story Golding had mentioned about the sailor marooned on Rockall – 'I wonder if you ever finished it'. Avoiding this question, Golding replied rather glumly that he was feeling 'moody' about novels because people seemed to think he had demonstrated a 'certain clever eccentricity', but now ought to set to and write a twentieth-century 'tea-cup novel'. In fact he had 'an idea, and a good one' about 'the present cosmic mess' (this was probably what became *Darkness Visible*, the first draft of which, as we shall see, was written in October 1955). But for some reason he found himself 'sneering at it unconsciously', and was happier with 'a less promising idea about pre-dynastic Egypt' (which was to become *The Scorpion God*).

He still felt pessimistic about *The Inheritors*. When Monteith wrote to say he had been 'enthralled' by the repeat of the BBC *Lord of the Flies*, Golding agreed it made 'terrifying radio' but added, 'If only the ripples of *The Inheritors* would spread a bit wider! I have an uneasy feeling that it's flopped.' Not at all, Monteith insisted, it was selling more than 100 copies a week and total sales were well over 3,000. Probably Golding was more comforted by the Christmas Day *Sunday Times*, in which Arthur Koestler, one of the guest celebrities rounded up to name their books of the year, wrote that *The Inheritors* 'gave me the impression of an earthquake in the petrified forests of the English novel'. It was 'beautifully written' and 'both complex and simple, as a novel should be'. The death of Lok was 'the most moving scene I have read for a long time'.

The reaction of American publishers was, by contrast, conservative and provincial. The novel's originality caused them shock and bewilderment. Peter du Sautoy sent it first to Coward-McCann, who had published *Lord of the Flies*, and they speedily rejected it: 'in the opinion of all of us the book would die aborning' (that is, in the process of being born). Attempts to persuade them failed. 'I am morally certain it will get nowhere,' T. R. Coward affirmed, 'It would be disasterous [sic].' He added that they had sold only about 2,500 of the 5,000 copies of *Lord of the Flies* they printed. John McCallum of Harcourt, Brace & Co expressed an interest, and du Sautoy sent a copy along, but McCallum replied that, though it was 'brilliant' and 'breathtaking', it would damage Golding to have a failure, as this would be. However, they would undertake to publish *The Inheritors* at some unspecified time in the future, provided they could have an option on Golding's next book. Du Sautoy replied politely that he was afraid he must treat this as a rejection. But nothing better was forthcoming. Not surprisingly, when du Sautoy met Golding in March 1956, he found he was 'rather sensitive about *The Inheritors* and about American reactions generally'.

So *The Inheritors* remained unpublished in America. When early copies of *Pincher Martin* became available, du Sautoy sent one to McCallum, who replied that he was 'overwhelmed' by such a 'remarkable' novel. But he was sure it would not sell in America. At least, though, it might be a bit more saleable than *The Inheritors*, so he proposed that Harcourt, Brace might publish *Pincher Martin* as Golding's second novel, and leave *The Inheritors* for later. There would be a clause in the contract to say that as soon as one of Golding's books sold a minimum of 7,500 copies in America, Harcourt, Brace would publish *The Inheritors* within six months. Du Sautoy tried to get better terms, but McCallum refused to budge. They would not publish *The Inheritors* yet, he insisted, because they did not feel, 'after the sales failure in America of *Lord of the Flies*', that they 'could do the best publishing job for William Golding' by publishing a book that would get only 'ivory-tower appreciation', as *The Inheritors* would. With that du Sautoy had to be satisfied. He recommended acceptance of the Harcourt, Brace terms to Golding, who innocently expressed 'complete confidence in your wisdom'. The result of du Sautoy's thirteen months of negotiation was, accordingly, that Harcourt, Brace would not publish *The Inheritors*, and would not let anyone else in America publish it either. This was not Fabers' finest hour, and readers may wonder whether Golding would not have done better to have an agent arrange his American rights. So it is only fair to add that de Sautoy did indeed get MCA Artists Ltd, an agency with a New York office at 598 Madison Avenue and a London office at 139 Piccadilly, to negotiate with McCallum, and they were no more successful than he had been. The trouble was that as yet Golding had no reputation in America, so Harcourt, Brace could have everything their own way. For now.

14

Pincher Martin

Golding told Monteith in his letter of 21 January 1955 that the story he had written over Christmas 1954, while typing out *The Inheritors*, was about 'a sailor who manages to reach Rockall in mid atlantic after his ship has gone down', and that it was called 'The Rescue'. This story has not survived, but its title, and Golding's statement that the sailor does reach the rock, seem to indicate that it was in a crucial respect different from, and less dark than, *Pincher Martin* – though 'The Rescue' may have been an ironic title, and Golding's letter may have deliberately concealed the novel's surprise ending.

It seems likely that the germ of the story was the real-life rescue of one of his colleagues at Bishop Wordsworth's. The physics master during most of his time there was Vivian Trewhella, and during the war he had been on board an LCT between Tilbury and Ostend when it struck a mine and caught fire. Trewhella managed to persuade another man to discard his sea-boots and jump into the water with him, but a third man, who could not swim, stayed behind. After floating around in the water for a time Trewhella lost consciousness – in effect, he said, he 'drowned'. He was pulled out unconscious, one of only twenty-eight survivors from a complement of three hundred, and at Bishop Wordsworth's his ordeal became a subject of staff-room conversation. Had memories of his past life flashed before him as they were supposed to do during drowning? Trewhella said they had – memories of cricket teams and games and other people and events. Golding was an eager listener at these exchanges, indeed it occurred to Trewhella that he sometimes steered the conversation round to the subject so as to glean information.

Monteith was eager to see the new story before anyone else did, and early in February Golding agreed to send it – but not yet. The subject had 'limitless possibilities', he thought, 'just as *Lord of the Flies* had', and he wanted to 'leave it and occasionally brood and see if it creates itself'. After that the excitement of getting *The Inheritors* finished and published took over, and the shipwrecked sailor story was not mentioned again in their correspondence until 26 October, when Monteith wondered if it had ever been finished, but got no reply.

In December Golding wrote that he had 'got torn between two novels' but had 'ended by writing neither – so far', and was very depressed about it. However he had returned to 'Rockall', for which his current alternative title was 'The Chinese Have X-Ray Eyes' (a sentence still in the final version of the novel), and it had run out at 37,000 words – 'an impossible length'. So he was going to 'take a couple of weeks off and think'. Monteith was delighted to hear it was back in production, and longed to read it, but Golding's next letter, on 29 December, announced a change of direction. He had had 'violent second thoughts' about 'Rockall'. He was now sure that it really would be a full-length novel, 'because there is one theme, only hidden. Sorry to sound obscure.' He wanted to have another go in January and February, as he had with *The Inheritors*, 'and that *might* be good'. At the moment it was 'rather an un-splendid torso. It's typed, but only because I did the first draft that way instead of in longhand. And it peters out at about 37 thousand from sheer exhaustion. I wrote the lot in seven days. Silly.' On a personal tack he added that he had taken David, now aged fifteen, to Oxford the previous day, 'to give him a preview'.

Monteith was naturally excited to learn that a third novel was on its way, but his spirits may have been dampened a little by Golding's next letter, on 24 February 1956. He had finished the second draft, he reported, and thought it 'pretty bad'. A certain amount was 'worth saving', but it would take 'a good month's work', and he wondered what the latest possible delivery date for autumn publication would be. He is somewhat downcast, he adds, that *Lord of the Flies* 'is a financial flop' in America, but he takes a robust line: 'Never mind, so is Godot; which I've now seen and enjoyed immensely.' Despatching a copy of the Faber edition of Beckett's play, Monteith gave the end of March as the cut-off date if the new novel was to get into their autumn catalogue. Golding promised he would try. He had heard, he added (and Monteith confirmed) that the first edition of *Lord of the Flies* was now a collectors' item: 'This makes me feel very distinguished – rather like a piece of Chippendale.'

Well within the time limit, he sent the typescript of *Pincher Martin* to Fabers on 19 March. It was 'a sanguinary mess', he feared, and he would be grateful if Monteith 'could spot the essential weaknesses'. He wondered, incidentally, if Monteith knew of anyone with a four-berth cabin cruiser for sale at £500 or less, 'my family are goading me into buying one to take the place of our old wreck' (the old wreck being the stolen or strayed *Seahorse*). At heart a solemn man, Monteith had not yet learnt to identify Golding's jokes, and he wrote back regretting that he knew of no boats for sale. Golding had to explain that he had meant to be funny. About *Pincher Martin*, however, Monteith was in no doubt. It was 'absolutely tremendous', and he offered the same terms as before – 12.5 per cent royalties on the first 4,000 and 15 per cent after that, with an advance of £200 (as against £120 for *The Inheritors*). In a private note to Peter du Sautoy, he reported that Golding had accepted these terms, and he suggested that 'we put a new option clause into our contract giving us an option on his next two books on the same terms as for *Pincher Martin*. He can, of course, be given an improvement; indeed, he always has to date; but this procedure will give us a firm hold.' It is a good example of the hard-headedness that lay behind Monteith's suave exterior, and it is doubtful whether, given the favourable critical reception of Golding's first two books, an independent agent would have advised him to sign such a contract. Nevertheless, he did.

Having just read *Pincher Martin*, Monteith can hardly be blamed for wanting to make sure he would remain Golding's publisher, for it is one of the most profound and original novels of the twentieth century. By examining the predicament of a modern Prometheus, a lone sailor exposed on a rock, it raises fundamental questions about consciousness, identity and language, and how they interconnect. The whole novel is made out of seeing-things-differently, or defamiliarization. As Pincher struggles through hallucination, dream and delusion, his body and everything else on the rock assume monstrous shapes. The flying reptiles that attack him are seagulls, the terrible red lobsters beside him are his sunburnt hands. It would be too simple to say that Pincher is

Golding, but the life he has lived, revealed in flashbacks, is Golding's life, or a version of it. Pincher remembers his childhood nightmares, which are Golding's nightmares about the cellars at 29 The Green. The hag from the corner of the cellar who haunted little Golding is on the rock with Pincher. Pincher went to Oxford, and remembers its church bells, as Golding did, and we can tell he read English from the abstruse quotations that float around his brain – 'Care charmer sleep', for example, from a sonnet by Samuel Daniel. Pincher was an actor, joined the navy, and became a sub-lieutenant. He plays chess. He even has a scar on his right thigh, which is Golding's scar from the MDI explosion. Nathaniel, the tall, ungainly, pious friend Pincher met at Oxford, who is now an ordinary seaman on the same destroyer as Pincher, is clearly Adam Bittleston, and the young woman Mary Lovell, whom Pincher is in love with, and who, to his fury, has married Nathaniel, is Mollie Evans, the girl who sat in front of him in class at Marlborough Grammar School, and whom he was engaged to before he married Ann. Every detail of Mary matches the description of Mollie in *Men, Women & Now* – her 'incredibly small waist' (Mollie's was eighteen inches), her pursed-up mouth and too-high forehead (an Evans family trait), her 'mousey' hair, her large, beautiful eyes, her 'little, guarded breasts' and her 'impregnable virtue'. Her purity arouses in Pincher the same urge to 'break' her as Mollie aroused in Golding, and the consequent chaos of love and hatred remind Pincher of the same Catullus poem, and of his attempt to write about his love-torment as Golding had attempted to write about his: '*Odi et amo*, like that thing I tried to write.'

So Pincher, like Geoffrey in *Circle Under the Sea* and Philip in *Short Measure*, is a self-defaming self-portrait. Pincher, 'born with his mouth and his flies open', embodies what Golding saw as his own greed, lust, egotism, cruelty and ambition. Pincher tries to rape Mary, and attempts to terrify her into yielding by driving her at reckless speed in a car. This is based on a scene in *Those Barren Leaves* by Aldous Huxley, young Golding's favourite author, and though it may bear no relation to anything Golding did to Mollie, it is worth remembering that Eileen, his adopted sister, said that he crashed Mollie's parents' car twice. In any case, whether or not he submitted Mollie to the Huxley fast-car ordeal, he did seduce, betray and abandon her. Pincher intends to murder Nathaniel – the ship hits a torpedo just before he can do so – and that is far from anything Golding did to Adam. But, despite their friendship, he knew that a part of him was contemptuous of Adam and his Steineresque credulity, and he was prepared to exploit him. He once told Judy that he had sold one of Adam's books to buy a ticket for Gielgud's *Hamlet*. This hardly amounts to attempted murder. But Golding depicted not what he had done, but what he believed he had the capacity to do. He told Stephen Medcalf that he thought all wickedness could be found in his own heart.

The surviving notes for *Pincher Martin*, in a green hardcover Bishop Wordsworth's School exercise book, include, along with chapter plans, a rigorous moral scheme:

> Basic. He is utterly selfish. Risking anything to preserve his life.
>
> Q. Why is he what he is?
>
> A. Because he has been running away from God (The old woman in the cellar).
>
> This is no answer. Somewhere he went wronger than most. That must have been pre-natal.
>
> Running away from God is running away from helplessness and death towards power and life.
>
> Life then means power over things and power over the most expensive things called women.
>
> The greatest power is to break the opposite thing an innocent and holy being.
>
> He finds two of them (they are Nathaniel and Mary).
>
> He devours his way upwards. He is about to devour Mary when she and Nathaniel meet, marry. Now she is untouchable. The war. The others (query? Producer and wife) whom he thought to eat now eat him. He is with navy. Officer. But so is Nathaniel. An illness holds Nat back and he gets him into his own ship. Plans to bump him off in one of the safe ways that war makes easy. Who would suspect? Best friend!

As *Lord of the Flies* reverses *Coral Island* and *The Inheritors* reverses Wells on Neanderthals, so *Pincher Martin*, too, is a reversal, though Golding may not have realized when he wrote it. A book called *Pincher*

Martin O.D. had been published in 1916 by 'Taffrail', the pseudonym of Henry Taprell Dorling. By contrast with Golding's Pincher, Taffrail's Pincher is a loyal, brave, patriotic British seaman. He is torpedoed and flung into the sea, and struggles to remove his sea-boots, like Golding's Pincher, but he 'dies' as he does so. He meets death calmly, committing his soul to God with Christian fortitude, unlike Golding's Pincher who shouts, 'I spit upon your God.' It was the writer and scholar Ian Blake who first noticed these resemblances, and he wrote to Golding about them. Golding replied that he 'vaguely remembered' reading Taffrail's book in, he thought, 'the early 'twenties', and Blake 'received the distinct impression' that he 'might not have been pleased that I had come upon this source'. However, since Golding had on two previous occasions gone out of his way to name the book of which his own book was a reversed version, there seems no reason why he should have intentionally suppressed any reference to Taffrail's *Pincher Martin* in his own novel. More probably he had just forgotten reading it.

Taffrail's Pincher does not in fact die: he is rescued by a fisherman. Golding's does. As in his two previous novels, there is a viewpoint switch at the end. In the last chapter the scene changes to the shoreside homestead of a fisherman, Mr Campbell. A naval officer, Davidson, arrives, to pick up the body of Christopher Hadley Martin (his real name: 'Pincher' was his nickname) which has been washed ashore. When Campbell worries about whether the dead man suffered, Davidson reassures him: 'You saw the body. He didn't even have time to kick off his seaboots.' This comes as a surprise to the reader, for we are repeatedly reminded, in the course of the narrative, that Pincher had been able to remove his sea-boots before scrambling onto the rock. It now seems that his whole ordeal on the rock – everything we have read – did not happen, or not in our world. Golding explained what he had intended in a letter published in the *Radio Times* on 21 March 1958, to coincide with a Third Programme adaptation of *Pincher Martin*:

Christopher Hadley Martin had no belief in anything but the importance of his own life; no love, no God. Because he was created in the image of God he had a freedom of choice which he used to centre the world on himself. He did not believe in purgatory and therefore when he died it was not presented to him in overtly theological terms. The greed for life which had been the mainspring of his nature, forced him to refuse the selfless act of dying. He continued to exist separately in a world composed of his own murderous nature. His drowned body lies rolling in the Atlantic but the ravenous ego invents a rock for him to endure on.

This was the interpretation of the story that Golding stuck to: Pincher dies at the beginning of the book, the rest takes place in purgatory. Stephen Medcalf remembers a woman student at a lecture in Sussex asking Golding, 'How long does it take Pincher Martin to die?' Golding replied, 'Eternity.' 'But how long does it take in real time?' she persisted. He paused, and then said, 'Eternity.'

For readers who do not believe in purgatory or eternity there is, however, a let-out. At the end of Chapter ii Pincher feels along his teeth with his tongue:

His tongue was remembering. It pried into the gap between the teeth and re-created the old, aching shape. It touched the rough edge of the cliff, traced the slope down trench after aching trench ... understood what was so hauntingly familiar and painful about an isolated and decaying rock in the middle of the sea.

The geography of the rock is the geography of an old tooth. That, we gather, is how the idea of the rock and the pain he suffered on it got into Pincher's mind. For Golding, as his *Radio Times* letter makes clear, Pincher's ordeal on the tooth-shaped rock takes place in purgatory. But we may believe, if we wish, that in the brief moments it took to drown there flashed through Pincher's mind not only the memories of his past life but the whole imagined future ordeal of defiance and survival prompted by his will to live and shaped by the memory of his tooth. The text is ambivalent, despite Golding's proclaimed intentions, as texts tend to be. Those who discussed literature with him, such as Frank Kermode and Mark Kinkead-Weekes, found that in time he relaxed his early view that an author's interpretation of his text was the only definitive one. However, there is no evidence that he changed his mind about the meaning of *Pincher Martin*. The memory of the aching tooth, we might add, was, like other of Pincher's attributes, Golding's own. His son David remembers that on the 1955 Cornish holiday, when they were out sailing together, his father finally gave in and decided the tooth would have to be looked at, and they came home and went over to Fowey to have it out. In his journal eighteen years later Golding still recalled the operation with some bitterness. It was a wisdom tooth, and the dentist who extracted it was 'an exhibitionist'.

While Charles Monteith was digesting this brilliant and astonishing story, Golding's mind was set on finding a seagoing craft to replace *Seahorse*, and he wrote at the end of March that they were 'off to see our boat, which we have almost bought'. This was *Wild Rose*, a thirty-seven-foot converted Whitstable oyster smack with two masts. She had been built in 1896 so, Golding joked, should by rights be in a maritime museum, but she turned out to be enormously strong, when put to the test, as well as very fast. David remembers her once outstripping a modern Bermuda-rigged yacht on their way back from France. She could sleep four, or six if they put in extra bunks. By 4 April they had bought her. She seemed 'huge', Golding told Monteith, 'I'm terrified of her.' They were now at Rochester and had to get her to Southampton, and if he could have afforded it he would have taken her by road. However, they sailed. 'We left last Tuesday and got to Southampton on Friday afternoon without a single panic.' There had been good weather except on the last day, and even then the wind was in the right quarter and simply blew them home. 'Wild Rose now sits demurely among a lot of flashy and expensive yachts – like a Salvation Army lassie who has strayed into an expensive joint by mistake.'

In his 4 April letter he had asked for the typescript of *Pincher Martin* back because he had 'thought of one or two extra sentences that ought to be inserted'. Monteith obliged, and Golding sent it straight to the printers once he had made his additions. Proof copies were ready by the end of July. On 28 August, however, Monteith arrived in the office to find that he had almost lost his author. 'What a turn we had this morning – headlines in every paper we picked up. It must have been an absolutely appalling experience.' The dailies all carried the same story. The Goldings had set out from Yarmouth on the Isle of Wight the previous Saturday, planning to arrive in Cherbourg the same evening, but had been overtaken by a Channel storm. For nearly three days *Wild Rose* drifted battered and helpless with her canvas ripped and her engine and radio dead. Late on Monday, when the storm abated, they managed to limp into Le Havre. The *Evening Standard* was particularly struck by their culinary deprivation. 'Four Adrift in Yacht. No Food for Three Days' was its headline. However, as Judy recalls, there was plenty of food but they were too seasick to eat.

Her memories highlight the risks the Goldings took. They had no lifejackets, and she is not even sure they had distress flares. Their radio was just a transistor on which they listened to the shipping forecast. But it broke down before they got to Yarmouth, so they got a forecast from the people on the boat moored next to theirs, and had no update, once they set sail, to warn them that a Force 7 gale was coming. The waves were enormous; they were nearly swamped; the engine died. The dinghy filled with water and threatened to drag the stern down, so Golding cut it adrift. He and David, not yet sixteen, took turns steering through the night, as neither Ann nor Judy was strong enough to hold the tiller. At the end of each spell of steering the one coming off watch did half an hour's pumping with the bilge pump, a metal rod in a three-foot cylinder which, after great effort, lifted a column of muddy water onto the deck that washed away through the scuppers. Being 'a fabulously strong boat', *Wild Rose* held together: 'We were lucky.' They turned south-east into the Baie de la Seine, and anchored on the Monday evening. They awoke to a dead calm, but were too weak to get the anchor up, and a passing French fishing boat helped them. The trawler skipper, David remembers, said it was 'L'amitié de la mer'. It was David who had dissuaded his father from trying to get into Cherbourg in the dark, surrounded by rocks, and Golding told the *Daily Mirror* that his son had been 'magnificent' in taking his turn at the helm. David's own recollection is that he was thinking about homework, 'so steering in a storm was fun'. Ann's postcard to her parents-in-law from Le Havre on 30 August was a model of restraint. It had been a rough passage over, she said, but 'not as bad as it sounds'. The children were surprised to find that everyone in France spoke French, and Le Havre was an easygoing sort of place that, said Ann, 'just suits Bill and me'.

Golding's report on their ordeal was almost equally stoical: it was 'not half as perilous as the papers made out. However, it was quite bad enough.' Monteith had just heard from the BBC that *Pincher Martin* would be discussed in their Home Service arts programme *The Critics* on Sunday, 28 October, and he lost no time in passing this on to Golding, together with a tentative inquiry about the future: 'I long to know what the next novel's going to be. *In Search of My Father*, or something quite different?' Golding's reply expressed an agitation that was perhaps not wholly feigned: 'How exciting and terrifying – the Critics! Please bribe everyone immediately.' The Arts Council, he added, had drawn him into writing a play for them, which he hoped to work off by Christmas. Then, 'after a couple of weeks walking round the Marlborough Downs', he thought he ought to be able to finish off a novel he had started, provisionally titled 'The Horizontal Man', which he would try to get to Fabers in time for their autumn 1957 list, 'if you decide to accept it'. What became of these two works is unclear. There is nothing in the archive that seems to correspond to them, and they may simply have been abandoned. Golding still carried a full teaching load at Bishop Wordsworth's and pressure was beginning to tell. 'I'm finding doing two full-time jobs a strain', he warned Monteith, 'and both suffer. I do neither.'

On Friday, 26 October, six days after Golding wrote this exhausted letter, *Pincher Martin* was published in an edition of 5,000 copies. The initial critical response was devastating. In the *Daily Telegraph*, on publication day, M. R. Ridley called it 'a perverse misuse' of its author's 'rare powers'. John Metcalf in the *Sunday Times* regretted that Golding had lost the vividness of *Lord of the Flies*, and was now merely 'straining after differentness'. 'Sadly the salient fact about *Pincher Martin* is that you can't read it.' Though 'brilliantly written', it is a 'wrong-headed bore'. Even John Davenport in the *Observer*, who had been enthusiastic about *The Inheritors*, was thrown by the new novel's ending – 'Mr Golding is too deep for me.' But the most cutting assessments were uttered on the BBC's *The Critics*. The chairman, T. C. Worsley, started inauspiciously: 'This is, I think, endurance week on *The Critics*. It seems to me we've got a good deal to endure, and I think this book is pretty tough going.' Nowadays T. C. Worsley is best known for what Noël Coward said about him. When Sheridan Morley was writing Coward's biography, *A Talent to Amuse*, Coward wanted the references to his homosexuality omitted, and Morley attempted to change his mind by pointing out that T. C. Worsley had openly referred to his own homosexuality in a memoir published in 1967. Coward replied, 'There is one essential difference between me and Cuthbert Worsley. The British public at large would not care if Cuthbert Worsley had slept with mice.'

However, this was far in the future when Golding sat listening to *The Critics* on 28 October 1956. What he was likely to know about T. C. Worsley was that he was an old boy of the despised Marlborough College, and a close friend of Stephen Spender, W. H. Auden and Christopher Isherwood – a member, in other words, of the literary establishment from which he was excluded. C. A. Lejeune, film critic of the *Observer* and the only woman member of the panel, quickly took up the chairman's lead: 'To me it belongs to a class of reading that I deplore, which looks at nothing except what I call the underbelly of the human body, and it sees nothing but the nasty side of it, the horrid side of it.' The writer and critic Eric Keown attempted to stem the tide, urging that Pincher's sufferings were 'marvellously described'. But Lejeune would not have it. 'No. I consider they're very badly described – they're described in sentences of one word, which to me is not grammar, it is not writing and it is very deplorable English.' Besides, Pincher was a 'beastly' man, and the sixty-year-old Lejeune appealed with little-girl ingenuousness to her male colleagues 'You're not all as beastly as that, are you?' Mischievously she added, 'What I would like to say is that the most beautiful thing to my mind in the book is the wrapper. Am I wrong in saying this?' No one told her she was. The playwright Lionel Hale and the academic Walter Allen both had their own grumbles about the book, and Colin MacInnes, whose first novel *City of Spades* came out the next year, was the only panel member who saw what Golding intended, remarking that Pincher is dead by the time the story begins, and that what takes place on the rock happens either in his imagination or in purgatory. Worsley, however, was not to be sidetracked by such subtleties, and pronounced with chairman-like authority that 'some of us might feel' Golding should use his imagination 'in a little more clear way'.

Understandably Golding was in no mood for letter writing on the day after this onslaught. However, he had recovered enough by the Tuesday to renew contact with Monteith, acknowledging that the reviews had not 'been pleasant', but trusting they would reduce his head to 'reasonable proportions'. By this time he had read the 26 October *Times Literary Supplement* which praised the book's 'brilliantly' intense imaginings – 'just within the limits of fantastic nightmare' – and Richard Mayne in the *New Statesman* of 27 October, who found it 'shaking and compelling', despite the 'flaw' of the 'trick ending'. He may, too, have seen Philip Oakes's 30 October *Evening Standard* review which, though also doubtful about the ending, found the book 'further evidence of an exciting and original talent'. The favourable reviews did something to 'restore the balance', Golding felt. 'But no one seems to realize that Martin is torturing himself and that he was a murderer – at least in intention! Nothing burns in hell but the self.'

Rescue came two days later when Frank Kermode gave a talk on *Pincher Martin* on the BBC Third Programme. Kermode was to become the most influential literary critic of his generation. In the late sixties, as Lord Northcliffe Professor of Modern English Literature at University College London, he organized a series of seminars which introduced contemporary French literary theory to Britain. But in 1956 he was little known. The book which first made his name, *The Romantic Image*, did not come out until the following year. Still, no one listening to the Third Programme at 7.50 p.m. on 1 November 1956 could have doubted that they were encountering an intelligence of a different order from C. A. Lejeune's and T. C. Worsley's. Golding, Kermode stated, was a philosophical novelist, 'fascinated by the ubiquitous evidence of a natural law: that human consciousness is a biological asset purchased at terrible price – the knowledge of evil'. The great theme he had rediscovered was the Fall of Man. Pincher was a modern Prometheus, and the novel's 'dense interweavings of image and reference' meant that much rereading was necessary. Its full import depended on the 'most accomplished narrative device' on the last page (what other critics referred to as the 'trick ending'). In its 'intense imagining and minute technical control' *Pincher Martin* was 'greatly superior' to Golding's two previous novels. It showed his kinship with Wordsworth, whom Coleridge had called a 'philosophic writer'. To say that the novel lacked compassion would be untrue, Kermode concluded, because Pincher represents us all, and pity would be self-pity.

Golding brightened. Kermode's broadcast 'turned all my adrenalin into glucose'. At the same time, he was worried that he had minded so much about the adverse notices: 'How incredibly dependent I find myself on praise or blame – quite revoltingly so.' Recognizing his weakness was not the same as curing it, though. He would remain extremely sensitive to criticism, and was evidently relieved when the November reviews, partly perhaps as a result of Kermode's intervention, improved on those of 'Black Sunday'. His letter to Monteith drew attention to three favourable notices, though he modestly refrained from quoting them. Ronald Bryden, in *The Listener*, concluded that in *Pincher Martin* he had done 'memorable justice to his shabby Prometheus and his high theme'; Francis Wyndham, in the *London Magazine*, detected 'imaginative gifts of astonishing quality', while in *The Spectator* the young Kingsley Amis predicted that the novel's 'utmost inventiveness, assurance and power' would ensure no reader would soon forget it. There was also an anonymous review in *The Times* which found the book 'remarkable and terrifying in its power of despair'. When the broadsheets came out with their Christmas books-of-the-year choices, Arthur Koestler declared that in *Pincher Martin* Golding had shown he was set to reclaim 'cosmic awareness' for the English novel – 'He has both the spiritual and technical equipment to succeed' – and Kenneth Tynan in the *Observer* pronounced it 'irresistible' – 'The shock ending, which throws a new and doubly alarming retrospective light on the whole book, is technical wizardry of the first order.'

Yet there were still hostile voices. The reaction to his third novel revealed for the first time a rooted antagonism in some readers to everything Golding represented – his originality of style, his pessimistic view of the human species, his experiments with structure. In a letter of 13 December Monteith had given notice that *Pincher Martin* would be discussed on the BBC Third Programme on Boxing Day, and if Golding listened it cannot have done much to augment his festive cheer. The three members of the intellectual elite chosen to debate his book were the Oxford philosopher Anthony Quinton, the old-Etonian editor of the *Times Literary Supplement* Alan Pryce-Jones, and the university don Graham Hough. They did not like it. For Hough, Martin 'never became a person'. For Quinton, the writing was 'too noisy', 'contorted' and 'knotty'. He did not 'frankly think' it came off. The matter of Pincher's sea-boots upset them all. It was, Hough complained, 'a gratuitous puzzle'. For Quinton it made the book 'extremely difficult to enjoy at all'. After some discussion they managed to work out that it meant that Pincher was never on the rock, and, with the air of someone making an intellectual breakthrough, Pryce-Jones triumphantly concluded, 'the scene at the end of the book doesn't really accord with the beginning'. So it was thumbs down so far as the big brains of academe and the book world were concerned. Another influential man-of-letters who joined the anti-Golding camp at this time was Arthur Calder-Marshall. Broadcasting on the BBC European Service a fortnight after the Boxing Day debate, he deplored a 'tendency towards turgidness and unclear expression' in all Golding's novels. *Pincher Martin*'s ending 'seems to me to defeat the book by overcleverness'. The puzzling thing about these adverse critics is their failure to notice the simplicity and immediacy of Golding's writing. Here, for example, is the moment when Pincher discovers in the pocket of his oilskins the crumpled wrapping from a bar of chocolate:

> He unfolded the paper with great care; but there was nothing left inside. He put his face close to the glittering paper and squinted at it. In one crease there was a single brown grain. He put out his tongue and took the grain. The chocolate stung with a piercing sweetness, momentary and agonizing, and was gone.

Can Lejeune, with her complaints about 'deplorable English' have read that?

Peter du Sautoy, sending the Harcourt, Brace contract for Golding to sign on 20 November 1956, ventured encouragingly that 'there have been some excellent reviews after that miserable Sunday', and Golding concurred: 'Yes, Sunday was a day of wrath, sackcloth and penitential psalms, but as you say the outlook now seems a little brighter.' In America, however, it was hardly brighter at all. The title, not surprisingly, gave trouble. All persons with the surname Martin in the British navy are called 'Pincher', just as all Clarks are called 'Nobby' and all Millers are 'Dusty'. The original Pincher, it is said, was Sir W. F. Martin (1801–95), renowned for being a strict disciplinarian, who did not hesitate to 'pinch' ratings for minor offences. Americans could not be expected to know or understand this, and John McCallum of Harcourt, Brace wrote in March 1957 to say that the book's title had 'absolutely no meaning in this country'. He suggested *The Rock*, or (from Milton's *Paradise Lost*, Book 2) *Where Time and Place Are Lost*. Du Sautoy passed on these possibilities to Golding, who returned six of his own:

1. *Crustacean.*
2. *Aftermath*
3. *Epilogue*
4. *The Chinese Have X-Ray Eyes*
5. *Perchance to Dream*
6. *What Dreams May Come*

Golding said he liked numbers 4 and 6 best, but would prefer to stick to *Pincher Martin*, perhaps with an explanatory foreword. Du Sautoy agreed that it would be 'nice' to have number 4 (which was a quotation from one of the novel's flashback scenes), but he pointed out reasonably enough that Harcourt, Brace were unlikely to accept it if they boggled at *Pincher Martin*. To McCallum he confided that they had been 'quite relieved' when Golding had dropped it in favour of the relatively straightforward *Pincher Martin*. At length, on 5 April, McCallum came up with *The Two Deaths of Christopher Martin* as the book's American title. Both du Sautoy and Golding agreed to it, and it was under that title that it was published by Harcourt, Brace on 26 August 1957. McCallum wanted T. S. Eliot to write a puff for the cover, but du Sautoy regretted that, though Eliot had met Golding, he had not read *Pincher Martin*. 'He does not read many novels.'

Elaine Greene of MCA, the agent du Sautoy was using in America, sent along an early review from *Time* magazine with a glum letter ('This I am afraid is the other side of the American press reaction'), but compared with the adverse English reviews *Time*'s unsigned piece, published on Monday, 9 September 1957, is positively upbeat. Admittedly, it begins by saying that Golding writes 'like a French existentialist who has wandered into the Manhattan offices of *True* magazine'. But it credits him with making clear 'a subtle philosophical notion – that one can change the past by what one thinks about it', and it welcomes the rare spectacle of 'an English writer indulging in over-statement'. After what he had put up with, Golding would be unlikely to complain. In any case, Norman Podhoretz's review in the *New Yorker* of 21 September put informed American opinion beyond doubt. For Podhoretz *The Two Deaths of Christopher Martin* was 'one of the most remarkable books of recent years', exhibiting 'as grim a philosophical scepticism as is to be found in literature'. East-coast critical acclaim was not, however, matched by any improvement in American sales. *Lord of the Flies* had not sold anything approaching the 7,500 copies that the Harcourt, Brace contract required before they were obliged to publish *The Inheritors*, so Golding's second novel remained unknown in America.

15

The Brass Butterfly

In 1955 Fabers had received from Elaine Greene at the MCA Agency in New York a stage version of *Lord of the Flies* by the American playwright Carolyn Green. It was called *The Wonderful Island*, and the William Morris Agency, who acted for Green, were keen to get Golding's approval. In this they were conspicuously unsuccessful. Having read it, he fired off a diatribe itemizing the many aspects of his novel Green had misrepresented or failed to understand. That was the end of *The Wonderful Island*, and for the next thirty years he was to resist Faber and Faber's urgent and persistent attempts to get him to write a dramatic version of *Lord of the Flies* or allow someone else to.

In 1956, however, for the first and only time, he did set about turning one of his works into a play. It was the short story 'Envoy Extraordinary' and the play was *The Brass Butterfly*. It had been commissioned by Alastair Sim, who was to take the leading role. Sim's widow Naomi recalls that if he admired any new novelist he would get in touch, on the off chance that they would write him a play. Michael Gilbert, the thriller writer, and William Trevor had both been spotted in this way, and soon after *Lord of the Flies* was published Sim contacted Golding to suggest a collaboration. In 1956 he was at the height of his fame. He had appeared in a string of classic films including Alfred Hitchcock's *Stage Fright* (1950), *An Inspector Calls* (1954) and *The Belles of St Trinian's* – the first of the St Trinian series, in which he played the headmistress, Miss Fritton, and her brother Clarence. His most famous role was Scrooge in the film adaptation of Dickens's *A Christmas Carol*. In 1950 he had been voted the most popular film actor in Britain.

Writing for a star had its drawbacks. After his first meeting with Sim in London Golding told Monteith that it had gone 'swimmingly'. He was a 'most charming man'. Only on his way home did it occur to him that he had been told 'exactly the sort of play he would like written for him and the limits he would accept'. Sim was at an advantage because Golding still felt a provincial. Invited by Monteith to lunch at the Travellers Club, he accepted, 'provided I can find Pall Mall'. Adapting his story for the stage turned out to be more time consuming than he had anticipated. When Monteith wrote (with apologies for 'pestering'), to ask if there would be a novel for the 1957 autumn list, he replied that he saw little chance because he was tied up with his 'perfectly lousy play'. Don't rush it, wait for the spring list, was Monteith's patient advice.

'Envoy Extraordinary' had been published in 1956 in a volume called *Sometime, Never,* along with stories by John Wyndham and Mervyn Peake, and is a comic scherzo on Golding's persistent theme of the conflict between science and religion. An eager young Greek inventor, Phanocles, arrives at the court of a cynical but benign old Roman emperor and displays his inventions – a steamboat, a bomb, and a pressure cooker. Only the pressure cooker takes the emperor's fancy. However, the other two inventions allow him to defeat his heir apparent, Postumus, an 'insensitive bruiser' who is jealous of the emperor's favourite grandson Mamillius, and has arrived at the harbour mouth with a battle fleet. There are witty dialogues between the emperor and Phanocles on subjects such as warfare and slavery, both of which, Phanocles prophesies, will be made obsolete by his inventions. After the defeat of Postumus, Phanocles reveals his final invention, the printing press, which at first arouses the emperor's enthusiasm ('A public library in every town!') but then appals him as he envisages the endless multiplication of books. Also, he perceives that Phanocles's science is inhuman and 'could go near to wiping life off the earth'. So he sends him as envoy extraordinary to China.

There were difficulties turning this into drama. The steamboat and the destruction of Postumus's fleet could not be shown on stage, and as Golding wrote the story it had no proper love interest. Mamillius falls in love with Phanocles's sister Euphrosyne, but she is so modest that she will not lower her veil below her eyes, and when she does it transpires she has a hare lip. This was quickly put right in the play: Euphrosyne has no hare lip, and marries Mamillius at the end. To introduce dramatic tension, Golding makes her a Christian, which means that by rights she should be put to death, especially as the emperor is ex officio High Pontiff of Jupiter. However, Mamillius gladly converts to the new religion, and the emperor regards all religion as a mere matter of form. The play's best moment comes when, at the approach of Postumus's fleet, he dons his full High Pontifical regalia and performs the sacred rituals, praying 'Thunderer destroy our enemies' just at the moment when, down at the harbour, Phanocles's bomb goes off. Sim's look of surprise at the unusual success of his invocations was apparently the high spot of his performance.

To Golding, the chance of a West End hit must have seemed very alluring. Income from his novels was still modest. In 1957–8 he received £1,100 from Faber and Faber as against his schoolmaster's salary of £1,150. Other activities, including book reviewing, brought the year's total income up to £3,082. A new source of profit was the BBC's *The Brains Trust*, a popular discussion programme that began on radio in 1942 and transferred to television in the 1950s. Its producer was John Furness, and the usual drill was for the four panellists, the question master and the producer to meet at noon on Sunday at Scott's restaurant in Piccadilly Circus. After a good lunch with a fair amount to drink they were driven to the television studios at Lime Grove in time for a 4.15 start. A fee of £50 was paid – generous for those days, especially as it was supplemented by lunch, drinks after the programme, and free transport home. Regular panellists included A. J. Ayer, John Betjeman, Rebecca West, Marghanita Laski, the Reverend Mervyn Stockwood, Alan Bullock, and Jacob Bronowski – a line-up rightly described by the *Radio Times* in September 1958 as 'some of the finest intelligences in the country'. Golding's first appearance was on 20 January 1957, and he told Monteith that it had been 'most amusing and exciting'. 'It's I should think the easiest way of earning money in the world … I hope to get asked again some time.' He was, in June 1957, and four more times, the last of them on 17 January 1960, seven months before the programme was chopped. Unfortunately no transcript or film of his appearances has survived.

Meanwhile he was having 'a searing time' with Sim and *The Brass Butterfly*. The real trouble was exhaustion: 'The truth is I've overworked these last three years and need to slack,' he admitted to Monteith. 'Have you a small Greek or Italian island for sale?' This time Monteith did not reply that he was afraid he had no knowledge of the market in islands, but countered with a joke of his own, though not one he had made up, which was that *Lord of the Flies* had won third prize in a science-fiction book competition, the International Fantasy Award. The winner was Tolkien's *Lord of the Rings*. Golding was surprised, as he had never heard of the competition, but the award is a reminder that, as his friend Brian Aldiss recalls, many people at this stage in his career regarded him as a science-fiction writer. Each of his first three novels could, in their different ways, be classed as science fiction, and his lifelong impatience with research into such matters as Neanderthal man matches the unshackled creativity that science fiction allows.

Resigned to not getting a new novel for their 1958 spring list, Faber and Faber decided that they would publish *The Brass Butterfly* instead to keep his name before the public, and in December 1957 du Sautoy wrote asking for a typescript. Golding replied that the play needed revising and he had no time to do it as he was 'slap in the middle' of his next novel. However, du Sautoy, who was always less patient with his diffidence than Monteith, decided to print the play as it stood, and get him to make any needful revisions in galley proof.

The Brass Butterfly opened at Oxford's New Theatre on Monday, 24 February 1958. The other big name in the production, beside Alastair Sim, was George Cole, who played Phanocles, and two film stars of this magnitude on a provincial stage ensured an enthusiastic reception. The *Oxford Times* applauded an 'entertaining and unusual' play and 'highly amusing' performances. The Goldings had pre-theatre drinks in Monteith's room at All Souls, and joined the Simses and the Coles afterwards for a celebration at the Randolph Hotel. The next day Monteith sent 'torrential congratulations! It went superbly well – a most tremendous success,' and Ann wrote thanking him for the 'splendid start' he had given to the evening. Neither of them, she admitted, had felt they could make an overall judgement of the play, being too tense and too involved. They must try for 'disengagement' when they saw it again on Saturday with the children. There was an extensive provincial tour – the Royal Court Liverpool, the Grand Theatre Leeds, the Theatre Royal Newcastle, the King's Theatre Edinburgh and the Alhambra Glasgow, all in March, and the Opera House Manchester on 7 April. Golding reported jubilantly on 30 March that the play was continuing 'to do enormous business'. In April *The Sphere* carried a double-page spread showing scenes from the production and the sets, rightly described by Naomi Sim as 'exquisite', and designed by one of the outstanding British painters of the twentieth century, Edward Seago.

In March *Books and Art* published an interview with Golding by Owen Webster – a mark of the public attention he was arousing – in which, with *The Brass Butterfly* and *The Inheritors* in mind, he talks about his yearning for direct communion with the people of the past. 'I would give all the Egyptian treasures ever discovered for one cedar box of papyri. Documents are what count; they speak to you, and there are too few of them.' The two things that have given him most pleasure in the past year, he says, have been 'the Sputniks, and the excavation of Jericho, which revealed a walled city of 7000 B.C., the earliest civilization yet'. As a boy, he tells Webster, he could 'understand hieroglyphics before he could read'. If, as he later told Stephen Medcalf, his interest in ancient Egypt was first aroused by reading Rider Haggard's *Cleopatra*, then this cannot be true. But what is interesting is how quickly he goes from thinking about the past to imagining it. Imagining himself reading hieroglyphics as an infant, and imagining the 'cedar box' in which papyri might be found, show his creativity getting to work – the same creativity that produced, on the one hand, say, *The Scorpion God*, and, on the other, the childhood hallucination of being present at the unwrapping of a mummy.

In the same interview he speaks feelingly of the conditions he has to work under. *The Inheritors* was 'written in a month' in the hubbub of a school staff room between breaks. 'We've always been extremely poor. I've never had a study and I don't know what it's like to have silence to write. But I find I write in complete inner solitude, one part of my mind is occupied all on its own while the rest of my life continues more or less uninterrupted.' Writing *Pincher Martin* left him 'exhausted for months' and he has only recently recovered. The task of a writer, he insists, is to free the mind from the shackles of habit and creed. Belief systems such as Christianity and Marxism impose 'rigid patterns' on reality, which deaden the mind. 'The difference between being alive and being an inorganic substance is just this proliferation of experience, this absence of pattern.' Accordingly, a writer must have 'an intransigence in the face of accepted beliefs – political, religious, moral – any accepted belief'. If he takes an accepted belief for granted then 'he ceases to have any use in society at all'. In effect his job is to 'scrape the labels off things', exposing the reality beneath. The eventual aim is to understand yourself, and understand what makes different creeds and ways of seeing things attract you. 'The greatest pleasure is not – say – sex or geometry. It is just understanding. And if you can get people to understand their own humanity – well, that's the job of the writer.'

On 17 April 1958 *The Brass Butterfly* had its West End premiere at the Strand Theatre, arousing nervous anticipation and simultaneous self-mockery in its author. 'It's all ridiculously exciting and absurd,' he confessed. He and Ann had to hurry away from the cocktail party Monteith gave for them beforehand, and declined his invitation to dinner afterwards because they would be partying with the cast. But the evening was a disappointment. The pace was too slow and the theatre too large, and the applause at the end was mixed with boos, which the press made much of. 'Author's Wife Hears Boos' was the *Daily Sketch* headline. The play found its staunchest defenders a fortnight later in the BBC's *The Critics*, chaired by Dilys Powell. The screenwriter Paul Dehn, one of the panel, regretted that 'our wretched colleagues on the national press' had 'trounced it in an extraordinarily philistine and blinkered way'. Only Alan Dent in the *News Chronicle* and Kenneth Tynan in the *Observer*, he noted, had written encouraging reviews. As for the boos, they had come only from 'about six dim-witted people', but 'straight away you could see the spectacle of some of our professional dramatic critics racing from the theatre to catch the last editions, and to get those boos into the headlines'. It had been, Dehn felt, 'scandalous'. The other BBC critics agreed, Dilys Powell and C. V. Wedgwood were both enthusiastic, and Lance Sieveking, one of the leading names in early radio drama, was reminded by the play's originality and wit of the experience of seeing Shaw's early comedies. 'As fresh as a spring morning, going from strength to strength to a dazzlingly funny third act', it was 'the best play I've seen for years, and I hope it will run and run'.

But it did not. The newspaper reviews killed it. *The Times*, one of the less adverse, pronounced it 'lukewarm', and even Kenneth Tynan, whose relative approval Dehn had singled out, thought that the first half was an 'uphill plod' and that, 'as often happens when novelists enter the theatre', the writing was too wordy to be dramatic. T. C. Worsley in the *New Statesman* called it 'slack'. Sim's wife Naomi thought it would have been better as a film than a play, because that would have solved the problem of off-stage action. Whatever the reasons for the failure, it seems clear that Alastair Sim's performance was not to blame. Tynan considered it one of the best he had ever given, and turned his review into a 'prolonged genuflexion' to the veteran comic actor, returning to the West End stage after an eight-year absence, who can still 'convulse us with a single twitch of his eyebrow'. Golding's daughter Judy, who was twelve at the time, remembers Tynan coming to dinner in their new flat, but whether this was before or after his review appeared is uncertain. At all events *The Brass Butterfly* closed after a month, and Golding attended the last performance wearing a black tie. His 1957–8 accounts show that he made £383 from his theatrical venture.

16

Free Fall

When Golding told Peter du Sautoy in December 1957 that he was 'slap in the middle' of a new novel he was being over-hopeful. The novel eventually became *Free Fall*, but by January 1958 all he had was a 'chaotic' draft about 65,000 words long. He now realized, he told Monteith, that he could either condense it to one volume or expand it to four. Would Fabers be willing to publish one volume in the autumn, knowing more would follow, 'or is a four-decker out'? He adds that he has just finished reading Ted Hughes's first collection, *The Hawk in the Rain*, which Monteith had sent him, and admires it greatly. By comparison, he pictures himself 'sitting sadly on a pile of my own threadbare verses ... Prose feels like the ground floor somehow – stuff written by the poor fellows who can't climb the stairs.'

Monteith replied speedily that he had no qualms at all about a four-decker. Fabers, he pointed out, were indeed currently publishing Lawrence Durrell's *The Alexandria Quartet*. However, he would need the first part by 31 March if it was to be in time for the autumn list. Golding replied that he would send a typescript before that, though he did not know if it would be a first volume or a condensed version of all four. However, he seems to have doubted whether he could manage anything at all. He wrote, on the same day, to du Sautoy to say that he was afraid 'novel No. 4' was going to be late: 'I just don't seem to be able to work as hard as I did.'

His doubt was well founded. Three days before the 31 March deadline Monteith wrote to say he was sorry to hear Golding had been unwell, and that he had been enormously impressed by the wireless adaptation of *Pincher Martin*. Tactfully, he refrained from mentioning the new novel, but Golding could hardly mistake the purpose of his letter, and he replied on 30 March that he had completed a draft, with 'some fairly good bits', of novel No. 4, which, 'for reference', he would call *Free Fall*. It would need rewriting and reorganizing. 'But what *really* is the matter is me.' He was so tired that he didn't really care whether it was a good book or not. 'It seems to me that I must put it by and forget it for a bit, as I did Pincher.' It was trying, he continued, that he had reached the point where people seemed to expect 'sombre mandates' from him, whereas 'in a better world' he would like to write something funny, or poetry, or perhaps both. 'And then again, I can't go on doing two jobs for ever. Etcetera.' As ever, Monteith's response was patient and upbeat. He must not worry, and should hang on to the manuscript of *Free Fall* until he was completely satisfied.

Perhaps Golding's fatigue was a symptom of physical illness. In June he was rushed into hospital for an emergency appendicitis operation. His daughter Judy remembers him wandering round the flat, bent with pain, in his old green dressing gown, and kneeling on the sitting-room floor, trying without success to drink a cup of tea. Eventually he and Ann disappeared and the couple in the flat upstairs gave Judy and David their Sunday lunch. Judy has the impression that it took her father a while to recover, which ties in with a letter du Sautoy wrote to John McCallum of Harcourt, Brace on 11 August, reporting that Golding's operation had 'set him back a good deal'. On 24 June Monteith sent his condolences, and some science-fiction books to while away his convalescence.

In the same letter he congratulated him on the award of a travel scholarship which, he gathered, he was undecided whether to accept. Golding replied that he was going to accept it. They had been planning a family holiday in Italy at Easter 1959, and now, with an extra £200 to spend from the scholarship, they might 'duck into Yugoslavia' as well. The award was made by the Society of Authors, who had set up their travelling scholarships in 1944 to keep British creative writers in touch with colleagues abroad. John Lehmann, who chaired the Scholarship Committee, had written on 19 June to say they wanted to nominate Golding for their 1958 award. In the event he could not use the money until 1959 because, as he explained to du Sautoy, he had splashed out 'such an appalling amount of money' on *Wild Rose* that the family must spend their summer holidays on her so as to recoup it. In the same

Paul Joyce's portrait study of WG in 1977: 'a cross between Captain Hornblower and Saint Augustine' (Michael Ayrton)

WG's maternal grandparents: Thomas Curnoe, veteran of the gold rush, and Mary Elizabeth. It was said she and Thomas would have murdered each other had they lived together for long

WG's mother Mildred with WG aged 2, Polly and Jo Golding, his paternal grandparents, and brother Jose looking over their shoulders. Taken in Savernake Forest where WG later saw a spectral stag

WG's father Alec at 22, 'a lonely, embittered, alienated young intellectual'

WG's mother Mildred on her wedding day in 1906; a 'leggy, gaunt, intelligent girl, high-spirited and witty'

29 The Green, Marlborough: a 'map', WG said, of his 'personal mythology', which came back to him in dreams and nightmares

Alec Golding reading to his sons Jose and 'a fair-haired, blue-eyed, sturdy little rascal called Billy' (WG), *c.*1914–15

Jose and WG in Marlborough Grammar School blazer, *c.*1923

WG playing the piano at 29 The Green; 'its yellow ivory keys were for ever embedded in his memory'

Ordinary Seaman Golding with Ann and their first child David, January 1941

WG deep in thought at the weapons research establishment MD1, 'Mr Churchill's toyshop', 1942

An LCT(R) in action. WG captained one on D-Day and at Walcheren

WG in uniform as a Lieutenant RNVR, with Ann, October 1944, just before the Battle of Walcheren

Lieutenant Golding RNVR (on right), senior officer of the Bishop Wordsworth's School Sea Cadets, with an unidentified Royal Navy Captain and the headmaster, Dr Frederick Happold

WG in an amateur production of *A Winter's Tale*, 'simply explosive. Though in a minor part he dominated the whole show'

WG and Ann on holiday in the early 1950s

WG, nicknamed 'Scruff', at the teacher's desk in a classroom in Bishop Wordsworth's School, *c*.1960

WG with son David in the garden of 29 The Green, 1945

WG with daughter Judy near Lamorna Cove, Cornwall, summer 1953

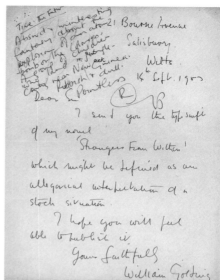

Charles Monteith at All Souls, early 1950s

WG's submission letter for *Lord of the Flies*, annotated with Fabers' reader's comments

Front cover of the original edition (illustration by Anthony Gross)

Photo for *Vogue*, 1954. 'It makes me look as if I were seated in the police station trying ingratiatingly to explain away my possession of a packet of dirty postcards'

Seahorse, with WG aboard, being hoisted onto a lorry for repairs, 1947/8

Ann and Judy trimming WG's beard and hair, aboard *Wild Rose, c.*1959

WG at the helm of *Wild Rose* with (l to r) Pauline Lewis, David and Ann

WG on the foredeck of *Wild Rose, c.*1957

Tenace, a Dutch racing hoogaart. For WG she had 'the clumsy beauty of a double bass'

WG at Hollins College, Virginia, 1961–2. America brought him 'fame, wealth and the adulation of the young'

Aboard the river steamer Maxim Gorky on the Goldings' 1963 Russian trip; (l to r) the ship's captain, Ann (steering), WG and their Russian translator

The Cannes Film Festival 1963, James Aubrey (Ralph) and Hugh Edwards (Piggy) with WG

At the Booker dinner in 1980 when *Rites of Passage* won. 'Goodness me what a night at the Stationers Hall,' WG wrote the following day

First edition covers of *Pincher Martin* and *Free Fall*

WG with Melvyn Bragg on the Dorset coast during filming of the South Bank Show, 1980

With Charles Monteith at the Royal Society of Literature, celebrating WG's installation as a Companion of Literature, 1983

In Stockholm for the Nobel Prize, 1983; (l to r) Charles Monteith, Ann, HM Queen Silvia, HM King Carl XVI Gustav of Sweden, WG

WG and Ann with crew members aboard the *Hani*, Egypt 1984

WG in his water garden at Ebble Thatch (left); Cobber, with WG up (right)

WG (on right) with his friend Heinrich Straumann walking in the garden at Tullimaar, the Goldings' Cornish house, *c.*1988

letter he thanks du Sautoy for successfully putting him up for the Savile Club. Situated in Mayfair, and founded in the mid-nineteenth century, this was among the most prestigious of London's gentleman's clubs and traditionally drew members from literature and the arts – Hardy, Kipling, Stevenson, Wells and Yeats had all belonged. But it was not a normal haunt of provincial schoolmasters, and Golding expressed half-joking trepidation when du Sautoy told him he had been elected: 'Was it touch and go?' He was to show the same nervousness about clubs, status and acceptability a few years later when he wrote in his journal that he was thinking of moving on from the Savile, but had 'reflected that Alastair [Sim] would black-ball me at the Garrick and Charles [Monteith] wouldn't want me at the Travellers'.

If he felt fed up in August 1958 about being stuck over *Free Fall* he may have been heartened by two published tributes that appeared that month. In the *New Statesman* V. S. Pritchett, the distinguished author and critic, acknowledged him as 'the most original of our contemporaries'. The important thing, for Pritchett, was not so much his fables or their meanings, but the force with which they engaged the reader's emotions: 'the pressure of feeling drives allegory out of the foreground'. Two weeks later, in *The Spectator*, Frank Kermode used the paperback publication of *Lord of the Flies* as the occasion for a celebration of the whole oeuvre: 'The texture of Mr Golding's writing is highly individual and proper to the heroic scale of his fictions. He keeps one aware of many contexts, his men live in a world of rock and sea and amoebae heaving in the pull of the moon, refusing to be locked fast by human imaginings of good or evil.'

Meanwhile, however, another reader of *Lord of the Flies* was scanning it with some dissatisfaction. This was the Academy Award-winning film producer Sam Spiegel, renowned for *The African Queen, On the Waterfront* and *Bridge on the River Kwai*. On 17 October 1958 the *Salisbury Journal*, Golding's local paper, published an interview with him about the rumour that Spiegel ('one of the world's top-ranking producers') was considering making a film of *Lord of the Flies*. Golding, it reported, had never heard of Spiegel or of *Bridge on the River Kwai* ('the most successful British picture yet made'). He rarely visited the cinema. Also, he had finished the novel five or six years ago: 'It's dead to me now.'

Nevertheless, the rumour proved true. It was the British theatre and film director Peter Brook who brought the novel to Spiegel's attention, having been alerted to it himself by Kenneth Tynan. Brook's idea was that he should collaborate on the film with Spiegel, who duly signed up Peter Shaffer to write a script (while, for some Machiavellian purpose, secretly engaging Richard Hughes to write a rival one). To Spiegel's way of thinking, the story needed basic readjustment before it could transfer successfully to the screen. He wanted to have girls as well as boys on the island, and to make them all American, not English. Brook was present at a meeting (the only one) between Spiegel and Golding at the Connaught Hotel, at which, as he recalls, the conversation went roughly as follows:

SPIEGEL: Mr Golding, I think it would be a much better story if there were girls as well as boys ... young girls ... ??? ...

GOLDING: Mr Spiegel, I wanted the film to be an allegory on the human race. 'Man' suggests all, 'boy' equally – if you bring in boys and girls you're forced to bring in secondary side issues, sexual attractions, conflicts, problems of puberty ...!

SPIEGEL: (very disappointed) Mm ...

In fact, Brook knew that Spiegel's friend, the Hollywood director and writer Joe Mankiewicz, had already suggested a scene in which one of the girls began to menstruate. Fortunately a distraction was provided by the Connaught Hotel's coffee. Spiegel pronounced it undrinkable, and it emerged in the ensuing fuss that it was made only once every two or three days and kept in great tureens waiting to be used. This deflected everyone's attention, the subject of the film was not raised again, and soon afterwards Spiegel abandoned the project.

A far greater upheaval was about to disrupt Golding's life. For the family holiday in August they had sailed round to Poole and Weymouth and then across to Cherbourg in *Wild Rose*. Ann, Judy and David were aboard, and a schoolfriend of David's from Bishop Wordsworth's called Glenn Collett, and they also took with them Golding's eighty-one-year-old father Alec. Judy remembers him sitting on deck with her in the dusk and pointing out the constellation Cassiopeia. On the way out they went round a headland where there was a fearsome tide rip.

Golding sent them all below because it was so rough. But Alec stayed on deck, watching, and during the next few minutes, as they tossed around in the rip, Golding saw him turn deathly white, then grey. He said later that he thought his father had probably had a slight heart attack. However, they reached France safely, and Alec went ashore with them, and said that it smelt just the way it had sixty years earlier. He declined to have dinner with them, though, saying he had a mouth ulcer – which they thought, in retrospect, may have been an indication that something was wrong. When they took him back to Marlborough afterwards it was, Judy recalls, very poignant, because her grandmother met him, in tears, and came towards him 'with her arms outstretched like a child (she was very small)'. She remembers him saying, 'There, there,' in an embarrassed way when he embraced her. It had never struck Judy before that she loved him, 'but she evidently did' – and perhaps she already knew, or guessed, that he was mortally ill. In November he was diagnosed with cancer and, following an operation, he died suddenly of a heart attack on 12 December.

It was the greatest grief of Golding's life. Years later he wrote that he had wept for Alec 'the most of tears I have ever had'. It hurt him to think of his father's atheism, because it meant that he had 'died in no hope'. He had been an atheist only because he could not bring himself to believe in the cruel God of the Old Testament, so he had chosen the 'dry, indifferent universe of rationalism' as the only alternative. 'He was thus a profoundly religious man who remained a grieving atheist until the last days of his life.' Recalling his father in a 1959 broadcast it was his range of knowledge and expertise, coupled with his unworldliness, that he emphasized.

> I never met anyone who could do so much, was interested in so much, and who knew so much. He could carve a mantelpiece or a jewel box, explain the calculus and the ablative absolute. He wrote a text book of geography, of physics, of chemistry, of botany and zoology, devised a course in astro-navigation, played the violin, the 'cello, viola, piano, flute. He inhabited a world of sanity and logic and fascination. He found life so busy and interesting that he had no time for a career at all.

Another disturbance, though far less shattering, in the autumn of 1958 was the Goldings' move from their Salisbury flat to the cottage called Ebble Thatch in Bowerchalke, where they had lived briefly in 1940. Since then the Walkers had added a big kitchen with a second bathroom and lavatory above it. In time the Goldings were to add a spacious sitting room with a picture window and electric underfloor heating (which, David remembers, you could feel tingling in your feet). They also eventually had the cottage rethatched in reed (reputed to last for sixty years). However, when they moved in they had no spare money for improvements and could, as Golding told Peter du Sautoy, 'hardly afford' their new home – though they had managed to get it for £4,250, which was £250 below the asking price. Bowerchalke was a gentle, remote, rather straggling village, about nine miles west of Salisbury, with a church, Holy Trinity, and (then, but no longer) a post office, school and shop. There was a thatched pub called The Bell, run by the same family as long as anyone could remember, where the landlady, Mrs Gulliver, kept strict lookout for any rowdy or drunken behaviour as well as outlawing jukeboxes and other modern abominations. Like most English villages it was socially segregated. The Bell had a saloon bar, frequented by a couple called Dawkins, who considered themselves the squirearchy of the village, and a public bar which the Goldings and their friends shared with the farm labourers. The countryside around was steeped in history and prehistory. A Celtic tribe called the Durotriges, who gave their name to Dorset, lived there before the Roman occupation, leaving behind gold and silver coins and rings that were and still are dug up from time to time. The Bowerchalke Barrel Urn was excavated in 1925 from a barrow on Marleycombe Down.

By the time Golding moved to Bowerchalke he was enough of a celebrity for prominent local people to want to know him. First to make contact were Wayland Young and his wife Liz, who were to remain family friends for life. Young, twelve years Golding's junior, had been to Stowe School and Trinity College Cambridge, and joined the Foreign Office after war service in the navy. On his father's death in 1960 he inherited the title of Baron Kennet. He started his career in the Labour Party, then joined the SDP. The topics he wrote about included Italian politics, arms control and London churches, and in 1964 he published

Eros Denied, a manifesto of the sexual revolution. He and Liz had six children, one of them the future sculptor Emily Young, and they owned a cottage called The Lacket in the countryside west of Marlborough, with an ancient sarsen stone in the back garden, as well as a beautiful, rambling London house in the Bayswater Road, where David remembers playing the harpsichord as a teenager.

Another new acquaintance was Lord David Cecil, the Goldsmith Professor of English Literature at Oxford, and through the Cecils they met Eddie Sackville-West (cousin of Vita, the sometime lover of Virginia Woolf) and Raymond Mortimer, editor of the *New Statesman* and later chief book critic of the *Sunday Times*. A close neighbour was Cecil Beaton, the society photographer and companion of the Bright Young Things, who lived in some splendour at Reddish House, which was only, as Golding put it, a few watercress beds away from their cottage. Beaton epitomized several of the things he hated about arty people – notably vanity, narcissism, snobbery and social privilege. He had known of him for years, because in the 1930s Beaton had leased and restored Ashcombe House, a Georgian manor set in a thousand acres on Cranborne Chase, near Salisbury. For Golding it was a part of 'that world I had lived *under* and not known, that interlacing, interwoven pattern of important people, aristocrats, gentry, artists who had a solid being in the very county where I (almost hopeless of my own craft) seemed to have no more place than my own reflection in a window full of real, expensive things'.

Now they were neighbours, and one afternoon Beaton rang up to ask them to come to tea and meet some people. Golding said they were gardening, but Beaton replied so was he and they were to come as they were. They did, and found that Beaton, clad entirely in green, was wearing gardening costume 'in the sense that Louis XIV might have been said to wear a hunting costume when hunting'. The other guests were Diana Cooper in blood-coloured velvet, Iris Tree dressed as Hamlet, and the young Lord and Lady Pembroke. Some time later Beaton rang again to say he had two friends who were 'dying to' meet him, could they look in? Golding watched his approaching guests with hostility. 'I saw them (all three of them) laughing wittily and dirtily as they came down our buckled asphalt drive.' Nothing untoward happened. They drank sherry, talked and left. But Golding felt that he was being patronized, and exhibited as a 'monster' by Beaton and other of the local notables. Perhaps he was. Frances Partridge, the Bloomsbury groupie, recorded in her diary that she had met Golding while staying with the Cecils at Cranborne Manor, 'a short, squarish, bearded man, smelling rather like an old labourer'.

All this lay in the future when the Goldings moved into Ebble Thatch, but it gives a sense of the unaccustomed social milieu they found there. Despite the move and Alec's death, the typescript of *Free Fall* was in Monteith's hands by 26 January 1959. With his usual diffidence Golding asked for advice about what to do with it, and Monteith was in no doubt. The novel was 'enormously powerful'. It needed no further work and should be published right away. His only query was over the use of the words 'fuck' and 'fucking' – not that Faber and Faber objected but the Book Society might, and 'if so we can think again'. The terms he offered were an advance of £400 with 12.5 per cent royalty on the first 4,000 copies sold and 15 per cent after that. These figures seemed 'generous' to Golding and he accepted them immediately. He had intended the book, he explained, 'as a bit of imagery for a whole baffled generation, meant to convey planlessness, chaos and impotence'. But he seemed to have ended it 'less certain of what it's about than when I started'. The typescript he had sent 'was never meant, I repeat, as more than notes towards a novel I was going to write. Perhaps a bit more than that, but not final, certainly.' This accounted for the 'gay abandon' in the use of swear words. 'Like you I should think twice about "fuck" and "fucking" for publication. The only trouble is I felt them as right in the context. However, lets leave them for now. If I can keep the power of the speeches without using them I certainly will.'

With *Free Fall* off his hands, Golding shared some of his thoughts with Brian Glanville, already making his name as the leading English football writer, whose 1956 novel *Along the Arno* had recently received critical acclaim. The popular paper *Reynolds News* published the interview on 22 February. Golding tells Glanville that he 'utterly rejects' Marxism because it is over-optimistic. Humanity does not improve. Civilized man externalizes in war what uncivilized man externalizes in personal violence. 'That is what *Lord of the Flies* is about.' He avoids reading contemporary novels, he admits, so as to prevent him imitating them. Indeed, he reads 'almost nothing but Greek ... You're pretty safe with Homer'. But he does not consider this makes him a highbrow. 'I've never understood the frantic fuss about highbrow and lowbrow. If you happen to like Greek you read Greek. If you happen to like tennis you play tennis.'

Some dissatisfaction with *Free Fall* continued to nag, and on 11 March he sent Monteith an amended typescript, 'the last few pages are new – can it be retyped?' He felt drained – 'I've dazed myself with this confounded book' – and intended to set to and write 'a play of some sort' and return to novels in the autumn. 'How would you like a large historical novel?' Monteith's reply was less than eager – 'I think there would be room for a large historical novel' – but he had no misgivings about the amended *Free Fall*. He had read the whole novel again the previous night and was 'completely bowled over'. He considers it 'superb', and thinks the 'new pages at the end are wonderful'. He realizes the Goldings are off to Italy very soon, so he will send *Free Fall* straight to the printers and let him have proofs as soon as they are ready.

By the time Golding received this letter he had gone down with a bad bout of flu – bad enough for him to have to cancel his appearance on the *Brains Trust*. Ann and Judy succumbed as well, so David, who had escaped because he was a boarder at Michael Hall, was the only one fit to do the map-reading when they set off for their long-awaited holiday in Italy, partly funded by the Society of Authors scholarship. A picture postcard showing some rather gloomy mountains, sent two days later by Ann to Golding's recently widowed mother, kept her up to date with events. They had landed at Le Havre, left it in the early morning, driven 600 miles down through France and Switzerland, traversed the St Gothard tunnel by train, sitting in the car perched on a flat truck – all in one day – and found a 'very nice pension' in Airolo, at the southern end of the tunnel, where they were just off to bed after a good meal. Next day they set off for Ravenna, where they saw the great Byzantine monuments – the Mausoleum of Galla Placidia (Judy sent a picture postcard of one of its mosaics to her grandma saying how lovely the colours were), the Basilica of San Vitale, and the Basilica of Sant'Apollinaire in Classe, with its green mosaic of meadows and sheep.

They stayed in a new hotel on the coast in Marina di Ravenna, where the patron had a little son called Claudio, whom Golding mystified by telling him that it was the name of an *imperatore*. Florence was next, where they spent a day in the Uffizi. Then came Rome, which gave them 'a certain sense of horror', with its monuments to cruelty such as the Colosseum. Judy remembers that her father was 'rather silent about it all'. They were disappointed by the Sistine Chapel, on several counts. The dense crowd of tourists turned it into 'a sort of fairground' and the ceiling was 'gloomy'. Ann thought the Moses 'cheesy and contorted', and the doom at the east end was, in Golding's view, 'melodramatic'. They agreed that they never wanted to see it again; reproductions were just as good. Golding favoured a 'travelling Sistine' exhibition where spectators would lie on beds or a moving belt, earphones plugged in, and watch the Sistine roof move past as an informed voice spoke to them. Admittedly this would lose the 'spirit of the place', but you could squirt dust and the smell of age and decay, and even arrange for some parts to be authentically difficult to see.

Ann was taken ill in Rome. She later confided to Judy that she thought she had had a miscarriage, and she was still far from well when they started their drive northwards. At Lake Trasimene, scene of the annihilation of a Roman army by Hannibal and the Carthaginians in 217 BC, they saw a farmer ploughing and Golding remarked to him that there had been a big battle there. He said yes, and some of his neighbours had been killed in it. In Pisa Judy terrified her father by walking solemnly round the outside of each layer of the leaning tower. In Milan they looked hopelessly for somewhere to stay, and fetched up in a 'very dubious outfit' with doors banging and many young women. Judy could not believe her parents did not realize what it was, but she later came to see they had been shielding her, imagining her ignorant. They had gone to Milan to see whether Golding's Italian publishers could let them have any money, as they were running low, but they said, very charmingly, that they had not sold any books. So they staggered home living on boiled eggs.

'We had a wonderful time in Italy. All superlatives exhausted,' Golding told Monteith's secretary Rosemary Goad on 23 April. Monteith himself was on holiday, and by the time he got back there had been a family crisis. Ann was taken into hospital with a small lump on her breast, and Judy thinks her parents feared it would mean a mastectomy. However it turned out to be a benign cyst – she had already had some removed a few years earlier. Monteith sent sympathy and some books for her to read in hospital, but his more immediate concern was *Free Fall*. While he was away Golding had asked du Sautoy to send the typescript back for revision, and had not yet returned it. Monteith apologized for 'pestering' but emphasized that time was short. 'Peter tells me that you're still a little worried about the last chapter. Can I assure you that I myself think it's absolutely first rate.' This letter crossed with one from Golding sending back the corrected typescript. In fact little had been altered. 'With the exception of one or two insets it's mostly details of grammar I'm afraid. I always have great plans for a completely new version but never seem to be able to do more than niggle.' Ann was 'rearing up out of convalescence' and consuming the books Monteith had sent 'at her accustomed furious pace'. He apologized that he had been 'a bit authorlike and difficult in the grand manner' over *Free Fall*. 'I suppose I couldn't really believe that if you start out to write a shapeless book, that's what you'll end up with. I hope I haven't strung you along too far, that's all.'

Monteith was too wise to be put out by authors being authorlike and he wrote cheerfully on 12 June to congratulate Golding on his appearance in the *Brains Trust* the previous evening, which he had unfortunately missed seeing – 'But everyone tells me you were a wow.' Meanwhile Ann's 'furious pace' at reading was to prove useful in another area. On 6 June 1959 *Smith's Trade News* announced that 'Tony Godwin of Bumpus has picked the panel for his new purchase, the Book Society', and their first meeting would be on Friday, 19 June. Godwin was a publisher as well as the owner of the bookshop Bumpus, and the aim of the Book Society was to pick 'good but saleable' books each month and recommend them in the Society's periodical *The Bookman*. He chose Golding as a member of his panel, the others being the poet and critic Richard Church, the novelist and journalist Penelope Mortimer, married at the time to John Mortimer, the novelist, critic and philosophical and political writer Kathleen Nott, the naturalist and ornithologist James Fisher, the historian J. H. Plumb, and the classical scholar Peter Green, who became a close friend of the Goldings. He was to write many books on classical subjects, as well as novels and a biography of Kenneth Grahame, but in 1959 he was working as a literary journalist in London.

Apparently du Sautoy had recommended Golding as a panel member. 'I can't thank you enough for the Book Society break,' he wrote, 'the steady money is a God send.' They were using it for repairs to the thatched roof of their cottage, which sparrows constantly eroded. Actually having to read books for the Society was less welcome than the fee. He joked that he had joined the panel only on condition that he did not have to read any novels, and it seems that Ann's phenomenal reading speed (it was family lore that she had read *War and Peace* in 'about nine hours') was called into service. In later years Ann and Joanna Mackle at Fabers had to advise him which books to choose for his books-of-the-year selections, because he read little contemporary literature himself. In the library at Tullimaar, the house Golding later moved to in Cornwall, there is still a copy of Allen Drury's anti-Communist novel *Advise and Consent* (Doubleday, 1959) with a note attached from Tony Godwin's secretary Jill Teasel: 'Please will you return *Advise and Consent* as soon as you have read it as we have only 2 copies for the whole committee.' Perhaps Golding was at the end of the line, or perhaps those further down never got *Advise and Consent*. It was to win the Pulitzer Prize for fiction in 1960.

Since money was tight, keeping some of it from the tax collector seemed a good idea. Could the advance on the American contract be paid into a Swiss bank account, he asked, so that they could use it for travel in Italy? He felt awkward making this request ('Ann says it reminds her of Goering') but made it all the same. There is no reply in the Faber file. In July he breezily implored du Sautoy to 'sell about half a million copies of Free Fall. I want to retire' (that is, from school-teaching). But du Sautoy was having a tough time selling the new novel to the Americans. Jean Detre at the MCA Agency doubted whether it would be 'strong enough' for the American market. 'I don't honestly feel it is likely to do well.' However, MCA were committed to getting the best terms they could, and Detre objected to the contract Harcourt, Brace offered. Their marketing of *The Two Deaths of Christopher Martin* had, she complained, been negligent, hence the poor sales. Simon and Schuster would be a better publisher.

Apprised of all this, du Sautoy wrote to McCallum at Harcourt, Brace and back came a squeal of rage. How dare MCA's new 'bright young lawyer' question the contract? Du Sautoy must know 'how committed we are to Golding'. Clearly du Sautoy should have replied, and perhaps did, that their commitment amounted, in effect, to refusing to publish *The Inheritors* and refusing to let anyone else in America publish it – even though other publishers wanted to. Mrs Helen Wolff of Pantheon (who was 'overwhelmed by this extraordinary writer'), Seymour Lawrence at Atlantic Monthly Press, and Farrar, Straus and Cuhady all expressed a keen interest. Du Sautoy had to turn them down because he had conceded, in a letter to William Jovanovich at Harcourt, Brace on 7 January 1959, that they did indeed have a 'continuing option' on *The Inheritors*. In the same spirit he now caved in and accepted their contract for *Free Fall*.

He was also having trouble with Coward-McCann, the American publisher of *Lord of the Flies*. They had let the hardback go out of print and not published a paperback. Du Sautoy wrote in January and February 1959, threatening to terminate their contract, and in April J. Stewart Johnson at Coward-McCann wrote that they had authorized Capricorn Books to bring out a paperback, the terms being a $500 advance against 7.5 per cent royalties. On 11 August 1959 du Sautoy was at last able to send an advance copy of the American paperback to Golding.

Free Fall was to be published in October and as a lead-up to it Golding gave a long interview to Frank Kermode which was recorded on 2 June, broadcast on 28 August 1959 as a Third Programme Feature, and published in a shortened version in *Books and Bookmen*. Golding reiterates that his mission as a novelist is to see things differently: 'If it is the way everybody else sees them, then there is no point in writing a book'. But exactly how he does see things, particularly religious things, is a point upon which Kermode respectfully but firmly presses him. Golding professes himself a 'religious though possibly incompetently religious man', and insists that Simon in *Lord of the Flies* is a saint, 'somebody who in the last instance voluntarily embraces his fate'. But, Kermode objects, Simon does not. He sees the body of the parachutist and comes down the hill to tell the other boys all is well. He has no idea what is going to happen to him. The point clearly disconcerts Golding, who replies rather lamely that it is 'a question of scale'.

Kermode then cites his letter to the *Radio Times* about *Pincher Martin* which, by using the terms 'hell' and 'purgatory', seems to accept Christian beliefs. Golding replies that hell and purgatory are not Christian but 'things that you make yourself'. However, in a passage excised from the published version of the interview, he goes on to interpret the novel in a way that seems unquestionably Christian. Pincher's real name, Christopher, he explains, meaning 'he who bears Christ in him', represents 'what he was at the hands of God'. That is why 'when God, the Angel of Days addresses him and in the storm at the end he says "Have you had enough Christopher?" he doesn't call him Pincher. He's been Pincher all the way through till then, but God calls him by his right name. And he denies that name straight away, (yes) he won't answer to it.' Earlier in the interview Golding had dismissed D. H. Lawrence's dictum 'Never trust the teller, trust the tale' as 'absolute nonsense'. The teller, he insists, always knows what his story means. But his wavering in the face of Kermode's questions helps to explain the ambivalence that readers find in the novels, which he himself was, as yet, unwilling to acknowledge.

For readers of *Free Fall* the most interesting part of the interview was neither broadcast nor printed but survives in a BBC transcript. His new novel is, he says, 'a confession'. In it he takes a man who has 'committed a crime when he is young, or at least a sin' – a sin that he was forced to commit 'by his nature'. He suffers 'the hammer blows of fate' and comes to understand that he will always carry the knowledge that 'I did this, and therefore this later terrible thing has happened.' So it is 'a twentieth-century equivalent of the Dante and Beatrice story'. He sees his Beatrice and realizes he can 'either take her as an ideal or as the opposite'. Dante took Beatrice as an ideal and she led him to paradise. But 'my Dante finds his Beatrice and doesn't take her as an ideal to be reached at, but as the very concrete present to be achieved, conquered and beaten'.

When Golding said the novel was a 'confession', Kermode no doubt understood him to mean a confession by *Free Fall*'s narrator. But its plot is in certain respects so close to Golding's own biography that it is tempting to take 'confession' more personally. The story is told by Sammy Mountjoy, an artist. He falls in love at school with a girl called Beatrice Ifor, who is clearly modelled on Mollie Evans. She has the same grey eyes and demure manner, and her parents, like Mollie's, are tradespeople in a nearby village. The school is evidently Marlborough Grammar School and the saintly, atheistic science master Nick Shales is a portrait of Golding's recently dead father – he performs exactly the same experiment to show the relativity of sense impressions that Golding described his father performing. The prurient, devout teacher Rowena Pringle is modelled on Golding's least favourite schoolteacher at Marlborough, Miss Pierce. Sammy falls wildly in love with Beatrice and, meeting her again when they are both students, tries desperately to win her. She is chaste, however, and keeps him at bay until he has bought her an engagement ring. When she finally yields, he finds she is frigid, as Golding says Mollie was. She lies awaiting his caresses as if it were a medical operation. Once they are lovers she becomes limply subservient, which exasperates him and makes him sadistic. The Second World War is approaching and, like Golding, he goes to Marxist meetings where he meets an upper-class young woman, Taffy, who is an intellectual and a communist, like Ann, and for whom he abandons Beatrice, as Golding abandoned Mollie.

Mollie had been Alec's pupil and he thought his son had acted dishonourably in abandoning her. Curiously, Golding's conduct echoed an incident in Alec's own past. His journal for May 1904 records that a young clergyman called Lintern has thrown over Alec's cousin Beatrice after borrowing money from her to pay his college fees, and she has been ill for months from the shock. It seems possible that cousin Beatrice's name had come up in angry exchanges between father and son over Mollie, and that this was why Golding adopted the name Beatrice for Mollie in *Free Fall*, and constructed or reconstructed the novel around her as a version of Dante's story. In the earliest surviving draft of the novel the girl Sammy falls in love with is called Maisie Ifor, not Beatrice, so it seems that the connection with Dante was not part of Golding's original design.

When war breaks out Sammy Mountjoy becomes a war artist, is captured, sent to a prisoner-of-war camp, interrogated, and locked in a dark cell where, to his horror, his exploring fingers come upon something soft and slimy on the cell floor, which he takes to be a 'fragment of human flesh'. Released from the cell, he emerges, as if washed clean, into a world that seems aflame with glory, where even the dust into which his tears drop is 'a universe of brilliant and fantastic crystals'. This vision of a luminous world is based on the *Meditations* of the seventeenth-century mystic Thomas Traherne, which Golding had probably read at Oxford in the selected edition by Bertram Dobell. Sammy now realizes that he misjudged Beatrice. She was 'simple and loving and generous and humble'. However, he cannot make reparation. On his return to England he finds she is in a lunatic asylum, hopelessly insane. The doctor tells Sammy that heredity may be a factor in her condition, recalling Golding's reference, in *Men, Women & Now*, to hereditary madness in Mollie's family.

Of course, Sammy Mountjoy is not William Golding. Apart from the Beatrice episode and the Marlborough Grammar School scenes there is little in *Free Fall* that corresponds to his life. Sammy is brought up in a slum by a drunken mother. After an episode where he is caught desecrating a church he is adopted by a paedophile clergyman, Father Watts-Watt, whose inclinations give Golding an opportunity to challenge usual attitudes to paedophilia: 'He might have kissed me and welcome if it would have done any good,' Sammy comments. 'For what was the harm? Why should he not want to stroke and caress and kiss the enchanting, the more than vellum warmth and roundness of childhood?' This is evidently the Golding who told Owen Webster that the true writer must have 'an intransigence in the face of accepted beliefs'. Like Golding, too, Sammy wants to be a girl, and it is one of his adolescent masturbation fantasies:

> With added intensity came the scent of talcum, the difference of a breast, glitter of brooches in Woolworth's, round, silk knees, the black treacle of their celluloid mouths, their mouths like wounds. I wanted to be one of them and thought this unique as self-abuse and very shameful.

The black celluloid mouths are those of the black-and-white silent-film stars of Golding's boyhood that he writes about in *Men, Women &*

Now. Sammy's longing to know what it would be like to be a girl ('How do they react in themselves, those soft, cloven creatures?') is another example of Golding's desire to see things differently. Sammy asks Beatrice, 'What is it like to be you?' But her response is, as usual, annoyingly unhelpful: 'Just ordinary,' she says.

Three typewritten drafts of *Free Fall* survive and they allow us to trace its growth, and see what lay behind Golding's indecision about the ending in his March and April exchange of letters with Monteith. It is clear that at some point in the novel's evolution he decided on a major and challenging structural innovation. A feature of the published novel is its disrupted time scheme. Events are not related in the order in which they occur. The narrative jumps from Sammy leaving Beatrice for Taffy, to Sammy being interrogated in the prisoner-of-war camp and locked in the dark cell. Then it jumps back to little Sammy living with Father Watts-Watt, then forward again to grown-up Sammy in the dark cell and being released from it, then back to Sammy at school and his encounters with Miss Pringle and Nick Shales, then forward to Sammy finding Beatrice in the lunatic asylum after the war. In the final chapter Sammy visits Nick, who is dying in hospital, and Miss Pringle, who seems not to remember how she victimized him. The concluding sentences jump back to Sammy's release from the dark cell and his realization, when the door opens and the light floods in, that what he had taken to be a fragment of human flesh was just a damp floorcloth.

The earliest of the three surviving typescripts shows that Golding did not originally consider these time-jumps necessary for his purpose. It relates the events of Sammy's life in straightforward chronological order, and differs in many other respects from the published text. In place of the flamboyant first paragraph, Sammy, as narrator, explains in this early version that he does not want to be wholly understood ('I shall try to bore you. Why? ... I am full of shame and would remain if I could in our common human isolation'). The ending was also different. After visiting Beatrice in the lunatic asylum Sammy sits on a bench in the sun and reads a letter from his agent telling him one of his paintings has been bought by the Tate. Then he goes out into the street and looks critically at his reflection in a tailor's window, seeing himself as representative of contemporary man, caught between belief and unbe-lief, as if floating free in space beyond the pull of gravity:

> We are the modern men. We bear the dark burden through chaos. The scaffold has been taken away; the figure stands free. Gravity has been taken away; the figure floats in a void. We are the masters of ignorance, proud, frightened and god-haunted. We have no country and no home. The worst terror is that we have a past behind us that is with us. The next to the worst is that the present will become the future.

In the published version this is replaced by the final chapter in which Sammy visits the dying Nick Shales in hospital, which Golding sent to Monteith on 11 March 1959. As Nick is a portrait of his father, it seems probable that Alec's death on 12 December 1958 occurred after the first version of the ending had been written, and was one reason Golding wrote the second. Possibly, too, he felt able to substitute the name of Alec's cousin Beatrice for Maisie only after Alec's death.

There are two other major differences between the early version and the final text. When Sammy gets back from the war in the early version he confesses to Taffy that when he was stationed in Egypt he was driv-ing back to camp drunk one night and, seeing a figure crossing the road, deliberately ran the unknown person down. Golding had a spell in Egypt after docking his minesweeper in Alexandria, but what relation Sammy's story bears to anything that really happened there it is impos-sible to say. The other difference relates to Sammy's ordeal in the dark cell. In the early version he has a religious vision. A circular aperture opens in the wall and he sees blue space and, against it, the head and shoulders of a man in 'living black'. As he watches, the head falls sideways onto the left shoulder, and the vision vanishes, 'as though I had been shown all that was needed'. From what follows it is evident Sammy takes this as a vision of Christ's death on the cross, and it brings about a religious conversion. He feels afraid, when he gets home, about telling Taffy that he has 'got religion', but she proves understanding and they pray together. Just after his vision he is released from the dark cell, and the camp commandant makes a kind of apology for the behaviour of the interrogator (called, in this early version, Dr Heidenzeit): 'Go. Der Herr

Doktor does not know der peepols.' It was this brief scene that Golding later lifted out of chronological sequence and placed at the end of his novel, with a slight adjustment of the last line: 'The Herr Doctor does not know about peoples.'

The other two surviving typescripts differ much less from the published text. They have the final version's disrupted time sequence, and the later of the two is marked up as the printer's copy. In the earlier Golding has scribbled a note to himself on the back of one of the pages from the dark-cell episode: 'Of course exit from cell and dismissal by commandant must be the end of the book!' Clearly this records the actual moment when it occurred to him that he must rewrite the ending. Why he did it we can only guess. He never, so far as I know, explained it. It seems probable, though, that he meant his new final chapter to work on the principle of significant juxtaposition. It juxtaposes Nick, the good atheist, Miss Pringle, the bad Christian, and Sammy, the redeemed sinner. It would, of course, be easier for readers to pick this up if they knew about Sammy's vision of the crucifixion while he was in the cell. But Golding had cut this out of the printed text. It seems to have been because he was worried about readers not understanding the new last chapter that he got du Sautoy to send the typescript back after submitting it. Perhaps he eventually decided to keep the new chapter as it was because he hoped that the principle of significant juxtaposition would be familiar enough to the reader by this time. It is, after all, the principle behind the disrupted time sequence throughout the novel, which juxtaposes things separate in time (such as Sammy's fear of the dark in the cell and his childhood experiences with Father Watts-Watt) but connected in other ways. Disruptions of time sequence should not have been baffling to critics in the 1950s. They had been a common modernist technique since the time of Joseph Conrad. But Golding's hesitation over the last chapter suggests that he feared he had made his novel too difficult, and the critical reaction was to prove him right.

One detail which he felt later had been misunderstood was the wet shape in the middle of the cell floor. Most critics and many readers have assumed that Sammy, touching this in the dark, thought it was an amputated human penis – a horror relating to his sin of lust and his treatment of Beatrice. Golding, however, later denied this.

W.G. himself when writing FREE FALL never, but never, *consciously* intended the wet floor cloth to be taken by Sammy as a severed cock. But never! I know that critics say that's what he thinks it is; but the author didn't! It was an infinite possibility of horror, I think, but not specific. Isn't this strange? I mean by that, that the thing is, of course, what the reader decides it is; but this oddly uniform idea doesn't include the author!

He wrote this in 1976, admitting that he had not read *Free Fall* since its publication, and that in the printed text 'Sammy *may* have been more explicit than I remember'. What he meant at the time is, of course, irretrievable. But it is worth noting that Sammy's thoughts about the shape are rather different in the first of the three typescripts. He remembers reading a story about a man in a small cell with a ceiling that came slowly down (it was probably Conan Doyle's Sherlock Holmes story 'The Engineer's Thumb'). Sammy imagines that there is a 'smashed body clung to the ceiling' high above his head, 'an unseen ruin from which one piece had fallen and from which other pieces might fall before the ceiling came down to crush me'. Of course, he might think that the piece that had fallen was the penis, but the anatomical reference is less specific than it seems in the later versions, and more like the 'infinite possibility of horror' Golding remembered.

Awaiting publication day, the Goldings took *Wild Rose* across the Channel in August to revisit the scenes of some of Golding's wartime experiences – a trip he later wrote up in 'Through the Dutch Waterways'. Ann's postcard home to her mother-in-law from Boulogne on 10 August reports that they have had a smooth but rather slow crossing and that with their friend Viv Lewis on board the engine is working perfectly. David is growing a beard. On the 15th she writes from Middleburg that they sailed up from Boulogne in twenty-four hours with perfect weather conditions and a nice steady wind, and arrived at Flushing on the morning of the 14th. Now they have come up the canal across Walcheren in glorious sunshine. What she does not mention is that they had a brush with Dutch customs officials at Flushing, because their three guests (Viv, his wife Pauline Lewis, née Kelly, a friend of Ann's from Maidstone days, and David's friend Glenn Collett) had somehow managed to leave their passports at home. As Judy (fourteen at the time) recalls, the customs men put them on their honour ('very Dutch', she thought) and they were allowed to proceed. After a day or two in Middleburg they pushed on northward to the ancient fishing village of Veere, with its castle 'that hangs on the side of the dike like a disused wasp nest'. Then they headed for the open sea again and raced up the flat, dyked coast to Ijmuiden at the seaward outlet of the busy North Sea Canal, with its strings of barges and ocean-going steamers. They followed the canal to Amsterdam, where they moored near the Central Station, and ate a huge Indonesian meal in a restaurant on the Leidsestraat. A day and a night's sailing across the old Zuider Zee, which the Dutch were in process of draining, brought them to the sleepy port of Hoorn, and a breakfast of sausage and cheese. Then they sailed on up the coast to Einkuizen, and across to Staveren in Friesland, where they 'dawdled in winding canals not much wider than our boat, through an Arcadian country, a land of woods and shallow lakes, and sunshine and flowers'. After that it was time to go home.

They were back by 12 September, and later that month Golding was interviewed for a BBC TV *Monitor* programme, to be broadcast on 25 October. Nigel Mussett, who was in the Science VIth at Bishop Wordsworth's, remembers the camera crew filming him 'in pensive mood' in the garden of No. 11 Salisbury Close. Other shots showed him on *Wild Rose*, at Ebble Thatch, taking a class with boys asking questions, and strolling around the cathedral and Old Sarum. The relaxed relations with the media that this programme and the long interview in August with Frank Kermode exemplify came to an end in 1959. After that he was much more wary about giving interviews, and twenty years were to pass before he would again consent to be the subject of a television programme, the *South Bank Show* in 1980. It seems clear that the reason for this change of attitude was his shock and hurt at the *Free Fall* reviews.

They were the worst he had ever had. On publication day, 23 October, friend and champion Frank Kermode pronounced it a failure, though a 'fiercely distinguished book', in *The Spectator*. The scene in the dark cell and the interrogation scene both verged on 'mental bombast'. Sammy's philosophizing and theologizing were written with 'a kind of dry heat, a brittleness'. 'For the first time, Mr Golding's invention seems to ebb.' In the *New Statesman* the following day Peter Duval Smith jeered at the book's ideas: 'Sammy is no great shakes as a thinker.' Golding 'pitches his voice too stridently', so that 'the congregation look curiously at the preacher ... "Why is he shouting?"' On 25 October Philip Toynbee in the *Observer* pronounced it 'a failure in almost every direction'. It was 'dull, and dull in the most disturbing way'. The language was 'large and noisy and out of all proportion to the work it is doing'; chronology was played with to no purpose; the prison cell chapter was 'pretentious'. The only redeeming feature was the Beatrice episode with its 'brilliant seduction scene'. In the *Sunday Times* J. D. Scott felt that Golding had overreached himself by seeking 'universal significance'. The torrent of complaint went on in the weeks that followed. Daniel George in the *Daily Telegraph* found the style 'incontinent', like a weak bladder; Graham Hough in *The Listener* regretted that 'Mr Golding's moral insights are not particularly original or striking', and the *Irish Times* shuddered that the whole thing was 'astonishingly and often brutally unpleasant'.

There were, however, dissenting voices. John Beddoe in *Tribune* gave it a rave review: 'one of those rare books that should be read by people who don't normally read novels'. He admitted that the prison-camp scenes were unconvincing, but the relationship between Sammy and Beatrice was supreme – never since Stendhal had there been so moving a picture of a man confronted with 'the nullity of his ideal'. Brian Aldiss in the *Oxford Mail* was also positive, and Roy Perrott in the *Guardian* reckoned it 'in some ways his most interesting novel so far'. The stoutest defence was mounted by Ian Gregor in *The Tablet*, though even he judged it 'less sure in its touch than the novels that preceded it'.

At the time Gregor was a young university lecturer, and he and his friend, another young lecturer, Mark Kinkead-Weekes, discussed *Free Fall* while Gregor was reading it for his review. They grew increasingly indignant as they watched the adverse notices coming out. 'I got very cross,' Kinkead-Weekes remembers, 'I thought they really didn't know what they were talking about, especially Toynbee in the *Observer*, whom I took a great scunner to.' So 'being young and cocky and stupid', he and Gregor wrote an article called 'The Strange Case of Mr Golding and his Critics', which they published in the *Twentieth Century* in February 1960.

It is, in fact, rather a tangled account of the novel, but at least it expresses unmitigated contempt for Golding's detractors and a conviction that *Free Fall* is part of the same exploration of the nature of man as the three novels that preceded it.

Monteith got in touch with Kinkead-Weekes and Gregor to say that Golding had liked the article very much and wanted to meet its authors. He also asked them to do an annotated edition of *Lord of the Flies* for use in schools – which they did, following it with a similar edition of *The Inheritors* and, in 1967, the standard work on Golding's oeuvre, *William Golding: A Critical Study*. They became friends and occasional convivial companions. Kinkead-Weekes remembers Golding's first meeting with them when they got off the train from Edinburgh (where they both had university posts) at Salisbury station. He had been expecting 'two Scotch moralists', but after one look at them said, 'My God, I'd better get some more beer in.' It was a condition of their friendship that they never talked about Golding's writings unless he himself broached the subject.

Monteith wrote on 26 October saying that he was 'incoherent' after reading 'those bloody stupid reviews'. It was good of him to be so concerned, Golding replied, but 'the antis are right. Free Fall remains magnificent in places, inflated and anxious in others.' To du Sautoy on the same day he protested that he was 'not suffering a bit' over the bad reviews. He just wanted the book to sell. And, despite the critics, it did. Its sales in the first year were 6,823 – almost twice the first-year sales of any of his previous novels.

17

Journalism and Difficulties with *The Spire*

Though Golding put a brave face on it, the *Free Fall* reviews were a blow. He wanted to give up the drudgery of schoolteaching, but could he provide for his family just by writing? He was worried about money. Admittedly, he always was, even when he had a great deal of it. But in 1960 his worry was reasonable. His commitments were piling up. There was *Wild Rose*, and Judy's fees at Godolphin, and because Bowerchalke was some way out of Salisbury they had to have a car. David, after his year at Michael Hall, had gone to a technical college in Southampton to take his A-levels – Judy later did the same – and he stayed with Golding's adopted sister Eileen. But his father naturally footed the bill for his upkeep and college expenses. Also, Alec's death had removed a sort of safety net. Judy thinks that Alec and her grandma had telegraphed them the occasional five pounds when they got stuck, but she remembers thinking, when they were in Italy, that they could not just send a telegram for help, because Alec was dead. Now they were on their own.

Promoting a career as a novelist clashed with school duties. On 5 January 1960 the *Guardian* reported on the fourth of a series of lunchtime lectures arranged by Manchester booksellers. It had been given by Golding, who had talked about his fruitless attempts to get published prior to *Lord of the Flies*, and about the experiment he had carried out at school, deliberately allowing the boys in one of his classes more and more autonomy until '*Lord of the Flies* was there with all its savagery and occasional beauty'. It went down well. But, Golding told du Sautoy, the Bishop Wordsworth's headmaster, Dr Happold, had 'created a certain amount of fuss' about letting him have the time off. 'I'm a schoolmaster after all.'

Another anxiety was that David had not yet got into a university. Golding had written, at Monteith's suggestion, to Maurice Bowra at

Wadham, who had been 'very nice and thank you very much – but I'd left things too late as usual. For two pins I'd go and live on sixpence in Greece.' His friend Peter Green did go off and live in Greece with his family a couple of years later, and perhaps Golding and he had been mulling over the pros and cons of becoming expats at Book Society meetings. Du Sautoy was anxious about his son Stephen, and Golding, as the father of two adolescents, sent his sympathy and his own paternal tidings: 'David is cheerful. It's something when they aren't suicidal.' Three months later he was able to announce that David had been accepted at Brasenose for the following October. 'He keeps saying that it is the *last* place in the world he really wants to go – but I think he'll go.' It meant, however, yet more expense. 'You'll probably catch sight of my name in a number of strange places in the future; I'm having to accept anything with money attached'. Meanwhile 'the thought of not going to Italy this Easter is like a pain in the side'.

In April another difficulty arose. 'My ancient mother now wants to come and live with us; and as she has to live on the ground floor and more or less be nursed, you can imagine what a difference that is going to make.' For a start, it meant they could not come to a Faber cocktail party on the 21st, 'what with getting another room furnished and rushing about we simply haven't time to come up to London'. Mildred nearly died at Ebble Thatch, and Eileen and her husband Bill Hogben rushed up from Southampton to be with her. But she recovered enough to go down to Eileen's by ambulance, and Eileen cared for her until her death that August. In November Golding published his childhood memoir 'Billy the Kid' in *The Spectator* – a tongue-in-cheek tribute to his mother in which he recalls how she rhapsodized over his infant beauty – 'eyes like cornflowers and hair like a field of ripe corn' – and how, nobly but mistakenly, she had taken his side when, entirely as a result of his thuggish behaviour, he had become unpopular with the other children at nursery school.

By the time he wrote this he was well on his way to becoming a full-time literary journalist, as he had warned du Sautoy he might have to do to make ends meet. He had not attempted much in that line before. In May 1957 the *London Magazine* had sent out a questionnaire asking to what extent writers should be interested in topical events, and he had written a short reply, which they published, insisting that writers should concentrate, rather, on 'the basic human condition'. That Christmas he reviewed a round-up of twenty-seven new children's books for *The Listener* – taking as his criterion that 'a great book for children must be a great book by any standard'. But that was the limit of his labours in Grub Street in 1957, and he did no reviewing at all in 1958. Halfway through 1959, though, he started reviewing regularly. The Book Society published a monthly magazine called *The Bookman* from its address at 6 Baker Street, which was sent out to members, and carried on its inside cover the titles of the Book Society monthly choices. It was beautifully produced, elegantly illustrated with photographs and drawings, and packed with reviews of current books by leading writers. Its editorial committee comprised Richard Church, James Fisher, Peter Green, Penelope Mortimer, Kathleen Nott and J. H. Plumb, and Golding joined it in July 1959. From then until October 1961 he wrote for it frequently, sometimes reviewing as many as three books in a single issue.

His reviews by no means bear out the contention that writers should concentrate on the basic human condition and ignore current events. His first, in the 1959 July-August issue, was of Gavin Maxwell's *The Ten Pains of Death*, which exposed the corruption and destitution in modern Sicily, an island where, as his review puts it, 'Sanitation is a hole behind the door. Water is rationed and not infrequently stinks. A stale crust of bread is a whole meal for a whole family.' His second review, of Sir Fitzroy Maclean's *Back to Bokhara*, observes how hard it is for Westerners to get a true picture of life in the Soviet Union, and optimistically takes Maclean's word for it that, from the perspective of ordinary Russians, communism has meant 'More of everything. More smiles. More freedom.' In the same issue he wrote an enthusiastic account of Peter Goullart's *Princes of the Black Bone*. Goullart, a naturalized Chinese and Taoist, had travelled through China and the Tibetan borderland, carrying only a walking stick, despite the wild animals that, quite literally, crossed his path. One of them, a leopard with wonderful amber eyes, pink jaws and white teeth, was only five yards away and – presumably – unhungry when Goullart noticed it. Golding's other 1959 reviews were of books about ships and the sea – Eric Hiscock's account of round-the-world yachtsmen, *Voyage Under Sail*, Fred Majdalany's history of the

Eddystone lighthouse, *The Red Rocks of Eddystone*, and Adrian Hayter's *Sheila in the Wind*, which described Hayter's bid to sail single-handed to New Zealand in an unseaworthy boat and with almost no experience. Golding's review makes it sound roughly the equivalent of trying to get to New Zealand in *Seahorse*. But though he frowns at the 'terrible risks' Hayter took, admiration creeps in, for Hayter did sail single-handedly to New Zealand twice, once east to west and once west to east.

Profits from writing in 1959 were boosted when Golding – or Curtis Brown, the agent who looked after his writing apart from novels – sold a short story to *Queen* magazine, which was published on 22 December. Titled 'The Anglo-Saxon', it is, in effect, a modern version of the encounter between Lok and *Homo sapiens* in *The Inheritors*, and may owe something to its author's observation of Wiltshire farm labourers in the bar of The Bell at Bowerchalke. The main character is George Smart, an old drover, who is driving his employer's heifers home when he comes across a figure standing by a gap in the hedge, cradling a stick.

As George stumbled forward, mouthing now, he saw the figure stood impossibly in a shadow like indoors and that the stick was a strange sort of gun ... The shadow like indoors was because of the roof. Out here, on the downs, a roof. It was metal with letters on, stretched away over the hedge, over the vegetable patch, away into the mist.

It gradually penetrates George's brain that it is the wing of an American bomber that has overshot the runway and come to rest in his vegetable patch, and the figure with the gun is one of a group of American soldiers guarding it. Later, in the pub, he meets the Americans again, gets drunk, and, outraged by the damage to his vegetables, punches one of them. He is arrested and fined £5 by the magistrates. However, a kindly American sergeant pays his fine and later, in the pub, when the landlady, Mrs Williams, refuses to serve George, the sergeant persuades her to relent and buys George a pint of bitter. It is a long time since anyone has been kind to George, and it has an unintended effect.

George understood that the twisted body inside his clothes was shaking with hangover. He did not understand the hot tides that seemed to be taking his chest and throat and eyes and filling them with water. He turned away, clutching his tankard, and blinked out of the warped window.

So 'The Anglo-Saxon' is *The Inheritors* with a happy ending. It is also beautifully subtle and uncensorious about the psychology of the villagers, the Americans and George.

His last 1959 piece for *The Bookman* was a survey of the year's titles in which he chose Maxwell's *Ten Pains of Death* as the non-fiction winner, but could think of no novels worth remembering. However, despite what he had told the *London Magazine*, several novels attracted him in the following year precisely because of their concern over social issues. The first, James Barlow's *The Patriots*, was about an ex-paratrooper, sent to prison after a pub brawl, who plans a train robbery when he comes out. Like *Free Fall*, it focuses on the generation disoriented by the Second World War, and perhaps that is why Golding liked it. These were men who, as he puts it, had been taught that, 'because certain papers had been signed, children could be blown to pieces or burnt to death. Then, high over their heads, the establishment signed other papers. Immediately to shoot or burn or knife or strangle was a fearful crime.' Social concern also marked out G. W. Target's *The Teachers*, about a day in the life of a slum school, and John Stroud's *The Shorn Lamb* (which Golding rightly guessed was based on personal experience) about a child-care officer's efforts to save the children of a destitute family from crime and prostitution. The courage and self-sacrifice of social workers commanded his admiration again in H. S. Turner's *Something Extraordinary*, a real-life account of the creation of an adventure playground for poor children on a London estate.

His reviewing does not suggest a wide knowledge of contemporary fiction. He finds Brian Moore's novel *The Luck of Ginger Coffey* gloomy, but seems unaware that Moore had made his name four years before with the even gloomier *Judith Hearne*. Reviewing Iris Murdoch's *A Severed Head* in May 1961, he was astonished by the book's sexual permutations, and called up Peter Green. 'Look, old boy,' he remonstrated, 'surely she can't be serious.' Green, who was reviewing the novel for another paper, agreed that it must be a send-up of Freudian psychoanalysis and liberal humanism, and they both reviewed it on this assumption. Only later did they discover that Murdoch was being perfectly serious. Two block-busters that he seems to have scanned rather hastily were a translation from the French of Jean Raspail's *Welcome, Honourable Visitors*, about the inscrutability of the Japanese (his review carried an illustration by Ronald Searle – typical of *The Bookman*'s high-grade artwork), and the American James A. Michener's *Hawaii* (which, perhaps as a result of rapid reading, he seems to think is a history of Hawaii rather than a novel). His interest in ships and the sea made him the obvious reviewer for Barrie Pitt's *Coronel and Falkland*, about two epic sea battles in the First World War, S. W. Roskill's *The Navy at War*, Francis Chichester's *Alone Across the Atlantic*, Alexander McKee's *The Golden Wreck*, which told of the destruction of the clipper *The Royal Charter* by a hurricane in 1859, and Dan Mulville's *Trade Winds and Turtle*, an account of crossing the Atlantic with one companion and little knowledge or equipment. In sympathy, he admits to having himself 'navigated more confined but not less dangerous waters with the aid of a wetted thumb and an outline of northern Europe printed on a teacloth'.

His tally of reviews for *The Bookman* in 1960 was completed with pieces on Lesley Blanch's *The Sabres of Paradise*, a biography of the nineteenth-century Caucasian warlord, Imam Shamyl, and Hesketh Pearson's *Bernard Shaw, His Life and Personality* – a review that acknowl-edges the 'immense debt' his generation owed to Shaw, who 'made us examine every foundation of our belief'. In his year's-end round-up he recommends, besides books he has reviewed, Margaret Irwin's por-trait of Sir Walter Raleigh, *That Great Lucifer*, James (later Jan) Morris's *Venice*, Giuseppe Lampedusa's *The Leopard* and Jerzy Andrzejewski's *The Inquisitors*. 'It's a bad thing', he admits, 'to read books when you want to write them' – but needs must. In addition to reviews, stories and articles helped to pay bills. 'The Ladder and the Tree', his mem-oir of childhood terrors and joys, had been published in *The Listener* in March 1960, and 'Miss Pulkinhorn', the story about the sacrament he had shown to Monteith, came out in *Encounter* in August.

During 1960 and 1961 he also wrote regularly for *The Spectator*, which had as its literary editor the young Karl Miller, a Scot of keen percep-tions and granite integrity, respected and feared in the literary world.

Golding's first review for him was of Raleigh Trevelyan's *A Hermit Disclosed*, a book based on the diary of Jimmy Mason, who had lived in the village of Great Canfield, Essex, at the turn of the century. Jimmy was a simpleton and had a harmless passion for little girls, but Golding's review extricates him from scandal and comedy and finds in his life 'the hallmark of an effective mystical experience'. Jimmy was a beekeeper, and a villager once saw him praying on his knees among his hives, with the bees crawling over his coat and face. It was an image that stayed in Golding's mind, linking up with his interest in saints such as Vianney, the Curé of Ars. The seriousness of the review clearly pleased Miller, and he soon sent Golding another book, *John Paul Jones* by the American Samuel Eliot Morison, the biography of a swashbuckling captain in the American navy who raided the English coast during the War of Independence. A letter from Miller about this review survives: 'I am sending you a galley for correction and I have marked a couple of points in the text where I am not quite clear about the wording. I enjoyed reading your review very much.' This astringent, appreciative scrutiny was just what Golding needed to put him on his mettle, and his reviews for Miller are more challenging and substantial than the *Bookman* pieces, which he seemingly edited himself. Miller cannily sent him books that tapped into his prejudices – in August 1960, T. W. Bamford's *Thomas Arnold*, and in November Christopher Hollis's *Eton: A History*. Arnold, father of the poet Matthew, is often celebrated as the high-minded creator of the English public-school spirit, but Golding, in his review, sees him as an impetuous and choleric man whose confidence in his own rightness led him to cruelty and dishonesty. As headmaster of Rugby he illegally closed down the primary school, which had been open to local children, in order deliberately to foster an elite, and so 'prised open the gap that still lies between the public schools and the rest'. Moreover the inbred sense of superiority Arnold encouraged connects directly, Golding argues, with imperialistic subjugation of other races – the pattern of colonialism which 'gave a convulsive shudder in the tragedy of Suez'. His review of Hollis's adulatory history of Eton again puts an opposing view. The vital thing in education, he observes, is the staff–student ratio. The average grammar-school master, such as himself, is not jealous of the corporate life of the public schools, but is jealous of the expensive system that can afford to devote a whole master to ten or twelve boys. State schools must have the same staff–student ratio if they are to compete. Snob value draws people to Eton, not intellectual eminence. It is not so much a school as a channel for social privilege, and he would contemplate its destruction without dismay. 'If a Royal Commission should ever find its conclusions in line with mine, they can provide me with a mile or two of wire, a few hundred tons of TNT, and one of those plunger-detonating machines which makes the user feel like Jehovah.'

The length of the *Spectator* reviews, twice that of *The Bookman*'s, gave space for anecdote, reminiscence and personal revelation that Miller evidently encouraged. In a piece on Gavin Maxwell's otter-saga *Ring of Bright Water* Golding recalls some of his own experiences with wild creatures – a red squirrel in a Welsh valley, dolphins off Cape Trafalgar, and 'migrant starlings coming in over the downs, a gossamer, a scarf, then a whole sky-concealing blanket and a tempest of song. They dropped on part of Savernake Forest and the bare trees seemed to be covered at once with an abundant and noisy foliage.' But his point is that, though he watches animals and birds, he does not love them. 'The positive *love* of animals has always amazed me.' As for Maxwell and his pets: 'A man's bed seems a preposterous place for an otter.'

Sometimes his memories have little connection with the book under review. Writing about a study of modern archaeology, Grahame Clark's *World Pre-History*, he remembers his mother saying that her sense of the world as a risky place dated from the day she heard the *Titanic* had sunk. Before that, life had seemed sunny and placid. More pertinently, reviewing a collection of essays on Rudolf Steiner, *The Faithful Thinker*, edited by his senior ex-colleague at Michael Hall, A. C. Harwood, he praises Steiner for trying to find a bridge between the world of the physical sciences and the world of the spirit. 'Most of us', he ventures, 'have an unexpressed faith that the bridge exists' – a claim surely connected in his mind with Sammy's conclusion in *Free Fall*: 'Both worlds are real. There is no bridge.' Also relevant to *Free Fall* is a review of the Arco paperback edition of the complete Jules Verne. He is sad to find that stories thrilling to him as a boy now seem 'turgid and slack'. But an illustration from the original edition of Verne's *Round the Moon*, showing three astronauts hanging helpless in mid-air inside their space-craft, jogs his memory: 'It is a, or rather *the*, moment of free fall – not the modern sort which can be endless, but the nineteenth-century sort, the point where earth and moon gravity is equal.' Understood as a point of equipoise between two gravitational fields, the worlds of science and spirit, 'free fall' makes sense as a title for his novel, and also as a label for Sammy's predicament, and Golding's.

A book Miller signed him up for in advance, knowing of his addiction to science fiction, was Kingsley Amis's history of the genre, *New Maps of Hell*, and Golding's review amounts to a semi-facetious analysis of his own maleness. Science fiction appeals to men, not women, he contends, because men are obsessed with machines and ideas, and avoid profound experience and emotion. They – and he – are 'androids', whereas women, being involved in nature's 'improbable and downright fantastic' side, have no wish to read about it. A young woman friend of his wife's was, he claims, carried from the delivery room after the birth of her first child 'crying in anguish to a shut sky, "It's pure science fiction."'

To exploit this anecdotal vein, Miller increasingly encouraged Golding to write personal pieces for *The Spectator*, rather than book reviews. The first, published on 7 July 1961, was 'It's a Long Way to Oxyrhynchus', an account of clearing out an old house (in fact 29 The Green, relinquished in the autumn of 1959 when his mother fell ill). Among discarded papers he finds a piece he had written years before, when successive books had been turned down by innumerable publish-ers. It plays with the idea of taking his manuscripts up the Nile to Oxyrhynchus, a site in Upper Egypt that has yielded many ancient papyri, and burying them in the desert sand, so that they might be excavated in AD 5000 by Peking University and published in their 750-volume *Vestiges of Western Literature*. Coming across this long-forgotten, wry fantasy among the lumber in the old house reminds him of the 'desperate, cruel, bloody business' of believing that he could write when no one else thought he could. His last review for Miller was of a new translation of Homer's *Odyssey* by Robert Fitzgerald. Though he read and reread Homer more than any other author, this is the only critical piece he wrote about him, and it characterizes Homer as 'the most unliterary of authors'. Fitzgerald's translation is 'eminently readable' but nothing like Homer, because it 'destroys the formality of the epic language', replacing the stock phrases of oral tradition with a diversified, up-to-date vocabulary. The only way to 'get alongside Homer', he concludes, is to learn Homeric Greek – and fortunately the stock phrases make that easier.

In the two years that he spent on reviewing and other literary journalism, from mid-1959 to mid-1961, he made no headway on a novel. Would there be one for spring 1961, Monteith inquired in August 1960? 'If all goes well', the reply came, 'I shall have a novel for you to decide about for next autumn – not spring.' All the same, he added, he had been 'working dashed hard but mostly at odd jobs (reviewing and suchlike) which brings in ready money. I suppose it holds up novel writing a bit, but there it is.' To du Sautoy he admitted, 'I've simply allowed myself to take on too much journalism, and am chasing desperately towards a moment when I can free my arm for a novel.' His agents, Curtis Brown, had an inquiry from America about the TV rights for *Lord of the Flies*, and he wrote excitedly to du Sautoy, 'There may be *gold* in them thar hills.' But the disappointing answer was that Fabers had already leased the rights to Ealing Studios. Though he was working 'dashed hard', the proceeds seemed inadequate. In the same month, May 1960, that he asked about TV rights he sent a discontented letter to the Society of Authors, which he had joined in 1955.

Dear Sir,

It has been borne in on me more and more, recently, that I have a considerable reputation in the literary world; and yet the fees I obtain from the BBC are much as they were.

I believe you give your members advice on this subject and if so I would be glad if you would look at the figures below.

For a forty-five minute dramatic piece I am offered £105.

For a fifteen minute film of Salisbury, with a running commentary consisting of what I think of it, ITV (Southern) offers £21.

For a five-hundred word review (Spectator) I am given £8.8.0.

Are these satisfactory? If not, what figures should an author of my reputation stick out for?

In reply the Society advised that the BBC tended to continue offering the same fee to writers unless they complained, and that he was right to query it. The ITV offer was 'very poor', and should be rejected. No opinion was offered about *The Spectator*.

Monteith, though no doubt disappointed about the absence of a new novel, was eager to maintain friendly relations. He spent the weekend of 14–16 October as a guest at Ebble Thatch, and on 3 December had Golding to dine with him at All Souls and stay the night. On 24 January 1961 he arranged a dinner at his club, the Travellers, for Golding to meet the novelist John Bowen, who was thinking of making a TV play of *Free Fall*, and when Ann was rushed into Salisbury hospital, later in January, to be operated on for an acute appendicitis, he sent a lavish bunch of flowers and get-well wishes. By 1 February Ann was, her husband reported, 'looking very transparent and fragile, but convalescing'. He, however, was still entangled in journalism and schoolteaching, and felt depressed about the future. In a specially commissioned piece entitled 'On the Crest of the Wave', written for the *Times Literary Supplement* in June 1960, in a series called 'Limits of Control', he set out the reasons why the alternatives of continuing to teach and becoming a full-time novelist both seemed unappealing. His essay sketches the history of working-class education in England, starting a century back with the publication of the *Hundred Best Books*, a library designed to bring the worthiest that had been thought and written within reach of everyone, and purchasable at sixpence a volume. A Cornish ancestor of his, a miner and lay reader, had mastered the whole library, book by book, getting up in the winter dawn and rigging up a contraption that allowed him to work the bellows with his foot so that the fire glowed enough for him to read by. Golding imagines him peering at the 'slabs of small, grey print' and memorizing whole paragraphs of abstruse authors such as Herodotus. Then came universal education, and children who would never have got to school could now attend. He remembers grammar-school boys in the 1920s, 'smaller, half-starved, some of them, often dirty, thin, bitter, lively', who 'fought swarmingly for a place in the sun'. But universal education assumes that everyone is educable, and it has become apparent that this is not so. The supply of teachable material is as limited as the supply of people who can teach, though no one is supposed to say so, just as no one is supposed to say that a pupil is unintelligent, and it will be taken as an 'irremediable insult' if they do. The aim of education has changed also. 'Science' has become a bandwagon on which everyone has jumped – parsons, TV stars, politicians. But science is not the most important thing. Philosophy is more important, so is history and courtesy and aesthetic perception. 'Our humanity rests on the capacity to make value judgements' – what is right or wrong, ugly or beautiful, just or unjust. Science cannot teach this, only philosophy and the arts can, and since they take second place to science the 'amiable majority' of people, 'not particularly intelligent or gifted', are left with a mass of undigested facts and some 'scraps of saleable technology'. 'I do not see how literature for them is to be anything but simple, repetitive, and a stop-gap for when there are no westerns on the telly.'

These disenchanted convictions, which Golding never relinquished, made continuing to teach and becoming a serious full-time novelist almost equally depressing prospects, and coupled with the frustrations of constant hand-to-mouth journalism they clouded the two years that followed the publication of *Free Fall.* The family's 1960 summer holiday in *Wild Rose* was less enjoyable, too, than their Dutch trip the year before. They spent most of the time, Golding lamented afterwards, 'beating back against foul winds', and Glenn Collett, who had been appointed engineer in Viv Lewis's absence, had difficulty getting the engine to work. They had planned to sail to Norway, but got no further than Boulogne, where, Glenn recalls, they were woken early in the morning by 'an almighty revving and banging as the fishing boats made ready'. Whether by accident or design, one of them bumped their stern, and Golding marched off to the harbour office to remonstrate. He and Ann had a 'fairly heated discussion' with a harbour official, and after the official had left Glenn noticed that they continued to discuss the incident with each other, still in French, 'with a lot of Gallic arm-waving'. Soon a carpenter appeared and repaired the damage, but the return trip was 'pretty rough', the engine conked out again, and they had to skim past the harbour wall at Ramsgate under sail, and then turn sharply into the entrance. In the course of this manoeuvre they carried away 'quite a few fishing lines', and some 'shocking language' came their way from anglers fishing off the harbour wall.

A happier experience awaited them the following spring. For twenty years Golding had dreamed of going to Greece, poring over ancient maps, and at last in 1961 the dream came true, thanks to the American magazine *Holiday*, which helped with the expenses in return for a series of travel articles. *Holiday*, launched in 1946 and published by Curtis Publishing of Philadelphia, was the first big post-war American magazine. Its editor Ted Patrick aimed at a high-quality product that would reintroduce Americans to foreign travel. Its artwork became famous. Picture editor Frank Zachary introduced a galaxy of European artists, among them Ronald Searle, who was sent all over the world by the magazine to capture the exotic and esoteric from German brothels to the Alaskan wilderness. Celebrated writers commissioned by *Holiday* included John Steinbeck, who did a series about rediscovering America, and S. J. Perelman, whom it sent to Bali for a series entitled 'Westward Ha! Or Round the World in Eighty Clichés'. By March 1947 its sales had reached 605,000 – the biggest circulation a fifty-cent magazine had ever reached in a single year. It paid $1,500 or more for an article, and Golding wrote fourteen between 1961 and 1967.

In April 1961 he drove across Europe with Ann and the children, then down through Yugoslavia, which, he told Monteith in an excited letter, 'was full of proper Gypsies holding fairs, and there were a few women in Turkish trousers and veils, carrying plastic buckets to the well'. When they got to Thessalonika they followed the eastern coast road down, beneath Mount Olympus to the little town of Lamia, which lies to the north of Thermopylae, the narrow pass between the mountains and the sea where Leonidas and his Spartans made their epic stand against Xerxes's Persian horde. There, his *Holiday* article recounts, they lunched off Easter lamb, a 'repulsive, naked thing' spitted and roasted over hot coals, drank ouzo and Turkish coffee ('one third black liquid and two thirds sludge, a delightful combination'), and then drove to the historic pass, which was deserted except for a goatherd and his flock, 'a tumultuous jumble of horns, of black and brown fur with ruffs and edgings of white, and staring, yellow, libidinous eyes'. Golding clambered up the cliff for a panoramic view, disturbing lizards, and a snake patterned in green and black, and drifts of white, yellow and brown butterflies, and felt, standing there, that 'a little of Leonidas lies in the fact that I can go where I like and write what I like. He contributed to set us free.' They moved on to Athens and made it the centre for various trips. One of them was to Tolon, which was then, as Judy recalls, 'an orange plantation which happened to be beside the sea'. There was just a ramshackle café, a deserted beach, and 'these incredible trees with oranges hanging off them'. It was at Tolon that Golding saw a baby girl run into the sea, and 'shriek with laughter and with sheer happiness at the behaviour of the water'. It was, he felt, like the meeting of lovers, and it made him think that, as long as there have been human beings, children must have 'played with exactly those ripples, and delighted in them'.

At Marathon, where the Athenians defeated Darius and his Persians in 490 BC, he gave his family an account of the battle, and a small crowd of tourists gathered round to listen. At Delphi, then a sparse, quiet village, they found that the chasm of the Oracle had been blocked by an ancient earthquake, but 'we got some kind of answer to our queries'. They were waylaid by an excited Greek, 'having one word of English two of French and three of German', who finally managed to convey to them that the Russians had put a man into orbit. This was Yuri Gagarin, who became the first man in space on 12 April 1961. They went to Olympia, which was then a tiny settlement with a dirt road to it, and found that the site of the original Olympic Games was just a jumble of stones, with the grass knee high in places. There was, as Golding later wrote, 'nothing but the thunderous stridulation of the cicadas' to remind them of 'the applause that resounded here for a thousand years'. They had driven to Olympia from Mycenae via, as Judy recalls, the road to Patras and then south. Arcadia was 'stunning and deserted and green and wooded', and as they passed what Golding told them was the River Ladon, he quoted from Milton's *Arcades*:

> Nymphs and shepherds, dance no more
> By sandy Ladon's lilied banks.

'We are back', he wrote to Monteith on 24 April, 'and fairly sun-soaked. Greece, as you might suppose, was out of this world – another planet almost.' They might, he added, buy 'a summer shack in the Peloponnese one of these days'. A couple of months later the euphoria had faded, as he contemplated his inability to write. 'As you have guessed, I'm bogged down in – or passing through – a state of creative impotence.' It was partly 'sheer lack of time' and partly 'sheer funk at being subjected, inevitably, to a close critical examination'. Memories of the *Free Fall* reviews evidently still hurt. Altogether he was 'most unhappy'. However, some notion of what the next novel would be had emerged, and his provisional title for it was 'Barchester Spire'.

This is the first glimmer of what was to become *The Spire* – for some, Golding's greatest novel. The daily experience of watching the rebuilding of Salisbury cathedral's spire from his classroom window must have been part of the book's gestation. But another memory was probably at work too. In 1946, shortly after he returned to Bishop Wordsworth's from the war, the school dramatic society, the Bishop's Players, performed Dorothy Sayers's play *The Zeal of Thy House*. There is no record of whether he helped in the production, but, given his interest in school drama, it would be surprising if he did not. The play centres on the architect William of Sens, who was chosen to rebuild Canterbury cathedral's choir in 1174, after it had been destroyed by fire. Though a supreme architect, William is debauched, corrupt and consumed by pride so overweening that he declares, 'We are the master craftsmen, God and I.' During the rebuilding operations he suffers a crippling fall, and is at last brought to repent and seek reconciliation with the wealthy widow Lady Ursula, whom he has seduced. A character mentioned in the play is called Jocelyn. There is also a moment when the archangel Raphael (who, along with Michael and Gabriel, is a member of the cast, and comments on the human characters) says of William's building work, 'the shafted columns rise/ Singing like music'. Quite a lot of this seems to have lodged in the mind of the author of *The Spire*.

But when he wrote to Monteith about being in a 'funk', his ideas about the new book were still wildly unlike the novel he eventually wrote, and still affected by fear of the critics who had attacked *Free Fall* for being strident and pretentious. 'Barchester Spire' was 'meant to be funny', he assured his editor, not 'savage/tragic stuff'. It 'wouldn't aim high', so it would be less frightening to write. Most of it, indeed, was already 'in longhand and the rest in my head'. It would be modest in length, too – just a 'long-short', so he proposed publishing it in a volume with 'Envoy Extraordinary', 'Miss Pulkinhorn' and 'The Anglo-Saxon'. Monteith accepted this idea, but wanted a completed typescript by 14 September, because on that date a new phase of Golding's life was to start. He was going to America.

18

America

Golding's stay in America in 1961–2 was a turning point. It lifted him out of stagnation and brought him fame, wealth and the adulation of the young. It also spurred him to give up, at last, his hated teaching job. The idea of the American trip originated with Professor Louis Rubin, head of the English department at Hollins, a small liberal arts college for women in Virginia. Acting on the suggestion of a colleague, John Rees Moore, he wrote to Golding in June 1960 suggesting he should come out as writer-in-residence in September 1961, and teach in Hollins's recently established MA programme in Creative Writing, Literary Criticism and Contemporary Literature. A reply came by telegram on 12 June 1960: INTERESTED STOP HOPE WE CAN MEET = GOLDING. Later that summer, when he was lecturing in France, Rubin flew over and visited the Goldings at Ebble Thatch. Judy, then fifteen, remembers him as very jolly and upbeat and 'slightly transgressive' compared with the Englishmen she knew – though that, she adds, would not have been difficult. He was quickly convinced that Golding would fit in admirably, and offered him the job there and then. The terms were $10,000 for the school year, together with a guest apartment, and the understanding that he would be free to accept lecture appointments elsewhere throughout the two semesters.

Rubin offered to set up reading engagements to help fund a trip to California and back for the Goldings during their stay. But, though he wrote to universities and colleges 'across the length and breadth of the continent', he had few takers. Golding, he found, had only a limited 'highbrow' reputation in America, and his works were not easily available. Coward-McCann had allowed *Lord of the Flies* to go out of print, and Harcourt, Brace had still not published *The Inheritors*, though they had brought out *Free Fall* in February 1960. The Capricorn Books paperback of *Lord of the Flies* had appeared in August 1959, but Rubin seems not to have known about it when he met Golding, which suggests it had made little impact as yet. This was soon to change. By the time the Goldings' stay began in September 1961, *Lord of the Flies* had become, as Rubin recalls, 'very much the rage among college students everywhere'. Undergraduates at the Ivy League colleges were especially taken with it, and in the months before he left England Golding began to be deluged with invitations to speak, and offered fees well in excess of what Rubin had been able raise for him. His editor at Harcourt, Brace, John McCallum, got wind of the growing enthusiasm and set about arranging additional lecturing engagements, which caused Golding some alarm. 'I didn't realise how fully John McCallum would throw himself into the fray,' he wrote to Rubin on 27 April 1961. 'I'm writing him by this post to tell him to lay off a bit. Obviously he can have no idea what I can accept and when.'

In the same letter he lists the novels he would like to cover in his course: H. G. Wells's *The First Men in the Moon*, E. M. Forster's *A Passage to India*, D. H. Lawrence's *Sons and Lovers*, Aldous Huxley's *Brave New World*, Robert Graves's *I Claudius* and *Claudius the God*, Graham Greene's *Brighton Rock*, Ivy Compton Burnett's *Pastors and Masters*, C. P. Snow's *The Affair*, Alan Sillitoe's *Saturday Night and Sunday Morning*, Lawrence Durrell's *The Alexandria Quartet*, and any novel of Iris Murdoch's that students can get hold of. He explains that he has restricted himself to books that he imagines will be cheaply available in America, and would otherwise have stuck to post-1950 novels. Rubin's reply does not survive but he evidently vetoed the earlier items in the list, and in his next letter, on 14 May, Golding suggested a 'compromise' by confining himself to post-1945 fiction. His new list is: Kingsley Amis's *Lucky Jim*, John Braine's *Room at the Top*, William Cooper's *Scenes from Provincial Life*, C. P. Snow's *The Masters*, Iris Murdoch's *Under the Net*, Anthony Powell's *The Acceptance World*, Alan Sillitoe's *Saturday Night and Sunday Morning*, Graham Greene's *The Quiet American* ('or *The End of the Affair*, if you prefer, in the interests of UK/USA accord') and Angus Wilson's *Anglo-Saxon Attitudes*. Rubin had evidently jibbed at *The Alexandria Quartet* on grounds of length and, perhaps, availability, but Golding insists that something by Durrell is 'a must', and suggests having *Justine* instead. He is, he says, 'prepared to hand round my own copies! (Actually they're Ann's own copies)' if the students have trouble tracking any down. He also puts in a personal plea for T. H. White's *The Once and Future King*. The examination paper ('English 350: British Post-War Novelists') that he set at the end of the course indicates that his second list, including *The Quiet American, The Alexandria Quartet* and *The Once and Future King* was eventually settled on, though one of the Hollins students who did the course recalls that they never got round to *Scenes from Provincial Life*.

His letter of 14 May expresses complete bewilderment about the lectures arranged for him in other universities – 'I'm now quite bogged down ... I simply don't know where I am ... Sorting the various letters I can't make out what the state of the poll is.' So he asks Rubin (who must by now have deduced that forward planning was not his new friend's strong point) to write and accept invitations on his behalf for the dates he thinks best: 'Then if I don't agree later, it'll be my fault and I'll have to put up with it.' He adds that he would like to do the Ewing Lectures 'whenever you think is most convenient'. These were annual public lectures at the University of California at Los Angeles – the 1960 lectures had been given by Angus Wilson, whose book *The Wild Garden or Speaking of Writing* (1963) was based on them. For Golding, agreeing to give them was a shot in the dark, as he had never given an academic lecture, let alone at a top American university. 'Could you tell me how many words constitute a public lecture?' he asked Rubin, adding, 'If I do the Ewing lectures I'd talk about Euripides which I should enjoy doing, even if the audience found it presumptuous.' As we shall see, he did not talk about Euripides but about himself, and perhaps Rubin was instrumental in steering him towards this more acceptable subject.

He and Ann left England on 14 September on the *Queen Elizabeth*, and he sent back to Karl Miller at *The Spectator* an account of the voyage that was published on 27 October. He jokes about the strict class divisions observed on board, and the comparative dullness of the middle class, to which he and Ann belong. When a gala night is proclaimed, a festival for the whole ship, he imagines the third-class passengers swilling Guinness and dancing 'Knees Up Mother Brown', and the film stars and tycoons in first class indulging in 'Lucullan orgies and Neronian debauch', while the middle class, on sitting down to dinner, find that they have been issued with small paper hats, which they bashfully don, avoiding all eye contact, and 'a confused, British silence' ensues, 'broken only by the steady champing of 400 sets of false teeth'.

After docking in New York they took an overnight train to Roanoke, of which Hollins is a suburb, and Rubin, who drove out to fetch them, recalls finding them next morning, seated in Roanoke's Norfolk and Western Railway passenger terminal, looking 'somewhat beleaguered'. Though it was a warm September morning, Golding had his overcoat on. However, Rubin was pleased at how quickly they adapted. 'Within a few days' they were becoming 'fully a part of the college community'. A letter Golding wrote to du Sautoy headed 'Monday 1st November' (though actually 1 November 1961 was a Wednesday, which suggests he was still rather disoriented) brims with excitement about their new life.

> We have learned to drink bourbon, smoke cigarettes with filters, say 'you all', and accept an attitude which is surely as near as nothing to pernicious Anglophilia. We have so much time! Two lectures a week on the modern British novel (hard going) and the rest of the time for writing, if it weren't for the parties, the mountain climbs, the trips to Williams Burg, the parties, the skyline drive, the parties, the local customs, the parties – but we have really settled down.

Ann, he adds, 'can't find anything to do'. She is 'stunned' by the siestas, and 'the general feeling that there are forty eight hours in any one day – and then another forty eight tomorrow'. He is off to lecture at Union College, Schenectady, on the 6th and 7th, Mount Holyoke College, South Hadley, Massachusetts on the 8th, and Dartmouth College, Hanover, on the 9th and 10th (these were the first three engagements on the list drawn up by Rubin and McCallum), and since du Sautoy is over in New York seeing publishers he hopes they might meet up – though he admits that 'we haven't yet got used to the scale of things, and at the moment just have an idea that we shall be in the top right hand corner of America'.

The account of Hollins he sent back to Miller, published in *The Spectator* on 24 November, was just as enthusiastic. It was an 'ineffably peaceful' place, 'lapped about by fields and set down in a fold of the

Alleghenies'. They had arrived in an Indian summer. Every leaf was loaded down with cicadas. Eagles and buzzards floated high in the hot air. Blue jays played in the fields, and a mocking bird balanced on a fence by their window, 'like a lady with a parasol on a tightrope'. A mountain bear had wandered into the town the day they arrived, but was anaesthetized and taken home. The Hollins estate covered several hundred acres. The architecture was colonial – 'white pillars and porches' grouped round a grass quadrangle with splendid trees. Drifts of girls 'pathetic and charming, giggling or absorbed', pass to and fro along the paths. 'Like all women students they are inveterate, comically obsessive note-takers, who hope by this method to avoid the sheer agony of having to think for themselves'. They are rich – it costs £1,000 a year to keep a girl here – and 40 per cent of them leave to get married before completing their studies. Servants in the college are all black, and live in a nearby hamlet. They seem proud of the college, and there is goodwill on both sides – yet, he observes, north of them is an area where public schools have shut down to avoid integration, and to the south the railway has segregated waiting rooms.

Hollins students remember their surprise that Golding was on their campus. By autumn of 1961 he had become 'a literary superstar', and they had a feeling that if he had anticipated the enormous popularity of *Lord of the Flies* with American students he might not have pitched up at Hollins at all. They could see he was in great demand and 'spent a lot of time lecturing at other institutions all over the States'. But he was not standoffish, and he joined in student activities. It was a Hollins tradition that on 'Tinker Day', in October, bells rang, classes closed, and the entire college climbed Tinker Mountain, part of the Blue Ridge Hills that nudge the campus. There were 'picnics, songs and general silliness'. When Golding, in a 'bold knitted jumper', arrived at the top looking 'somewhat bemused', Professor Rubin, perched on a rock, tried to get the girls to sing 'Rule Britannia', not with entire success. On another occasion Golding swept his class off to the library to play them his LP of Flanders and Swann's *At the Drop of a Hat*. At the time none of the Hollins students knew of Flanders and Swann (though they toured America in 1960–61), and one of them recalls that her greatest pleasure was seeing Golding relish the songs himself – 'especially the Gnu'.

None of the Hollins students was familiar with contemporary English writers either, and Golding's reading list was 'a delight'. His lectures were formal. In Professor Rubin's course on the Modern Novel he spoke on *Lord of the Flies* and suffered evident 'discomfort' when a naïve girl in the front row praised the book effusively. On the other hand, when an opinionated male graduate student began pointing out what he saw as flaws and contradictions in the symbolism, imagery and thematic development, Golding hit back, citing passages and images, and making it clear that he had thought out every detail and implication in the book. In another lecture he expressed his passion for classical Greek, 'evoking the joy of learning and reading it'. His classes, as opposed to lectures, were fairly loose – he discussed the books and encouraged questions. The students were told to write a paper, on any subject they chose, of any length, at any time they felt like handing something in. At the end of the semester he asked them to write on whichever of the authors they would like to pursue. One of the four male graduate students (the one with the only beard on campus apart from Golding's, which Golding was thought to resent) answered by explaining why he did not want to pursue any of them – and got the only A in the class. They gathered that Golding did not like teaching. He frequently looked at his watch. 'When the bell rang, he shot out the door like a mad thing.'

Then there were the creative writing classes on Wednesday evenings in the Rubins' basement on Faculty Row, where students took it in turns to provide pretzels and beer, and read and criticize manuscripts. At one of these a student, Betsy Payne, was sketching him while he spoke, and he stopped in mid-sentence and demanded to see the drawing. She 'wasn't too embarrassed' because she thought it 'pretty good'. 'Is that how you see me?' he demanded, 'Santa Claus?' After that they became friends. Judy remembers Betsy, whom she met a couple of years later when she visited Ebble Thatch with her parents, as 'tall, leggy, good looking (an understatement)', with 'a splendid head of red-gold hair', and she thinks her father was 'smitten'. His journal shows that he was still dreaming of the 'strangely glittering gold of her hair' ten years later. With another student, who was thinking of applying for a Fulbright, he took the trouble to arrange a consultation where he suggested Thomas Traherne's poetry as a dissertation subject.

In the next few months he was to sit in on creative writing classes in several American universities, and his general impression was not good. The average class, he estimated, contained a few students who had no business to be there at all, then there was a section, 'bearded and jeaned', with ambition and no talent. The rest tended to have a spark of ability which was, however, no more than a part of general intelligence – they would be fairly good at anything. Very occasionally he would come across a 'genuine, bumbling, fettered, uncertain, groping writer' whose work might well lack the smoothness and finish of less-gifted classmates. The account of a typical creative-writing session he sent back to *The Spectator* is comic, characterizing the professor as a mealy mouthed creep, cringingly tactful towards the arrogant young male whose work is under discussion. But to live with a class, rather than dropping in on one in passing, is, he admits, a different experience, and he avows that he never felt his own students – 'Mark, Anna, Jane, Ben, Betsy, Geneli' – could 'commit anything like these idiocies'.

In December another round of visiting lectures began. On the 1st he was in Nashville, Tennessee, to talk at Vanderbilt University, then on the 10th he found himself waiting at a fog-bound New York airport – alone: he was travelling without Ann – for a flight to Los Angeles where, the next day, he was to give the first Ewing Lecture. As he wrote it up for *The Spectator*, this trip was a three-day cultural helter-skelter, with jet-lag so severe he felt his body and soul had come apart. They eventually took off at midnight – his first ever flight, apart from those distant days in an Avro Avian. He sinks two bourbons before dinner, and is flattered to be recognized, from English TV, by an air hostess who speaks 'Kensingtonian'. He arrives, sleeps, wakes, is driven to the 'Del Monica heights' (presumably the Santa Monica mountains) to see film-star mansions razed by forest fires, and swimming pools on stilts over a gorge, takes a look at the Pacific, lunches, learns that the university has its own police force and bus service, gives his first lecture, goes to a party after dinner where there are original Beerbohm cartoons on the wall, sleeps, wakes, is taken to see a Mormon temple, a colossal medical centre, a beach, gives his second lecture, pleads for an evening in bed but sneaks off to dine alone on a filet mignon and a bottle of burgundy-type wine, sleeps, wakes, is taken to see the San Gabriel mountains with snow on them, and the Chinese Theatre, and pavements with film-stars' hand- and footprints set in them, and Hollywood, and Mae West's hotel, and the William Andrews Clark Memorial Library, where for 'ten ridiculously exciting seconds' he holds the manuscript of *The Importance of Being Earnest* in his hands, gives his third lecture, goes to a faculty party, is taken to an English-type restaurant where, to make him feel at home, the bartender and all the waiters are dressed in full hunting kit, is rushed to the airport, and flies back to New York.

Unlike Angus Wilson, he never turned his Ewing Lectures into a book, but they survive in a recording as well as a transcript. An American voice introduces him ('today only seven years after the appearance of that first novel Mr Golding is recognized as one of the major contemporary novelists of England'), then, when the applause has died down, Golding's voice takes over. Nervousness makes him sound clipped, slightly sardonic, and very British. A surprise is his 'BBC' accent ('beckground' for 'background'), though no doubt it was common enough among educated speakers in 1961. The first lecture is called, indeed, 'Background', and aims to explain how he has become the sort of writer he is – interested in ideas rather than people, and in seeing mankind in a cosmic perspective rather than an everyday social setting. He describes his parents as high minded, preoccupied with the nature of the universe, women's rights, and the future of the League of Nations, but also victims of 'that vicious system that grades people socially'. They had to keep up appearances on a small income or, as he puts it, they endured 'the dreadful poverty of a position which was just that bit more costly than we could afford'. Consequently they kept themselves to themselves and he grew up 'detached from society'. There were certain children he was not allowed to play with, and vice versa, so 'the nature of Man with a capital M' came to seem 'a more urgent matter to me than actually meeting people'. When he read Dickens's *Pickwick Papers* as a child he could see that Dickens was, by contrast, actually interested in people, and since he assumed that this was the only way to write a novel it put him off trying. To ask which previous novelists he is indebted to would be meaningless, therefore – and is, indeed, he maintains, always meaningless: 'no novelist is influenced in more than his punctuation by any other novelist'. What nourishes the novel is poetry, and what novelists try to do is capture in their writing those moments that poets and poetic dramatists 'seem to enjoy as by divine right'. The most potent influence on him has been not the English novel but ancient Greek, and the peculiarity of the Greek language, as he sees it, is its transparency: its words 'seem to lie right against the face of real things'. Also the Greeks were, as he is, occupied with man in a cosmic setting: Aeschylus, with divine, cosmic and human law, and Sophocles, in *Oedipus Rex*, with causality. Euripides, however, destroyed belief in the old gods with a sort of Shavian savagery, and subjected their myths to the withering, reductive power of the intellect. This was, Golding contends, mistaken, for he sees myth as the highest of forms, and its power lies in its ability to outrun the intellect. 'Myth is a feeling towards something which we know to be significant and cannot tell why.' If myth can be explained intellectually it becomes allegory, which is 'a dead thing', as evidenced by 'the rather boring poems of Edmund Spenser'. Myth is vital for life, not just literature: 'Where there is no mythology the people perish.'

Contentious, highly personal, and reflecting his own disappointment at not being a poet, this lecture was also oddly out of key with his second, which was called 'Fable'. For 'Fable', later published in *The Hot Gates*, explicates *Lord of the Flies* in terms that seem indistinguishable from allegory – the dead airman represents 'history', and Simon is 'a Christ figure', much as Golding had told Frank Kermode in the June 1959 interview. However, he goes on to admit that he no longer thinks (as he thought at the time of the Kermode interview), that the author knows best what his work means. Readers, he now believes, may know better, and this wide range of interpretability may make fable, he implies, as inexplicable as myth. Also new in 'Fable' are the autobiographical passages. He recounts that he used to believe, before the war, in the perfectibility of social man – that all social ills could be removed by reorganizing society ('It is possible', he adds, perhaps thinking of his happiness among the young Americans at Hollins in the last few months, 'that today I believe something of the same again'). However, the Second World War and its atrocities destroyed that trust, and he came to see that 'man produces evil as a bee produces honey'. He wrote *Lord of the Flies* out of a belief in original sin, derived not from books but from watching how people behave. He lays claim, too, to a kind of myth-ical or mystical experience while writing the book. The words spoken by the pig's head to Simon were dictated to him by something beyond himself: 'The pig's head spoke. I know because I heard it.'

He includes in 'Fable' an anecdote to illustrate how history distorts human emotions. Ann and he had, he says, recently been driven down through Virginia by a scholarly southerner, an 'educated and rather cynical man', who explained, while driving at moderate speed, the events of the American Civil War in the area. But when they came to the place where Lee's Confederate Army had surrendered to Grant their guide grunted, 'Aw, shucks!' and sped past at 75 mph. History of this kind, felt in the blood and bones, is, Golding concludes, always pernicious.

The scholarly southerner was, in fact, Louis Rubin, whose own account of the incident differs markedly. In the fall of 1961 he had to drive from Hollins to Williamsburg, and invited the Goldings to come along. The route passed a Virginia State Police station on Highway 460, then turned north on a less travelled road. Highway 460 was always well patrolled so he kept to the 50 mph limit, but after the turn-off he accelerated to 60–65 mph, and was going at that speed when they passed the entrance to the McLean House, so he had to explain its his-torical significance rapidly before they had left it behind. The Goldings began laughing, which puzzled him, so he asked why, and it became clear they thought his atavistic impulses had kicked in. Golding embroidered the incident when he wrote it up – the 'Aw, shucks!' and the 75 mph were invented – and four years after *The Hot Gates* came out someone sent Rubin a book entitled *Brain Storms: A Study in Human Spontaneity*, by Wayne Barker MD, in which his behaviour, as described by Golding, is treated as a neuropsychiatric episode exemplifying 'those sudden whirls of spontaneous activity by which the brain copes with threats to the continuity of our everyday living'.

Golding was diffident and disliked pontificating, so turning his lectures into stories, or tall stories, came naturally to him as lecturing did not. By the time he got to his third lecture, entitled 'Prospect', he was running out of new things to say. The first part of it is virtually a repeat of the essay about the decline of education and of culture that had been published in the *Times Literary Supplement* in June 1960 as 'On the Crest of the Wave'. Having come to the end of that material he falters, or pretends to: 'the next word I have written down here appears to be "drink". I can't think what...'. That gets a laugh, and he goes on to imagine a mural painting of a more hopeful scene than the British one he has been outlining. He depicts an American 'army of education', with creative writers in the van, and he would like, he says, to think of his own books as ammunition for that army: 'I saw in the New York Times on Sunday that I am required reading in more than fifty colleges in the United States.' He has started a new novel, he tells his audience, and is going to take them completely into his confidence, 'so if it never gets written, or is a flop, it will be your fault'. The novel will 'explore a symbol' – Salisbury cathedral and its spire. Anecdotes about the cathedral follow – about Lord Ferrars who was hanged for murdering his steward in a fit of pique and used to have a wire noose on his tomb; about the sixteenth-century organist who chased the Dean down the aisle and cut his throat in the cloister. Then come anecdotes about the spire – which Trollope in his novels about Barchester (alias Salisbury) did not stop to consider. It is a wonder. It has no foundations, but floats on water meadows. It tries all the time to burst apart the tower under it (as 'must be obvious to anyone who listens to it talking'), and across the room at its base is a gigantic steel tie. If you take a tuning fork and a mallet, and hit the tie with the mallet and the stone with the tuning fork, they should emit the same note. If they do not, you should vacate the building. It is not vertical, but leans, though no more than it did in the seventeenth century when Sir Christopher Wren measured the angle. Even before that the piers at the bottom, 'four immense pillars of Purbeck marble', had begun to bend. Visitors do not always like this being pointed out, and organists hesitate before letting go with their thirty-two-foot pipes. Having dissolved his lecture into stories, he tells his audience that, though very little of his new novel is written, and what is written may not be in the published book, nevertheless he will read them, as the conclusion of his lecture, the first two pages. The 1,000-word introduction he reads is quite different from anything in the published novel. It is spoken by a twentieth-century narrator, 'at a hot point of the Cold War, when nothing is even as certain as usual', who describes the spire as it appears in various weather conditions – when 'dry heat and light bleach the stones to a bone white against blue sky', or when it is 'lit from below by the reflection from twenty acres of open daisies'. He remembers how its lightning conductors 'glittered like a chain of emeralds against the smoke from burning Dunkirk', and he thinks of how it has loomed over the lives of various local people – the Dean of Barchester, 'with the spire as his pride and headache', a surveyor, a painter, a housewife, a garage-hand, a consulting engineer. 'Whoever we were, within the radius of that influence, we had the heart of some indefinable matter standing at our shoulders.' Perhaps these were to be the characters in the version of *The Spire* he never wrote.

One person who would have been relieved to hear that *The Spire* was in production was Charles Monteith. Golding had not let him have a typescript before leaving England, as he had hoped, but had written on 3 September to say that 'Barchester Spire' would ultimately be two long short stories, or possibly three, or even four. On 28 October he wrote from Hollins, starting 'You are going to hate this letter' and explaining that he had written the first part of 'Barchester Spire' three times, but had at last seen what 'the proper scope of it is'. There is 'a proper book there', but it 'needs concentration, discovery, and even love: all of which I mean to give it'. He adds, 'this seems right to me – I mean, not snatching at quick returns as I did with The Brass Butterfly'. 'I don't hate it at all,' Monteith reassured him: it was excellent news that 'Barchester Spire' was going to be a real book, and he must not worry about missing the spring 1962 list – it will 'tower over the autumn one'. There was even better news in February. On the 28th Golding wrote from Hollins, 'After shilly-shallying and mucking around, I got down to the book and wrote it (between fifty and sixty thousand words) in a fortnight and am properly flaked out'. He would need to reconsider and rewrite but it would be in time for autumn publication, and he had thought up 'a gorgeous title, though Ann says she doesn't see how you can use it. What do you think? AN ERECTION AT BARCHESTER.' Monteith diplomatically feigned mirth ('AN ERECTION AT BARCHESTER rolls us in the aisles') but suggested an alternative might be necessary. More sincerely he greeted *The Spire*'s completion as 'absolutely wonderful' – though it had, in fact, already missed the deadline for the autumn list. On the family front he reported that David had had a drink with him in Oxford the weekend before last and seemed 'in excellent form'. 'I had Brian Aldiss in at the same time and they talked SF to each other like mad.'

Meanwhile Golding's punishing schedule of off-campus lectures and readings continued. In February 1962 he talked at Smith College and Williams College, both in Massachusetts, and at Yale, where he received a standing ovation. In March he was at Johns Hopkins University, Baltimore, and at Pennsylvania State. Towards the end of March David, on vacation from Oxford, and Judy flew out to join their parents. Golding bought a Chevrolet that had belonged to an old lady and not clocked up many miles, and the day after the children's arrival they set out westwards through the Texas panhandle, and on across the continent from Virginia to San Francisco. He lectured at Stanford University on 3 April, and at the University of California at Berkeley on the 4th. It was while they were in San Francisco that William Golding Ltd was formed. The first meeting of directors (Golding, Ann, David and Judy) took place in a Chinese restaurant – a rather consciously bohemian choice, Judy suspects, to offset her father's misgiving that he was joining the capitalists. David and she initially blocked the election of a chairman, until Golding decided that Ann, as secretary, had a casting vote. From San Francisco they drove across the Golden Gate Bridge and north to Seattle, where they stayed from 9–13 April and he lectured at the University of Washington. Then came another marathon drive across the Rockies and the Dakotas, stopping off on the way at the site of the Battle of Little Bighorn, where the Cheyenne Indians annihilated a detachment of US cavalry in 1876, and where the Goldings bought a book by American Indians saying what really happened. This brought them to the University of Minnesota at Minneapolis, where he talked on 18 April, and down to Chicago and across to Ohio, where he had engagements at Ohio Wesleyan University, Delaware, on 27 April and at Kenyon College on the 28th. David and Judy flew home from Cleveland, but Golding and Ann headed for New York, where he gave the Harcourt, Brace Lecture. On 8 May he lectured at the University of Kentucky in Lexington, and on the 10th at Purdue University in Lafayette, Indiana, before returning to Hollins. It is hard to estimate exactly how much ground they covered on this trip but it was certainly not less than 6,500 miles and they did it inside five weeks, fitting in nine reading or lecturing engagements on the way.

His new popularity in America put Faber and Faber in a better position for bargaining with American publishers, and he was soon spurring them to do so. On 3 January 1962 he wrote to du Sautoy's assistant Giles de la Mare that wherever he went on campuses sales of his books were good and everyone seemed 'very interested'. Further, the *New York Times* in December had reported that paperback sales of *Lord of the Flies* had reached 48,000. Yet *Pincher Martin* was out of print, bookshops were having to import English copies of *The Inheritors*, and *Free Fall* seemed unobtainable. De la Mare and du Sautoy evidently consulted over this. It was becoming clear to both of them that other American publishers were eager to promote Golding if Harcourt, Brace were not. Du Sautoy had heard from Ellis Amburn at Coward-McCann that they wanted to publish an American edition of *The Inheritors*, and were bringing out a new de luxe hardback of *Lord of the Flies*, to celebrate its paperback sales, with drawings by Leonard Baskin and an introduction by (they hoped) T. S. Eliot (in the end it was written by E. M. Forster).

Coward-McCann were not the only interested party. On 18 January du Sautoy wrote to Golding to say that the Atlantic Monthly Press had offered a $5,000 joint advance for *The Inheritors* and Golding's next novel. He had phoned John McCallum at Harcourt, Brace, but he would offer only $3,500 (and thought this 'generous'). Did Golding, du Sautoy asked, want to stay with Harcourt, Brace or go over to Atlantic Monthly? His own advice, rather surprisingly, was to stay with Harcourt, Brace. Golding replied that he would take du Sautoy's advice but felt Harcourt, Brace were asking for his 'academic prestige' without being prepared to pay for it. They had been 'very casual so far' about promoting him. 'Sorry to sound so sordid, but wherever I've been people have complained of not being able to get my books.' 'I'm living the kind of life I've never lived before,' he added, 'lectures, travel, parties, more travel – I can see my ego getting monstrous ... thank God I'll be a normal cottage-dwelling, pen-pushing, respectable citizen in no more than five months.' 'We'll give Harcourt, Brace one more chance to pay $5,000,' du Sautoy decided. 'They have plenty of money and are planning to build their own skyscraper in New York.' So, on 30 January, he wrote to McCallum to say that, though Fabers would like Harcourt, Brace to remain Golding's American publisher, they could not accept 'a cent less than $5,000' for *The Inheritors* and his new book. After all, Golding was, du Sautoy pointed out, a 'good investment for the future' with his appeal to the rising generation in colleges and universities. 'In the meantime, even a genius has to exist!'

The letter that came back from McCallum was breathtaking. Actually, on research, he had found, he said, that Harcourt, Brace already had a contract to publish *The Inheritors*. So they would offer a $5,000 advance but it would be for 'Barchester Spire' and Golding's next novel after that. He added that he had recently dined with Golding and Ann after his lecture at Yale, which had received an 'extraordinary' reception, and was proposing, with Golding's approval, that Princeton and Harvard should invite him to teach during the 1963–4 academic year. The implication that Golding's success was due in no small part to him was eventually spelt out quite baldly: 'As you know many of the lectures Golding is now giving across the country were arranged by me.' Faced with this effrontery, du Sautoy consulted Richard Gilson at MCA Artists Ltd, Fabers' agent in New York, who advised him that it was not true that Harcourt, Brace had a contract for *The Inheritors*. Their contract for *Pincher Martin* obliged them to publish *The Inheritors* when hardback sales of *Pincher Martin* had reached 7,500, but, as they were still far short of that total, Fabers should stick to their guns and insist on $5,000 for *The Inheritors* and 'Barchester Spire'. At the same time du Sautoy received a letter from Golding describing his dinner with the ingratiating McCallum ('he was amiable – so much so that I felt a bit of a swine'), and confirming that his reception at Yale ('boys sitting in the aisles and a crowd outside who couldn't get in') had made his market value among American students quite apparent.

Armed with this information du Sautoy wrote to McCallum on 16 February, repeating his demand for a $5,000 advance for *The Inheritors* and 'Barchester Spire', and McCallum accepted defeat with an ill grace. That was the end of Golding's and du Sautoy's trouble with American publishers for the time being. Harcourt, Brace published

The Inheritors on 25 July and McCallum wrote to du Sautoy on the 30th to say that the early reviews had been 'splendid'. In November Golding got a letter from Walter J. Minton, president of G. P. Putnam's Sons, who published Capricorn paperbacks, to say that the paperback of *Pincher Martin* had sold 35,000 since publication at the end of June, and that the plates of the *Lord of the Flies* paperback had literally worn out, so they had had to reset the whole book, and of the first 60,000 of the new printing only 10,000 remained. Scores of colleges and high schools had placed orders for it during August and September for their survey-of-literature courses.

In the following months various accounts of the extraordinary American publishing history of *Lord of the Flies* appeared in the English and American press. The hardback published by Coward-McCann in 1955 had sold only 2,383. The 1959 Capricorn paperback sold 4,300 by the end of the year, 15,000 in 1960, 75,000 in 1961 and, according to some estimates, half a million by the end of 1962. Several cultural commentators noted that Golding's novel had replaced Salinger's *Catcher in the Rye* as the bible of the American adolescent. The celebrated American critics Lionel and Diana Trilling declared that the transference from the woes of Salinger's spoiled, self-pitying teenager to the rigorous confrontation with original sin in Golding's book amounted to nothing less than a 'mutation' in American culture. Whatever the reasons for this, it seems clear that the anti-war tenor of *Lord of the Flies* helped to ensure its profound impact on the young at a time when (as *The Spire*'s narrator in the third Ewing Lecture had noted) the Cold War was hotting up. Construction of the Berlin Wall began in August 1961, the month before Golding arrived in America. The Cuban Missile Crisis erupted in October 1962. By that time Golding and Ann were back home. On 9 June he told Monteith that he was sitting down to rewrite 'Barchester Spire' with 'an immense feeling of freedom out of having given up teaching'. He felt 'a new man, in fact, which may be a bad thing'.

19

The Spire

Golding's 'immense feeling of freedom' had its downside. Suddenly finding his days empty, after sixteen years of schoolteaching, gave limitless scope for perfectionism and self-doubt, and *The Spire* had a more tormented birth than any of his previous novels. The three years between mid-1961, when it was first conceived as a 'funny' short story, to the publication in April 1964 of what Rebecca West in the *Sunday Telegraph* greeted as a 'superb tragedy', were fraught with reconsideration, exasperation and near despair. When, in February 1962, he had put an end to 'shilly-shallying and mucking about', and written a fifty- to sixty-thousand-word draft in a fortnight, he was buoyed up by daily contact with the admiring young students at Hollins. He was still full of confidence in May, and feeling triumphant after giving his Harcourt, Brace lecture in New York, when he told John McCallum that he could have the final typescript, for simultaneous American and English publication, by December 1962. 'A six-month period in quiet waters' at Ebble Thatch would, he reckoned, be just what he needed to finish it off. His 'new man' letter to Monteith in June still sounds optimistic. But by November 1962 he confessed that he was in 'a state of misery' over the novel.

It is not clear what had gone wrong. But a return of his terror of adverse criticism was a factor. The eager young admirers at Hollins had vanished, and, in the silence they left, he was reminded of how much he liked praise. On 14 November he wrote to du Sautoy about a letter from G. P. Putnam's Sons in New York which suggested they might publish a book of scholarly essays on *Lord of the Flies*. 'It *would*', he confessed, 'be rather fun to be treated as a defunct immortal (do you remember Armada Philip used to have requiems sung for him while he lay in his coffin?) ... If you want the honest truth, I *like*

reading about myself provided the verdict is good or at least respectful.' Besides his misery over the stalled novel there were other irrita-
tions. Monteith was pestering him ('since you have thrown off the
shackles of schoolmastering') to edit an anthology of modern poetry
for schools, and to write an introduction and notes to a school edition
of *The Brass Butterfly*. He replied grumpily that he had not kept up with
modern poetry and, as for *The Brass Butterfly*, 'oughtn't we face the fact
squarely that this play was a flop which when produced bored even the
author'. Instead of dropping the anthology idea, Monteith came back
with the suggestion that Golding might co-edit it with W. H. Auden. In
addition to these distractions, Ebble Thatch was no longer ideal for
concentration. Building work was in train, including the resiting of the
kitchen and the construction of a panelled dining room. 'We are
slightly hysterical here,' he told Monteith, 'workmen march through
everywhere like the kings in Macbeth'. Perhaps, too, he was disappointed by his editor's rather dry response to his suggestion that he
might publish a book of his own poems. 'About the poetry', Monteith
had replied, 'I would counsel caution.'

The stress of all this probably explains the unfortunate conclusion to
a dinner in All Souls to which Monteith invited him at the end of the
same week, on Saturday, 1 December. What actually happened is
unclear, but it sounds, from his letter of apology, as if it was nothing
worse than getting drunk and falling down some stairs, which cannot
have been an unprecedented event at an All Souls dinner. But the
letter, written on 6 December, is deeply contrite. He promises to 'act
like a civilized person' in future: 'My cracked nose and ribs I have
passed off by airy reference to the fog, ice, and the nearness to me of
the steering wheel ... It is all very humiliating. I beg that we may never
refer to the actual circumstances again.' December was the month by
which he had promised delivery of *The Spire*, and there was plainly no
chance of that. 'We are having the *devil* of a time here, what with
having the house altered and difficulties with the children – or young
people, as I suppose I should now call them,' he complained to du
Sautoy. Things were no better by January 1963. He had, he admitted,
lost du Sautoy's last letter amid the 'wreckage of house alterations and
general uproar ... I am just going through a black period and can only

hope to come out the other end'. The novel 'stands there, remote and mocking. I *must* do what amounts to a half-rewrite heaven help me.'

Meanwhile the business of a projected collaboration with Auden had dragged on. Had he thought any more about it? nagged Monteith in October 1962. Golding suggested in reply that he and Auden might meet in Oxford. If so, he could take the opportunity to give David a square meal, 'which judging by his ghastly digs the poor chap probably needs'. Seemingly this did not work out, so Monteith proposed a meeting at a Faber party on 19 October. In the event, he immediately took against Auden, privately comparing his gouged face (which its proprietor described as a 'wedding cake left out in the rain') to the 'new map of the Indies' in *Twelfth Night*. They disagreed over schoolboy behaviour in *Lord of the Flies*, Auden opining that the older boys would have taken the young ones under their wing and protected them, a view Golding would certainly have regarded as both sentimental and ignorant. He managed to miss a second meeting with Auden in New York in March 1963 and a third in London in April. After that Monteith gave up.

A bigger obstacle to progress on *The Spire* was another lecturing trip to America in February and March 1963. As before, he sailed out on the *Queen Elizabeth*, and Monteith caught sight of his picture on display in the Cunard offices in Lower Regent Street, among those of other distinguished people disembarking in New York. But this time Ann did not accompany him. Judy was suffering from what she describes as a nervous breakdown, and her mother stayed behind to look after her. Golding felt lonely, seated in a corner of the restaurant with a table to himself, 'unless you count three chrysanthemums which decorate it', but he found that there were twenty-six Hollins girls on the same ship, Betsy Payne among them, travelling back from the first semester of a year-abroad programme, spent mainly in Paris. They were in tourist class, but some of them managed, strictly against Cunard regulations, to sneak up to the first class to see him, and he invited Betsy to dine with him one evening. He admitted in a letter home to Ann and the children that this had been a foolish thing to do, but he had to go through with it despite his embarrassment and the conspiratorial grins of the stewards. Betsy was too seasick to eat anything, but the grandeur of the first class impressed her ('even tourist was pretty amazing to us'). They kept in touch when she returned to finish her year in Paris, and for several years after that. When her parents came to visit her in October 1963, all the way from Shreveport, Louisiana, the three of them crossed to England and drove out to Ebble Thatch for lunch. For her twenty-first birthday he sent her a copy of *The Two Deaths of Christopher Martin*, inscribed 'For Betsy, who is old enough to vote, and to have a latch key, and to read this book. With the author's love. William Golding'.

When they docked at New York he got 'very frightened and lonely waiting at the barrier', but was delighted to find that Ann Logan, wife of the Principal of Hollins College, had come to meet him. 'I hugged her with what amounted to a cry of Mother!' and she saw him to his hotel. But almost as soon as she had left him he succumbed to a severe attack of flu, his temperature soared, and what followed was a 'sheer terrible fantasy, a Pincher-ish fantasy'. The phone kept ringing, 'there were television people, photographers, publishers, Esquire, Harpers, Holiday, Stage people, who rang and rang'. He felt helpless to say anything but 'yes', and he would find himself sitting 'between two men at a bar with my coke in front of me and they would be putting a proposition to me with rectangular grins'. Late one night he was dropped off near his hotel and got lost and wandered deserted streets, bemused by the 'strange, undulant screaming' of police and ambulance sirens, which he imagined were 'like one of Blake's terrifying horizontal angels'. John McCallum wanted to get him a doctor, but when he discovered it would cost $1,000 he decided to make do with a bottle of aspirin, and Edith Haggard, the Curtis Brown New York rep ('a delightful lady of sixty-five or so, who smokes cigarettes in a sort of lorgnette held delicately between two fingers') showed him how to fix the phone so that no one could get through. When he felt well enough he took a train to the Institute of Contemporary Arts at Washington, but after a single lecture he had to give up and flew to Roanoke, where the kindly Logans (who were to remain friends for life) 'coddled' him until he was fit to go back and complete his programme. He sailed home on the *Corinthia*, docking on 15 March. The whole ordeal brought out the extent of his dependence on Ann. 'My hands are still shaking slightly', he told Monteith, when announcing his return, 'from the terrors of an unwived journey through the eastern states.'

Progress on *The Spire* was no easier when he got back. He was, he admitted 'excruciated' over 'this damned book'. 'I've written it four times, each time getting a bit worse – now I'm writing it backwards.' He is 'looking for motives and God knows what they are'. Even Ann cannot help. She is as confused as he is 'after all these drafts'. But he expects to finish the version ('rough, at least') that he is currently writing by the end of the week, and asks if he may send it for an opinion. Monteith replied at once that he was 'more than willing' to read it, and Golding posted it on 9 May. 'Herewith this stuff. At the very best it is still wildly imperfect; but perhaps there is something there; at the worst, it must be scrapped. I've just tried this time to find a story line; and a lot is first-time cobbling.' His worries were not only about the run of the narrative ('How great are the irrelevancies?') but also about the reaction of contemporary readers ('Does a story of this sort have any right to be published at this day and age?'). As often, it was his wife's opinion that he valued most and, in this case, found heartening: 'Ann thinks some of it is good. I hope so. God knows, I don't know myself.'

Quite what worried him about the sort of story *The Spire* is remains uncertain. But perhaps he feared that modern readers would be impatient with a historical novel or with the moral struggle at its core. It is about the building of a cathedral spire (evidently Salisbury, though it is not named) – an enterprise that, in Golding mode, pits science and reason on the one hand against faith on the other. Science and reason are represented by the chief builder, Roger Mason, who points out that the foundations cannot bear the weight of a spire. It will fall and destroy the building. The spokesman for faith is the dean, Jocelin, but his motives are questionable. His passion has been aroused by a young woman, Goody Pagnall (whose shining red hair perhaps recalled Betsy Payne's) and he has arranged for her to be married to the cathedral caretaker, who is, he believes, impotent. The ruthless willpower with which Jocelin drives on the spire's 'erection' is, it is suggested, a sublimation of his lust as well as – or rather than – an expression of pure faith.

Setting the novel wholly in the Middle Ages was not Golding's original intention. He planned it as partly historical and partly in modern times. Three manuscript pages survive, of which the second and third are notes for his second Ewing Lecture, so can probably be dated in December 1961. The first page contains a plan for *The Spire*:

Jocelin – puts up spire against dictates of commonsense.
    He has experienced an astral (?) vision of the cathedral. But it becomes a symbol of human endeavour.

N.B. Jocelin's sermon is only revealed when the spire falls. It is rotted and excerpts only can be made out.

His last years writing a homily in preparation for a sermon – but he gets less and less inclined to do it as he finds fewer and fewer people do anything but recoil in horror.

(Ask Lamar what in the 14th century a man would have called the cosmos – totality.)
    Is buried at last – his monument a cadaver.

N.B. West window blowing in might be keyed into removal of west front and shortening of the nave.

Part one   Jocelin   Spire built.
[...]es   Martyrs   training.
Part two   Hannah & Paul.   Spire leans.
Part three   West window – Edward VIIth?   Ithyphallic.
Part four   The spire falls.
Epilogue – the dream   Spire fixed.

The bracketed question mark after 'astral' is in the manuscript, and 'Lamar' was Lamar Crosby, a faculty member at Hollins College. He and his wife may, it seems, have been, in part, models for Roger Mason and his wife Rachel. Though parts of this plan are enigmatic, the novel was plainly, at this stage, going to extend to modern times and, indeed, to the future when Salisbury spire will fall.

Having got the typescript of *The Spire* off his hands, Golding took Judy to Cannes to see the world premiere of Peter Brook's film of *Lord of the Flies*. 'She's been miserable lately, poor child,' he explained, 'and I hope she'll convalesce a bit.' Brook's project had started back in 1959.

When collaboration with Sam Spiegel did not work out, he found a young American, Lewis Allen, and he and his partner Dana Hodgson bought the rights for £50,000 plus a third of the producer's profits. Though they managed to attract a couple of hundred Washington backers, the budget remained tiny. They could not afford to bring boys out from England, so they cast from English boys who happened to be closer to hand. They found Ralph (James Aubrey) in an army-camp swimming pool in Jamaica and, in answer to an ad, Piggy (Hugh Edwards) sent 'a sticky *Just William* letter on lined paper. "Dear Sir, I am fat and wear spectacles ..."' Their jungle paradise was the island of Vieques off the Puerto Rican coast, owned by Woolworth's, who lent it in exchange for a screen credit. During filming they lived in what had been an old canning factory. Golding himself was not involved with the casting, script, or any element of the production.

Brook abandoned the six-hour epic script that Peter Shaffer had written for the Spiegel project and returned to the original, improvising as he went along. Roger Allan (who played Piers), remembers that while they were on the island Brook was constantly consulting a paperback copy he kept in his back pocket. They ended up with sixty hours of rushes and then spent a year editing. Brook's experience with the boys confirmed, for him, the truth of Golding's fable. Their off-screen relationships paralleled the story. Piggy, for example, came close to tears, because the other boys told him his death was going to be for real: 'They don't need you any more.' Golding's only falsification, Brook concluded, was the length of time the descent into savagery took. In the novel it is about three months, whereas, in Brook's view, if the constraints of adult presence were removed, 'the complete catastrophe could occur within a long weekend'. His dark, terrifying film has long been recognized as a masterpiece and it introduced Golding's fable to thousands who never had and never would read him.

Prior to the film's release, Golding's opinion of it seems to have vacillated. He wrote to du Sautoy from America on 5 May 1962 to say that Brook was pleased with the rough cut, and he had been shown some stills, which seemed 'very much to the point'. But in December, despondent about *The Spire*, he grumbled that he did not know when

the film would be out 'and to tell the truth, I'm not particularly interested'. His doubts vanished, though, when he first saw it, with Ann and
Judy, on 30 May 1963 at a private preview in the Hammer Theatre,
Wardour Street, and he was soon discussing with Brook a film version
of *Pincher Martin* (which never materialized). The Cannes trip in June,
was not, Judy recalls, entirely enjoyable. They had a two-bedroom
suite in a 'vast pale yellow hotel on the sea front', and there were lots
of 'hangers-on types' so that Golding got rather desperate without
Ann to act as buffer. As a 'silent and mournful teenager', still recovering from her nervous breakdown, she felt she was no substitute, so
'it was heavy going for dad, and I'm afraid he hit the bottle rather'.
However, they all went to a party on a yacht, Sam Spiegel's, she
believes, and she felt that her father was very impressed by Brook's
film, 'perhaps even astonished'. It was well received at the festival, but
did not win. The judges preferred Frank Perry's *David and Lisa*, about
two young people in a mental hospital.

Meanwhile Monteith and du Sautoy had read the typescript of what
was still provisionally titled 'Barchester Spire', and were impressed,
though both felt 'a certain amount of unravelling' was needed.
'Relieved and delighted' by their verdict, Golding asked Monteith to
keep the typescript for a few weeks and make suggestions. He agreed
to do so, and at the same time offered terms (£500 advance on 15 per
cent royalties) which Golding accepted at once. Having read and
reread the typescript, Monteith sent his promised suggestions: the
novel should not be a long continuous narrative as at present, but
divided into chapters; possible titles might be 'Dust in the Air' or 'The
Earth Creeps'; what seemed to be traces of earlier drafts should be
removed. Actually the bits Monteith picked on turned out not to be
oversights, and they remain in the printed version. But Golding
thanked him for his 'labours', and invited him down to Ebble Thatch
for the weekend of 12–14 July, when they discussed the novel. On the
17th he told Monteith over the phone that he had reshaped the first
three chapters, and hoped to have the whole book in a new form by the
end of the month – though this might not be its final form. He planned
to go to Greece in September and wanted to postpone sending the
new version till his return.

There was another duty to fulfil before his Greek holiday, however. He had agreed to be a member of the British delegation at a conference in Leningrad organized by COMES, the European community of writers. The other Britishers were Angus Wilson, John Lehmann and the Catholic intellectual Bernard Wall. The Irish novelist and playwright Kate O'Brien travelled with them. France was represented by Nathalie Sarraute and Alain Robbe-Grillet, joint promoters of the *nouveau roman*, together with Sartre and Simone de Beauvoir. The Italians sent the poet Giuseppe Ungaretti, and the Germans the poet and essayist Hans Magnus Enzensberger. The British team flew out via Hamburg and Helsinki, changing planes twice, and were accommodated in the faded luxury of a nineteenth-century hotel with vast red-curtained bedrooms and heavy marble and brass fittings. Golding and Ann's room had a grand piano, on which he played 'The Mountains of Mourne', hoping that Kate O'Brien might hear its nostalgic cadences through the wall. There were six days of round-table discussion of the high-minded, vacuous kind usual at such gatherings. Among the Russians, Ilya Ehrenburg (author of the novel *The Thaw*, which gave its name to Khrushchev's relaxation of some Soviet policies) and Aleksandr Tvardovsky (editor of the magazine *Novy Mir*, in which *The Thaw* had been published in 1954) spoke for freedom. But otherwise the standard Russian line was condemnation of modernism and other bourgeois degeneracies. There was a concluding press conference in Moscow on 9 August, at the same time as a nuclear test ban treaty was being signed by the Americans, British and Russians. After that some went home, but a select few including Golding and Ann, Wilson, Lehmann, Sartre and de Beauvoir were invited by Khrushchev to his villa by the Black Sea in Pitsunda, Georgia. They flew out next morning (without, de Beauvoir complained, so much as a cup of coffee) and were driven to the Soviet leader's estate through subtropical vegetation. He appeared wearing a Russian blouse and wide beach pyjamas, looking, Wilson records, 'like a silent-footed lumbering bear or even more a giant panda', and delivered a rambling harangue by way of a welcoming speech: 'You intellectuals of course support and serve your bourgeoisie, but *we* spat on all that ... You may call us barbarians, but we're not about to make our policies to suit you. So keep that in mind and don't try to change our minds.' After that Khrushchev gave a broad smile and the mood changed. He showed off his swimming pool, retracting its enclosing glass walls by pressing a button, and provided bathing costumes for anyone who cared for a dip. Luncheon followed (caviar, smoked salmon, trout, duck and many fine wines), then came a forty-minute reading in Russian of a satirical poem by Tvardovsky, the boredom relieved only by a break for smoking (which was not allowed in Khrushchev's presence). They were then whisked back to Moscow, and so home.

Getting back to revising *The Spire* after this magic-carpet episode cannot have been easy, but by 27 August Golding told Monteith that he would be 'home and dry' in ten days, and would then leave for a month's holiday in Greece. However, no typescript arrived in Russell Square, and when Monteith phoned Ebble Thatch on 13 September he learnt from Judy that her parents had left for Greece on the 10th. Their host was Peter Green, who, in the spring of 1963, had given up being a literary journalist, sold his London house and decamped with his wife Lal and their small children to the coastal village of Molyvos, the ancient Mythymna, on the island of Lesvos in the Aegean. Molyvos, as Green remembers it, was 'a scatter of pink, white and red houses rising in a shallow cone from the harbour, and crowned with a crumbling Genoese castle'. He moved into a 'vast and sprawling house' high on the hillside, with a view over the sea and the little square, 'where black-clad women would gather to exchange gossip as the sun went down'. It was here that the Goldings came to stay. There was a sizeable colony of expats – painters, sculptors and writers, as well as, Green recalls, 'deadbeats and eccentrics'. Freya Stark, Patrick White and Gore Vidal were among those who came and went. Golding soon established a routine. He worked at *The Spire* in the morning, and moved, around noon, to his favourite *kapheneion* to drink. Ice-cold bottles of the Greek beer known as Fix would appear, together with assorted *mezes* – grilled octopus, tomato salad, fried eggs – and the empties would soon be lining up on the table in front of him in, Green recalls, a 'soldierly row'. Among the locals he became known as 'King Fix'. The lunchtime *Bierfest* was followed in the evening by ouzo and cheap Greek brandy, and Golding would start to hallucinate. His 'visions', so far as Green could make out, were usually 'ecstatic, not demonic', and they were more likely to occur if Green played music, especially Sibelius's 7th Symphony. Drink occasionally sparked altercation. His guest, Green found, was a man with 'a perilously volcanic temperament'. Years later Golding recalled, in his journal, throwing a man onto the cobbles at Mythymna by using a Cornish wrestling hold called 'the flying mare', which allowed you to toss your opponent over your head. Green does not remember this, but he recalls that Golding 'liked provoking explosions', and once egged Green and 'the village no-good boyo' to fight. They ended up reeling out onto the balcony like a 'rolling hoop', and the next day the police sergeant asked them to keep it indoors in future.

Frustration over *The Spire* probably lay behind Golding's anger and drinking. Back from Greece, he sent Monteith 'yet another draft of this ghastly book' on 16 October, asking him to have it typed and return both typescript and manuscript, so that he could 'exercise some sort of final judgment on the whole ludicrous thing'. His letter suggests that an inner dispute between religion and reason was what caused him to be so dissatisfied with what he had written, since, whichever side prevailed, its opposite would inevitably feel thwarted. Or, as he put it to Monteith: 'I seem to have written the whole thing with one hand tied behind my back. I will *never* try to be portentous again.' The inner dispute was still active when he sent back the corrected typescript in November: 'I've cut something like two thousand words out, and ought to cut the rest, too. But this is all I've the guts to do.' In January, returning heavily corrected page proofs, he was still concerned about what he saw as the novel's 'portentous' elements. It contains, he feels, 'too much weeping ... These technicolour, vistavision cutouts are as leaky as an unstaunched wench, to quote the disgusting bard. Don't you think? Oughtn't the dustcover have a handkerchief in it somewhere?' His jokey quotation from *The Tempest*, and his questions, convey his indecision, as do the comic titles he tried out on Monteith: 'The Old Man and the See'? 'Room at the Top'? *The Spire* would 'do admirably', Monteith soberly replied.

In November 1963 Golding flew to San Francisco to speak at the National Council for Teachers of English, and stopped off in New

York on the way back. A note by Monteith of a telephone conversation they had before he left, dated 28 November, records that he was going to see 'four people who are writing books about him – Prof. Baker, Mr Hein from Swarthmore – can't remember other two'. 'Hein' was Samuel Hynes, later to become one of America's most distinguished critics and cultural historians, whose short introductory study *William Golding* came out in the Columbia Essays on Modern Writers series in 1964 (on 7 January 1964 du Sautoy sent Henry Wiggins at Columbia University Press an uncorrected proof of *The Spire* so that Hynes could mention it in his book). Golding had met Hynes when he lectured at Swarthmore, where Hynes was then teaching, and they had clearly got on well. He sent answers to questions about his life and work for Hynes to use in his book, and, in a letter of 16 October 1963, recalled a late-night party at which 'we discussed American liquor in every sense of that word'. The other two academics mentioned in Monteith's memo were probably Bernard Oldsey and Stanley Weintraub, whose *The Art of William Golding* (Harcourt, Brace, New York), appeared the following year. Together with James R. Baker's *William Golding: A Critical Study* (St Martin's Press, New York, 1965) these were the first three full-length studies of his work. They had many successors. The Gekoski-Grogan bibliography lists 103 books with him as subject published up to the year of his death. Another 285 had articles or essays about him.

It seems to have been on this trip that he attended an uncut version of Wagner's *Tristan and Isolde* at the Metropolitan Opera, for which his hosts had thoughtfully obtained tickets. It lasted four hours, and he later described it to a shocked Fiona Brown as like toothache. He also met Paul Scofield for a drink at the bar in the Algonquin, but found that they had nothing to say to each other. On the Americans, however, he made a good impression. Writing in the *New York Times Book Review* of 22 December 1963, Lewis Nichols reports that 'Here a year or so ago' (on the flu-plagued Washington visit) 'at an egg-head gathering, Mr Golding seemed detached, remote; this time he was a thing of jokes, laughter and earthy stories. He had promised to address a convention of English teachers in San Francisco and flew over to do so.' On 5 December Julian P. Muller of Harcourt, Brace told du Sautoy that he had 'lunched with Bill Golding yesterday, and he seemed in great form. He's on his way back to England at the time of this writing.' Du Sautoy wrote welcoming Golding back from his 'trans-polar flight'. It was the first time he had gone to America by air.

The Spire was due to be published on 10 April 1964, and in January he was already getting nervous. But he received, he told Monteith, a 'very nice letter about the novel from Forster' that 'almost reconciles me to publishing it, and waiting for the boys' (that is, the critics) 'to operate'. His friendship with E. M. Forster had begun in June 1962 when he wrote to thank him for the introduction he had written for Capricorn's celebratory edition of *Lord of the Flies*. Forster sent a welcoming reply and wrote again in August and September. In October he invited Golding over to lunch in King's College Cambridge (or alternatively, he added, 'I could meet you in London and lunch with you a little drearily in the Reform Club'). Golding chose King's, and the two men evidently got on well. In June 1964 Forster came over and stayed two nights at Ebble Thatch. Mark Kinkead-Weekes remembers Golding saying that Forster was so small and frail he was terrified the wind might blow him away. Forster's long, friendly, discriminating letter about *The Spire* (which Monteith had evidently sent him in page proof) is dated 4 February 1964, and written on a torn-out sheet from a 1955 desk diary – probably a sign that this is a serious letter and not a bit of social graciousness. It is, he says, a 'wonderful novel' and 'its great (literary) merit' is 'the sense of weight – stone weight', which he has come across only once before in a novel called *The Nebuly Coat* by John Meade Falkner (best known for his 1898 novel *Moonfleet*). In Falkner's novel, though, it is 'only incidental – the central pillars groan to each other despairingly in the night – but in *The Spire* it is continuous'. 'But how', Forster adds, 'I do deplore Christianity. A Hindu or Egyptian building wouldn't have created half that trouble or been so riddled with that sense of sin.'

This may have been the kind of reaction Golding anticipated when he wondered whether the book would appeal to contemporary readers, and it perhaps strengthened his determination not to give interviews about his new work. 'Bill says he's going to get out of the country before *The Spire* actually appears,' Monteith told Julian Muller in January, and

Golding and Ann did get away at the end of February – 'greatly daring', Golding joked, 'and actually going by train to Salonika. It's the influence of all those spy novels'. Maybe he really felt pursued. Hilda Lindley of Harcourt, Brace wrote to du Sautoy on 2 March that the editors of *Life* and *Time* had been anxious to fix interviews to coincide with publication of *The Spire*, and were 'highly distressed' and 'astonished' to learn that 'after weeks of fruitlessly trying to make a date with Bill Golding', he had gone off to Greece. On 19 March Mary Kersey Harvey, having vainly attempted to get a reply from Golding, wrote desperately to du Sautoy explaining that she was due to file a piece for the *Saturday Review*, and including twenty-eight questions for Golding to answer. Du Sautoy cabled back 'William Golding giving no interviews at present. Regrets cannot reply questionnaire'. The BBC's invitation to introduce and read selected passages from *The Spire* was also turned down: Golding limited himself to a reading without any commentary (the programme went out on the Third Programme on Sunday, 15 March). In America the book received a pre-publication airing in *Show* magazine. Curtis Brown's New York office sold the rights for a three-instalment serialization for $10,000 (an increase on the magazine's original offer of $8,500).

Reviews began to appear on 10 April and it soon became clear that there was radical disagreement among the critics. V. S. Pritchett in the *New Statesman* found 'obscurity, monotony and strain ... His inventiveness is dulled. His clear narrative is choked and his sense of character and human conflict is paralysed'. Francis Wyndham in the *Sunday Times* also complained of 'strain': for him Golding's sentences signalled 'a state of mystical exultation which their sense cannot support'. Richard Lister in the *Evening Standard* complained that it was 'a closed-shop of a book, strictly for members of the Symbol-Lovers-Union', and an unsigned review in *The Times* pronounced it 'wilfully tough to read'. In *Tribune* Robert Nye dismissed both the 'cult' of Golding, which he deemed 'insufferably pretentious', and *The Spire*, which amounted, for him to 'a hopelessly obscure tract on, I presume, the nature of pride'. 'Pretentious' was an epithet used also by Robert Pitman in the *Sunday Express* ('pretentious and joyless ... but fine fodder for intellectual cocktail talk') and by Kenneth Allsop in the *Daily Mail*. Golding's 'always costive' prose, Allsop opined, had 'here swollen to an incoherent bombast'. It was 'false-heroic, solemn and dull', 'a terribly bad book'. In the *Financial Times* Arthur Calder-Marshall quite lost patience: 'He is an infuriating writer, devoid of felicities, striving with a clumsy force for subtleties that occur in few other novelists' work, but that are cluttered with imprecisions a greater stylist could avoid.'

All these reviews, in their different ways, recoiled from what was original and daring about Golding's novel. They must have hurt. But if Golding had bothered to count up, which is unlikely, he would have found they were outnumbered by favourable notices. For John Wain in the *Observer*, *The Spire* was 'almost in the class of Dostoyevsky and Kafka'; for Rebecca West in the *Sunday Telegraph* it 'should become a classic'; for Isobel Murray in the *Scotsman* it was 'brilliant' and 'enthralling'; for P. N. Furbank (E. M. Forster's friend and biographer) in *Encounter* it was 'masterly'. Martin Seymour-Smith in the *Birmingham Post* predicted that it would be 'read and re-read' for its 'haunting power'. David Lodge in *The Spectator* judged it 'superbly written', and suggested that critics took against Golding because his attitude to life was uncongenial to their prejudices. Golding was the 'least facile' of writers, observed Terence de Vere White in the *Irish Times*. His writing was 'like Cezanne's painting', and he was 'touched with genius as are none of his contemporaries'. There were other enthusiastic notices in *Tatler* (Michael Ratcliffe), the *Daily Express* (Peter Grosvenor), *Country Life* (Geoffrey Grigson), *The Listener* (Elizabeth Jennings), the *Times Educational Supplement* and the *Church Times* (both unsigned). Ian Gregor in the *Guardian* pronounced it 'a great dare, coming off finely'.

Disagreement about the novel caused a spat among *The Critics* on 12 April. Karl Miller championed it, despite its 'perplexing, thorny, exalted style', and the chairman, Jack Lambert, was also positive. But Edward Lucie-Smith reported that an American critic had said Golding's book 'touches the Wuthering depths', adding that those were his 'sentiments' too: 'this is a very, very, very bad book'. Another panel member, Riccardo Aragno, chimed in, disparaging it as 'mock Gothic', but Harry Craig came out strongly in favour, and Harold Hobson ticked Lucie-Smith off for his tasteless joke. He was unrepentant, however: 'I made a joke about the book because it strikes me as being ultimately a ridiculous book'; its sexual symbolism was 'crude'. Not until Miller had ruled frostily that the American critic had been guilty of 'disgracing himself' by making 'cheap puns' did Lucie-Smith pipe down. It later turned out he had been mistaken anyway, for the American critic had made his joke about David Storey's *Radcliffe*. However, it was true that the American critical reception was, like the British, wildly inconsistent. The *New Yorker* dismissed the novel as 'a slick and lifeless equation of symbols', and Paul Picknell in *Harper's* complained that it was 'excessively didactic' with 'a curious opacity in the writing'. *Time* found it 'sometimes brilliant, sometimes tedious', and in *Newsweek* it inspired 'respect, even a kind of awe, but not love'. By contrast, Douglas Haskell in *Life* thought the descriptions 'wonderfully vivid' and the last page 'tremendous'; for Frank Kermode in the *New York Review of Books* it was 'potent, severe, even forbidding', but 'a marvel'; and for R. W. B. Lewis in the *Washington Post* 'a puzzle, a challenge, and a very considerable triumph'.

Knowing his author's sensitivity, Monteith wrote encouragingly about the reviews, highlighting the good ones and ascribing Pritchett's and Wyndham's reaction to 'temperamental incompatibility'. Besides, he pointed out, the literary editors of their papers, Karl Miller and Jack Lambert, had spoken up for the book on *The Critics*. As for 'the unspeakable Allsop' and 'the equally unspeakable Lucie-Smith', he offered to recruit 'a small but efficient underground organization' to assassinate them. Comforted, Golding wrote quite cheerfully from Scotland, where he and Ann were visiting Mark Kinkead-Weekes and Ian Gregor. He agreed that the reviews were 'for rather than against' on the whole and, changing the subject, reported that Edinburgh Castle and the Trossachs were shrouded in mist, and that the Scots really did say 'a wee while'.

Monteith was supportive again in May when George Steiner wrote a review of *The Spire* in the New York *Reporter*, regretting its 'religiosity', and implying that Faber and Faber had urged Golding to publish an earlier version. He alleged that *The Inheritors*, too, had been 'written and rewritten'. On this second point, Monteith checked with Golding, who confirmed that it was untrue. 'I wrote a longhand first draft in a month or less ... Then I typed the draft which got published straight from that in another month or less. It was the quickest book I've ever written.' This reply was, of course, rather misleading, for it omits to say that there were many differences between the manuscript and the typescript. However, Monteith was not to know that, and armed with Golding's assurance he wrote to the editor of *The Reporter* denying both Steiner's points. *The Inheritors* had not been 'written and rewritten', and though *The Spire* had been 'rewritten and reshaped very considerably and several times' in the five years since the publication of *Free Fall*, Faber and Faber did not urge Golding to publish it earlier, nor had they seen any version of it till Golding sent a typescript on 9 May 1963. This letter was published on 18 June 1964 along with Steiner's reply which insisted that 'a senior editor' at Fabers had told him he had seen an earlier draft of *The Spire* and been 'very excited' about it. In a second letter to the editor Monteith reasserted (correctly) that no draft had arrived at Fabers before 9 May 1963. He courteously sent copies of both his letters to 'Dear George' at Churchill College, Cambridge, as well as to *The Reporter*. What his letters do not say is that the novel was indeed partly rewritten in the interval between 9 May and the submission of the final typescript in November, that this rewriting was, to an extent, a response to his criticisms, and that it would have been perfectly possible for Steiner to hear from someone at Fabers, during this interval, that the novel was being rewritten. However, his letters to *The Reporter* were perfectly true so far as they went.

For many readers, as for E. M. Forster, the nerve-racking evocation of the actual construction of the spire is the novel's most memorable achievement. As the spire grows higher, the four great pillars at the crossing that bear its weight begin to bend and 'sing', and fragments of stone come 'skittering' out of them across the paving like bits of smashed ice across a frozen pond. Then, high up on the spire among the scaffolding, Jocelin feels it start to tilt:

He felt the solid stone under him move – swinging sideways and out. The dunce's cap a hundred and fifty feet tall began to rip down and tear and burst, sliding with dust and smoke and thunder, faster and faster, breaking and sheering with spark and flame and explosion,

crashing down to strike the nave so that the paving stones danced
like wood chips till the ruin buried them ... He fell with the south
west column that swung out over the cloister bent in the middle like
a leg and destroyed the library like the blow of a flail ...

But it has not happened:

He opened his eyes, sick with falling through the air. He was
clutching the parapet and the cloisters were moving below him.

It is often assumed that, to write about the building operations as he
does, Golding must have undertaken intensive historical research. But
he trusted his imagination and did not care for research. One day Frank
Kermode, who had read several treatises on medieval building in an
attempt to trace *The Spire*'s sources, asked him how he had managed
to find out so much about cathedral construction. When he put this
question they happened to be in Salisbury cathedral, standing at the
crossing beneath the spire. 'Oh,' Golding replied, 'I just came here and
said to myself, "If I were to build a spire, how would I go about it?"' 'He
was', Kermode recalls, 'very proud of that handy-man side of him.' The
critic Virginia Tiger was given a similar explanation. Golding told her
he had briefly consulted an architectural book on tower building in
Harvard University Library, but then abandoned it, preferring to trust
his own knowledge of seamanship, which included lifting heavy
weights by primitive means such as blocks, tackle and levers.

The disagreements among the critics may have stimulated public
interest in *The Spire*. In America it had sold 32,000 by 5 June, and was
'firmly entrenched in all the best-seller lists', as a jubilant Julian Muller
told du Sautoy. In Britain it topped the best-seller lists in May, and sold
nearly 13,000 by 1 October, a far better first half-year performance than
any previous Golding novel, 'despite', as Monteith remarked, 'all the
horror stories'. Golding remained wary of discussing his work, however.
He 'somewhat regretfully' declined to take part with Malcolm
Muggeridge and Donald Soper in the BBC1 TV programme *Meeting
Point* on 26 July 1964. Soon he would get away to Greece again.

20

The Hot Gates and *The Pyramid*

Before he left for Greece his next book would, if Faber and Faber had had their way, have been safely with the printer. This was the selection of his essays and reviews eventually published as *The Hot Gates*. The original idea seems to have come from America. When he was in Washington in December 1963 he heard from Walter J. Minton, head of G. P. Putnam's Sons, that they would like to publish a book of his critical essays, and he told du Sautoy that Harcourt, Brace were also interested. He was quite content to leave decisions about what should and should not be included to Monteith, aided by Kinkead-Weekes and Gregor, and sent them a batch of possible items early in 1964. The reception was not good. Both academics were in favour of abandoning the project. Gregor said it would amount to 'book-making', and Kinkead-Weekes doubted whether a volume could result 'of the standard one wants to see under Golding's name'. Monteith did not pass these views on to Golding, but suggested, in February, that the selection should be 'stiffened up' with 'one or two other major pieces'. He offered at the same time an advance of £250 on royalties of 15 per cent, with a delivery date of 3 June 1964. Meanwhile his academic advisers were sent two and a half guineas (to be divided, it seems, between them) for their trouble.

Golding took their criticisms 'very well', Monteith thought, and wrote to say that he was working on a piece called 'Egypt from My Inside', and would probably send three more, on Delphi, Olympus, and the cathedrals of southern England. 'Egypt from My Inside', the only piece to be written specially for *The Hot Gates*, is where he first tells of his hallucinatory boyhood adventure with the mummy and the museum curator. The other three items did not materialize, but the first and third of them were published in *Holiday* magazine in December 1965 and

August 1967, and reprinted in his 1981 collection *A Moving Target*. He sounds, in his reply to Monteith, ashamed of writing for *Holiday*. It 'limits one from elaborate language', he regrets, and 'frees one into the perilous swamps of outright journalism'. He did not even bother to keep copies of his *Holiday* pieces. Yet they include some of his best writing, outside the novels – vivid, variegated, full of personal reminiscence. 'Digging for Pictures', for example, published in *Holiday* in March 1963, and included in *The Hot Gates*, is about his passion for archaeology, which was stimulated by living near the Wiltshire downs, and inspired *The Inheritors*:

> For me there is a glossy darkness under the turf, and against that background the people of the past play out their actions in technicolor. Sometimes I feel as though I have only to twitch aside the green coverlet of grass to find them there. Might I not come face to face with that most primitive of Europe's men – Neanderthal Man – who once loped along the track where I used to take my Sunday walk?

He tells how he once took part with other archaeologists in a 'rescue dig' at the site of an Iron Age settlement that was to be bull-dozed and concreted over for an airstrip, and how he found the bones of an old woman with a 'beautiful skull' in which 'the pits that decay had made in her teeth had been cleaned out by time to a gemlike perfection'. He does not say when or where it happened, but it can be identified from the details he gives. It was an excavation in advance of a new runway at Boscombe Down in April and May 1949 under the supervision of Dr Marcus Stone, and Golding took David, who was eight at the time, along with him. David remembers the 'pot-boilers', not mentioned in the piece, which his father explained to him were stones, heated by the fire, and then dropped into the cooking pot to heat it. In the same essay Golding remembers visiting the ruins of Clarendon Palace, a medieval royal residence in the countryside near Salisbury, where Henry II confronted Thomas à Becket:

> When my daughter could just about walk, she found a piece of medieval glass here, a fragment iridescent as a soap bubble, and my

mind fogged out with the effort of realizing that the King or the Saint might have drunk from it.

Like the Boscombe Down rescue dig, this must have been in the late 1940s, when he was still an obscure schoolmaster. Judy recalls how she and David would play among the Clarendon Palace ruins, foraging for scraps of encaustic tile. The transformative power of Golding's imagination turns these memories into one of the most vivid and enticing essays on archaeology ever written, and it increases one's regret that he never got round to writing a book he proposed to Monteith in October 1963 – 'a set of four long essays (might call it FOUR ENTHUSIASMS) on Greek, Sailing, Music, Archaeology'.

Unsurprisingly he did not meet the June 1964 deadline for *The Hot Gates*, or even sign and return the contract, despite du Sautoy's pained reminders, until 5 January 1965. At the end of July 1964 he set off for Greece again. This time it was a family holiday. David and Judy came, and a girlfriend of David's, as well as Ann. They went in their brand-new white 3-litre Rover, flying it over, David recalls, from Lympne to Le Touquet in an old Bristol freighter with cars on the lower deck and passengers above. The car broke down in northern France in a small town called Hesdin, and they had to stay there for three days while it was repaired. This put their schedule out and they drove night and day to get to Brindisi and the ferry. Peter Green remembers watching them manoeuvre their 'vast and shiny' car out 'of the bowels of the *Karaiskakis*' onto the quayside at Mytilene. This visit seems to have been more sober than the previous year's, partly, perhaps, because the children were there, and partly because things did not work out well between David and his girlfriend, and the situation called for tactful handling by the adults. Judy celebrated her nineteenth birthday during the holiday, and Green organized a party. The event that summer that he remembers best illustrates Golding's (and David's) love of risk. They hired, David recalls, a 'rackety old boat', with worn paint, to sail anticlockwise round Lesvos into Mytilene harbour. People warned them the east coast was dangerous, and Green thinks that 'Bill checked out with the Met office and found a storm was forecast, but said to hell with it'. The storm – one of those known locally as a *phourtouna* – duly blew up, and there were fears for their safety, but skill and daring saw them through.

At the end of August Golding drove them all back via Athens, Naples, Assisi, Florence and Venice, arriving in England, as he told Monteith on 2 September, 'very brown', to find that Judy had got 'top marks' in her A-levels and was 'all set' for the University of Sussex, having 'refused Oxbridge on the grounds that they make poor girls *work*'. (Judy comments: 'I'm afraid this was a bit of window-dressing by my old dad. I didn't turn Oxbridge down – I declined to apply.') Golding was feeling more cheerful about money too, as proceeds from American sales of the *Lord of the Flies* paperback were coming through. 'Your accounts department keeps sending us *incredible* quantities of money,' he wrote in November, enclosing a new batch of essays and articles for consideration. 'I like it so much, and can only hope you'll keep it up.' Having read the newly submitted items, and mulled over the possible contents of *The Hot Gates* yet again, Monteith, Kinkead-Weekes and Gregor drew up a report covering five sides of double-page spread and arranged in columns, which lists each item to be considered, forty-two in all, followed by its publication details, their critical comments on it, and a mark on the alpha, beta, gamma scale. Monteith sent this document, with apologies for its 'schoolmasterly' appearance, to Golding in December.

As he had agreed beforehand to accept their verdict Golding did not demur, but thanked Monteith good-humouredly for his 'termly report'. Nevertheless his three advisers made some bad mistakes. The worst was excluding 'Thinking as a Hobby', one of his funniest and most incisive essays, published in *Holiday* magazine in August 1961. They decided, ineptly, that it did not 'make out its claim for a place in the book', so it has never been seen in England, though in America it has regularly been reprinted in writing manuals as a model of thought and expression. Another blunder was omitting Golding's review of Christopher Hollis's *Eton: A History*, which they dismissed as an 'agreeably irrelvant [sic] squib'. Presumably they felt timid about reprinting a piece in which their author offered to blow up Eton with a few hundred tons of TNT. But an article that demands the same student–teacher ratio for state schools as for public schools cannot be brushed aside as a squib, and omitting items like this diminished the volume by making it appear charming but toothless. Leaving out his review of Raleigh Trevelyan's *A Hermit Disclosed*, central to his interest in sainthood, was another misjudgement, as was turning down his analysis of science fiction and of his own obsession with it in his review of Kingsley Amis's *New Maps of Hell*. Any of these pieces merited inclusion far more than laboured potboilers like 'Crosses', which, in the event, provided easy targets for the anti-Golding brigade's reviewers.

On 4 January 1965 Golding sent Monteith the final agreed copy for *The Hot Gates*, with the news that he and Ann were off to a Pugwash conference in Manchester in February and would then visit Mark and Ian in Edinburgh, prior to a 'cultural jaunt' in London. Pugwash is an international scientific organization, dedicated to reducing nuclear weapons and seeking co-operative solutions to global problems, which was formed following the publication of a manifesto by Bertrand Russell and Albert Einstein in 1955. Golding's interest in the anti-nuclear movement went back to at least 1962 when Frank Kermode was asked by a group of worried scientists, headed by Professor Brian (later Lord) Flowers, to seek Golding's help in finding a way to bring home to the public at large the proximity and horror of the nuclear threat. Golding proposed taking an advertising slot on ITV where, every hour or so, a man would appear carrying three dice, which he would throw, and then he would say, 'As you can see, they have not come up with three sixes. But one day they will.' The scientists were, Kermode recalls, not very impressed. 'They were expecting something more spectacular, perhaps a piece of writing.' So the idea fizzled out. But as his attendance at the Pugwash conference indicates, Golding's concern did not.

Ecology was another global problem that engaged his attention in the mid-1960s, and this came about through his friendship with Professor James Lovelock, propounder of the Gaia hypothesis. Lovelock had moved to Bowerchalke in 1964. At the time he was working at NASA's jet-propulsion laboratory at Pasadena, California, but refused to live there ('dreadful place') so commuted from rural Wiltshire. He met Golding on one of his frequent walks to the post office, and soon they were both regulars at The Bell, where they would spend whole evenings 'chattering away'. Lovelock found that Golding was 'quite educated in science', and was up to discussing jet propulsion with him, though it was 'very hot physics'. They found they were both science-fiction addicts and shared an admiration for the wit and ingenuity of the great Robert Sheckley – the master, they agreed, of 'what-if?' situations such as, 'What if the population explosion reached impossible proportions? Would people start hunting each other?' Lovelock first broached his new 'big, big idea about the earth' when they were walking to the post office and Golding got so interested that he said, 'Let's go the long way back.' So they did, and Lovelock explained how he had been challenged to find whether there had ever been life on Mars, and it had struck him that, if there had been, it would have changed the atmosphere of the planet. By using an instrument that analysed the infra-red spectrum coming from Mars, he could identify every gas there was in its atmosphere, and he found it was almost entirely carbon dioxide. Comparing this with the earth's atmosphere led him to conclude there had never been life there, but it also led him to think about the earth's atmosphere:

I looked back at the earth, in my mind, so to speak, and thought, God, we've got such an incredible atmosphere – it's the kind of explosive mixture that goes into the intake of a car. Why is it stable? What makes it stable? It's so out of equilibrium that something must be regulating it. And what else than life, because life makes the methane and it makes the oxygen. Life on the surface has been regulating the composition of the atmosphere ever since life formed on earth. And not only that, but it would make the climate, because the climate depends on the atmosphere. And that was quite a big idea, and I was quite excited telling Bill about it, and he got excited too and he turned to me and said, 'Look, if you're going to come up with a big idea like that you'd better give it a proper name,' and I said, 'What do you suggest?' And he said, 'I suggest you call it Gaia.' I thought he had said 'Gyre', not having a classical training, after all, and what with atmospheric circulation my mind was naturally on 'Gyre'. But Bill said, 'No, no, no, no, I mean Gaia, the Greek goddess of the earth.'

Lovelock adopted Golding's suggestion, but at first it made him 'a bit of a hostage to the biologists', because they assumed he was just 'another

New Age person coming up with a freaky theory, Gaia, mother earth, crystals, ley lines, and all the rest of it'. 'But then', he remarks philosophically, 'all ideas take about forty years to be accepted.'

Golding's readiness to leave the choice of pieces for *The Hot Gates* to Monteith and his aides suggests that he had other things on his mind. One was tax. 'Money is *very difficult*,' he wrote on 2 February, 'not because we haven't any but because we have too much. I now have a solicitor and accountant fighting the Inland Revenue. I *ought* to live in Greece and not answer any post except Faber and Faber. Moan, moan, moan.' A more serious concern was the next novel. Mention of any new work is ominously absent from his letters to Monteith during 1965, but they met on several occasions. In April he was at Russell Square to award the Geoffrey Faber Memorial Prize to Frank Tuohy for his novel *The Ice Saints*. His thank-you letter for the dinner afterwards, and Monteith's reply to it, are written in modern Greek – a language they were both learning, using the Linguaphone method. Despite the bravado of his Greek letter, Golding found spoken Greek problematic:

> I'm all right so long as the conversation follows predictable lines, since holiday situations tend to repeat themselves. I can even do some car stuff – explain that I have had a *travma* with my *elastiko*, *dhexia*, *mprosta*, resulting, I consider, in a *tripa*. But to sit at a table with a real Greek, not a record, and with all the resources of mind on either side, is a sort of linguistic purgatory.

He wrote this after a holiday in the Greek islands with Ann in May. They went to Rhodes and 'cased the outer islands', but finished, on Monteith's recommendation, in Corfu, which they loved.

> Corfu – as you told us it would be – was wonderful. In a strange way it was Keatsian. I suppose we all got our first idea of Greece as a separate place, from Keats. But this abundance, this fertility, this lushness; this heat and beauty – It's fashionable, I know, to like the bare austerity of Attica and so forth; I've said that myself. Well then, I – we – have been seduced into enjoying a rich island more than the poor ones.

This was part of a long, chatty, comforting letter to Monteith, who was in hospital having an intestinal polyp removed. He did not return to work until mid-July, so it was du Sautoy who arranged terms for the American publication of *The Hot Gates* ($2,000 advance on a royalty of 10 per cent on the first 5,000 copies, 12.5 per cent on the next 2,500, and 15 per cent after that). Tactful inquiries about the next novel must have accompanied these negotiations, but there is no sign of any reply, and it seems likely that it was during this year that, at Ann's suggestion, Golding tried to prepare the ground for a new novel by writing the memoir called *Men, Women & Now*, out of which he was to carve *The Pyramid*.

Men, Women & Now has never been published, or even typed. It is about 35,000 words long and occupies seventy packed, closely written pages of a lined exercise book. It is meant, he says at the start, as an answer to critics who say he cannot write about relations between men and women, or 'deal with adults deeply'. One reply is that he sees no use in writing that does not 'involve the reader with the cosmos'. However, he concedes that some writers – Shakespeare, for example – can do this and also portray characters in depth, and he determines to try to learn from his critics. 'I am said not to stand with Dostoyevski and Kafka. I haven't read either so can't tell; but I know myself not to stand with Euripides and Shakespeare and take that roughly to mean the same thing. Perhaps this analysis will help me to move a little nearer to D and K if not the others.' He acknowledges that he is 'deficient in intuition'. He has intuitions, but they are seldom about people. The only being in his books who 'took over off his own bat and dictated to me' was the pig's head in *Lord of the Flies*. He admits, too, that he is not good with characters, in the sense of making people into 'cards, or proper cautions'. His characters are 'universal'.

Next he considers men and women and the difference between them, and determines to try to do so with complete objectivity. It is an exercise in seeing things differently, rather like the passage at the end of *The Spire* where Jocelin sees mankind as a strange species of creatures made of pipes and struts covered in brown parchment and wearing the skins of dead animals on their feet. So sitting in his car in Salisbury, waiting while Ann has a driving lesson, he tries to view the passers-by dispassionately, as a 'Martian' might. The males, he concludes, are geometrically more beautiful than the females. The human female is 'far more clearly a four-legged thing pulled upright'. She has been 'rotated through ninety degrees, her bottom tucked into the tops of her thighs, her cunt pulled round in front, he breasts now going against gravity instead of with it'. Her 'broad base' and 'shelflike bosom' would be 'ridiculous' if the observer were not sexually conditioned, as the human male is but a Martian is not. The same goes for female thighs and legs, which are 'very seldom objects of beauty in themselves'. The human female physique is really a kind of joke, which is why women incorporate the 'whimsical' or the 'frivolous' into their clothes. 'It is a kind of apology for not being a total and exact harmony.' Further observation allows the Martian to conclude that women's bodies are 'far nearer their minds than a man's body is to his'. Essentially, women *are* their bodies – or rather, 'there is hardly a distinction that may be made between mental, physical, emotional – in this sense they are a totality'. They defend their grace and beauty 'as a child defends a sandcastle against the tide'. Intellectually their principal lack is 'an indifference to the nature of things in general'. But this is more than compensated for by their prime virtue, which is 'a passionate absorption in the being and fate of people as individuals'. Because they have this virtue, women 'stand between us and the two terrible male concepts of a world destroyed or a society of ants'. On the other hand, their 'near-fatal' weakness is the 'desire, perhaps the need, to submit', which results in men running the world. 'The worst product of the female soul is the instinct to believe that a man is right.'

Quite a few women readers would probably be able to overcome that instinct on reading Golding's – or Golding's Martian's – view of their sex, as he no doubt realized. He was writing *Men, Women & Now* for Ann to read, and at one point the manuscript incorporates her criticism of it. But after its contentious early pages it settles into an autobiographical account of his own relations with the female sex – his mother, the girls at school, his music teacher Miss Salisbury, Mollie, Dora, Sheila – and the early chapters of my biography have drawn on this material.

He may have still been writing *Men, Women & Now* in October 1965 when *The Hot Gates* was published. The reviews of it included a fine tribute in *New Society* by the Cambridge critic Tony Tanner, who applauded the book's 'singularly attractive' tone: 'It is highly individual yet profoundly modest; it has an unusual, slightly angular candour, full of painful knowledge and a beautiful humanity; it couldn't be pretentious if it tried.' Even its slightest piece, Tanner observed, bore the mark of Golding's 'rare austere mind' and 'remarkable imagination', reminding us that 'there is not, at the moment, a writer to touch him'. There were appreciative reviews too by Frederick Laws in the *Daily Telegraph*, Douglas Hill in *Tribune* and Bonamy Dobrée in the *Yorkshire Post*, and brief, unsigned recommendations in *The Times*, the *Sunday Times* and the *Observer*. More than one reviewer found the pieces of childhood autobiography, as in 'Egypt from My Inside', especially attractive. John Daniel in *The Spectator* thought that the boy's apprehension of the world, 'stripped of the adult husk', was Golding's 'most fruitful territory', and the anonymous *Times Literary Supplement* reviewer urged that Golding 'should be badgered into getting down to the task' of writing a full autobiography.

The adverse reviews were fewer but outspoken. Both Douglas Sealy in the *Irish Times* and Robert Nowell in *The Tablet* felt the book could have been written by anybody. Anthony Burgess in *The Listener* conceded that Golding had the 'skill of a true fabulist', but reckoned his talent 'deep and narrow'. He had 'hardly an original idea in his head', and once his prose lost the charge of a 'terrible message' it became 'cosy and whimsical'. The *New Statesman*'s brilliantly acerbic young critic Christopher Ricks, an admirer of Golding's fiction, berated the book. He deplored the 'huge gulf between the distinctive vitality of *Lord of the Flies*' and the 'thin obviousness' of the commentary on it in the essay 'Fable', and found much of the rest 'sententious, overwritten, trivial and lumpishly jocose'.

If Golding read these assessments he could hardly have felt much heartened as he set to work on his new novel, and there is some indication that he was aware of hostile currents in the air. In the 1966 New Year's Honours list he was awarded the CBE and, thanking du Sautoy for his congratulations, he struck a defiant note: 'Let *them* say what they like, an honour is an honour is an honour.' To Monteith he was more light-hearted: 'I feel at once proud and shy like a girl with illegitimate triplets.' The elevation had 'put our credit up in the valley. I've even been invited to join the darts team.' Perhaps the honour gave him a creative boost, for on 10 March he sent Monteith what turned out to be the first instalment of his new novel: 'Herewith my *NOVELLA* (!!), INSIDE A PYRAMID. I'm sending it imploring your help. This sort of thing is a new departure for me, and I don't know whether I'm barking up the wrong tree – or indeed whether there's a tree at all. Ann and I have now written and read three successive versions of the thing, and I still don't know what it's about. It's growed, like Topsy.'

These protests seem largely neurotic, for there is not much question what the new work is about. It is a fictional development of people and events in his own youth, based, sometimes verbatim, on *Men, Women & Now*, and its subject is social class and its power to distort and destroy human relationships. When a young Australian student, Robert Scoble, wrote in 1968 to ask whether the title referred to 'the class pyramid', Golding left him in no doubt: 'the Pyramid is the English Social pyramid, a particularly crippling and terrible structure'. Some readers were confused because Golding chose an epigraph for the book from the maxims of the ancient Egyptian vizier Ptah-Hotep, which naturally set them thinking about a real Egyptian pyramid. But the maxim evidently seemed relevant to him because it points to the human value that social class obliterates: 'If thou be among people make for thyself love, the beginning and end of the heart.'

The first of the novel's three episodes is a retelling, with alterations, of Golding's affair with Dora Spencer. She is re-named Evie Babbacombe, and Golding's fictional surrogate is Oliver, son of the local doctor's dispenser. Marlborough becomes 'Stilbourne'. Oliver is eighteen, has just left the grammar school and is about to go up to Oxford to read Chemistry, like Golding. But the action takes place in the late rather than the early 1930s, and Golding's first encounter with Dora, which he describes in *Men, Women & Now* as attempted rape, does not happen in the novel. Evie is quite willing ('Get on with it then,' she urges the inexperienced Oliver) and she is already having an affair with a public-school boy Robert Ewan, the doctor's son. Other-wise events fall out much as they did in life, but Golding emphasizes the class barriers that fragment Stilbourne society. Oliver is terrified when he believes Evie may be pregnant because he knows it would kill his parents to be related by marriage to the Babbacombes, who are marginally lower than them on the social scale. Only at the end, when it is too late, does Oliver realize with 'shame and confusion' that Evie is an 'undiscovered person', not just a social inferior whom he can trifle with, bully and exploit.

The second episode owes less to *Men, Women & Now*, but is based on Golding's and his parents' involvement with the Marlborough Operatic Society. Its Stilbourne counterpart puts on a musical, *The King of Hearts*, and Oliver, now at Oxford, is cajoled into a walk-on part. His parents are in the orchestra, and a professional from London, Evelyn de Tracy, has been hired to direct. De Tracy is gay, and hearing Oliver rail against the lies that Stilbourne society is built on, he risks, when they are having a drink together, showing him some photographs of himself dressed as a ballerina. Oliver roars with laughter, and de Tracy, shocked and hurt, gets drunk and goes back to London. Like the Evie episode it illustrates how – as Golding put it in his letter to Scoble – Oliver is 'limited' by the social pyramid. The third and final episode centres on Golding's frumpish piano teacher Miss Salisbury (renamed Miss Dawlish). But it considers, as *Men, Women & Now* does not, the stifled longings behind her respectable exterior, and invents a love-story for her in which class-boundaries are crossed, with disastrous results.

It was this third episode that Golding sent to Monteith as his novella 'Inside a Pyramid' on 10 March. Monteith wrote back that he was 'immensely moved and impressed' by it, but that it would need 'one or two stories of the same length' to make a viable book. To Golding, his approval clearly came as a relief, for *The Pyramid* was, as he acknowledged, a 'new departure'. Simpler in style and technique than his previous novels, it was an answer to the critics who maintained he could not write about everyday life or relations between men and women. The day after receiving Monteith's letter he wrote back enthusiastically that he was at work on the Evie episode, which was called 'Midsummer's Eve', and was 'beautifully sexy and really rather scabrous, I'm glad to say'. He thinks, too, that he can see his way to a third story. He has found he can work hard again, and feels 'rather happy, as if I'd come through a narrow door, or opened out in some way. It's middle age now securely established or something.' He suggests calling the book 'Stilbourne Stories' (which Monteith tactfully pretends to applaud, 'a super title'), and by 25 April he has finished a second draft of 'Midsummer's Eve', and started the middle, operatic-society episode ('It contains a *sophisticated character*, which will be such a relief!'). The first draft of this is finished by 3 May. He is adamant that he does not want Ian Gregor, currently at work with Kinkead-Weekes on their *William Golding: A Critical Study*, to be told about 'Stilbourne Stories'. It 'is going to alter my IMAGE! Ian will be *mad*!' 'Up to the end of The Spire is a period, and apt for criticism. This is a new life, or book, or what not ... So Ian can be left to roll up all that period like a rug and tuck it away.'

The typescripts of the Evie and the operatic-society episodes were with Monteith by 17 June, but he told the Faber Book Committee on the 24th that Golding wanted them back for polishing, and final drafts were unlikely before the end of July. Meanwhile he assured Golding they were 'absolutely super' and offered an advance of £500 on 15 per cent royalties, which was accepted. As he might have guessed, however, the end of July proved too optimistic a delivery date, and there were numerous toings and froings before *The Pyramid* was safely with the printer. For one thing, Harcourt, Brace, who were to publish the book in America, were not keen on 'Stilbourne Stories' as a title ('Bill does have a way of sending shivers along the editorial spine even before the arrival of a manuscript,' observed Julian Muller ruefully), and *The Pyramid* was settled on only after Golding had pondered various unlikely alternatives – 'The Music Makers'? 'Three Women'? 'The Best of British Luck'? 'Three Sisters'? 'Judy O'Grady'? He liked *The Pyramid* best because of its 'overtones of weight and deadness and suffocation'.

Muller also argued that the book was not three separate stories but a novel, and wanted to publish it as such. Monteith agreed, but Golding demurred at first, insisting that the stories, though 'deeply, inextricably connected', were 'three separate blocks of stone', and he might some day want to 'heave another block into place'. However, Monteith, egged on by Muller, prevailed. Golding cut some repetitions that had made the stories seem more separate, and the blurb was reworded to claim that the three episodes 'form an organic and satisfying whole'. By this time it was December, and on the 29th Golding wrote to say he had sketched out another story for *The Pyramid*, though he realized there was no chance of adding it to the other three now. But still, he persists, he has the 'gay, gaudy idea' of using the book as a 'holdall for Stilbourne stories', perhaps publishing them first in magazines and ultimately adding them to the book. 'I like the idea so much of having something infinitely extensible', though he quite sees it is 'bad economics'. Monteith replied patiently that, with publication fixed for 1 June 1967, it was indeed too late for major changes, but there was no reason they should not publish another Stilbourne book as soon as he had enough new stories.

In the course of these transactions Golding had several other things on his mind. One was an 'enormous' new sailing boat, *Tenace*, bought to replace *Wild Rose*. She was Dutch, a racing hoogaart, built in Walcheren, where Golding's comrades fought and died, and fifty-two feet long, as against *Wild Rose*'s thirty-nine. For Golding she had 'the clumsy beauty of a double bass', and he was immensely proud of her. His first cruise in her, with the family, was in August 1966, and he wrote to Monteith afterwards that she was 'a WOW'. She was also a possible means of escape. The Inland Revenue, he complained to Monteith in the same letter, were 'blistering my neck with fiery breath'. He was thinking more and more seriously of living abroad, 'because I can't go on buying the country H bombs'. However, he could not go quite yet, because *Tenace* had to spend the winter in a boatyard 'having bits of wood put into her to keep the water out'. But after that perhaps Monteith would like a book titled 'Sideways Through Europe in a Racing Hoogaart'. Monteith replied soberly that, if he did consider writing a travel book, Fabers would be 'delighted'.

Another plan was to revisit Russia the following year, and perhaps find a market for his books there, particularly *The Pyramid*, which, as an exposure of the British class system, might appeal to the Soviets. In April he had given an interview about the new book to Professor Valentina Ivashova of Moscow University, and in September he was visited by Boris Ryurikov, the editor of the magazine *Foreign Literature*, which had a Moscow office at 41 Pyatnitskaya Street and a circulation of 170,000. Ryurikov wanted to publish a translation of *The Pyramid* in his magazine and, having no English, he brought along a simultaneous translator to help with the negotiations, though Golding tried to make do with his 'kitchen German'. 'I'm a bit excited,' he confessed to Monteith, 'because it might mean more pounds for Faber and Faber and roubles for me, so that we could come back from Russia next year with Ann swathed in sables and carrying a couple of ikons.' Then, at the end of September, he and Ann went to Greece for a month – not, this time, to Lesvos, because Peter Green, with his children's education in mind, had moved to Athens in August and the Goldings joined him there. Green had taken a flat at 10 Tsimiski Street, on Mount Lycabettus, where the landlord wore a French beret and bred canaries and the Green family's elegant calico cat sat and sunned itself in the front window. This delightful retreat was, however, too small for visitors, so the Goldings stayed at a small hotel on Odos Ermou, below Syntagma Square, near the cathedral. As the Greens were still busy moving in, the Goldings were left to their own resources, and how they spent their time is not recorded.

A glimpse of how Golding seemed to a chance acquaintance in the 1960s comes from Ruth Inglis, a journalist who buttonholed him on a day-visit to London. She found herself confronting 'a short, twinkly-eyed man with a grizzled beard which rambled purposelessly from temple to moustache and back again'. He was modest – showing 'the humility of the great' – but also defiant and assertive, decrying the idea that human life was a jungle; it was far worse: 'In what jungle could you find six million people being processed through a death chamber?' Despite this blackness, he held out the hope that nuclear war would not happen: 'This monstrous creature, this biological irrelevance, will not blast himself off the face of the earth because he's too scared.' Throughout he chain-smoked furiously, 'stabbing at the air, cigarette sparks flying. A live coal settled comfortably on the cork floor near his armchair and began to smoulder.'

How he seemed to his friends can be gathered from the BBC World Service programme *The Masters*, broadcast at the end of March 1966, in which the sculptor and painter Michael Ayrton was asked by Arthur Calder-Marshall what sort of a man Golding was. Ayrton and Golding had met at the Savile Club and enjoyed arguing with each other about myth, Marxism and related topics, sometimes in the company of their mutual friend, the psychiatrist Anthony Storr. They fell out in 1967 when the fascist colonels took over in Greece, and Ayrton vowed not to visit the country again, whereas Golding maintained his right to do so (though in fact Ann eventually vetoed any further visits). Their argument took place in the Minotaur restaurant, and both stalked off in high dudgeon. However, this parting of the ways was still in the future when Ayrton was asked to describe his friend in *The Masters*. He described him as 'a cross between Captain Hornblower and St Augustine'. Physically he was 'stocky, heavily built, short, very thick in the shoulders, with a slight nautical roll', and temperamentally he was extremely changeable. 'He can be in a single day dramatically and exuberantly cheerful, and tragic to the point of desperation.' He felt the world's evils as if they were a personal guilt. 'I don't know any man', Ayrton attested, 'with a more intense and passionate sense of sin.' He was struck, too, by Golding's unpretentiousness. Though he had made 'a great deal of money', he had 'not found it necessary fundamentally to alter his way of life. The only extravagance Bill has is his car, of which he is extremely proud.' This was not quite true. *Wild Rose* and *Tenace* would count, for most people, as extravagances, and in his 1986 journal Golding recalls buying three Savile Row suits 'about a quarter of a century ago', which must mean some time in the early 1960s. In 1961 he told du Sautoy that he had bought a piano 'that even Mollie' (du Sautoy's wife, a music teacher) 'might consent to play on'. This was a Bechstein grand dated 1912, that said to have been one of Paderewski's practice pianos. All the same, Ayrton was right about Golding's relatively modest lifestyle. It was Ann who was the extravagant one. Her love of spending was a family joke. Whenever Golding worried about his finances, as he often did, her response was to take him out shopping or engage his interest in the Harrods catalogue.

The frugal upbringing that Alec and Mildred had given him probably accounted for his sparing ways. A reminder of his days of youthful poverty came at the end of 1966 when Brasenose, the college that had hitherto largely restricted its official communications with him to demands for payment of debts, made him an honorary Fellow. Golding was rather nonplussed: 'When I look back on my academic career I can't help feeling it's a Turnup For The Book.' David, who had not enjoyed Oxford, and whose politics were of the left, surprised his father by approving: 'It even touched my Mao-ist son, who said "Congratters, Pater".'

21

Disaster

With *The Pyramid* due to appear on 1 June 1967, Golding followed his usual plan of refusing to talk about the book, and staying out of the country as much as possible prior to publication. He returned a prompt no to BBC Television's invitation to discuss his new novel on *The Lively Arts*, hoping that his refusal did not seem 'stuffy or haughty'. Quite apart from pre-publication nerves he felt that he was, he told Monteith, 'in a writing slump'. However, once he was abroad his mood brightened. A chatty letter on 1 March from Peter Green's Athens address, 10 Tsimiski Street, reports that he and Ann have settled in, 'and very nice too. You can see the ACROP and everything – also the noble descendants of Hellenus necking under the olives in every possible combination of the sexes. It's a very classical area.' They are, he adds, off to Russia, 'next Tuesday, we think, for a fortnight', and he wonders whether Monteith has any spare proof copies of *The Pyramid* ('that exposé of the class system'), since the Russians might publish it, and then they would have 'lovely roubles to spend on Furs, Ikons, old, unwanted Czarist junk that would otherwise corrupt the Socialist Sixth'. In preparation for their trip they have bought a record 'with two hundred words of Russian', of which they have already learnt four. 'I don't believe in Russian at all. Nobody, but nobody, could make noises like that.' Monteith hastened to get a proof copy to them before they left for Greece: 'Do let me know how the Russkies react to it.'

Having got over the turmoil of their move from Lesvos to Athens, the Greens had more time to spend with their visitors on this holiday than in 1966. One day, after an 'excellent and discursive lunch' in the old quarter known as the Plaka, Green asked what they would like to do, and Golding replied resentfully, 'See the bloody Parthenon, I suppose.' It was a miserable, rainy afternoon, and the historical site was swarming with tourists. As Green remembers it, after a brief glance at 'the Western world's biggest cultural cliché', Golding seated himself on a block of stone, with his back to the Parthenon, and peered out through the industrial smog that hung over Piraeus at the dirty white mushroom cloud ascending from the Eleusis cement works. '*This*', he observed moodily, 'is what I call the right way to look at the Parthenon.' After a spell of glum silence he added, with evident contempt, 'Did you know who invented that phrase about "the glory that was Greece"? Edgar Allan Poe.' At that moment there was a clap of thunder and rain deluged down, scattering the tourists, to the satisfaction of Green and Golding who remained where they were sitting, taking swigs from a hip flask – two 'laughing, nipping, sodden Olympians in mortal guise'.

This not-entirely-pleasing account was perhaps coloured by Green's own feelings, for it diverges markedly from Golding's. 'The odd thing', he commented, 'is that I remember it for a quite different reason. As the huge raindrops fell, splat, splat, splat, they struck a smoothed bit of the sacred rock between my feet, and I saw at once why it was sacred – it became (because it *was*) translucent like a quartz pebble in a pool, and I saw that the whole rock was semi-precious stone.' This sense of sacredness, that Golding was always on the watch for, was disappointingly absent from another of their excursions on this holiday – an overnight trip to Delphi, written up for the August 1967 number of *Holiday* magazine and later reprinted in *A Moving Target*. Though they had Green as their expert guide, and though they reminded themselves that this had once been the spiritual centre of the Western world, the place seemed dead. Present-day Delphi was, Ann remarked, 'nothing but archaeology'. In addition, Golding felt that he could not reconcile the calm, austere face of the bronze charioteer in the museum – the great treasure of Delphi – with the dark, Pythian mysteries of the Oracle. They seemed to represent the two alien worlds of reason and religion – the poles between which his own experience endlessly shuttled – and he wondered how the Greeks had ever brought the two together.

Their longest expedition on this holiday was to the long, narrow mountainous island of Euboea in the western Aegean They made a joint decision to forgo ouzo and retsina for the day – 'Clear, bright heads at sundown,' Ann decreed – so when they stopped, on the way back, at a hilltop *kapheneion* they resolutely ordered tea. While they were waiting for it to arrive Golding disappeared briefly, and on his return the waiter was setting out cups, sugar, lemon slices and two teapots. 'Is ezpecial,' he said, pointing to one of them, 'For the *aphendis* – how you say, boss.' Golding helped himself from his special pot and Green, watching him, noticed something odd – his special tea had no steam. It was, in fact, retsina which, during his absence from the table, Golding had persuaded the waiter to smuggle into the pot. The others did not notice, and Green kept quiet, but the conversation, he recalls, 'picked up wonderfully'.

Of the Goldings' fortnight in Russia which followed their Greek holiday, almost nothing is known. It failed to register with Judy, who was working hard for her finals at Sussex, that her parents had ever paid this second visit to Russia. What is certain is that they spent some or all of the time in Tbilisi, capital of Georgia, which Golding refers to by its old name, Tiflis. He remembers in his 1972 journal seeing a Byzantine angel in an ancient church 'near Tiflis', and when he is thinking, on another occasion, about naïve art he recalls 'the Georgian artist we saw in Tiflis who painted shop signs with cuts of beef seen against the jet black of ignorance, incomprehension'. He seems to have maintained cultural relations with Georgia for some years. His journal records in 1982 that 'a Georgian (USSR) professor wants to visit'. However, the 'Russkies' did not publish *The Pyramid*.

A new relationship began for Golding when he got back to Ebble Thatch. On 29 March he received a letter, written the previous day, from a Canadian graduate student, Virginia Tiger, who was working on a doctoral dissertation about his novels at the University of British Columbia. She and her husband Lionel, an anthropologist, were, she explained, in London until September, and he was writing a book about the relation between human phylogeny and the political behaviour of male groups, which she thought might interest Golding. Several mutual friends, among them the publisher Marion Boyars, had encouraged her to write, assuring her that he would not be averse to discussion with a serious student of his work. Now that her thesis was all but finished, 'I discover, with warmth, that my interest in meeting you has become as much a matter of encountering the author as engaging in a literary discussion'. It would be 'a trifling, indeed enjoyable, matter' to journey to Salisbury to see him. He replied immediately to say that he would be in Salisbury 'for an hour or two' on the coming Wednesday, 5 April, and that though he was 'less amenable to interviews' than he once was, he would give her lunch in a pub. There was a train from London that got in 'some time after eleven', and she should let him know whether she would be on it. 'I'll be sitting outside the station in my car. It's a white Rover number DMW 402 – or maybe 402 DMW, I forget which.'

She came. He took her to Salisbury, where they went round the historical museum, and to Old Sarum. They had lunch at the Red Lion Hotel, where he made her sit on a particular chair, saying that it touched 'two out of three obsessional strands'. But the visit was not, from her viewpoint, a success. It seems that he had taken the opportunity to ridicule the kind of academic literary criticism in which she was engaged. She wrote on 10 April, complaining sturdily that he had treated her as 'whipping boy for the whole world of scholarship', and that his persistent 'disclaimers' and 'disavowals' had been at first puzzling, then annoying. She confessed, however, that she had found him 'aware, warm, and I think disturbed however you may have tried to conceal these things behind diffident spectacles and Achillean armour'. She added a request – apologizing for the inconvenience – that he would send her a note authorizing her to consult transcripts of interviews he had given in the BBC archives, and an invitation to 'you and Mrs Golding' to ring her on Bel 1404 if they were ever at a loose end in London. Golding's reply was quick and generous: 'I think the wrong person is apologizing.' He should not have ridden his 'hobby-horses' so exclusively, and is 'deeply sorry' to have 'disappointed' and 'wounded' her. He encloses the BBC authorization, gives her permission to write with questions about his work if she wants, and wishes her luck with the thesis.

It might have ended there, but Tiger quickly took up his offer to answer questions, writing on 15 April to say that his letter had 'warmed' and 'delighted' her, and to ask about his comment, in a number of essays and interviews, that his characteristic mode of thought was pictorial. His reply, written on the 22nd, is disinclined to go into the 'mechanics' of writing, but ends with an affirmation.

I'd say I'm passionately interested in *description*, the exact description of a phenomenon. When I know what a wave looks like or a flame or a tree, I hug that too me or carry the thought agreably as a man might carry a flower around with him.

This – written, the misspellings suggest, rapidly and intensely – is the first sign of what was to prove a rich co-operation between Tiger as critic and Golding as author. She was to write two books about his work and they contain explanations and insights derived from letters and conversations with him that can be found nowhere else. Their next meeting was at his instigation. He wrote on 2 May (addressing her for the first time as 'Dear Virginia', rather than 'Dear Mrs Tiger') to say that he would be in London the following week and would phone, hoping they might meet for a drink or a meal. 'It's a great pleasure to a man of my age', he confessed, 'to find someone of your age prepared to be friendly and argumentative once my foolish fear of the Scholar has vanished.' Being 'so old and weatherbeaten' he will bring, as a 'passport', a 'paper or two that might be useful in your work'. But he is careful to banish any hint of flirtation: 'One other thing. Could we include your husband? This isn't only because I am deeply, not to say avidly curious to find what man you choose to share your life with but because I have a sense that his preoccupation must be deeply connected with my own.'

Whether Lionel came or not is not clear, but in the weeks that followed Tiger recalls that she and Golding met more than once. She would get a train to Basingstoke, he would drive up from Salisbury, and they would sit and talk about his work. Basingstoke is roughly halfway between London and Salisbury, which may be why it was chosen, but it has always had a slightly comic ring in English usage, ever since Gilbert and Sullivan used it as a byword for tedium in *Ruddigore*, so perhaps there was an element of self-mockery in Golding's choice. Because he was late on one occasion, and Tiger had to wait at the station for him, he dubbed her 'Griselda of the Iron Horse', referring to Chaucer's Patient Grissel. This friendly jocularity continued to characterize his letters to her in later years. It is clear that he enjoyed her company, respected her intelligence, and was flattered by her admiration. A 'hasty note', undated, but written on a Saturday probably at the end of May, invites her down to Southampton the following Tuesday to show her his boat *Tenace*. 'Very presumptuous of me to assume you'd like to – but you're writing about me and the boat is part of me ... Make it an early train! It's a big boat!' This letter is signed, for the first time, not 'William Golding' but 'Ever, Bill'.

The even tenor of this friendship was disrupted on 3 June when Lionel and Virginia drove to Ebble Thatch for the weekend in their elegant white Alfa Romeo. Judy was there, but not David, and the Tigers were the only guests. Several aspects of the visit grated on Virginia. She was astonished at how much the Goldings drank (she heard, for the first time, the phrase 'The hair of the dog that bit you'), and Golding insisted on playing chess with her, beating her easily, as she was only a beginner. But it was what seemed to her Ann's undisguised animosity that upset her most. She came away with the clear impression that Ann angrily resented her association with her husband, and was suspicious of its nature. When she got back to London she wrote Ann a bewildered and placatory letter, hoping the Goldings would visit her and Lionel in London. It is not apparent how far this reassured Ann, nor whether she had known of her husband's meetings with Virginia. But it seems that she was hurt by the discovery that he had shared his creative life with another woman, and one whose youth, looks and education transformed her into an imagined rival. 'It made my mother very unhappy, alas,' Judy recalls. Golding, for his part, may also have been surprised by Ann's suspicions. He went out of his way to assure Judy that his relationship with Virginia was not sexual – a distraction which, in the middle of her final examinations at Sussex, she could have done without.

It was through Judy that Golding met, at this time, Stephen Medcalf. Born in 1936, Medcalf had read Classics and then English at Merton College Oxford, and had been among Judy's tutors at Sussex. He was a gentle, loveable, pathologically untidy bachelor, and his profound knowledge of Greek, several literatures, and the byways of Christian theology, chimed with Golding's fields of interests. Their conversations over the years, fortunately noted down in some detail by Medcalf, are unparalleled as a register of Golding's extraordinary range and vitality as a talker. He recalls that on 10 July 1967 Judy entertained him to supper on board *Tenace*, and two days later he met her parents at the Sussex graduation ceremony. They had intended to leave England before this, so as to escape the reviews of *The Pyramid*, but they kindly stayed on until Judy got her degree result. In the event she just missed a first, but did well enough to qualify for a state scholarship that would allow her to read for a BLitt at Oxford.

The reviews of *The Pyramid* were, in any case, not terrifying enough to justify flight. The book was widely welcomed as an entirely new development, and Golding's most approachable novel so far. Martin Seymour-Smith in *The Spectator* proclaimed it his 'finest', and in *The Listener* Hilary Corke, who had thought *Lord of the Flies* 'in a profound sense *untrue*' about human nature, found the Golding of *The Pyramid* more 'grown-up, less noisy, and much more truly himself'. A. S. Byatt in the *New Statesman* praised its 'unstrained throwaway brilliance', and Frank McGuinness in *The Queen* judged it subtle and penetrating, 'full of vivid and totally convincing characters'. It was, wrote Fred Urquhart in the *Oxford Mail*, 'so good that I was afraid to finish it ... a seemingly slender but steel-centred tour-de-force that appreciative readers will return to again and again'. Paddy Kitchen in the *Tribune* observantly noted that Golding 'feels and hears his meaning through the shape of his sentences better than any contemporary novelist'. The book's third episode, about Miss Dawlish the music teacher, was particularly admired. Julian Jebb in the *Financial Times* thought it the profoundest, 'as puzzling and disturbing as one expects from this writer', and Montague Haltrecht in the *Sunday Times* and Colm Brogan in the *Yorkshire Post* both shared his preference. Even John Bayley in the *Guardian*, who was upset by the 'slapstick' of the first two episodes, thought that Golding had 'never written more movingly' than in the last section: 'It is impressive how the plainness suits him.' The BBC's *The Critics* (broadcast during the Tigers' ill-starred weekend at Ebble Thatch) were almost unanimously enthusiastic. Dilys Powell, Alexander Walker and Basil Taylor all liked it very much, and Edward Lucie-Smith, who had so hated *The Spire*, found *The Pyramid* 'rich, subtle, human and humane' and an 'enormous pleasure to read'. The praise extended across the Atlantic. John Wakeman's perceptive analysis in the *New York Times Book Review* noted that it differed from Golding's previous novels in its treatment of free will.

They regard it as absolute, whereas in Stilbourne free will can be still-born, limited by class and family, which makes *The Pyramid* 'more humane, exploratory and life-size than its predecessors, less Old Testament, more New Testament'. In December Virginia Tiger, back in British Columbia and reviewing it for CBC's *Critics on the Air*, deemed it 'winning', though 'less important than the other novels', and revealed that Golding had told her he had 'the shape of the sonata in mind' when he wrote it.

The adverse reviews were, however, decidedly adverse. 'The worst has happened,' trumpeted John Wain in the *Observer*. 'We have Golding as social commentator writing about everyday life ... Disgust, contempt, an utterly withering east wind blowing through every paragraph. I never read a book that took more effort to finish.' Gavin Ewart in the *Evening Standard* pronounced it 'middlebrow' and 'pretty awful', and Barbara Bray in the *Scotsman* was sad to find that the 'experimental novelist' in Golding had been 'snuffed out by the critics'. Paul Barker in *The Times* and Robert Baldick in the *Daily Telegraph* were more measured, admiring its subtle skills but feeling it was below par as a Golding novel – 'a pausing kind of book', as Barker put it, 'before the next move forward'. The anonymous *TLS* reviewer and Terence de Vere White in the *Irish Times* both took a side-swipe at Mark Kinkead-Weekes and Ian Gregor's *William Golding: A Critical Study*, which was published at the same time. The *TLS* questioned their admiration for Golding as a thinker, and blamed him for encouraging such excesses in his 'celebrants', while de Vere White feared that Golding's tendency to take himself too seriously would 'not be cured by a book about him by two dons'.

But the reviews, good and bad, passed Golding by. His sensitivity to criticism was by now so acute that he could not bear to read them. Rosemary Goad, Monteith's secretary, wrote a memo for Peter du Sautoy on Tuesday, 13 June 1967:

Before C[harles] M[onteith] left for Greece he rang William Golding on Thursday evening and spoke to Ann. Golding is in fact still at home, although very much in hiding and Ann said he was in a very nervous state, not reading any of his reviews and refusing to speak to anybody at all on the telephone. They hope to leave England in about ten days time (as soon as they have heard whether or not Judy has got a degree from the University of Sussex) and are planning to make in a leisurely way for Greece. Their only address is the Royal Hellenic Yacht Club, Piraeus, Athens, but Ann said she had no idea when they would reach there. If a more concrete address crops up before then she will let us know.

In the event it was another month before they got away. At 3.00 in the afternoon of 13 July *Tenace* left Shoreham harbour and headed out to sea. Aboard, besides Golding himself, were Ann, Judy, Viv Lewis, who had been their engineer on the Dutch waterways holiday, Paulette Sainsbury, a college friend of Judy's, who was the daughter of Lord Sainsbury, head of the supermarket chain, and a young man who later became Paulette's husband, twenty-three-year-old James Anderson, a useful crew member because, after a short service commission in the Royal Artillery, he had done some sailing in the Caribbean. As James recollects, it was not just a holiday Golding was embarked on. 'In Bill's mind it was the start of a brighter future – go down through the French canals to the Med, cruise among the islands, live another life with no end in sight.' *Tenace* was 'a big, roomy Dutch racing barge, very nice boat, traditional wood. Suited the romantic in Bill.' The romanticism, and pride in his boat, are evident in the first of a series of articles that Golding had agreed to write for the *Guardian* about the voyage: 'She is three-inch oak throughout, cutter-rigged in the Dutch manner with a curved gaff, enormous staysail, and a bowsprit that can be cocked up to 45 degrees and gives her the air of dating from the 17th century.'

At five o'clock the next morning *Tenace* was about five miles south-east of the Nab lighthouse. It was foggy, and there was a light wind. Ann had the dawn watch, so she was in the cockpit steering and the others were below. Paulette was with James, and for some reason she felt uneasy, so the two of them went up on deck. They were just in time to see an enormous steel bow looming through the fog. James flung himself on the tiller and they started to go about – 'Ann's reflexes were slower, so James saved us,' Paulette thinks – but he could not entirely avoid a collision. 'Everything happened very quickly,' he remembers, 'They clouted our stern, holed us, and disappeared into the mist. Our wooden stern was stove in and we started sinking very quickly'. The ship that had hit them was the 6,489-ton Japanese freighter *Heian Maru* (inappropriately, the name means 'Peace', or, more literally, 'Quietude-Safety'). She was on her way from Durban to Rotterdam with a cargo of bauxite. An English pilot was on board and her radar was switched on. Years later Paulette received a letter from the pilot, telling her how the accident had preyed on his mind, because he had not seen them, and they had not shown up on the radar.

On the sinking *Tenace*, after the *Heian Maru*'s disappearance, reactions differed. Judy was sure she would die, but felt strangely unafraid, seeing her approaching death 'like a glass of wine suddenly clearing and becoming water'. By contrast Paulette, who knew nothing about sailing, had not 'the remotest idea' she might die. At twenty-one she was 'too young to think such a thing'. There was a brief discussion about whether they should get into the inflatable dinghy, but even Paulette realized that 'bobbing around in a major shipping lane they wouldn't stand much chance'. Golding, like his daughter, remained calm. Judy later told Stephen Medcalf that he quoted (from *Hamlet*) 'Too much of water hast thou, poor Ophelia' as he surveyed their 'farcical situation', and finding his throat 'a trifle dry', requested a glass of water, which Ann fetched 'wading thigh-deep through the main cabin to get to the galley'. What they might do to summon rescue was an urgent question. Ann later said they sounded a foghorn. Judy remembers that Viv found a distress flare, 'not something that shot into the sky – it just burnt like an old-fashioned wood torch'. Her father lit it, held it up, and got slightly burnt – 'we were all pretty ignorant about such things'. She estimates that forty-five minutes elapsed before the freighter reappeared. It did 'a huge circle, much bigger than its minimum turning circle', and was 'going slowly for obvious reasons'. Paulette guesses it was thirty minutes, but cannot really say: 'Time was suspended.' James feels the same. People were 'dashing around with no realization of time'.

The *Heian Maru* found them by using its radar. Paulette saw 'little heads peering over the side', a ladder was let down, and 'the girls', James remembers, went up first, followed by himself and Viv. 'Bill insisted on being last.' *Tenace* was brought alongside and there was an attempt to get a chain under her. But it failed, and she sank. The Japanese crew were 'very good'. They plied them with whisky and coffee, gave them dressing gowns, and tried to get them to sign a document saying it was not their fault, 'which we resisted'. James noticed that the gramophone on the bridge was playing *Madam Butterfly*. Then a Trinity House launch was summoned and took them off, putting them ashore at the Red House Hotel in Bembridge, where they were offered breakfast. Paulette managed a boiled egg, but the others were too traumatized. 'My husband is still very upset,' Ann told a reporter. However, she thought they might get another boat and 'try again'. 'Almost the first thing he said when we were all sitting round the table on the Japanese tanker [sic] was: "Will you all sail with me again?"'

But he did not get another boat, or ever sail again. Friends agree that the *Tenace* disaster had a lasting effect on his confidence and self-esteem. After long legal wrangles the Japanese owners of the *Heian Maru* admitted responsibility, and compensation was paid. But this was not, for Golding, the main issue. The loss of *Tenace*, as James Anderson saw it, 'stopped him in his tracks. He was always sensitive, nervous about writing, intimidated by the sight of a hard-back notebook. A dreamer in a lot of ways. He had built a persona around the achievement of a young naval officer in command of a ship. It gave him status and validity. In that world, which was not Bill's world, to be brutally demoted from that – even if he did all the right things and was in command till the end – it was all taken away from him.' Wayland and Liz Kennet believe, too, that the collision 'haunted him' and 'robbed him of his self-respect'. Virginia Tiger saw him only once in the immediate aftermath of the accident, in a pub near Piccadilly Circus, and she got the impression he was 'devastated'. She remembers him watching a young woman serving drinks, and quoting the last lines of T. S. Eliot's *The Love Song of J. Alfred Prufrock*:

> We have lingered in the chambers of the sea
> By sea-girls wreathed with seaweed red and brown
> Till human voices wake us, and we drown.

In a letter to her of 31 August he says that he has a sense of marking time: 'visualise another boat; play the piano badly; read good bad books; ... feel my identity like a lump of stone'. Her husband Lionel had written immediately offering help, and, thanking him, Golding reported that everything was under control ('forms in septuplet'), though 'the elder members of our quondam crew are still rather shocked'. He excuses his 'scrawl', but has no typewriter: 'The floor of the channel is thick with typewriters, seeing what a literate lot we are.' Not only typewriters. He told his lawyer that his 'notes and diaries for a forthcoming novel' had gone down with *Tenace*, which constituted 'a major part of his work towards his next book, and without them the book cannot be written'. Also lost was a gold ring that had belonged to his mother, allegedly made out of the only bit of Thomas Curnoe's gold to survive.

Ann, thanking Peter and Mollie du Sautoy for their letter of sympathy on 20 July, apologizes for her 'shaky writing' and admits that 'Bill and I have taken some time to recover' from the 'terrifying experience'. But Golding maintained a more cheerful front. Stephen Medcalf was invited by Judy to Ebble Thatch for 15–17 August, and Golding, who had been visiting his tailor, picked them up in London in his car. Medcalf was awestruck, but quickly put at his ease by Golding's 'immensely companionable personality'. He seemed by no means depressed. They discussed the construction of the scaffolding in *The Spire* on the way down and, later in the evening, the nature of the universe, which, Golding opined, could not be put into words: 'I don't know what can do it. Music perhaps.'

All the same he was longing to get away to the healing remoteness of Greece, and he went off by himself at the end of August, leaving Ann to shepherd Judy off to Oxford and join him later. They rented a house in the Arcadian coastal resort of Paralion Astros from an American lady, but the weather was the worst for twenty years and the roof leaked, so they packed up and returned to Athens in their hired 'fiddling Fiat', which leaked as well. In Athens, at last, the sun shone. Writing to Judy from the Hotel Esperia on 6 November, Golding reports that they sit in the American Bar in the afternoon and watch the mini-skirted young women going back to work, and muse 'very lovingly' about what she must have looked like when she was in Athens on holiday earlier that summer. They are 'dry, comfortable, clean, and perhaps in my case at least, a little unwilling to face the future'.

22

'The Jam' and a Breakdown

The future had to be faced, and in the early months of 1968 Golding seems to have started to pick up the threads. He probably talked to Monteith on the phone after the loss of the *Tenace*, but he did not write, and no letters passed between them during the remainder of 1967. Monteith sent a many-happy-returns telegram on 19 September, which was not a thing he usually did, as if in an attempt to re-establish contact. They met again the following January, though, and a letter Golding sent in February shows every sign of being back on form and making plans for the future (and was perhaps designed to give just that impression). He would, he says, prefer his Italian royalties to be kept in Italy, 'so that I can pick them up on my way through to Greece'. He has met someone at the Hungarian legation who has told him he is 'Top Author' in Hungary, and could live like a rajah on the piles of money his books earn there. The prospect of living 'like a Hungarian rajah' appeals, but it would be awful to go there and find it was all untrue. 'Could F&F find out what money would be available to me in Hungary for the purchase of Apes, Ivory and Peacocks?' On the writing front he reports that he has 'notes towards a book and even a provisional title HERE BE MONSTERS. I'll keep you posted as to progress. I hope it'll be a big baggy book as little like the others as possible.' ('Here Be Monsters' was his provisional title for *Darkness Visible*, but ten years were to elapse before it was published.) His letter adds that he is continuing his struggle with modern Greek, 'but honestly seem to make absolutely no progress. Too late! Too Late!' He rounds off with an inquiry about sales of *The Pyramid*.

Monteith replied that it had sold nearly 12,000 since its publication the previous June ('which isn't at all bad, I think'). But he had hardly sent off his letter when he received another financial query from

Golding, this time complaining that he was going to get only half of the $20,000 advance on the mass-market American paperback of *The Pyramid* (which Pocket Books were to publish), while his American publishers Harcourt, Brace would take the other half, having done nothing to deserve it except sign the agreement with Pocket Books. This struck him as 'rather steep'. Monteith handed the letter to du Sautoy, who wrote back assuring his indignant author that a 50/50 split was usual. But Golding's protest suggests he was less satisfied than he used to be with Fabers' management of his affairs, and, as we shall see, he employed an agent to negotiate the next contract they offered him. Meanwhile a further sign that he felt he could face the world again was his appearance on 13 March in an episode of BBC's *Viewpoint*, in which he discussed original sin and the modern novel with Mark Kinkead-Weekes, Ian Gregor, Frank Kermode and the Irish literary critic Denis Donoghue.

In his correspondence with Virginia Tiger, too, he seemed his old self. Some time during the summer of 1968 she got in touch asking him to write her a reference for a Canada Council Grant. He wrote it, she got one, and a chatty letter to her in the autumn ('Dear Griselda') is full of banter, and includes a mock-Taoist poem:

> The leaves fall
> Float brown from
> My calendar
> Take Epitone for
> Loss of appetite
> Lowered vitality
> And nervous stress.
> Have your heart
> Transplanted.

The letter also reports cheerfully on the slow progress of 'Here Be Monsters': 'The monsters dance; and the book looms; nearer. But not yet.'

Fabers, on the other hand, heard no more from him for some months after the exchange of letters in February, which perhaps suggests he felt disgruntled about the American paperback deal. But the

picture postcard that arrived from the Hotel Loti, Istanbul, in October
was as jovial and friendly as ever:

> We came willing to be fair: have just seen Santa Sophia and are
> now irrationally, passionately, and indignantly philhellene.
> It's most amusing when one cools off, to watch how one's
> hackles automatically rise.
> Love from us both, Ann and Bill

The sixth-century Byzantine basilica of Sancta Sophia in Istanbul
had been converted into a mosque in 1453, with the addition of
minarets and other Islamic features, and Golding's joke mocks his and
Ann's pro-Greek, pro-Christian prejudices. It was on this Turkish
holiday that, at Monteith's prompting, they first tried snorkelling. It
revealed 'a completely new world, and we are hooked', they told him.

Replying to their postcard, Monteith suggested dates for an Oxford
lunch party ('it seems far too long since we last met'), but Golding
pleaded that he was too busy ('*ghastly* post et cetera'). Soon he was
engaged on a new project, as a December letter revealed. 'I've got
mixed up in a film script, and rather excitedly so – it feels almost as if
some faculty, some muscle were toning up again'. Consequently he
had put the novel on one side, though he might 'one day' continue it.
Meanwhile, would a film script be something Fabers might consider
publishing? Yes indeed, Monteith replied, thanking him for his 'very
exciting' letter. 'Is it the same idea, I wonder, that Anthony Simmons
spoke to Rosemary Goad about earlier this year – the vast traffic jam?'

It was. The film was to be called 'The Jam', and one of Golding's two
collaborators was the British-born writer and director Anthony
Simmons. He had recently had a success with his film *Four in the
Morning* – a bleak kitchen-sink drama following the parallel stories of
two couples in crisis. Released in 1965, it won Judi Dench a BAFTA
award as the most promising newcomer to a leading film role. It had,
too, a haunting score by John Barry. It was Barry, Simmons recalls, who
originally brought him the idea of a film about a traffic jam, and gave
him a script. But at that stage it was a 'very small concept' – just some
notions about what people would do if they were held up on the road
for a few hours. Simmons saw that it could be a 'fantastic opportunity'

for an allegory about the human condition, and they both agreed Golding was the obvious choice for writer. They got in touch, were invited to Ebble Thatch for lunch, and found Golding happy to join the project. By 1967 the thirty-four-year-old Barry was already rich and famous, having written the music for four James Bond films, and he undertook to pay expenses in the early stages of the collaboration.

Over a period of six months they met several times in London, usually in Barry's flat, which occupied the whole top floor of a block overlooking the Thames opposite the Tate Gallery. They took the Bayeux tapestry as their 'beginning', imagining their film as six huge murals with Golding describing what was happening in each. Barry's previous film work had meant writing a score for films that already existed, but he wanted this to be different. He would write the music first and the film would follow. Golding's job was to write a 'concept', 'a basic something that would inspire John to write a symphony, or a symphonic poem about a jam with a kind of structure we could follow'. 'Sounds crazy,' Simmons admits, 'but it was mid sixties, and it could've been great.' He felt it was 'an important project philosophically', and so did Golding. They wanted to say 'this is our view of what has happened to the world'. Golding wrote numerous versions, 'one every week or so', and meanwhile Barry met with Leopold Stokowski to get him to conduct, and he and Simmons had drinks with the film distributor and producer Joseph E. Levine, who liked the idea and talked about shooting it in Brazil.

Nine synopses of the film survive, varying in length as new characters and situations are introduced. In each, the action is realistic to begin with, later becoming 'super-real'. It starts on the southbound lanes of a motorway. A note suggests Golding had in mind a complex of overpasses and underpasses near Milan, but 'The Jam' has no specific setting. Another note points out that English will account for only a minor proportion of what is said in the film. French, German, Italian and Spanish will also be heard, and various 'impenetrable' languages 'Hungarian, perhaps, and Icelandic.'

On the motorway the traffic runs freely at first, then slows and jams. It is near a big city ('Megalopolis'), where there are scenes of wild, unexplained rejoicing – massed bands and drum majorettes. As the jam inches forward it passes a graveyard and the mourners run out and applaud. The people in the cars seem just a random selection of men, women and children, but we then start to distinguish groups and individuals. There is a car full of armed crooks. There is a preacher who, when the jam jams, passes among the cars handing out leaflets. There are a stuck-up couple in a Bentley, a quartet of teenagers, an old couple worried about being late to see their children, a pregnant woman, a young man in a Lamborghini, a beautiful Chinese girl whom he chats up, a man who listens to tapes of his own diaries on his car's cassette player and a busload of American girls (Golding's note reads 'Hollins abroad?') being lectured to by a professor.

During periods when it is stationary, the jam turns into a sort of temporary township, and personal dramas evolve. The four teenagers put up a tent and make love. A pop group plays. The pregnant woman gives birth. The old man who was worried about seeing his children dies of a heart attack. An unknown woman wanders among the cars shouting 'Heinrich! Heinrich!' A husband and his jealous wife quarrel about a letter from a girl that has dropped out of his map book. The woman in the Bentley plays peekaboo with a child in the car in front. The jam is not allowed into Megalopolis, nor can it get into the 'Jamdrome' (which Golding annotates as 'a huge enclave full to bursting with cars and every amenity for the full life', adding, 'But consult with John Barry whose idea the Jamdrome is').

Further on the jam enters a plain, empty and menacing, and stops under a viaduct. Some travellers climb up, only to find the viaduct is another motorway full of derelict cars. One of them, the Lamborghini driver sees, is exactly like the Chinese girl's. As the jam moves on, one driver has the idea of leaving the road and steering across the plain, but he soon returns, screaming to be let back in. A man who walks out onto the plain is shot by an invisible sniper. In some versions there are more shots and grenades are thrown. Then the jam moves into the mountains. Snow falls. There is privation and desperation. The preacher, using the loudspeakers on top of his minivan, calls on them to repent. Violence breaks out. Cars are set on fire, and by the light of their burning the travellers find they are on an enormous bridge. They throw the burning cars off. In one, the child who played peekaboo is still waving through the back window. The preacher's is the last to go, its speakers screaming in the flames. There is a launch on the river with a searchlight and loudhailers, but no one can understand what it says.

The jam moves off the bridge into a ravine, then into a tunnel, where it stops again. It is warm and softly lit, and the travellers sleep and dream. In their dreams the past is made better. The plain was not menacing but fertile and full of friendly people. The child was not thrown off the bridge. They could understand what the loudhailers on the launch were saying. Restored by their dreams, the travellers move out of the tunnel into the 'Spring Country', where they drive fast against a background of flowers, music and rejoicing. Then, far ahead, the hooting of car horns is heard and it gradually increases, coming nearer, until it sweeps over the jam and passes away. Golding admits, in one version, that he is not sure 'what it all means'. But he insists that the last scene of 'indiscriminate and baseless rejoicing' is not just an empty effect. 'I feel it means what I mean, whatever I do mean; and whatever I do mean, I mean savagely.' Simmons remembers the 'Spring Flood' ending as meaning that it is 'all going to start again'.

But the project foundered. No screenplay or score evolved, and Simmons realized it 'wasn't going to happen'. There were several reasons. Barry was in demand and went off to New York to do the music for John Schlesinger's *Midnight Cowboy*. He wanted Simmons and Golding to work out a script, whereas they wanted him to do the music first. Golding's drinking damaged their working relationship. He resented Barry's youth and success and the way women flocked round him. Barry remained respectful and courteous, but Golding would get so drunk that Simmons had to take him back to the Savile Club and 'pour him into bed'. He seemed to think that history had treated him badly, Simmons gathered. He resented *Lord of the Flies*, because it meant he owed his reputation to what he considered a minor book. It had made him a classic in his lifetime, which was 'a joke', and he called the money it made 'Monopoly money', because he had not really earned it. Beset with these difficulties, the project 'kind of disappeared from under us as we went'.

Golding's drinking was a sign of stress. For some time now a shadow had been falling across his life. He wrote to Monteith about it on 8 March 1969.

I write to you first as a friend simply to let you know how we get on.

You may or may not have known that our poor son David has found it increasingly difficult to settle – and later still, for the last 18 months, by contrast, impossible to leave home. All this ended as we ought to have known it would in what as a blanket phrase I will call a severe 'Nervous breakdown'. He has been under treatment for the last six weeks and we begin to dare to hope that he may improve, if slowly, and maintain the improvement. I cannot describe what he has gone through nor what we have gone through. You were kind to him at Oxford; and I think it reasonable for his sake to tell you that his intransigence and 'difficulty' (which you must have noticed) was very probably the sign of his slowly developing sickness. We can hope, but cannot tell what the future will bring.

On 20 March he mentioned David's illness, more briefly, more optimistically, and less specifically, in a letter to Virginia Tiger. 'I've – we've – been much preoccupied with the health of our son David and thought of little else. He's been sick, and convalesces.' Among the manuscripts of 'The Jam' is a sheet with four lines of poetry, which, he later told Tiger, were about David's breakdown.

> I do not know how deep it is
> Nor where it is from
> This thing that lies under my house
> Like a rusting bomb.

A letter to du Sautoy on 4 May reflects how continuing anxiety about David drives out all other thoughts. 'It's difficult to concentrate on anything else, or summon up the energy to do anything. Even a letter seems like a mountain ... David convalesces, or that's what we hope it is. Ann's not too good, run down, eyestrain, a floater, whatnot. I'm, I'm, I don't know what.' As for 'The Jam', 'The main thing is I have to find the energy somewhere to go on writing the thing and don't know where it's to come from.'

The manuscript memorandum in which Golding writes of David's birth, his shock at his son's club foot, the pillow fight and other childhood incidents, ends with a section written on 10 February 1969 which brings the story up to date. It was to get away from the strain of David's illness, he reveals, that he and Ann had gone abroad for three months the previous summer (the holiday from which they sent Monteith the Sancta Sophia picture postcard). When they got back they found David 'withdrawn, having lived by candlelight when the electricity was cut off'. They consulted their psychiatrist friend Anthony Storr, who made a diagnosis, and got in touch with Chris Brown, their GP. 'Three and a half weeks ago' (that is, in mid-January 1969), 'David was taken, against his will, into the Old Manor Hospital.' The manuscript ends on a note of hope.

> The treatment is being very successful (though I am not such a fool nor so ignorant as to be unaware of what the future probably holds for David and us). The treatment returned him to childhood, forgetting suspicion and hatred, forgetting most things. I had come in my frustration and human imperfection nearly to hating him. We went to the hospital and David had just woken up, not knowing where he was and why. The nurse told him we had come. I saw him, floundering, running, stumbling down the corridor towards me. He flung himself into my arms and I hugged him. Then he hugged Ann, sat at a table between us, stroking us to make sure we were real, and as he said, for reassurance ... I am changed because now I can love David. I can only hope that he is changed because now he can love me.

Golding's letters to Monteith, Tiger and du Sautoy about his son's breakdown were all written in the following weeks, and indicate that, despite the joy in his apparent recovery, anxiety about his health continued. Perhaps in an attempt to restore his confidence in himself, Golding drove him up to Oxford on 1 May to take his BA degree at one of the regular graduation ceremonies in the Sheldonian theatre. David's tutor Eric Collieu wrote a welcoming letter, confirming the arrangements, on 29 April. As Judy recalls, the ceremony proved rather an ordeal for a young man recently out of hospital.

Work on 'The Jam' struggled on in the midst of the family tragedy. Golding's 8 March letter tells Monteith that he has finished a first draft 'in a kind of automatic trance'. It is in the shape of a novel from which he and Simmons 'will ultimately cut out a film script'. The manuscript of this survives, written at the back of a Bishop Wordsworth's School hardcover exercise book (of which Golding seems to have retained a supply, after giving up teaching). It is about 20,000 words long – much longer than the eight copies of the film version – and Golding went on to enlarge it. He explains in his 20 March letter to Tiger that he has written 'The Jam' 'novelwise' so as to 'find out what it's all about', and it is 65,000 words long. There is a typescript of this version, too, in the archive – or of a version that corresponds closely in length. The playful, affectionate tone of his letters to Tiger suggests that he found their relationship a respite from the burden of guilt and apprehension that David's illness imposed, and also that he enjoyed sharing his intellectual life with her. In the 20 March letter he tells her he is reading four Dostoyevsky novels at once, and has finished Gogol's *Dead Souls* ('not as funny as Pickwick').

Uncertainty about David's future made him even more worried than usual about money, and he impressed on Monteith and du Sautoy, when they sent him a draft contract for 'The Jam', that terms must be settled not in the usual gentlemanly way but through negotiation with the agent he used for film and magazine work, Curtis Brown. So Monteith sent the proposed terms to Curtis Brown, and on 6 May 1969 Graham Watson at the agency sent back a tactful but firm letter. He was, he admitted, 'slightly embarrassed' to intervene, knowing of the 'extraordinarily close relationship' between Golding and Monteith. Nevertheless he must point out that, for an author of Golding's distinction, it was 'a bit unrealistic' to offer an advance of £500 on 15 per cent royalties. An advance 'ten times' what Monteith proposed would be 'more equitable', and royalties of 17.5 per cent. Also the paperback advance should be split 60/40 in Golding's favour. 'As for your acquiring world rights, I quite honestly cannot see what argument you would advance for this suggestion.' This letter must have shaken Monteith, but he replied with aplomb. On the question of world rights he yielded at once. But he contested the paperback split, and agreed to a 17.5 per cent royalty only after sales at 15 per cent had reached 10,000. As for the advance, he insisted that with Golding's income-tax worries a large advance was the last thing he needed, so he suggested an 'accrued advance' that Fabers would hold and

Golding could draw on as he wished. After some further bargaining, Fabers signed the contract with Curtis Brown on 10 June. This altercation might suggest that Golding's publishers had, in the past, taken advantage of him. But such a conclusion would be over-simple. Golding was by this time earning very large sums. By July 1969 UK sales of *Lord of the Flies* had reached 2 million and US sales 2.5 million. The tax he had to pay seemed to him exorbitant (the top rate in 1969 was 50 per cent; in 1964 it had been 91 per cent), and Monteith's point about restricting the size of any advance was an attempt to spread the tax burden over future years. It is worth noting that, although Golding was aware of the Curtis Brown correspondence, he opted to stay with Fabers, and never used an agent again. He assured du Sautoy that he had no intention of changing publishers, and apologized to Monteith for putting 'everybody's back up'. Monteith assured him that he had done no such thing.

Meanwhile Ann and he decided they would try to aid David's recovery by taking him away on holiday. On 4 July Rosemary Goad left a memo for du Sautoy to say that she had spoken to Golding on the phone that morning and he was on the point of going through the front door for a three-month break. It is not quite clear where they went or by what route, but it seems they stopped off in Italy (Golding's 1972 journal refers to the 'Hotel de la Ville, Florence' – a four-star hotel five minutes from the Duomo – 'where we were with David'). Then they made their way to Turkey and up to Bulgaria – a substitute, presumably, for Greece, which Ann's political sensitivities would not now allow them to visit. The picture postcard Monteith received from Slantchev Briag (Bulgarian for 'Sunny Beach') showed a greyish seaside scene.

> We arrived a little botched and bewildered from Turkey: but Bulgaria at last, the people's paradise! Very fertile, clean and well organized, from the splendidly amplified band at dinner to the queues for breakfast. The sea does not look good for snorkelling, however. Nevertheless it's good to have got out of the decadent S.W. Balkans with their lonely beaches and run-down hotels to a forward-looking economy. David is happy to be in a genuinely socialist country at last. I believe tomorrow we may all visit a collective farm. Our love and fraternal greetings. Bill.

The sarcasm seems rather heartless in the circumstances. But it may simply show that he is less worried about David than he was, and can allow himself to joke. On 2 October he writes to du Sautoy, 'We're back. I think David enjoyed it and is better.' He adds cautiously, 'tho' with these things nobody really knows what may happen'. David's health did indeed remain precarious, but at least the immediate crisis was over.

The collaboration on 'The Jam' was still ongoing, in a 'time-wasting way', he reported in January 1970, but he was 'deadly tired of the whole thing'. He realized he was an 'unsatisfactory contributor' to the Faber list, but 'the truth is, I live a surface-life, because in the circumstances it's less painful that way'. He was also unwell. He told Virginia Tiger in a letter of 14 May that he was suffering from gout – 'ludicrous from the outside, painful from the inside' – and attributed it to drinking too much coffee. He was on 'a diet and pills' and they seemed to be working, but he felt like something 'out of Charles Addams'. He feared he would not be able to see her, especially as she now had a little son, born the previous year, unless perhaps she could come down to Salisbury for lunch in a pub. It was difficult for her to get away from London, but she was able to leave her baby in the care of her hostess's au pair, and meet Golding for lunch in the Rose and Crown in Salisbury, to give him a finished copy of her thesis. He wrote on the 25th explaining that he had not been able to read it immediately because he had left his glasses in the pub, and had dashed back there with Judy to retrieve them, 'thus setting an all time record for boozing there twice on the same day with a ravishing young thing!' 'Am hungover,' his postscript reads, 'hence dizzy vagueness of this note.'

By July it was clear that there would be neither a film script nor a novel for Fabers to publish. 'The Jam is a jam,' he confessed to Monteith. He had tried twice to make a novel of it, but it 'turned out to be a load of junk'. A note from Monteith to du Sautoy regretted that 'The Jam' was 'a write-off', and du Sautoy broke the news to Harcourt, Brace, who had hoped to publish it in America. The day Golding wrote his despondent letter, 15 July 1970, he also received an honorary DLitt from the University of Sussex. Professor David Daiches, in his address, remarked how, though Golding had kept experimenting with different forms and themes, all his novels 'implicitly challenged facile orthodoxies about the relation between good and evil'. Monteith, in the audience, must have felt dejected that there was not going to be a new one for Fabers' 1971 list. But he tried to look on the bright side. 'I thought you looked smashing in that yellow robe,' he wrote.

The most powerful version of 'The Jam' to survive is an 8,000-word short story narrated by the tape-playing diarist. Simmons thinks of this as the final version and it has episodes and characters other versions lack. The Jamdrome, for example, has now become the Pandrome, an enormous, obscene shopping mall offering everything from prostitutes to cut-price funerals, and in addition to the arid plain there is a fertile plain with flowering trees and fruit, that seems welcoming but turns nightmarish.

> There were three children, two little girls and a boy who were climbing the wire of the fence and reaching out at the apples hanging beyond it. The sound of the combine harvester stopped. The little boy managed to touch an apple, hang on to it, pull. There was a quick series of bangs and the three children were blown raggedly away from the fence, scattered across the road and the verge and the cars like litter.

At once crueller, more thoughtful, and more brilliantly written than the previous drafts, this version is, even more evidently than they are, a godless, science-fiction parody of *Pilgrim's Progress*, both marvellous and horrifying, in which the modern world becomes 'a shouting, screaming trap of too many people in too little space'. In what seems to be an acquiescence in his father's Darwinian belief that all life issues from random mutation, Golding concludes that 'the name of our God is Random'. Life is chance, and those who survive are not 'the ruthless or the compassionate, the moral or the immoral', but simply those who survive. Simmons, who was a Marxist, and believed in progress, took issue with this. But Golding insisted that history was indeed random. 'The Jam' is one of his blackest works, and perhaps an index of the despair he felt over his son's cruel and unmerited illness.

23

The Scorpion God and 'History Of A Crisis'

Despite the eclipse of 'The Jam', Monteith did get a book from Golding for Fabers' 1971 list. It was *The Scorpion God*, described on its title page as 'Three Short Novels'. He had written the first draft of the title story seven years before. On 6 February 1964 he told Monteith he was just finishing his 'predynastic Egypt Long/Short. Provisional title TO KEEP NOW STILL. It's most unsatisfactory, flat as ditchwater and not at all what I intended. I'll have another go.' Three months later, having finished the first draft, he confirmed that he was 'most disappointed' and would 'probably re-write'. After that he seems to have set it aside and forgotten about it.

Whatever the first draft was like (and, as usual, it is hard to take Golding's obsessive self-deprecation at face value), the finished story is a masterpiece. From its very first sentence ('There was not a crack in the sky, not a blemish on the dense blue enamel') its style is flawless, and its revelation of an imaginary civilization beautifully subtle. The enigmatic provisional title, 'To Keep Now Still', means 'To keep the present moment always' or 'To live for ever', and it is the phrase the ancient Egyptians in 'The Scorpion God' use about embalming and mummifying a pharaoh so that he joins the immortals. In the story the pharaoh, Great House, has a favourite slave he calls Liar, who entertains him with fantastic fictions. Liar is, we gather, a captive from a northern land, and his fantastic fictions are his attempts to make Great House understand what life is like in a cold climate. In his homeland, he explains, if a man 'lies down in the white dust which is water, he stays where he is. Presently he becomes stone.' This is Golding in his Martian mode, showing familiar things from an alien viewpoint, and the point of 'The Scorpion God' is that different cultures seem alien to each other, though they are so familiar to those who live inside them that they appear natural. To Great House and his subjects it is obvious that the pharaoh is a god who holds up the sky and makes the Nile flood, and that when he grows weak he must be killed and mummified 'to live now still' and continue these vital functions. It is also obvious that after Great House's death Liar will want to be killed and mummified and enjoy eternal life with his god, and his disinclination for this supreme honour is greeted with incredulity.

It seems likely that somewhere at the back of Golding's mind when he wrote 'The Scorpion God' was another masterpiece: H. G. Wells's 'The Country of the Blind'. In Wells's novella a mountaineer called Nunez discovers an isolated community of blind people in a valley in Ecuador. Their blindness, originally caused by an epidemic, goes back many generations, and they have now no knowledge that there is such a thing as eyesight. They dismiss Nunez's attempts to describe it, and the outside world, as lies. Nunez falls in love with a young blind woman just as, in Golding's story, Liar falls in love with Princess Pretty Flower; and just as Liar resists the benefits of mummification, so Nunez resists his hosts' benevolent plan to take his eyes out to cure his unhealthy illusion of 'sight'. Golding's debt to Wells was probably unconscious, but the fact that, in 'The Scorpion God', the little prince, Pretty Flower's brother, is going blind, suggests that a residual memory of 'The Country of the Blind' was hovering somewhere.

In his letter to Monteith of 8 March 1969, in which he told him of David's breakdown, Golding added that he had 'turned up' a 25,000-word novella about pre-dynastic Egypt which he had forgotten. 'Ann says it's good and needs not much more than revising.' Would it, he wonders, make a book together with 'Envoy Extraordinary'? His letter to Virginia Tiger a couple of weeks later carried the same news – that he had 'come across' a short novel that he 'must have written between FREE FALL and THE SPIRE and completely forgotten. Ann says it's good! That's rather like getting an unbirthday present.' This suggests he had forgotten not only the story but also when it was written, for its first draft actually postdated *The Spire*. The point is worth making only because it illustrates how Golding, perhaps through diffidence, or through a belief that his imagination would go on working at a story if he removed it from his conscious mind, chose to make his creative life into a kind of fertile chaos, in which drafts that any other author would have gladly published were abandoned, set aside, forgotten or subjected to endless, periodic rewriting. Even though Monteith replied to his 8 March letter with an eager request to see the Egyptian novella, no copy was sent, and more than a year passed before any more was heard of it.

'Any word, I wonder,' Monteith ventured on 10 July 1970, 'about TO KEEP NOW STILL?' Golding's reply seemed unhurried. He had just completed the fourth draft but was 'not wholly satisfied – indeed far from it. I'll have another and I hope final look.' Perhaps a little exasperated, Monteith seems to have phoned to try to pin down what the contents of the new book would be, and the next day he left a memo for du Sautoy to say that, in addition to 'The Scorpion God' and 'Envoy Extraordinary' there would be 'two new short stories, as yet I think unwritten – one on the fall of The Spire and the second on the building of Stonehenge'. 'So', he added unconvincingly, 'this looks reasonably promising.' In the course of 1970 he had been renewing his luckless campaign to wrench an acting version of *Lord of the Flies* out of his reluctant author ('As I mentioned to you two or three months ago ...'), and having heard nothing from Golding for a further three months he attacked on both fronts: 'I *much* look forward to reading The Scorpion God and hearing what you eventually decide about the dramatization of *Lord of the Flies*.' For good measure he enclosed the typescript of a novel about Stonehenge by Harry Harrison and Leon Stover (eventually published in 1972 as *Stonehenge: The Search for Atlantis*), in case it might help with the promised new Stonehenge short story. He cannot have found Golding's next letter, written on the same day as his own, entirely encouraging: 'I have vague ideas of setting the explosive anarchy of FLIES in the framework of ritual', Golding mused. But first he had to 'brace' himself to reread his novel, which he dreaded. However, the same letter at last enclosed a typescript of 'The Scorpion God': 'You may remember you were going to be generous and explain to me why I find it so unsatisfactory. Other than this story', he added, 'I have thoughts round several more, but seem to lack self-confidence.' The last phrase is a reminder of what the loss of *Tenace* and David's breakdown had inflicted.

Reading the Harrison–Stover Stonehenge typescript, which he sent back with criticisms five days later, induced further nervousness about his own story: 'As for The Scorpion God, I wish I could send it to you in triumph. But having just read Stonehenge, my doubts multiply. I've cut out tushery and forsoothness, reduced archaeology to a minimum, and used history as my humble obedient servant – i.e. bent it where necessary – but what began as a joke has stretched beyond it and become nothing in particular.' Monteith swept aside these ditherings. Having at last been able to read Golding's Egyptian novella, he assured its anxious author that it was 'absolutely tremendous' – though he found the title puzzling. Might the other two stories in the volume, he wondered, be 'Miss Pulkinhorn' and 'The Anglo-Saxon'? Golding, it seems, really had been worried that his new story was no good, and he declared himself 'cheered no end' by Monteith's enthusiasm. The title, he explained, was historical. 'One of the vague pharoahs' (which he corrects to 'pharaohs', adding 'I can *never* spell that word') 'of the first dynasty (or just possibly predynastic) was called Scorpion', so he decided to use that name for the pharaoh of his novel. As for the other stories in the volume, he is against including 'Miss Pulkinhorn' and 'The Anglo-Saxon' because 'they were both written with the right hand while SCORPION and ENVOY were written with the left, if you see what I mean. Also the left hand might very well write another so that we could publish A TRIVIAL TRILOGY'.

Monteith, blenching, one imagines, at this suggestion, hurriedly assured him that *The Scorpion God* was 'a very good title so let's keep it', and that he quite saw the point about the other two stories. However, he was anxious to have a book for autumn 1971 publication, and 28 February 1971 would, he insisted, be the last possible delivery date. He heard nothing for two months, and phoned on 25 February to discover that Golding had just finished the first draft of a new story and needed more time. So he gave him till 22 March. This story, 'Clonk, Clonk', was the funniest thing Golding ever published, and is, improbably enough, a comic version of Euripides' *Bacchae*, the tragedy that depicts the tearing to pieces of Pentheus by his mother and the other maddened women whose secret rites he has intruded upon. He delivered the typescript personally on Monday, 22 March and was rewarded with lunch and a tour of Faber and Faber's new premises at 3 Queen Square. Three days later Monteith wrote to say that 'Clonk, Clonk' had kept him 'happily dazzled all Monday afternoon'. It was 'brilliant', 'William Golding right on form'. With that the contents of *The Scorpion God* were complete.

'A Trivial Trilogy' would have been an inaccurate title. 'Envoy Extraordinary' is relatively slight, but the other two stories are about things Golding took seriously. 'Clonk, Clonk' is about women's superiority to men, and their cleverness in concealing it, and 'The Scorpion God' is about tyranny. He made this clear in an interchange with Monteith in April and May about the book's cover design. After consulting the head Egyptologist at the British Museum, Fabers sent along a cover picture for Golding's approval showing an unidentified male figure from an ancient Egyptian wall-painting. He thought it all right, but had a 'far better idea'. One of the pharaohs associated with Scorpion, he pointed out, and possibly identical with him, was Narmer, the first king to rule over both Upper and Lower Egypt, and the famous Narmer Palette, discovered in 1898 in Hierakonpolis, is in effect, Golding suggests, 'the first press release', showing Narmer 'inspecting rows of decapitated prisoners'. 'History! History! It's the beginning of us all – it's Hitler, Redvers Buller [a British VC in the Zulu War of 1879], Stalin, Westmoreland [US Commander in Vietnam], it's where we came in.' 'I'm stunned,' Monteith replied. 'I had no idea you were such a dab hand at Egyptology.' However, as they were in a rush they were sticking to the picture they had got. So Golding's intervention was in vain. But it showed that there was nothing 'trivial' about the subject of 'The Scorpion God'.

His other communications with Faber and Faber in 1971 were mainly about money. In March he asked them to get in touch with his accountants, Malpas and Simmons of Salisbury, to discuss ways of easing his income-tax burden – which they did. In May he urged du Sautoy to insist on a $5,000 advance for *The Scorpion God* from Harcourt, Brace. Lamenting the poor market for short stories in the States, Julian Muller had offered only $3,500 – a steep decline from the $10,000 paid for *The Pyramid*. Golding was having none of this. When du Sautoy tentatively suggested they might ask for $5,000, he replied robustly.

'Yes, of *course* Julian Muller must pay £5,000 for *The Scorpion God*. His sky-scraper is much bigger than yours.' He felt sure his new volume would do well in the States, not just in bookshops, 'but also in drug-stores et al' – and 'Clonk, Clonk' had been 'half designed with Playboy in mind'. 'A thought', he added: 'Am I becoming contaminated with commercialism? Watch this space.' This awkward attempt at a joke reveals an unease that was not merely his usual fretfulness about money. David's illness had brought home to him that his son might remain dependent on him, and might need to be supported after his own death. Writing to du Sautoy the previous year he had touched, for the first time, on 'the necessity of leaving some sort of post mortem income', and in this context the failure of Curtis Brown's representative in New York, Emilie Jacobson, to place either 'The Scorpion God' or 'Clonk, Clonk' with any American magazine was a disappointment. It made it more imperative that Harcourt, Brace should up their advance. So du Sautoy was firm, Muller yielded, and the advance was raised. '$5,000 is *much* nicer,' Golding observed appreciatively. However, Fabers' terms for *The Scorpion God*, which he accepted, were the same as for *The Pyramid*: £500 advance on 15 per cent royalties.

Worryingly for Fabers, there was no mention of a new novel. The only plan Golding came up with during the year was for a long short story called provisionally 'I Said: Ye Are Gods' (a quotation from Psalms 82.6). Like 'The Jam', it was to be about overpopulation and pollution, but a distinctive feature would be its typography. Its first and last pages would be black, but in between the text would start normally and become, as the story went on, 'an illegible mass of the smallest (diamond?) print possible', graphically illustrating population explosion. He outlined the idea in a letter to Monteith of 16 November and discussed it over lunch with him on the 21st. But, though Fabers thought they could handle the typography, Monteith and his fellow directors were 'pretty much against it'. The reviews of *The Scorpion God*, which started to appear in October, must have pleased them, however. Golding, as usual, avoided reading them, but the snippets Fabers quoted in their *Sunday Times* advert had him 'purring gently', and Monteith assured him there were plenty more like that. All the critics seemed to admire it. William Cooper in the *Daily Telegraph* said the writing was so brilliant, fluent and stylish that 'the stories read themselves like a dream', and Isobel Murray in the *Financial Times* hailed Golding as 'a colossus'. 'Like H. G. Wells', said Valerie Jenkins in the *Evening Standard*, he was 'almost too clever to be believed'. There was not a 'slipshod sentence', not a page 'without some felicity', testified Christopher Wordsworth in the *Guardian*. Stephen Wall in the *Observer* praised the 'brilliant demonstration' of Golding's ability to 'make a world anthropologically remote from us physically immediate', and in *The Listener* P. N. Furbank, who had long been an admirer, concurred: 'the disciplined anthropological and archaeological dreaming' were 'marvellous'. In the *Sunday Telegraph* Anthony Quinton, a more recent convert, admired the way the stories held 'the exotic and the permanently human in mutually illuminating balance'. They were the work of an author, declared Julian Symons in the *Sunday Times*, with 'a wholly original and disturbing view of man's place in the world'. Malcolm Bradbury's searching review in the *New Statesman* focused on Golding's 'distinctive but variable language' that 'enacts perceptions not quite fully formed', and A. S. Byatt on BBC Radio 4's *Now Read On* found that the 'marvellous thing' about the book, as always with Golding, were the descriptions. There was no one like him for 'shifts of light and new angles of vision and consciousness'. A week later on Radio 3's 'Arts Commentary' Frank Kermode recognized in the book's 'intense imaginative concentration' a return to the manner of *The Inheritors*. Almost the only dissenting voice was Auberon Waugh's in *The Spectator*, who deemed the first two stories 'the purest gibberish', and feared Golding had reached the stage in life when writers 'start to mistake themselves for St John'. But this was so clearly the voice of a Young Turk eager to make a splash that it was unlikely to bother even Golding very much.

The most important event of the year in the Golding family had been Judy's wedding on 6 January 1971 in the register office at Oxford. Her husband was an American student Terrell Carver, and they had met at Holywell Manor, a joint Balliol–St Anne's annex. Terrell was twenty-four, had done his AB, majoring in Government, at Columbia and a BPhil at Balliol, and was writing his DPhil thesis. Judy was at St Anne's writing a thesis on Percy's *Reliques*, an eighteenth-century collection of ballads and popular songs. Their first married home was a cottage in Ramsden, a Cotswold village with a rail connection to Oxford. On 9 January there was a party for them in the big, recently enlarged living room at Ebble Thatch, with about seventy guests. 'It seemed to go on most of the night', Tim Brown recalls; 'we drank, danced and talked'. He was astonished next morning that he had no hangover. 'Bill said that it was because the best brandy, the best champagne, the best everything else, had gone into it.' Guests dossed down on floors and sofas, and next morning a bunch of them got up early and went to see dawn at Stonehenge. Stephen Medcalf was among these, and he and Golding spent the rest of the day drinking cans of beer and talking. It was a Sunday, and Stephen lamented not being able to go to church, saying his upbringing had accustomed him to doing so. Golding replied genially that we all have these difficulties with our upbringing, but must learn to overcome them.

At the end of July he and Ann left for a long Italian holiday. Du Sautoy phoned Ebble Thatch on 24 August, and David told him his parents had been away for three or four weeks and would not be back for another three or four. They spent the early part of August with Wayland and Liz Kennet, who had rented a house for the summer at Bracciano, a little town with a lake and a medieval castle thirty kilometres north of Rome. Liz remembers that 'Bill was having a writing block', and talked about it quite freely. 'He said he couldn't write but he had these amazing dreams.' They both encouraged him to keep a dream diary. It was not something they had done themselves, though Liz sometimes had spectacular dreams, and wrote them down. They remember little else about the holiday except that they all swam in the lake, and Ann screamed because she saw a snake that was swimming too, but it turned out to be harmless. 'Had a spotty holiday,' Golding told du Sautoy on 30 September, 'operatic weather and poisoned feet' (the latter probably, he thought, due to the lake shore being dirty).

He started his dream diary that November, and kept it for the rest of his life, though over the years dreams feature in it less and less and it becomes a daily journal of his writing, reading, thinking, plans for stories, memories, meetings, conversations and travels. On an undated early page, under the heading 'History Of A Crisis', he writes his own personal account of 1971. The crisis in his life may have begun earlier, he thinks, perhaps as early as 1954 when *Lord of the Flies* was published, but by 1971 it was 'unendurable'. Life seemed pointless. There was a kind of 'raw intensity' about daylight perception, and his nights were sleepless. The remedy he took to was drink. He cannot remember how many times he was 'dead drunk', but it was at least once a week. Once or twice he was drunk for more than a day. He said 'unforgivable things' to Ann, and 'pulled her about on at least three occasions'. He would play records all night, or sit at the piano 'drooling non-music'. The inability to write 'fretted' him. Only when he was writing 'The Scorpion God' and 'Clonk, Clonk' could he do without drink. In August he and Ann drove south – to France, Italy, Switzerland and Yugoslavia, and in Rome on 19 August, after their stay with the Kennets, he had a dream that was 'as near as I have been to a great dream'. He wrote an account of this dream, which survives. It was set on the Spanish Steps in Rome, near where he and Ann were staying. The place was full of beautiful young people, and one of the long-haired young men was his father, who explained to him mathematically why the Norse gods 'couldn't build a proper temple at Asgaard' and why it was possible to build 'the proper temple of Santa Euphemia at Spoleto'. There was also a very old man, a maker of folk songs and ballads, who may have been Yeats. He sang as he went down the steps, and all the young people rushed to the railings to listen. 'I woke up happy and moved to tears at the memory of the old man's voice.'

However, this dream 'did not make much difference', according to 'History Of A Crisis'. On the boat coming home he got 'beastly drunk, piss, sick, shit, the lot'. Ann had a 'terrible and dangerous time' driving him back to Bowerchalke. Two days later they saw their GP Chris Brown about his drinking, and he put him on a half tablet of Antabus a day and a Mandrax at night. (Antabus is the trade name for the drug disulfiram, used to treat chronic alcoholism by producing an acute sensitivity to alcohol; Mandrax is methaqualone, a sedative used for the treatment of insomnia.) This, he hopes and believes, in 'History Of A Crisis', has helped towards a resolution of his problem. He can sleep at night and has stopped drinking. Also, he has 'started to read Jung again', and finds it has 'an immediate and most powerful relevance'.

Adam Bittleston, Tony Brown and Anthony Storr had all discussed Jung with him in the past, but his interest now was far more personal and engaged. With Ann's help and encouragement he decided to go to Switzerland by himself in October and see the places where Jung had lived. He left on Wednesday the 20th, returning the following Wednesday, and during that week he had 'one of the most exciting, fruitful and also happy experiences of my life'. He went to Bollingen, the village on the north bank of Lake Zurich where Jung built his country retreat, and there he carried out a sort of ritual of discipleship. During this week he feels that he perhaps learnt to give up 'the follies of an old man who will not admit his age' – 19 September 1971 had been his sixtieth birthday.

Interpreting the 'History' and the fragmentary jottings that lead up to it in the journal is difficult. But they seem to record an urgent need to find some kind of belief that will replace the bleak Darwinian randomness of 'The Jam'. The connection, in the dream, of his rationalist father with religion (the church of Sant'Eufemia) suggests that, to satisfy Golding, it must be a belief that unites rationality and spirituality. On an early page he outlines the origin of the universe as a rationalist with a knowledge of modern physics might describe it. There was 'density beyond all densities, heat beyond all heat', leading to an explosion, 'blind, dumb, ignorant, without sense or awareness'. Then, after millions of years, 'the rules of the game invent nerve ends to feel, eyes to see, and a tiny flicker of pale flame – consciousness so that the universe can be aware of its own futility'. If this is how omnipotence created the universe, he concludes, 'I don't believe it's possible to think of anything of sublimer cruelty.'

What attracted him to Jung, it seems, was Jung's belief that life has a spiritual purpose beyond the material. He deduced from his reading that Jung did not believe in the objective existence of God, but only in a god-image 'buried somewhere in the unconscious of all men'. The one Jungian concept that seemed to him 'inconsistent with the world of science' was the collective unconscious. But he suspected Jung might not mean that the unconscious is shared, rather that it is identical in everyone, much as a scientist might point out that every hydrogen atom is identical. However, he resolves to investigate further what Jung 'really means by collective unconscious'. Meanwhile the idea that 'God', and other such concepts, have 'psychological validity', not objective existence, seems 'more than enough' for him, promising 'a rich inner life' and an 'end to aridity'. As for the afterlife, 'on the whole I don't *want* an after life but prefer oblivion'.

Evidently Jung played a vital role in helping him to recover from his 1971 crisis. He read Frieda Fordham's *An Introduction to Jung's Psychology* and Jung's *Aion: Researches into the Phenomenology of the Self*, and started the first volume of the eighteen-volume *Psychiatric Studies*. In early November 1971 he deliberately stopped reading Jung because he thought it was influencing his dreams, and he wanted to dream his own dreams. But he got Ann to read Jung instead, and to discuss his theories with him, and he soon returned to his Jungian studies. On 9 April 1972, for example, he was reading *Man and His Symbols*, and two years later he reread Jung's paper 'The Phenomenology of the Spirit in Fairy Tales'. There are scores of references to Jung and his ideas in the journals. The majority of them, however, are in the early 1970s, and it seems that his belief in Jung may have gradually lost some of its intensity. After a time he gave up trying to interpret his dreams with strict regard to Jungian archetypes. In dreams about his naval experience, for example, he came to think that the sea might just be the sea, rather than a symbol for the collective unconscious. All the same, Jung continued to interest him. As late as 1981 he bought a paperback of Jung's interviews. Criticizing a thesis that analysed the Jungian influence on his work, he complained that the author had underestimated Jung's 'Merlin-like quality, the magician, weird, numinous, holy. He is far more than his writings.' A Jungian idea he found no difficulty accepting was that of synchronicity. This has seemed to some to be among the least 'scientific' of Jung's theories, and it involves the belief that seeming coincidences are not coincidental but reflections of some governing dynamic underlying all human experience. (The mysterious way in which the stories of the different characters interconnect in *Darkness Visible* may perhaps be an illustration of this.)

The 1971 drunkenness he describes in 'History Of A Crisis' seems sometimes to have had, in his imagination, its own spiritual dimension, like the 'ecstatic' drunkenness Peter Green remembered on Lesvos. A friend who saw him regularly in the 1970s was the writer Andrew Sinclair. They had met in the early 1960s, when Sinclair was on a trek from Glastonbury to Canterbury and got caught in a deluge. He knocked at the door of Ebble Thatch and was welcomed, dried, and entertained with chess, red wine and Liszt on the piano. In 1967 Golding reviewed Sinclair's translations from the *Greek Anthology* in the *Guardian*. Later he owned several mews houses in Hanover Terrace and would put Golding and Ann up when they came to London, and give dinner parties for them. Other guests included Harold Pinter and his wife Vivien Merchant, and Gregory Peck. Sinclair had a puppet modelled on Bob Dylan, which was in the Goldings' room when they came to a dinner in 1971. As usual, Golding got very drunk, and the next morning Ann broke the news to Sinclair that her husband had destroyed the Bob Dylan puppet. He had woken in the middle of the night, attacked it under the impression that it was Satan, and buried it in the back garden. Sinclair subsequently retrieved it, and it still bears the marks of Golding's diabolic encounter.

Although Carl Jung and Dr Brown's Antabus solved the immediate problem in 1971, they did not cure Golding's writer's block. He tried to start the first draft of a new novel, but put it off. 'I'm frightened of not being able to,' he admitted in March 1972. 'I need a little magic.' It would be years before his confidence was restored.

24

Gap Years

From March 1971, when he finished 'Clonk, Clonk', until October 1975 when he restarted work on what would become *Darkness Visible*, Golding's creativity hibernated. Once or twice it stirred briefly, but for the most part it lay inert through a winter of self-doubt. Meanwhile he occupied his time with various displacement activities. The most regular was his journal, which he wrote up every day, usually before 10 a.m., recording everything from metaphysical speculations to the weekly trip to Salisbury for Ann to get her hair done. He realized that the journal was 'little but an effort to relieve the sorrow, the grief, the pain' of not being able to write a book, and its pointlessness often dismayed him. 'I don't seem to do anything else', he fretted. He invented comic nicknames ('Pewter' and 'Bolonius') for the 'ridiculous and wearisome' everyday self who filled its pages with reams of mundane detail. But at least his daily stint made him feel he was still, in some sense, a writer. At the present rate, he worked out in April 1972, he would clock up 182,500 words in just half a year, 'the equivalent, more or less, of all the books I've written'. Eventually the journal stretched to two and a half million words.

Gardening absorbed time and energy almost as effectively as the journal. In 1971 the Goldings bought a field adjoining their Ebble Thatch property that stretched down to a stream or 'winterbourne' (so called because it dried up in summer) and a bridge called Applespill bridge. This provided endless alternatives to writing a novel. 'There's massive work to be done on all sides,' he estimated with satisfaction, 'hedge repairing, bourne clearing, planting of all kinds, drystone walling, to say nothing of all the waterworks. God knows how we'll get it done.' The waterworks were his swamp garden, a source of pride, frustration and exhaustion in the years to come. He planned it, dug it out and planted it almost single-handed, and fought a long battle with a reluctant stream that was supposed to supply it with water. Like his writing, his gardening relied on imagination rather than research, and he recorded his mistakes with wry resignation. He omitted to weigh down his water-lily pots with bricks, and found them floating upside down. He stocked his pond with decorative fish and they were eaten by herons. He bought an innocent-looking aquatic fern called azolla and it spread with such monstrous vigour that he was soon dredging it out by the wheelbarrow-load, and feared it might end up damming the English Channel.

Photography was another diversion. Because of his swamp garden, he was particularly keen to take underwater pictures. But cameras, like most other machines, tended to malfunction soon after coming into his possession, and their instruction manuals baffled him. 'My underwater camera is with the mechanic and God knows when it will be back,' he laments in January 1972. In its absence he decides to 'fake up' an underwater housing for his 16mm cine camera with polythene and sealing wax, and goes in search of a projector on which to display the results. He leaves the shop with a projector, a speaker, a transformer, a test film, and a feeling of total bafflement as to how the film fits into the projector. 'It must practically tie itself in a knot inside the machine.' The man in the shop promises to send a booklet, but just looking at his new purchase terrifies him. 'Even the spare lamp is a ghastly looking thing, with a filament that looks like a diagram for a computer or something arcane and electronic.' A couple of months later he buys an expensive Eumig cine camera with underwater housing, and instructions that are not too difficult to understand, 'even for me'. But it proves less co-operative than he hoped ('The rewind stuck *again*') and he admits that his relationship with photography has struck an all-time low. For a while he sulks, protesting that he has no desire to become a 'camera-buff festooned with expensive equipment'. But this is a passing mood, and his struggle with recalcitrant cameras continued for years. Complaints about their behaviour punctuate the journals: 'When I came to wind back the film once more it jammed'; 'The close-up thing on the camera is useless for portraits of fish', and so on.

He was far too keen an observer of his own motives not to realize that these activities were essentially time-wasters. Even piano playing, which he had always enjoyed, he now recognized as a wilful distraction. He finds that a Hindemith piano sonata is easier to play than it used to be, and wonders whether 'all that labour at the Chopin studies' accounts for the improvement – but then reprimands himself: 'What time I waste – and there is another book that has to be written.' Other possible distractions did not advance beyond the planning stage. He thought of taking up flying again, drove out secretly to a local airfield to watch the planes, passed a medical examination and got a provisional pilot's licence. But when Ann found out there was a terrible row, and he dropped the idea. He felt an urge to learn to dive with air cylinders, and to take up gliding, but these schemes, too, ran up against terminal family opposition. Considerable thought went into planning another boat to replace *Tenace*. She would be called *Viola*, and have a 'vast owner's lady's cabin' with a shower or bath 'to tempt Ann aboard again'. This desirable craft was never built, but she served the purpose of keeping his mind occupied with something other than his inability to write.

Travel was the most absorbing distraction of all, and he and Ann did a lot of it in the gap years. In August 1972 they took a cruise up the Rhine to Basel, with guided tours to Cologne, Bonn, Heidelberg, and Strasbourg on the way. Then they drove to Rapperswil on Lake Zurich, and up into the mountains to the Braunwald to see Adam Bittleston and his wife Gisela. At the start of September they drove down through Italy, crossed to Sicily and found a hotel on the coast under Cape San Andrea, near Taormina, where they slowly unwound, agreeing that 'one gets less and less able to cope with the wear and tear of travel'. They enjoyed the snorkelling, but Golding, ever alert for class distinction, noticed there was a 'posh inner circle' of hotel guests from which they were excluded. It cheered him a little when he saw the beach attendant's son beat up a 'soft rich kid', but the contrast between the dark brown satin-smooth bodies on the beach and his own 'middle-aged bloat' upset him. This was a perennial concern. His journal repeatedly laments his 'porcine' shape, his 'white sow's belly', and the 'disgusting' amount he eats, and he periodically vows to diet and take more exercise. Over the years his weight varied from rather over 13 stone ('obscene') to 11 stone 2 lb, more or less an ideal weight for a man of his height (5 feet 9 inches). But on bathing beaches his 'great sagging bulge of fat' was, he felt, humiliatingly conspicuous, and towards the end of September he and Ann took the ferry to the Aeolian Islands, first to Lipari, then Vulcano, where the beaches were emptier and the water was so clear that 'you were flying rather than swimming'. On their leisurely journey home they took in Palermo, Cefalù and Monreale before crossing to the mainland, and dawdled in Rome where they had a happy day at Hadrian's villa among the wild flowers and butterflies. In France they made a slow circuit of the Loire châteaux – Nevers, Bourges, Blois and Chambord (the 'one building', Golding thought, that made him understand why the French Revolution happened) before landing in England on 9 October. He brought back 45,000 words of foreign atmospheres and keen social observation in his journal. But it did not help towards a novel, and a sense of aimlessness pervades the whole narrative of their travels.

They were off again in March 1973, driving down to Provence and the Pyrenees in their new light-blue Daimler Sovereign. They felt out of place in the mountains among the skiers, so 'drifted off' to do a circuit of mountain passes and look at the snow. On the way back through the Pays Basque the Daimler, true to the traditions of Golding machinery, needed attention at a garage. It broke down again on the way to Chinon and they had to proceed by taxi, but were home by 12 April. Their next trip was more extensive. On 4 September they crossed to Le Havre and drove to Verbier in a single day, though the temperature in Switzerland was in the nineties. From Verbier they enjoyed some spectacular mountain walking, and met a retired professor from Zurich, Heinrich Straumann, who had known Jung and Joyce, and was to remain a friend. A three-day drive eastwards through the Furka and Loibl passes brought them into Yugoslavia, where they headed for Rijeka, on the Adriatic, and took a ferry to the island of Krk, which they drove round before moving on to Rab, another island in Kvarner Bay. But it rained and the hotel was substandard, so they took a boat back to the mainland, and stayed briefly in Makarska before embarking again for the island of Korčula, further down the coast. It reminded them of the Greek islands, 'donkeys everywhere, and grapes hanging among the deep green leaves like swarms of purple bees', and the water was warm for swimming. It seemed their stay would be idyllic, but it was spoiled because they met a young English couple who persuaded them to come to a night club, where Golding drank three bottles of a 'ghastly plonk called "Blato"' (he had been drinking again, on and off, since their 1972 summer holiday) and got so drunk that he fell over. He has no recollection of who got him home or how, but he records as much of the fiasco as he can remember precisely and remorsefully in his journal, so that 'Ann will be sorry for me rather than bitter as she, and all women married to drunks have a right to be'.

However, he recovered, and on the following days they drove round the island and enjoyed snorkelling at the fishing villages of Lumbarda and Brna, before moving on first to the Hotel Excelsior at Dubrovnik, then to the exclusive Island Hotel at Sveti Stefan, favoured by international celebrities. Two weeks of luxury living took their toll. They had hangovers and stomach upsets, culminating for Golding in 'a terrific upheaval of diarrhoea and vomiting' one night. 'High living becomes a real bore when you have too much of it,' he remarked ruefully. They drove home by way of Split, and through the Loibl Pass again, to the medieval city of Lienz in the Tyrol, where they walked up through pinewoods for a view of the Dolomites. Golding had 'ragged nerves' from all the driving, but consoled himself that he had accumulated 20,000 words of 'factual stuff' during his two months away, which might, just possibly, help towards a book. It did not.

In 1974 they took David to France in March, and had a walking holiday in Switzerland in June. But these excursions paled beside their trip to Australia the following spring. They went as guests of the Fellowship of Australian Writers and the Australian Society of Authors, which meant that their six-week stay, from 1 March to 10 April, was packed with official gatherings, television interviews, broadcasts, and talks at schools and universities. Australian students seem to have been rather overawed by their visitor. At a lecture in Melbourne town hall, one participant recalls, the audience, mainly high-school students, listened dutifully to the 'lion-maned writer speaking in a gruff, low register', but when the convenor asked for questions there was absolute silence. Finally, one of the teachers asked if he had had reason to change his views since writing *Lord of the Flies*. 'Not at all,' he replied. There was another silence, and the session ended.

Besides Melbourne, their programme took in Canberra, Sydney, Brisbane, Hobart, Adelaide and Perth, and it was exhausting. But it also reawakened Golding's sense of fantasy. Australia's trees and birds astonished and delighted him by their strangeness. In the Melbourne Botanic Gardens he and Ann found the tree trunks – silver, smooth and tactile – even more extraordinary than the foliage, 'like the trees of nowhere else'. At Ballarat, where he visited his grandfather Curnoe's old mine workings, the tree ferns brought home the 'terrifying age' of Australia. Walking among them was 'like walking straight back into a coal measure'. In Canberra the araucarias seemed like elephants, grey and 'slackly wrinkled', more animal than plant. The strange bird noises also came from a realm of make-believe. He would not be surprised, he felt, if one of them turned out to be a pterodactyl. The cry of the kookaburra birds was 'cackling, maniac laughter'. From Brisbane they were helicoptered to the Great Barrier Reef and Heron Island for two days of snorkelling in 'a world of utter and alien fantasy'. A shark 'flittered away, furtive as a fox', a shoal of stingrays swept past 'like a vaultful of Draculas'. He could find no words for the coral and fish colours, and asked them aloud, 'How do you praise God?' They were Gaia's children, he concluded, and lived in a different universe from him.

Australian light also seemed otherworldly, clearer than he had seen anywhere, even in Greece. Athens was 'a blurry place compared to Sydney'. At Ballarat they were taught how to pan for gold, and they found one or two bright specks among the gravel, 'gleaming like a bit of sun'. In 'this country of clear light and clean emptiness', European ideas seemed irrelevant. He tried playing the piano only once and was ashamed at how alien it seemed. He was taken to a performance of *Hedda Gabler* in Sydney, with Glenda Jackson as Hedda, and dismissed it as 'a lot of old rope', an intruder from another culture. He met many Australians, some of them distinguished – the poet A. D. Hope, the novelist Patrick White – but it was hard for them to compete with Australian trees and birds. White seemed a 'spiritual sea urchin', needing to be told he was the world's greatest author three times a day. During his stay Golding met no aborigines, but he was shown a photograph of an aboriginal man which made him weep, 'out of sympathy for its sheer, unhealable sorrow', and he met the artist Russell

Drysdale, who gave him a print of his painting of an aboriginal rain-maker. Golding had already seen a copy of this back in England, and had described it as 'the portrait of an aboriginal with an extraordinary mist or cloud in his face so that he wasn't a modern, sharp or blunt featured man at all'. It would later be used in the cover design of *Darkness Visible*.

Egypt had been part of his imagination since childhood, so it was natural he should include it in his travels while trying to rediscover his creative self, and he and Ann spent two months there in 1976. They landed in Alexandria with the Daimler early in February, after one of their usual punishing drives across Europe, and seem to have thought they could simply motor up the Nile, enjoying the winter sunshine and making hotel bookings on the way. The reality was a shock. Alexandria was a nightmare of traffic jams, noise and dirt, and the weather was vile. Since they had no Arabic, even making a phone call or getting a taxi was a baffling ordeal, and when they tried walking they quickly got lost in slums. The tourist industry was organized around package tours, and individual travellers were treated as an oddity. It was almost impossible to book a hotel room, and bookings could be cancelled mid-stay without warning. An elaborate and impenetrable system of bribery governed all transactions. In their first few days they were both ill with stomach upsets – creeping to the loo every hour, as Golding put it. The plumbing and sanitation were primitive, and they came close to despair. It was a week before they could get to Cairo and see the pyramids, and all he could think when he at last set eyes on them was that 'at least sixty percent of the people who see the pyramids do so while wondering how long they can hold out against diarrhoea'. As for the famous Cairo museum, it was 'a disgrace', dark, dirty and dismal. Besides, they had little time for antiquities. Just living, moving, eating and finding somewhere to stay took up all their time and energy. 'How down-to-earth', he reflected miserably, 'have become all my pretentious approaches to Egypt.'

Luckily they had met an American couple called Eddie and Pauline Blair on the boat from Venice. Eddie worked in Cairo, and evidently felt concern for the helpless, elderly Goldings. Chaperoned by the Blairs they did the usual tourist walk through the tunnels inside the

Great Pyramid, which they had not felt up to doing by themselves. Eddie introduced them to a professor at the American University, who in turn got in touch with Dr Kent Weekes, the director of the University of Chicago's archaeological project, housed in a comfortable modern building at Luxor. When they arrived there they were put up and made welcome, and Dr Weekes gave them an eight-hour guided tour of the Valley of the Kings, where they saw the tombs of Tutankhamun, Seti I and Ramesses II, and the two massive stone statues of Pharaoh Amenhotep III known as the Colossi of Memnon. These had, Golding thought, 'the splendour of all gigantic, ruined things', but their guide's outflow of archaeological knowledge was overwhelming, and left him 'speechless, wordless, without an idea in my head, almost without feelings'. The next day Dr Weekes showed them the temple complex at Karnak, and two days later he and Golding got up early to visit the gigantic Temple of Horus at Edfu. Ann opted out, but later in the week they went by taxi to the Valley of the Nobles, with its rock-cut tombs decorated with murals of everyday life, and on 5 March they drove to Aswan, where Dr Weekes had managed to find a room for them twelve floors up in the New Cataract Hotel.

By this time their archaeological enthusiasm was waning. They felt it a relief to be alone, and not have to admire some 'deathless wonder'. On the other hand they were no longer defended against the rapacity of the 'festering baksheesh children', or the bogus guides and peddlers of fake antiquities. Golding reflected that Egyptians had depended on fleecing the traveller since the time of Herodotus, but this did not reconcile him either to the exploitation, or to the 'slow, inevitable balls-up' of any Egyptian attempt at organization. The delays and mismanagement they encountered in getting tickets for their short flight to Abu Simbel exasperated him, and when they got there they were caught up in the 'stampeding, rushing and crushing' of the package-tour groups. Besides, the gigantic rock temples with their 'circus-size, Coney-Island' statues of Ramesses II on the façade, and more statues of the warrior king 'bragging along the walls' inside, seemed to him tasteless monuments to enormity and egomania. His disillusionment increased the next day when two friendly archaeologists took them to a burial site across the Nile, where white bones fanned down the hillside and some of the corpses were not even buried – just a 'sad heap of rags and sticks and tatters with a skull at the further end'. It was, he felt, 'less creepy than insanitary', and driving back to Cairo a few days later he found he was 'in a state of mutinous disagreement with my earlier self', 'wondering, perversely, exactly how important Egyptian history really is'.

Ann was ill during their last weeks in Egypt and on the way home, and they both felt so shattered by their holiday that when they got to Menton they stayed there five days recovering. It was the end of Golding's obsession with ancient Egypt, and the end, too, of his old, freelance idea of setting off for far horizons, as he had in his sailing days. In future when they ventured into unknown regions it would be under the aegis of some organization that could provide local guidance and, if necessary, medical care. No new novel grew out of the journal of his Egyptian travels, but in February 1977 he gave two lectures, incorporating passages from it, at the University of Kent (where he had been made an honorary DLitt in 1975), and these were printed as 'Egypt from My Outside' in *A Moving Target*. This public version is, however, prudently toned down, and lacks the spleen and jaggedness of the journal.

From time to time during his life Golding would feel that he had had a religious experience, linking up with the visionary white cockerel and the phantom stag of his childhood, and two of these revelations seem to have occurred while he was in Egypt. The first was in the early morning of 16 February when he was in Cairo and listening to the muezzins starting up from various minarets near their hotel, the Longchamps on the Nile island of Zamalek. He was 'suddenly swamped by a feeling of the comedy of *not* believing in God'. It was as if 'some kindly power had lent me an intelligence greater than my own', and he saw so clearly that 'positively *not* to believe in God' was 'preposterous' that he 'came near to laughing out loud'. A month later when they were on their way back through Cairo he lectured to some students at the American University to repay the kindness of the professor who had put him in touch with Kent Weekes, and found that for the first time ever he could talk about 'redemption' because of the 'experience' he had had on 16 February.

The second occurrence was on 24 February, when he and Ann drove Pauline Blair to the vast ancient burial ground of Sakkara, thirty miles south of Cairo, and they went down into several of the tombs. When they came up into the light there was a 'coppery column of cloud' and a 'blast of hot air' and a sandstorm, and they rushed for the car and cowered in it till the storm was past. Golding writes excitedly about this, saying that it 'gave us a glimpse of the spirit of the place', but it is not clear from his journal that he attaches any supernatural significance to it. However, Andrew Sinclair later took part in, and jotted down notes on, a conversation at a Faber party between Golding and P. H. Newby, the novelist whose *Picnic at Sakkara* had appeared in 1955. In Sinclair's account Golding says: 'The devil smote me out of Sakkara. He came up, higher than the sky, and pelted me in the back. We ran to our car. He tried to kill us – the spirits at Sakkara.' Newby replied: 'It's like that. The dead do rise there.'

Between foreign holidays, life at Ebble Thatch was routine. Never a sociable man, Golding at this time was even less interested than usual in meeting new people. He played chess regularly with Tony Brown, and the Browns and Goldings met for meals occasionally. It was not always comfortable. Sally Brown remembers how, early in 1971, she and her new husband Tom met the Goldings for dinner in The Bell at Bowerchalke. Golding, at the head of the table, got very drunk, grabbed a container of chips and threw them over his head, shouting, 'Oh for heaven's sake, there's Ann talking crap, and Judy talking crap, and Sally talking absolute complete crap.' Sally remembers his 'sloppy wet lips'. Ann remained 'slumped and silent, waiting for it to blow over'. Sally and Tom left. Tim Brown tells of another time when Golding, while drunk, was 'incredibly rude and cruel' to Tim's sister Iona at a dinner party at the Browns, calling her 'a whore' in front of both families and Iona's first husband. Golding's relations with Iona seem to have been complicated. In his journal for January and February 1972 he records two vivid erotic dreams he has had about her, and annotating them he recalls that she made 'a pass' at him 'a few years ago, when she had been doing for some years what she still does, that is play the violin and sleep around'. In the event, he writes, he turned her down, because the Browns were family friends. But he did so with 'genuine regret', and she still 'hangs there in the top left hand corner of my mind, as it were, a faint possibility. She stands, then, not just for music, but directly, for fucking.' He may, of

course, have misinterpreted what he took to be Iona's 'pass'. Sally Brown
was dubious when told of the claim he made in the journal. Golding, she
felt certain, 'would be one of the last people Iona would want to go to
bed with'. He was not her physical type, and, besides, Iona thought he
was gay, as Tony did. Perhaps the mixture of antagonism and desire in
Golding's thoughts was affected by Iona's popular success. It was in 1972,
the year he had the two dreams, that she first caught the attention of the
record-buying public with her recording of Vaughan Williams's *The
Lark Ascending* with Sir Neville Marriner and the Academy of St Martin
in the Fields.

Mark Kinkead-Weekes and Ian Gregor were friends Golding saw
more rarely, but he could relax in their company, feeling secure in their
admiration. By this time they were both teaching at the University of
Kent at Canterbury, so could be visited more easily than when they
were in Edinburgh. In 1974 they and the Goldings went to Sissinghurst
Castle, with its famous garden created by Vita Sackville-West and
Harold Nicolson. Kinkead-Weekes remembers how Golding 'got this
sort of impish, clown thing on, and he went into the White Garden and
said very loudly to tweedy ladies, "I do like a bit of colour myself," and
he sat in the Tower and denounced Bloomsbury and all its works'. That
night they stayed up till 3 a.m. drinking, and Golding's journal records
that he was 'fairly frank and rude', and wounded Gregor by calling him
inhibited and withdrawn. The Kinkead-Weekeses confirm that he was
'always fairly frank and rude', but deny that he was ever 'personally
insulting'. It was more a matter of being 'drunk and slightly bumptious'.
What they remember most is the laughter. On a later visit to Wilton
House, Golding 'kept on disappearing behind box hedges, and coming
out as one caricature of a Shakespearean character after another; he
knew them all; so he would come out and spout Richard II, and then go
back and be someone else. It was very funny.'

Another friend he did not see often enough was Stephen Medcalf,
Judy's ex-tutor at Sussex. When they did meet they would talk late into
the night on topics ranging from classical literature and theology to
anthropology and cosmology. They also drank a good deal. Of a meeting
in 1977 Medcalf notes, 'Very much to drink. Golding sat on the floor,
missing the couch.' But drink had the advantage of encouraging Golding

to air some of his more unorthodox religious thoughts. Talking of God and the Creation, he said 'that he could imagine a longing for absolution so great that you would create the world'. The idea of God wanting absolution seems bizarre, and when Medcalf told me of this I asked him what he thought Golding had meant. He said he had no idea, but was sure that was what he said. Less strangely, he told Medcalf he could not endure the crucifix. It was 'a horror to be veiled'. On the first of two visits in 1974 Medcalf was accompanied by Tom Braun, an Ancient-History don at Merton College Oxford. Braun spent the night in a room full of Golding's writings, and at breakfast the next day he remarked; 'Last night you said you weren't a Christian: but it strikes me your novels are much more Christian than those of many who would claim to be.' 'Oh Bill,' Ann interjected, 'You didn't say you weren't a Christian, did you?' 'That was last night,' Golding replied.

Not seeing people was partly his own choice. He grumbled that he met no one in Bowerchalke except the milkman and the people who kept the shop. 'Of friends, I have practically none.' Yet when he did meet new people he did not bother to find out who they were, or remember their names. One Sunday in June 1975 he and Ann drove over to Oxford for lunch with Anthony and Catherine Storr. Among the other guests, the journal records, were 'a professor and Mrs of unknown name except that his Christian name was Stewart'. This was in fact Stuart Hampshire, at the time one of the most famous philosophers in the Western world, whose work in the 1950s and 1960s had helped to change the nature of moral philosophy. It is inconceivable that he and Golding would not have had interesting things to say to each other. But whether through diffidence or self absorption or both, Golding made no contact. He did not care about people, he announced defiantly in his journal, unless they had 'the spark of God' in them – the implication being that most did not. He frequently misspells proper names, even familiar ones. W. B. Yeats is 'Yates', George Eliot, 'Elliot'. There are occasional other misspellings ('illiterate' comes out as 'ilitterate') but those of proper names are the most frequent, and perhaps this specialized form of dyslexia reflects a measure of indifference to people.

It should be added that his lack of interest in people was understandable. His fame had made him a target. He received huge quantities of fan-mail, which he dubbed 'grab-mail', because the senders, frequently students, demanded prompt replies to their lists of queries, or help with their academic assignments, or confirmation of their idiotic theories about his work. Increasingly often as the years went by he simply tore their letters up, though sometimes he steeled himself to grind out an answer. Requests for interviews from academics and journalists were also frequent, and it never seemed to occur to those who made them that they were simply being boring and intrusive. He usually refused, and regretted it when he did not. In September 1976, for example, Jack Biles and his wife came to lunch. Biles was an American admirer who had published *Talk: Conversations with William Golding* in 1970, so it was difficult not to see him. But it was a mistake. 'Jack Biles who describes himself as a Golding Specialist is a fool. He is also loud, imperceptive and boring,' Golding noted. 'He is even more awful than I remembered.' Another unwelcome visitor was the dissident Russian poet Yevgeny Yevtushenko, who arrived with his companion Jeanette Butler on the morning of 9 October 1975, explaining that they must hurry away as they wanted to see Stratford. In the event they stayed for lunch and dinner, and a great deal of drink was consumed, while Yevtushenko held forth about Khrushchev, Solzhenitsyn and Pasternak. 'I can't remember much of the evening,' Golding grieved.

He had never sought to be part of the London literary set, so his feeling of isolation persisted when he and Ann made their occasional visits to the capital. In November 1972 they went up to town for the Booker Prize dinner, and joined other guests at a big party in the Café Royal. But there was no one there they knew, so 'after a bit we went and sat down as wallflowers, plainly indicating that we opted out of the whole thing'. They generally went to London three or four times a year, usually for a weekend, and they always stayed at Brown's Hotel in Mayfair. A morning or afternoon in Harrods for Ann to shop was a necessary part of the schedule, and they would try to fit in one or two shows. On a midweek visit in February 1973 they saw *Krapp's Last Tape* at the Royal Court, *Cowardy Custard* at the Mermaid, and a John Osborne play so bad that Golding had already forgotten its title when writing up his journal (it must have been *A Sense of Detachment*). The Chelsea Flower Show was the one London event they tried not to miss, and they also took in any exhibitions that happened to be on. In December 1973 they went to the Chinese Exhibition at the Royal Academy, and Golding reacted adversely to the famous jade burial suit of Princess Tou Wan, which incorporated 2,160 plates of solid jade sewn together with gold wire. In all the excitement over this 'huge assembly of gold and jade', he complained, no one had stated the obvious, namely, that it was 'quite staggeringly grotesque and ugly', and would fit well into a horror film if surrounded with 'glass tubes, beakers, retorts, and some nineteenth-century wiring'. He wrote up his opinions for *The Listener*'s 'Langham Diary' the following month.

In April 1976 he was elected to the Athenaeum, the grandest and also the most intellectually distinguished of the London clubs, with a magnificent Doric portico overlooking the Duke of York's column on Waterloo Place, and several great novelists among its past members including Scott, Dickens and Thackeray. He could hardly be indifferent to the honour, but typically he had reservations about his fellow members. The first time he stayed there, in September 1976, he tried to find his way around the library, but 'failed fairly dismally', and then had tea and buttered toast in the huge drawing room, where 'half a dozen of the eldest club members in London' were 'shaking over their volumes'. It occurred to him that he must look just like them, and the thought depressed him so much that he went out, bought a hamburger from a barrow in Regent Street and 'ate it greedily but glumly all the way to the Athenaeum'. It rather spoils this story, but must be added in the cause of truth, that between leaving the Athenaeum and buying the hamburger he had dinner at his old club the Savile. Even in this diluted form, though, it illustrates his wariness of new faces, and his misgivings about being hooked into the establishment.

Back at Ebble Thatch, TV and reading occupied a lot of his time, and his choices in both bring to mind his remark to Brian Glanville, back in 1958, that he could never understand the frantic fuss about the distinction between highbrow and lowbrow. He watches every kind of TV sport available – tennis, cricket, *Match of the Day*, snooker. But at the same time he reads Homer, Plutarch, *The Epic of Gilgamesh*, Rabelais ('almost as boring as Ulysses'), *Paradise Lost*, *Paradise Regained*, *La Chartreuse de Parme* and Henry James's *The Golden Bowl* (which he likens

to 'foam rubber or expanded polystyrene'). Along with these serious
concerns he gets a lot of pleasure from Georgette Heyer, and thinks of
writing to tell her how much he enjoys her books. On Christmas Eve
1975 he watches *Carry On ... Up the Khyber* ('very good, and made me
laugh myself silly'), then, waking at 5 a.m. next morning, goes downstairs
and reads Corneille's *Le Cid*. A novel he often reread was Richardson's
Pamela, admiring its 'absurdity, touchingness, and slight, oh ever so slight
but nevertheless real and pervasive salaciousness'. He thought of making a TV series of it, and wrote a pastiche of it in a letter to Judy (after
she had 'uncharacteristically', she says, sent him a cheque, relating, so far
as she can remember, to an insurance claim):

Hovel Thatch
November 14th
1774

Dear Daughter,
Yeſtereven John Coachman on his way to yᵉ Great Houſe
delivered yᵉ monies you was ſo good as to ſend us for which we
praise God. Your mother, good creature, unknotting yᵉ ſtuff in
which it was tied, Father (cried ſhe) is not this a piece of yᵉ frieze
petticoat our deareſt child had of Widow *Beſt* five years ago come
Lammas? Oh *Pamela* our hearts miſgive us that you should bee ſo
changeable in your attire and poſſeſſed of ſuch wealth! We are
perſuaded that you have a good and kind maſter but bid you
conſider moſt earneſtly what ſins and ſhames and ſorrows are
ſpread for yᵉ careleſs. Your mother is coming to you when ſhe has
hid yᵉ money in yᵉ privy. Squire *Scrooge* (good kind gentleman)
hath a dung cart to Baſingſtoke tomorrow in which he ſays ſhe
may ride, and thence ſhe will go afoot it is but fifty miles. The kale
and onions are well ſet. The rats have ate yᵉ new baby but God
will provide.
Your unctious and loving,
Father

This letter is a reminder that Golding was not persistently sunk in
gloom during the gap years, and that he took pleasure in his children.

Judy had started work at the Clarendon Press in Oxford in 1971, and moved to Jonathan Cape in March 1974. She left in August 1975 when her husband Terrell was appointed to a lectureship in Politics at Liverpool University, and their first child, Nick, was born on 10 September 1976. Three years later they came south again to Bristol, when Terrell got a job in the university there, and their second child, Laurie, was born on 1 December 1979. Judy recalls that her parents were 'very sterling' during these transmutations, undertaking duties ranging from childminding to a 'seriously large' bridging loan so that they could buy 'the house of our dreams' in Bristol before selling their Liverpool one.

David was still living at home, and in 1973 he bought a canal boat, *Sans Souci*. His father helped him to fit it out, and in August 1973, and again in 1974 and 1975, Golding, David and Ann went on canal holidays in it. It was difficult for Golding to be on a boat without assuming he was captain, and this led to some tensions. But the canal holidays, with their rough-and-ready accommodation and pub meals at tie-ups along the route, seem to have suited him better than more luxurious continental jaunts, and the stretches of lonely waterway allowed contemplation of unspoiled nature. In a wooded cut near Berkhamsted on the 1974 holiday they saw a kingfisher which flew up the cut 'like a brilliant arrow', and was still visible a quarter of a mile ahead, 'for the cut was dark; but here and there the kingfisher found and flew through a gleam of sun, thus exploding like a firework'. In April 1976 David was received into the Roman Catholic Church – not an institution Golding had much sympathy with, but he thought it would be good for David's peace of mind. He and Ann presented him with a silver wine goblet, and David's card for their thirty-fifth wedding anniversary was inscribed 'To the best Mum and Dad in the world'.

These were not, however, the happiest years of the Goldings' marriage. It was partly that they had too much money. In the old days, he reflected on Ann's birthday in 1974, spending money was a 'breathless adventure', and Ann 'could feel herself valued by the extent to which I dared to do it'. But now, thanks to the worldwide sales of *Lord of the Flies*, money was so plentiful that 'the only thing to do was waste it', and no present he gave meant very much. Then there was his friendship with Virginia Tiger, which still rankled in Ann's mind. In June 1972, Golding's journal records, he received a letter from Tiger accusing him of being 'brutal', because he had written to say he did not want to meet her again, as 'it would be pointless'. When he showed Tiger's letter to Ann she 'suggested that only the brutal and determined can react so'. Much later, in 2003, when both Goldings were dead, Tiger printed as the Epilogue to her book *William Golding: The Unmoved Target*, a love sonnet by Golding:

> What fever is it in our monstrous blood
> That brings a crazed serenity of love?
> What absurd germ found entry where it could
> And fed and bred and multiplied and throve
> Till you whose years are shorter than this beard
> Fewer in number than these broken teeth
> Could share the instant brilliance of the bird
> Then rage against my necessary death?
> We'll call it living in a world of wars
> A world of pointless ambiguity
> Of angel-apes, of shit and quasistars
> Of bad good luck that flashed your face on me.
> Come lovely then with young Medusa's hair
> Sweet monster, come – who are already here.

There is no knowing whether Ann saw a manuscript of this sonnet in the 1970s, or, if she did, whether she knew to whom it was addressed. But she had already made it clear, when the Tigers came to Ebble Thatch in 1967, that she resented Virginia's relationship with her husband, and evidently her disquiet continued. In June 1973 when she was having a 'down', Golding asked her why:

> she said it saddened her to feel that we lived with life 'papered over the cracks'. She also said a terrible thing: that it is tragic to take away someone's past.
>
> I don't know what to do.

At any rate he did not see Tiger again. But bitterness between husband and wife lingered. When they had the row about his secretly obtaining a pilot's licence, Ann declared she had known 'for the last ten years' that he 'regarded marriage as a trap', and in his 1975 journal he reprimands himself for saying 'the usual unforgivable things' to her when drunk.

On 4 June 1976 Ann noticed a lump in her breast and Golding took her to their GP, Chris Brown, who referred her to a surgeon they both knew called Shemilt. He saw her on the 16th, and on the 29th she went into Salisbury hospital for an operation. Later that day Shemilt phoned to say that he had had to perform a double mastectomy. Golding was distraught. He felt an 'empathy' as if his own flesh had been cut. 'Half a dozen times a day or more I realise my poor Ann's operation with a pang and sometimes a localised one at that.' He had 'bouts of strange and I dare say irreligious outrage and grief for her', he told the Belgian academic Jeanne Delbaere. But at the time, he could not bring himself to write much about his thoughts, though he found that Ann's suffering 'made me bitterly aware of and sorrowful for the people I may have injured whether it was necessary, as at Walcheren or not'. Four years later he recalled how he had sat in the garden through the hours of darkness, unable to come to terms with Ann's plight, 'and oscillating between grief and sheer rage at blind nature'. Yet he felt that her suffering had cemented their marriage: 'I knew then she was *my Ann* which was perhaps a good discovery from my point of view but no cure for her.'

Ann was soon sitting up and demanding a 'big book' to read. She was allowed home on 3 July, and when she saw Shemilt a week later for a check-up he was 'enthusiastic' about her scar, comparing it to 'the one Boadicea had' ('I suppose he meant Hippolyta', was her husband's caustic comment). She had a twice-a-week course of radiation therapy at St Thomas's hospital in London, and in April 1977 Shemilt pronounced her 'in the clear'.

Anxiety about Golding's own health, as well as Ann's, nagged him during the gap years. He was haunted by 'a tremendous feeling of looking towards the last lap of life'. Ann and he were both told – perhaps by their GP – that their bone structures were degenerating because of age, and they arranged a course of treatment with an osteopath, which does not seem to have been wholly successful. Golding complained that the osteopath's rough handling of his neck had caused 'a roaring' in his right ear, and though his neck showed some improvement it was 'at the cost of making my shoulder worse'. He was aware that these pains were partly psychosomatic. He felt the loss of *Tenace* as 'a kind of castration', and his writer's block had an almost physical dimension. He called it a 'paralysis'. He was tormented, too, by the thought that nothing he had written was of a stature to compare with the world's great novelists, and that his next book, if there was one, might be his last chance. 'Dear God', he petitions, 'if you are indeed One who can properly be supplicated on this question – let me write a major novel!' Despite his prayers, he still felt, in April and May 1975, 'grey and empty', 'without even the memory of talent', and 'further from writing a book than I have been for thirty years'.

He took up book reviewing again in the gap years, partly as a displacement activity and partly because it kept him going 'as some sort of wordsmith'. Otherwise, he was afraid, he 'might drop right out of the game'. Most of his reviews were for the *Guardian*, and a few of the books the literary editor, Bill Webb, sent him were of real interest. Norman Cohn's *Europe's Inner Demons*, about the sixteenth- and seventeenth-century witch-craze, and Paul Fussell's *The Great War and Modern Memory* were works of historical and literary scholarship worthy of his attention. He reprinted his Fussell review in *A Moving Target*. Another book he gave time and thought to was the second volume of Samuel Eliot Morison's mammoth *The European Discovery of America*. It was, he noted, the seventeenth book by Morison he had read, and he was gratified to find, when he and Ann went to a *Guardian* party hosted by the Webbs at the National Liberal Club in November 1974, that Geoffrey Grigson, among others, had admired his review. But mostly his reviewing was hack work – knocking out a thousand words on some ephemeral publication that Webb thought appropriate for him because it had to do with sailing or the navy. He realized he was being typecast. When Webb phoned asking him to review Piers Paul Read's *Alive*, a book about cannibalism among survivors of an aircrash in the Andes, he grumbled in his journal that he got 'lumbered with these survival things' just because he was the author of *Pincher Martin*. It was a matter of, 'If you've got a good corpse let Golding deal with it.' All the same he said yes to Webb, 'since it keeps me feeling I'm still a writer'.

Several fragmentary ideas for novels are jotted down in the journal during the gap years. One that recurs is about a father and son who wake in a ward after ECT treatment. The father is a writer who has lost his talent. A homosexual male nurse cares for them. When off duty the nurse meets a 'spiritual man' (one, that is, who has had contact with 'spirits'). This man conceives the idea of a club or society that will give up the use of written language. They will communicate only by 'the touch of one body against another, the sound of one mouth in another ear'. The spiritual man will have 'no name because he had given it up. One day he might be called this and the next day that.' To join his society 'you must bring a murder as your initiation'. Another idea, seemingly connected with this embryonic story, concerns a man who has murdered a girl. He fears visiting her grave, but when he does so he finds it has been empty for years, and is just 'a blurred hollow in the woods'. This may relate, in turn, to another idea, about a man who 'finds more to despise in himself' with each woman he meets, and 'projects it on them'. He ends by murdering one, 'as a final gesture of contempt'. Everyone says he is mad, because his crime is pointless. 'Unfortunately I understand him,' Golding adds. 'Perhaps that makes me mad.' Some of these motifs were to find their way into *Darkness Visible*. Others seem to relate to Golding's private life. Still others remain mysterious. He felt frustrated because, though the ideas mattered to him, he could not make anything of them. 'I am throwing ideas together, I have been for months – and I still haven't a core or attitude. What is it *about?*'

In September 1974 he began to rewrite the historical novel *In Search of My Father*, about Telegonus' search for Odysseus, that he had abandoned twenty years earlier, when he started *The Inheritors*. His journal entries plot his plans and progress. This new version will be set not in Homeric times but in the twentieth century. Telegonus will be called Niki, and he will have 'scandalous' adventures in the 'stews of some middle-eastern seaport', before landing up in the Greek islands among the expats. These will include a 'theosophical lady' and a 'gentle old homo' who will be based on Roger Senhouse, the ex-lover of Lytton Strachey, whom Golding had met on Lesvos. He started writing at the end of September and continued regularly until 22 December, when he gave up, having completed 60,000 words. He decided that it was too obscene ('it is so boring to imagine and *dwell* on dirt'), and that there should be a 'ceremonial burning' of the manuscript, because he would not wish anyone else to see it. However, though it was 'a load of rubbish', there were, he felt, 'one or two tiny bits of growing stuff among the rocks'.

Two items that relate to this burst of creativity survive in the archive. One is a set of notes about Middle-Eastern brothels, recording stories he heard in the navy and elsewhere, which may well, he concedes, be fantasy or wish-fulfilment, since his informants were 'uneducated sailors with exceptionally dirty minds'. In one homosexual brothel, he was told, 'naked boys and men sat round, and in front of each was a peg of the same size as the one they sat on to keep their assholes open for the clients. The pegs were of varying sizes to accommodate all clients.'

The second item bears no relation to this at all. It is Niki's story, spoken into a tape recorder by him for his son Yiorgis. Niki is now a wealthy shipowner, with seven tankers, his own private island, houses in New Smyrna and Volos, and a flat in Kolonaki, a fashionable district of Athens. But his earliest memory is of being an abandoned child, whom the captain of a *kaiki*, trading among the islands, finds on the quay at Lesvos trying to steal food. The captain, a kind and gentle man, takes him aboard, and he becomes the captain's lover. When he is seventeen Niki stabs and kills a drunken English naval officer because the officer makes advances and calls him a bastard when he resists. It was at the time when the Germans were taking Crete, and the officer was trying to escape from them. The captain does not blame Niki. The stabbing was clearly an honourable deed, and admirably quick. But it may cause unpleasantness for the *kaiki*'s crew if the authorities investigate, so he regrets he must put Niki ashore. On their last night of love together he gives Niki advice about how to survive. In peacetime, he explains, American and English women come to the islands. They are no longer young or beautiful, but they are rich, and they have strange ways. For example, they feed cats and birds, buy books, and think they can speak Greek. The captain advises Niki how to select one of them and ingratiate himself with her. He must make out that he cannot speak English, so that she can teach him, and he must pretend to like children:

'You may allow her to find you playing with children; with three little boys, shall we say.'

'Then she will think me mad as she is.'

'No, no. Do you know any games that children play?'

'Few. How should I know them, master? But wait. There is one. I saw this in Astypalaea. You catch a bird, being careful not to damage it. Then you pull out all its feathers, and let it go. It is most amusing to see how the naked bird scuttles here and there and beats its wings and cannot understand why it is not flying. I could be playing that with the little boys.'

My master considered for some time, twisting his moustache. At last he pursed his lips, lifted his chin definitely, and lowered his eyelids.

'It is unsubtle, that one. The English and to a lesser extent the Americans have a religion of animals. I do not think it would be the correct thing. It would be better to play with a ball of some sort.'

This whole cynical, cruel, affectionate scene, illustrating how incomprehensible one culture is to another, is one of the funniest things Golding ever wrote. It is also his most sympathetic treatment of homosexuality.

The second part of the story concerns Niki's early steps towards profitability and success – a narrative of callous exploitation, recounted by him in a voice of entire self-righteousness and reason. At the conclusion the ice-cold humour gives way to a gentler mode. In Lindos at the end of the war Niki finds a starving boy called Andreas, whose family have been killed by the Germans. He cares for him and gives him a meal, which causes him to vomit and collapse, since he has not eaten for many days. So he finds a spare bed for him in a brothel and, while Andreas sleeps in his arms, Niki remembers his own mother and what it was like to know love. It is almost inconceivable that this wonderful story could have been written in the gap years when Golding was lamenting his aridity. Yet it seems that must be so, for there is no mention of Niki in the journal after 18 December 1974. It is equally astonishing that, having written it, he did not publish it, or even let

Monteith at Fabers know of its existence. Perhaps he thought it unfinished – and clearly it could be expanded. The theosophical lady and Roger Senhouse have not appeared by the time the story stops. But it is 20,000 words long, it has its own shapeliness, ending, as it began, with the finding of a starving boy, and it is a masterpiece crying out for publication.

Correspondence with Faber and Faber more or less dried up during the gap years, but relations between Golding and Monteith remained friendly. There was jubilation in April 1974 when Golding wrote to announce a breakthrough in the Case of Piggy's Spectacles. Ever since *Lord of the Flies* was published a steady trickle of letters from scientifically minded schoolboys had been arriving at Ebble Thatch and Fabers' offices, pointing out that it would have been impossible to light a fire using Piggy's spectacles, because lenses to correct myopia are concave and so cannot concentrate the sun's rays. Monteith always wrote back politely saying how clever they were, and how only a few other boys had spotted the error. He was less charitable in private, and so was Golding. 'What a horrible little boy. Let's hope he takes up drug smuggling in Turkey,' he wrote after Monteith had sent on yet another know-all communication. 'I originally thought of the spectacles as those worn by people after a cataract operation when the inside lens is removed as well as the cornea – but little boys seldom have cataracts. Damn. Bill.'

However, in April 1974 Barry Bullen, who knew Judy and Terrell in Oxford, alerted Judy to a footnote in J. P. Stern's book *On Realism*, published the previous year. Piggy's spectacles are convex not concave, Stern argues, because Piggy is hypermetropic. This is confirmed by his inability to see either at a distance or close up, and it fits in with his obesity, his asthma, and his underdeveloped physique (his hair, for example, hardly grows while he is on the island, though the other boys' hair does). Piggy's spectacles could, then, concentrate the sun's rays and they exemplify 'the compelling logic set in train by Mr Golding's fiction'. Even in a trivial matter like bad eyesight he follows out 'the consequences of his choice'. Golding was delighted to find he had been right all along, and so was Monteith who, at Golding's request, supplied him with photocopies of Stern's solution to be sent to future schoolboy savants.

The two picture postcards that arrived on Monteith's desk from Australia the following year also indicate that friendly relations were being maintained. They were couched in Golding's cheery approximation to the native argot ('My bloody oath, it's hot!'), and one of them, clearly chosen for its unattractiveness, showed the main street of Gladstone, Queensland, and bore the message 'Not very many people include Gladstone in their itinerary'. There was an exchange of letters later in the year about some studio photographs of Golding taken by Cecil Beaton (the occasion of much embarrassed jocularity on Golding's part). He happened to mention, in passing, Yevtushenko's visit, and Monteith responded chattily: 'Is Yevtushenko really nice – only met him once – held lift door open for him after he visited TSE[liot] – swept by without a look – realized what it must have felt like to be a serf – and why the revolution happened.' In October Monteith heard that Golding had been invited to Rouen the following year to address a conference of French school and university English teachers, and he arranged for Faber and Faber to have a stand at the conference selling his novels, with blown-up prints of the Beaton photos.

His interest suggests that he interpreted Golding's public appearance as a sign he was emerging from dormancy – as, indeed, proved to be the case. The Rouen conference was the first of many foreign events organized for Golding by the British Council, and it was an encouraging success. He travelled out, without Ann, on 14 May 1976 and was modestly pleased with the lecture he gave ('It was ham, but not your ordinary ham. Parma ham, perhaps'). He still thought lecturing 'whorish', though, and was ashamed of the self-importance it implied. Geoffrey Hitchcock, director of the British Council in France, and Ian Scott-Kilvert, the Council's literary director, looked after him, and took him to Paris on the 16th for a question-and-answer session with twenty senior French academics. Despite his escorts' meticulous arrangements, Golding managed to land up in the wrong hotel on the evening of the 16th. He had been booked into Le Colbert but could not find it and spent the night in the Hôtel Richelieu-Mazarin ('a sleazy dump'). It was a sign of how hopeless he was at managing without Ann, and the British Council decided that it would be well worth paying for her to accompany him in future, as he was 'not himself' without her.

All the same, Monteith must have been pleased to hear how well the trip had gone. Golding was a huge asset to Faber and Faber, but he was also, to Monteith, a personal friend, about whom he cared deeply. He had recognized his greatness as a writer when no one else did, and he retained his confidence in him through the gap years. He was undoubtedly disappointed that Golding never wrote a dramatized version of *Lord of the Flies*, and the only moment of asperity in the whole of their forty-year correspondence relates to this. 'Oh dear, oh dear, oh dear,' Golding wrote in January 1972, 'I *dread* reading the book. That's silly but true.' 'If it really is going to be such a dreadful imposition,' Monteith replied tartly, 'do please forget all about it.' His impatience was understandable, but it failed to take into account Golding's complicated and resentful feelings about his first book's enormous success, which had dwarfed everything he wrote afterwards. When, in April 1972, he did bring himself to reread it for the first time in ten years, his verdict was hostile. 'I found it boring and crude. The language is O level stuff.' But Monteith kept trying, and also proposed alternatives. Might Golding do a children's book for the 9–13 age group, he suggested in October 1975, perhaps set in ancient Greece and retelling legends? Four days later he got Golding's reply, which was far more interesting: 'I am working towards the first draft of a book; or rather I am writing a mass of words to find out if there is a book in there and, crossing fingers, believe there may be.' He had given this 'mass' or 'wodge' the provisional title of 'the QUARRY' and hoped to have it 'ended rather than finished' by the end of the year, after which he might start turning it into the first draft of a novel in the winter and spring. 'What marvellous exciting news,' Monteith replied. The novel that was to be built from the quarry was *Darkness Visible*.

25

Darkness Visible

Golding would never talk about *Darkness Visible*. It was the one book he refused to discuss either in private or in public. However, his manuscripts tell us a good deal about why he wrote it and what he thought it meant. His journal entries from 1975 to 1979 amount to an authorial commentary on the novel, plotting its daily progress, and revealing the changes of plan, additions and deletions from which the published work emerged. They are far too numerous and detailed to record here, but the main developments can be summarized.

First, though, the plot – which is rather harder to summarize, and readers should take the next few paragraphs slowly. The novel has three parts. Part One, called 'Matty', begins during the London Blitz, when incredulous firemen see a small boy walk out of an inferno of blazing buildings. He is naked, and badly burned on the left side, but otherwise unharmed, and walks with a kind of 'ritual' gait. Since the fire is of such intensity that it melts lead and distorts iron, it seems impossible any human could have survived. To one of the firemen the boy does not appear at first to have a human shape but is 'a bit of flickering brightness'. What sort of being the boy is remains the novel's central enigma. He is taken to hospital and undergoes several years of plastic surgery, which partly restore his face. But the left side of his head stays bald and his left ear is a hideous purple stump, so other children shun him. He cannot speak at first but gradually learns English. He is given the forenames Matthew (shortened to Matty) and Septimus by the hospital authorities, but his surname is mysteriously unstable. The official responsible for allocating surnames writes down a name and then alters it, he does not know why. 'The name had first jumped into his mind with the curious effect of having come out of empty air.' It appears in the book as Windrove, Windgrove, Windgraff, Windwood, Wildwort and other variants.

Matty is sent to a Foundling School in a home-counties market town, Greenfield. He is devout and literal minded, and knows much of the Bible by heart. One of the masters, Sebastian Pedigree, is a paedophile, who has a pet among the boys called Henderson. When Pedigree ironically calls Matty a 'treasure', Matty takes it literally and believes Pedigree values him. Soon after, Henderson is found dead at the foot of a fire escape, with one of Matty's gymshoes beneath his body. Questioned, Matty mumbles what the headmaster later realizes is a primitive curse from the Old Testament, 'Over Edom will I cast out my shoe' (Psalms 60.8). Pedigree, called in for questioning, blames Matty for what has occurred and shouts, 'It's all your fault,' which fills Matty with remorse and anguish.

Leaving the school he finds work in an old-fashioned ironmonger's called Frankleys (Golding based this on an ironmonger's in Castle Street, Salisbury, called Woodrows). However, he is tormented by lust for the young woman who serves in the plastic-flower department, so he leaves and emigrates to Australia. Here he gets casual employment in Melbourne, Sydney and Gladstone (the town from which Golding sent Monteith his comic picture postcard), where he works as a gravedigger. Trying to get to Darwin across the outback he is attacked by an aborigine who drives a spear though his hands in a kind of crucifixion and jumps on his groin. In hospital it is feared he has been castrated, though it later turns out he has not. But his lust is quietened for the time being, and on his release he becomes a sort of preacher – not speaking, but performing symbolic acts, such as lighting a fire under an earthenware vessel to illustrate Ecclesiastes 7.6 ('The laughter of fools is like the crackling of thorns under a pot'). He also performs a strange, lonely ritual at night, wading through a deep pool naked, loaded with chains and metal wheels, and holding a lamp over his head.

He returns to England in 1966 and works for a time in Cornwall before getting a job as a handyman at a boys' public school called Wandicott House, near Greenfield, where the pupils include the sons of foreign royals and oil sheiks. We learn of his doings from his journal, where he tells how he is visited periodically by two spirits who give him instructions (not spoken but 'showed'). Like George Fox's *Journal*, which may have been in Golding's mind, Matty's journal can seem ridiculous in its mixture of the mundane and the supernatural, leaving the reader unsure how to take it.

The novel's second part is called 'Sophy' and is about two other inhabitants of Greenfield, the twins Sophy and Toni Stanhope. Their mother has left home and their father, who writes and broadcasts on chess, neglects them, taking up with a series of mistresses. Both twins suffer from his rejection. Toni goes to Afghanistan, gets mixed up with people who are running drugs and is jailed. Extricated with some difficulty, and brought home, she becomes politicized and makes off again, sending back a defiant postcard from Cuba. Sophy drifts into casual sex, and discovers she is a sadist when she digs a penknife into a boy who is having sex with her and it gives her an orgasm. She meets Gerry, an ex-subaltern who has resigned his commission to get out of Northern Ireland, and Bill, once a private in Gerry's regiment in Ulster, who got too fond of killing and shot several civilians. To keep them in funds and drugs, the trio rob shops, using a replica gun. But Sophy aims higher, and plans with them to kidnap and hold to ransom a pupil from Wandicott House School.

The novel's last part brings the various characters together in June 1978. Toni turns up, disguised, in Greenfield. She is now a member of a terrorist organization and Sophy lets her in on the kidnap plan. Meanwhile Matty sees Sebastian Pedigree in the park, using a brightly coloured ball to lure children. We learn from Matty's journal that his spirits have told him he is responsible for guarding a boy at the school, and he is to be a 'burnt offering'. The meaning of this becomes clear when he surprises a man (who is actually Bill, Sophy's accomplice in the kidnap plot) planting a bomb by petrol tanks at the school's garage. The man knocks Matty out, the bomb goes off, and the place is engulfed in a tide of blazing petrol. In the confusion that follows Bill grabs a child, and is carrying him off, struggling, when a strange thing happens to the fire. It seems to organize itself into a shape of flame that rushes out of the garage doors and whirls round Bill, who drops the unharmed child and flees. The flaming shape is Matty, sacrificing himself to save the child — or perhaps Matty transformed into a fiery angel, we cannot be sure which. Sophy, back in Greenfield, sees the blaze in the sky and has an orgasmic vision of herself knifing the kidnapped boy. But when Bill arrives, she learns the kidnap has failed and she has been fooled. Gerry is in league with Toni, they have taken hostages, forced the authorities to give them a plane and escaped to Africa, from where Toni later appears on television delivering a speech about freedom and justice.

As Pedigree sits alone in the park at dusk, clutching his brightly coloured ball, Matty appears (perhaps in spirit form, perhaps just part of Pedigree's dream). Pedigree explains to him that he is terrified he will eventually kill one of the children he molests, just to keep it quiet, and he begs Matty for help. Whereupon Matty becomes a golden angel with peacock feathers and a smile that is 'loving and terrible'. He seems to speak the word 'Freedom', though not in human speech, then he reaches out his great hands, grasps the brightly coloured ball, and pulls it away, leaving Pedigree lifeless.

At the Court of Inquiry into the kidnapping Sophy presents herself as an innocent victim and gets away with it, selling her story to a newspaper. It turns out that the security forces had bugged the Stanhope home, but all they had managed to record was a kind of séance where Matty, Sim Goodchild the local bookseller, and Edwin Bell, a teacher at the Foundling School, joined hands, and Edwin spoke in a strange tongue, like music. This is described in great beauty in the narrative, but is ridiculed at the Court of Inquiry.

Synopsis does *Darkness Visible* no favours. It makes it sound muddled and improbable, with twice as much plot as is good for it. In reality, quite apart from the power of its writing, it is a technical marvel, uniting the Matty story and the kidnap story into a single narrative that is at once gripping and elusive. Matty's final appearance to Pedigree is Golding's greatest piece of religious writing, yet it allows the reader no fingerhold in certainty. Everything is as you interpret it. Pedigree may have been dreaming, or he may have had a vision of celestial reality.

Getting the novel's structure right did not come easily. It was a bitter struggle, often bringing Golding close to despair, and it lasted twenty-four years, the longest incubation period of any of his books. It began between 10 and 15 October 1955 (he put the dates at the tops of the pages), when he started writing a story in a Bishop Wordsworth's School exercise book labelled 'The Vertical'. Those dates were a Monday and a Saturday, so possibly this was the school half-term. The story is set in the future. The world is divided into two armed camps, and both have been stockpiling atomic weapons. These are, however, not old-style ICBMs but small devices, easily carried by a single person, yet more powerful than an H-bomb. Many of them have been planted by each side in the other side's cities throughout the world, and they can be activated by remote control. Now the flashpoint is thought to be imminent. The world's populations are terror-stricken, many are committing suicide. The story focuses on a schoolmaster called Henry Eustace Manderson who has just been released from prison where he was sent, we gather, for child-molesting. He is clutching a football, which he has stolen, and is fleeing from an angry crowd of (curiously) Boy Scouts. He is rescued by a girl who takes him to an upper room where there are two men, called Windrove and Pete. Windrove is some kind of spiritual leader, and he calms Manderson and gently takes the football from him. Pete explains that Windrove distrusts words, especially written words, because they are 'dead'. They are always yesterday's words and today needs today's words. So Windrove says little and Pete is his 'talker'. The story is unfinished, but a synopsis Golding wrote at the start indicates how it would have continued. The girl would fetch the Foreign Secretary, who would come and seek Windrove's help. He however, would be more interested in helping Manderson. Leaving Manderson in safety, he would go out and be 'martyred making a speech to the crowd'. Later the girl and Pete would listen to the Foreign Secretary on the radio. Manderson would leave at dawn and be killed by a bus.

For whatever reason, elements in this strange story were profoundly important to Golding. A spiritual being called Windrove who distrusts words; a paedophile schoolmaster clutching a ball; and the moment when Windrove takes the ball from him – these things stayed in his imagination for twenty-four years, demanding to be fitted into a story. And something else: he was sure from the start that the story must have a national or international political dimension. The Foreign Secretary, the radio broadcast – these details would change with time, but the political context they represent remained a vital part of the imaginative nexus. One element that did not survive was Manderson's name. There had been a real Manderson. He was a friend of Golding's father and used to play the cello at musical evenings with Golding's parents. Nothing is known of his sexual leanings, and he died in 1917 when Golding was six. Perhaps the use of his name was arbitrary, and perhaps changing it to Pedigree, with its suggestion of genetic inheritance, seemed more meaningful.

The elements of this story stayed in his mind through the 1960s and he mentioned it under its provisional title 'Here Be Monsters' (words used on unexplored parts of the world in old maps) in letters to Monteith and Virginia Tiger. Some notes at the end of his 1973 journal show him trying to fit the different ideas together. Windrove's name now becomes 'Windover': 'How does Windover get killed? Martyred? Yes but how?' he asks himself. The 'idea of the new book', he decides, will be to 'meld' Windover's religious society that shuns written words (called 'the Unwritten Love') with the 1973 oil crisis. This had come about when the OPEC countries, united by the 1973 Arab–Israeli war, sought to coerce the industrial nations into intervening on the Arab side by cutting down their oil supply. Golding, in his 1973 notes, contemplates making Windover a Jew who is wanted by the Arabs, and is handed over to Syria by the Foreign Secretary, showing 'our willingness to do *anything* to get oil and avoid terrorism'. Windover's 'Society' will be bugged so that 'all the stuff about *speech only* comes out in court'. But he remained undecided about what political events to link the Windrove (or Windover) story to. 'Windover I now think is possibly a coloured gent,' he notes in January 1974, who will be 'extradited' to a country that will 'do him', perhaps Portugal. Two days later he reminds himself that 'the proper person for the British Government to sell for oil would be a Jew', so perhaps Windover could be a 'coloured Jew' who is 'framed' by MI5 and maybe the CIA as well.

His decision to ditch these ideas and make international terrorism his political subject seems to have been a response to events. On 30 January 1972 in Derry thirteen civil rights protestors were shot dead by members of the 1st Battalion of the Parachute regiment in the atrocity that became known as Bloody Sunday. Golding, in his journal, admits that he shares a common British prejudice against the Irish, but he feels 'personally humiliated and stricken' at the 'ghastly news'. A national demonstration of guilt is called for, he maintains, and he would himself be perfectly willing 'to walk to St Pauls in a white sheet and carrying a candle'. His notes for *Darkness Visible* (though not the published book) identify Bill, the 'brute' who kidnaps the child, as one of the soldiers who opened fire on Bloody Sunday.

But the Provisional IRA's terrorist campaign following the massacre kindled his anger and hatred, particularly the kidnappings. In December 1973 the German industrialist Thomas Niedermeyer was kidnapped and murdered; in June 1974 Lord and Lady Donoughmore were taken and held to ransom. 'I do so passionately hope that somewhere, some time, a kidnap victim will kill his or her kidnappers,' he wrote in his journal, adding that he would wish them 'to die slowly and in pain'. Contemplating current events, he felt a surge of impatient anarchy. 'The best work for an anarchist today', he wrote, would be to explode a bomb big enough to trigger a natural catastrophe such as the melting of the polar ice caps.

How agreeable to sacrifice most of England in a last splendid assassination of the assassins! I would drown happily if my last moments could only be consoled by the thought of the tiresome, half-witted Irishry all sitting on Ben Bulben or the mountains of Morne. And to hear on one's transistor of Moscow reduced to an island and eight hundred and fifty million Chinese climbing into Tibet! Oh the thunder of sea water down those thousands of missile silos, the hesitant questing of ships among the high rise flats! And presently the atomic submarines would come, nosing curiously among the tree tops of a wilderness of drowned forests.

Terrorism in the 1970s was by no means an IRA monopoly. At work on his novel, he keeps track of terrorist outrages in his journal – the seizure of eighty-five hostages, including children, on a train in the Netherlands in May 1977; the 'sadistic and inhuman' kidnap and murder of the Italian politician Aldo Moro by the Red Brigades in March 1978. In an attempt to understand the mentality of terrorists he reads *The Angry Brigade*, an account of the British urban guerrilla group of the 1970s, by Gordon Carr, John Barker and Stuart Christie, but he concludes that the group were 'paranoid'.

The decision to make his terrorists female also reflected what was happening around him. The first woman terrorist to receive global media coverage was Leila Khaled, a member of the Popular Front for the Liberation of Palestine, who organized the simultaneous hijacking of four airliners in September 1970. Other women who came to prominence during the terrorist decade of the 1970s included Ulrike Meinhof, co-founder of the Baader-Meinhof Gang, and Margherita Cagol, co-founder of the Red Brigades. Khaled, who was exceptionally beautiful, underwent plastic surgery to alter her appearance after the hijackings, and was probably in Golding's mind when he brought the equally beautiful Toni back to Greenfield facially changed.

Toni's earlier history – running off to Afghanistan and risking years in jail because she accepted a lift from people who were running drugs – drew on a closer acquaintance. Emily Young, the daughter of his friends Liz and Wayland Kennet who is today one of Britain's leading sculptors, had left home in 1969, when she was eighteen, and landed up in Afghanistan with her Sioux boyfriend who was a draft dodger and into drugs. Through her association with him she was sent to an Afghan prison, which was, she recalls, 'not that terrible – it was just like living in a compound – lots of children, goats, chickens. It was icy cold so it wasn't smelly or anything.' When she was eventually fetched home her father told her that Golding would like to talk to her about her experiences. She had known him since early childhood and thought of him as 'Blake and God and Michelangelo' rolled into one – 'a very serious creature, golden and inspired and inspiring'. So she was astonished that he wanted to know anything about 'my pitiful little shenanigans'. But he came and asked her why she had gone and what it was all about, and she explained as well as she could.

It was probably because he had watched Emily grow from child to rebellious teenager that, as the journal shows, he found it so imaginatively stimulating to write about his 'girl terrorist' (there was only one at first, called Beryl; the realization that the plot would require a twin sister came relatively late, in December 1975). He had understood from the start that his 'main constructional problem' in writing the novel was 'getting what could well be two separate books into one plot', and the more he was drawn to the girl-terrorist story, the more he felt tempted to jettison the Matty story altogether. This possibility attracted him because concentrating just on Sophy's story would give him space to describe 'more of the ordinary pains and pleasures of being a girl', and allow the reader to sympathize with Sophy's predicament. 'I am approaching a crisis in this damn book', he acknowledged at the end of April 1978, after a four-month spell of almost daily labour. 'Somehow I have to reach a decision over the strategy of the whole. Is it to include nineteen forty one and the ponderous portentous relationship between Matty and Pedigree? Or is it to be smaller and ray out from the two girls?'

He got to the stage of thinking that the story of the two girls would 'turn out to be novel length', and could be titled 'Sophy and Toni'. It would be a riposte to critics who charged him with neglecting female characters. One of the impulses behind the book, he told Monteith, 'was to prove I could write about women as well as men'. The scene, for example, where Sophy washes herself out after sex could be seen as a deliberate attempt to answer Sammy Mountjoy's question in *Free Fall*, 'How do they react in themselves, those soft, cloven creatures?'

> she washed herself out as in the films and was faintly repelled by the mess of blood and spunk, and – reaching far in, her lower lip hurting between clenched teeth – she felt the pear-shaped thing stuck inside the front of her stomach where it ought to be, inert, a time bomb, though that was hard to believe of yourself or your body. The thought of the possible explosion of the time bomb started her even more elaborately probing and washing, pain or not, and she came on the other shape, lying opposite the womb but at the back, a shape lying behind the smooth wall but easily to be felt through it, the rounded shape of her own turd working down the coiled gut and she convulsed, feeling without saying but feeling every syllable – *I hate! I hate! I hate!* There was no direct object to the verb, as she said to herself when she was a little more normal. The feeling was pure.

What changed Golding's mind about limiting his novel to the girl-terrorist plot was the idea of including in his narrative parts of Matty's journal – a possibility that occurred to him on 4 May 1978. He saw at once that this would allow him to open up Matty's mind to the reader, conveying 'the terror of his vision together with his sense that great things are to follow'. After the 'repellent' story of Matty's early life, his journal, he thought, should put us 'if not on his side at least in a state of pity or compassion for him, since we are bound to think him deluded'. As soon as he started writing the journal he felt relieved, as if he were 'hauling a great load' of what the novel was about 'into the daylight'. At the same time, giving Matty a journal ran counter to part of his original conception of Windrove as a man alienated from the written word. So in this new version it is Windrove's avoidance of speech that is stressed, climaxing in the beautiful episode where Edwin Bell, under Matty's influence, gives voice to what is more like music than speech – which Golding in the journal refers to as 'speaking with tongues'.

His journal also records, in September 1977, that his son David has become involved in the charismatic movement – a branch of Christianity that practices glossolalia, or speaking with tongues, on the pattern of the Pentecostal events described in Acts 2.1–4. This coincidence naturally prompts speculation about how far Golding's remodelling of Matty was influenced by his observation of his son. David was devout. He had been received into the Roman Catholic Church, and later confirmed. Unlike his father, who worried constantly about money, he was careless of worldly goods, and gave away his possessions to a degree that caused his parents some anxiety. When he moved into a small house in Salisbury in July 1978, he generously took in two young women as lodgers, one of them an unmarried mother. Golding was sometimes exasperated by his son's piety and angered by his unworldliness, but it may have struck him that these qualities had an aspect that might almost be called saintly. If so it would match his thoughts about Matty. Writing to Charles Monteith after the publication of *Darkness Visible*, he explained that he had intended Matty as a 'saint' – like, he said, Simon in *Lord of the Flies*, St Jean Vianney, the Curé of Ars, and St Thérèse of Lisieux. 'It's a figure I've tried for again and again and I suppose Matty in Darkness Visible is as near as I shall ever get.' Monteith rightly saw this as an extraordinary revelation, in view of Golding's usual adamant refusal to comment on the novel, and he was properly grateful: 'your mention of Matty is immensely illuminating and helpful'.

Apart from David's religious nature, the intensive medical treatment he had to undergo in his early years to rectify his deformed foot might also suggest a connection with Matty. Mark Kinkead-Weekes, to whom Golding spoke about David's breakdown, as he did to very few others, is sure that Matty was to some extent inspired by Golding's son. So is Tim Brown, whose flat, in Duke's Lane off Kensington Church Street, David had shared for six months after coming down from Oxford. At the time he was in his Marxist phase, and had a job washing up in the Dorchester. Emily Young, who knew David at the time his father was writing *Darkness Visible*, remembers him as having 'a quality of intensity – of someone who is thinking hard and none of it coming out'. He seemed to be 'in a very, very private place'. That would fit Matty. But the question of David's influence remains unanswerable.

At the end of June 1978 Golding finished yet another draft of his troublesome novel (the previous draft had been finished early in March), and he wrote to Monteith announcing his 'return to the light'. True to form, however, he cautioned that the book he had written was 'a mess'. It was 'jumbled, inconsistent, wallowing', and trying to get it right had exhausted him. '*Honestly, I don't know what to do.*' Awkwardly jocular, he added: 'I don't suppose, said he, with partly pretended diffidence, you'd want to read the book in its present stage? I think not!' Monteith, only too accustomed by now to Golding's nervous contortions, did of course want to see it. He phoned as soon as he received the letter, arranging to come and stay at Ebble Thatch for the weekend of 22–23 July, and asking him to send his manuscript at once. It came, and after reading it he passed it to Kinkead-Weekes and Gregor for their opinions. Kinkead-Weekes remembers being handed a large 'box of manuscripts', and told 'we think it's tremendously good, but it's big'.

Golding waited anxiously, unable to sleep at night, and watching out for the post each morning. So when Monteith turned up for his weekend visit it must have been a relief to learn that Fabers would publish the novel as it stood if he liked. However, they discussed its problems 'at great length' that afternoon and on the Sunday morning, and back in London on the Monday Monteith put a report before the Faber and Faber Book Committee. He and his two advisers were agreed, he said, that it was an 'immensely powerful' novel. They also agreed about its

'weakest passages', and, unlike Golding, they preferred the part about
Matty to the part about the twin girls. After their weekend talk,
Monteith concluded, Golding had promised to get to work on the book
again and send a final draft by 31 October.

   So that is what happened. He set to and, after much private grumbling
('How fatuous it all is. What a relief it will be to get it over!'), he finished his
novel with a few days to spare. The differences between it and the June 1978
version can be deduced from the letter he sent with his October typescript,
as well as from his journal entries and Monteith's memo to the Book
Committee. The final version is 30,000 words shorter, and most of the cuts
were made in the part relating to Sophy and Toni – not without a pang. 'It
did rather hurt me to leave out so much,' Golding lamented. A sermon to
the dead that the spirits give Matty permission to preach was cut too, on
Kinkead-Weekes's advice. It was 'marvellous' and 'astonishing', he thought,
but not 'doing anything that led anywhere'. The June 1978 version had also
been much more violent. It gave more coverage to Toni's terrorist organization, and ended with a 'pile of corpses', among them the corpses of
Sophy and of the kidnapped boy whom she murders. It was Ann's idea that,
in the rewrite, Sophy should be kept alive, and that instead of murdering
the boy she should have a 'vision' of herself doing it. Since the boy died in
the earlier version, there was no place there for Matty's fiery rescue. This
moment, both horrifying and triumphant, is the point when the two plots
at last come together, as Golding had been trying to make them do for
years. It is so obviously the climax of the novel that it seems inconceivable
it could have been such a late addition. Yet he was still wondering, with
only two months to go to Monteith's October deadline, how he could
arrange things so that Matty would 'spoil the op' for the terrorists. 'More
thought here,' he counsels himself. Six days later, he has solved it: 'I have
now tidied up Matty at the end, burning him alive as they [the spirits]
always predicted'.

Matty's adventures in Australia were also new in the rewrite.
Monteith had been keen to have Drysdale's picture of an aboriginal
man on the cover, so Golding obliged with an Australian section. 'You'll
be entertained to hear', he wrote, when sending the final copy, 'that I've
worked Tassy Drysdale's RAIN MAKER into Matty's adventures,
principally to bolster your opinion that the picture was the perfect dust

jacket. Can writer's devotion to publisher go further?' The episode where Matty wades through the pool takes place in Australia in the printed version. But Golding had written it months before he had even thought of setting part of the novel in Australia. 'I am now with Matty in the swamp,' he noted on 20 May. Then, having written the account of Matty's Australian adventures between 2 and 4 August (drawing on his journal of 'the Goldings in Aussie-land'), he reminded himself: 'I have to join it to Matty in the pool.'

The mysterious pool episode may have had a relatively homely origin. During the spring and summer of 1978, while doing daily stints on *Darkness Visible*, Golding was engaged in major operations in his swamp garden. In May he hired a pump to empty the pond, prior to attacking its bed with a hired 'Kango Hammer' road drill, as part of his campaign against the invasive azolla weed. He started the pump early on Saturday, 6 May, but soon after H-hour it got clogged with mud and stopped working. Exasperated, he waded into the pool and engaged in hand-to-hand combat with the weed, searching for his missing water lilies. But his boots sank deeper than he expected and, though he struggled to keep his balance, he fell in. There was a plus side. His fall dislodged a quantity of mud below the water, and four lost Sagittaria bulbs bobbed to the surface with him. Perhaps Matty's mystical descent into the pool, which has perplexed commentators, was the artistic outcome of this recent immersion, and the strange nocturnal ritual somewhere in northern Australia began as an encounter with aquatic plants at Ebble Thatch.

He packed up his novel (or, as he cautiously persisted in calling it, his 'advanced draft' of the novel) and sent it off to Fabers by registered post on 27 October. Then he took Ann to Crane's restaurant for a 'triumphant dinner'. With the book out of the way they were both so 'free-feeling' that they decided to prolong the celebrations and 'shove off for a day or two' to Cornwall. Which they did. When they got back there was the title to settle. 'Darkness Visible', as an alternative to 'Here Be Monsters', had first occurred to him in April, 1977, and it turned out to be what Fabers' Book Committee preferred, so it was selected. It is a quotation from Milton's description of the hell that the fallen angels find themselves in in *Paradise Lost* – and it inevitably raises the question of whether Matty is a fallen angel, though not necessarily one who has fallen, as Satan's followers do, through his own fault. Matty's spirits tell him, 'The cry that went up to heaven brought you down,' which suggests that he was once a heavenly inhabitant, and the fireman who, at the novel's start, saw him as a flame, not a human, may have seen him in his true shape. His 'ritual' gait, too, does not suggest a human being escaping from a fire. Thinking about the orders of angels in his journal in March 1979 Golding wrote: 'Might not Matty's nature be that of always (eternally) being consumed by fire? That would make a seraph of him.'

It may be that, as had happened before, an idea from H. G. Wells was lingering in his mind. In a Wells story called *The Wonderful Visit*, a country vicar, out shooting, accidentally wounds an angel and brings him to earth. The shocked and contrite clergyman, finding he has bagged one of the heavenly host, accommodates him in the vicarage and sets about nursing him back to health. He is naked, as Matty was when he walked out of the fire, but the vicar persuades him to wear clothes lest the villagers should be scandalized. He also explains to him about pain, food, death and other human interests. In the village the angel is thought to be a hunchback because of the bulge under his clothes caused by his wings, and he is accounted a simpleton because his opinions, especially on political issues, are so outrageously naïve. The schoolchildren pelt him with nuts. Of all the humans he meets the only one to arouse his affection is the vicar's servant girl Delia, and she fervently returns it. One day the vicarage catches fire and the angel, returning from a walk, learns that Delia is inside. He rushes in after her, and there is a sudden blinding glare that shoots upward to an immense height. That is the last anyone sees of Delia or her angel. 'Delia Hardy' and 'Thomas Angel' are inscribed on two little white crosses in the churchyard. But beneath them lie only the remains of the vicar's stuffed ostrich, for no human remains were found. The resemblances between Wells's story and *Darkness Visible* seem to extend even to occasional verbal parallels, and the witty absence of a surname for the angel might remind us of the strange fluidity of Matty's surname. But in the interests of scholarship it seems right to add that on an evening in March 1990 I found myself sitting next to Golding at dinner in Trinity College Oxford, after he had given the first Hillary Lecture. I was eager to test out my theory about Matty and the Wells story, but I knew of Golding's embargo on any discussion of *Darkness Visible*, and realized that a direct approach would be impossible. So instead I steered the conversation round to Wells, about whom he talked with enthusiasm, and towards the end of the evening I commented nonchalantly, 'Then there's that early story, isn't there, about the angel who comes to earth – *The Wonderful Visit?*' 'Ah!' replied Golding quickly, 'I don't think I remember that one.'

In the blurb for *Darkness Visible* that Monteith got him to write, he leaves Matty's nature as a string of unanswered questions: 'Who was he? What was he? What was he for? Was he more than human or less?' There is a suggestion in the blurb, too (though later excised by a Faber editor) that Matty's encounter with Sophy and Toni may have taken place in some other dimension than the earthly: 'Perhaps the three were enemies in an ancient war with a child for a prize.' The blurb also puts in a word for Sebastian Pedigree, 'thought by all to be the wickedest of men but proving in the end less harmful than those who thought they held the one truth firmly in both hands'. The editor cut this too, but it chimes with Pedigree's eloquent insistence in the book's last chapter that paedophiles do little harm compared to bombers, kidnappers and hijackers, all of whom act from 'the highest motives'.

The blurb's unanswered questions reflect Golding's state of mind about the novel. 'The basic difficulty is that *I* don't know what the damn thing is about either,' he told Monteith. He had written so many different versions that 'I can't remember what is which'. His refusal ever to discuss the book may relate to this inner bewilderment. The Latin epigraph he chose, 'Sit mihi fas audita loqui' (May it be rightful for me to speak what I have heard) was meant, too, as an admission of ignorance, or, as he put it to Monteith, 'a modest disclaimer of any personal knowledge of spiritual matters'. It is taken from Virgil's invocation to the gods in *Aeneid VI*, where he asks for divine help before writing his description of the Underworld, the classical equivalent of Milton's hell. Golding had come upon it by chance when reading *Aeneid VI* on his summer holiday in 1978 (not, one imagines, common summer-holiday reading, but typical of his eclectic tastes), and it had immediately struck him that it should 'stand on the title page of the book'. Monteith felt they ought to print a translation underneath, but Golding protested that it would be 'no good with a translation', adding despondently, 'Can't we rely on what used to be called "the spread of universal education"? No, probably not. Ah well.' Monteith let him have his way, but asked, a little huffily, where the quotation came from: 'An ignorant question, I am sure, but I don't know.'

The years 1977 and 1978 which brought *Darkness Visible* to an end, also saw the end of two lives that had been of significance to Golding. On 5 April 1977, Tony Brown died of cancer. Golding had spoken to him on the phone two days before, when he was already 'slow and confused', and what he now wanted to say, but could not, was 'Go on without fear, my old friend. You left the world a more musical place than you found it.' A death that touched him less closely came in February the following year, when Jose's wife Theo rang to say that May Golding, the daughter of Alec's brother, George Walter Raleigh Golding, had died. He reflected that he had not seen his cousin May since he was six, and for that matter had not seen his brother Jose for several years. 'We are an odd withdrawn family.' He went, unwillingly, to May's funeral in Kingswood, and was upset by the dilapidated churchyard, and by the family grave, so full of dead Goldings that there was scarcely room for May's coffin on top. It was 'Dickensian', he thought – evidently reminded of the burial of Esther's father in *Bleak House*.

Getting back to writing had given him confidence to undertake more speaking engagements, much as he always detested them. In February 1977 he and Ann went to Lille, where he gave a lecture on 'Utopias and Antiutopias', later printed in *A Moving Target*, to a symposium of *Anglicistes*. In the Musée des Beaux Arts they were charmed by a genre painting of the wolf that St Francis converted being given a morsel of meat by a butcher and wearing a halo.

In October they took the Daimler across the channel and drove down through France for a British Council tour of Spain and Portugal. He and Ann were both tired out by the driving, and there were mishaps. He lost the key to the Daimler boot, and was held up for two days finding a locksmith. Then he left his camera in a hotel and his Visa card in a restaurant. As usual, they seem to have done no pre-planning to find out what might be worth seeing en route, so they drove past Salamanca, seeing only its industrial outskirts. They were eating and drinking too much and both felt ill. He reflects that it is 'odd and sad' to think of himself as a 'common drunk, oh God have mercy!' He would never have suspected it would happen, he adds, though he might have predicted he would have a taste for young men. They decide to cut Cadiz and make straight for Seville, where he gives two lectures, and is not over-pleased with their reception. No one laughs at the first, he has a bad cold for the second, and only a trickle of buyers turns up at his book signing.

Moving on to Lisbon, he is grumpily unimpressed by Mike Eltenton, head of the British Council in Portugal, on the grounds that he seems not to have heard of de la Mare's 'The Traveller'. However, more than a hundred people turn up for his question-and-answer session, and his lecture the next day is crammed, with standing room only. Sightseeing, he and Ann are enchanted by the gardens of the Estufa Fria, especially the great hothouse, where the central pool has 'golden carp, blue lotuses, and pink flamingos'. He takes many pictures but is 'devastated' to find next day that, as so often, his film has somehow not wound on. On their leisurely way home they take in Santiago de Compostela, and find it astonishing, 'a fantasy of old buildings, huge concoctions rising like full-rigged ships' from huddles of ancient tiled and plastered houses.

In December he drove to Bangor for a lecture at the university but complained that the questions afterwards seemed to assume he was a theologian or philosopher, not a story-teller. The drive home was not a success. He had left the light on in the Daimler, so the battery was flat, and then he lost his way, arriving in Manchester before he discovered his mistake. His sense of direction was never strong, and even familiar journeys foxed him. Whenever he and Ann visited London, John Bodley of Faber and Faber would guide them out of the metropolis afterwards, going ahead in his own car, until they reached a point where error was, at least in theory, impossible. More enjoyable than the Bangor excursion was a trip to Cambridge in May 1978 to give a talk at St Catharine's College, and meet up with two undergraduate nephews, Jose's son John and Martin Brookfield.

There was a family summer holiday in September 1978, with Ann, David, Judy, Terrell and, for the first time, Nicky, aged two. They rented a house in the grounds of a château at Varennes, near Vichy in the Auvergne, and Nicky was the centre of attention. Golding's fondness had become apparent soon after Nicky's birth. A new movie camera was bought to capture the child's achievements, and seeing him in his bath brought home to his grandfather 'with a shock that what other men have said is true, and that people are beautiful'. On holiday, Nicky learnt to play Pooh-sticks, and was taken to see a tractor ploughing the golden stubble. When he said 'Oh!' in his sleep, it seemed to his grandfather 'the most affecting and strange kind of grief, as if it were the natural expression of our human condition'. He looked 'enchanting' in his Joseph's-coat dressing gown, and David sang to him at night to soothe him. There was general consternation when he developed an ear infection and required some injections. However, he came through his ordeal valiantly. The only thing that vied with Nicky for Golding's attention during the holiday was Anatoly Karpov's first defence of his world chess title against Viktor Korchnoi in the Philippines, a bizarre thirty-one-game drama of scandal and histrionics, which Karpov won 6–5.

With Tony Brown's death Golding had lost his own chess opponent, and in December 1977 he ordered a Chess Challenger, an early chess computer manufactured by Fidelity Electronics, which proved, like gardening, a welcome distraction from the agonies of writing. His machine was probably Chess Challenger 3 (the figure refers to the number of levels at which it can play), and he was rather scornful of its capabilities at first ('I don't see the machine beating me very often'). But quite soon it held him to a draw, and on 18 January 1978 beat him for the first time. In October 1978 he bought Chess Challenger 10, an improved model with 4KB memory, which offered tougher opposition. One game lasted for ten hours, until 3 a.m., and left him dizzy and rocking on his feet. In retaliation he set it chess problems from the *British Chess* magazine and timed how long it took it to solve them. At the end of August 1979 he records that he has just finished his fifty-sixth game with the machine, and has played it once a week for a year, 'not bad going'.

Another diversion into which he put serious effort during the struggle with *Darkness Visible* was relearning Latin. He worked his way through his old schoolbook, Francis Ritchie's *Second Steps in Latin*, three times, and embarked on a reading programme, starting with Caesar's

Gallic War, in which he took strongly against Caesar's self-righteousness, and his refusal to see anything from 'the barbarian point of view'. He tried, but gave up, Cicero's *Of Friendship*, feeling it irrelevant since he had (he grumbled) no friends, and graduated to Virgil's *Aeneid*, which he found difficult but 'lovely stuff'. The suspension of meaning that inflected languages like Latin allow fascinated him, and he thought of taking a complex Latin sentence and working out the process of comprehension that must have taken place in the mind of a Latin-speaker reading it. Ambitiously, he decided to teach himself to write Latin elegiac couplets, and picked up a second-hand 1919 reprint of a Victorian schoolbook *Clivus* by a Victorian Eton-master, A. C. Ainger. After an introduction explaining the metrical structure of the couplet (alternate hexameters and pentameters, made up of dactyls and spondees), Ainger's book consists of sixty exercises. Each is a piece of English prose, with those words that do not need to be translated into Latin placed in brackets, and those sets of two or more words that will translate into one Latin word hyphenated. Also supplied are lists of Latin poetic words that will be needed. The translator has to turn each piece of Ainger's English prose into twenty-four lines of Latin verse, deciding which Latin words to use and which grammatical forms the context requires. He must also know which syllables in each word are long, and which short, so that it will fit into the metrical structure.

Perhaps this testing task recommended itself to Golding because it was rather like trying to fit the different elements of *Darkness Visible* into a coherent whole. Equally, it may have seemed a more relaxing alternative. He compared it to filling in shapes with crayon or paint in a child's colouring book, but 'more fun'. Did it attract him, he wondered, for reasons of social class? Was he simply 'trying to catch up with Marlborough College?' Or was it something more aesthetic, a pleasure in the sound of words: 'the hexameter that was once a thornbrake has now become a limber line that can loiter or race along'? At all events, he persevered. Ainger's sixty exercises start with pieces on the seasons of the year and the Greek gods, then draw on fables, Greek myths, and stories from Homer. Golding began on 17 December 1977, writing his verses in a W. H. Smith & Son A6 hardcover notebook, and finished the last exercise on Saturday, 14 April 1979. There can be few twentieth-century novelists whose oeuvre includes 1,440 lines of Latin verse.

The publication date for *Darkness Visible* was 1 October, and as it approached Golding made clear his determination to remain incommunicado. He would take no part in any 'promotion' of the book, he assured Monteith, and would never again tolerate the kind of 'malarkey' he had put up with publicizing the film of *Lord of the Flies*. Besides, he could no longer bear adverse criticisms ('No, that's an exaggeration,' he conceded, 'but I ask myself, why put up with them?'). American publication was fixed for 5 November, and requests for magazine interviews soon arrived. Monteith sent on one from *Atlantic Monthly* in July, but met with a flat refusal. *Darkness Visible* was 'the one book of mine I'm never going to talk about'. His American publishers 'regretfully' told their publicity department, 'it is no on Golding interviews for the US press'. He was 'something of a recluse these days', Monteith's secretary, Rosemary Goad, explained to Rosalie Swedlin of Anthony Shiel Associates, who wanted the film and TV rights. All this did not stop TimeLife phoning to say they were sending a photographer to Ebble Thatch, 'but', Golding rejoined, 'as I have told them I am not, repeat not, discussing Darkness Visible with anyone, they may think again. Damn them all'. The BBC's request to broadcast a radio adaptation was also summarily refused.

Just to make sure he would be out of contact on publication day, he and Ann left at the beginning of September for a two-month holiday in the south of France. David, Judy, Terrell and Nicky came for the first month. They stopped on the way down to see the prehistoric cave paintings at the Grotte de Pech Merle near St-Cirq. But having imagined himself 'a thousand times' in a prehistoric cave, experience of the real thing was 'a bit dim by comparison'. He carried away a memory of the tap root of an oak that stretched down through the cave roof into the clay floor. They rented a holiday home near Puivert, a village with a small lake and a ruined Cathar fortress on a hill. (The address, sent to Monteith on 7 August, was c/o M and Mme A. Roux, Le Pla de Fa, Fa, 11260, Esperaza, Aude, France). It was surrounded by peach orchards and vineyards, and in sight of the Pyrenees. But for some reason the holiday was not as happy as the previous year's. There were family tensions, David's mental health was not good, and Nicky was no longer quite so angelic. Observing human nature down by the lake, his grandfather watched him go into paroxysms of rage when a little girl purloined his bucket. With the same observant eye he watched an elder brother bullying a younger, covertly and unmercifully, eventually hitting his head from about twenty yards away with a quite large stone, then rushing up to comfort him 'with many an indignant glance round for the assailant'. In addition, he found the novel he had brought for holiday reading, Sterne's *Tristram Shandy*, boring and unfunny.

At the end of September he and Ann had been married for forty years. 'I don't think anyone would have foreseen it,' he reflected, noting that Ann still looked 'very fetching with her powder'd wig tied *en queue* with a pink and silver scarf'. She had taken up painting, and he decided to have a try himself, thinking privately that he might be quite good, 'in a careless, amateur, slapdash way'. But he considered his first attempt hopeless, and threw it in the dustbin. When the Carvers and David left, he and Ann headed for Andorra, but they had failed to bring a road map and got hopelessly lost in the Pyrenees. They eventually made it into Spain, and drove down to Tortosa, but found it was too cold for bathing. Golding's journal account has a desultory feel, as if their only purpose was to stay out of England. They drove long distances, ate and drank too much, and slept a lot between meals. As usual, they were not interested enough in where they went to find out anything about it beforehand. On their way back through France Golding was 'stunned' to find that Aigues Mortes was a walled town with gates, towers and battlements. They went to Aix-en-Provence to see Cézanne's paintings, only to be told in the tourist office that there were none in the town. Home on 22 October, Golding admitted that they had run out of energy, 'let alone money and inclination'.

It was understood in the family that reviews of *Darkness Visible* must not be mentioned. When her parents phoned Judy from France, she said she knew it was a forbidden subject, but added that the book looked well. This was taken, rightly, as a hint that the notices were favourable, and when they got home Ann persuaded him to listen to her reading out some of the good bits. They were not hard to find. John Bayley in the first issue of the *London Review of Books* thought it his best novel to date, confirming him as 'a master craftsman in his particular sort of magic'. It 'restores a living force among us', said Frank Tuohy in the *Times Literary Supplement*, displaying 'an intensity of vision without parallel in contemporary writing'. A thoughtful appreciation by A. S. Byatt in the *Literary Review* identified Matty as 'the incarnate Second Coming' as well as the Egyptian god Horus. For her the book was 'spattered with clues and signs, clotted with symbols and puns' – an observation intended as praise, not blame. The quality of the writing attracted widespread attention. It was 'unique and marvellous', reported Myrna Blumberg in *The Times*, 'on some pages every line is poetry'. She ranked it as 'one of the most moving books I've ever read'. Golding's struggle to find a structure that would hold the reader's attention was rewarded by Ronald Hayman's verdict in *Books and Bookmen* that, more than any of his novels since *Lord of the Flies*, it made you want to find out what happened next. As always there was some dissent. Lorna Sage was sniffy in the *Observer*, and Christopher Booker in *Now! Magazine* dismissed it as 'a rather unpleasant, disordered, and not particularly well-written nightmare which Mr Golding might have done better to take to his psycho-analyst rather than to his publisher'. No one was likely to mistake that for intelligent criticism, but a more considerable figure, George Steiner, thought the book derivative, detecting, in his *Quarto* review the 'strong presence' of Patrick White's *Voss* and J. C. Powys's *A Glastonbury Romance*. Golding was not amused. 'According to Ann', he noted, 'some damned reviewer derives me from Patrick White and the Glastonbury Romance. The silly sod cant see that I derive from knowing Australia and Glastonbury.'

Ann told him *Darkness Visible* was 'a break-through', and he began to believe in its success. 'So it is real! Out there they are all reading it and muttering *yes, yes, we are like that*'. Judy congratulated him on being in the best-seller lists, 'with', his journal notes, 'Dick Francis and a man called Forsyte'. At the end of October Rosemary Goad sent a batch of 'marvellous' early American reviews – Peter Prescott in *Newsweek*, a rave on the cover of the *Los Angeles Times*, and a piece from *Village Voice* nominating him for a Nobel Prize. On American publication day a telegram arrived from Monteith congratulating him on the 'ABSOLUTELY

SMASHING' reviews, and reporting that a third American printing had already been ordered. There was a fourth in December, bringing the total to 45,500. In Britain in the month after publication Fabers sold 15,000 and printed another 10,000. There was academic recognition too. In April 1980 Peter McIntyre, editor of the *University of Edinburgh Calendar*, wrote to tell Monteith that *Darkness Visible* had been awarded the James Tait Black Prize for fiction on the recommendation of Professor Alastair Fowler.

The American publisher of *Darkness Visible* was not Harcourt, Brace. Their treatment of Golding over the years, though outwardly cordial, had not been generous. Back in the 1950s and early 1960s they had refused to publish *The Inheritors*, while preventing anyone else from publishing it by insisting on their contractual option. The decision to sever relations with them, despite their having a similar option on *Darkness Visible*, was taken by Matthew Evans, who was soon to succeed Monteith as head of the firm. He did not consult Golding or anyone at Faber and Faber and, looking back now, wonders at his own 'irresponsibility'. The alternative he chose was Farrar, Straus and Giroux, a literary publisher of great distinction. They had been founded in 1946 by John Farrar and Roger W. Straus, who later hired Robert Giroux, a close friend of Evans, from their rivals Harcourt, Brace (the authors he brought with him included T. S. Eliot). Monteith gave a lunch for Giroux to meet the Goldings at L'Etoile in Charlotte Street, which Giroux found 'delightful', and Golding, after expressing some anxiety about the morality of ditching his old publisher, gathered that it was 'sewn up' already and acquiesced ('that's all a jungle and I propose to keep out of it').

Evans, on Giroux's suggestion, got Golding to sign the contract personally. It might be 'helpful', he explained, 'when we break the option with Harcourt, Brace'. Farrar, Straus and Giroux's advance was $15,000 (the Faber advance had been £5,000) and they committed themselves to bringing Golding's other titles back into print if Harcourt, Brace would release them. Evans warned Golding that he might get a 'tough letter' from the president of Harcourt, Brace, William Jovanovich, when the news broke, in which case he should hand it over for Fabers to deal with. In April Jovanovich did indeed seek an injunction in the Supreme Court, New York County, to stop Farrar, Straus and Giroux publishing *Darkness Visible*, as Evans had suspected they would, and he issued a writ against Evans claiming $1m in damages. Evans was invited to the American embassy in London, so that the writ could be served (an invitation he declined), and meanwhile, as he gratefully recalls, Roger Straus 'hired the best lawyers in town and paid for them'. When the case went to court the Harcourt, Brace injunction was thrown out, and the law relating to option clauses was rewritten.

26

Rites of Passage

It would be hard to think of two novels more unlike than *Darkness Visible* and *Rites of Passage*, but they were written in tandem. From May 1976 to the end of 1978 the two books fermented together in Golding's mind, to such an extent that on at least one occasion the name of a character from *Darkness Visible* strayed into his notes for *Rites of Passage*. Perhaps that should make us think again about their apparent dissimilarity. For both novels are, though different in tone and period, about despised victims who are redeemed and justified. Golding seems to have turned to *Rites of Passage* as an escape from his struggles with *Darkness Visible*, as if it were an easier variation on the same theme. He wrote the first draft between 12 July and 31 October 1976, and the second between 30 November 1976 and 26 March 1977. Then he set it aside and knuckled down to his penultimate and final versions of *Darkness Visible*. Once that was out of the way he went back to his new novel, writing the third draft between 4 December 1978 and 14 March 1979, and the final between 17 July and 25 November 1979.

Rites of Passage is set in the closing years of the Napoleonic Wars and takes place on board an old, barely seaworthy warship (we never learn her name) that has been converted to take passengers and cargo, and is en route to Australia. The narrator is Edmund Talbot, a young man with aristocratic connections who is on his way to join the colonial government. His narration takes the form of a journal he is keeping at the request of his godfather, an unnamed nobleman, about whom we learn little except that he has translated Racine into English. To entertain this grandee, Talbot pens amused and condescending accounts of the other passengers. There is Mr Prettiman, a noted atheist and rationalist, who parades the deck with a loaded blunderbuss, hoping to shoot an albatross and so disprove the superstitious notion, spread by Coleridge's

Rime of the Ancient Mariner, that such an act would bring bad luck. There is Miss Granham, a sharp-tongued bluestocking, resentful at having to earn her living as a governess, who becomes engaged to Mr Prettiman during the voyage. There is Mr Brocklebank, a corpulent, drunken marine artist and portrait painter, accompanied by two women of easy virtue whom he passes off as his wife and his daughter Zenobia. Talbot, seeing through this pretence, grasps the opportunity to pleasure himself with the far-from-unwilling Zenobia while the other passengers and crew are up on deck watching the carnivalesque ceremony that celebrates the crossing of the equator.

But the passenger who comes most forcibly to Talbot's attention is a young clergyman, Robert James Colley. He is gauche and lower middle class, and Talbot find his coarse appearance and obsequious manners repellent. However, his sense of fair play is aroused when Colley is publicly humiliated by the ship's choleric commander, Captain Anderson. Determined to protect Colley if he can, Talbot lets slip in conversation with Anderson that he is keeping a journal of the voyage that his noble godfather will eventually read. Fearful that his petty tyranny will come to the notice of those in power, Anderson moderates his persecution of Colley and even makes a kind of apology. Unfortunately this gives Colley the confidence to don his ecclesiastical regalia and venture into the forecastle, the part of the ship where the lower-class emigrants and the crew are accommodated, intending to lead them in worship. Catastrophe ensues. Raucous laughter and applause are heard, and Colley emerges, drunk, scantily clad, and evidently ecstatically happy, clinging to a half-naked sailor, in full view of the assembled gentlefolk.

Nothing is heard of him in the days that follow. He lies face down in his bunk, seemingly unconscious. Anxiety about his condition mounts. Lieutenant Summers, an officer who has risen from the ranks, and is undervalued at first by the haughty Talbot, persuades Talbot and even, eventually, Captain Anderson, to enter the stricken young clergyman's cabin and speak words of comfort. It does no good, Colley remains motionless, and dies, overwhelmed by shame.

On his visit to the dead man's cabin Talbot notices some sheets of manuscript and, out of curiosity, takes them. They prove to be Colley's journal of the voyage, written as letters for his sister. By contrast with Talbot's worldly Augustan superciliousness, what Colley has written is ablaze with romantic ardour. We could almost be reading the young Coleridge. He glories in the sun, the sea, the ship and her bronzed young crewmen, especially a beautiful youth called Billy Rogers, whose soul Colley hopes to save. As he reads, Talbot learns more of Captain Anderson's cruelty and of the public degradation Colley endured at the hands of two other officers in the crossing-the-line ceremony.

What happened while Colley was in the forecastle remains a mystery until Mr Prettiman and Miss Granham overhear some gossip among the crew to the effect that Billy Rogers is boasting that he 'never thought to get a chew off a parson'. Prettiman and Granham innocently infer that this means Colley was in the habit of chewing tobacco, and gave some to Billy. But Talbot and Summers know better. They realize that, as Talbot explains rather awkwardly to his noble godfather, Billy must have encouraged the drunken, infatuated clergyman to perform a 'ridiculous, schoolboy trick' – 'the *fellatio* that the poor fool was to die of when he remembered it'.

Golding got the idea for his story from the first volume of Elizabeth Longford's biography of Wellington, which he had read in July 1974. A very minor incident in this very large book evidently stuck in his mind, and two years later, on 26 May 1976, it became the germ of *Rites of Passage*. He wrote in his journal:

> Hippolytus says according to Racine 'ainsi que la vertu le crime a ses degrés/ Et jamais on n'a vu la timide innocence/ Passer subitement a l'extrême licence'. Whenever I read this I think of that poor devil of a chaplain who sailed for India in the same ship as Arthur Wellesley. He got drunk and wandered into the fo'castle, or wandered into the fo'castle and got drunk. He spent a long time there carousing with the people. Presumably, once his defences were down, he was an object on which all their care, and all his own care, could be lavished. When he came to in his bunk he stayed there, neither moving nor speaking. Despite all that anyone could do, he simply stayed there and died. It is the only case I know of which contradicts Hippolytus.

The lines quoted from Racine's *Phèdre* (which translate roughly: 'Vice has its degrees, like virtue, and timid innocence has never been known to turn suddenly into extreme debauchery') turn up on the last page of *Rites of Passage*, translated into pompous Augustan poeticisms by Talbot's godfather. Golding, in his journal entry, goes on to wonder whether Lady Longford understood the 'true depth and love/hate cruelty of what very probably happened'. The shame that killed the chaplain, he feels certain, was caused not by 'carousing, but what he found out about his own nature, as we so tritely say'. To write a story about this, he thinks, 'would be to write a piece of complete anti-pornography. It would be a story of *orifices* (Histoire d'O). I wonder if the chaplain ever saw an octopus hauled out of the water. I mean by its vulvar mouth.' The main difficulty of writing such a story, he concludes, would be the selection of a narrator: 'It is always difficult to give a first person account of a suicide, or even of a death.' Perhaps the chaplain could leave a manuscript, to be discovered after his death. 'Part of it could be in letters to his sister.'

The references in this pregnant journal entry to pornography and an octopus both relate to recent events in Golding's life. Only the week before, on 17 May, when he had landed up in the wrong hotel on his British Council trip to Paris, he had found that his bedroom wardrobe contained a 'vividly pornographic magazine' and a half-empty box of liqueur chocolates. He imagined that 'some poor devil', probably 'from Leeds', had left them behind in an onrush of resolve or disgust. He did not, he adds, touch the liqueur chocolates, but 'enjoyed the vivid pornography more than I ought, and I mean, more than I ought'. So Colley's shame in succumbing to sexual temptation may owe something to a momentary shaming lapse on his creator's part in a Parisian hotel. The octopus relates to an earlier incident. On his 1973 holiday in Korčula he had seen an octopus killed and, just a month before his 26 May thoughts about the doomed chaplain in Longford's book, he had vividly recollected the horror of it in his journal.

I was reminded of the hideous occasion there [in Korčula] when a fisherman caught a large octopus and hauled it up, the wretched writhing creature hanging by its mouth from the hook. The man

hauled and the creature reacted. There was a shouting crowd. The
man took out a sheath knife and drew the creature nearer. It saw
the knife, understood and reared up, threatening with its tentacles,
and the mouth part was visible, a flash of tender vulvar pink,
vulnerable, hideously scared, then savaged as the knife went in. I
have seldom seen pain so vividly. What was particularly dreadful
was the – I come back to the words – particularly vulnerable,
vulvar, sensitive flash of the pink mouth area.

'Vulvar' means relating to the female genitals, so Golding's connection
of this incident with Colley may indicate, as may the memory of the
pornographic magazine and the reference to Pauline Réage's sado-
masochistic classic *Histoire d'O*, that his first idea was to make Colley's
fall from grace heterosexual. Longford's book does not say that the
chaplain was homosexual or, indeed, that he performed any sexual act
at all. In her (and Wellington's) account he merely gets drunk and runs
about naked, 'talking all sorts of bawdry and ribaldry and singing scraps
of the most blackguard and indecent songs'. However, Golding's reference, in the same 26 May journal entry, to the chaplain finding out
about 'his own nature, as we so tritely say' suggests that the possibility
of constructing his story around a homosexual act was already present
among his preliminary thoughts, and it was the one he chose to pursue.

Why, is impossible to say. But his journal, and especially his accounts
of dreams, show that he was acutely aware of his own 'homosexual component', as well as of his tendency to deny it. 'I pretend to be immune to
such bent delights as homosexuality and transvestism', he remarks, after
dreaming of dressing up in his mother's clothes. But his unconscious
tells him otherwise: 'My dreams won't let me get away with standard
attitudes about myself.' Though he reckoned himself 'wholly heterosexual', his dreams, he believed, restored him to the 'human situation of
being omnisexual'. 'You are always trying to hide the fact that you are a
homosexual,' a dream figure tells him. He has vivid dreams of making
love to Oxford undergraduates, among them his BNC contemporaries
J. A. C. Pearce and C. G. Allen. He stresses that he never did go to bed
with an undergraduate, 'either at Oxford or out of it', although on one
occasion 'it was what the Duke of Wellington called a damned close run

thing'. The dreams represent his unconscious, not his conscious life. Some of them have exotic settings. One takes place in a ramshackle village in Abyssinia, where a small black boy invites Golding's 'dream ego' to bugger him, and he declines 'with a gloomy sense that he has missed the only thing the place has to offer'. In another he is about to have oral sex with a naked, handsome young man on the roof of a bistro. A third dream is of being buggered in 'an extraordinary ritual of homosexuality', which he feels 'embarrassed and ashamed to record', though he thinks it is 'submerged wish-fulfilment'.

Lying awake at night he wonders 'what homosexuals brood about, dream about – what invented persons and situations they fill the darkness with'. He may have followed this train of thought not just because of his own divided sexuality, but because men he liked and admired, among them E. M. Forster and Angus Wilson, were openly homosexual. Charles Monteith, too, was widely believed to be homosexual, and in the years when Golding was writing *Rites of Passage* he was undergoing persistent public persecution at the hands of a former friend Robin Bryans (also known as Robert Harbinson). Bryans was Belfast-born, like Monteith, and had been a shipyard worker before he became a writer. He had published a series of travel books and several volumes of autobiography with Faber and Faber in the 1960s. But he evidently fell out with Monteith, and arrived outside the Faber offices in Queen Square one day with a sandwich board bearing insulting slogans. Having gained entrance, he threw a bulky piece of telephone equipment at Matthew Evans – apparently the only Faber representative deemed able-bodied enough to tackle him – and was arrested. However, he was released without charge, and began a campaign of harassment, sending lurid letters to judges, MPs, ministers and other prominent figures, denouncing Monteith as a sodomite. One was sent to Golding who, understandably, did not reply to it and, equally understandably, took Monteith's side. In April 1979 Fabers were awarded damages, and Bryans was sent to prison for three years for contempt of court, after throwing a water carafe at a barrister during the hearing. The papers made a joke of this. But for Monteith, the whole long-drawn-out scandal was devastating, and the fact that he had been put through purgatory on account (if Bryans was to be believed) of his sexual nature, which he was ashamed to acknowledge, but had unwisely revealed to Bryans, can hardly have failed to have some effect on Golding's decision to write a story about homosexuality and shame. It may be, too, that he felt his own homosexual 'component' had increased with age, for he reflects in the journal that people generally 'move a bit closer to homosexuality' as they get older, 'not merely through chemistry, but by finding young things attractive because they are young things, irrespective of sex'.

At all events, to judge from the journal, the division he found in himself between his conscious and his unconscious attitudes to homosexuality affected his depiction of Colley. His feelings about the unfortunate clergyman were so ambivalent that he was at a loss to decide what his true position was. Working on his second draft, on 17 December 1976, he noticed that in describing the scene of Colley's disgrace he had made him naked rather than clothed, as he had been in the first draft. 'I don't know which scene (if either) is the right one. Oddly enough, the precise scene casts a glare over the rest of the book so it must be what I want, or I shall fail. But I don't know what I want.' He refers to the scene as Colley's 'theophany or perhaps morophany'. 'Theophany', meaning the showing forth of a god, was the word he had used years before when writing to Monteith about Simon and the supernatural element in *Lord of the Flies*. 'Morophany', on the other hand, means the showing forth of folly (from the Greek *moria*: in his journal Golding writes the first four letters of the word in Greek characters: 'μωρο-phany'). Colley's behaviour could be seen as either. As he emerges from the forecastle, ecstatically happy, shouting 'Joy! Joy! Joy!' and lovingly embracing a stalwart young seaman, he might be construed as a divinely uplifted being ushering in a new world order where natural desires are no longer crushed. Or he might be seen as a fool. Golding's journal entry suggests that he could not choose between these alternatives, which may be one reason why his novel is so deeply ambivalent – tragic to some readers, comic to others.

Perhaps the ecstatic, new-world, 'Joy! Joy! Joy!' version of Colley reflects events that were going on while Golding was writing. On 8 August 1976, three days before he finished his first version of Colley's journal, he writes excitedly in his own journal about the landing of a space capsule on Mars. NASA, he reports, believe they have detected some 'primitive life form' on Mars, and it is 'the most startling and exciting news' of his life 'or anyone else's life'. For it could mean, as he sees it, that the universe is not dead matter but, in embryo, a living organism, and this would give the moral and spiritual life that human beings have developed a universal, scientifically valid significance.

The universe might thus be seen as a mode of being that becomes conscious of itself. There are sky-meadows; and next-to-infinite pastures for unconscious life as it moves towards awareness: and then, then, what one thinks and feels, and perhaps above all what one does becomes in some way as important or even more important than whether a star explodes or collapses.

His euphoria did not last long. On 16 August came the news that organic compounds had not, after all, been found on Mars. But for a few days, while finishing the first version of Colley's journal, he believed they had, and that the discovery presaged a new moral universe.

The other aspect of Colley, apart from his homosexuality, that was Golding's innovation was his social class. In the story as recounted by Longford, there is no class tension. The chaplain who dies of contrition is a gentleman, the nephew of Wellington's friend Mr Scawen. When he shuts himself away and refuses to eat it is Wellington himself who goes to his cabin and talks to him 'like a father', in a bid to save his life. Golding's decision to make Colley lower middle class reflects his own class consciousness, dating from his resentment of the privileged young gentlemen at Marlborough College. However, he makes his hero, Talbot, just such a privileged young gentleman, and this is another source of ambivalence in the novel. For Talbot, despite the good qualities Golding gives him, remains alien to his creator. The biggest 'hurdle' he has to surmount in *Rites of Passage*, he notes, is 'conveying a vivid scene to a reader through the mouth or pen of a character wholly unlike myself'. The decision to have Talbot in the novel at all was a second thought. He began by writing Colley's journal, and had been working at it for a week when it struck him that he 'should perhaps have one more person to be the "I" of the reader'. Three weeks later he has decided that his second character will be a 'toff', and his working notes in the following weeks and months show him refining his concept of Talbot. There is a danger, he suspects, of a likeness between the Talbot of his first draft and Flashman (George MacDonald Fraser's raffish hero) which must be avoided. 'Edmund must not be a *parody* of an eighteenth century or regency gentleman'. He must be a man of 'courage, intelligence and will', and believe in his right to rule. At the same time, he must learn that his class attitudes are distorted, and that his haughty contempt for Colley was mistaken. 'I intend Edmund to find from the [Colley's] journal what a friend he missed or rather what a help he might have been.'

Once the novel's basic design had clarified in his mind, its composition seems to have been relatively easy. As usual there are outbursts of exasperation and boredom as he thinks his way through the four successive drafts. But the adjustments he makes relate mostly to the management of individual scenes and speeches, and there is no large-scale replanning, as there had been with *Darkness Visible*. His notes show him planting mysteries in the novel, as if to shield it from complete comprehension by any reader. An early decision was that the name of the ship should remain unknown. He was amused, in the months after publication, that various people claimed they had guessed it, and an American couple even went so far as to publish their 'discovery'. The 'real joke', he noted, was that he did not know it himself. He also constructs an enigma around the ship's purser: 'We must build up this very mysterious, framed, magical picture, the purser at his high, brightly candlelit desk.' There is no point to this, it seems, beyond mystification: 'it is nice to think of puzzling everyone legitimately'. Mystery also surrounds the disappearance of Talbot's servant Wheeler. Golding explained to Monteith that Wheeler had been acting as a spy and informer for Captain Anderson, and was accordingly murdered by the crew. But it is difficult to extract this from the text. The nature of another mystery remains mysterious. 'I know something about someone in the story that I shall never reveal,' he told his journal on 11 March 1977. He was probably thinking of Conrad's advice (which he cites in his essay 'Rough Magic') that, to give his work depth, a novelist must know something about each character that he will not put in the book.

While he wrote, he was reading books that gave him a feel for the novel's historical period. Boswell's *Life of Johnson* took him into Talbot's world of Augustan propriety; Wordsworth's *Prelude* into Colley's Romanticism. He supposed he must have read the *Prelude*, or part of it, at Oxford, but its proclamations of hope and rebellion, and its denunciations of wealth and privilege, seemed new to him when he reread them in 1978. The social comedy of the novel, as in the scene between Talbot and Miss Granham, clearly draws on Jane Austen. In sleepless nights during 1979 he reread all six of her novels, and read *Emma* three times: 'Each time it has become lovelier.' He was worried that he ought to do some specialized reading in naval history, to get his nautical details right, and decided to join the London Library, for which du Sautoy wrote him a letter of recommendation. But this foray into the world of research was not a success. When he visited the library he felt shy among the scholars, and could not understand the catalogues. He found three promising titles in a subject index and, choosing the 'smallest most bespectacled and most mousey girl' among the assistants, he explained it was his first day and asked whether '4°' meant the book was on the fourth floor. She explained 'with fairly well disguised contempt' that it meant quarto and referred to the size of the volume. 'Collapse of elderly novelist disguised as a scholar.' He could not find any of the three books, so went to the Athenaeum library, but failed there too, since there seemed no connection between the catalogue and the books on the shelves. Eventually he gave up, and had dinner and drinks with Angus Wilson and his partner Tony, who happened to be in the club.

That was the extent of his specialized research. However, his own eclectic reading was in fact quite sufficient to supply the information he needed. In Australia he had met the great Australian historian Manning Clark and his wife Dymphna (the Clarks visited the Goldings at Ebble Thatch in 1978) and he found that he had among his own books the first volume of Clark's *History of Australia*, with details of an old warship, the *Guardian*, that had been converted to take stores and convicts to Australia. To create the ship in *Rites of Passage* he took hints from this, and from the description of the Manila expedition (on which the unfortunate chaplain died) in Longford's Wellington biography. He also discovered in his library Michael Lewis's *The Navy in Transition* ('just what I want'), and in December 1976 he bought J. H. Plumb's *The First Four Georges* 'to remind myself of what the eighteenth century was about'.

News of the novel's progress was received with pleasure and relief by Monteith at Faber and Faber. 'It's clear to me that getting *Darkness Visible* finished and complete has broken some sort of creative log jam', he told Roger Straus. Golding had seemed 'immensely relaxed and confident' at their last couple of meetings. At the Faber Book Committee in August 1979 he announced that he had extended the deadline for *Rites of Passage* to 15 December. Golding realized, he said, that the main fault of *Darkness Visible* was 'a certain untidiness and incomplete organization' due to the 'immense amount of time' he spent on the book, and he was anxious to avoid this in his new novel. That might not seem the best reason for allowing him more time for *Rites*. But apparently no one on the Book Committee felt like pointing this out. In fact Golding sent off what he cagily called the 'penultimate version' of *Rites* on 10 December, along with a mock-despondent or perhaps genuinely despondent letter: 'Herewith this load of old rope. I hope you can make head or tail of it.' No word came back for more than a week, and he began to worry. But on the 19th Monteith rang, 'full of enthusiasm'. He wrote to Giroux the same day to say that the new book was 'immensely powerful', and that he had discussed final queries with Golding on the phone. One of these was about 'what precisely had happened to Colley in his cups'. Monteith did not know, or professed not to know, what 'getting a chew off' meant, so Golding agreed to insert the word 'fellatio' in the text: 'if the reader doesn't know what "Fellatio" means, that's his bad luck, so to speak!' The terms Monteith offered were an advance of £7,500 on a 15 per cent royalty, but Golding must have, unusually, stuck out for more and the advance was upped to £10,000.

In the midst of these negotiations there was joyful family news. Judy gave birth to her second son, Laurie, on 1 December 1979. Golding drove Ann to Bristol, and reported that the baby was 'very neat and calm'. He wondered how Nicky was feeling and 'to keep his head up in the sibling situation' he phoned through a message when he got back to Ebble Thatch: 'Tell Nicky Bill loves him very much and is thinking of a new story for him.' At the end of January he and Ann took the car across to Brittany to spy out a family holiday venue for the summer, but the weather was depressing, with 'low filthy clouds' dragging across the landscape. The decay of his body also saddened him. He spent a 'painful half hour getting an incisor out', and as he looked at the 'misshapen fragment of bone' he had extracted he reflected ruefully that 'tongues have licked round it and not just mine'. However, a new hobby helped to lift his gloom. Ann had been buying orchids in a small way since 1977, but their love affair with orchids really began in February 1980 when they drove over to Keith Andrews's nursery near Plush in Dorset. Golding found the orchids there so 'utterly gorgeous' that his bad temper disappeared at once, and they brought back a large cymbidium with one spike already in flower. They returned at the end of February to buy a 'fine zygopetalum' with a blue tip and a heavy scent. Orchids appealed to Golding's thriftiness because they stayed in flower for so long. When the cymbidium had been flowering for four weeks he calculated that it worked out at only forty pence per day. He started to plan an orchid-house, which he would call his study, so that it would be tax deductible. 'I have always pictured myself working at a white table among greenery.' Construction began in October 1980, and it was finished the following March, by which time they had thirty plants. The machinery of the new structure gave trouble, as was to be expected. The carpenter pointed out that the automatic openers on the windows were the wrong sort, so they had to be replaced, and the thermostat switch went off 'like a rifle shot' every quarter of an hour. In summer their orchidarium overheated, even with the windows open, and frequent watering was needed to keep the plants alive. To improve the air circulation Golding ordered tubular aluminium staging, but found that assembling it was 'like trying to play a trombone at the same time as you are making it'. He hurt his hand, lost his temper, and broke a flower off a miltonia. Despite these setbacks, watching over, photographing and documenting their orchids gave them both a great deal of pleasure.

Lonelier, but more intellectually absorbing, was his developing relationship with chess computers, which took a step forward in January 1980 when Ann bought him the latest Voice-Sensitive Challenger from Harrods for £250. He did not much like the way it pronounced words, and when he pitted it against his old Challenger 10 it lost. It was returned to Harrods in disgrace, and its replacement, set the same task, won after a game that lasted all night and most of the next day, with Golding, as usual, noting down every move. It was, he said, 'a kind of fantasy fun'.

The computers were like the little figurines in the tombs of pharaohs, who worked for their masters in the other world: 'my ushabtui playing chess for me in a never never land'. They were not entirely reliable. He complained from time to time that one of them had 'gone phut' or made a foolish or illegal move, or that its complex controls had confused him. Nevertheless their cold, impersonal skills were irresistible, and he graduated from the Voice-Sensitive Challenger to a Competence Mephisto II in 1982, an Excellence in 1986, and a Novag Super VIP in 1991. Though he preferred playing with machines, he did not entirely give up human opponents. In November 1980 he joined a group of enthusiasts, organized by Tony Curtis of the *Financial Times*, who played chess by post. One of his opponents was the poet and novelist John Fuller, who found him an 'imperturbable and patient' player, unfazed by Fuller's 'grandly' choosing the Tarrasch Defence against his habitual Queen's Gambit. 'However terribly I played,' Fuller recalls, 'he never rashly overstretched himself.' Nor would Golding resign even if his position was hopeless – partly, he explained, because resignation 'denies the opposition the savage joy of the coup de grace!' It sounds like the kind of relentless persistence, and aversion to risk, that systematically refined each novel, version by version.

On 9 April 1980 he flew out with Ann and Monteith for a brief British Council trip to Hamburg and Copenhagen. Ann had almost not come. A few days after Christmas 1979 he had got terribly drunk, drinking whisky as well as wine, which he thought he had weaned himself from. He was overcome by shame – 'What a melancholy and humiliating business it is! Is it my ancestry, or have I done it all on my own?' – and Ann said that, though she pitied him, she could not envisage coming to Hamburg and Copenhagen and being responsible for him. Nevertheless, she evidently relented. His lecture, in the Congress Hall, was packed, with people standing at the back and sitting on the floor, and the book signing at Reuter and Klockner's was crowded too. Less enthusiastic was a 'narrow headed little man', with 'pebble glasses and sticky out ears', who opined that the lecture (later printed in *A Moving Target* as 'Belief and Creativity'), verged on 'subjectivism'. This (cogent) criticism was ignored by Golding at the time. Only later did he find himself experiencing 'the slow burn which makes me want to blast him alive'.

A pleasure on the trip was meeting Tom Stoppard, who was lecturing in the afternoon. 'Stoppard is one of the few wordmen to whom I give best,' he had noted in his journal the previous year, 'God knows what he will do. He is a genius.' As it turned out, their meeting was brief. Stoppard was said to be 'terrified' because he had not prepared a lecture. He refused lunch, and spent the afternoon in his room with 'the shakes', deciding what to say. Golding was sympathetic, but sceptical: 'I bet he has a fair idea. We are all showmen and tears.' Next day they flew to Copenhagen, where a reception was given for them ('smorgasbord and drink with the accent on drink') by the British Council representative Douglas Pickersgill. By this time he was feeling 'worn', and lunch the following day at the British embassy, to meet the Danish Society of Authors, dragged. However, he thought his recorded interview with Danish TV went well. It may have tipped the scales towards his agreeing to do a *South Bank Show* with Melvyn Bragg later in the year.

A few weeks after getting back from Copenhagen, though, depression hit him. 'Having a crisis', he acknowledged, 'an acute sense of failure'. None of his novels was 'any good', and he was powerless to start another. Every time he looked at a page it was 'like facing a white-washed wall'. He knew the novel he wanted to write. It would be about an old man in love with a young woman, and it would include the 'great dream' about his father and the Spanish Steps recorded at the start of his journal. In the novel as he imagined it, the dream 'positively whirls the man round to face away from the girl and towards his own death, and of course he finds when he faces it that he becomes young again'. Perhaps he was thinking of himself and Virginia Tiger. The book would be called *The Goat and Compasses* – 'the perfect title', he thought. But it was only 'a music in my veins that I do not at the moment hear more than faintly', and it was never written. 'Shall I ever write anything again?' he wondered. There were other causes for melancholy. The osteopath had forbidden him to lift anything 'heavier than a newspaper', so he could not garden. Angus Wilson had been given a knighthood and Margaret Drabble a CBE, so 'I have got myself well left behind in that particular race'. He had recorded himself playing the Hindemith Piano Sonata and 'it was horrible'. 'After sixty years or more at the keyboard I cannot play a *single* piece of piano music without a mistake.' A video of his 'pontifications' at Copenhagen had arrived: 'I thought it so good at the time and it is so bloody awful.' He had hit his left temple on the door and it had affected his eye. This was no new thing. He was always hitting his head on doors, car boots and other projections. It was a family joke, and may have been symptomatic of some basic deficiency in his co-ordination. But as he aged it got less funny: 'one cannot go on for ever hitting one's head without permanent damage'.

His depression lifted temporarily in July when he and Ann went by train to Switzerland to see Heinrich Straumann, the retired professor they had met while holidaying in France in 1973, and his wife Ursula, first to their home in Zurich, then to their sixteenth-century country house in the woods at Mühlebach. It was quiet, they slept well, and took healthy Alpine walks. The flowers were wonderful: violas, campions, Alpine dianthus, 'lush and brilliant with all their wet colours', two sorts of wild orchid, macula and green, gentians and bearded campanulas. The Straumanns' youngest son Hans Pieter cooked raclette for dinner one night, and played chess with Golding, winning their third game. Ann did a lot of painting. Despite the rain and his despondency, it seems to have been one of their happier holidays.

They flew home from Geneva on 16 July, and it was soon time to get ready for the family holiday in France. They took three cars, the Daimler, the Carvers' Ford Escort, and David's Mini, and drove to their holiday let in Léchiagat on Brittany's south-west tip. The children were not at their best. Nicky was 'rowdy and violent and attacking everybody' at first; Laurie, teething, yelled solidly for hours. But the beach was 'a brilliant sight, under a hot sun, with blue sea, white gravelly sand, and every plastic colour of the improved rainbow'. Nicky made friends with a little French girl called Aurélie, though communication was a problem, and Golding bought an inflatable PVC boat to give his grandson 'prestige' among the French children, which it did. He found the amount of exposed female skin on the beach a little troubling: 'some of it would have defeated St Anthony – or so I think'. His holiday reading was Zola's *Thérèse Raquin*, in French ('pretty hot'), and when he finished it he bought René Boylesve's *La Leçon d'Amour Dans le Parc*, hoping it would be 'delicately improper', but it proved 'contrived and scented from end to end'. At the beginning of September the weather broke, and he swam alone in a stormy sea, dancing naked afterwards under a freshwater shower on the deserted beach.

Back home he faced his first (and last) prolonged ordeal by television. Melvyn Bragg recalls that he had tried previously to interest him in making a television film, but failed. His letter of refusal was 'cheerful and aggressive'. He was fed up, he said, with seeing writers on TV, and 'someone had to put a stop to it'. But in January 1978 the first *South Bank Show* had been aired, and Bragg thought there might not be many more, so he should try to get the writers he really wanted while it lasted. He wrote to Golding in March 1980, proposing an hour-long film to co-incide with the publication of the new novel. Golding refused at first, but changed his mind at the beginning of May, and Bragg went down to Ebble Thatch for lunch on the 23rd. It was rather sticky. Golding seemed morose, and Bragg suspected his host wished he had not come. But Ann was welcoming and smoothed things over. Both Bragg and Golding got quite drunk, and in the garden afterwards Golding insisted that they should walk tightrope style along a low wall. By the time this had been safely accomplished Golding was more relaxed, and insisted, more perilously, on driving his departing guest to Salisbury station, despite Ann's pleas. When they got there Bragg realized his train would come in at the opposite platform so, instead of using the bridge, he hopped down ('extremely foolishly') onto the rails, walked across, and hauled himself up the other side. Golding stood grinning with delight, waving his arms, and shouting encouragement. He soon wrote to say that it was the custom among the ancient Assyrians to discuss all serious matters twice, once drunk, once sober – so he and Bragg should meet in London for a cup of tea. They did, and from then on things went like clockwork. Golding's co-operation was 'terrific'.

Filming began on Monday, 15 September 1980 with an interview lasting an hour and twenty minutes. The next day they filmed at Stonehenge, an archaeological dig, Old Sarum and Marlborough, and on the Wednesday in Salisbury cathedral cloisters and at Portland Bill, with lunch at the Red Lion in Salisbury for Golding, Ann and the crew. On Thursday, filming was at Ebble Thatch, with shots of the lily pool and swamp garden, and Golding read some pieces, mostly from his essays. His journal records that he had already felt 'deadly tired and exhausted' after the second day, but he kept going with 'booze and sleeping pills'. The Friday was his sixty-ninth birthday, and he felt 'lucky to get there'.

A fortnight later came two pieces of good news. Putnams phoned to say that sales of *Lord of the Flies* in America had passed the 7 million mark, and would he do a down-the-line interview with Herbert Mitgang of the *New York Times* (he did on 1 October). Then John Bodley phoned from Fabers to say that *Rites of Passage* was on the shortlist for the Booker Prize. The news was in the papers the next day, the other shortlisted books being Anthony Burgess's *Earthly Powers*, Anita Desai's *Clear Light of Day*, Alice Munro's *The Beggar Maid*, Julia O'Faolain's *No Country for Young Men*, Barry Unsworth's *Pascali's Island* and J. L. Carr's *A Month in the Country*. The winner would be announced on 21 October at a reception at Stationers' Hall, and Monteith, writing to Robert Giroux, predicted that it would be 'a fairly nail-biting evening', with the main competition coming from Anthony Burgess. Golding spent the night of 4 October 'evolving angry speeches of rejection or acceptance of the Booker', and in the run-up to the Stationers' Hall event he gave interviews to Vicky Glendinning for the *Sunday Times* and Bill Webb for the *Guardian*. He told Webb how his mother had taken him to see Nelson's *Victory* when he was little, and how the petty officer showing them round gave him a splinter of wood from the ship, and how, fearing to lose it, he ate it. The splinter of wood, though not his eating it, also features among his memories in the journal. Talking of *Rites of Passage* he emphasized how the class feeling in it reflected the 'ghastly' stratified society in which he grew up, and specifically his 'red-hot' resentment of Marlborough College, which was 'indelibly imprinted' in his 'emotional, almost my physical being'. Speaking to Glendinning about Colley, he said that he felt 'desperately sorry' for anyone whose 'innate folly catches up with him' – a curious way to talk of homosexuality, but true to one side of his feelings about it.

Rites was published on 16 October (the Booker judges had been sent early proof copies) and there was a party at Fabers that night, followed by a dinner at the White Tower, hosted by Roger Straus. Reviews had begun to appear on the 15th and were almost all favourable. Melvyn Bragg in *Punch* thought it Golding's 'best and most accessible' novel since *Lord of the Flies*. Blake Morrison in the *New Statesman* found its first hundred pages the funniest Golding had ever written. It was a 'brilliant achievement' that should banish for ever the notion of him as a 'glumly serious' writer. T. J. Binyon in the *Times Literary Supplement* agreed: 'Readers who know only the earlier Golding will be surprised by its humour'. 'The work of a master at the full stretch of his age and wisdom', was Andrew Sinclair's verdict in *The Times*, and Paul Bailey in the *Observer* found himself 'deeply moved and as deeply delighted'. Bill Webb in the *Guardian* praised its 'magical' descriptive passages, and judged it 'a profound and subtle comedy of the darker kind about class and power'.

By 20 October Burgess and Golding had emerged as front runners for the Booker Prize, at least in bookland gossip, and Golding set aside part of the day to practise tying his black tie, as he always had to. On the 21st he and Ann caught the 1.10 from Salisbury and were at Brown's by three o'clock, 'wishing the whole thing was over and done with'. Meanwhile the Booker judges – Ronald Blythe, Margaret Forster, Claire Tomalin and Brian Wenham, with Professor David Daiches in the chair – had assembled for their final session. Tomalin found the atmosphere 'rather odd', and got the impression that Daiches and Forster had made 'some sort of compact' that the winner was going to be Anita Desai. She herself had spent the night before 'agonising over whether it should go to Burgess (flawed but terrific) or Golding (excellent but slightly musty work)'. Her main determination had been to get Alice Munro onto the shortlist, though she realized no one would give her the prize. Daiches began by saying, 'Well, I imagine nobody here wants to spend much time considering Burgess.' She was shocked, and launched into an impassioned plea about his merits. When she had finished she saw she had no support and decided, at that moment, to put herself behind Golding. So the vote went in his favour. During the afternoon the judges were told that Burgess had said he would not attend the dinner unless he had won – so he had to be told he had not.

The other contestants remained in the dark, but as soon as the proceedings at Stationers' Hall began, at least one of them, J. L. Carr, felt sure Golding would win. He thought: 'That man is going to get the £10,000. He not only has written a much longer novel but he has a very much longer beard. And a white one. He looks a SEER.' Carr's publisher John Spiers, of the Harvester Press, got a less elevated glimpse of the victor. 'I went to the loo with Jim, and William Golding, who'd clearly had a lot to drink, came in, fell flat on his face and said "Fuck."' When the announcement was made, Claire Tomalin was standing in the crowd quite close to Golding, and she saw that tears came into his eyes. 'I was touched by the sight, and felt happy for him.' His own record of the evening in the journal is disappointingly brief. 'And so it happened! We have won the Booker prize!' Perhaps he did not remember very much about it. 'Goodness me what a night at the Stationers Hall,' he wrote the following day, adding thankfully, 'I didn't get too bad a head out of it.'

Winning the Booker Prize ensured high sales for *Rites of Passage*. A wrap-around band announcing the award was added to copies in the shops, and on 28 November Monteith sent the good news to Giroux that *Rites* was heading all the British best-seller lists. Giroux reported that some early American reviews had been disappointing, but later ones were superb. He enclosed an encomium by Robert Towers from the *New York Review of Books*. By the end of March 1981 British sales had reached 50,597. After all the excitement, Golding received a sad letter from Charles Monteith, saying that he had been having 'a bit of heart trouble' for the last three years, and would go into 'half-retirement' from 1 April 1981. He would continue to look after 'my' authors, 'you, of course, are eminent among them', but Matthew Evans would take over as chairman. In reply Golding expressed his gratitude, 'not just for recent events and editorial support but for a process that may well – I forget the exact date – have started in 1953'. There was, he said, 'a way in which I am as a writer at least partly your creation'. He counted Charles as one of the three people who had 'been of major importance and influence in my life'. The other two, presumably, were Ann and his father. On 6 December 1980 he was Monteith's guest at the Chichele dinner in All Souls, and they were both cheered next morning to see that the *Sunday Times* and the *Observer* had *Rites* among the year's book choices.

In November Golding and Ann had flown to Portugal for a week, hiring a car in Lisbon and driving to the Algarve, where they were thinking of buying a house. It was not a success. The coast, they found, was fast being built over with high-rise hotels. They were both ill and unable to eat. They quite liked the coastal plain around Faro, and the agent showed them a house near Paraiso with three square kilometres of land among pinewoods, and a swimming pool and sandy beach, which attracted them. But Ann guessed from her husband's silence that he had no real intention of buying it or anything else in Portugal. The trip was, however, an indication that they wanted a change from Ebble Thatch and from what Golding was accustomed to refer to (Terrell Carver recalls) as 'this fucking awful Wiltshire village'. Another source of frustration at the year's end was his feeling of barrenness as a writer: 'I'm right back facing a long blank period I believe.'

27

A Moving Target and *The Paper Men*

For Golding, 1981 to 1983 were years of worry and indecision. Those were quite frequent states for him. But in 1981 to 1983 they were more acute than usual. He felt old. He was anxious about Ann's health and the health of one of his grandchildren. He did not know what novel to write next, or whether he could write one at all. The first glimpse of what was to be *The Paper Men* had come to him back in January 1979. He and Ann had been rereading the account of Hemingway's decline in Carlos Baker's *Ernest Hemingway: A Life*, and suddenly there appeared 'in the air', as it seemed, 'the idea of a writer watching his *biographer* coming apart at the seams'. One 'clip' from the sequence he visualized showed 'the demented biographer stalking the writer's house from the woods with a rifle'. This would eventually be the last scene in *The Paper Men*, where the novelist Wilf Barclay, sitting at his desk writing, catches sight, through the window, of his would-be biographer Professor Rick L. Tucker leaning against a tree and taking aim at him with a gun. The first title for the story that occurred to Golding was 'A Question of Egos'. Three months later, while still at work on *Rites of Passage*, he noted in his journal: 'Perhaps I sh'd nibble at another story some how. I c'd call the one about the biographer (Atherton P. Walters) *The Other End of the Binoculars*.'

Atherton P. Walters was presumably just a stuffy-sounding name thought up on the spur of the moment. But a real-life model for Golding's fictional biographer soon occurred to him. Like Hemingway's, he was called Baker. In 1965 James R. Baker, who taught English Literature in San Diego, California, had published *William Golding: A Critical Study*, with effusive acknowledgements of Golding's 'good will and patience' in its preface. Ten years later the patience was wearing thin. Baker, Golding complained, kept writing him letters, 'as if he had a sort of God-given right to my few works and the understanding of them simply because he wrote a bad book on them about fifteen years ago'. Worse followed. Baker planned another study of Golding and requested an interview. In May 1979 he flew to England and spent a night at Ebble Thatch. The visit was, as his host recorded, 'disasterous'. They had nothing to say to each other, and on leaving Baker said he had found the encounter 'formidable'. This did not deter him from coming over to England again, with more questions, in June 1981. But during his first visit something about his body language lodged in Golding's mind, and it bore fruit: '*The Other End of the Binoculars* is a concept only,' he noted, 'but having seen Baker with his bowed and drawn-back jaw and his curious indomitable timidity I might well use him for the prof!' In *The Paper Men* the 'bashfully determined' Rick L. Tucker is given Baker's mannerism: 'that drawing back of the chin into the neck, that look up under lowered brows'.

Not that Rick resembles Baker in other respects. His university is different, for one thing, and that, too, went back to the first glimmerings of the novel. In March 1978, while Golding was strolling round his garden, it struck him 'like a bolt from a stun gun' that 'some pussy-footing graduate student from Ashcan' might one day write his biography, and he contemplated writing it himself to pre-empt this possibility. 'Ashcan', in this context, seems to have been just Golding's rude name for a low-grade American university. But it survives in *The Paper Men*, where Rick Tucker (who is surprised at the start of the novel scavenging in Barclay's dustbins, or 'ashcans') wears a T-shirt with the legend 'OLE ASHCAN', an affectionate sobriquet for his alma mater, the University of Astrakhan, Nebraska.

Despite these preliminary ideas, the story was slow to clarify. '*The Critic*', as Golding now called it, was 'drifting', he feared. He was just 'doodling' with the 'lousy thing'. At the end of January 1981 he abandoned it, 'at least for the time being'. Instead he began putting together a selection of his essays and lectures. Over the phone Monteith did not sound too keen on this new project. But after Golding had anxiously suggested that they should 'cancel the whole thing', he sent a reassuring letter, blaming a bad telephone line, and protesting that he had 'admired and immensely enjoyed' the pieces sent so far. He would gladly read any other items and 'make a final selection'. Getting the contents of the volume together was not easy. Golding did not have enough material from the recent past, and he had mislaid several pieces he had written in the 1960s for *Holiday* magazine. Judy was despatched to the British Museum library to find them, and friends in America joined the search. It was well worth the trouble. Colourful, happy, and spiced with out-of-the-way knowledge, the *Holiday* pieces ('Wiltshire', 'An Affection for Cathedrals', 'Through the Dutch Waterways' and 'Delphi') are for many readers the most winning things in the collection, for which Golding chose the title *A Moving Target*.

Book reviews from the *Guardian, The Spectator* and *The Listener* written in the 1960s and 1970s made up another section, though only four survived Monteith's 'final selection' – a piece on a book of photographs of the earth seen from the air, by Georg Gerster, and reviews of Robert Fitzgerald's translation of the *Odyssey*, Iona and Peter Opie's *The Classic Fairy Tales*, and Paul Fussell's *The Great War and Modern Memory*. Golding's review of Christopher Hollis's *Eton*, expressing his wish that class sizes in state schools should be the same as those in public schools, and his willingness to blow up Eton with high explosive, had been vetoed by Monteith when selecting items for *The Hot Gates*, and he banned it again this time round. It was a timid misjudgement, resented by Golding, who resolved, in retaliation, to rewrite and enlarge his polemic, though he never got round to it. Monteith also rejected, as 'too slight', a virtuoso talk given to the Arts Association in Melbourne, two days after Golding had landed in Australia, which compares the English language with French, Spanish and Chinese.

Only one piece was written specially for *A Moving Target*. Titled 'Intimate Relations', it is in his best unstuffily erudite, book-chat vein, and surveys a selection of English diarists – Pepys, Johnson, Queen Victoria and the swashbuckling Vice-Admiral Augustus John Hervey, third Earl of Bristol. Economically, it reuses part of his review of Raleigh Trevelyan's *A Hermit Disclosed*, written for *The Spectator* twenty years back. Monteith suggested he might write another new piece 'on, say, Australia or somewhere else fairly remote', and he agreed to, 'if the urge comes' – which it evidently did not. The only other recently written item was 'My First Book', first published in *The Author* in July

1981. It is about the sad, unnoticed little volume of *Poems* Macmillan had published in 1934, and he felt 'strangely moved', he told Monteith, recollecting his teenage poetic aspirations. A copy, he noticed, was now up for sale in America for $4,000.

The rest of the collection consists of lectures, mostly written for British Council trips in the previous four years. Taken together with the book reviews and travel pieces, they amount to a more personal declaration of Golding's thoughts and beliefs than anything he had published before, and his stance is combatively irrational, rejecting reductive intellectual systems and uncompromisingly asserting, in 'Belief and Creativity', his belief in God – a rare occurrence in an academic lecture. Not that his God resembles the orthodox Christian one. At many points *A Moving Target* comes close to science fiction – a genre that always fascinated him, and that now reappears in the guise of religion. 'Gaia Lives, OK?', his review of the Gerster photographs, puts forward the theory that the earth is not a 'lifeless lump' but a conscious female organism. When irritated she wrecks cities with earthquakes and volcanoes. We know that human consciousness consists of electrical discharges in the brain, and we should realize, Golding suggests, that the electrical discharges in the clouds, which we call lightning, are also signs of a consciousness. A mind may be 'staring out at us from the unimaginable violence of the sun', and as our science improves we may be able at last to see our mother, Gaia:

> Surely eyes more capable than ours of receiving the range of universal radiation may well see her, this creature of argent and azure, to have robes of green and gold streamed a million miles from her by the solar wind as she dances round Helios in the joy of light.

In his review of Paul Fussell's book he pursues an alternative science-fiction idea, suggesting that the universe, far from being a conscious organism, may be a figment created out of our own souls. The atrocities of the Second World War – Belsen, Hiroshima, Dachau – are, he argues, unimaginable. They are gaps in history, 'black holes', and they may be the origin of the black holes astronomers think they have discovered in outer space: 'Did we discover black holes out there because we had already invented them in here? Do we create not only our history but our universe?' Modern science fiction's tendency to encompass theology also attracted him, because it allowed him to rewrite religion as well as science, and the overlap between science fiction and theology, in writers such as C. S. Lewis, becomes his focus in the lecture 'Utopias and Antiutopias'. In 'Rough Magic' he suggests that the power great novelists have over us – Stendhal, Dickens, Eliot, Austen, Dostoyevsky – defies rational explanation and can be accounted for only by following another science-fiction pathway into 'that curious region of the occult, of psychokinesis, extrasensory perception, second sight'.

The last piece in the book, the lecture called 'Belief and Creativity', is the most defiantly anti-rational. The 'glum intellect of man', he argues, has constructed iron cages for the human spirit – the main culprits being Marx, Darwin and Freud, 'the three most crashing bores of the Western world'. It seems unlikely that he knew these writers extensively at first hand. He never mentions having read Marx, and he told Jack Biles he had never read any Freud. The only book by Darwin he certainly read was his treatise on the pollination of orchids – a subject in which he had a practical interest. In condemning them he had in mind, rather, the general, vague notion of their ideas that had become part of the modern Western mindset. Truth, he asserts, is to be found not in such reductive theories, but in art. The novelist – or painter, or poet – reaches down into 'the magical area of his own intuitions' and comes up with something new, and this, he believes, proves that 'beyond the transient horrors and beauties of our hell there is a Good which is ultimate and absolute'. Further, there 'must be' infinite universes and infinite hells, because 'it would deny the nature of our own creativity, let alone the infinitude of God's creativity' if there were not.

This challenging rejection of reason was unlikely to appeal to the agnostic Monteith. Writing to Roger Straus on 15 July 1981, he remarked archly of this lecture that it was an account of Golding's '*Weltanschauung*' (or world-view), and that it included, 'en passant, his present opinion that we are, all of us, at this very moment, in hell'. Monteith had heard the lecture when it was first delivered in Hamburg the previous year, and perhaps that accounted for the tone of voice which, thanks to a bad telephone line, had sounded so like lack of enthusiasm when Golding first rang him about a book of lectures and essays. Nor could Monteith have failed to notice that impatience with the limits of rational thought permeated other pieces in *A Moving Target*, from the apprehension of a spiritual presence or *mana* in 'An Affection for Cathedrals' to the affirmation, in the review of the Opies' fairy-tale book, that the real world is 'the magic one'.

Golding was himself far too complicated to be entirely satisfied with the person who got up on platforms and voiced these improbable ideas. In calmer moments he attributed them to 'Bolonius', the foolish alterego of the journals. 'Bolonius has sounded off all round the world about Belief and Creativity,' he observed gloomily. He had misgivings about the lecture from the start. It was originally called 'Thoughts on Creativity', and when he changed it to 'Belief and Creativity' he noted scathingly that the new title was 'even more portentous' than the first, 'but more like the damned lecture as it is written'. Although he enjoyed the applause when lectures went well, he also felt that it was ridiculous for him to be lecturing at all. He insisted that he was just a story-teller, not a thinker. In a letter to a French academic who had inquired about his beliefs, he stated: 'I claim the right not of the philosopher or psychologist but of the story teller – that is, to be impenetrable, inconsistent and anything else he likes provided he holds the attention of his audience. That I appear to do and it is enough for me.' Ann, reading the letter, said this statement should be his 'banner', and he used it, with a few verbal changes, to round off 'Belief and Creativity'.

The root of his dilemma, as always, was a division between reason and faith. He had reacted against his father's scientific rationalism, but had something of it in his own nature. He said he was just a storyteller, but he argued and propounded opinions about the nature of man. A similar duality shows up in his attitude to critics. He was fond of pointing out that the critical books and academic theses on his works occupied more shelf space than the works themselves. 'I am the raw material of an academic light industry' he told lecture audiences. This was a boast but also a complaint, because by fixing on the thought-content of his books the critics failed to treat him as a story-teller. He resented their appropriation of his writings and their attempts to get inside his mind. He jeered at them for subjecting him to 'Freudian analysis, neo-Freudian analysis, Jungian analysis,

Roman Catholic approval ... protestant appraisal, nonconformist sur-
mise, Scientific Humanist misinterpretation'. He wanted their attention yet, at the same time, he disdained it. It was out of this tangle that
The Paper Men grew, and the fact that it was a tangle, exposing a
contradiction in himself, made it a hard novel to write. He 'couldn't
even imagine how to begin', he confessed.

As often when he felt frustrated, he was tempted to drink, and he got
so drunk at the Faber party in July that he frightened himself. A period
of self-questioning ('Do *all* writers drink to excess?') and vows of absti-
nence followed. Meanwhile, life held out some compensations. By the
end of January 1981 his royalties from Faber and Faber during the
current financial year amounted to £74,000 – an increase, he worked out
on his electronic calculator, of 54 per cent on the previous year. The
total at the end of the tax year was over £90,000. 'I love money,' he
observed semi-ironically, but in fact there were plenty of things he
valued more than money – among them, loyalty to Faber and Faber. In
May Penguin offered him £30,000 for the paperback rights of *Rites of
Passage*, but he turned it down. Matthew Evans sent him, as a token of
their gratitude, a gold krugerrand – 'value', Golding noted drily, 'about
two hundred and thirty pounds'. (Evans, it should be said, has no recollection of this, though Golding records his receipt of the gift.) Later in
April he traded in his old Daimler for a new model, 'white, and a very
superior job, with electrically controlled windows and locks and aerial,
and any number of refinements'. Getting the refinements to work was a
struggle ('most of them escape me altogether'), and within weeks something went wrong with the windscreen wipers. However, even the new
car's peccadilloes were a kind of diversion.

There were also academic engagements. At the end of April 1981 he
drove to Canterbury to lecture at the University of Kent. Ann did not feel
well enough to come, so inevitably he got lost on the way ('I entered
Hayward's Heath a number of times'). But the lecture, which was 'Belief
and Creativity', 'seemed to go over big', with the audience sitting in the
aisles and on the floor. He signed books for an hour and a quarter non-
stop in the university bookshop. In May he gave the same lecture at the
University of Sussex, but it went less well and he drank too much at
the reception afterwards. Hung over the next day, he wondered, not for

the first time, what to do about his drinking. 'If there *were* anything to be done about it there would be no alcoholics but happy ones. I am not a happy one. Nor is Ann, alas, alas, a happy wife.' In July he went to Coventry to get an honorary degree from the University of Warwick. The acoustics in the cathedral prevented him hearing any of the speeches, except one by Lord Scarman, which referred to him as 'Simon Golding'. So he came away disillusioned. 'Oh my God, what a load of malarcky. I must consider quite seriously not doing this sort of thing again.'

It was on this trip that he first met Rick Gekoski, an American academic who had done a DPhil at Oxford, and taken up a lectureship at Warwick in 1971. As chair of the arts faculty he looked after Golding during his visit, and had the idea of compiling a bibliography of his works. Golding advised him to consult his publishers, which he did, and he wrote in September 1982 to say that Faber and Faber had agreed to give him sole access to the relevant material. He adds that he is about to become a bookseller, and will send his first catalogue in a week or two – it contains, he explains a little uneasily, four of the books Golding signed for him while he was at Warwick. Golding subsequently co-operated with Gekoski on the bibliography, inviting him over for meals or overnight stays on four occasions, the first in May 1986. When *The Paper Men* came out, however, Gekoski suspected that Golding had been thinking of him when he called Barclay's bothersome biographer 'Rick'. It may be so. But Golding's journal shows that it was as early as 8 July 1983 that he decided to change his character's name from 'Jake' to 'Rick'. 'What I want', he wrote, 'is a name for the professor which would be possible for a poor white from the wrong side of the tracks. He has now become Professor Rick L. Tucker, the L, we think, standing for Lindbergh'. When Golding wrote this he had met Gekoski only once, and some years were to pass before the rather fraught encounters took place between them which Gekoski describes in his book *Tolkien's Gown*. So Golding's adoption of the name 'Rick' for his character may have been coincidence. This is made more likely by the fact that when he first mentions Gekoski in his journal he (characteristically) gets his name wrong, calling him 'Nick'.

The first part of 1981 brought family sadness. In March Bill Hogben, husband of Golding's adopted sister Eileen, died aged sixty. They had not known he was ill. He had been suffering from cancer for six months but would not have anyone told. Golding, at Eileen's request, gave the address at Bill's cremation in Southampton. Then in May came the tragic news that Martin Brookfield, the son of Ann's youngest brother, had been found dead in his rooms at Cambridge on the eve of his exams. 'He was beautiful and witty and eccentric and he was all his mother had,' Golding wrote. Almost exactly twenty years before, Martin's father John had gassed himself, and Martin's mother Marion told Judy that to Martin suicide had been 'an ever-open door'. It struck Golding as 'an illuminating phrase'. The inquest recorded an open verdict, and the Goldings went down to Maidstone for Martin's funeral.

At the start of August they all got away for a family holiday on a remote farm (the Ferme du Creac'h) at St-Yvy near Concarneau. It was hot, they drove to beaches, and got sunburnt, despite buying a huge beach-parasol. Nicky had tuition in swimming, archery, and the background of the Trojan War from his grandfather, who was delighted by the beauty of children on the sands. 'I quite lost my heart to a little girl of ten whose animal assurance and dexterity let alone agility was an enchantment.' He had always felt this way, and years before, in Greece, had written a poem about just such a little girl, possibly Peter and Lal Green's daughter Sarah:

> I read the book you could not understand.
> You squatted on the beach to build in sand
> A hollow, pointed shape, and there beside,
> Mounds to confront that sea without a tide.
>
> Thin arms, pale hair, voice like a wren's, short dress,
> Of olive grey and worked with crocuses:
> Your hands were fumbling at a ship, and all
> The colonnades of Troy before her fall.

His holiday reading was the poems of Alexander Pope, and when Ann was painting their farmhouse he painted her, seated at her easel, backed by a little wood, and inscribed it 'Trees where you sit Shall crowd into a shade'. A tiny image, beautifully accomplished, it now hangs in one of the bedrooms at Tullimaar. Less happily, he felt the touch of age. He fell downstairs, shaking himself up badly. Walking over the rocks he had to be careful because of his game leg, and when he was snorkelling his false teeth got in the way of the breathing tube. The biggest excitement came on a trip to Concarneau, when his 'incredulous eye' fell on a *Guardian* headline and he 'rushed with a kind of headlong limp' back to Ann to tell her England had won the Ashes. As was to be expected, Nicky and Laurie were often fractious and noisy, so at the end of the holiday the two older Goldings had three days to themselves at the Manoir du Vaumadeuc in Pléven, from which they drove through the forest to explore Lamballe and the ruined castle of Hunaudaye.

Back home he still felt unable to make any advance with *The Paper Men*, and it did not improve his temper. In September the print unions called a strike which temporarily stopped publication of *The Times* and the *Sunday Times* (a foretaste of the strike that began in January 1986 and lasted more than a year). Golding evinced little sympathy with the workforce, which he characterized as 'a handful of illiterate bastards'. He toiled through the Booker Prize winner, Salman Rushdie's *Midnight's Children*, pronouncing it 'beastly'. Physical decrepitude did not lighten his mood. In the Farthing Gallery in Salisbury a picture of an old frigate being broken up caught his eye. 'I feel much like her,' he admitted, and bought it for himself as a seventieth birthday present. He found relief in planning and writing a first draft of *Close Quarters*, the sequel to *Rites of Passage*, which he finished by 1 December 1981. Then that too was set aside to mature.

The new year brought proofs of *A Moving Target*, and reading them through in cold blood he was aghast at the self-importance of the lectures and their 'high level of complacency'. They seemed to him to 'resound with modest disclaimers which let through gleams of awful pride'. He was clearly in a nervous state, and sleeping badly. News stories of old people being robbed, and left bound and gagged, alarmed him. He thought of getting a sword stick and a handgun, or perhaps a shotgun. In the end he settled for a powerful air rifle which he propped beside his bed. He would shoot an intruder 'without a qualm', he decided. But he found himself going over the idea and becoming more 'elaborate and savage' about it, which he knew was 'absurd and unhealthy'. Probably worry over the stalled novel was behind it all. 'I don't seem to be getting back on the Paper Men,' he regretted. It was 'as far away as ever'. Thinking about the air rifle did help, though. It was never used against intruders, but it appears in the first scene of the novel when Wilf Barclay, waking early one morning, and hearing some creature out in the garden ransacking his dustbin, assumes it is a badger, grabs his 'ancient but powerful airgun', and goes outside to shoot it, only to find that it is Rick L. Tucker searching for discarded manuscripts and suchlike treasures.

In March Golding and Ann went for a week's holiday to St Ives, staying at the Tregenna Castle Hotel. It was no ordinary holiday. They had signed on for a week's riding lessons at a nearby stables. Ann found it too physically demanding, and gave up after a few days – which increased her husband's concern about her health. But for him it was a revelation. He found riding a physical and intellectual challenge, far 'more complex and difficult' than he had expected. When they got home he contacted Vin Crocker, who owned some stables near the village of Corton, and arranged to continue his lessons. Then, in September 1982, he heard about a riding school called Hoofprints nearer to Bowerchalke, and he began taking lessons there regularly three times a week. Two months later he bought his own horse, a piebald, measuring fifteen hands and three inches and called (by his previous owners) Cobber, for the prosaic reason that he was technically a cob. He was not a glamorous animal. Golding thought he looked rather like a carthorse with his 'very hairy fetlocks'. But buying a horse gave him a tremendous thrill: 'I haven't found myself in such a state of mixed terror, pleasure and excitement since we bought Wild Rose'. When purchased, Cobber was not in good health. The vet detected a heart murmur, so the buying price came down to £600. But Betty Saxon, the owner of Hoofprints, where the horse was stabled, advised that with regular feeding he would grow stronger, which he did. Quite soon she allowed Golding and Cobber to go off by themselves, and he discovered the 'profound pleasure and exhilaration of hacking'. He got to know the woods, farms, plantations and prehistoric barrows in the countryside around – Knighton Wood, Grimsdyke, Toyd Down, and Blagdon Hill, which was a 'riot' of tall grasses and May blossom in early summer, with 'a view for twenty miles in every direction' from the top. He wrote to Monteith that he was discovering ancient burial mounds, and 'orchards remaining where the monastery was dissolved'. Riding through fields of mead-owsweet, past hedgefuls of wild roses, he felt how 'visibly marvellous' creation was. His rides were 'either a refuge from the real world, or an excursion into the real world, I am not certain which'. There were mishaps. In May 1983 he had a bad fall and was concussed, arriving back at the stables shaken and bewildered. But he was in the saddle again only a day later. He determined to learn to jump and, despite more spills, eventually persuaded Cobber to tackle jumps three to four feet high. A fringe benefit was that riding encouraged him to lose weight, since extra pounds affected Cobber's performance. 'Slimming is the order of the day or the wretched beast will founder,' he cautioned himself. He had never been fond of animals, rather the contrary, and he formed no sort of sentimental bond with Cobber. Nor did Cobber with him. After some months on Betty's improved diet he demonstrated his returning strength by trying to bite his owner. For all that, a relationship of mutual respect seems to have developed between them. As Golding's *Wild Rose* comparison suggests, the pleasures of riding were akin to the pleasures he had got from sailing – risk, loneliness, adventure, a link with the his-torical past, physical effort. It lifted him out of despondency, and helped him to overcome, for a time, his nervous dread of writing, and in that respect Cobber may be said to have contributed more than most horses towards the advancement of English literature.

The improvement did not happen all at once. Months were to pass before work resumed on *The Paper Men*, and in the interim he had three foreign engagements to fulfil. Ann's increasingly uncertain health kept her at home, so he was alone each time. In bad moments he attributed this to his alcohol problem: 'I am tired of me, and I think that Ann must be tired of me also.' His first excursion, at the end of March 1982, was to Milan as the guest of his Italian publisher Longanesi. There were TV, radio and press interviews, and a meeting with the local British Council reps, and on the way back he stopped off in Zurich for lunch with the Straumanns. The next trip, a month later, was more enjoyable. He flew to Paris, and was much taken with the British Council literary officer Christine Jordis, in whose care he was put ('she *is* charming'). For her part, she was impressed by his modesty and courtesy. She was late meeting him at the airport, and feared he would be cross or disturbed. But she found 'this little man leaning against a wall and reading quite peacefully. I looked between the big hat and the white beard, and there was William Golding, quite calm.' When she apologized for her lateness he said: 'Time is important to me when I write, but when I don't write I don't mind what I do with my time.'

His lecture, in the British Council's biggest room, was packed, partly because *The Spire* was on the syllabus for the Agrégation, the competitive examination for teachers and professors. Even the anteroom and the foyer were crammed, and eminent professors from the Sorbonne were sitting on the floor. He was introduced by Sylvère Monod, the translator of Dickens, Conrad, Scott and Shakespeare. In the whirl of British Council engagements Golding often met people whose names and achievements he failed to catch, and he seems not to have realized who Monod was. Monod, however, was obviously much impressed by him and wrote to him charmingly about their meeting. Christine Jordis recalls that Golding's reading of 'Belief and Creativity' was very slow, out of consideration for his non-Anglophone audience, and took nearly two hours. Everyone was exhausted at the end, though they were 'absolutely delighted' by his saying that Marx, Darwin and Freud were the biggest bores in the Western world. What Golding particularly recalled was the reception afterwards, where an 'elderly but charming lady' explained to him that there could not have been a cedar in the close at the time of *The Spire*, and a man defended logic on the grounds that it had developed over two and a half thousand years. He riposted that religion had developed over at least twenty thousand years. This was greeted with puzzled annoyance, and when he added that 'logic was a structure internally satisfying, but no more than a loftier game of chess', his interlocutor swept away as if he were beneath notice.

Next day he managed to fit in visits to the Ste-Chapelle and the Jardin des Plantes. At a lunch given by the director of the British Council in France, Bryan Swingler, he sat next to the British ambassador, who talked of nothing else but how it had cost him £20,000 to stock the embassy wine cellars. In the afternoon he went to buy a present for Ann, and Christine Jordis, thinking it her duty to make sure he was not left alone, caught up with him in the Place du Palais Bourbon and asked him back for a drink, to which he replied, 'Ten years ago I would have said yes to this kind of adventure.' She was rather surprised. On the way back to his hotel he met an American walking his dachshunds and remarked, on the spur of the moment, 'The more I see of dogs the more I like men.' 'Why am I fool enough to do this sort of thing?' he asked himself in his journal.

His British Council trip in May was to Greece. As soon as he landed in Athens he was overcome with nostalgia for the place – 'everything slightly cheap and noisy and friendly'. An old friend, the poet and travel writer Gilbert Horobin, and his wife Maryke entertained him, and Michael Bootle, the British Council rep, provided conscientious back-up, despite which Golding managed to leave his briefcase, containing his lecture, traveller's cheques and air ticket, in a café where he had paused for a midnight drink. Bootle snapped into action and got everything back, and the lecture was listened to politely ('a procession of young women came up and thanked my eminence warmly'). But he was bored and homesick. A question-and-answer session at the British Institute lasted an hour and ten minutes, 'despite my imploring glances'. The next day he flew to Thessaloniki, where chanting crowds of communist students were demonstrating against Greek membership of NATO. He hoped this would mean his engagements were cancelled, but the British Council's Jim Potts decided to go ahead. 'Belief and Creativity' had a 'muted' reception, and when he 'slanged' Marx three young men got up and walked out. He managed to get a taxi to the archaeological museum to see the treasures of King Philip of Macedon, and worked out from the evidence of several pairs of greaves that Greek warriors were five feet tall ('small but plaguey fierce').

The Falklands War had begun when he was in France and it filled him with 'dread and incredulity', though he considered the British 'strong arm' response just. While the landings were taking place he went to see *The Persians* performed in Greek at Bradfield College and found Aeschylus's gloating over a defeated enemy repulsive. A more immediate concern were the reviews of *A Moving Target*, which was published on 24 May. He did, it seems, bring himself to read them, though he had long ago given up reading reviews of his novels, and they were overwhelmingly positive. William Shawcross in the *Sunday*

Times, D. J. Enright in the *Observer*, Frank Kermode in the *London Review of Books*, Allan Massie in the *Scotsman*, Richard Luckett in the *Evening Standard*, Patrick Skene Catling in the *Sunday Telegraph* and Ronald Blythe in the *Guardian* all had complimentary things to say. Clancy Sigal in *The Listener* affirmed that he would like to see the lecture on the mechanics of narrative, 'Rough Magic', printed as a pamphlet and pinned above the typewriter of every practising novelist. 'What an amazingly good writer and splendidly awkward and original man he is,' enthused Edward Blishen in the *Times Educational Supplement*. Jan Morris in the *New York Times Book Review* expressed 'envious admiration' of the lectures but thought the travel pieces 'amateurish', whereas David Montrose in the *New Statesman* took precisely the opposite view: the lectures were 'affectingly old-fashioned', the travel pieces 'excellent'. There was a division of opinion, too, on BBC Radio 3's *Critics' Forum*, with Blake Morrison and Marghanita Laski, both strongly pro-Golding, versus Edward Lucie-Smith and John Higgins, who thought the travel pieces 'geriatric', 'Georgian', 'carpet-slippered' and 'naïve'. All the same, even Golding cannot have felt that *A Moving Target* was anything but a success, and he confessed his 'astonishment' at its popularity.

In June there was worrying news from Judy. Laurie, aged two and a half, would have to go into hospital for an operation in August. He had been diagnosed with an inflamed hiatus hernia, and she was told he could have died in his sleep within a few weeks. Anaemia caused the tissues in his nose and his tonsils to become enlarged, so after the operation he had a tube through one nostril down into his stomach and a tube through the other into his lungs. He was in intensive care for two weeks. Meanwhile Golding, Ann and David took Nicky away, for what had been planned as a family holiday, to the farm near St-Yvy where they had stayed the previous year. Anxious phone calls to Judy about Laurie's progress were made from any available phone box, but it was difficult getting through. Apart from worry, giving Nicky a semblance of a happy seaside holiday engaged all their energies.

Some progress on *The Paper Men* had been made before they went away, but not much, and concern about Laurie halted it. He resumed work at the end of September, but was soon in difficulties. None of his novels left him feeling more dissatisfied than *The Paper Men*, and the reasons can be pieced together from his journal and his letters to Monteith. The plot, as he first formulated it, was simple. The action would shift around Europe, as the author Wilf Barclay fled from his would-be biographer Rick Tucker, and they would 'fuel each other's paranoia'. But turning this idea into narrative raised the question, why should Wilf object to having his biography written? The true answer was because Wilf was William Golding – private, secretive, and irritated by years of harassment by critics and academics. But he could not give this answer in the novel, because it would expose himself and his feelings to just the kind of public scrutiny he wanted to avoid. Ann warned him that he must 'establish very clearly' that the novelist in *The Paper Men* was not him.

However, since the novelist *was* him, insofar as the novel had begun in his personal feelings about critics and biographers, the autobiographical element proved impossible to hide. Wilf Barclay has much in common with his creator – his physique, his beard, his drink problem, his fear of heights, and the fact that his first novel outsells everything else he has written, keeping him in funds. To counteract all this, Wilf is supplied with rather flimsy non-Golding attributes – education at a minor public school, an early career as a bank clerk, a mother who keeps a riding stable. Golding even considered including a scene where Wilf, on his travels, meets William and Ann Golding, but decided against it. Whereas his own objection to having a biography written was due to his instinctive privacy, he felt that, to explain Wilf's objection, he must have 'a real criminal past to cover up'. Inventing this proved troublesome. Wilf might, Golding thought, have written obscene love letters to a married woman, who might now be blackmailing him, and he might employ a crooked solicitor who might hire a burglar to get the letters back, and the woman's baby, or maybe one of her twin babies, might be killed, or maybe just brain damaged, during the burglary, because the babysitter might hit its head on a door jamb as she rushed out of the house – and Rick L. Tucker might find out about these misadventures, or Wilf might fear he would. Not much of all this survives in the finished novel, but tangling with it was frustrating, and drained Golding's energy. His letters to Monteith complain of exhaustion.

A second problem was humour. In essence the story is not humorous. Wilf taunts and humiliates Rick, dangling before him the hope that he will be allowed to write his biography, then flitting to some other European city so that Rick has to hunt him down and be taunted and humiliated all over again. The most powerful scene is the one where Wilf makes Rick lap wine from a saucer, like a dog. It was a novel, Golding told Monteith, about how a writer and his critics 'destroy each other'. Yet he wanted it to be funny. This was partly because of the favourable reviews of *A Moving Target* – a book he considered lightweight, but which people evidently liked. 'Perhaps', he thought, 'I try too hard in my novels. Perhaps my metier is *Rites of Passage*' (which he evidently, in this context, thought of as comic). So the new novel 'must be comedy', too. His attempts to inject comedy into it caused Monteith some discomfort. 'I don't think', he wrote, after reading Golding's second draft, 'that KNOCK KNOCK or WINNIE THE POOF (though I like that joke) will do.' These were titles Golding had thought up for Wilf's novels. Monteith also advised against 'the funny names, Jane Fruitcake, Angina Thomas etc.'. Golding omitted them. But the novel that resulted was darker than he had wished. It was 'Black on Black which isn't what I meant'.

All the same, the black parts, such as the saucer-lapping scene, are the most powerful. Wilf's ruthless malice, and the build-up of murderous rage in Rick, have a cumulative force that grips the reader. They are also true to the novel's original impulse, which was Golding's anger at pests like Baker and the whole intrusive academic-critical industry. Wilf's wish to humiliate Rick perhaps expressed something he recognized in himself. Terrell Carver, his son-in-law, felt that 'putting other people down and humiliating them' was part of Golding's nature. In the 1980s he used to taunt Terrell with predictions that he would never be made a professor. On another occasion, when drunk, he pelted him with small clods of earth because Terrell had cared for some stray kittens that had taken up residence in one of the outbuildings at Ebble Thatch. No doubt these were meant as jokes. Nevertheless it is possible that by presenting Wilf Barclay as such a deeply dislikeable character Golding was engaging in self-reproach.

Another part of the novel that might be read as self-reproach are the scenes between Wilf Barclay and Rick's wife Mary Lou. Rick sends her to Barclay's room in hopes she will seduce him and so secure the biography contract. Mary Lou, a naïve, ignorant, guileless young woman, is rigid with fear and embarrassment. Her every movement bespeaks revulsion, and Barclay feels rage and self-loathing that, even though he can see she shrinks from him, desire for her makes his heart lurch and the blood pound in his ears. The scenes are masterly, and hard to read without almost physical discomfort. They may bear no relation at all to any actual experience of Golding's. But they are a searingly disillusioned portrayal of an elderly, famous novelist, such as himself, who enjoys flirting with young women. Like Barclay's scenes with Rick, they show how little the novel needed, and how awkward it was for it to assimilate, any comic element.

The third difficulty was the supernatural material. Like the humour, this had no place in the novel as it was first conceived. But Golding was worried that if his story was simply one of persecution and revenge it would be too 'shallow'. He had 'an awful feeling' that he might come across as 'the thinking man's Dick Francis'. This was not a matter of intellectual snobbery. Highbrow–lowbrow distinctions were completely alien to him. But a story without some spiritual depth was not, so far as he was concerned, worth writing. The spiritual elements he included in *The Paper Men*, however, have no real relevance to the Wilf–Rick story, and their meaning is not clear. In an argument with an Italian woman friend Wilf denies the authenticity of the Italian priest Padre Pio's miraculous stigmata, but later stigmata appear on his own hands and feet. In a cathedral in Sicily, he has a kind of mystical seizure (or perhaps just a slight stroke) when confronted with a statue of Christ, and he realizes that he is one of the 'predestined damned'. The millionaire called Halliday, who funds Rick's research, but whom neither Rick nor Wilf has ever seen, is, it is strongly suggested, not merely a human being but (as Monteith put it, commenting on Golding's draft) 'a sort of deity (second division)'. Golding admitted that Halliday was supernatural, though he was unsure of his status – 'God or devil or demi-something'. These features bring to *The Paper Men* that element of the irrational and inexplicable that the essays and lectures in *A Moving Target* had so valued, yet they do not seem integral to the novel. Near the end Wilf has a dream about the Spanish Steps in Rome, with young people on them, and it has a redemptive effect ('It turned me round'). This was the 'Great Dream' Golding had had in August 1971, which had helped, he thought, to save him in his crisis. He had meant to use it as the turning point in *The Goat and Compasses*, the novel about old age and renunciation he never got round to writing. Its inclusion in *The Paper Men* suggests he was incorporating elements from the unwritten novel, which is perhaps why they seem extraneous.

These difficulties made the struggle with the recalcitrant novel unusually arduous. But there were relaxations. At least three days a week he was out in the countryside on Cobber, exploring secluded tracks and byways. In October he and Ann had a break in Canterbury with Ian Gregor and the Kinkead-Weekeses. They dined, drank, talked literature, and argued about which five Shakespeare plays they would preserve if the rest had to go. Golding's choices were *Antony and Cleopatra, Hamlet, A Midsummer Night's Dream, Twelfth Night* and (surprisingly) *Love's Labour's Lost*. In January 1983 he went to Paris to receive an honorary doctorate at the Sorbonne. Sylvère Monod had nominated him, and the official eulogy was delivered by another giant among French *Anglicistes*, Robert Ellrodt. Golding judged the ceremony 'brilliant. Trust the French!' Next day, the 8th, he and Ann went to the Fantin Latour exhibition, and that evening Christine Jordis and her husband Sacha took them to dinner at La Coupole in Montparnasse. He scribbled a Blake poem on a paper napkin as a memento for her:

> He who binds to himself a joy
> Does the winged life destroy;
> But he who kisses joy as it flies
> Lives in eternity's sunrise.

Signed 'Bill Golding, 9 Jan 83', it indicates that joy went on till after midnight.

He had been anxious for months about Ann's health, and it was this as much as anything else that accounted for his spasmodic progress on *The Paper Men*. In April he took her into hospital for an X-ray and blood test. She had difficulty breathing, and evidently he feared that cancer might have spread to her lungs. But on 21 April Chris Brown their GP called to say that the X-rays showed she was 'in the clear'. They both felt great relief and happiness. 'I hadn't known what a dark cloud it was', he acknowledged, and on the very next day he managed a 'huge' writing stint that took the second draft of the novel to 40,000 words. In *The Paper Men* Wilf's wife Liz, whose toughness and intelligence resemble Ann's, dies of cancer, and the account of her emaciation as death nears ('There stood before me a skinny old hag. The life had gone out of her famous hair and it hung in nondescript wisps') may give some idea of the fears that had been tormenting Golding in the previous months.

Reading the draft through when it was finished, he feared it lacked 'the obsessive qualities of passion, drive and commitment'. However, Monteith wanted to see it, so he sent it off, with misgivings ('I dread Charles reading it. Sort of'). Waiting for his editor's verdict made him jumpy, and when an unexpected parcel arrived at Ebble Thatch he opened it behind a stone trough in the garden, suspecting it was a letter bomb. Ann crouched loyally nearby. But it turned out to be a copy of John Fowles's *History of Lyme Regis*. Monteith came to stay for a weekend in May, and insisted that *The Paper Men* was 'very powerful and must be done'. The suggestions he sent along a fortnight later, though, show there was much he thought should be changed and clarified. He was puzzled by Wilf's stigmata, and Golding explained it meant Wilf was a 'hysteric'. He also thought advice was needed on Rick and Mary Lou's American idiom, and suggested W. H. Auden's friend Ed Mendelson might be consulted, though it seems he never was. Monteith's private note in his editor's file stressed it would be a 'big copy-editing' job. 'Mis-spelling, mis-typing. Sometimes words are *wrong*.' In this respect things did not improve. In August, when Monteith had read the fourth draft, he warned Liz Bland, head of Faber's copy-editing, that it was a 'terrible MS', full of slips and mistakes. 'The character called Rick used to be called Jake and Golding forgets to change it etc.' Even Faber's copy-editing could not cope, and 'Rick' appears as 'Jake' three times in the first edition. The state of Golding's typescript is an index of the unusual perplexity that lay behind it, and of his anxieties during its evolution.

The summer brought two honours. The secretary of the Royal Society of Literature, Pam Schute, wrote in May to tell him that he was to be made a Companion of Literature. There are only ten Companions at any one time, and the other two appointed with him were Samuel Beckett and Graham Greene – so it was a serious distinction, and he was duly impressed ('Golly'). In June he went to Oxford to be made an honorary Doctor of Letters. The Encaenia procession was led by the Chancellor of Oxford, Harold Macmillan, 'who, being ninety, inched along. In rain it would have been impossible. As it was we were in danger of sunstroke.' At the garden party they met Anthony and Catherine Storr, and Anthony, who had been David's psychiatrist, said he was pleased with him. This must have been a very happy moment for the Goldings, who watched their son's progress with eager affection. The previous September they had been enormously cheered when David, who had been taking gliding lessons, came home to tell them he had flown solo for the first time. 'Wonderful news!' Golding recorded, 'He has impressed us and himself too.'

To round off the Encaenia celebrations Golding had to dine, without Ann, in Christ Church, which brought back some of the things he disliked about Oxford. 'The duke of Norfolk made a quite appalling speech which was greeted with servility by the dean who capped it with a worse one of his own. I have never heard such a load of self-congratulatory clap-trap.' Being honoured was exhausting. Next day when they got home they had a quick lunch and went to bed. A couple of days later he rode Cobber and said to Betty how good it was to get back in the saddle. She replied, thinking of his honorary degree, that he had been doing something much more important. '"No", said I, quite spontaneously, "this is worth ten of that – a bit of paper and some dressing up."'

On 31 July they left for the usual month-long family holiday in France, sailing from Plymouth to Santander, and driving to Hossegor, about twenty miles north of Biarritz on the Côte d'Argent, where they had taken a house called Al Sola on the Boulevard de la Dune. First impressions were not good. It was part of a 'most dreary development of the get-rich-quick kind', and the roads were choked with cars. However, the sun was blazing hot, it was a fine beach, and behind it was a shallow lagoon, ideal for Nicky and Laurie (now quite recovered from his operation), apart from 'a little human scum from make-up, piss and *ambre solaire*'. Golding, still scatter-brained from concentration on *The Paper Men*, had left behind in Bowerchalke a big box of foods unobtainable in France, the pump for the inflatable boat and the books he had meant to read to Nicky. Instead he read him a simplified version of the English translation of the *Aeneid* from the Loeb edition. His own holiday reading was *The Death of Virgil*, a complex, Joycean, stream-of-consciousness novel by the acclaimed Austrian modernist Hermann Broch, which he dismissed at first as 'the higher rant', but reread back-to-front so that he could savour each poetic phrase, and began to wish he had written it himself. His own language skills disappointed him. 'It's the French who can't speak French,' he joked, 'They twitter incomprehensibly.' On the boat back to Plymouth, as a change from Broch, he read Octave Mirbeau's French-decadence novel *Le Journal d'Une Femme de Chambre*, but it turned out to be 'dull and dirty and bad-tempered rather than salacious – a pity'.

He got home to find two letters from Monteith. The first announced that he had reread the fourth draft of *The Paper Men*, thought it 'marvellous', and was 'more than happy' to accept it as the final version. The second, written a day later, offered terms: an advance of £10,000 on 15 per cent royalties. Golding was 'agreeably surprised', but also alarmed. He felt far from satisfied with the novel and, as Monteith was away in Greece, he immediately phoned Rosemary Goad to retrieve his typescript from the copy-editors. The 'main theme', the relationship between Wilf and Rick, had to be 'brought out more clearly', he told himself, and the subsidiary material reduced. But he felt it was a losing battle, and worked with 'increasing gloom'. At the end of September he gave up, and sent Monteith a final draft. 'What will be will be. I suppose. Perhaps. Now the thing to do is forget it!'

28

The Nobel Prize and *An Egyptian Journal*

At ten o'clock in the morning on Thursday, 6 October 1983 Golding was phoned from Stockholm by an unknown journalist (referred to in his journal as 'Ingmar whatsit') who told him that he had a fifty–fifty chance of winning the Nobel Prize for Literature, and might get a call about it in a couple of hours. The recipient of this unasked-for alert was far from pleased. It seemed to him that it was mere 'thoughtless selfishness', typical of journalists, to inflict two hours' anxiety on him, and then probable disappointment. 'I am shaking with quite unnecessary excitement,' he noted – adding, 'No I'm not – I'm dismissing the idea and being calm.' At one o'clock the news was on radio and television – he had won the Nobel Prize. After that the phone rang more or less continuously. He left Ann to answer it, and took Cobber out for a ride. When he got back to the stables a television crew was waiting. Then more television people, photographers and journalists turned up. It was 10 p.m. before the last of them left.

He gathered from the news that one of the judges on the Nobel jury had 'disagreed violently and said I was a small British phenomenon of no importance'. This was the first time in eighty-two years that any Nobel judge had broken ranks, and the next day's papers made much of it. The dissident was seventy-seven-year-old Swedish poet Artur Lundkvist, described as 'the grand old man of Swedish letters', and he clarified his position at a press conference in Stockholm on the 8th. He had merely said something to a friend, he protested, and a reporter had eavesdropped on them. He had nothing whatsoever against Golding or British authors in general. He had reviewed several of Golding's novels favourably and met him at the 1963 COMES conference in Leningrad. However, the more Lundkvist talked, the less it sounded like the 'retraction' that the British press welcomed it as during the next few days. His first choice for the prize had been Léopold Senghor of Senegal, he explained, and when he realized he could not gain the necessary support he opted for the avant-garde French novelist and philosopher Claude Simon. 'I simply didn't consider Golding to possess the international weight needed to win the prize, but that doesn't mean I am against him. He is a good author.' Asked about his alleged opposition to Graham Greene as a Nobel candidate, he said that he had admired *The Power and the Glory*, but the novels that followed were 'just light entertainment'. Most modern British novelists left him cold, 'but I admire Anthony Burgess very much. He is of far greater worth than Golding and is much more controversial.' Golding was 'a little too "nice" for my taste'.

In essence Lundkvist's opposition to Golding, as to Greene, was the common highbrow disdain for writers who appeal to a wide readership. An austere intellectual, who had reputedly taught himself English by translating Virginia Woolf's *Orlando*, he had virtually dominated the Nobel Committee since the 1940s, in alliance with the poet Anders Österling. Together they were credited with selecting some of the more startlingly obscure Nobel laureates in the post-war years. However, Österling died in 1982, aged ninety-six, and Lundkvist began to sense that he had lost his power base. Hence his outburst. His fellow committee members did their best to lessen the damage. Lars Gyllensten, the permanent secretary of the Swedish Academy (the institution that awards the Prize), insisted that it was all a storm in a teacup, and that 'Artur must have been provoked'. However, he allegedly told the *New York Times* that Lundkvist had 'the soul of a magpie'. Though judges were supposed to remain silent for fifty-five years, once Lundkvist had gone public his colleagues became copiously communicative. The author Lars Forssell revealed that Golding's name had been on the list of Nobel candidates for the last three years. 'Committee sources' informed the *Daily Telegraph* that two voting sessions had been needed to make the award to Golding. In the first he had received seven votes, Claude Simon five, and five had been cast for other authors. The result of the second session was not known but, according to the same sources, Golding's vote had increased. Lundkvist, meanwhile, claimed that the Academy had 'carried out a coup' by excluding him from the second session. Another academician, Knut Ahnlund, broke the secrecy rules in order to reassure Golding, in a confidential letter, that, despite popular misconceptions, the choice of a Nobel laureate was almost never unanimous. The winner often had only a small majority, and 'I think yours was well above the ordinary'. It was simply bad luck that 'one of the members should lose his wits in the wrong moment'.

There is no doubt that Golding was hurt by the controversy surrounding his award. But he shrank, as always, from publicity, and hid his feelings. He remarked pointedly to one reporter that Lundkvist had probably been stung into committing his indiscretion 'by having journalists down his neck'. 'Any assessment is subjective,' he told Michael Davie of the *Observer*. 'That panel chose me. Another panel would have chosen someone else. So I am not in the least distressed by a dissentient.' In the same interview he expanded on more personal topics. He assured Davie that he believed in God, and, asked if he went to church, replied, 'No. I don't know that God does either. I am in the odd position of not being a believer in any particular direction.' He was 'delighted and flattered' to have won the prize, but also apprehensive, because he did not want respect: 'It turns you into a mummified person.' On the contrary, he welcomed disagreement, and he recalled an incident (not, it seems, recorded anywhere else) that happened when he had been lecturing in an American university and a banner saying STOP SOCIALIZED MEDICINE had been strung up in the hall. In his lecture he maintained that Christianity should have more influence on politics, and when a sceptical questioner asked for an example of when and where Christianity had ever influenced politics, he replied firmly 'The British Health Service'. Davie also interviewed Ann and learnt that she was a Kent cricket supporter who reverenced Frank Woolley. She demonstrated his late cut in the Ebble Thatch kitchen. A high point in her career, she told him, was when she played hockey for Kent at the Oval. Davie refrained from asking them what they would spend the £125,000 prize money on.

Several of Golding's fellow authors publicly applauded his success. Doris Lessing was 'absolutely delighted', so was Gabriel García Márquez, and John Fowles thought Golding 'a wonderful choice'. His publishers backed him robustly. Matthew Evans's assessment of

Lundkvist was reported in several newspapers: 'The guy is an idiot.'
Brian Dixon, Fabers' production manager, got Carr's Ales in Buckinghamshire to brew a special Celebration Ale in Golding's honour.
Others were less happy. Francis King, in common with many admirers
of Graham Greene, seemed to blame Golding for taking the prize
from their favourite. A snide piece by Paul Gray in *Time* magazine
presented Golding as appealing chiefly to adolescents. He was just a
'comfortable Englishman with no extreme political opinions'. Seeing
him preferred to Gordimer, Grass and Greene must 'give pause to
even the staunchest defenders of the Nobel experiment'. Auberon
Waugh pitched in, with the accusation that Golding, in *Lord of
the Flies*, had plagiarized an obscure novel by Waugh's grandfather,
W. L. George, called *Children of the Morning*. Golding replied that, as
far as he could recollect, he had never heard of the author or the book.

According to a gossip item in the *Observer* of 23 October, the Prime
Minister's Office had phoned the Arts Council when news of the Nobel
award came through, saying that Mrs Thatcher would like to write and
congratulate the author, but a few things had to be cleared up first. 'He's
all right, isn't he?' was the question, 'I mean he's not divorced or anything
like that. You're sure there's nothing, well you know, odd about him?' The
Cecil Parkinson 'love-child scandal' had just broken, so a degree of prime
ministerial caution was understandable. Once Golding's normality had
been vouched for, a communication duly arrived from Number 10: 'I am
delighted at the recognition given to you and English literature by the
award of the Nobel Prize. It is due reward for novels which are known
and admired throughout the world. My warmest congratulations.' This
was followed by an invitation to meet President François Mitterrand at 10
Downing Street on 20 October. 'It's a proper case of swaying about,' commented Golding, remembering his mother's cutting remark when he was
on the point of going up to Oxford. He and Ann accepted, but he did not
enjoy the occasion much, partly because he was too nervous to understand the torrent of French with which Mitterrand greeted him, and
partly because he was exasperated by the titled lady seated next to him:
'How does one answer such silly people?'

The aftershock of the Nobel rumbled on for two months. At the end
of October he and Ann flew to Paris for a conference of Nobel laureates

('full of persons so distinguished I felt a proper tramp'). Jacques Chirac, then Mayor of Paris, presented all the laureates with parchment scrolls and medals – except Golding, whose had somehow been mislaid. He thought afterwards he should have quipped 'Je pense, mais je n'existe pas', but in fact 'grinned sheepishly' and murmured that it didn't matter. Meanwhile scores of congratulatory letters were arriving at Ebble Thatch, which he conscientiously answered. There were seemingly endless foreign press and television interviews. He was filmed riding Cobber for Portuguese TV, and spoke for twenty-five minutes in French for Swiss TV – 'a breakthrough', he felt, in his contest with the French language. In November they went to London for a reception at the Swedish embassy, where he was introduced to the Duke of Edinburgh. Prince Philip observed that it was a pity there wasn't a Nobel Prize for Engineering, and Golding replied that 'we didn't want to spread the prizes too wide, which caused paroxysms of Royal Mirth'. Long before their departure for the award ceremony in Stockholm, he was feeling 'sick of all this Nobel stuff'.

On 20 November he was brought briefly into contact with things that really mattered when Judy gave birth to her third child, Roger Alec. Driving down to Bristol with Ann, he found that the new arrival was 'a fine little baby', Judy looked 'positively blooming', and Nicky and Laurie were delighted with their brother. A much less momentous though still gratifying event in November was his debut (and, as it turned out, also his swansong) as an exhibiting artist. An American dealer called Wylma Wayne, who had a gallery in Old Bond Street, had written to the Goldings in October to say that she was putting on an exhibition of 'art done by prominent and distinguished writers, actors, directors, and politicians', and would be delighted if they submitted one work each. So they did, or, rather, they both submitted two, of which only one was for sale. Golding's were his holiday painting of Ann at her easel, against a background of trees, with the quotation from Pope as caption (not for sale, and now at Tullimaar), and a work entitled 'Christmas Celebrations' which shows three dustbins full of empties and other rubbish and with flies (or possibly small birds) hovering above. It is on ordinary lined loose-leaf paper and seems to have been done with felt-tip pens. The private view was on the 30th, just before the Swedish embassy party, and he found to his 'surprise and horror' that someone had bought the picture he now referred to as 'La Chasse de la Sainte Poubelle' for £150. The mystery buyer was, in fact, his friend Andrew Sinclair, who still owns it. At the private view they ran into the portraitist Felix Topolski, who had already drawn Golding once and said he would like to again.

On Monday, 5 December they flew to Stockholm and met up with Charles Monteith for the sumptuous and protracted Nobel celebrations. Each laureate had a personal attendant allocated by the Swedish Ministry for Foreign Affairs, and Golding's was Karin Oldfelt ('a charming girl'), who took them to Spånga on the first morning to see a twelfth-century church with runic inscriptions. At lunch Charles told them a French limerick which seems to have pleased Golding quite as much as any of the splendid events that followed:

> Il y avait un jeune homme de Dijon
> Qui n'avait que peu de religion.
> Il dit, 'Quant à moi
> Je déteste tous les trois,
> Le père et le fils et le pigeon.'

On the Wednesday evening he gave his Nobel Lecture. Writing it had been a chore. It had seemed to limp 'from the trite to the turgid', and big pompous platitudes kept rearing their heads. ('Oh God another bromide!') In the end it became a plea for Mother Gaia, and a wish that literature might show the rape of our planet to be 'preposterous folly'. He thought it went about as well as it could, given that the audience were following it in translations and made a deafening noise when they turned their pages. Rick Gekoski was keen to publish the lecture and, finding that Faber and Faber had no inclination to do so, he brought it out in 1984 as the first publication from his newly founded Sixth Chamber Press (a name derived from Blake's *Marriage of Heaven and Hell*).

After the lecture there was a dinner with reindeer steak ('rather good'). On Thursday it was snowing. They had a 'splendid' lunch with Golding's Swedish publisher, Bonnier, slept in the afternoon, had drinks at the British residency with Sir Donald and Lady Murray, and were taken to a performance of the *Dream of Gerontius* ('which I have heard done better'). On Friday they 'met all the same people again' at a residency lunch and a reception at the Swedish Academy. Then they had an hour in bed, and went to another concert, where 'the Nutcracker Suite was fun and soothing. I went to sleep in the middle.' In the interval they were introduced to 'a royal highness', so Ann did her curtsey and 'I my nod'. 'I found nothing to say but it didn't seem to matter. It's all very interesting psychologically.'

Saturday was the big day. There was a rehearsal of the presentation ceremony in the grand auditorium of the Stockholm Concert Hall at 11 a.m. and the ceremony itself began at 4.30 with the entrance of the Swedish royal family, followed by the procession of the Nobel laureates (in Physics, Chemistry, Medicine, Literature and Economic Sciences). The podium was decorated with begonias and roses from San Remo, where Alfred Nobel died in 1896, Swedish flags were draped above it, and behind it was the Stockholm Philharmonic Orchestra and the Swedish soloist Sylvia Lindenstrand. There were musical interludes after each speech and the presentation of each prize. In previous years the music chosen had related in some way to the laureates, but as 1983 was the 150th anniversary of Nobel's birth, the music played was from Sweden, Russia, France and Italy, the countries where he had lived. After King Gustav had handed Golding his gold medal and diploma the orchestra played the Farandole from Bizet's *L'Arlésienne*, Suite No. 2.

'The Nobel ceremony was very boring I'm afraid, though the music made up for the impenetrable Swedish,' was Golding's verdict. The banquet afterwards was 'ghastly'. They assembled at 7 p.m. to be introduced to the Swedish royal family, the prime minister and members of the government. On meeting the author of *Lord of the Flies*, King Gustav remarked that he had had to read the book at school – not the most enthusiastic endorsement. Then they all processed to the Blue Hall, each laureate paired with the royal who would be next to him at table. Golding accompanied Princess Christina 'for about a quarter of a mile thro' halls and steps and couldn't find anything to say to her'. The meal went on 'for ever', his dress-shirt studs 'didn't work', and over coffee each laureate had to make a three-minute speech from a special pulpit. 'I was bored and furious.' Then a procession of university students entered the hall with banners and a choir to pay tribute to the laureates, after which King Gustav and Queen Silvia led the way to the Golden Hall, where there were more refreshments, and the laureates were taken off to give interviews for Swedish television. Then there was a ball. The Goldings left earlier than anyone else, and he felt that he had earned 'a considerable slice of that hundred and twenty thousand' during the evening.

Things got better after that. In Sweden on Santa Lucia's day, the shortest day of the year, girls dress up in white with crowns of candles, and there are beauty contests in which the year's 'Santa Lucia' is chosen. Golding had been selected to crown the 1983 winner, Yvonne Ryding (who was later chosen as Miss Sweden and, in July 1984, as Miss Universe). It was dark, and snowing steadily, and Karin took him to a hut in the woods. Soon a procession appeared, led by the saint 'wearing a crown of electric candles and a very low cut dress', with little girls singing and bearing candles behind her. Golding's task was to emerge from the hut and put a necklace round her neck, while she smiled 'a smile so wide it eclipsed her earrings'. It was being filmed, and he had to do it three times before the publicity people were satisfied. When he finally got back to the hut with the saint, he found that she was 'a charming girl who confessed that her feet and her candles were killing her'.

That evening there was a banquet at the Royal Palace, where he sat between Princess Lilian and Queen Silvia ('very decorative, and as for her parure – my, what rocks!'). She spoke, he gathered, 'about eight languages and has a degree in something – it could be maths'. He took the liberty, contrary to protocol, of drinking her health, because she was so beautiful – 'an excuse which was accepted very cheerfully'. On the Tuesday there was a book signing – five hundred people queued, and the till was ringing for an hour and a half. He was asked for his autograph in the loo, 'a first, I think'. Then Karin took them to the Vasa Museum, which was wonderful: 'You really *can* walk in a seventeenth-century ship.' That evening the students gave a banquet for him at the university ('Fun, rather, though hot') and he made a speech in English, Latin, Greek and Swedish, which 'went down well but nobody understood'. Next day there was an hour's book signing in the civic library, and they were driven to Gothenburg, Sweden's second city ('distinctly provincial compared to Stockholm'), where the audience at his lecture were not, he felt, as quick on the uptake as in the capital. Then they flew home. Back in Ebble Thatch on the 16th he felt 'sad, nostalgic, flat and near to tears without understanding why'. Ann thought they were both close to clinical exhaustion.

They were ill over Christmas, and Ann stayed in bed the whole of Christmas Day. Golding began to be seriously worried about his 'genito-urinary-anal' system ('Old men's sorrows as my father said') and resolved to see a doctor. In the interim, some photographs that arrived of him crowning the Santa Lucia queen did nothing to improve his mood: 'They make me look a fool, and feel one as well.' His GP booked him in for a medical examination on 31 January, with a barium enema and X-rays, and he awaited it 'with crossed fingers', reflecting wryly that it was sad to find himself so concerned about his bowel movements, given that his 'private conversation with himself' had always been 'erotic rather than scatological'. To his great relief, the examination found nothing that needed surgery. He was suffering from diverticulosis, a common condition in men of his age, requiring no treatment beyond a high-fibre diet. To cheer him further, Camilla Horne at Fabers sent along two favourable reviews of *The Paper Men* (published on 6 February), from *Vogue* and *Books and Bookmen*.

She must have looked hard to find them. The book's general reception was, at best, lukewarm and puzzled. Even Malcolm Bradbury in *Vogue*, who called it 'a complex literary comedy from an extraordinarily powerful writer', conceded that it was not one of Golding's best. Others were franker. Derwent May in *The Listener* recognized Barclay as a condemnatory self-portrait, and deemed it 'a public self-abasement of a particularly unpleasant and unnecessary kind'. David Hughes in the *Mail on Sunday* revealed that Monteith had told him Golding was anxious Barclay should not be taken as a self-portrait, and he consequently found the book 'muddling' and its message 'hazy'. Anthony Burgess in the *Observer*, evidently still smarting from his Booker Prize defeat, admitted that 'the brilliant word-magician of *Pincher Martin*' was sometimes present, but concluded that the novel was 'banal' and gave the lie to 'the great claims made for Golding's genius'. Others were merely dismissive. Graham Lord in the *Sunday Express* reported, inaccurately, that it had been 'rattled off by Golding in just one month'. Janice Elliott in the *Sunday Telegraph* found it a 'hollow creation'. Michael Ratcliffe in *The Times* and Harriet Waugh in *The Spectator* both expressed disappointment. There were, though, loyal friends who rallied round. Melvyn Bragg in *Punch* and Anthony Curtis in the *Financial Times* were upbeat, and Victoria Glendinning in the *Sunday Times* tried hard not to say anything unpleasant. *Time Out* was sturdily in favour ('A minor work? We think not'), and Nina Bawden in the *Daily Telegraph* gave it its solitary rave review ('hugely enjoyable'). A long, thoughtful piece by Frank Kermode in the *London Review of Books* was critical of Barclay's 'epiphany' and pointed out that Rick was not a credible American professor (Paul Bailey in the *Standard* had called Rick's idiom a 'tin-eared disaster'). But Kermode still thought it 'an extraordinary composition' even if minor – 'a concerto for piccolo'. By far the most subtle and profound review was John Bayley's in the *Guardian*. While conceding that the novel was sometimes (and sometimes deliberately) boring and unfunny, he found that Golding's 'equivocal magic' was still present. It flickered through the 'awfulness' of Wilf Barclay as it had done through 'the wearying elegance of the period narrator in *Rites of Passage*'. Both novels were 'stylized studies in humiliation', and both left the reader 'more impressed by a *tour de force* than imaginatively satisfied'. Golding was one of those rare novelists – Thomas Hardy was another – who was at his best in 'a more blundering kind of book' like *Free Fall* or *Darkness Visible*.

Almost certainly Golding did not read this or any other review apart from the two Camilla Horne sent. He might not have been much concerned had he done so for, whatever critics thought, *The Paper Men* sold 95,000 in hardback in its first six months. At a book signing in Oxford the queue coiled out of Blackwell's and back down the Broad past the White Horse, and an American tourist, impressed by the crowd, mistook Golding for George Bernard Shaw. In any case, preparations for his next book were soon occupying all his attention. It was to be an Egyptian travelogue, and had been first mooted back in June 1982 when he received a letter from David Roberts, then a director of the publishers Rainbird. Roberts's letter introduced Rainbird as the major international publisher of illustrated books – Lawrence

Durrell's *Greek Islands* had been one of their best-sellers – and he invited Golding to write a 50–60,000 word essay on a place with particular associations for him – perhaps Egypt. Rainbird would provide a first-class photographer to take the pictures.

As Roberts explained to me, Rainbird tended to approach authors who felt they were unappreciated by their publishers and offer them the prospect of making a lot of money for very little work. Fabers were not best pleased, but Golding jumped at the chance, and over the next eighteen months the details were thrashed out. Rainbird would pay an advance of £30,000 on a 15 per cent royalty. They would also cover travel costs and provide a 'minder', approved of by Golding (who at first stipulated that the minder must be able to ride, since he proposed seeing Egypt from horseback – an ambition soon abandoned). Fabers would act as Golding's agents with Rainbird but not charge a fee. It was agreed that John Bodley of Fabers should seek out a suitable minder, and he introduced Golding to a young Egyptian writer living in London, Ahdaf Soueif, who was the wife of the poet and critic Ian Hamilton, founder of the *New Review*. Golding found her 'very appealing' and thought she 'could have come straight off an Egyptian fresco, probably offering the big man a lotus'.

More to the point, she had a brother, Alaa Swafe, who would clearly make an excellent minder. He was an electronics engineer who had set up a small radical publishing house in Cairo. On 16 November, while Ann stayed at Ebble Thatch waiting for Judy to have her baby, Golding flew to Cairo for a couple of days to meet Alaa and hire a boat on which he and Ann could make their journey up the Nile. After several disappointments they found a cabin cruiser, the *Hani*, named after the son of the owner, a Dr Hamdi, which seemed ideal for size and accommodation, and had a diesel engine that would do eleven knots. So they hired her for the month of February for 4,500 Egyptian pounds. Before he flew home Golding got in touch with Eddie Blair, the young American who had been so kind to them on their first visit to Egypt, only to find that Eddie's wife Pauline had returned to America some three years before, because she could not stand the Middle East any longer, and had been murdered by the man she was living with. Golding could not get the tragedy out of his mind, and kept thinking of what Pauline had said once when she got back to Alexandria: 'I'd forgotten how awful it was.' It was rather what he felt about Egypt.

However, there was no backing out of it now. On Sunday, 5 February 1984 he and Ann flew out to Cairo, where Alaa had booked them in to the Sheraton, and the next day they dined with Dr Hamdi, Alaa and Ahdaf, who let them leave some of their luggage in her Cairo flat. On Tuesday they went aboard the *Hani* and met her crew. It was not a reassuring experience. There was an engineer with a Ronald Colman moustache, a cook with a lute, a frail old Nubian with, it emerged, a deep hatred of the English, and a boy in a star-bespangled tracksuit who, they thought, would do excellently in the part of Aladdin. A haughty bigamist from Qena acted the part of captain. Having no Arabic, the Goldings depended, for contact with these mariners, on their interpreter Alaa, who seems to have wisely decided that what he did or did not translate from either side was a matter for his own discretion. On exploring their new home the Goldings soon found that the *Hani*'s lavatories did not work, and that she carried no sheets or blankets to shield them from the chilly February nights. She made snail-like headway upstream and, despite her panoply of navigation lights, was apparently quite incapable of motion after dark. When Golding remonstrated, through Alaa, about their slow progress, the captain grandly rejoined that 'He who rides the Nile must have sails woven of patience'. For those riding the *Hani* this apophthegm proved entirely reliable.

She began to reveal her extensive repertoire of mechanical defects within hours of casting off. On the second day out the water pump failed, and a crew member returned to Cairo for spare parts. Then the cable connecting wheel and rudder parted, necessitating frantic midstream manoeuvres with nylon string. As the *Hani* approached Qena, where the captain's wives lived, she became capable of considerably increased speed, producing a cloud of black smoke astern which hid much of the Nile from the voyagers' view. This effort quickly destroyed her engine bearings. The crew phoned the owner to report the calamity, and were advised to press on. Thenceforth the propeller shaft bounced deafeningly beneath the Goldings' cabin, and the black smoke became white steam. On the credit side the bone-jarring vibration at last unblocked the lavatories. Drawing on his wartime naval experience, Golding was able to compose, during these operations, some vivid comparisons between British and Egyptian maritime practice, which fortunately his lack of Arabic prevented him from sharing with the crew. Only once does his nautical lore seem to have let him down. When the *Hani* tied up at one of the towns en route, he noticed that the foreshore was alive with rats, and petitioned, in vain, that the gangplank should not be lowered lest the creatures should swarm aboard. In this he failed to credit the rats with their proverbial wisdom. None of them, in the event, was so foolhardy as to set paw on the *Hani*.

Even without the *Hani*'s faults Golding would have been in trouble. He had failed to realize that a cabin cruiser, unlike the big tourist boats, is not tall enough to allow passengers to see over the Nile's high banks. Consequently he found himself sliding hundreds of miles along a soupy grey ditch, with no view beyond the mud escarpments on either side. This might have daunted another writer, but it proved just the thing to set Golding in his true vein. Seeing things differently had always been his forte, and just as *Lord of the Flies* had been a black *Coral Island*, so *An Egyptian Journal* becomes a grimly hilarious send-up of the realm of the Pharaohs. The tourist sites, when he bothers with them at all, get short shrift. The temple at Luxor has 'the air of having outstayed any welcome the town was prepared to give it, and of waiting only for the arrival of the removal men'. They go ashore to see some tombs near Beni Hassan, but he decides that unless you are a professional archaeologist there is more interest to be found in an illustrated book about a tomb than in 'the comfortless rock-hewn thing itself'. He had promised himself a thrill at seeing the Bahr Yusef – the canal that, according to legend, the biblical Joseph built for Pharaoh. But he is 'moodily and quite illogically vexed' to find that they have been chugging along in sight of it for twenty kilometres, and that it is just a canal like any other. From Qeda, Alaa manages to get a car to drive them to the Red Sea, which turns out to be 'a flat stretch of the usual stuff and not very colourful either'. The one monument to pass muster is the pyramid of El Meidum. He likes it, he explains, because it is the only pyramid that ever did anything, other than weather slowly. What it did was to fall down. Tourist police shoo him away as he nears the disgraced pile, but he has already loaded his memory and his camera with pleasing images of collapse.

Let loose in the Cairo museum he is jubilantly disparaging. 'I think that mummies are at once disgusting and pitiable.' When the experts have done their job of examination, they should be burned. 'There was good sense in using mummies for fuel in the earliest Egyptian railways.' The Tutankhamun loot is mostly just a lot of old furniture, and the famous shrines that guarded the mummy are 'tinselly'. As for the celebrated goddesses who stand round it spreading their arms protectively, they are only about eighteen inches high, and 'doll-like'. The carefully guarded jewel room is also a let-down. 'The truth is that jewellery dies if it isn't worn. There is a curious dullness that comes over gold in a showcase as if it knows it's in the wrong place.' People say that gold does not tarnish, but if so what accounts for the difference between 'the gold of your wife's wedding ring and the stale pieces of yellow metal exhibited in museums'. Perhaps gold gets its gleam from the body's natural oils, in which case there should be a ball every so often for curators and their wives and girlfriends when the ancient stuff is 'given an airing, and a chance to resume its former splendour'.

While neglectful of the accredited marvels, he insists on noticing bits of Egypt to which any respectable tourist would turn a blind Kodak. He ambles with indecent glee through dreadful souvenir shops, jammed with plastic busts of Nefertiti. He muses on the hideous Cairo high-rises outside his hotel window. They look papery, rather as Egyptian temples look like brown cardboard. Or they look like the fitments for an electronic system, where you slot bits in. Or the flimsy balconies give them the look of a corncob that has been gnawed all the way down, leaving the seed sockets jutting. As he goes on you realize that he has turned the high-rises into a poem, lending the imagination's colour to the defamed and disgraced, as his novels do. He watches labourers staggering under loads of bricks that are stacked on hods strapped to their backs, 'hands clasped tightly at their chests as if to prevent the rib-cage from bursting'. He watches women taking water from the Nile in huge metal bins, like rainwater butts, then walking in procession, 'red and blue and black', all stepping with a 'graceful and majestic pace'. They remind him of the famous ancient Greek sculptures of female figures that act as supporting columns in the porch of the Erechtheum on the Acropolis at Athens. The statues represent the daughters of Caryas, enslaved by the Athenians and set to carry burdens as a punishment, and the sight of these Egyptian peasant women seems to him lovelier than the caryatids, 'and as cruel'. He asks repeatedly to meet one of the poor of Egypt, one of the *fellahin*, a peasant farmer 'with half an acre and no cow'. But somehow it can never be arranged, and he suspects that his conductors feel shame at the poverty and wish to conceal it.

The battered old Nile sailing barges, called 'sandals', come in for close scrutiny. Are there, he asks the crew, different names for small sandals and big sandals? Yes, they reply, they are called small and big sandals. Is there a special name for a big sandal with two masts? Yes, it is called a big sandal with two masts. His dissatisfaction with the Egyptians culminates in two episodes which form the twin peaks – or, at any rate, twin molehills – of this wryly low-level venture. He visits the Gournawis, descendants of medieval tomb robbers, who live among the graves near the Valley of the Queens and smuggle the spoil from ancient burials, known only to them, onto the international market. An elegant modern village has been built for them nearby, using traditional adobe mud bricks and designed by Egypt's best-known modern architect, Hassan Fathy, whom Golding meets in Cairo. But the new village has stood empty for years, and nothing is done about it. Then, in the desert near Fayoum, he comes upon four greenhouses, tended by a Dutch scientist and his Egyptian assistant. Together they comprise 'The Institute for the Multiplication of Mango and Olive Trees', which, the scientist explains, could supply Egypt with a million olive trees, and an industry even more valuable than sugar. But it is doomed, because of bureaucratic obstruction. The Dutchman is going home, fed up, and the infant olive trees will all die. The two episodes stay in his mind as symbols of the inefficiency of a country that (as he admits in his notes but not in the printed text) 'alternately bores and disgusts me'.

No other book, not even *A Moving Target*, brings the reader so close to Golding the man as *An Egyptian Journal*. It is unpretentious and funny, it bulges with abstruse knowledge – about geology, papyri, the ancient method of disposing of night soil – and it continually defies received opinion. It makes no claim to objectivity, but freely admits its prejudices. He realizes, he says at the end, that anything he writes about Egypt will not be about Egypt but 'about me, or if you like, us, middleclass English from a peaceful bit of England, wandering more or less at will through infinite complexity'. He feels the Englishness in himself 'like a wall', cutting him off from the Egyptians. He knows he should have got to know the crew of the *Hani* better, but the truth is 'I was *shy*'. He simply could not bring himself to 'catch their eye in a matey way'. He realizes Ann managed much better. She made friends with them and learnt bits of Arabic from them and they loved her. He simply could not do it.

It is natural to imagine that *An Egyptian Journal* is the journal he kept while in Egypt. But that is not so. The journal he kept day by day on the *Hani* is cursory, consisting of disjointed notes with occasional out-bursts of impatience ('One feels really more and more like giving up'; 'My God. The silly sods have run out of fuel'). *An Egyptian Journal* was commotion recollected in tranquillity. Turning his notes into a book took months. He talked it over with Ann, and decided that what was needed was 'a sort of complex sewing-job', amplifying his jottings, and interspersing new material to 'make it vivid'. Some of the most mem-orable incidents are not mentioned in the notes at all. On their way back downriver they pass a green patch of onions on the bank – 'Is there any crop quite as beautiful as a patch of onions?' The wash of the *Hani* nudges into it, and a young woman squatting nearby jumps up, screaming, and hurls a stone after them. 'You could see her eyes flash long after the rest of her features were a pale blur.' This leads him to think how Egyptian women have relied on their eyes for glamour for thousands of years, as the tomb paintings show, and how an undiseased pair of eyes in ancient Egypt must have been rare, and how even fab-ulous Nefertiti had one blank eye. Then he thinks how most of Egypt's population has been helpless for millennia, exploited, tortured and worked to death, and how this explains their tempests of violence, and how the woman hurling her stone was expressing her pent-up rage at rich foreign tourists, and at the Golding party in particular for insult-ing her onion patch with the wash from what must have looked, to her, like a 'sumptuous toy'. The passage reads as if his thoughts are arising as he writes – which was what he wanted. He typed the first draft at top speed to make it seem 'fast, eloquent, oral'. But there is not a word about the woman and her onion patch in the journal he kept on the voyage. That is not to suggest that he just made her up. She was probably, like a lot of *An Egyptian Journal*, an imaginatively reconstructed memory. He wrote to Monteith on 16 April that he was 'busy trying to get down An Egyptian Journal before I forget the day-to-day events'.

He finished the first draft by the 19th. But then an interruption loomed. He had agreed, back in January, to propose the toast of the guests at a banquet in the Mansion House to celebrate the centenary of the Society of Authors. He only had to give a six-minute speech, but it was the kind of occasion he dreaded: 'God curse all dinners, speeches, toasts, and may the manipulators of such carnivorous festivities sit out a red hot eternity of courses in hell.' To calm himself he took Cobber up through Knighton Wood, where there were 'pools and lakes of bluebells', as well as a few early purple orchids. The dinner, on 21 May, was a grand affair, with the Duke of Gloucester proposing the toast of the Society and the president, Sir Victor Pritchett, replying. But it merited only a couple of lines in Golding's journal, recording that the minister of culture 'made some amiable references to my work but I forget what they were'. He adds, bitterly, that (as Ann learnt in conversation with Margaret Drabble) it was only when Patrick White won the Nobel Prize that he discovered what enemies he had.

On 4 July he sent the second draft of *An Egyptian Journal* off to Monteith and, while waiting for a reply, drove over to Bristol to collect an honorary DLitt from the university. There was a distinguished bunch of honorands – L. C. Knights, Peter Maxwell Davies, Sir David Piper – and he thought the ceremony was very well done 'as these things go', though he did not much care for his official eulogy, 'and would not have given myself an hon degree on the strength of it'. He heard nothing from Monteith for a fortnight, and began to worry: 'He is probably submitting it to the critical opinions of Anthony Burgess and Jan Morris.' But all was well. Monteith rang on the 16th to say he liked it and John Bodley had 'laughed his head off'. Whether Rainbird would like it was another matter. They had been expecting a 60,000-word book about the glories of ancient Egypt, and were getting a book nearly twice that length about exactly the opposite. Monteith put this to Golding over the phone and was surprised when he replied that he was quite prepared to write a book about the glories of ancient Egypt, if Rainbird insisted, but they would have to wait a while before they got it. He wondered whether, if that happened, Fabers would publish *An Egyptian Journal* as it stood, and Monteith instantly said yes, though he thought it would be tactless to tell Rainbird that just at present. As it happened these machinations were unnecessary. Elizabeth Blair, who had replaced David Roberts at Rainbird, rang on the 25th to say that she was 'over the moon' about *An Egyptian Journal*. She had a few bits of rewriting to suggest, but thought his personal voice came through perfectly.

The objections came from quite another quarter. Alaa and his wife Soheir lunched at Ebble Thatch in September, bringing his photographs, which Rainbird were to use as illustrations. A few days later Elizabeth Blair sent him a copy of the typescript, and Ahdaf phoned on the 21st to say she was 'enjoying it immensely'. Her pleasure was short-lived. Both she and her brother found what Golding had written offensive. In October Alaa sent ten pages of corrections and comments, and said that he wished to dissociate himself from the project. Golding accepted the corrections, but disagreed with some of the comments, and set about trying to compose 'a telex to cool Alaa down'. Meanwhile he asked Monteith to put him in touch with an Arabic scholar: 'I want a bit of clout on my side in a mild punch-up with our Egyptian minder'. However, Alaa did not relent. Only one of his photographs appears in *An Egyptian Journal*. Almost all the rest are Golding's own. Ahdaf made her feelings clear in an angry denunciation in the *London Review of Books*. She objected to a passage where Golding imagines that Alaa had 'quaked' in the presence of a government official. This was not the brother she had known for twenty-eight years, but a 'stereotype' of a downtrodden Egyptian. The scene on the quayside on the first morning, when Golding represents Dr Hamdi turning up 'together with the females of Alaa's apparently extended family', is a gross misrepresentation. These 'females' were herself and Soheir, and far from just turning up they had used their cars to transport the Goldings' luggage from the Sheraton to the Ma'adi Yacht Club. No acknowledgement is made in the book of the help she had given during preparations for the trip, for which Fabers had offered her a fee which she had refused. She accuses

Golding of 'chauvinistic sourness' and 'idle condescension'. It is only fair to say, she adds, that having received Alaa's detailed comments on his typescript he removed some of the 'more blatantly offensive material', but what remained was bad enough for her brother to end his co-operation.

The only answer to this (and it is not an excuse) is that Golding was an imaginative writer. *An Egyptian Journal* is not reportage but a literary creation. It is understandable that real people, caught up in its comic invention, should feel insulted, but Golding did not present it as truth. He knew before he started, and acknowledged in the book itself, that 'whatever I wrote would not be about Egypt, it would be about me'. He seems, in fact, to have liked Alaa, who comes across in the book, and in Golding's notes, as firm, knowledgeable, helpful and tactful. Seven years later, thinking about how easy it is for people to be insulting across national boundaries, Golding conceded: 'Probably I was so, in the Egyptian Journal, the consolation being that few Egyptians will read it. I wonder how Alaa is?'

For their family holiday in August they took one of M and Mme François Lahuec's lets in Brittany, as they had in 1981 and 1982, but it was rather dismal. It rained a lot. Nicky got tonsillitis, Laurie bronchitis and Terrell cystitis. Of the menfolk only Roger, not yet a year old, remained healthy. Terrell's illness was a blow for the others, because on holiday he did the cooking. Under his aegis the huge old-style English meals the Goldings normally consumed, rich in butter and lard, were replaced by a healthy diet, which the senior Goldings scarcely recognized as food at all. 'Oh but of course we only had snack meals in France,' Ann once let slip, to Terrell's fury. Now that he was indisposed, his share of the childcare, as well as the cooking, fell on the others. 'I should very much like a holiday from this holiday,' Golding grumbled. However, his vacation reading, Ovid's *Metamorphoses* (in Latin, of course), cheered him a little. So did what struck him as the 'science-fiction' behaviour of their washing machine, which vibrated so fiercely that it moved from its corner out into the centre of the room, stopping only when it had pulled its own flex out and turned itself off. Towards the end of the holiday, while playing a kind of makeshift tennis with the children, he fell off the terrace and cut his leg quite deeply. Ann made him see a doctor, and he was prescribed antibiotics and forbidden swimming – 'a great bore'. Another irritation was a paragraph about him and the Nobel Prize in the local paper *Ouest France*, 'containing the usual implication that I'm small beer', to which the well-meaning Lahuecs drew his attention.

In October he and Ann flew to Thailand for a fortnight, where he gave the prizes at the Southeast Asian Award ceremony. They had the Noël Coward suite ('full of orchids') at the Oriental Bangkok Hotel, which sponsored the awards, were presented to Queen Sirikit ('very lovely, lovelier than her photographs'), met Princess Sirindhorn and lunched with the British ambassador Justin Staples ('and missus'). They also went on a river trip, were taken on a tour of the royal palace and the ruins of the old city, watched Thai dancing ('spectacularly graceful') and drank milk from green coconuts through straws. Of the writers to whom he presented the awards he records nothing at all in his journal, nor did he mention them in the speech he made at the ceremony, though at least three of the five, Budi Darma from Indonesia, the Malaysian poet and philosopher Latiff Mohidin and the Filipina playwright Virginia R. Moreno, were and are of great distinction in their own cultures. This might seem neglectful, but it is more probably an index of how out of place and embarrassed Golding felt on such occasions. On the night after meeting Queen Sirikit he had a horrible dream. It was a version of his most commonly recurrent dream, which he had been having all his life, in which he is about to be executed. The method varies, but is usually by hanging, and is so on this occasion, though the apparatus on which he is to be hanged looks rather like a shower system. Near it is his coffin, painted red, and he points out to the 'man of authority' who is in charge that this is 'unnecessarily distressing'. Ahead of them are 'dark children' who laugh at him, and his hands are 'full of his own shit that he is eating'. The man of authority wears a tall brimless hat, and he thinks he may be a Turk.

The dream seems to show that although – or perhaps because – he is being honoured and bestowing honour, mingling with royalty and officiating at a grand occasion, he feels acutely, at a subliminal level, guilt, humiliation and self-disgust. If that interpretation is correct it may clarify his discomfort over the publicity and celebrity that the

Nobel Prize had involved. It would be congruent, too, with his mockery of the self who held forth from lecture platforms, and also with his sensitivity to adverse criticism. Despite his obvious eminence in the real world, in the world of dreams he does not identify with authority figures, but constructs them as inherently alien, hostile and punitive. Perhaps these are the feelings we should imagine accompanying him when, a week after their return from Thailand, he and Ann attended a state banquet at Buckingham Palace, and 'met all the royals except the prince and princess of Wales'. The occasion merits only the most cursory mention in his journal, with a dash of wholesome scepticism: 'We are pressed to stay at the embassy should we find ourselves in Paris again – a likely story!'

29

A Move and *Close Quarters*

Towards the end of April 1985 Charles Monteith received an excited letter. It was typed on Ebble Thatch paper, but was not from Ebble Thatch. At the time of life, Golding announced, when sensible couples might think of retiring to a bedsit in Knightsbridge or a timeshare in the Algarve, he and Ann had bought a 'devastatingly beautiful house in the middle of a flowering wilderness'. It was a 'piece of inspired lunacy', and after a fortnight's residence they were even more pleased with it than they had been at first.

This happy find was a Georgian mansion called Tullimaar (meaning 'House on the Hill'), with five acres of gardens and woodland, a cottage and a lodge, near the tiny Cornish village of Perranarworthal (or 'St Piran's by the Creek'). The house had been built in 1828 by Benjamin Sampson, who had been manager of the Perran Iron Foundry and made a fortune from a gunpowder works at Kennal Vale and from investment in the Tresavean copper mine. Golding imagined him as 'one of the hard-faced men who did well out of the Napoleonic wars'. In Sampson's day Perranarworthal was quite a lively little centre, with Norwegian ships tying up at its wharf to unload timber for the mines. The Norway Inn, named as a tribute to these traders, was built in the same year as Tullimaar. But Cornish mining declined, the creek silted up, and the village went to sleep. In 1870, not long before the Perran ironworks closed, the Reverend Francis Kilvert spent three quiet weeks on holiday in Tullimaar, and admired the pool with its gleaming fish and the sunlight through the trees. Local legends accumulated about the house. It was said that some time in the nineteenth century a mysterious old lady lived there, and when she died a royal hearse turned up and took her away to be buried at Frogmore because she was the illegitimate child of one of George III's daughters. In the later stages of the Second World War Tullimaar was occupied by American soldiers, and after the war it was bought by the Franco-Romanian writer Princess Marthe Bibesco, who lived there from 1958 to 1973. She caused some embarrassment to the Goldings by putting up a plaque in the hall (still in situ) claiming that Eisenhower planned the Normandy landings in the house. Local historians doubted this, and the Goldings hung a tapestry over the possibly mendacious plaque. However, not long after they moved in they were contacted by an American who had been stationed at Tullimaar during the war, and confirmed that Eisenhower and Churchill met there, and were driven down to King Harry Ferry in the Fal estuary, which was the embarkation point for the locally based American troops.

The Goldings paid £200,000 for their new home, which they could well afford. In the 1985-6 tax year alone income from Faber and Faber amounted to more than £100,000. They did not even need a bridging loan while they were waiting for the £120,000 for which they sold Ebble Thatch. However, Golding admitted to Monteith that he was 'terrified' by the expenditure, and jokingly blamed Ann: 'women have that type of natural frivolity which enables them to spend huge sums of money as if they were in government or something'. Actually Ann had preferred another house. Tullimaar was his choice. Perhaps its remoteness attracted him. At Ebble Thatch they had been increasingly annoyed by the fans and students who would stand shamelessly in the road waiting for him to emerge. But the approach to Tullimaar is up a long curved drive through dense woodland that hides it from the Falmouth–Truro road, and you come upon the house in what seems like a forest glade. The big trees around it make it look gentle and elegant rather than grand. In spring and summer its tall, round-topped windows, which reach to within a foot or so of the floor, flood it with light and greenery. Every time Golding looked out at the trees, he wrote, he was filled with delight and satisfaction. The space and quiet relaxed him. He noticed a 'lack of strain', not felt before. 'You have a little bit of heaven up here,' said the girl who drove over with the Sunday papers, and he agreed. Three months after moving in he stopped drinking, and stayed off alcohol for more than a year.

But there was a great deal to be done. The woods and gardens had been 'let go for thirty years', he told Monteith. A major problem were the rhododendrons, which had grown enormous and were choking everything else. On hearing of their purchase, Monteith had confessed himself a secret member of the Anti-Rhododendron Society, pledged to destroying one a year, and Golding wrote back that Ann fully shared his antipathy. Many of theirs did not flower at all, and the others only briefly: 'For one week they look like the house of the lord and for the rest of the year like the tents of the ungodly – or do I mean it the other way round? A good question.' The woodland trees had been neglected too. Many were dead or dying, and the tree surgeon's estimate came to more than £6,000. But there were ample compensations: magnolias, camellias, a vast fern-leafed beech, an 'awesomely exotic' collection of azaleas and, a favourite of Golding's, a big holly with clusters of berries 'the size of a small fist' symmetrically sewn all over it, reminding him of something in a French Book of Hours. Some of the specimen trees and shrubs – among them three *Ailanthus altissima* or trees of heaven – had been swamped by the general profusion and became visible only when clearance began.

The huge walled garden on the south-facing slope was a jungle, and had to be flailed and ploughed to clear it of nettles and brambles. Its ancient stone walls were crumbling under a densely knotted carapace of ivy. Golding favoured demolishing them, and was 'sick with rage' when English Heritage and the Department of the Environment vetoed this suggestion. He attacked the ivy himself with a saw and an axe, and the immediate result was that he ricked his back and had to spend the rest of the day in bed. But that was only the opening round. His battle with the invasive parasite was to last for years, and became a major preoccupation. Meanwhile he planted the whole walled garden with rows of bush apple trees of different varieties, so that Ann would be able to walk among them in spring and enjoy their blossoms. They have flourished, and are now weighed down with fruit each autumn. His sole ally in these works was his gardener William Rose, who lived with his wife Di and her two children in the West Lodge rent free, and was paid £88 for a four-day week. Over-generosity was not among Golding's faults as an employer, and the record of William's labours in the journal suggests that he earned his keep. In October 1986 he was engaged in planting 1,000 white daffodils which Ann envisaged flooding down the hillside and forming a pool at the edge of the wood. New specimen trees were planted too, including a ginkgo and a tulip tree, and a big new bed of mixed shrubs and herbaceous plants was constructed for Ann, which had to have the pH level of the soil changed so that lime-loving plants would grow there.

Golding's happiness at Tullimaar was reflected in his happiest novel, *Close Quarters*, a sequel to *Rites of Passage*, which resumes the story not long after the death of Colley. The ship continues on its way to Australia, but a mishap occurs. Because of the negligence of Lieutenant Deverel, who was supposed to be on watch, it is hit by a fierce squall and almost capsizes. In the panic, Talbot behaves gallantly but receives a blow on the head and is concussed. When the ship has righted itself it is found that its foremast has been damaged, which reduces its speed. This makes it the more alarming when a sail is sighted on the horizon. It is thought to be a French warship, and the crew take up battle stations.

But it is an English ship, *Alcyone*, captained by Sir Henry Somerset, and it brings news that the war is over and Napoleon is on Elba. Merrymaking ensues. The two ships are roped together and decorated with lights and artificial flowers. To Talbot, still rather dazed by his blow on the head, it seems like a floating village, with excited passengers passing to and fro. He is introduced to Sir Henry and Lady Somerset, and to Lady Somerset's protégée, Marion Chumley, with whom he falls instantly in love. She continues to charm him at the grand dinner and the ball that form part of the celebrations, and, wild with passion and concussion, he tries to persuade Captain Anderson and Sir Henry that Marion should come with him to Australia. He even moves out of his cabin into the one recently occupied by Colley to make room for her. Because of his rank and his head injury he is treated indulgently, but in the end has to be manhandled off *Alcyone* and taken to his cabin, where he is dosed with paregoric.

When he wakes, *Alcyone* has gone, continuing on her way to India and taking Marion with her. Talbot is frantic at losing her, but can do nothing. He finds that there is a new officer on the ship, a Lieutenant Benét, of French extraction, who has been exchanged for Lieutenant Deverel, now on *Alcyone*. This arrangement suited both captains. Lieutenant Benét had made advances to Lady Somerset, with her encouragement, so Sir Henry was glad to be rid of him, and Lieutenant Deverel's conduct towards Captain Anderson had become outrageous. Reprimanded by Anderson, he had responded with breathtaking upper-class arrogance, and even challenged him to a duel. Anderson was on the point of having him clapped in irons when *Alcyone* appeared and a way out of what, in the early nineteenth century, would have been a perilous imbroglio for Anderson, presented itself.

It is not a happy novel for everyone. A friendship develops between Talbot and Lieutenant Benét, who has the great advantage of being able to talk to him about Marion. Their friendship arouses the jealousy of poor Lieutenant Charles Summers, the risen-from-the-ranks officer who behaved so humanely in the Colley affair, and who, it is evident (to the reader, though not to Talbot), is in love with Talbot. The book's saddest character is Wheeler, the steward who disappeared at the end of *Rites of Passage* and was assumed to have been thrown overboard by the crew. When *Alcyone* arrives, Wheeler is aboard her. After suffering agonies of exposure and deprivation so dreadful that he can only hint at them, he was picked up by *Alcyone* and he now returns to his duties as Talbot's steward, sticking close to him because he is terrified the crew will try to murder him again. Talbot's treatment of him is far from sympathetic, and shows us how much progress he still has to make in transforming himself from an Augustan gentleman into a human being. He tells Wheeler he is a 'lucky dog' to have been picked up, and reprimands him for being so 'devilish long in the face'. When Wheeler confides, 'I'm in hell, sir,' he pays no attention. At the novel's end we have one of Golding's seeing-it-differently moments, when Talbot returns to his cabin and catches sight of Wheeler through the louvred door.

His head tilted and lifted. His eyes were shut, his expression peaceful. He raised towards his lips a gold or brass goblet. Then his head exploded and disappeared after or with or before, for all I know, a flash of light. Then everything disappeared as a wave of acrid smoke burst out of the louvre. My left eye was, or had been, struck and filled with a wet substance.

Wheeler has blown his brains out with Mr Brocklebank's blunderbuss.

It seems as if, at one stage, Golding intended to connect Wheeler more closely with the novel's homosexual undercurrent. At the end of Chapter 14 in the printed version Talbot reveals that he got Wheeler to tell him the true story of what happened to Colley in the forecastle, and the information 'was of such a nature that I do not propose to commit it to this journal'. That is all we hear. But in his jottings for the novel Golding sketched the scene of Wheeler 'spilling the Colley beans' more explicitly.

> night, the noise of creeping and then the confession in darkness
> with Wheeler's hands feeling at Talbot in his bunk, the whole
> foetid, salacious, perverted, disgusting, mixed with Talbot's rising
> excitement and – disgust – and shot through it Wheeler's
> religiosity acquired by three days in the water.

The mixture of excitement and disgust suggests an ambivalence about homosexuality in Talbot that Golding decided not to include in the finished novel. Instead, he brought out a clear parallel between Talbot and Colley. Like Colley, Talbot falls so wildly in love that he seems to others to have taken leave of his senses. His love, like Colley's, flies in the face of his previously rational and decorous behaviour. Like Colley's, too, it crosses a class barrier, for Miss Chumley is a penniless parson's daughter and would not have seemed at all a suitable match to his aristocratic godfather. To reinforce the parallel, when Talbot moves into Colley's cabin we are told that it is a mirror-image of his own. The difference, of course, is that Talbot's love is socially acceptable whereas Colley's is not, so the novel implicitly questions the prejudice against homosexuality in Talbot's and Golding's society.

Wheeler's suicide is not the only shock in the closing pages. The ship has become clogged with masses of weed below its waterline which slow its progress, and at Benét's suggestion a dragrope is passed under the keel and drawn by gangs of sailors along the ship's length. It detaches vast swathes of floating weed, but something else comes to the surface – something that, Talbot says, has returned to him in nightmare many times. It looks like the crown of a head pushing up through the weed, or a fist, or 'the forearm of something vast as Leviathan'. The sailors drop the dragrope in horror as the huge shape towers black and streaming above them. Someone screams. Then the shape slides sideways and disappears. Was it a sea monster? Or flotsam? Or, as Lieutenant Summers thinks, part of the bilge keel – a subsidiary keel attached to the side of the ship to reduce rolling – that has become detached? The function that the unknown apparition serves in the novel is spelt out by Talbot: 'Its appearance cancelled the insecure "facts" of the deep sea and seemed to illustrate instead the horribly unknown.' We are reminded, in other words, that beneath the surface glitter of life – the lights and the artificial flowers, and beyond the reach of human intellect, lies something fathomless that only the imagination can enter. This is close to what Golding had proclaimed in 'Belief and Creativity', and it is a reprise of his theme of two worlds with no bridge between them, articulated in *Free Fall*. The 'awful creature' from the depths could be taken as a kind of symbol of his rejection of his father's scientific rationalism, for it is something that scientific rationalism cannot explain.

There are other things in the novel that relate to Golding's own life. Askew, the plain-spoken gunner who reprimands Talbot for his haughty manners, alludes to 'the swaying about. The hoity-toity,' and so recalls young Golding's chagrin when his mother accused him of 'swaying about' in anticipation of his grandeur as an Oxford under-graduate. A senile old midshipman called Martin, in attendance when Talbot and Askew talk, sings 'Down to the river in the time of the day', which was the song Golding heard his great-grandmother sing when he was three years old. After Marion's departure Talbot consoles him-self by writing Latin elegiac couplets about her beauty, and discusses short and long syllables and the mechanics of Latin metre, drawing on what Golding had learnt from working through the exercises in A. C. Ainger's *Clivus, Part I*. Early in the novel the passengers see a whale spouting, and it looks 'for all the world like the strike of a can-non ball', as did the spouting whale that ordinary seaman Golding saw off Iceland during the hunt for the *Bismarck*. 'Grommet', naval slang for buggery, a word he had picked up below decks on *Galatea*, is used in conversation with Talbot by Mr Gibbs the carpenter.

Though *Close Quarters*, as it evolved, was a Tullimaar book, Golding had written a first draft of it back in 1981 as a relief from his struggles with *The Paper Men*. This draft has not survived, but his notes about it give some inkling of the contents. It was to be called 'The Village' or 'The Siren Rock' or 'The Great Day' and, as in the published novel, the central event was to be the two ships coming together in mid-ocean. This would lead to 'the mingling of two quite different societies' and the introduction of a new character, 'A girl? She has been desperately seasick and transfers to the larger vessel.' So in the story's original conception, it seems, Marion, or Marion's prototype, would have come aboard Captain Anderson's ship as Talbot wanted. There would also have been 'a clergyman aboard the frigate – a rip-roaring companion of Edmunds'. So perhaps a mid-ocean marriage would have taken place. Or perhaps 'Edmund could fall desperately for the new girl and have finally to give himself a talking to on paper – the reasons for and against marrying the girl'. The girl could be 'a flirt and very pretty, but a husband hunter!' A few days later in this pre-planning stage Golding seems to have abandoned the idea of the seasick girl, and thought instead of making Edmund fall hopelessly in love with a virtuous Quaker lady, Mrs East. The story's lack of action was a worry to him: 'Can we not get someone shot or hanged? The only possible candidate w'd be Deverel.' Several weeks later, when he had started writing his first draft, he found that 'it's coming out that Deverel is going downhill: and I think, mad ... I believe the death and midnight burial of Deverel will have to come – what a pity Wheeler went overboard – damn, damn!' A further note suggests that Deverel commits suicide.

Golding had finished this first draft on 1 December 1981 and these notes indicate that it was a darker story than the one he eventually wrote. In *Close Quarters* Deverel does not die but is exchanged for Benét (the unfortunate Wheeler being brought back from the dead and then killed again in Deverel's place). Marion is not a husband hunter but a lovable girl to whom Edmund is devoted. A postscript, added on the advice of Ann and Monteith, reveals that the story will eventually have a happy ending and that the ship will reach Australia safely. This optimism coincided with the move to Tullimaar with its new joys and challenges. Golding started writing his second draft (on his new Sharp ZX-500 electric typewriter) on 9 June 1985, finished it and began a third in March 1986, finished that and sent it to Monteith on 13 May, finished a fourth draft, taking his criticisms into account, on 14 September, and sent the final version off, after some further tinkering, on 5 November. Provisional titles for the new book included 'Hornpipe', 'The Entertainment' and 'A Peculiar Providence'. 'Close Quarters' is first mentioned as a possible title in July 1986 and seems to have been a memory of something far in Golding's past. In 1947 a book called *Close Quarters* was published by Michael Gilbert, then unknown, but later to become a prize-winning crime writer and founder of the Crime Writers' Association. It is about a murder in a cathedral close (hence the title), which is evidently Salisbury. In the late 1930s Gilbert had taught in Salisbury cathedral's choir school, where Golding's great friend Tony Brown taught piano. Tony had a copy of Gilbert's book, now owned by his son Tim, and Tim remembers his father mentioning it in relation to Golding in the days when they were both teaching at Bishop Wordsworth's School. Given this set of coincidences, it seems unlikely that *Close Quarters* was a title Golding invented, though he may not have realized he was remembering it.

While Golding was in the process of turning *Close Quarters* into a happier book he had another horizon-widening experience, besides the move to Tullimaar. On 14 October 1985 he and Ann flew to Montreal for a two-month reading tour of Canada arranged by the British Council. The 'wonderful sense of endless space' that Canada offered impressed them even on their sightseeing tour of the city. But their stay in Montreal was short. After a reading at Concordia University on the 17th they caught a train the next day to Toronto for the Harbourfront International Festival of Authors. 'One comes to an early love for the earth rock and water of Canada,' Golding noted, looking out from the train at the 'clean deserted sandy beaches' of Lake Ontario. Literary festivals were not exactly his thing: 'I'm not really a groupie,' he conceded. All the same he seems to have enjoyed seeing old friends and making new ones in Toronto, and they met up there with Monteith, who had come out to join them for part of their trip. They heard Les Murray, Julia O'Faolain and James Baldwin give their readings, and joined the 'buffet scrum' with Brian Aldiss and his wife and Malcolm Bradbury. At dinner he sat next to Alison Lurie and discussed what they would have guessed the gathering was if they did not know it was a bunch of writers – deciding they would have taken it for 'a charity home for broken down circus personnel'. They were driven to an Indian reserve where a woman was teaching Indian children ballet, which he found 'quite absurdly moving'. At his own reading on the 26th ('Billy the Kid' and part of 'Belief and Creativity') the audience 'roared its collective head off' and gave him a standing ovation – the first since he read at Yale in 1962.

The next day they flew to Halifax for a reading and were driven afterwards through the forest to see the fishing village of Peggy's Cove. On the 29th they flew back to Toronto and took a sleeper train to Winnipeg. Here and there fires had broken out in the hundreds of miles of birch forest they sped through, and the surviving trees, Golding wrote, stood 'starkly, perfectly white against the shadowy woods, like ghosts of themselves'. They lunched at the university, where the student waitresses were dressed as bunny girls, and his reading received another standing ovation. A short afternoon flight on 2 November took them to Regina, Saskatchewan, where the Canadian playwright Ken Mitchell and his wife Jeanne Shami drove them out onto the prairie. They both sensed the Goldings were overawed by the vastness. 'People feel exposed,' Mitchell explained, and he noticed that Ann was nervous about getting out of the car. At the Moose Jaw Wild Animal Park the massive rack of antlers on a bull elk attracted their admiration. The elk was less favourably impressed, and charged their station wagon, with Mitchell yelling to Golding to get back inside and, as he recalls, 'elk semen spraying in all directions'. Golding's journal shows that he was intrigued, too, by a ship which a homesick Finn had built, high and dry in the middle of the prairie – the subject of one of Mitchell's plays, *The Shipbuilder*.

On the 4th he and Monteith did a double-act seminar discussion about how they had co-operated on *Lord of the Flies*. Then on the 5th they flew to Calgary and were driven out into the Rockies for some mountain views. His reading on the 6th was a sellout, and on the 7th they flew to Edmonton, where the temperature at night was minus 20 degrees, and he wore his fur hat for the first time. Ann said it made him look like Ivan the Terrible on a bad day. His lecture at the University of Alberta went well, and seeing the indoor student mall, a sort of heated, undercover village thronged with eager young people, made him 'suddenly hopeful for the future'. They watched the ice floes on the North Saskatchewan river from their hotel window, had a Mennonite meal in a log house at Strawberry Creek, and were taken to see three beaver dams and a beaver lodge – a 'wonderful visit'.

On the 10th they left Edmonton by train (the Super-Continental, Dome Car De-Luxe) and arrived early the next afternoon in Vancouver, where their hotel overlooked English Bay. There were the usual TV and radio interviews, and a radio show where he was asked to choose three pieces of music. He chose Chopin's Op. 25 No. 1 in F minor, Benjamin Britten's 'The Splendour Falls', and the last movement of Beethoven's 5th Symphony. The pianist in the recording of the Chopin was Ashkenazy, and Golding noted critically that his rhythm was shaky. 'In one place he squared the triple time as incompetently as I can myself. It was very heartening.' He did a seminar with graduate students at Simon Fraser University on the 12th and a reading at the Vancouver Institute on the 16th. It was in the medical centre, with two overflow rooms both packed with people. Next day they took a ferry to Victoria, where the first event, on the 18th, was a reading at the Faculty Club, chaired by the poet Robin Skelton, who, perhaps in a bid to upstage his distinguished guest, was dressed as a magician, wearing three huge rings and a pentangle on a chain. On the 19th there was a question-and-answer session after lunch, and a creative writing class attended by about 150 people. A reading on the 20th rounded off the 'over-full' Victoria programme, and they took to the airways yet again.

This time, though, it was for pleasure not duty. Judy, Terrell and the children were in Richmond, Virginia, because Terrell had arranged a temporary exchange of jobs with an academic from Virginia Commonwealth University. The Goldings flew via Calgary and Washington for a reunion with them, and then Terrell and Judy drove them 300 miles south to Myrtle Beach, South Carolina, to see Terrell's parents – Terrell senior and Harriet – whom the Goldings had met in England but never encountered on their home ground. They were given a room with a balcony facing the Atlantic and an endless beach of white sand,

and could at last relax. They needed to. It had been a gruelling two months. Golding felt 'clobbered' and Ann was showing signs of being seriously unwell. She had been suffering from swollen ankles since they were in Winnipeg, and had been taking Dyazide regularly. Work was not quite over even now for Golding. He had agreed to do a reading at the Library of Congress in Washington, and was dreading it ('Have I a great thought? No, I haven't. Have I a small thought? Not that either'). It seems, though, to have gone well. He flew to Washington on the 25th and stayed in the Cosmos Club, and his reading was in the Coolidge Auditorium at the Jefferson Building next day. He was pleased to see Librarian of Congress Daniel Boorstin again ('still as much like a bull-dozer as ever'), and even more pleased that Boorstin seemed rather at sea when they discussed Homer ('my impression is he doesn't know any Greek'). Back at Myrtle Beach the temperature was 80 degrees even at the end of November. He bathed in the sea and watched skeins of pelicans 'wallow' overhead. On the 30th Judy and Terrell drove them back to Richmond. But there Ann was taken ill. She had a nosebleed that could not be stopped, and fainted from loss of blood. They drove her to St Mary's Hospital, where a consultant, Dr Kriestler, stopped the bleeding and stabilized her blood pressure. He and the hospital refused to take any payment and in gratitude Golding gave a talk at Kriestler's son's school, Godwin High.

Ann's illness postponed their departure for home, and gave Golding time for reading. In the house Judy and Terrell had taken over he found a copy of Dryden's translation of Virgil's *Aeneid*, and tucked in ('I've been wanting to read that for years'). He finished it before they left, remarking how odd Virgil seemed in seventeenth-century dress. 'I can hardly think in anything but heroic couplets.' For Talbot and Talbot's translator-godfather, Dryden's *Aeneid* would have seemed the acme of Augustan decorum, which may explain Golding's inter-est. Before leaving for Canada he had been rereading Homer's *Iliad*, and liking it less than before. He was 'appalled, not to say disgusted' this time round, by the bloodlust and cruelty. 'What a bastard Achilles is!' For Canada he chose something gentler, the pastoral *Idylls* of Theocritus, which had 'a strict sophistication of which Homer never dreamed'.

They were back at Tullimaar on 13 December, after two months away. One absence from Golding's new life was Cobber. Riding in Cornwall does not seem to have attracted him, though he made some inquiries, so Cobber remained in Wiltshire. He made sure, though, that his old steed did not come to want, arranging with Betty at the stables that he should be hired out, but assuring her that he would make up any shortfall in Cobber's earnings. Meanwhile a new interest was a weekly French-language class that he and Ann joined. It was run by a young French woman, Françoise Bowyer ('*bretonne* tall red haired from Brest and not large', he noted appreciatively). They began in January 1986, and the journal records his ups and downs and occasional blunders ('made a proper cake of myself'). Speaking French and understanding it when spoken were both difficult for him, though he could read it fluently. The class, being almost entirely oral, helped, and so did tuning into French radio, which became habitual. In September they were both promoted to the advanced class, which entailed writing essays in French on such subjects as what is to be done about terrorism.

Though Golding had moved to Cornwall partly to avoid people, he seems to have enjoyed a fuller social life there than at Ebble Thatch. Matthew Evans and his wife Liz had recently bought a house by the sea in a secluded part of St Mawes, and they introduced Golding to another local resident, Pete Townshend of The Who, who was a colleague of Evans at Faber and Faber. ('He is a pop star,' Golding reminded himself in his journal after their first meeting.) Townshend liked and admired Golding, and found Ann 'witty, mischievous and a real match for Bill'. He owned 'a small, safe local boat called a Falmouth Bass Boat', and one day in September 1987 he took Golding and Liz Evans out in it. They sailed up and down Carrick Roads for two or three hours and, watching Golding's silent concentration when he was at the helm, Townshend felt that it was the kind of focus that wins races, 'but also – I imagine – the degree of concentration that allows new fiction to develop and grow with powerful roots over a period of time'. It was the first time Golding had been at sea since the wreck of *Tenace*, and both he and Ann thought it a milestone. 'One gets hooked again,' Golding wrote in his journal. He came ashore 'exhilarated', Townshend recalls, and Ann said to Evans, 'You have no idea how significant this is.' Some years before, he had suddenly been gripped by terror on seeing a television picture of waves coming towards the camera, and had speculated that it showed the *Tenace* disaster haunting his unconscious. It seems the Townshend trip helped towards recovery.

Another friend only a car-drive away was the Tudor historian, poet, maverick Shakespeare scholar and perennial enfant terrible A. L. Rowse, whom Golding had got to know when dining at All Souls with Monteith. Rowse lived in a beautiful old greystone house, Trenarren, with a spectacular view to the south where the lawn dropped away into a combe, with tall woods framing a headland and the distant sea beyond. Golding was a little jealous of its situation, remarking to Stephen Medcalf on their first visit in August 1985, 'Rowse lives in front of a visual cliché.' At tea that day they were regaled with heavy fruit cake and non-stop talk from Rowse, which Medcalf rather resented but Golding excused. 'We are all pretty good yakkers,' he remarked on the way home. The other guest was Colin Wilson, who had shot to fame as a young author in 1956 with the publication of *The Outsider*, and whom, Golding worked out, he had not seen for twenty-eight years.

Meeting those he already knew was all very well, but he was keen for new acquaintance and he asked Raleigh Trevelyan to arrange some introductions. Trevelyan had made his name as a writer with a classic account of the Battle of Anzio, in which he served with the Green Jackets, but it was his second book, *A Hermit Disclosed*, that Golding particularly treasured. He had reviewed it in *The Spectator* in 1960, but they did not meet until they were both guests at the Evanses in 1985. As a guide to Cornish society Trevelyan was ideal. He was in publishing, and knew everyone in Cornwall with even the remotest links to the book world. He also knew those with showpiece houses and gardens. His own house, St Cadix, is beautiful and remote, set among gentle hills beside a tidal creek, and built on the site of an old Cluniac priory. The Goldings lunched there in September and were instantly smitten, though Golding conceded that its ninety acres would have made it rather large for them.

Close friends of Rowse that the Goldings soon came to know through Trevelyan were Christopher and Charlotte Petherick of Porthpean

(Charlotte was president of the Cornish Garden Society), Donald Adamson, who dealt in rare books in Polperro, and Diana Colville, widow of Norman Colville, who lived at Penheale Manor, Launceston – a house partly designed by Lutyens, with a distinguished collection of paintings. Among authors Trevelyan introduced them to were John le Carré, whose books Golding quickly came to admire ('How good le Carré's prose is!') and the crime and thriller writer Jessica Mann, wife of the archaeologist Charles Thomas. In June 1987 they lunched with two other new friends, Robin and Luella Hanbury-Tenison, at their house Maidenwell, eight hundred feet up on Bodmin Moor – a site that, Golding noted, had been naked moorland 'till Robin twenty seven years ago planted conifers then deciduous'. An explorer and prolific travel writer, Hanbury-Tenison was also a leading light in the Royal Geographical Society, and his ecological concerns chimed with Golding's reverence for Gaia. He was to become founder and president of Survival International, the world's leading organization supporting tribal peoples, and to lead the RGS expedition to study rainforests. The current international concern about their disappearance was sparked by his book *Mulu, the Rainforest*. In May 1986 at St Cadix the Goldings met another much-travelled writer, Penelope Tremayne. As a *Sunday Times* journalist she was used to seeking out trouble spots – Cyprus at the time of Makarios, the Falklands, Afghanistan – and in the 1960s she had gone, by herself, into a danger area in Sri Lanka and been captured by the Tamil Tigers. She gave Golding a vivid account of 'how one reacts to the fact of facing death – in her case a firing squad in an hour or two'. Reciting 'How Horatio kept the Bridge', which took thirty-five minutes, had, she found, prevented her thinking about her children and shedding tears, which would have pleased her captors. Like Golding she had a semi-mystical passion for Greece, which is apparent in the book she wrote about her captivity, *Nor Iron Bars a Cage*. She and her husband Tony lived at Kestle Farm, but her own family house was at Croan, and the Lost Gardens of Heligan – now one of the most popular gardens in Britain, with its fabulous collection of rhododendrons and camellias – was originally part of the Tremayne estate.

Through Trevelyan the Goldings also came to know Rowse's close friend David Treffry, and at Treffry's house, Place, in Fowey, as at

St Cadix, they met members of the Cornish horticultural high-priesthood. These included Charles and Caroline Fox, whose house Glendurgan has one of the great sub-tropical gardens of the south-west, and Sir Richard Carew-Pole, owner of Antony House, near Torpoint, which is set in twenty acres of landscaped gardens. Simon Boyd, son of Alan Lennox-Boyd, and Simon's wife Alice belonged to the same circle, and Alice was on the committee of the Royal Horticultural Society. Their home, Ince Castle, has a famous garden, but when the Goldings visited them they were not living there, because Simon's mother had inadvertently burned it down while smoking in bed. Some of the garden-owning grandees were interesting apart from their gardens. David McKenna, for example, who, with his wife Lady Cecilia had a house, Rosteague, on the Roseland peninsula, was a keen amateur musician and harpsichord player. Others, however, had little to recommend them except their possessions, and Treffry, when sending out invitations, would warn of occasions to which only 'the snob lot' were coming, so that the more cerebral could stay away.

Golding's attitude seems to have been tolerant. When he and Ann lunched, dined and partied with members of the Rowse–Treffry circle, he enjoyed talking to the interesting ones and put up with the others. True, he noted of one patrician couple who turned up at Tullimaar that they 'could not be more ignorantly philistine than they are without making the Guinness Book of Records'. But that was a rare asperity. He liked visiting beautiful houses and gardens, though he could be critical of them, as of their owners. He judged Lanhydrock, for example, 'pretentious and pointless', and its gardens 'no great shakes'. These opinions would have pained another of the friends introduced by Trevelyan, Giles Clotworthy, who was head of the National Trust in Cornwall, based in Lanhydrock. The Goldings' transition to a new social set was viewed with disfavour by some. In an article published in 2006, the novelist D. M. Thomas, another Cornish resident, referred rather sniffily to Golding and Ann being 'fawned on by Cornwall's minor gentry'. But this seems a jaundiced view. Golding met stimulating people in Cornwall and took pleasure in their company, as they did in his. Jessica Mann recalls that, 'in the role of country gentleman or literary pensioner', he seized the chance to talk about things that interested him, 'without being recorded for posterity'. He was 'witty, caustic, sensitive, perceptive, frank', and he did not mind being contradicted. Once, in a conversation about politics, he said 'he did not give a damn about what politicians got up to', and she retorted that that was 'the *trahison des clercs*'. Ann, 'who was an old-style socialist', was delighted that she dared to argue with him, and Mann realized that 'they'd rather have disagreement than deference'.

Judy, Terrell and their children loved Tullimaar and were eager visitors. They continued to spend each August abroad with the Goldings and David, though the 1986 holiday was rather a washout. They went, as before, to Mme Lahuec's domain in Brittany, this time taking a house called Les Tritons. But it rained and the sea was too cold for swimming. One day they made a trip to Vannes, which, Golding noted, was in the territory of the Gallic tribe called the Veneti, who had sailed with leather sails. 'F. M. L. Caesar toughened them up, in his inevitable civilizing mission. He killed the elders and the elite and enslaved the rest.' Field Marshal Lord Caesar was his disrespectful pseudonym for the author of the *Gallic War*, one of his least favourite books. His holiday reading included N. A. M. Rodger's *The Wooden World: An Anatomy of the Georgian Navy*, which he was reviewing for the *Guardian* and which *Rites* and *Close Quarters* gave him a particular interest in. Rodger defended the Georgian navy against the popular assumption that its motive forces were, as Churchill put it, 'rum, sodomy and the lash'. He argued that the 'flogging captains' of fiction were not to be found in the records, that sodomy was almost unknown, and that, though a lot of alcohol was consumed, men did not get drunk at sea because it would put others in mortal danger. Golding, in his review, accepted most of this but questioned the point about sodomy: 'There is vast oral evidence in naval speech, custom and lore that where men are cooped up in a wooden world for weeks and months at a time unnatural acts take the place of natural ones.' No doubt he was thinking of his own experience on *Galatea* as well as of Billy Rogers and his ilk.

Back home he embarked on a 'final tidy' of *Close Quarters*, but his interest was waning. 'I have to admit that the days are conditioned by the snooker on television'. Friday, 19 September was his seventy-fifth birthday and celebrations started the day before with a dinner party at

Andrew and Sonia Sinclair's Chelsea house, attended by Princess Michael of Kent and her husband. Antonia Fraser sat between Prince Michael and Golding. 'The former', she recalls, 'never once looked at me or Miriam Gross on his other side but into his plate, closer and closer and closer.' Golding, however, 'rubicund, cheery and at seventy-five much more lively, made an extremely hearty meal, I was glad to see'. The next night Faber and Faber gave a grand dinner in his honour at Brown's Hotel. He was still on the wagon, so he resisted the Laurent-Perrier at the reception beforehand and the Montagny Tête de Cuvée and the Château La Croix Bellevue served with the smoked salmon and best end of lamb. Among his presents were an Imari ginger jar from Ann, a 1534 *Iliad* from Stephen Medcalf and a *Magnolia campbellii* and a tree fern from Karen and Pete Townshend.

It was because of his seventy-fifth birthday that I came to know Golding. Fabers had decided a couple of years before that they would publish a *Festschrift* to mark the occasion, and Charles Monteith asked me to edit it. Golding came to lunch with me in Oxford in April 1984 to talk it over, and I went down to Tullimaar in July 1985 to do an interview that was published in the book. It was not hard to find writers eager to contribute. Ian McEwan wrote about reading *Lord of the Flies* for the first time, aged thirteen; Craig Raine identified some putative Golding sources and showed how Golding outshone them; Ted Hughes investigated baboons and Neanderthals; John Fowles admired Golding's refusal to become a celebrity; Seamus Heaney sent a new poem, 'Parable Island'. An ex-pupil recalled what it was like to be taught by Golding's father, and another what it was like to be taught by Golding. I included appreciations by critics – John Bayley, Barbara Everett, Ian Gregor, Mark Kinkead-Weekes – and by friends, Peter Green, Anthony Storr and Stephen Medcalf. I had wanted to call the book 'Golding Olding', but Monteith gravely demurred, so it was called *William Golding: The Man and His Books*. Writing to thank me for it, Golding said that he preferred to call it his Birthday Book, 'better than *Festschrift*, don't you think, and easier to spell! Anyway the German makes it sound as if we all danced in heavy boots round a foaming barrel or two.'

During our interview he had laughed quite a lot in a self-deprecating way, and to show this I put 'laughs' in square brackets when I transcribed it. On seeing the typescript, he asked me to take these interjections out – which I did. It was only when I read his journal, years later, that I discovered why he had felt awkward about them. '[Laughs]' was 'a dead give-away', he wrote. 'I suppose that basically I despise myself and am anxious not to be discovered, uncovered, detected, rumbled.' The only other thing in the Birthday Book that gave him pause was Charles Monteith's account of the original typescript of *Lord of the Flies* and of the collaboration between them that produced the published text. Monteith had sent him a draft of his essay on 18 April 1985, and it evidently came as rather a shock: 'Lord, Lord,' he replied, 'it's a time capsule and you've dug it up from the foundations of the Laureate's monument.' He admitted that the account had 'its painful side for me', because he now realized that, as a result of the repeated rejections of his novel, he had 'fallen desperately sick psychosomatically'. After one rejection he remembered shouting furiously, 'It's Good! I know it's good!' There was 'a kind of delirium all bottled up in that pursed, bearded, well-conducted schoolmaster'.

He conceded that Monteith had written 'a marvellously accurate account'. But then, in the same letter, he suggested one or two corrections, and ended up with an apology for 'all this self-pity'. He clearly continued to feel unsettled about it, and after a phone conversation Monteith agreed to send a second draft of his essay, which he did on 15 May. Golding wrote back to 'place on record my acceptance in full of your piece', and to thank him for emending it: 'yet another debt on top of many years of help I've had from my editor. A thousand thanks.' Even after this, and after the Birthday Book's publication, though, he went on feeling slightly aggrieved, as his journal records: 'I'm not happy either, if the truth is to be told by Charles's article on *Lord of the Flies*.' The original manuscript of the novel was safely locked away in Barclays Bank, and he thought of getting it out to check on Monteith's accuracy. He seems, though, to have decided that reading what he had penned thirty-five years earlier might be too much of a shock: 'I might do myself a mischief.'

His boyhood admiration for Tennyson's poetry must have given a special piquancy to an invitation he and Ann received, at the end of the year, to dinner with Pete and Karen Townshend at their house in

Twickenham, for it was the house where the young Tennysons had lived when they were first married. Joanna Mackle at Fabers hired a Daimler with a telephone for them, so that they should arrive in style at the star's residence. The other guests included Michael Foot and Jill Craigie and, Townshend recalls, an altercation ensued between the two 'fiery men', first over the number of words Golding wrote in a day (he claimed 3,000, which in fact he very rarely achieved, and which Foot declared impossible), and then over whether you could, as he insisted he had, learn classical Greek in a few months. An entire bottle of malt whisky disappeared and a second was begun in the course of this discussion, and Townshend (who was off alcohol himself at the time) was 'terrified', though Ann and Jill Craigie ('somehow a sex-bomb at seventy years old', Townshend attests) just laughed. Golding's verdict, noted in his journal next day, was that Foot 'drank a great deal of whisky and got rather drunk but was good-tempered and managed by Ann who talked back and accepted his clumsy approaches in the spirit in which they were meant'.

When *Close Quarters* was published the following June the critical accolade was almost unanimous: 'thrilling' (David Hughes in the *Mail on Sunday*), 'wonderfully enjoyable' (Barbara Everett in the *Independent*), 'overwhelmingly successful' (Chloe Chard in the *Financial Times*), 'even more enchantingly readable than its predecessor' (John Bayley in the *Observer*). Bernard Levin in the *Sunday Times* wrote glowingly about its social tensions, A. S. Byatt in the *Evening Standard* declared that no other living writer 'represented the fragility of man's enterprises so marvellously', Ronald Blythe in the *Guardian* judged the final chapters 'as good and strange as Conrad at his finest'. For Stanley Reynolds in the *Sunday Mirror* it showed Golding was a humorist as well as a great writer. There was a small band of antis, the most disgruntled of them being women – Barbara Hardy and Hilary Spurling.

Despite the general acclaim, Golding still thought of critics as hostile by nature. 'I've got to the point in my life where I don't care as much about a lot of things, including what people say about my books,' he told Blake Morrison in an *Observer* interview. 'In *The Paper Men* I put my tongue out at the whole literary world and told it to go piss up a rope. So now I'm pleasing myself.' What he regarded as the apathy in Britain about his Nobel Prize irked him. It had attracted eager attention abroad, he complained, but 'it really means nothing in this country whatsoever – but then being a writer here means nothing either'. This was hardly fair. He had continually chosen to avoid publicity, so could not reasonably complain about being ignored, and in any case he was not ignored but argued over and written about, besides being studied by a considerable proportion of the world's schoolchildren. What his bitterness ultimately reflected was the pain that lingered from his early years of neglect and rejection – the pain Charles Monteith's essay in the Birthday Book had reawakened.

30

Fire Down Below and Globe-Trotting

In the three years from 1987 to 1989 Golding wrote and published *Fire Down Below*, the concluding part of his sea-trilogy. As usual the final text emerged from a tangled sequence of redraftings, changes of plan and outbursts of exasperation, recorded day-by-day in his journal. Yet far from seeming laboured, the finished book is taut with excitement. He never wrote anything more knuckle-biting than the sequence where the battered ship, with a smouldering peril eating at her timbers, is driven southwards and trapped among the towering ice cliffs of the Antarctic. In addition, the novel reaches a level of seriousness in its treatment of Edmund Talbot and his journey towards self-knowledge that is different from anything Golding had tried before, less schematic, less clear-cut, more compromised, lifelike and adult.

He had started on the third volume in August 1986, soon after finishing *Close Quarters*, and had written 40,000 words before concluding that it was 'all to hell' and abandoning it. At that stage he intended to make the book 'a critique of the hopes of the enlightenment'. By the time he started the second draft in June 1987 he had decided that, on the contrary, Mr Prettiman, the disciple of Voltaire, who plans to found a utopian colony in Australia on enlightenment lines, should be the book's hero, and that the principle behind the rewriting must be 'the up-marketing of Mr Prettiman and his nobility'. What happened between the first and second drafts was that he and Ann went to India, and it seems possible that their experiences there changed his mind about what he wanted to do with his book.

The Indian trip, sponsored by the British Council, had originally been planned for January 1985, but Golding pulled out following the assassination of Indira Gandhi in October 1984. Sikhs were being targeted after the killing, and Harriet Harvey Wood, the Council's literary director, recalls Golding saying, 'How can they tell one man with a beard from another?' So it was not until 22 January 1987 that he and Ann landed in Delhi, and they were in India for two months. Many Indian universities and cultural organizations were eager to host the new Nobel laureate, and Golding had agreed to an itinerary that would have been strenuous in itself, even if he had not been giving interviews, readings, lectures and press conferences everywhere he went – with sightseeing fitted in between. In their three days in Delhi there were two sessions at the university, plus interviews, official receptions and discussions with his British Council hosts, which left him in no doubt that he was in for a 'desperately busy time'. Then they were driven to Agra to see the Taj Mahal (its minarets, he thought, 'not quite right'), and to the Khajuraho temples, famed for their erotic sculptures, which he scrutinized approvingly, while observing that the ancient Hindus must have been double-jointed. At Varanasi on the 29th they saw the burning ghats, and sunrise over the Ganges (or would have done had it not been hidden by fog).

They arrived in Calcutta on the 1st for another round of interviews, press conferences, a public reading and events at the university, then they flew down to Orissa, where they visited the great temple of Jagganath at Puri (closed to non-Hindus, so they saw only the outside) and the sun temple, in the shape of a huge black granite chariot, at Konark. Another flight brought them to Madras on the 15th, where among the official functions they managed to fit in a drive to the Tirupara Kundran rock temple in the Alagar hills. Hyderabad was their next stop, with a lecture at the university, a session at the library, and a trip to the Golkonda fort. Then they moved on to Bangalore for another university lecture, a reading and a talk at the science institute. Robert Bellarmine of the British Council took over as their minder at Bangalore, and drove with them to Mysore for a talk at the Dhvanya Loka literary centre, followed by an eight-hour drive to the sea at Kochi. On the way they stopped off, at Golding's request, to look at some enormous ant-hills built by white ants. By this time the temperature was in the nineties, and they flew down the coast to Trivandrum ('white sand, blue sea, dazzling surf') for a free day, before meeting academics and students at the University of Kerala.

A bumpy flight took them to Bombay on 5 March, where British Council officer Clive Brasnett welcomed them. Under his guidance Golding saw two of India's greatest archaeological treasures, the Ajanta caves, carved out of the sides of a wooded ravine and adorned with Buddhist masterpieces of painting and sculpture, some dating from the second century BC, and the Buddhist, Hindu and Jain cave temples and monasteries cut out of the face of the Charanandri hills at Ellora. As they left the site, Golding said wonderingly to Brasnett that there was nothing in the Valley of the Kings at Luxor that surpassed what he had seen at Ellora. On the 8th they flew to Pune for a lecture engagement, then back to Bombay for another, at the famous Taj Mahal Hotel. Robert Bellarmine joined them once more for a flight to the University of Karnataka at Dharwar, followed by a drive to Goa. They had a couple of days' relaxation there by the hotel pool (Golding was tempted to try wind-surfing, but thought 75 rupees – £3.50 – an hour too pricey). Back in Bombay, he flew Ann to Aurangabad to see the Ellora caves, as 'traveller's tummy' had prevented her going with him before. On the 20th, they took a plane to Udaipur in Rajasthan, 'the Venice of the East', and were ferried out to the vast marble Lake Palace, with its endless courtyards and fountains and life-size marble elephants, and, Golding noted with astonishment, a separate 'monsoon palace' on a mountain top for the Maharaja to use when the city was flooded. That was their last excursion. Two local flights brought them back to Bombay, where they were woken at four in the morning on the 22nd for the flight home. Golding, exhausted, 'came over a bit queer' in the airport lounge, but perked up as soon as he was on the plane.

His journal of the trip packs in, higgledy-piggledy, social chat, academic engagements, food and drink consumed, bouts of illness (several) and occasional mishaps (as when, at Goa airport, he sat in a pool of coloured water, left behind by Holi revellers, and, wandering out onto the blazing tarmac, dried off by placing his behind against the scalding metal cylinder of a parked steamroller). The beauty and strangeness of India continually astonished him – the harsh calls of tropical birds, the 'chuckle' of the Indian cuckoo, the huge black, red and white butterflies that flapped so much more slowly than any European butterfly, the monkeys and the peacocks, the elephants 'plodding vastly along' – one of them, he noticed, with its fanned-out ear turned into a 'yellow rose' by the rays of the setting sun. ('I did not know the fabulous creatures had such subsidiary talents.') The trees were a wonder – the palms so beautiful he could not resist stroking them, the yellow-flowered happiness tree, the mauve-blossomed jacaranda, the coffee bushes with a chain of white stars along each branch. The shapes of plants, birds and animals were imitated in the sculptures of Hindu temples, and he found himself instinctively making obeisance before them. 'I am a natural idolator', he concluded. 'India is the smile on the face of Mother Earth.'

Like any Western visitor he noticed the poverty too – a beggar woman on the pavement, 'carrying on quite a complex life with tins and rags and strings'; girls in blue and red and green bearing burdens on their heads, 'thin and straight as laths'. But in the 1980s, India was already making strides towards the modern world, and he sensed the change. At Ellora he saw a crowd of little schoolgirls, all dressed Bengali-fashion in white, and chattering 'like a flock of starlings' – as gay, irreverent and noisy as schoolchildren anywhere. 'May they be happier than their mothers,' he wished. He felt surrounded by hope and idealism, and was ashamed of the cruelties of the past. Robert Bellarmine remembers how, when they visited Tippu Sultan's palace in Bangalore, Golding stood looking at a picture of British soldiers with the head of a young hostage they had decapitated, then walked slowly away, moved to tears. He was amazed when he learnt that some families had travelled twenty-five kilometres in a bullock cart to hear him talk. At lectures, he was asked continually about the 'philosophy of pessimism' in his novels, and he repeatedly denied he was a pessimist. It was just, he said, that pessimism showed up more, as red would show up more if you wound strands of red and blue together.

It was not only the eagerness of his hearers but the depth of their interest that impressed him, and nowhere more so than at Bangalore, where the grace and intelligence of a young Indian academic Susheela Punitha won him over. She had drilled and rehearsed her colleagues for the panel discussion with Golding, as he realized. 'I'm sure the whole thing was rigged. I could hear your voice in every question,' he told her afterwards with a mischievous look. The result, preserved on

CD and published in the British Council Madras Division periodical *Literature Alive* for June 1988, is the best surviving record of a Golding question-and-answer session, and the only place where he publicly criticized Monteith's cutting of Simon's supernatural dimension from *Lord of the Flies*. 'Some things', he declared, 'should've been left in, which went.' He ought to have stood up to Monteith. 'Simon should've been a lot more. It's my fault that he wasn't.'.

He did not make a good impression everywhere in India. The literary critic Mohan Ramanan recalls that in Hyderabad he came across as 'supercilious and arrogant', and Clive Brasnett noticed that at signing sessions he would sign only copies of his books, not autograph books or loose pieces of paper – failing to take into account that most Indian students could not afford books. One difference between Western and Indian assumptions was brought home to him by the response of audiences to his reading of 'Billy the Kid'. In Europe, America and Canada the account of his bullying other children at primary school had always been greeted with roars of laughter, especially his juvenile admission that he enjoyed hurting people. But in India it was met with 'the silence of incomprehension or shock'. He felt that they took the whole thing as 'a psychological problem for which the West may find no answer'.

It was when he got back to work on *Fire Down Below* with these experiences in mind that he decided to reorientate the book, making the idealistic Prettiman its hero. 'The real point of the whole thing is Prettiman of course,' he noted in his journal. At the start, the cynical, worldly-wise Edmund Talbot still regards Prettiman as a fool – a starry-eyed, lower-class rabble-rouser who had attracted the attention of the authorities back in England. But in the course of conversation it gradually dawns on Edmund that Prettiman and the ex-governess Miss Granham, who is now his wife, are not only as well educated as he is, but more intelligent, more perceptive about people, and nobler in their aims. As their talk goes on, he seems like a boy in the company of two adults. They both urge him to join them in their utopian enterprise when they reach Australia, and he feels ashamed of his cowardly failure to respond to their altruism or share their hopes for mankind.

The book ends in a dream that Edmund, years later, has of the Prettimans – or perhaps a vision. He says he hopes it was no more than a dream, 'because if it was, then I have to start all over again in a universe quite unlike the one which is my sanity and security'. In the dream, he is buried up to his neck in the sand, so he sees the Prettimans from ground level.

They rode past me a few yards away. They were laughing and chattering in a high excitement, the men and women following them with faces glowing as in a successful hunt for treasure. They were high on horses – she leading, astride with a wide hat, and he following, side-saddle, since his right leg was useless. You would have thought from the excitement and the honey light, from the crowd that followed them, from the laughter and, yes, the singing, you would have thought they were going to some great festival of joy, though where in the desert around them it might be found there was no telling. They were so happy! They were so excited!

I woke from my dream and wiped my face and stopped trembling and presently worked out that we could not all do that sort of thing. The world must be served, must it not? Only it did cross my mind before I had properly dealt with myself that she had said, or he had said, that I could come too, although I never countenanced the idea. Still, there it is.

When I first read that it occurred to me that Golding might have been thinking, when he wrote it, of his own parents – the two idealists who, in family legend, had stood on the steps of Marlborough town hall being pelted with overripe tomatoes, while forwarding the cause of women's suffrage and other worthy aims. This might explain why they were seen in the dream from a child's low-level perspective and, given the disagreements he had had with them over the years, why the tone was so poignant with regret. So when he was in Oxford in February 1990 I asked him, over lunch, whether this was so. He answered instantly that, yes, he had been thinking of his parents. So it might be said that his trilogy ends with the humble grammar-school master Alec Golding being shown as the moral and intellectual superior of the toff Edmund Talbot, a representative, as it were, of the young gentlemen of Marlborough College whom Golding had so detested as a boy.

Although he had decided, on his return from India, to put the Prettimans at the centre of his novel, there was still a lot of rewriting to do, and having finished the second draft in July 1987, he set to work on a third. By chance, while describing Edmund Talbot's painful acquisition of self-knowledge, he acquired some painful self-knowledge himself. 'I have learnt a great deal about myself in the last day or two,' he wrote, 'and none of it what I would have thought or wanted to know until I broke my shins over it.' What had happened was that he had to pay £52,000 income tax, and was shocked to find that writing the 'ghastly cheque' made him feel grief-stricken, as though he was mourning someone who had died. The grief was not as intense as he had felt for his father, he estimated – more like what he had felt when his close friends Tony Brown and John Milne died. He knew that it was 'terrible' to equate money with people, 'but my muddy soul does it'. So, though he lost £52,000, he gained self-knowledge – 'as usual, the bitterest myrrh to drink'.

It seemed possible that he might recoup some of the money by selling the manuscript of *Lord of the Flies*. According to Golding's journal this suggestion came from Rick Gekoski, who advised him that the manuscript was so valuable they could not afford to insure it, and that as it was not earning anything they should sell it. 'He mentioned a figure of a million.' Later, the journal records, Gekoski adjusted his estimates and 'turned up possible valuations' of the manuscript varying from £60,000 to £250,000. Gekoski's recollections, published after Golding's death, are quite different. In his account the idea of selling the manuscript came from Golding, who said to him one day, 'If you can find a nice rich American or Japanese I would take a million for it.' Gekoski asked if Golding meant pounds or dollars, and when Golding replied pounds he advised that no buyer would pay that price, and that the only twentieth-century literary manuscript that had raised such a sum was Kafka's *The Trial*. Golding, Gekoski relates, was undeterred, so he sought the advice of leading dealers and came up with figures ranging from £50,000 to £250,000. 'I conveyed this information to him gingerly and he snorted with contempt.' Whatever the truth, Golding evidently worked out, as he notes in his journal, that after tax and agent's fees the manuscript could not be expected to yield much more than £100,000, and 'We don't need a hundred thousand that bad!'

In August the Goldings had their usual summer break with the children in Brittany, staying, as before, in one of the Lahuecs' lets near the beach at Le Cabellou. But bitterness about the tax cheque quite spoilt the holiday for him. It was a 'rooted sorrow'. Besides, the house had too many mirrors in it, so all too often he caught sight of 'an ancient decaying slob'. When he got home yet another tax demand, for over £40,000, awaited him, together with a VAT demand. It meant, he calculated, that in a period when he had earned just over £70,000 he was expected to pay £105,000 in taxes. On 19 September he reached his seventy-sixth birthday, but he felt there was 'nothing to rejoice at'. He could not work for worry. 'I really am investigating tax-havens,' he recorded morosely.

In reality, though, he was far too attached to Tullimaar to think of leaving it. It continued to provide physical challenges as well as joys. The battle with the ivy that covered the quarter-mile-long stone walls of the old kitchen garden engaged him more and more intensely. Ivy, he came to think, was 'very clever stuff'. It had not merely a pattern of habits, which a mathematician might codify, but something like intelligence. He had come to feel that he was more intelligent than his horse, Cobber, but with ivy he was not so sure. 'It is a draw.' As he disentangled the ivy, day after day, it seemed to integrate with his creativity, becoming 'conjunctive in the obscure reaches of this book-making'. The experience of fighting it was 'a contribution and a major one to the book'. People thought of ivy as soft, feathery stuff, lapping ancient ruins in cushions of green. But he knew this was an illusion.

There is bone beneath the feathers. As you wrestle with the stuff you come up against extraordinary and mysterious strength. Only when you have cut away the bitter leaves and torn or cut the vegetative tendrils that have not yet turned to wood do you come upon the hard heart of the matter, the bone. It is elbows tensed against blocks of masonry, wrists twisted, fingers thrust so deep in the crevices they have made it evident that wood and stone are now an equation of forces in which the hidden roots and the visible leaves are constantly feeding in strength to the one side.

The wall's destruction, as the ivy pushes the stone blocks sideways and outwards, seems a 'slow catastrophe', but seen in 'the time-scale of generations' it is a swift one. As he clambered into the ivy's 'bitter and dusty ambience', he came upon 'not wood – but apparently the antlers of stags, mysteriously thrust through crumbling stone', or 'narwhale's tusks', or 'rhinoceros horn'. It could be frightening, like being lost in a jungle and feeling yourself unarmed 'as something stirs in the scrub'.

Another invasive presence in the walled garden, though less dramatic, were rabbits. Fearing that two elderly people in a remote house would be a likely target for armed robbers, Golding had bought a shotgun, and, though never used against humans, it provided a measure of anti-rabbit defence, as he records.

> I have just been to the walled garden with my gun for rabbit, but there were none. I killed a rabbit some days ago on almost my first visit and perhaps the rabbits are wiser now. It was extraordinary. The rabbit I shot was on watch. The range was about thirty yards. He heard the click of the safety catch going off. I was in hiding with the gun supported and the bead sight right on his head. He never stood a chance. He stood up to see what was happening and was right in the blast of small shot. It knocked him over of course. Every time I think of it I see his expression as he was blown back, a combination of astonishment and outrage – I am a live thing being violated! I suppose this is imaginary and I am importing my own feelings but I see it clearly.

As often in Golding's fiction you sense pity and ruthlessness joined together, and feel like asking, 'How can he bear to write this?'

Apart from the ivy and the rabbits the Tullimaar wildlife was generally friendly. There was a nightingale that sang before dawn in the fern-leafed beech to the south of the house, and a vixen and two fox cubs who were holed up in the trees near the drive. In sunny weather the cubs played 'charmingly' on the asphalt, and it occurred to him that they, rather than his shotgun, were deterring the rabbits. In the time left over from garden maintenance he finished the third draft of *Fire Down Below* (for which his provisional titles at the time were 'Utmost Despatch' and 'The Best of Friends') by the end of November 1987. On 1 January 1988 he sent a copy to Monteith, with a letter full of the kind of self-doubt that his editor was by this time thoroughly used to. The typescript was a 'load of cod's wallop', possibly 'publishable in the last resort', but possibly too long or too short or dull or muddled or worthless. 'You won't believe the contrivances I've been at even to get this far. Are you unretired enough to have a look?' Two days later he handed a duplicate copy to Matthew Evans at a party in Raleigh Trevelyan's house St Cadix. Then he and Ann went home and celebrated with fish and chips and Schubert's 9th symphony.

Monteith was indeed unretired enough, and came down to Cornwall the next weekend to talk about the book. They discussed the idea of having a postscript, added by Talbot thirty years after the events recorded in his journal. In a letter thanking Ann and Bill for their hospitality, Monteith suggests that Talbot might find himself sitting next to Benét, now an admiral, at a City livery company dinner, and that this might prompt his recollections, in the postscript, of 'the Prettimans and the Ideal City etc ... And then, that night, he has The Dream'. Golding did not adopt the suggestion about the meeting with Benét, but the rest is evidently the germ of the novel's brilliant, elegiac finale, in which everything that has been vivid and alive in the journal suddenly shrivels into history. However, he was too busy to consider Monteith's ideas for the moment. He had been invited by President Mitterrand to a conference of Nobel laureates in Paris, and he and Ann flew out on the 17th. The reception at the Elysée Palace was very grand, 'ruffles, fanfares, uniforms, in fact the full strength of the Pompiers', and Golding felt that his seminar paper on the 19th went well. The idea he put across was for an 'agreed' history of the world that could be taught to small children. Mitterrand's chief of protocol relayed this to the president, who mentioned it in his closing address and passed it on to UNESCO.

Mme Mitterrand gave a banquet in honour of the laureates on the 20th (*Roulades de filets de soles 'printanière' au Chablis; Mignon de veau sur coussin d'artichaut aux petits légumes; Fromages; Charlotte aux deux chocolats,* accompanied by Chablis 'La Chablisienne' 1985, Grand Listrac 1982 and Champagne Pol Roger). Golding was allowed to take one guest besides Ann and chose Christine Jordis, who had looked after him on previous Paris trips. It was, she recalls, 'great fun to see Bill sitting so straight, solemn and bored and silent and very stiff among all the laureates'. He told her that it made him think of an elephants' grave-yard. On the 22nd he gave a lecture at Sorbonne III, which took the form of a commentary on 'Belief and Creativity'. But by this time he felt he was going down with a stomach bug, or perhaps the after-effects of the banquet, and was glad to get home.

Not for long, however. On the 29th he and Ann flew to Singapore for a British Council-sponsored visit, where they met up with Mark and Joan Kinkead-Weekes. Mark was there on a nine-month teaching engagement, and he remembers that 'Bill was sweet with the students, and made them laugh. They were very respectful, and some of them were quite pretty, which helped.' Ann, however, had contracted a virus and was in a wheelchair. Mark and Joan took Bill to the orchid gardens and the botanical garden 'and he was very happy'. But Ann 'couldn't get out and simply stayed in the hotel, except for the last night of Bill's stay when there was a reception in Raffles Hotel, and Ann came, but she seemed irritated and annoyed'.

Apart from anxiety about Ann, who quickly improved with a course of antibiotics, Golding's account in his journal is upbeat. He was amazed to see orchids growing in clumps seven feet high, 'like sweet peas', and his lecture at the University of Singapore (one of four that week) 'went like a bomb, Mark presiding. Gales of happy laughter.' On the 7th they flew to Kuala Lumpur for more press conferences, read-ings and radio and TV interviews. Golding noted that the waitresses at their hotel, the Shangri-La, wore ankle-length skirts split right up to the thigh on one side, yielding 'a delectable vision of long legs' as they hurried past. He and Ann were taken on an excursion into the jungle, where they saw tree ferns, bamboos, wild bananas, and 'monstrous spiders with a leg span of six or eight inches, waiting at the centre of wide nets'. Before they flew home on the 14th, Ann gave an interview to Joan Lau of the *New Straits Times* in which she is reported as saying that she read science at London University. It would be easy to take this small falsehood as an indication that she sometimes regretted her lack of a university education. But Ann was, her daughter attests, 'the most terrifyingly truthful person', to a degree that was 'splendid but sometimes a shock', so it seems more likely that the interviewer simply misunderstood Ann's reference to the chemistry evening classes she attended after she left school.

Back home Golding was at last able to work at a final draft of the novel that took into consideration Monteith's ideas, and it was finished by 1 March. But as usual he almost immediately started having second thoughts. In London on 14 April he got to the stage of wondering whether he should 'hold back' *Fire Down Below*. There was 'reasonably good stuff' in it, but 'the connective tissue is bad'. Perhaps concern about the book explains what followed. They flew to Paris on the 15th for the Salon du Livre, the Paris Book Fair, and Joanna Mackle had arranged a dinner for the Faber contingent at L'Ami Louis the following night. When she and Matthew arrived at Le Méridien to pick the Goldings up, Ann answered the phone in tears. Golding was in a terrible state. He had cleared the hotel mini-bar and was, Evans recalls, 'legless'. They dosed him with hot coffee, and managed to get him into a bath. Joanna felt that Ann 'was no help, shrugging her shoulders and making big eyes'. By the time they got to the dinner Golding was 'drunk but under control' – or almost. Among the other guests was the South African novelist, poet and painter Breyten Bretenbach, who had spent seven years in prison under the apartheid regime. For some reason Golding singled him out and demanded, 'What makes you think you can write a novel just because you have been in solitary confinement?' Bretenbach made no reply and everyone else remained impeccably polite. 'I am entirely disgusted with myself,' Golding wrote in his journal for the 16th. In his letter of apology to Evans he said he had thought he had overcome his drink problem. 'A very nice letter indeed' came back in reply, 'far nicer than I deserve'.

A week later they were off on British Council travels again, this time to Hamburg for a reading, a press conference and interviews. The reading was a 'great success', with a bigger audience than the hall could hold and students 'hanging from the chandeliers'. Ann and he found time for an exhibition of Holbein drawings at the Kunsthalle – 'marvellous ... like walking straight into the sixteenth century'. But they agreed they were doing 'more quick travel than we can manage', and were glad to get home on the 27th. Particularly glad, as on the 29th they went to London for the launch party of *Moving Pictures* by Judy Carver (dedicated 'To My Parents'). They had known Judy was writing a novel for quite a while, and were delighted when Duckworth gave her a contract. Set in California, *Moving Pictures* centres on Angela, the daughter of a successful lawyer, who gets entangled with Sam, an ageing film star who is her father's oldest friend, and with a boy called Dave, who is an amateur bank robber. Kidnap, killings and gang warfare ensue. Angela's mother is shot by gangsters who mistake her for her daughter. Dave goes to prison. Angela, pregnant by either Sam or Dave, confronts her father and demands why he loathes his family. He reveals that he was in love with a man before he met her mother ('*Daddy!* You mean you're *gay?* Wow, I can't believe it!'). Returning to the family home at the end she finds two grey-haired men kissing each other in the kitchen – Sam and her dad.

Golding was delighted with Judy's black-comic extravaganza ('witty in a way I couldn't possibly manage myself'), and wrote proudly to friends about it. He was indignant when the *Observer* reviewer interpreted it as an 'anti-daddy' novel – 'If ever anything were further from the truth!' – and he told Jessica Mann that he would have liked to kill reviewers who were unkind to the book. Judy's facility made him feel even worse about *Fire Down Below*. Correcting proofs in June, a process he managed to spin out to October, he reflected how drastically it needed cutting and rewriting ('If I had the guts I'd get rid of thirty pages'). Meanwhile something cheerful happened: he got a knighthood. He had wanted one for a long time. In 1980, when Angus Wilson was knighted, he noted bitterly, 'I have got myself well left behind in that particular race.' He fancied he had been overlooked because he had persistently turned down invitations to royal garden parties, or perhaps because he had been 'very terse with the twit of a photographer who married Princess Margaret'. (This referred to an explosive incident with Antony Armstrong Jones, who had inadvertently assured him how much he admired *Lord of the Rings*.) Golding had badgered Monteith to lobby the great and the good on his behalf, and Monteith obliged by writing to Sir Keith Joseph, who replied that he would send his letter on to Richard Luce, the Minister for the Arts, 'so that he may follow it up as he sees fit'. When Golding met Matthew Evans in Cornwall, he entrusted him with the same mission, and followed up by sending him a card: 'Are you Kultivating my K?' A week later, at a publishers' dinner in Soho, Evans mentioned Golding's ambition to Kenneth Baker, who, besides being secretary of state for education, was editing a Faber anthology, and he had a word with the secretary of the Cabinet, Robin Butler. Golding's knighthood was in the honours list on 11 June 1988.

It gave him enormous pleasure. One of the first things he did was to phone Joanna Mackle about getting the names on their passports changed to Sir William and Lady Golding. He records, with satisfaction, in his journal the grovelling attentions he receives from hotel managers and head waiters. His response was understandable – this was, after all, the William Golding whom Oxford had labelled 'Not quite a gentleman' – but it was mixed with irony. He looked up Jane Austen's cool comment in *Pride and Prejudice* on the absurd Sir William Lucas and his knighthood – 'The distinction had perhaps been felt too strongly' – admitting that he felt 'a rueful sympathy' with Sir William. 'I even find in myself the merest inclination to *strut*.' The investiture was on 27 July. As the Queen was adjusting the ribbon round his neck, 'with the occasional maternal tuck', she asked, 'Are you still writing?' He replied, 'Yes, marm,' and she said, 'Good' – 'which I think exhibits a degree of critical insight'. They also, at last, went to a royal garden party, where they got a glimpse of Prince Philip's head and admired a royal herbaceous border: 'I have to declare, though, disloyal as it may seem, our pink mallow is better than Her Majesty's.'

For the French family holiday in August they took a house near Pornichet on the Atlantic coast. It was a shorter break than usual – only a fortnight – and not much of a holiday since he laboured each day at a lecture he had agreed to give in Japan in November. It was still not finished when they got home, and it had to be set aside for yet another British Council tour, this time to Spain. They flew to Madrid on 23 September for a flurry of TV, radio and newspaper interviews, saw the Goyas in the Prado, lunched in Toledo and toured the cathedral, did a colloquium with students at the university ('fun'), then flew to Barcelona for the book fair. Stephen Spender was there ('a slightly bent beanpole in gent's best suiting'); so was Kazuo Ishiguro, a writer Golding came to like and admire. Ishiguro was scheduled to read (from *The Remains of the Day*, which won the Booker Prize the following year) immediately after Golding, but three-quarters of the audience left when Golding had finished, and he felt so 'anguished' for the younger man that he stayed, asked a question, and led the applause.

The Japan lecture was a worry because its prescribed topic was conservation, which, despite his ardour for Gaia, he did not know much about. He had been a conservationist ever since reading a pioneering book on soil erosion called *The Rape of the Earth* which G. V. Jacks and R. O. Whyte had published in 1939, but he lacked up-to-date facts and figures. Robin Hanbury-Tenison helped, giving him information about Japanese big business and the destruction of rainforests, and Friends of the Earth sent him some material. He brightened up his lecture with personal touches (remembering his father showing him, sixty years back, photographs of receding glaciers in the Royal Geographical Society's magazine). But it remains a rather routine rehearsal of familiar threats – the greenhouse effect, depletion of the ozone layer, acid rain, rising sea levels. Logical exposition was not his thing, as he had noted many years before in *Seahorse*. He thought in pictures, and the only bit of his 'Conservation' lecture that comes alive is when he warns his Japanese audience, in a vivid science-fiction image, that unless the world changes its ways, 'Your descendants, few in number, will sit on the hills hoping that the sea will go back one day. And as the ozone layer will have been depleted they will all be negroes.' The first version of this passage had been even more dramatic: 'You young people who are going to be old in the new age – you are going to be negroes.' But he evidently decided, on reflection, that the change of skin colour would take rather longer, allowing time for natural selection to 'do its usual horrible work'.

On 4 November, the day before their flight to Japan, they drove over to Plymouth for Ann to get her fur coat out of cold storage – an annual autumn ritual not, he noted, entirely appropriate for a champion of conservation. From the 5th to the 10th he made no entries in his journal, something that had never happened before and a testimony to the severity of the culture shock they both felt on arriving in Japan. Only on the 11th did he fill in the missing days. They were guests, along with several other Nobel laureates and their wives, of one of the oldest Japanese newspapers, *Yomiuri Shimbun*. A limousine had fetched them from Tullimaar and they flew first class to Tokyo, where they were lodged in the 'immense and splendid' Imperial Hotel. There was a preliminary conference on the 7th, addressed by the Swedish author and physician Lars Gyllensten, chairman of the Nobel Foundation, then an opening ceremony, with a thousand people present, where they met the Crown Prince and Princess – 'practised and charming', Golding judged. The Crown Prince spoke so softly it was hard to hear him. 'I suppose the more cultured a Japanese is the softer he speaks and when the crown prince becomes emperor he will be completely inaudible – a lesson for our own royal house!' A dinner followed, 'but I can't remember it'.

On the 8th they all went to Nagoya by bullet train and there were lectures all day, then a banquet, where they sat cross-legged in Japanese style, with geishas sitting among the guests – 'large, coarse-faced wenches and embarrassing. I am sorry to sound so carping even to myself.' Ann asked them how long it took to put on their make-up and they said forty minutes, allowing time for wigs. The Goldings had two guides, a journalist and an interpreter, allocated exclusively to them, who were 'an enormous help'. On the 9th he and two other laureates gave their lectures in the morning to an audience of about fifteen hundred. His went 'far better than I had hoped', but he was so exhausted during the afternoon lectures that he started hallucinating. 'People came and stood by me who couldn't have been there, including Ann who at the time was in a museum some miles away.' The next day they went by chartered bus to the sleepy old city of Kanazawa, through forested hills with autumn-coloured maples. This part of Japan had not been damaged in the war, and the traditional houses looked like a Hokusai or Hiroshige print. The laureates held their forum in a school, surgically clean, 'like everything in Japan', where the children sat so still it was hard to believe they were real. Next day they were in Nara and saw the vast bronze Buddha in the Todai-Ji temple, and other temples which, in retrospect, became just a blur in

Golding's mind. Time blurred too. 'Now it is a quarter past seven in the morning of some day or other', he wrote. They caught the bullet train in Kyoto and saw, on the station, an elderly couple bent very nearly at right angles, their bones, Golding notes, ankylosed in that position by a life of planting rice. It was not, they were told, unusual among the older generation of peasants. On their way back to Tokyo for their return flight they caught a glimpse of Mount Fuji and thought it had a cindery texture, 'as though a celestial aga had had its ashes dumped there for an aeon or two'. On 15 December they were back in Tullimaar, 'whacked' and jet-lagged.

Golding had thought well of the 1980 *South Bank Show*, and he agreed to be filmed again by London Weekend Television early in the new year. On 14 January 1989 he was picked up and driven to Portsmouth for a two-hour interview with Melvyn Bragg in Nelson's cabin on board HMS *Victory*. It was cold and raw, and he felt 'chilled right through', but was glad to be aboard the legendary ship again after more than sixty years. Besides, the programme would be good publicity for *Fire Down Below*. It was broadcast on 24 March to coincide with the book's publication. He seems by now to have got over his fear of reviews, and could even face reading them. They were hardly intimidating. *Fire Down Below* brought the 'marvellous trilogy' to a happy conclusion, said John Bayley in the *Guardian*. 'When I reached the last page I re-read it instantly.' Penelope Lively in the *Evening Standard* thought it 'majestic and enthralling', and David Hughes in the *Mail on Sunday* agreed that it brought the trilogy to a 'breathtaking close', never losing 'the mood of dour significance that Golding has made his own'. 'Breathtakingly vivid' was Francis King's verdict, too, in the *Sunday Telegraph*. The iceberg incident achieved 'a surreal kind of poetry'. If Golding had lived when it was natural to tell stories in verse, judged Stephen Medcalf in the *Times Literary Supplement*, he would have been a great narrative poet. W. L. Webb in the *New Statesman* thought there was 'nothing quite like it in our literature'. The 'magnificent sea pictures' grabbed the attention, and the pastiches of Jane Austen, Fielding and Peacock made it almost post-modern. Victoria Glendinning in *The Times* found the evocation of the ship so powerful that it made her seasick. Peter Kemp gave it a rave review in the *Sunday Times*, noting, as other reviewers had failed to, Charles Summers's repressed homosexuality, apparent to the reader though not to Talbot. This was picked up again by Patrick Gale in the June 1989 *Gay Times*. The maritime novelist Patrick O'Brian reviewed it at length for the *London Review of Books*, calling it a 'truly noble achievement', while noting some nautical inaccuracies. Golding's ship should have had copper sheathing, as other ships of its class did, and should have carried spare topmasts and a surgeon. Its poop and quarterdeck seem to change levels in Golding's account, and some features he mentions, such as a 'mizzen mainmast buntline', did not exist. Disinclined to argue, Golding noted that O'Brian's corrections would be 'useful in a reprint'.

Martyn Goff, the administrator of the Booker Prize, had planned a volume of stories by previous winners to celebrate its twenty-first birthday, and Matthew Evans cajoled a reluctant Golding into agreeing to contribute. His story, called 'Caveat Emptor', which he sent to Goff in March, is appropriately about a novelist (at first called 'William', but later changed to 'Wilfred') who cannot think of anything to write. A friend offers him a true story for £50, and he accepts. The friend relates how, when he was on holiday in France, and snoozing by a stream, two cars sped by and a parcel thrown from the front car struck him on the head. Unwrapping it, he found it was a Van Gogh. He refrained from telling his wife, who was herself a painter, but used some of her paints to daub the Van Gogh so that he could take it back to England unrecognized. Later, however, while he was absent from home, the Van Gogh was stolen and his wife murdered. He worked out that the criminals who originally stole the painting had tracked it down and exacted vengeance, and that he was responsible for his wife's death. Wilfred does not know whether to believe any of this, so 'Caveat Emptor' ends, as it began, in uncertainty about what or whether to write – the recurrent Golding dilemma.

In March 1989 Joanna Mackle, in charge of Faber and Faber publicity, arranged for him to be interviewed by John Walsh for the *Sunday Times*. The result was exceptionally informative, particularly about his current religious thinking. One could only make a negative confession, he told Walsh, amounting to total ignorance: 'I believe in God, but

God is not even that which I believe in.' Belief did not mean you were a better person: 'It doesn't make anyone wise or any of the good things.' Nor did it entail expectation of an afterlife: 'I'd sooner there wasn't an afterlife really. I'd much rather not be me for thousands more years.' In conversation with Stephen Medcalf, who visited Tullimaar in April, he was marginally more definite, seeming to endorse belief in God as creator. Medcalf quoted the Hebrew blessing 'Blessed art Thou, our Lord God, King of the Universe, who hast made the creation', and Golding replied, 'There's nothing else to say, is there?' However, it remains unclear how his belief in God relates to his belief in Gaia. On his flight to India in January 1987 he had had a vision of Gaia, admittedly after drinking one and a half bottles of Lanson, and prayed to her: 'Glory to thee Gaia, our mother, first of Gods through whom men may come and be presented to that old one who created thee!' This 'old one' might possibly be Medcalf's King of the Universe. Or possibly not. Writing in his journal in December 1989, it occurred to Golding that, though he was sometimes called a theist, 'my own theology omits God', and he added: 'It is more glory to my father the sun and my mother the earth.'

As he implied to Walsh, his kind of faith, whatever it was, did not affect his conduct. Reading in *The Times* in June 1989 that the evangelist Billy Graham dismissed faith without works, he observed that his own faith was faith without works. Perhaps it was the death, the previous month, of his old friend Adam Bittleston that prompted these thoughts. Adam, it seemed to Golding, had believed that 'he was put on earth to help other people'. So Adam's faith affected how he lived. But his own case was, he acknowledged, different, and resulted in a different kind of God, or no God at all: 'Faith without works makes God irrelevant,' he noted in his journal.

Golding's interview with John Walsh sparked a disagreement with Pete Townshend, for in the course of it he berated popular music. 'I loathe it. Not just pop music, but show tunes – all that mock emotion.' His brother Jose, he recalled, had made him listen to the Savoy Orpheans on the wireless. 'I used to think it was immoral, the things they did with sound.' Townshend wrote a pained letter, trying to explain that pop music 'was not quite what it seemed, that it was art with a necessary function for my generation and although cathartic and apparently flippantly aggressive and shallow, was deeply reflective of the post-war condition of young people'. Golding replied diplomatically, but stuck to his guns: it was 'raging and distorted sound'. Townshend wanted to explain that 'the distortion was itself a part of the art', but felt it wiser to refrain, and to accept that those 'born either side of the D-Day divide would always see art differently'. Stephen Medcalf was staying with the Goldings when Townshend's letter arrived, and they discussed it. Ann accused her husband of being 'unreasonably dismissive of two and only two things, ballet and pop music'. But Golding said to Stephen, 'I, and I guess you, want a voice from on high. Pete doesn't understand that.'

Poetry, on the other hand, was a voice from on high, and in July, at the Stratford Poetry Festival, he and Peter Orr read a selection of their favourite poems. Writing to invite him to the festival, Orr had reminded him that they had met once before, at Ebble Thatch in January 1977, and that, greeting him at the gate, Golding had 'announced glumly that there was no gin in the house'. The 1989 encounter was happier, but Golding's choices were melancholy on the whole, including Tennyson's 'Break, break, break', parts of Eliot's *Four Quartets*, some of Blake's *Songs of Innocence and Experience*, and Larkin's 'The Trees' and 'Cut Grass'. He signed off, however, with a poem of his own about the body's irrepressible demands.

> Sophocles the eminent Athenian
> Gave as his final opinion
> That death of love in the breast
> Was like escape from a wild beast.
> What better world could you get?
> He was eighty when he said that.
> But Ninon de l'Enclos
> When asked the same question said no,
> She was uncommonly matey
> At eighty.
> And I?
>   When I die

Heap rocks over me
For what rest I can have,
Let concrete cover me,
Girls keep off my grave.

July 1989 also saw the Goldings in Cambridge for the British Council's annual Cambridge seminar – 'vastly international and polygot'. He read the perennial 'Billy the Kid', and Ann, in question time, asked, 'Where has all that aggression gone?' to which he replied, 'My dear, if you don't know, nobody does.' It provoked 'much amusement and acclaim'. The next day they drove to Oxford to see his recently completed portrait by Norman Blamey installed in Brasenose College hall. It seemed to Golding to be a picture of a middle-aged Edmund Talbot, 'a firm, hard, uninspired man, only able to stare up at ideas and selflessness which have got beyond him'. In October they flew to Berlin for a lightning visit, paid for by the international media corporation Bertelsmann AG. The evening they arrived they were taken to see the Leningrad Ballet dance *Petruschka* and *Le Sacre du Printemps* ('most enjoyable', he thought, despite Ann's accusation of anti-ballet prejudice), and the next day Dr Wildung, director of the Egyptological Museum, gave them a 'marvellous' conducted tour. The best thing, Golding thought, was an 'exquisite' bust of Queen Ty. By comparison the famous bust of Nefertiti was 'a gaudy piece of fairing'. He was nervous before his lecture; his head seemed 'full of cotton wool' and his answers 'fluffy'. He put it down to the increased drinking he did on such trips. To think it over, he went back to the hotel afterwards and 'drank three glasses of champagne slowly'.

Their last British Council trip of the year was in November, to Mexico, where they were looked after by the regional director Richard Watkins. As usual, it was no rest-cure. After two days in Mexico City they flew to Guadalajara on the 24th for the book fair – 'signings, interviews, television and other wastes of spirit', plus a lecture in the local theatre. Next day they returned to Mexico City for a dinner at the embassy, and on the 26th there were three and a half hours of interviews, followed by a talk to a packed auditorium at the Anglo-Mexican Institute. On the 27th came 'another dose of interviews', two of them televised, then a three-quarter-hour drive to a book signing at El Parnaso. He was told that the university he would speak in that evening was the biggest in the world, with 20,000 professors and 300,000 students ('What in hell shall I say?'). In the event it seemed successful, though with 'some elements of farce', because there was no simultaneous translation, so everything had to be said twice, in Spanish and English. Towards the end of their stay Richard Watkins took them to the vast archaeological site of Teotihuacan, where they saw the pyramids of the sun and moon. But Golding seems to have been too tired to pay much attention to these giant structures. Besides, he was worried about Ann, who was near to collapse, and might, he thought, need a wheelchair for their change of planes at Amsterdam. The only thing that really engaged his interest in the days before they left were the women in shawls and 'a kind of trilby hat', squatting on the ground in the cathedral square in Mexico City, with mats spread out, selling fruit, vegetables, honey, eggs, scarves, toy soldiers, strings of beads, and holy pictures and images.

Back at Tullimaar the Mexican trip seemed 'a fantasy', and he felt he had been 'a fool to take it on, and a careless if not cruel fool to inflict it on Ann'. So why had he? What impelled the marathon journeys – India, Singapore, Japan, Mexico? Was it restlessness? Or fear of having to face a blank sheet of paper? Or an appetite for applause and publicity which he felt he lacked in England? Perhaps all of these, but there was also, it seems, a kind of patriotism – showing the flag for Britain – though the very idea made him feel foolish. One day when, as the half-decipherable writing shows, he had drunk too much, he wrote in his journal: 'This has been a kind of ludicrous half-witted way of keeping some sort of duty of service of the crown ... I am a sad person. A craven and foolish person which fifty years ago might have meant something.'

His health held up rather better than Ann's on their travels, but there were some serious worries. In November 1989 he had a small black blotch removed from his nose, which it was thought might be malignant. Four months earlier he had been diagnosed with emphysema. Palliatives were prescribed, but there was no cure. 'So it seems', he wrote, 'I now know more or less what I shall die of.' But then, no one, he reflected resignedly, could have smoked as heavily as he had for so many years 'without doing himself a mischief'. His son's health was a much more immediate concern. 'I'm most terribly sorry to hear that David's going through a bad patch,' Monteith had written in October 1987. David's mental condition did not improve, and during 1989 he came to the attention of the social services and the police. In May 1990 he was compulsorily hospitalized for a time. The anguish his parents felt is evident from Golding's journal, and it may have been another reason why they sometimes felt the need to escape abroad.

31

The Double Tongue

The new decade started stressfully for Golding. The previous September Trinity College Oxford had invited him to give the first of a series of literary lectures in memory of the Second World War fighter ace Richard Hillary, author of *The Last Enemy*. He would not have to do it until February 1990, and it could be on any subject, so he accepted. But as the date approached, his agitation about the 'flaming lecture' intensified. He dared not 'risk a flop', but what should he talk about? Asked, in January, for a title, he proposed 'Aspects of Narration', to keep his options open. On 26 February, after weeks of anxious work, he drove to Oxford.

Dennis Burden, Trinity's English Fellow, welcomed him, and was touched when he asked, on arrival, if he could use his phone to ring his son David and say he had arrived safely. His other, less expectable, request was that Burden should take him to a shop in Oxford where he could buy some 'shells' for his shotgun. Presumably the defence of Tullimaar against possible marauders was on his mind, but they scoured Oxford for an ammunition supplier without success. The classical scholar Richard Jenkyns was lecturing next day on Cardinal Newman, and Golding asked Burden to take him along. Walking into the Examination Schools, he felt, he confided, a sudden chill, since he had not been there since he took his finals in 1934. The audience at Jenkyns's lecture struck him as 'fearsomely distinguished', and made him even more apprehensive about the approaching ordeal.

His lecture on the 28th was open to students from every Oxford college, as well as to the public, and the Gulbenkian Theatre was packed to suffocation. He had recently been rereading *Robinson Crusoe*, and he used Defoe and Homer, a writer he had now been studying for almost half a century, as entry points to an analysis of the story-teller's art. Attention was rapt, and the applause at the end tumultuous. Yet he entered in his journal that night: 'It was not as well received as I had hoped but better than I had feared.' Evidently his chronic diffidence would not allow him to recognize success, and it may have influenced a decision he took later in the year. He had agreed, in 1989, to give the prestigious Clark Lectures at Cambridge University during the academic year 1991–2. But in the months after the Hillary Lecture he persuaded himself that he was not a 'fit person to give mainstream lectures in the academic world', and in July 1990 he wrote to Sir Andrew Huxley withdrawing from his agreement.

What his next novel would be about was his overriding concern, and his failure to come up with any promising ideas generated a reservoir of dissatisfaction that spilt over onto his other activities. This was apparent in March, when he and Ann went on a cruise. It was work, not pleasure. The *Sunday Times* had offered him £1,800 for a travel piece and Cunard gave them a free trip (the normal cost was £8,500) together with 'first class (royal)' flights out and back. Their ship *Sea Goddess II* was, the brochure explained, more like a private yacht than a cruise ship, and the luxurious lifestyle she offered was 'designed for a very particular type of person'. Quite what type was suggested by the illustrations, which showed two splendidly bronzed young couples in evening dress sipping from champagne flutes at a bar. In the next picture they are apparently naked, but still holding their champagne flutes, in a Jacuzzi, and in the final snap they are gathered merrily at a roulette table. In fact the Goldings found, on going aboard at Bali, that most of their seventy fellow voyagers were well above retirement age. 'This ship is a geriatric ward,' he noted sourly as *Sea Goddess II* made her stately progress north along the east coast of Java towards their first port of call, the enormous Buddhist temple at Borobodur. Ann felt too ill to go ashore – fortunately, perhaps, since Golding found that the temple tour entailed a four-hour bus journey and the ascent of near-vertical steps. Neither of them saw the remains of Krakatoa the following day because they were asleep when *Sea Goddess II* sailed past, and they decided to give the next attraction, Ujung Kulon National Park (with rhinoceroses), a miss. Returning trippers reported that a tropical storm had turned the UNESCO World Heritage Centre into knee-deep mud.

As the ship nosed through the Sunda strait and up the west coast of Sumatra, Golding interviewed the captain, and what he discovered deepened his disillusionment. Calling *Sea Goddess II* a Cunard ship was stretching a point. She had been built in Finland and was registered in Oslo. Cunard did not own her, they merely hired her from the builders. The crew were of various nationalities, many of them Filipino, and the officers, all Norwegian, were not Cunard-trained but hired from an officer-supply company. It would be naïve, Golding admitted, to expect anything else in the modern world, but using the name Cunard in publicity material gave the cruise an aura of British maritime pride that was no longer appropriate. The low point was reached at the village of Bowomataluo on the island of Nias, billed as an unforgettable experience since the tourists would encounter native warriors untouched by civilization and be privileged to watch their war dances. In the event the villagers were evidently used to tourists and went through tired routines, while the children pestered and begged: 'One not-so-little girl manipulated my hand in that palm-scratching way that is sexually suggestive. A small boy kept repeating "money, money".' On the way back a fellow tourist told Golding that a girl had offered to sell him her baby brother. Several tourists bought 'ebony' artefacts that turned out to be soft white wood painted black.

Their last stopping points on Sumatra were Belawan ('a place only redeemed from complete ugliness by the sun') and Medan, with its Sultan's Palace ('sordid and vulgar') and a mosque which some tourists, 'head-scarfed and sarong'd and with their feet bare', entered. Golding, opposed to compulsory religious observance of any kind, waited angrily outside in the coach. After the crossing to Malaysia there was a day tour of Kuala Lumpur, but the Goldings stayed on board. The eleven-day cruise ended at Singapore, where they were picked up by the British Council for four days of official functions – a lecture ('Aspects of Narration'), a discussion at the Faculty Club of Singapore's National University, interviews, receptions, and lunch with the British High Commissioner at Eden Hall. On 21 March they flew home.

Turning his experiences into 2,000 words for the determinedly upbeat travel supplement of the *Sunday Times*, designed to attract advertising revenue from tour operators, was something of a challenge.

In the event, a measure of disgruntlement shows through, but most of the astringency of his journal account is expunged. Titled 'The Life of Lord Riley', his article celebrates 'a beautiful ship wandering in exotic places', and avows that 'everything that money could buy attempted to seduce me and to a large extent succeeded'. A cause of dismay on the cruise had been a phone call from Judy right at the start, on 6 March, to tell them that Tullimaar had been burgled. When they got home they found that several of their pictures, including an early nineteenth-century oil that Golding had bought with his James Tait Black Prize, had gone, as had other treasured items, including Ann's Royal Worcester coffee service, which had been a wedding present. Their eyes kept straying to the empty walls and shelves. 'There is no doubt that a burgled house tastes different from what it did,' he lamented. Worst of all, Mrs Humphries, their invaluable housekeeper, now went home each night, as she no longer felt safe sleeping in the house.

To guard what remained, they had a new alarm system installed before their next excursion, which was a six-day British Council trip to Rome in May. Their programme seemed 'desperately full' to Golding, though actually there were two free days, both with a car and driver at their disposal, on one of which they went to see ancient Ostia and its ship museum. This intrigued them, but their general opinion of ancient Rome remained negative: 'Roman ruins are singularly repulsive, at once gigantic and dull.' On the other free day they went to Keats's house by the Spanish Steps, and Golding mused how much easier writing poetry probably was than writing novels: 'This stuff, endlessly quoted, anal-ysed, dissected, written about for ever, obeys the single law of running down someone's arm and flowing out on to the page without benefit of second thoughts.' On the working days there was a public 'Incontro con l'autore', two press interviews, a press conference, a TV interview conducted by a female journalist who said things like, 'Tell me your view of life. Please make the answer brief,' and a dinner with the ambas-sador Sir Stephen Egerton and his wife. During the trip Golding read, 'with a kind of appalled enjoyment', A. N. Wilson's new life of C. S. Lewis, concluding, 'He was good, and awful.'

No glimmerings of a subject for a new novel appeared, so, back home, he occupied himself with incidentals. He wrote an introduction for Rick Gekoski's bibliography of his works, and adapted his sea-trilogy for a single-volume edition, called, on John Bodley's suggestion, *To the Ends of the Earth*. Monteith had told him the previous year that several people were eager to write his biography, and he assured him that one would be written whether he authorized it or not, so he started 'doodling' at an autobiography, called *Scenes From A Life* (which remains mostly unpublished) so that Monteith could fend off inquirers. He was also, as always, reading a lot. On the family holiday in Brittany in August he reread the *Odyssey* yet again, feeling how cruel it was, particularly the mutilation of the goatherd Melanthius and the hanging of the household maids after the slaughter of the suitors in Book 22. Other recent rereadings were Tennyson's *Princess* ('plush twaddle') and Gautier's *Emaux et Camées* ('much like the jewelled nonsense of Wilde'). He had discovered Virginia Woolf's journals and read them avidly, admiring her 'deadly accuracy', and speculating that such penetrating insight into character was a uniquely female attribute, developed in prehistoric times as woman's only defence against male muscle. He also read more contemporary fiction than before: A. S. Byatt's *Possession*, Julian Barnes's *Flaubert's Parrot* and *History of the World in Ten and a Half Chapters*, Ishiguro's *An Artist of the Floating World* and *The Remains of the Day* ('a quite seductive newness'). These were 'brilliant' young writers, and the English novel could, he thought, safely be left in their hands.

Ann, however, took a different view. 'What you have to do is publish a new novel in a year's time,' she admonished him on the day before his seventy-ninth birthday. It sounds stern, but no doubt she realized the only thing that made him unhappier than writing was not writing. However, he remained blocked. In October he did another poetry reading with Peter Orr at the Cheltenham Festival, and attended the Booker Prize dinner ('exactly the same as last time and a great bore'). *Possession* won, as he had predicted. December, though, brought something new: he went to see a dramatization of *Lord of the Flies*.

For years Monteith and du Sautoy had tried to persuade him that someone should make it into a play, with no success, but on 1 November 1989 he sent an apologetic letter to Monteith, explaining that he had changed his mind. Monteith would probably have heard, he wrote, that a new film was to be made of *Lord of the Flies*. 'I haven't seen it, have dissociated myself from it and propose to stay that way!' The new film, directed by Harry Hook, with a screenplay by Sara Schiff, was an Americanization of Golding's novel. It substituted a group of boys from an American military academy for Golding's English schoolboys, and made many other changes. His distaste for it was entirely understandable, and it spurred him to retaliate by at last agreeing to co-operate on a dramatization. As he wrote to Monteith, 'it occurred to me that my recourse, small as it may seem, was to have a play made of the book, preserving its Britishness et al'. He put the idea to Matthew Evans, and Evans approached a young Faber author, Nigel Williams, who jumped at the chance. *Lord of the Flies* was one of his favourite books. His father, a schoolmaster, had reviewed it for *The Times*, and given it to his son, who read it first when he was fourteen. He went down to Cornwall to discuss it with Golding and, like other first-time visitors, was surprised by the great author's 'Cap'n Birdseye' appearance and 'Yo ho, m'hearties' manner. At the same time, he felt instantly at ease as he took his seat in the 'battered old Daimler, with its dashboard full of conkers and apples' (soon to be replaced, in fact, by an almost-new 3.6 litre Jaguar Sovereign).

They talked about the book for several hours, agreeing that it should be acted by children, not adults, then dined, consuming what seemed to Williams a spectacular amount of wine. He left the next day, and fairly soon received a letter from Golding asking what had become of his dramatization. He hurriedly despatched a draft first act, which received a favourable response, then, when the play was finished, he sent it to Evans, who reported that Golding had 'had a wobble' and was not sure he wanted to go ahead after all. This hesitation was short-lived, and in December 1990 the play was given its world premiere by pupils of King's College School, Wimbledon, with the Williamses' son Jack in the part of Simon. Ann had flu, so could not come, but Golding was there and was clearly affected. Joanna Mackle recalls he had tears in his eyes. It was 'terrifying', he told Williams at the end of the first act, when Simon goes up the mountain. 'I don't know how you can let your son play a part like that.' In 1995 there was a Royal Shakespeare Company production at The Other Place, directed by Elijah Mijinsky, and many revivals have followed.

At the start of 1991 he was as far as ever from finding a subject for his next novel. He had been reading past volumes of his journal, and thought that a book could be made out of them, but decided it would be a job for his 'heirs and assigns'. He meditated destroying pages where he was 'hopelessly drunk', and the writing became illegible, but concluded they were needed as 'a kind of posthumous confession which a charitable reader might understand & absolve'. Then, quite suddenly, he began to write a story. It is not entirely clear what set it off, but he had been following TV coverage of the Gulf War, and had been shocked by pictures of the Iraqi dead – one, especially, of a driver in his cab which was 'almost tho' not quite as ghastly as an Egyptian mummy'. The Bishop of Durham was reported as saying that a victory parade for British troops would be obscene. Golding saw his point, but felt that the men who had fought deserved their parade, and that the bishop spoke 'not with the voice of men but angels', adding, 'I've no doubt that from the point of view of an angel a man's guts are obscene, inside the body or out of it.' On the question of who was to blame for the war, 'The real bottom line would be to sub poena Jesus of Nazareth and the Prophet Mohammed.'

Out of this nexus of thoughts came a story, set in biblical times, about the legendary Greek hero Herakles and an angel. Golding had been planning to write a comic story about Herakles since 1973, if not before, and in the summer of 1989 he had talked it over with Monteith, who said he would look forward to a Herakles novel 'in a year or two'. But it was only now, it seem, that Golding started to write it. The narrator, we gradually gather, is an angel who has come down to earth, rather like Matty in *Darkness Visible*, only much cleverer and more articulate. He refers to God as 'the Ineffable', and:

> all I can say of Him, Her, It, Them, is that the Ineffable Is. Of course, in saying that one has said nothing. All that has happened, I remind myself, in saying 'Is' is that one has said a word which people think they understand though of course they don't except in a limited sense. But that is better than nothing so let it stand.

The angel's appointed task is to be Herakles' guardian angel, an unenviable position, for Herakles is, from birth, a monster. The story that he strangled two snakes in his cradle was, we learn, a falsehood put about by his guardian angel to prevent scandal. In fact he strangled two babies who happened to be crawling near his cot. He quickly grows gigantic, an ugly, ferocious brute with scarcely any forehead and a body covered in thick hair. When he meets a young woman – the first female he has seen – she flees screaming and he pursues. The angel remains behind in contemplation. Herakles reappears, with the woman's bloodstained clothing in his hand, and the angel lectures him on the wrongness of rape, only to learn that Herakles did not rape her but ate her.

The next two people they meet are men, whom Herakles kills out of hand, though not before he and the angel learn that the land they are in is Philistia, and that it is being ravaged by the wandering tribes of Israel, who are in the habit of cutting off their enemies' genitals (the meaning, it is explained, of the biblical phrase 'smiting hip and thigh'). It emerges that, by contrast with the wandering tribes, the Philistines are intelligent and civilized and have invented the alphabet (as some modern histori- ans of language plausibly conjecture they did). The angel and Herakles come to a Philistine temple, sacked by the Israelites, with mutilated corpses and a smashed stone god inside. The god has a kindly face, and it occurs to the angel, with a terrible shock, that the barbarians respon- sible for this destruction are the Ineffable's 'Chosen People'. Why has He chosen them? Can He have made a mistake? For that matter, how could He have created such a monster as Herakles? As the guardian angel struggles with these questions, Herakles is supernaturally con- sumed by fire and a superior angel appears, who explains that Herakles was a faulty prototype, and that a new Herakles will be created. As for the Chosen People, they are clearly an embarrassment to the superior angel too, but he assures the guardian angel, with something less than total conviction, that, at the end of time, it will be seen that everything works together for good. There, unfortunately, the fragment ends. It covers twenty-eight typed pages (about 9,000 words) and is a little masterpiece of black comedy, raising, yet again, incredulity that Golding could create such work and then, seemingly, cast it aside.

In March he had another idea for a story, which he outlines in his journal. While he was in Mexico, the woman assigned to look after him and Ann had told him about how Muslims treated women. She recounted that she had been on good terms with an Arab, but was curious that he never introduced her to his wife. So she invited them both to dinner. They came, but the wife remained wrapped from head to foot in black and sat silent in a corner of the room. When Golding's informant tried to include her in the conversation the husband snapped, 'She'll say nothing – Let her be.' Golding writes that he had taken this, at the time, as an example of 'the extreme reserve practised by Moslem women'. But a few days later, in Mexico City, he was drinking with his publisher and told him the story, whereupon another member of their party had chipped in and said that 'under the dull black wrapping would be a girl dressed in the height of fashion and wearing a chastity belt'. Golding rejoined jocularly that he supposed she would be wearing a brassiere made of mild steel as well, but his publisher corrected him – no, it would be made of 22-carat gold. Further, the girl would have had a kind of clasp, made of gold, inserted into her mouth: 'he put his finger in the left side of his mouth – "there's a screw just here. The girl's husband fixes it in. That's why she was silent. She couldn't be anything else."'

Golding admitted to himself that, for all his outrage on behalf of women, he found this talk of female bondage 'exciting', and could not get it out of his head. It might all be untrue, and it was clearly 'porno-graphic', but his 'prurient mind' kept 'snuffling' around it, and around the possibility of making it into a story. It might start with a 'fashionably dressed and beautiful girl sitting and reading on a park bench', and it would also feature a 'naïve young man'. It might be called 'Of Bondage', and the gold mouth-clasp might be called, in the story, a 'hush-puppy' – which he realized was the name for a brand of shoe, but 'the name seems to fit on so many levels'. However, 'Of Bondage' remained unwritten.

In May he and Ann went to the Czech Republic on a British Council tour. Perhaps because of his anxiety over the absence of a new novel, it was one of their least joyful trips. A fair proportion of his rather terse record of it is given over to complaints about the food, the slow service, and the weather. In Prague they were taken to the usual tourist sights, but declined an invitation to see the old Jewish quarter, apparently unaware of its outstanding and tragic interest. After the usual round of interviews and academic events, they were driven to Bratislava in Slovakia, which was even less to their taste. The audience at his lecture was 'a frost', no one laughed, and they were taken to an opera, something by 'Dvorzac', which 'lasted three million years'. In the old Moravian town of Olomouc he delivered his fourth university lecture of the week, then they made an excursion to the battlefield of Austerlitz. The weather continued dreadful. 'It stinks, and we are ready to depart,' he grumbled, adapting Landor.

On their summer holiday in Brittany he had a scare. One afternoon he followed David, who was a strong swimmer, into the sea, but after a few yards he found himself breathless, and being carried out by the ebb tide. Alarmed, he struck out for the shore and was 'uncommonly thankful' to find his feet on gravel again. It was one of those signs of age that he got into the way of noting in his journal. His holiday reading was Madame de Sévigné's letters, in French, which he found 'very nearly contemptible', repelled by her 'fawning yet proprietorial "love" of her daughter'. Then he embarked on Marguerite Yourcenar's three-volume autobiography *Archive du Nord*.

For his eightieth birthday in September the *Guardian* printed an interview by James Wood. Lacking John Walsh's interviewing skills, Wood had evidently managed to get across Golding from the start. He represents the two of them as sitting together 'inside a little chamber of hostility and awkwardness', and he reports that Golding's face is 'curiously alive, yet also dead', that his eyes are 'shrewd' and 'cold', that his prose is 'stony', and that people 'ingest his books but are not nourished by them'. The author of this unusual birthday tribute was evidently an unfamiliar name to Golding, but on making inquiries he found that Wood contributed frequently to the *Guardian*, and concluded, 'It's time I left.' He had been reviewing for the paper for twenty-five years, but did not write for it again.

More enjoyable, in November, was a lunch with Prime Minister John Major ('Almost too amiable to be prime minister. Perhaps it is genuine'), where he met the president of Hungary, who happened also to be the translator of his books into Hungarian. Later in the month came a four-day British Council trip to Paris. Ann and he had dinner the first evening with Christine Jordis and her husband Sacha ('very cheerful'), and next day Christine, by this time working for French radio, recorded an interview with him in his room at the Hôtel Duc de St-Simon. At his lecture, the audience was timid at first, but he 'got them laughing in the end'. Afterwards, at the home of David Ricks, the British Council officer, he was glad to find Sylvère Monod, the French translator of Dickens's works, whom he had not met for years.

The year ended with what Golding called a 'Nobel Thrash' – a reunion and conference of laureates – in Stockholm in December, at which he was scheduled to give three lectures and take part in a quiz chaired by David Frost. It started well. After the opening ceremonies they flew to Karlskoga to visit Nobel's house. Then, while Ann, who was developing flu, returned to Stockholm, Golding flew to Umeå, where he got a standing ovation from an audience of fifteen hundred students. In the 'kissing goodbye session' that followed a woman said to him, 'You are loved,' and he felt elated. After that, age and exhaustion began to take their toll. Back in Stockholm, Ann's flu was no better, and he developed a 'filthy, sewerish, feverish cold'. A doctor was called, and he was 'stuffed with anti-biotics', but had to miss most of the remaining functions. He forced himself to attend a royal banquet, but the endless corridors and staircases were 'purgatory', and a member of the royal household 'about seven foot tall' had to grab him and hold him up when he tottered at the sight of a descending flight of steps. 'I am épuisé by it all and want to be home,' he confessed.

Once back in Tullimaar he felt better, but no nearer to writing a novel. The inside of his head seemed to contain a vacuum: 'nothing, in a state of chemical purity'. Their 1992 summer holiday was planned for Spain, and he and Ann started to learn Spanish, setting aside twenty-five minutes a day. They had a brief London visit in February – to Peter du Sautoy's eightieth birthday party and to the Mantegna exhibition at the Royal Academy. Then in May they drove to Hay-on-Wye for the literary festival, where he was to give a revised version of 'Belief and Creativity'. The audience were 'kind', but he was 'terrified' beforehand, 'debilitated by fear and drink', and for the first time in his life Ann exhorted him to 'be a man'. She was the only person, he reflected, who saw him clearly, and realized how 'weak and defenceless' he was. Later in the year, when they were on holiday, Ann thought, during the night, that she was dying, and she told him next day that she was concerned she had not made her last speech to him. She had worked it out before she fell asleep, and she confided that it had begun and ended with thanks. Surprised, he asked what for, and she replied, 'For being yourself.' He was moved to tears, though 'I did not ask what came between the end and the beginning.'

Ann was his mainstay, but the piano also helped save his sanity, as he acknowledged. He indulged himself 'shamelessly', playing Liszt's arrangements of Wagner's operas. 'It brings the worst out in all three of us.' Then, after 'revelling' in 'the cheapest most vulgar emotions', he would go 'pattern-making' with Bach, and 'it's like after you've cleaned your teeth'. Another redeeming distraction was the garden, which sparked a series of crises. Their gardener, William Rose, had departed in September 1990, saying the last three years had been hell. He was replaced by a father-and-son team who seemed competent at first but whose work soon deteriorated. Golding was torn between suspicion that they were cheating him and concern that he might be grinding the faces of the poor. After a final stormy exchange they drove off at high speed, showering the house and lawn with gravel. A young man called Nathan, assisted by Mrs Humphries' husband Ken, took over, and recommenced the battle with the ivy on the ancient stone walls. Working with them could be hazardous. An operation to fell a large tree, with Golding, at eighty, clambering up to tie a nylon rope near the top, ended with the tree almost falling on them. 'We moved faster for ten yards than I remember since the days of the air raids.'

In May he went, with Ann, to Oviedo in northern Spain to receive an honorary doctorate. The robes, which he had been measured for in England, and was allowed to keep afterwards, were of ecclesiastical grandeur, and the hat he wore for the ceremony was a 'coconut-shaped contraption' in Cambridge blue. 'It was fun.' Tom Maugham of the British Council drove him to Salamanca for an 'inquisition' by ranks of professors, and to Madrid for 'round-table questioning' by 150 literary critics. A week after their return they gave a big party in Tullimaar, for which he bought a new 'flaming red' bow tie. David was there, 'looking very well', and the children were elegant in their party clothes. Golding abstained from drink until the closing stages and felt better for it, and for once he did not worry about money. He estimated that it cost between £1,600 and £1,700, 'which is cheap, considering'.

David, his health much improved, came with them too on their Spanish holiday in July. They landed at Santander, and Golding was filled with wonder by the cathedral at León, especially when its mass of stone was 'dissolved' by floodlighting. It was strange to think it had waited a thousand years for this 'apotheosis'. It put him in mind of the resurrection of the body. By comparison the cathedral of Santiago de Compostela seemed 'brutal and faintly vulgar'. They were renting a house, the Casa Ofelia, at O Grove in the north-west corner of Spain, where the Carvers joined them. It had a naturist beach, which led him to reflect that naked humanity is not much like the sculptor's view of it. But the water was 'blue as butterfly's wings'. He was trying yet again, 'with less and less attention', to read Joyce's *Ulysses*. A large proportion was 'rubbish', he concluded, and the parodies, though clever, were 'grossly long'. He also read his first, and last, Agatha Christie, deciding that she had no compassion and played with her characters like toys. Both judgements were typical of his independence. Earlier in the year he had read Chateaubriand's *Mémoires d'Outre-Tombe*, famed as a beacon of the Romantic movement and a monument of Western culture, and had been unimpressed by its 'Rousseauesque load of malarkey'. On the other hand he had pronounced Jilly Cooper's *Polo* 'not half bad' – 'like Leonardo da Vinci's drawings – anatomically exact'.

Soon after their return home the police contacted them to say that some of the things they had lost in the burglary had been recovered. They were taken to the police-station cellars, then to a vast hangar at an army camp, where the floor was covered with the loot of years of robberies. Wandering through, they found their silver teapot and silver spoons and three of their oil paintings and Ann's Royal Worcester coffee cups. It was 'strange, a haunting, mysterious tangle. For these things had died. Here before our very eyes they were resurrected.'

He had agreed to go once more to Toronto's Harbourfront Festival, and told himself, too late, 'I *must* stop this madness and learn to say *no*'. The flight out on 15 October was just as awful as he had feared, and they both took several days to recover. 'My nerves are so jet-lagged I still can't write,' he scrawled on the 17th. But his reading on the 25th went well. 'People got so used to laughing that they laughed once or twice when there wasn't anything to laugh at.' They were home on the 27th but had to go to Norwich a week later, where he read Chapter 17 of *Fire Down Below* (the crucial conversation between Talbot and the Prettimans) to an audience of about 800 at the University of East Anglia. The queue for signing afterwards stretched 'coil on coil'. Scarcely had they returned home from that than it was time to get ready for the British Council seminar in Portugal, which began on the 11th. Harriet Harvey Wood recalls the playwright Arnold Wesker joking on the flight out, 'If the plane went down we would make the headlines.' Golding was not amused. Andrew Motion, the future Poet Laureate, met him for the first time at this seminar. He had been amazed to hear that Golding was coming: 'he seemed much too grand to bother with a trip such as this'. But he found him instantly likeable, 'Bluff, hail-fellow-well-met, loud and large, but with an unmissable intensity. I kept thinking of galleons and hearts of oak.' Golding's solo reading was in a 'gigantic, gladiatorial arena' at the Gulbenkian Centre in Lisbon, packed to the rafters with students. But they sat in absolute silence while he read the ice passage from *Fire Down Below*. He was a tiny figure on the brightly lit stage, 'but he filled it all right, reading very confidently and milling his arm about sometimes'. He looked as though he was enjoying himself, and it made Motion wonder if the trip was a kind of 'release and relief' for him. At the end, when he invited questions, a firm voice out of the darkness asked, 'Why aren't there more women in your books?' He laughed, shifted from foot to foot and said something like, 'Well, yes, there aren't many, are there? People are always asking me that' – and there was a 'welter of forgiving laughter'. Later Motion learnt it was Ann who had asked the question, and others at the seminar told him she often asked questions at Golding's public readings: it was a kind of arrangement between them. All the same, Motion wondered why she had chosen such a tricky question, putting him on the spot instead of helping him out.

In December, in tandem with Peter Orr, Golding read some of his favourite pieces of literature on the Radio 4 Arts programme *With Great Pleasure*, and the *Independent on Sunday* selected him as 'reader of the year', pipping Sir John Gielgud at the post. He had an apprehensive

Christmas, for the blotch on his nose, treated in 1989, had reappeared, and an operation was necessary. In hospital on the 29th the blotch was removed and a patch of skin from behind his ear grafted in its place. A biopsy revealed that there had been cancerous tissue, but it was not invasive. When he went for a check-up some weeks later, all was well, and he was told he had the blood pressure of an eighteen-year-old.

By that time he had started writing his novel. A 'splendid set of ideas' occurred to him on 14 January 1993, and he jotted them down in his journal. His novel would be about the Oracle at Delphi, and would be set in the first century BC. The central character would be a young woman who escapes from home to become the 'Pythia' or prophetess at the Oracle. What allows her to escape is the intervention of the head of the 'college of priests' at Delphi, and the journal-jottings sketch out a speech for him: 'Don't be frightened little girl. You are quite safe. I am, so to speak, the warden of all these souls – you must think of yourself as simply part of the establishment.'

This was the germ of what became *The Double Tongue* – a title that he noted in the journal on the 28th. In the novel the young woman, who is also the narrator, is called Arieka. She is the daughter of an aristocratic family living on the shore of the Gulf of Corinth, not far from Delphi. She is not attractive. There is something wrong with her face – one side is not properly balanced by the other – and she is rejected by her family. 'We don't want the girl any more,' says her brutal father. However, she is rumoured to have psychic powers, and this is what attracts the attention of the head priest at Delphi. He is called Ionides, and he takes her to Delphi as a trainee. He does not believe in the gods himself, but he wishes to restore the power and influence of the Oracle. He teaches Arieka to write Greek verse, so that she will be able to speak in hexameters to make her oracular answers more elevated. His job as priest is to interpret the answers the Pythia gives, and his plan is that, with Arieka's co-operation, he will be able to invent oracular utterances that will further his own political aim – which is to free Greece from Roman rule.

Things do not work out as he intends, however. For it turns out that Arieka really is inspired. When she enters the sacred cave she is possessed – 'raped' – by Apollo. He speaks through her, and it tears her mouth. In her prophetic trance she utters truths that she has no memory of afterwards. Unwilling to betray her sacred gift, she refuses Ionides' request to tamper with her answers for political purposes. The affection between them survives, though, and she is horrified to learn of his foolish revolutionary plans. With reason – for he is arrested and seems certain to be executed. But the Roman governor Lucius Galba decides it will humiliate him more simply to let him go, which proves correct. Ionides cannot stand the disgrace, and dies of shame. All this is long in the past when Arieka, eighty years old, relates it. By this time she is no longer sure what she believes in. Her certainty about the Olympian gods, particularly Apollo, has faded. When the Archon of Athens writes to say that, in view of her long service as Pythia, he wishes to erect an image of her among the altars on the Field of Mars, she asks that he should, instead, erect a simple altar and inscribe it: 'TO THE UNKNOWN GOD'. Those are the novel's last words.

One or two elements in *The Double Tongue* recall earlier books. Arieka's lopsided face and mystical inspiration are faintly reminiscent of Matty in *Darkness Visible*; Ionides dies of shame as Colley did in *Rites of Passage*. But, as usual with Golding, the story was completely different from anything else he had written, and he had never before used a female narrator. For the brilliantly realized details of his classical world he found help in Plutarch (who had been a priest at Delphi and wrote about the decline of the oracles) and in Euripides' *Ion*, set in Delphi, which gave him Ionides' name. Perhaps there is some autobiographical significance in the eighty-year-old Arieka deciding that, on the subject of God or the gods, nothing can be known – for that is what Golding told John Walsh he had come to think.

But is there anything else in Golding's life that could have suggested such a story? Do its key elements resemble anything that happened to him? It is a story about a man of authority who rescues someone who has great – indeed, supernatural – gifts, but has been rejected. The man of authority, by his intervention, allows those gifts to flower so that they bring to their possessor wealth and fame and a public voice that is heard around the world. Can this, at some perhaps unconscious level, relate to Charles Monteith rescuing the typescript of *Lord of the Flies* when Fabers' reader had rejected it, and so bringing Golding wealth, fame and a public voice? Once the idea of Monteith as Ionides presents itself, other elements fit into place. Ionides, an unbeliever, wants Arieka to fake her divine utterances, but she refuses. Monteith, on the other hand, had persuaded Golding to take all references to the divine out of *Lord of the Flies*, a betrayal of his original (and, as he thought, inspired) utterance which, as he told his audience in India in 1987, he later came to regret. It is made clear in *The Double Tongue* that Ionides is homosexual, as Monteith was widely thought to be, and when Golding jotted down his first ideas for the novel he referred to Ionides as the head of a 'college of priests' and the 'warden of all these souls'. True, Monteith was not Warden of All Souls, but he was a Fellow of the college, and when Golding first met him can have seemed only a little less grand than the Warden.

Perhaps all this is fanciful. We cannot know. What is clear is that once the outline of his story had occurred to him Golding worked with speed and enthusiasm. He was soon 'hammering out' 2,000 words a day, and by 16 February had reached 36,000. Ideas came to him like 'an illumination', and he grabbed them, 'otherwise they vanish'. He was cheered, as he wrote, by signs of early spring: the winter-flowering prunus out, the blue anemones 'all a-blow'. There was no more blockage. He found he could put a sheet in the typewriter, adjust it, and start writing straight away. He finished the first draft in just over a month on 18 February. Then he took a few days off to re-plan, and make the bookings for their family holiday in August – three weeks at the Casa Ofelia, as the previous year. He started the second draft on 8 March, adjusting the historical period. In the first draft young Julius Caesar comes to the Oracle. The second is set slightly earlier, in the time of Sulla.

He allowed himself a few interruptions. On 20 March he was John Fuller's guest at the Waynflete dinner at Magdalen College Oxford. They had been playing postal chess for years – and still were. Golding's moves would arrive in window envelopes, with post-its containing facetious or apologetic commentary ('Sorry for delay – I've been castling in Spain', or 'So sorry – senility', when his opponent pointed out he had made an illegal move). As Fuller recalls, he enjoyed the dinner 'in his quiet, bluff way', and joked that it was good to see Leonardo among the guests, referring to Magdalen's recent acquisition of the oil version of *The Last Supper*. Another break from routine was at Easter, when Judy, Terrell and the family came for three days. Ann and he had decided to have another party, since their last one had been such a success, and he spent the morning of 13 May writing invitations to about fifty guests. The fight with the ivy continued, and on 21 May he bought a fifteen-foot scaffolding tower, with a six-by-four-foot platform at the top: 'Now we really can get on with the walls. It's rather like having a new meccano set.' Gardeners Nathan and Ken were both disinclined to set foot on this apparatus, so it seems clear that Golding planned to use it himself, despite his fear of heights. Peter Green, with whom he had visited Delphi years earlier, and who was now a professor of classics at Austin, Texas, came and stayed the night of the 23rd. He remembers that 'Bill was on cracking form', and drove him over in his new Jaguar to see A. L. Rowse, 'sitting up in bed full of witty malice'. On the way back, Green asked what the new novel was about, but 'he gave me an old-fashioned look, and said: "You know the rule, Peter, never talk it away."' This was a reference to their times together on Lesvos, when they had seen too many young hopefuls who talked but never got round to writing. Apart from these brief distractions, though, Golding forged ahead, and finished the second draft on 6 June. Matthew Evans had asked if John Bodley could have a look at the first draft, but Golding did not want to show it to anyone yet. He thought a third draft might well be needed, but wrote in his journal on the 17th, 'I shall do no more to the story until after tomorrow's party.'

Judy thought he looked pale before the party, but he said he was fine and would put his rouge on. Harriet Harvey Wood recalls that he was in 'excellent form'. She talked to him for about twenty minutes, planning the next Cambridge seminar in the summer, and he told her that he had been up a ladder that day clearing out a blocked drainpipe. Jessica Mann was in a group that included Judy, John le Carré and the novelist D. M. Thomas, and Golding joked with them about being 'the fastest two-fingered typist in the world'. One always did write another book, he said, even after feeling it would never come again. D. M. Thomas stayed behind when everyone else had gone, and sat in the dining room drinking red wine with the family. He persuaded Ann to show him some photos of herself when young, and informed her she had been 'stunning'; he listened to an 'intimate though veiled' conversation between Judy and her father; he gathered that Golding was lonely, and offered to meet him in a pub sometime. Golding said politely that he would love to, and scribbled down his phone number on a scrap of paper. Even when Ann said she was off to bed, Thomas confesses he did not 'take the hint', but started singing the Beatles song 'Yesterday'. The Goldings exchanged 'uneasy smiles', and Thomas 'staggered out' to his car at one o'clock. The family waved goodbye.

A detail Thomas does not mention, but Judy remembers, is that at some point in the evening, while Thomas was still there, Golding recited a poem from the *Oxford Book of French Verse*. It was Ronsard's translation of the dying Hadrian's address to his soul (*Animula vagula blandula*), and the book in which he had first read it, still in the library at Tullimaar, is inscribed on the title page 'K. M. Evans'. It had belonged, that is, to Mollie, the girl he had fallen in love with when he sat behind her in class, and had been engaged to in the 1930s, and had abandoned when he married Ann.

By the time Thomas had gone everyone had had quite a lot to drink. Golding lay down in the empty bath, fully clothed but also wearing his dressing gown, and Ann pretended to turn the tap on. He did not seem to want to move, and Ann, Judy, Terrell and David agreed that he should sleep in David's room, next to the bathroom. Terrell loosened his collar before saying goodnight.

Next morning Terrell took him a cup of tea, and found him 'in a crouching position' on the bedroom floor. He went to fetch Judy, and when she saw his face she said at once, 'Is he dead?' But he could not bring himself to say yes: 'I did not want to be the one who ruins everyone's life. It was a bright sunny morning ...' They fetched Terrell's father, a doctor, who was staying in the house, and he and Terrell lifted Golding's body back onto the bed, while Judy kept watch outside.

Five days later, on Midsummer's Day 1993, Golding was buried in the churchyard at Bowerchalke. Ann was in a wheelchair, which Terrell and Matthew Evans manhandled over the rough ground. She had suffered a stroke, from which she never fully recovered, soon after learning of her husband's death. Judy was in shock, and could not manage the usual reception for mourners after the funeral, so Iona Brown threw open her house and received people on her behalf.

Golding's memorial service was in Salisbury cathedral on Saturday, 20 November. It was a dark, bitterly cold day. At the start, Tim Brown played the Prologue from the *Serenade for Tenor, Horn and Strings* by Benjamin Britten, and at the end he played the Epilogue. The cathedral choir sang Raymond Leppard's 'Kyrie Eleison' from the film score of *Lord of the Flies*, and Bishop Wordsworth's School choir sang Psalm 98. David read the lesson, I Corinthians 13, and Judy read a passage from *The Spire*. Wayland Kennet gave the address and spoke of Golding as 'the cleanser of the imagination and the guardian of mercy'. He was a 'theist', who believed in 'the crashing ascendancy of some sort of God' but did not think himself good enough to be a Christian. At about the midpoint of the service Ted Hughes read, unforgettably, from *The Inheritors*. As preface, he said that, though Golding wrote in prose, he was a poet with a 'tragic imagination' who sensed the presence of another life, a 'mythic life', behind our personalities. Then he read a long passage about Lok, bewildered and alone, and as he read his voice seemed to grow gigantic, and the raw, colossal syllables boomed and echoed around the cathedral's freezing columns.

Ann died on New Year's Day 1995, and was buried beside her husband at Bowerchalke. Later that year, in June, Golding's last novel was published. John Bodley, who prepared it for publication, chose to print Golding's first draft, so, as with no other Golding novel, readers can experience his writing as it came fresh from his brain, before revision and second, or third, or fourth thoughts.

The Golding family dedicated *The Double Tongue* to all those at Faber and Faber who had helped, encouraged and cared for him. 'Above all', the dedication ended, 'this book is for CHARLES'. At Golding's funeral Monteith had seemed 'stunned', Judy remembers. He said, 'I can't believe it.' She had never seen him at a loss before. Later that summer he was staying at Fowey with David Treffry, and they both came to lunch at Tullimaar. Ann was so upset she retired to bed, and Judy and Terrell entertained their two guests to 'a rather unexuberant meal downstairs in the dining room'. It must, she felt, have been 'a terrible contrast with all those convivial occasions' in the past.

In London Monteith continued to entertain friends at his flat in Randolph Avenue, St John's Wood. Rosemary Goad saw him quite often, and so did his nephew John, son of Charles's brother Ted. Charles still seemed to John to be 'fairly busy socially', though he had slowed down quite a bit and walked with a stick. When they met it was usually in the evenings and they would eat either at Charles's flat or in the nearby Café Rouge. John got the impression that Charles enjoyed 'the challenge of cooking', but by far his best contribution to the dining table was his huge range of stories, 'laced with humour and modesty', about writers and poets he had worked with, and about his life and travels. His knowledge of Europe was 'astounding', and he had often revisited India, a country he first came to know during the war. On his occasional visits to his native Ulster, John recalls, his relatives 'never failed to be amazed that he could answer all the questions on Mastermind or read a book in two hours'.

But his heart was a worry. He suffered from fibrillations – an irregular heartbeat – and his condition deteriorated after Christmas 1994. One morning in May 1995 he phoned Rosemary to say he was not feeling well. She was in Dorset, but left immediately for London. That afternoon he had a heart attack. He was found by his Spanish-American housekeeper, who was very devoted to him. She called an ambulance and he was taken to hospital, but by the time Rosemary arrived Charles had died.

Postscript

Nowadays mention of *Lord of the Flies* sparks instant recognition in a way that Golding's own name does not, or so my admittedly limited market research has indicated. This seems unjust, both to Golding and to readers, because it means that they remain unaware of the protean variety and inventiveness of his work. My subtitle is chosen with this in mind, and is both ironic and purposeful. I like to think that it will catch the eye of people who remember reading *Lord of the Flies* at school, or who maybe just saw the film, and whose curiosity will be sufficiently aroused for them to discover, through these pages, how much more Golding was than 'the man who wrote *Lord of the Flies*'.

Some questions remain. What would he have thought about his private journal being made public, as it is in this book? I think that he would not have been surprised nor, in the last resort, displeased. In the journal itself he anticipates its possible publication. Once or twice he considers burning it, but he dismisses the idea both because it is a 'treasure', 'closely written like coins in a chest', and because, at the deepest level, he knows that he has written it for an audience:

> For of course, there is always an audience. If you are a professional writer what else can you do but write to be read? Indeed I doubt very much if the man who has never published and never wanted to publish, the man who writes really for his own amusement exists or can exist.

He knows that some parts of the journal may cause pain and embarrassment if they come before an audience. All the same, 'I cannot deceive myself and pretend that I do not write for one.'

Would he have minded a biography being written? It seems clear he knew one would be, and in his journal he contemplates how it will be received, and what the chances are of its telling the whole truth. He is not optimistic on either count.

> One day, if my literary reputation holds up, people will examine my life, and they will come to the conclusion that I am a monster and possibly they will finally say *tout comprendre* and all that. They will think they know all but they won't. No matter how deep they dig they won't reach the root that has made me a monster in deed, word and thought. No one but I knows that, or suffers it. This is not guilt, it is self knowledge.

I do not know why he thought he was a monster. Perhaps it was because of his memories of how he had treated David as a child. Perhaps it was because of Mollie, the once-loved, once-worshipped woman, whose life he ruined. Perhaps it was because he had killed people, probably many people, in the war, both civilians and enemy combatants. Perhaps it was none of these, but something I have not discovered. My own guess is that it was because he was a deeply self-examining and self-blaming man who, as he said more than once, saw the seeds of all evil in his own heart, and who found monstrous things, or things he accounted monstrous, in his imagination.

Why, some readers may ask, have I called him 'Golding' throughout my book? To friends he was always 'Bill', and it would have made for a different and warmer biography if I had called him that. For me, however, that was never an option, partly because I would not have dreamed of calling him 'Bill' in real life – I admired and respected him far too much – and partly because the whole 'Bill' business seemed and still seems to me an element in the bluff, affable old sea-dog disguise which hid the real Golding. When I first met him I could not believe that this was the man who had written the novels. He seemed like a nautical caricature, and the opinions that issued from behind the beard were things he had said many times before – a kind of gramophone record put on for an interviewer, which is what I was. When I came to know him a little better – never very well – I sensed that this was all a shield with which he kept the world at bay. However, it was not until I read the journal that I discovered I was right.

How, then, would I characterize him as he comes across in the journal? The emotion he felt most vividly and often behind his disguise was, I think, fear, on a scale varying from mild anxiety to terror. He had been a sensitive, frightened child, and he grew into a sensitive, frightened man. Of course, his war record shows that he was also extremely courageous, and his courage in war was all the greater because, as he admits, he was terrified much of the time. The journal reveals that there was quite enough in ordinary peacetime life to bring on panic attacks. Some of his phobias were fairly common. He went rigid with fear if he had to have an injection. He was scared of heights – Peter Green, who drove him along mountain roads in Greece, was amazed to see him huddled in a 'near-foetal position' on the back seat with his hat crammed over his face. He was afraid of crustaceans, insects, and other creeping things. He had a fearful experience one night with an 'enormous' centipede, 'brown and hideous', that tried to get into his bed at Ebble Thatch. Spiders were a special dread. A 'vast' one, three inches across, once appeared on his pillow while he and Ann lay reading in bed. It was so big he could hear the 'dry tap and scramble' of its walk as it approached him. He catapulted himself out of bed in horror, and Ann had to shoo it out of the window with a copy of *Vogue*.

The unseen world was still more frightening. He was scared of being alone at night, 'even if I am in bright electric light'. The mere thought that he was alone, and that 'something' might appear, would send him scurrying to bed, where he could lie down beside Ann, hear her breathing and feel safe. Entering empty rooms at night was an ordeal. He would throw the door open loudly to give a 'warning' to whatever spectral beings might be lurking inside, in case he might 'see what I should not'. He felt 'sheepish' about admitting this, but fear of the supernatural had been with him since 'before I can remember'. Whatever his rational mind told him, his 'natural and irrational mind' was convinced that the dead are always present.

Of course, it is not surprising that an imaginative writer should be imaginative in this way, nor that he should adopt a sturdy male disguise to hide it. But the disguise was not Golding. Among the real Golding's terrors, terror of writing was perhaps the greatest, and this too is common with writers. Writing is a stressful occupation. It is not like living over the shop, or even living in the shop. It is being the shop. It means making your livelihood out of nothing. To control the fear, Golding tried various remedies. He drank. He wrote several drafts, so that he could tell himself he was not writing the frightening final one. He believed, or half-believed, that he did not actually do the writing – it was some other being inside him that did it. This removed the fearful responsibility, though it brought with it the new dread that the other being might decide not to write any more, leaving him barren.

He feared critics almost as much as he feared writing. This is not true of all writers, and with Golding the origins were partly social. He did not think of himself as belonging to the class that set critical standards in art and literature, and his natural self-distrust had been intensified by long years of having his work rejected. So the kind of adverse review that a less insecure writer would have simply shrugged off left him feeling hurt, ashamed and exposed to ridicule. His family learnt to keep reviews away from him. But even that was no answer, for it encouraged the bitter suspicion that the critics were defaming him behind his back. His prolonged writer's block in the 1970s was directly traceable to the reviews *Free Fall* received.

Although his fears and phobias could impede his writing, or sometimes stop it altogether, they were indispensable to it, because they were integral to his imagination, and he lived in his imagination to an unusual degree. Reading his journal confirms that what most people regard as the real world was secondary to him. This showed itself in a number of ways, some of them trivial. When travelling, for example, he tended not to bother with road maps or guide books, preferring to trust his intuition, with the result that he frequently got lost. He did not do research for his novels. Even when they were set in historical periods not wholly familiar to him, he relied on his imagination rather than consult authorities. He was not really interested in intellectual debate or engaging with other minds, because he was too intent on his own imaginative life. Dwelling in his imagination so much, he discounted logic, and contended that, though it was an internally self-consistent system, it amounted to no more, as a means of reaching truth, than 'a loftier game of chess'.

So far as I know he articulated this intellectually heretical belief in its extreme form only once, when fending off a pestering academic after a lecture. But it was, I think, a vital aspect of his mental life. He explained to an audience, when discussing *The Inheritors*, that his Neanderthals are unfallen because, though they can imagine, they cannot think. 'The Fall is thought.' The writer and psychiatrist Anthony Storr, who knew him well, was of the opinion that he had 'a profoundly irrational, anti-intellectual view of reality', and that he believed the imagination could penetrate what, in *Darkness Visible*, is called 'the screen that conceals the working of things'. It would be only a slight exaggeration to say that this is the subject of all his novels. All of them, at any rate, bring into collision, to some degree, two different ways of thinking about the world, pitting logic, reason and science on the one hand against religion and imagination on the other. The outcome is never simple, for Golding was himself divided. He had been trained as a scientist, as few modern novelists have been, and his religious belief seems to have become more and more tenuous as time went on, until it was simply belief in something that could not be known. Yet it was still belief. To express his dilemma he used the image, remembered from an illustrated Jules Verne he read as a boy, of an astronaut held motionless in space between the gravitational fields of the earth and the moon, at a point where they exactly balance each other.

It still seems an appropriate image for our predicament, caught between the vague but powerful residual pull of religion and the dominant disciplines of science. Curiously, it seems more appropriate now than it did when Golding wrote. For recent events have reminded us that any comfortable Enlightenment notion that religion, with its hopes and terrors, is on the way out, and must finally evaporate in the face of progress, is far from being shared by the world at large. Besides, some scientists now argue that adherence to a belief of some kind has been implanted in us by evolution and is necessary for our survival.

It seems wrong that biographies should end with deaths and burials, because bringing the past back, and breathing life into it, is what they are supposed to be about. So I thought I would end by finding and returning to a moment when I could be sure that Golding was happy. It proved more difficult than I supposed. He was happy when he moved to Tullimaar, but it was a happiness that brought with it new worries and responsibilities. He was probably happy at three o'clock in the afternoon of 13 July 1967, when *Tenace* left Shoreham harbour and headed out to sea. Ahead lay a new life of wandering among the Greek islands, and tying up in little harbours among the caiques, where no one would know him, or expect him to write another book, or sneer at him when it was written. But that dream ended in a shipwreck fourteen hours later, and he would never again take to sea to escape the pressures and terrors of writing. Perhaps, though, he did escape sometimes, temporarily, when he was on holiday. In the end I chose a day in September 1972 when he and Ann were in Rome:

> We had a lovely day yesterday. We visited Hadrian's villa at Tivoli where absolutely *no culture* is necessary and the wild flowers and butterflies are a wonderful and delightful riot. We saw one creature, that at rest was a grasshopper: but if you came too close it immediately took off and turned into a blue butterfly, as it might be a chalk blue. We were very happy and must have seen a dozen different sorts of butterfly – the large yellow and black, small yellow and black, white, yellow, orange, brown, blue – to say nothing of some splendid peacocks. Then we went on to the Villa d'Este, where I rather shame-facedly took a sheaf of photographs – but we have come to enjoy the place so much that it will be pleasant to have them.
>
> Today is our thirty-third wedding anniversary. That is much better than anyone ever expected. I must say, Ann has stuck it extremely well, seeing how much she's had to put up with. It might be a good thing to record in an unbritish way here, how much I love her, and how much she has done for me, from bed to books. For I would never have been as happy in the one with someone else, nor have written the others with someone else – or indeed, written anything.

What Happened to Mollie?

There is a gap in this story which I have now been able to fill. We saw in Chapter 3 that, some time in the 1930s, Golding got engaged to Mollie Evans, whose parents kept the village shop in Great Bedwyn, and that in 1939 he broke off the engagement and married Ann. In *Free Fall*, Beatrice, who is modelled on Mollie, goes mad when Sammy deserts her. Whether this was Mollie's fate, I had no idea. Then, in September 2009 at the Marlborough Literary Festival, a lady came up to me at the book signing and showed me a ring she was wearing, a large opal, set in gold. It was, she told me, Mollie's engagement ring, and she was Mollie's niece, the daughter of Mollie's sister Joan. She told me Mollie's story.

Mollie was born in June 1914, so she was three years younger than Golding. Her sister Joan was older, born in 1910. Their parents were Frank and Florence. Mollie was a bright girl and good at languages. There was a French lady called Mrs Egerton in the village, and Mollie went to her for language classes. On leaving school she trained as a teacher at Southlands Training College, Wimbledon, and in 1935 she got a job teaching English and History at Fairlop School for Girls, near Epping.

In the little cache of relics found among Mollie's things after her death, together with her engagement ring, there are two snapshots. Mollie's mother has written on the back that they were taken at Whitsun in 1937 on a family outing to Chastleton House in Oxfordshire. One shows Mollie and Golding. They are half-sitting, half-lying on the grass, both smiling happily. She is leaning back against him, and his right arm rests on her shoulder. The other photo, presumably taken by Golding, is of Mollie and Joan and their parents. It is posed so that Mollie is in the centre, looking glowingly happy, and her sister is turning her head to look smilingly at her. Perhaps it is an engagement photograph.

Certainly Golding and Mollie were engaged by the autumn of 1937. In the cache of relics there is a letter from him to Mollie's father Frank, written on Brasenose College Junior Common Room paper at the start of the 1937 academic year when he had gone back to Oxford to study for the Diploma in Education. He says how much he envies Joan for being 'settled and comfortable' (she had married in October 1937), while he is still a 'mere bachelor'. The thought of it makes him want to 'catch the first train to town and marry Mollie instantly'. Frank has been ill, though, so the marriage must wait 'until you are strong enough to give away the bride'. He guesses that Frank helped with the redecoration of Joan's house, and asks him not to use up all his bright ideas, 'because Mollie and I will need them for our cottage'. The letter ends on a playful note: 'By the way Mollie wants a King Charles Spaniel; whatever that is – can you dissuade her? A violin is much better company'.

A memorial of another day they had together, also found among Mollie's relics, is a small gold crucifix, pierced at the top for a chain. It was wrapped in paper annotated in Mollie's hand, 'Crucifix from Buckfast 1938'. Buckfast Abbey in Devon was destroyed at the Reformation, but rebuilt in the early twentieth century by a dedicated group of Benedictine monks. They used primitive building techniques, with wooden scaffolding lashed together with ropes, and no safety protection. One monk fell 50 feet, but survived. The final stone was put in place in 1937, the year before Golding and Mollie's visit. Perhaps his memory of that day, and his love for her, which later turned to guilt, and what he learned about the building of a medieval abbey and the dangers involved – perhaps these things stayed deep in his mind to emerge, twenty-five years later, in *The Spire*.

In July 1939 Mollie and Golding went on holiday together to France. Though he was teaching at Maidstone by this time he was hard up and still owed money to Brasenose, so it seems Mollie, who had been teaching at Fairlop for four years, lent him money for the trip. In her cache there is a 'Certificate of the Issue of a British Money Order' for £10, date-stamped 16 June 1939. The order is made payable at

Maidstone to W. G. Golding. Found with it was an envelope on which Mollie has jotted down some details of fares and journey times: 'Newhaven Dieppe £4.10.11' and 'Leave London 8.20 Grenoble 4.53 aft'.

Together with the certificate and the envelope is a picture postcard – a view of Grenoble – which Mollie sent back to her mother on 29 July 1939:

> Bill says I'm to say 'Arrived and exhausted – can't write any more'. That about sums up the situation at the moment – the train journey was the last word, but the crossing was marvellous. We haven't found anywhere to stay in Grenoble yet – I'm writing in a café – but we shall be here possibly for two days. I'm afraid I can't give you the next address because we haven't got a map yet. Love M.

What went wrong after that is a mystery. But according to Mollie's sister Joan, Mollie came back from France alone, and that was the end of the affair. She would never speak of Bill again. On the envelope with Mollie's jottings of the journey time and cost she has added eight lines of writing.

> There are two things which, tho' they cannot be heard by the physical ear a mile away, cry from end to end of the earth. The one is the crash of a tree that has been felled while it is still bearing fruit; the other is the sigh of a woman whom her husband sends away while she still loves him.

Mollie's niece had always thought that Mollie composed these lines herself as she made her sad and lonely return trip from France, but Dr Ian Patterson of Queens' College, Cambridge, has been able to identify them as a quotation from Willa and Edwin Muir's 1932 translation of Lion Feuchtwanger's historical novel *Josephus*. In Feuchtwanger's story Josephus divorces his devoted wife Mara, who shortly afterwards gives birth to his child. Mollie, who was presumably reading the novel on her holiday, and was struck by the aptness of the quotation she copied out, possibly thought she might be pregnant. In *Free Fall* Beatrice gets into the habit of putting a little cross on the top left-hand corner of her letters to Sammy – a secret code to tell him her period has begun. Her last letter, written after he has deserted her, has the reassuring cross.

And afterwards? Mollie did not go mad. She had a successful teaching career. As she was very patient, she was especially effective with children with special needs. She was offered the headship of Fairlop School, but she declined because she wanted to continue teaching, which she loved. She stayed single, though another ex-Marlborough Grammar School pupil, Howard Lansley, who later became Mayor of Marlborough, wanted to marry her. When she retired she lived in Great Bedwyn with a friend, Kathleen, who had been a probation officer in the East End. They read the same books and took an interest in politics. Mollie seemed to her niece very left wing. She was also an agnostic or atheist, insisting that when she died there should be no service and no mourners. Kathleen, who died first, had made the same requests, and Mollie saw they were carried out, and did not go to the crematorium. 'She said nobody and she meant nobody,' she insisted. Mollie died on 27 December 2004, and her niece put her ashes beneath a turf on her parents' grave.

Acknowledgements

My biggest debt is to Golding's daughter Judy Carver, who invited me to write this biography, gave me unrestricted access to the Golding archive, welcomed me and my wife into her home, photocopied many documents for me, and sent, over the course of three years, scores of informative e-mails in response to my queries. I am also greatly indebted to her husband, Professor Terrell Carver, for his hospitality and friendship and the memories of Golding he shared with me. Through Judy I was able to spend some days with her brother David at Tullimaar, and talk to him at length about his father. I am very grateful for his patience and understanding.

My other major debt is to the directors of Faber and Faber, who gave me access to their archive, containing hundreds of letters that document the remarkable, forty-year collaboration between Golding and his editor Charles Monteith. In the long days I spent labouring in the basement of 3 Queen Square I was given expert assistance by the Faber archivists, Victor Gray and his successor Robert Brown, and by John Porter, who also brewed many life-saving cups of tea.

Other archivists and librarians to whom I should like to record my gratitude are Simon Bailey, Emma Marsh and Alice Millea at the Oxford University archive, Elizabeth Boardman at the Brasenose College Oxford archive, Clare Hopkins at the Trinity College Oxford archive, Verity Andrews at the University of Reading Special Collections Service, Robin Davies Chen at the Manuscripts Department of the Library of the University of North Carolina at Chapel Hill, Camilla Hornby at the Curtis Brown Group archive, and Mark Le Fanu, who kindly showed me the Golding items in the archive of the Society of Authors. Thanks must go, too, to the safe-custody teams at Barclays Bank, Queens Road, Clifton, Bristol, and King Street, Truro, for their patience.

ACKNOWLEDGEMENTS

I owe a special debt to W. J. R. ('Jock') Gardner at the Naval Historical Branch (Naval Staff), Ministry of Defence, Portsmouth, who generously undertook research into Golding's naval service record for me, and into the fate of Midshipman Fisher.

Tim Brown, son of Golding's close friend Tony Brown, has been a constant source of information and encouragement, and gave me a rare CD of Golding's Ewing Lectures, delivered at the University of California in Los Angeles. Professor Louis Rubin, who arranged Golding's two semesters at Hollins College, and his American lecture tour in 1961–2, has given me unstinting aid, supplied copies of his correspondence with Golding, and put me in touch with Golding's former students Terry Herrin Andrews, Anna Sevier Morgan, Betsy Payne Rosen and Jane Gentry Vance, who have patiently responded to my questions. Soon after I began work, Andrew Sinclair, who had himself once contemplated writing a biography of Golding, got in touch, shared his very detailed knowledge with me and gave me copies of his large Golding correspondence, as well as a snapshot of the Bob Dylan puppet that survived Golding's anger.

Golding's old friend Professor Peter Green talked to me about their adventures together in Greece. Dr Ken Gibson shared with me the fruits of his research into the life of Adam Bittleston. Harriet Harvey Wood OBE put me straight on many details relating to Golding's British Council engagements. Virginia Tiger gave me copies of letters Golding wrote to her, and was tolerant of my expectation that events that took place four decades ago would be fresh in her memory. I am grateful to them all. The late Stephen Medcalf, whose knowledge of Golding and his works was eager and profound, sent me notes on or transcripts of their many conversations, and came to Oxford for two days of absorbing talk. His help has been invaluable, and I am very sorry he did not live to read my book. I hope he would have approved of it.

Others who have helped, advised, informed and encouraged me, and earned my gratitude, are Brian Aldiss, James Anderson, Paulette Anderson, David Angier, Julian Barnes, the late Terence Barnes, Robert Bellarmine, Dinah Birch, Sid Birch, Ian Blake, Irene Boston, Roger Bowen, Melvyn Bragg, Clive Brasnett, the late Thomas Braun, Keith Brocklehurst, David Bromige, Peter Brook, Marion Brookfield, Richard

Brookfield, John Browning, Felicity Bryan, Dennis Burden, David Butt, Roger Clements, Gunnel Cleve, John Coldstream, Glenn Collett, Joan Crisp, Joe Mordaunt Crook, Giles de la Mare, Colin de Souza, Pavritha Devadatta, Adelaide Docx, Heather Eason, Sam Eidinow, Willy Engineer, Howard Erskine-Hill, Matthew Evans, Cyril Eyre, John Farrant, Andrew Fitzpatrick, Lady Antonia Fraser Pinter, Patrick French, John Fuller, Shantha Gabriel, Rick Gekoski, Brian Glanville, Rosemary Goad, Theo Golding, Sally Hallam, Anne Hardy, John Harries, Ann Harrison, Andrew Harvey, Tim Heald, the late Norman Hidden, Misako Himuro, the late Eileen Hogben, Lizzie Hogben, David Hopkins, Ann Howard, John Hughes, Samuel Hynes, Kazuo Ishiguro, John Jacobson, Simon Jenkins, Christine Jordis, Wayland and Liz Kennet, Frank Kermode, Mark and Joan Kinkead-Weekes, Robin Knibb, Paul Laing, Jeremy Lewis, James Lovelock, Joanna Mackle, Derek Mahon, Jessica Mann, Robert McCrum, Mark Merrill, Uwe Meyer, Jeffrey Meyers, John Mills, Ken Mitchell, Ted Monteith, Andrew Motion, Peter Nichols, Ruth Padel, Mr and Mrs Robert Payne, J. A. C. Pearce, John Peter, Catherine Peters, Maria-Elena Pickett, Frank Pike, Jonathan Prag, Susheela Punitha, Craig Raine, Sally Rees, Bernard Richards, Adrian Risdon, David Roberts, Janice Rossen, Christopher Rowe, Mike Sammes, Robert Scoble, Jeanne Shami, Anthony Simmons, David Stedman, David Stooke, the late Elizabeth Suddaby, Andy Taylor, D. J. Taylor, John Thwaites, Michael Tillett, Claire Tomalin, Pete Townshend, Raleigh Trevelyan, Ken Walsh, George Watson, Edgar Williams, Nigel Williams and Emily Young.

At Faber and Faber, Stephen Page, Rachel Alexander and Julian Loose have listened encouragingly to my excited talk, and Julian, perhaps divining that I work best when left alone, has radiated a general air of benevolence while keeping his interventions to a minimum. I am grateful to all three. I am also greatly indebted to my matchless copy-editor Trevor Horwood for his care, patience and skill.

It is usual for biographers to apologize to their families for carrying on so tediously about their subject during their years of writing and research. My impression, though, is that my wife Gill has found Golding and his strange eventful history as engrossing as I have myself. She has co-operated on the project at every stage and I am truly thankful.

Sources

This book is based almost exclusively on manuscript materials in two archives, the Faber and Faber archive and the Golding archive, neither of which is catalogued or open to the public. It seemed to me, therefore, pointless to annotate it in the normal way, picking out a section from the text and directing readers to its source, since the sources are inaccessible. Instead I have listed all the sources I have drawn on for each chapter, making clear, in the case of archival items, their origin and how they can be identified. I hope this may be useful to future researchers. I have put the main archival source for each chapter first and the secondary source(s) afterwards. The following abbreviations have been used:

Invasion Notebook: An untitled notebook with mostly undated MS entries kept by Golding while waiting for D-Day.
'It was 1940': An untitled autobiographical MS in Golding's hand, chiefly about his relations with his son, which begins 'It was 1940'.
J: Golding's journals. Entries are identified by day, month and year.
MW&N: The MS of *Men, Women & Now*.
Scenes: The MS of *Scenes From A Life*.

The Golding items in the Faber and Faber archive are stored in seven boxes labelled 9/216, 9/217, 17/56, 17/96, 17/154, 17/155 and 221. There is also a file labelled 'William Golding 1955–9'. Most of the correspondence between Golding and Monteith up to December 1966 is in Box 17/56, and most of their later correspondence is in Box 17/96. Most of the correspondence between Golding and Peter du Sautoy is in the file. The contents of the boxes and file are not catalogued or arranged chronologically. I have identified letters by sender, addressee and date, and have used the abbreviations G for Golding, M for Monteith, PS for Peter du Sautoy, ME for Matthew Evans, RG for Robert Giroux and VT for Virginia Tiger.

Other abbreviations are:

Biles: Jack I. Biles, *Talk: Conversations with William Golding*, Harcourt Brace Jovanovich, New York, 1970
Billy: 'Billy the Kid', in William Golding, *The Hot Gates*, Faber and Faber, 1965
Gekoski: *William Golding: A Bibliography 1934–1995*, ed. R. A. Gekoski and P. A. Grogan, with a Foreword by William Golding, André Deutsch, 1994

Happold: Frederick Crossfield Happold, *Bishop Wordsworth's School, 1890–1950*, privately printed for Bishop Wordsworth's School, 1950

Ladder: 'The Ladder and the Tree', in William Golding, *The Hot Gates*, Faber and Faber, 1965

Poems: W. G. Golding, *Poems*, Macmillan, 1934

Tribute: *William Golding: The Man and his Books. A Tribute on his 75th Birthday*, edited by John Carey, Faber and Faber, 1986

WG at BWS: *William Golding at Bishop Wordsworth's School*, edited by John Cox, November 1993 (privately printed)

1 Beginning

These memories are from *MW&N* and *Scenes*. The cockerel episode is also in *J*, 23 Feb 1972.

2 Grandparents

Sources in the Golding archive: *J* 1971: 7 Nov; 1972: 26 Oct; 1974: 28 Mar, 12 Aug; 1975: 5, 6 Mar; 1980: 21 Jun, *MW&N*, *Scenes*, and Alec Golding's journal, 18 Jul 1904.

Other sources: Judy Carver's e-mail, 27 Feb 2007 and her notes on her conversations with Eileen Hogben on 26 Jan 2001 and a later undated occasion.

3 Parents

Sources in the Golding archive: *J* 1971: 8 Nov; 1978: 10 Sep; 1985: 12 Jun, Alec Golding's journal, *MW&N*, *Scenes* and a letter to Golding from Eric Edney, dated 26 Mar 1960.

Other sources: Peter Moss's essay in *Tribute*, two e-mails from Judy Carver, both dated 1 Mar 2007, and her notes on her conversations with Eileen Hogben.

4 The House

Sources in the Golding archive: *J* 1971: 10, 15 Nov; 1972: 1 May; 1973: 30 Jun; 1975: 23 Nov; 1986: 1 Jun; 1991: 6 Aug; *'It was 1940'*, and an untitled, undated 7-page MS in Golding's hand, starting 'I was then thinking about houses'. Sources for Golding's attitude to Marlborough College are *J* 24 Nov 1971, 10 Sep 1972, 22 Sep and 16 Nov 1974 and 11 Nov 1977.

5 Childhood

Sources in the Golding archive: *MW&N*, *Scenes*, and *J* 1971: 15 Nov, 13 Dec; 1972: 27 Jan, 3 Feb, 9 Jun, 13 Nov, 19, 30 Dec; 1973: 29 Jan; 1974: 24 Jan, 11, 14 Feb, 1 Apr, 10 Oct; 1975: 12 Jan, 13 Sep; 1976: 10, 19 Aug; 1978: 30 Oct; 1983: 9 Apr; 1986: 21 Aug; 1987: 11 Nov;

1988: 13 Apr; 1989: 1, 26 Jan, 27 Jun, 29 Oct; 1991: 10 Mar; 1992: 10 Dec; Alec Golding's journal and *'It was 1940'*.

Other sources: *Ladder, Billy*, Biles p. 94, and a CD of Golding's Ewing Lectures given to me by Tim Brown. Judy Carver's investigation of the U-boat episode is in *Areté*, No. 2, Spring/Summer 2000.

6 Growing Up

Sources in the Golding archive: *J* 1972: 12 Sep; 1974: 25 Apr; 1975: 27 Apr, 13, 21 Sep; 1978: 13 Apr; 1979: 25 Mar; 1980: 1 Sep; 1981: 4 Nov; 1982: 29 Mar, 18 Nov; 1983: 13 Feb; 1984: 18 Dec; 1987: 14 Dec; 1988: 7 Apr; 1989: 6 Jun; 1991: 11 May, 1 Dec; *MW&N, Scenes* and Golding's VIth-form diary. His school prize for drawing and his *Oxford Book of English Verse* inscribed by Jose are among his books at Tullimaar.

Note: 'Dora Spencer' is an invented name; her father's personal details are also invented. Correct identifications are given in *MW&N*, and are concealed here to protect the privacy of any surviving family.

Other sources: Judy Carver's notes on her conversation with Eileen Hogben, 26 Jan 2001, and her e-mail to me of 10 Feb 2007. I learnt of Golding's 10.8-second 100 yards from John Browning (interview, 18 Mar 2006) and of his aversion to concerts from Tim Brown (interview, 2 Oct 2006).

7 Oxford

Sources in the Golding archive: *J* 1972: 2 Apr, 20 Sep; 1973: 5 Aug; 1974: 21, 27 Jan, 4 Mar, 5 Oct, 9 Nov; 1975: 6, 13 Sep; 1976: 13 May, 21 Jul, 17 Sep; 1977: 21 Mar; 1978: 30 Nov; 1981: 5 Aug, 13 Oct; 1982: 3 Aug; 1983: 17 Jun, 15 Aug; 1987: 20 Sep; 1990: 27 Sep, 26 Oct; 1991: 4 Jan, 11 May, 28 Jun; 1992: 3 Feb; *MW&N*, Golding's VIth-form diary, *'It was 1940', Scenes* and *Invasion Notebook*. Golding's letter to his tutor Wrenn is an undated pencil manuscript draft, and his letter from his tutor Brett-Smith is on Hertford College paper with typed address and date, 19 Linton Road, 25 Jan 1935.

Other sources: Judy Carver's notes on her conversation with Eileen Hogben, 26 Jan 2001, and on her undated interview with J. A. C. Pearce, and her e-mail to me of 14 Jan 2008. Golding's remark about grammar-school boys feeling uncomfortable at Oxford was made in an interview with John Mortimer, *Sunday Times* magazine, 5 Feb 1984. The fellow student who reported on Golding lying about being Russian was Ken Walsh, who kept a diary while at Brasenose; his widow Ann Walsh sent the relevant entry from it dated 13 Feb 1932 to Judy Carver on 14 Sep 2005.

For information on Adam Bittleston I am indebted to Dr Kenneth Gibson (phone conversation, 11 Mar 2008, and letter to me, 16 Mar 2008). Bittleston's letter to Macmillan about publishing Golding's poems, dated 8 Apr 1934, is numbered 1089152/41 in Reading University's Special Collections. The Brasenose College tutorial lists, copies of *The Brazen Nose* published during Golding's years of residence, his application form, his letters to and from the bursar, and the draft letter to him from C. H. Sampson are all in the Brasenose College archive, and are quoted by permission of the Principal and Fellows. Professor Joe Mordaunt Crook advised me on the position of Stallybrass's college room relative to Golding's. Other material on Stallybrass is from *Time* magazine, 13 Oct 1947.

The Einstein story is in 'Thinking as a Hobby', *Holiday* magazine, Aug 1961; the hypnotism incident is in 'My First Book', reprinted in *A Moving Target*, p. 152, and, slightly differently recounted, in *J* 17 Nov 1974. The Oxford University Appointments Committee index cards are in the Oxford University archive.

8 Drifting

Sources in the Golding archive: *J* 1971: 11 Jan, 6 Dec; 1972: 2 Mar, 7 Jun; 1973: 4 Jan, 9 Dec; 1974: 13 Oct; 1979: 18 Sep; 1981: 27 May, 29 Aug; 1990: 11 Jun; 1991: 24 Jan, 3 Sep; *Invasion Notebook, MW&N, Scenes, 'It was 1940'*, a typescript of 'A Play of Persephone', and David Garnett's letter dated 30 Jul 1937.

A large white unlabelled envelope in the archive contains most of my sources for Golding at Maidstone Grammar School, including James Clinch, *Gaudeamus. An Account of Music at Maidstone Grammar School*, 1997, which records some of Michael Tillett's memories of Golding, the Old Maidstonian Society Newsletter for Spring 1995, the programme for the March 1939 production of *Julius Caesar*, and letters to Judy Carver from Old Maidstonians W. E. Foster, dated 8 Apr 2001, and P. S. Hedgeland, dated 14 Apr 2001.

Ann's appearance in Huxley's play is recorded in an undated cutting from the *Salisbury Journal* among Mildred Golding's papers in the archive.

Other sources: The review of *Poems* is in the *TLS*, 7 Feb 1935, p. 72. Golding's letters to Macmillan are in the University of Reading Special Collections, numbered 1089173/10 and 163/191. My account of Golding as actor draws on *Tribute*, pp. 171–89, John Mortimer's interview in the *Sunday Times* magazine 5 Feb 1984, Judy Carver's interview with Richard Brookfield, 28 Mar 2001, and my interview with Terence Barnes, 30 May 1985.

Sources for Golding at Michael Hall are Judy Carver's notes on interviews with David Stedman, 28 Jul 2004, and David Bromige, summer 2003. Golding's Appointments Committee index cards are in the Oxford University archive, and his correspondence with Brasenose is in the Brasenose College archive.

Sources for his pre-war teaching experience at Bishop Wordsworth's School are my interview with John Browning, 18 Mar 2006, my phone interview with David Hopkins, 23 Mar 2006, and Sally Hallam's e-mail to me, 22 May 2007; also Happold *passim*, Alan Harwood in *WG at BWS*, p. 15, and Judy Carver's notes on her undated interview with John Hughes. The incident of Happold, Golding and the unruly class was related to Judy by Professor John Harris (her e-mail to me of 2 Nov 2008).

There is additional material about Golding at Maidstone Grammar School in Judy Carver's notes on her interviews with Michael Tillett, 14 Mar 2001, and Richard

Brookfield, 28 Mar 2001. Other sources for this chapter are Judy Carver's notes on her interview with Eileen Hogben, 26 Jan 2000, her e-mails to me of 17 Jan, 6 Feb and 6 and 10 May 2007 and 18 Oct 2008, and my interview with her, 21 Mar 2007.

9 The War

For much of the information in this chapter I am indebted to my conversations and correspondence with W. J. R. Gardner of the Naval Historical Branch (Naval Staff), Ministry of Defence. He elucidated many entries in Golding's service record for me, supplied a copy of Golding's official report on the Battle of Walcheren (UK National Archive ADM 202/407 Enclosure No. 15 to the Commander Support Squadron Eastern Flank's letter No. 162/94/I dated 14 Nov 1944), and discovered what happened to Midshipman Fisher (Ref. National Archive ADM 267/124 15A/12). There are photocopies of Golding's service record, his application for a commission (dated 8 Nov 1941), and the Admiralty Certificate for Wounds and Hurts (dating his injury from the explosion 30 Nov 1942) in the Golding archive. Other archive sources are *Invasion Notebook*, *MW&N*, *Scenes*, the manuscript of *Seahorse*, an undated, untitled manuscript draft of 'Through the Dutch Waterways' (starting 'I have visited the Low Countries a number of times'), and *J* 1972: 6 Jan; 1974: 11, 30 Nov, 2 Dec; 1975: 25 Apr, 22 Jul, 15 Oct; 1976: 30 Oct; 1989: 18, 20 Dec.

On mines and the risk Golding took sailing across a minefield on D-Day I consulted W. J. R. Gardner, David Golding (8 Aug 2007) and Andrew Sinclair, who sent me the full text of his 'Bill and Ted Are Dead', which reports Golding's comments. Golding's memory of the Portsmouth air raid is in an interview with John Walsh, *Sunday Times*, 19 Mar 1989. Other sources are my interviews with Terence Barnes 30 May 1985, David Angier 8 Feb 2006, Professor James Lovelock 23 Feb 2006, Tim Brown 2 Oct 2006 and VT 24 Apr 2007; Judy Carver's e-mails to me of 21 May, 21 Jun and 3 Jul 2007, her letter of 23 May 2007, and her notes on her interviews with Richard Brookfield, 28 Mar 2001, and David Golding, 13 and 14 Aug 2002. Printed sources are: Capt. S. W. Roskill DSC RN, *The War at Sea, 1939–45*, 3 volumes, HMSO, 1954; J. D. Ladd, *Assault from the Sea: The Craft, the Landings, the Men*, David and Charles, 1976; R. Stuart Macrae, *Winston Churchill's Toyshop*, The Roundwood Press, Kineton, 1971; and Gerald Rawling, *Cinderella Operation: The Battle for Walcheren 1944*, Cassell, 1980; M. R. D. Foot, *Memories of an S. O. E. Officer*, Pen and Sword, 2009, p. 156.

10 Teaching

Sources in the Golding archive: *J* 1971: 11 Jan, 4 Nov; 1972: 1, 24 Jan, 4 Feb, 4 Sep; 1979: 24 Dec; 1980: 4 Mar; 1981: 16 Sep; 1983: 9 Jan; 1984: 15 Dec; 1990: 4 Sep; 'It was 1940', *MW&N*, a photocopy of the BBC typescript of *Break My Heart* (broadcast on 15 May 1966), the typescripts of 'Winter Night, 1945' and 'Words for a Sensitive Juryman', and the notebook with Golding's MS record of twenty-four chess games played against Tony Brown.

Other sources: Interviews with Terence Barnes, 30 May 1985, Ian Blake, 15 May 2007, Tim Brown, 2 Oct 2006 (and Tim's e-mail of 17 Dec 2006), David Golding, 6–10 Aug 2007, Sally Hallam, 14 Mar 2007, Liz and Wayland Kennet, 23 Nov 2005, and Stephen Medcalf, 12–13 Sep 2006, and my interviews and phone conversations with ex-colleagues and pupils of Golding – John Browning, 18 Mar 2006, Andrew Harvey, 15 Feb 2006, David Hopkins, 23 Mar 2006, John Jacobson, 19 Mar 2006, Mark Merrill, 13 Dec 2005, and Christopher Rowe, 22 Mar 2006. I have also drawn on a long reminiscent e-mail from Robin Knibb, 8 Nov 2006, the memories of ex-colleagues and pupils recorded in *WG at BWS* (David Chamberlin, Malcolm T. Cooper, John Cox, Donald Culver, Derek J. Dawkins, John S. Eyres, Brian Groves, Alan Harwood, J. L. Mumford, Nigel Mussett, Christopher Rowe, Norman Thorne, Robert W. Naish and Gerald Ponting), and Judy Carver's notes on her interviews with Richard Brookfield, 28 Mar 2001, and with David Golding, 13–14 Aug 2002. Golding's memories of the Bishop Wordsworth's School archaeological society are from Biles.

11 Unpublished Novelist

Sources in the Golding archive: The typescripts of *Seahorse*, *Circle Under the Sea* and *Short Measure* and Ann's postcards to her in-laws. The *Seahorse* typescript has a handwritten title page, reading 'SEAHORSE/ BY/ W. G. GOLDING/ HOME ADDRESS/ 21 BOURNE AVENUE/ SALISBURY/ WILTS', and is prefaced by two hand-drawn maps, one labelled 'Seahorse – First Voyage' and the other labelled 'Keyhaven'. Each has a dotted line showing the boat's course. The cover of the *Short Measure* typescript has a neatly handwritten label 'SHORT MEASURE/ BY/ WILLIAM GOLDING'. Under the title is added 'By the author of Chalk in My Hair' – perhaps a Golding joke. The typed title page reads 'SHORT MEASURE/ A Novel/ By/ William Golding/ (80.000 words, approx)/ Home Address/ 21 Bourne Avenue/ Salisbury/ Wilts'. There is an epigraph: '"Good deeds are better than knowledge, but without knowledge good deeds are impossible" The Emperor Charlemagne'. Mr Rackham's complaint about the 'yacht' is in *J* 3 Jun 1985.

Other sources: I am grateful to John Jacobson for lending me a copy of the 1946–7 Bishop Wordsworth's School photograph – the only photograph I know showing the adult Golding unbearded. I have drawn on my interview with David Golding, 8 Aug 2007. The description of *Circle Under the Sea* as 'Arthur Ransome for grownups' is in G to M 28 Oct 1955 in the Faber archive. Golding's assertion about saints was made to Stephen Medcalf and Pamela Gravett over dinner at the Royal Crescent Hotel, Brighton, on 23 Nov 1976. Pamela Gravett was the widow of Kenneth Gravett, a Fellow of Balliol and friend and chess-opponent of Golding's, who had committed suicide (letter to me from Stephen Medcalf, 15 May 2007). Cape's negotiations with Golding are recorded in Michael Howard, *Jonathan Cape, Publisher*, Cape, 1971, pp. 246–7.

The incident of the boys sniggering is recorded in an e-mail to me from Robin Knibb, 8 Nov 2006.

12 Breakthrough

Sources in the Faber and Faber archive: Correspondence about Monteith's appointment: 1953 John Sparrow to Geoffrey Faber 12 Feb, T. S. Eliot to Geoffrey Faber 14 Feb and 'Ash Wednesday', Geoffrey Faber to M 3 Apr, M to Geoffrey Faber 11 May. All these letters are in Box K44. Letters that chart the evolution of Golding's novel from submission to publication are: 1953: G to Faber and Faber 14 Sep, M to G 15 Oct, G to M 20 Oct, M to G 27 Nov, G to M 28 Nov, G to M 6 Dec, M to G 14 Dec, G to M 18 Dec, M to G 30 Dec; 1954: G to M 10 Jan, M to G 12 Jan, M to G 11 Feb, G to M 14 Feb, internal Faber memo by M 18 Feb, M to G 25 Feb, G to M 28 Feb, M to G 1 Mar, G to M 2 Mar, G to M 25 Apr, M to G 27 Apr, M to G 20 May, G to M 21 May, M to G 24 May, G to M 25 May, G to M 17 Jun, M to G 21 Jun, M to G 25 Jun, M to G 20 Jul, G to M 28 Jul, M to G 6 Aug, M to G 3 Sep, G to M 7 Sep, M to G 8 Sep, G to M 10 Sep.

Correspondence after publication: 1954: M to G 20 Sep, G to M 22 Sep, M to G 30 Sep, G to M 17 Oct, M to G 21 Oct, G to M 21 Nov, M to G 26 Nov, G to M 31 Nov [*sic*]; 1955: G to M 21 Jan, G to PS 20 Apr.

Correspondence about film rights: 1954: M to G 30 Sep, M to PS 6 Oct, M to G 21 Oct, G to M 27 Oct, M to G 28 Oct, G to M 31 Oct, M's memo about Hankenson's phone call 5 Nov, M to G 8 Nov, G to M 31 Nov; 1955: G to M 21 Jan.

On Golding and T. S. Eliot: G to M 2 Feb 1955, M to G 30 Sep 1955, and *J* 10 Apr 1972.

The publishers who rejected the book are listed in G to M 28 Oct 1955 in the Faber archive, and in an untitled manuscript in the Golding archive, which names the agent as Curtis Brown, as the letter to Monteith does not. Cape's response is cited in Michael Howard to PS 14 Jul 1969.

Rejections of *Lord of the Flies* by American publishers: 1954: Elliott B. Macrae of Duttons to PS, 25 Jun; Lynn Carrick of Lippincott to PS, 23 Aug; Robert Giroux of Harcourt, Brace to PS, 2 Dec; 1955: Ben W. Huebsch of The Viking Press to PS, 3 Jan; Charles Duell of Duell, Sloan and Pearce to PS, 17 Jan; Roger Machell of Harper & Brothers to PS, 25 Feb; Katherine King of Macmillan to PS, 22 Mar; Barbara Noble of Doubleday to PS, 18 Apr; Sidney Phillips of Criterion Books to PS, 7 Feb; L. H. Brague of Scribner's to PS, 24 Mar; PS to Sarah Childsey at Knopf, 7 Feb; Sarah Childsey to PS, 29 Mar.

Sources in the Golding archive: Golding's memories of the book's composition are in *J* 1 Nov 1975, 12 Sep 1976 and 2 Nov 1989; the *medias res* reference is *J* 16 May 1985.

Other sources: The talk to Indian students is in 'William Golding: A Panel Discussion', compiled by Susheela Punitha, *Literature Alive*, Vol. 2, No. 1, Jun 1988, published by the British Deputy High Commission, British Council Division, Madras. Pupils' memories are in *WG at BWS*, pp. 4, 9, 15.

My account of Monteith's career draws on M to Greg Gatenby 10 Jul 1985 in the Faber archive, and on my interview with his secretary Rosemary Goad, 8 Jun 2006 (who also identified the sales director as W. J. Crawley, in an e-mail of 7 Sep 2007).

I learnt of the opposition to Monteith's appointment at Faber and Faber from Matthew Evans in an interview on 9 Apr 2008. Faber and Faber's organization in the 1950s was explained to me by Joanna Mackle, e-mail of 29 Jul 2008. Monteith's account of the *Strangers From Within* typescript and his negotiations with Fabers and Golding is in *Tribute*, pp. 57–63. Rick Gekoski kindly checked his copy of the page proofs and confirmed (e-mail 22 Oct 2008) that 'A not-light' is omitted.

Dates of reviews undated in my text: 1954: *New Statesman* 25 Sep, *Guardian* 28 Sep, *Glasgow Herald* and *Scotsman* 30 Sep, *Spectator* 1 Oct, *Listener* 21 Oct, *Church Times* 26 Nov, *Daily Telegraph* 18 Dec, *Observer* 26 Dec (E. M. Forster), *London Magazine* Dec, *Vogue* Dec.

13 *The Inheritors*

Sources in the Faber and Faber archive: 1954: M to G 21 Jun, G to M 25 Jun, M to G 28 Jun, G to M 12 and 18 Jul, M to G 20 Jul, M to G 28 Jul, G to M 10 Sep, G to M 17 Oct, M to G 21 Oct, G to M 27 Oct, G to M 9 Nov, M to G 18 Nov, G to M 21 Nov, G to M 31 Nov, M to G 2 Dec; 1955: G to M 21 Jan, M to G 28 Jan, G to M 29 Jan, M to G 31 Jan, G to M 13 Feb, G to M 15 Feb, M to G 16 and 17 Feb, G to M 18 Feb, M to PS 28 Feb (gives contents of his letter to G of 26 Feb which is not in the file); G to M 28 Feb; M to G 1 Mar, G to M 2 Mar, M to G 3 Mar, G to M 7 Mar and M's undated reply, G to M 12, 16 and 20 Mar, M to Eric Hiscock at the *Evening Standard* 19 May, M to Sir Mortimer Wheeler 26 May, M to Leslie Harrison at the *Daily Mail* 27 May, M to G 14 Jul, G to M 19 Jul, M to Siriol Hugh Jones 3 Aug, G to M 18 and 20 Sep, M to G 26 Sep, G to M 28 Sep, M to G 30 Sep, G to M 1 Oct, M to G 3 Oct, G to M 15 Oct, M to G 18 Oct, G to M 22 Oct, M to G 26 Oct, G to M [reply to M's letter of 26 Oct, dated 'Wednesday'], G to M 28 Oct, M to G 2 Nov, M to PS 3 Nov (internal memo), M to G 28 Nov, G to M 30 Nov, M to G 2 Dec.
  Negotiations with American publishers: 1955: T. R. Coward to PS 14 Oct, 23 Nov and 30 Dec, John McCallum to PS 12 Dec, PS to John McCallum 15 Dec; 1956: PS to T. R. Coward 30 Jan, PS to Elaine Greene of MCA 7 Mar, John McCallum to PS 21 Sep, PS to G 1 Oct, G to PS 2 Oct, PS to Elaine Greene 1 Nov, reporting contents of John McCallum to PS 23 Oct. A copy of the *BBC Audience Research Department, Report to Readers*, Oct 1955, and a transcript of 'The Masters: William Golding', BBC World service, 28 Mar 1966 (containing Dr Calvin Wells on Neanderthals) are in the Faber archive.

Sources in the Golding archive: MSS of *Dionysius*, *In Search of My Father* and *The Inheritors* and a typescript of *The Inheritors*. Golding's thoughts on his 'daimon' are in *J* 25 Aug and 4 Sep 1985.

Other sources: On *artos* and Golding's 'daimon' see Stephen Medcalf in *Tribute*, pp. 30–44; Monteith's first impressions of *The Inheritors* are in the catalogue of *William Golding 1911–1993: A British Council Exhibition*, Craig Raine on Wells is in *Tribute*, pp. 101–9; for Golding's explanation of *The Inheritors* to VT see Tiger, *William Golding: The Dark*

Fields of Discovery, Calder & Boyars, 1974, pp. 91–5; dates of reviews undated in my text are: 1955: *Times* 22 Sep, *Truth* 7 Oct, *Daily Worker* 13 Oct, *TLS* 25 Oct, *Jerusalem Post* 4 Nov, *Melbourne Age* 12 Nov, *Encounter* Nov, *Tribune* Nov, *Twentieth Century* Dec.

14 *Pincher Martin*

Sources in the Faber and Faber archive: 1955: G to M 21 Jan, M to G 28 Jan, G to M 2 Feb, M to G 26 Oct, G to M 11 Dec, M to G 13 Dec, G to M 29 Dec; 1956: M to G 2 Jan, G to M 24 Feb, M to G 25 Feb, G to M 26 Feb, M to G 28 Feb, G to M 19 Mar, M to G 21 Mar, G to M 22 Mar, M to G 26 Mar, M to PS 28 Mar [internal memo], G to M [dated 'Tuesday', a reply to M's letter of 26 Mar], G to M 4 Apr, M to G 9, 24 and 30 Apr, G to M [dated 'Tuesday', a reply to M's letter of 30 Apr], M to G 28 Aug, G to M 15 Sep, M to G 18 Oct, G to M 20 Oct, M to G 22 Oct, G to M 30 Oct, G to M 5 Nov, M to G 8 Nov, G to M 9 Nov, M to G 16 Nov, PS to G 20 Nov, G to PS 22 Nov, G to M 12 Dec, M to G 13 Dec; 1957: John McCallum to PS 13 Mar, PS to G 18 Mar, G to PS 26 Mar, PS to G 27 Mar, PS to John McCallum 28 Mar, John McCallum to PS 5 Apr, PS to G 12 Apr, PS to John McCallum 23 and 24 Apr, Elaine Greene to PS 12 Sep.

The Faber archive has transcripts of the BBC Home Service *The Critics*, broadcast 28 Oct 1956 at 7 p.m., Kermode's BBC Third Programme talk, broadcast Saturday, 1 Nov 1956 at 7.50 p.m., the BBC Third Programme discussion of 21 Dec 1956, and Arthur Calder-Marshall's talk on the BBC European Service, 10 Jan 1957.

Sources in the Golding archive: An exercise book labelled 'The Vertical' containing notes for *Pincher Martin*, and *J* 10 Jul 1973 (on the 'exhibitionist' dentist).

Other sources: Ian Blake's letter to me of 18 Jan 2006, my interviews with David Golding, 6 Aug 2007, Stephen Medcalf, 12 and 13 Sep 2006, and Judy Carver, 21 Mar 2007, and Judy's e-mails to me, 25 Jan, 3 Feb, and 10 and 11 Sep 2007, and her notes on her interview with Eileen Hogben, 26 Jan 2001. Vivian Trewhella's story is in *WG at BWS*, p. 17.

Dates of reviews undated in my text: 1956: *Sunday Times* 28 Oct, *Observer* 28 Oct, *Times* 1 Nov, *Spectator* 9 Nov, *Listener* 29 Nov, *London Magazine* Dec, *Sunday Times* and *Observer* 23 Dec.

15 *The Brass Butterfly*

Sources in the Faber and Faber archive: 1956: G to PS 19 Dec (rejecting Carolyn Green's play and explaining the meaning of *Lord of the Flies*. There is a copy of *The Wonderful Island* in the Faber archive, and a correspondence between PS and Elaine Greene of MCA about it continuing to Mar 1957), M to G 8 Nov, G to M 9 Nov, G to M [dated 'Sunday', probably 18 Nov]; 1957: M to G 8 Feb, G to M 9 Feb, M to G 14 Feb, G to M 21 Feb, M to G 28 Feb, M to G 6 Apr, G to M 25 Apr, M to G 6 Sep,

G to M 11 Sep, PS to Kitty Black at Curtis Brown 18 Nov, G to PS [undated], PS to G 17 Dec [reply to previous letter]; 1958: M to G 27 Jan, G to M 3 Feb, G to M 11 Feb, M to G 25 Feb, Ann Golding to M ['Tuesday', probably 25 Feb], G to M 30 Mar, G to M 8 Apr, M to G 9 Apr.

A note of touring dates for *The Brass Butterfly*, a New Theatre, Oxford, programme, and a transcript of *The Critics*, BBC Home Service 4 May 1958, 12.10 p.m., are also in the Faber archive.

Sources in the Golding archive: Golding's notes on his 1957–8 income.

Other sources: Judy Carver e-mail, 20 Sep 2007; Naomi Sim, *Dance and Skylark: Fifty Years with Alastair Sim*, Bloomsbury, 1987, pp. 131–2; A. J. Ayer, *More of My Life*, Oxford University Press, 1984 (on the routine for *Brains Trust* broadcasts); *The Sphere*, 26 Apr 1958, p. 147; and *Brass Butterfly* reviews: 'Mr William Golding's First Play', *The Times* 18 Apr 1958, Kenneth Tynan, 'Golding Standard', *Observer*, 20 Apr 1958, T. C. Worsley, 'A Near Miss', *New Statesman*, 26 Apr 1958.

16 *Free Fall*

Sources in the Faber and Faber archive: 1958: M to G 16 Jan, G to M 26 Jan, G to PS 26 Jan, G to M 13 Mar, M to G 28 Mar, G to M 30 Mar, M to G 2 Apr, M to G 24 Jun, G to M 28 Jun, G to PS 28 Jun, PS to John McCallum 11 Aug, PS to John McCallum 21 Oct, William Jovanovich to PS 24 Oct, John McCallum to PS 25 Nov; 1959: PS to William Jovanovich 7 Jan, G to PS 26 Jan, PS to J. Stewart Johnson (Coward-McCann) 19 Jan, 27 Feb and 28 Jul, M to G 26 Jan, M to G 29 Jan, G to M 31 Jan, M to G 2 Feb, PS to G 10 Feb, G to M 11 Feb, M to G 17 Mar, PS to G 23 Mar, J. Stewart Johnson to PS 9 Apr and 22 Jul, G to Rosemary Goad 23 Apr, M to G 1 May, M to G 6 May, G to M 8 May, G to M 10 May, G to PS 14 May, M to G 12 Jun, Jean Detre to Elaine Greene at MCA 29 Jun and 10 Sep (internal memos), G to PS 1 Jul, Helen Wolff to PS 6 Jul, PS to G 11 Aug, G to PS 12 Sep, John McCallum to PS 5 Oct, M to G 26 Oct, David Jones (BBC *Monitor* programme) to M 28 Oct, G to M 31 Oct, G to PS 31 Oct, G to PS 8 Nov; 1961: Seymour Lawrence to PS 4 Dec, PS to Seymour Lawrence 13 Dec.

A copy of a BBC transcript of the Frank Kermode interview, with pre-broadcast deletions, is in the Faber archive.

Sources in the Golding archive: *J* 1972: 3 Feb, 12 May; 1975: 16 Jun; 1980: 18, 29 Jul (on Cecil Beaton); 1983: 11 Oct; 1987: 1 Aug; John Lehmann to G 19 Jun 1958; G to Jeanne Delbaere (the 'severed cock' letter) 26 Sep 1976; the three typescripts of *Free Fall*.

Other sources: V. S. Pritchett, *New Statesman*, 2 Aug 1958; Frank Kermode, *Spectator*, 22 Aug 1958; Peter Brook, *The Shifting Point: Forty Years of Theatrical Exploration 1946–87*, Methuen, 1988, and e-mails, 24 May and 19 Jun 2007; Judy Carver e-mails 31 Jan, 2, 4, 8, 12, 13 and 20 Oct 2007; my interviews with David Golding 6–10 Aug 2007, James Lovelock 23 Feb 2006, Mark Kinkead-Weekes 14 Sep 2006 and Joanna

Mackle 31 Aug 2006; Frances Partridge, *Life Regained: Diaries 1970–1972*, Weidenfeld & Nicolson, 1998, p. 245 (28 Dec 1972); 'Through the Dutch Waterways', *Holiday* magazine, Jan 1962; Nigel Mussett in *WG at BWS*, p. 12; *Books and Bookmen* Oct 1959, pp. 9–10 (a shortened version of the Kermode interview).

Dates of *Free Fall* reviews not dated in my text: 1959: *Oxford Mail* 22 Oct, *Guardian* 23 Oct, *Sunday Times* 25 Oct, *Tribune* 30 Oct, *Daily Telegraph* 30 Oct, *Listener* 5 Nov, *Tablet* 7 Nov, *Irish Times* 21 Nov.

17 Journalism and Difficulties with *The Spire*

Sources in the Faber and Faber archive: 1960: G to PS 6 Jan, G to PS 'Wednesday' [probably 20 Jan], PS to G 23 Jan, G to PS 31 Jan, M to G 26 Feb, G to M 27 Feb, G to PS 6 Apr, G to PS 18 Apr, G to PS 10 May, Giles de la Mare to G 13 May, M to G 26 Aug, G to M 12 Sep, M to G 4 Oct, PS to G 25 Oct, G to PS 9 Nov, PS to G 18 Nov, M to G 23 Nov, G to PS 30 Nov, PS to G 5 Dec, G to PS 16 Dec, PS to G 19 Dec; 1961: M to G 20 Jan, G to PS 1 Feb, Ann Golding to M 6 Feb, G to M 17 Feb, G to M 24 Apr, M to G 6 May, PS to G 10 May, G to PS 14 May, PS to G 14 Jun, G to PS 15 Jun, G to M 'Saturday' [probably in Jun], M to G 31 Aug, G to M 3 Sep, G to M 12 Sep.

Sources in the Golding archive: *J* 9 Mar 1972; Karl Miller to G 13 May 1960.

Golding's letter to the Society of Authors, 21 May 1960, and Ian Rowland-Hill's reply, 25 May 1960, are in the Society of Authors archive. Golding's letters to Louis Rubin of 27 Jun and 12 Sep 1960 are among the Louis Decimus Rubin Papers (#3899) in the Southern Historical Collection, Manuscripts Department, Wilson Library, The University of North Carolina at Chapel Hill.

Other sources: Judy Carver e-mails 30 Jan and 12 and 13 Oct 2007; Glenn Collett e-mail 15 Jan 2008; Peter Green, *Tribune*, p. 54.

Full references for Golding's articles and reviews mentioned in this chapter are in Gekoski, pp. 53–5.

I am indebted to the late Elizabeth Suddaby for bringing Dorothy Sayers' play to my attention.

18 America

Sources in the Faber and Faber archive: 1960: G to M 3 Sep, M to G 12 Sep, G to M 28 Oct, M to G 3 Nov; 1961: G to M 28 Feb, M to G 7 Mar, G to PS 1 Nov; 1962: G to Giles de la Mare 3 Jan, Ellis Amburn of Coward-McCann to PS 12 Jan, PS to G 15 Jan, PS to G 18 Jan, PS to Ellis Amburn 19 Jan, G to PS 21 Jan, Ellis Amburn to PS 22 Jan, PS to G 30 Jan, PS to John McCallum 30 Jan, Seymour Lawrence of Atlantic Monthly to PS 9 Feb, John McCallum to PS 9 Feb, G to PS 11 Feb, Richard Gilson of MCA to PS 12 Feb, PS to John McCallum 16 Feb, PS to G 23 Feb, John McCallum to PS 27 Feb, Richard Gilson to PS 27 Feb, G to PS 5 May, G to M 9 Jun, Walter J. Minton to G 16 Nov, PS to G 19 Nov, PS to G 20 Nov, PS to G 21 Nov.

Sources in the Golding archive: *J* 11 Jun 1972 (Golding's dream of Betsy Payne's hair).

Sources in the Wilson Library, University of North Carolina at Chapel Hill, Louis Decimus Rubin Papers (#3899): 1960: G to Rubin 12 Jun [telegram], 27 Jun, 30 Jun, 5 Aug, 12 Sep, 27 Oct; 1961: G to Rubin 6 Mar, 26 Mar, 28 Mar, 27 Apr, 14 May, 3 Aug, 21 Aug, 6 Sep; 1962: G to Rubin 13 Aug, 21 Oct; 1963: G to Rubin 'Thursday' [probably 3 Jan], 20 Mar, 14 Apr, 6 Sep.

Other sources: Professor Rubin shared his memories of Golding's stay at Hollins with me in e-mails of 23 Jan and 3 Feb 2007, and sent copies of the final examination paper Golding set his students, and of a list of the lectures at other colleges arranged for him while he was at Hollins. Other Hollins sources are e-mails from Terry Herrin Andrews, 25 Jan 2007, Anna Sevier Morgan, 8 Feb 2007, Betsy Payne Rosen, 28 Jan and 6 Feb 2007, and Jane Gentry Vance, 16, 17 and 20 Jan 2007.

Judy Carver's e-mail of 12 Oct 2007 and my interview with David Golding 6 Aug 2007; *Spectator* 24 Nov 1961, 19 Jan 1962, 7 Sep 1962; Lionel and Diana Trilling interviewed by Edward Lucie-Smith, *Sunday Times*, 27 Sep 1964; Lionel Trilling, 'Lord of the Flies', in *A Company of Readers*, ed. Arthur Krystal, New York Free Press, 2001. On the publishing history of *Lord of the Flies: Yorkshire Post*, 28 Jun 1962 (citing the *New York Publisher's Weekly*); Kenneth Allsop, *Daily Mail*, 27 Jun 1963.

19 *The Spire*

Sources in the Faber and Faber archive: 1962: G to PS 5 May, M to G 29 Jun, G to M 1 Jul, M to G 14 Sep, M to G 15 Oct, G to M 17 Oct, G to PS 14 Nov, G to M 19 Nov, G to M 23 Nov, M to G 26 Nov, G to M 6 Dec, G to PS 'Thursday' [probably 13 Dec]; 1963: G to PS 8 Jan, G to M 19 Mar, M to G 21 Mar, M to G 26 Apr, G to M 1 May, M to G 6 May, G to M 9 May, M to G 9 May, PS to M 17 May, M [internal memo] 20 May, M to G 21 Jun [misdated 21 Jul], G to M 25 Jun, M 9 Jul, 18 Jul, 27 Aug, 13 Sep [internal memos], G to M 16 Oct, M to G 21 Oct, G to M 19 Nov, M 28 Nov [internal memo], Julian Muller to PS 5 Dec, PS to G 17 Dec, G to PS 29 Dec; 1964: P. H. Newby (BBC) to M 1 Jan, G to M 2 Jan, G to M 6 Jan, M to Julian Muller 17 Jan, G to M 6 Feb [misdated 6 Jan], Alan C. Collins of Curtis Brown to PS 23 Jan and 5 May, M to G 24 Jan, Ernestine Novak of Curtis Brown to M 24 Jan, G to M 28 Jan, M to G 15 Apr, G to M 26 Apr, M to G 30 Apr, G to M 1 May, Julian Muller to PS 16 Jun, M 1 Oct [internal memo].

Sources in the Golding archive: *J* 1972: 27 Jan; 1974: 2 Feb; 1982: 28 Feb; 1992: 20 Dec; letters from Golding to Ann and his family, 31 Jan 1963 and 'Monday' [probably 4 Feb 1963]; an MS page of notes for *The Spire*; letters to Golding from E. M. Forster, 25 Jun, 25 Aug, 13 Sep and 5 Oct 1962, and 4 Feb, 1 Mar, and 16 and 19 Jun 1964.

Other sources: E-mails from Judy Carver, 7 Feb, 20 Nov and 2 Dec 2007; Betsy Payne Rosen, 28 Jan 2007; Peter Brook, 24 May and 19 Jun 2007; Samuel Hynes, 7 Dec 2007 (Professor Hynes also sent me copies of Golding's letters to him). Interviews with Judy Carver, 21 Mar 2007; Frank Kermode, 8 Sep 2006; Mark Kinkead-Weekes, 14 Sep 2006. For Golding in Greece I drew on a telephone interview with Peter Green, 23 Apr, and an e-mail, 27 Apr 2007, and *Tribune*, pp. 45–56.

Printed sources: Peter Brook, *The Shifting Point: Forty Years of Theatrical Exploration 1946–87*, Methuen, 1988, pp. 192ff.; Margaret Drabble, *Angus Wilson: A Biography*, Secker and Warburg, 1955, pp. 318–23; William Taubman, *Khrushchev: The Man and his Era*, Free Press, 2003, pp. 601–2; Virginia Tiger, *William Golding: The Unmoved Target*, Marion Boyars, 2003 p. 154.

Reviews not dated in text: 1964: *Listener* 9 Apr, *Daily Mail* 9 Apr, *Daily Express* 9 Apr, *New Statesman* 10 Apr, *Church Times* 10 Apr, *Guardian* 10 Apr, *Spectator* 10 Apr, *Irish Times* 11 Apr, *Sunday Times* 12 Apr, *Observer* 12 Apr, *Sunday Telegraph* 12 Apr, *Sunday Express* 12 Apr, *The Critics*, BBC Home Service, 12.10 p.m., 12 Apr, *Evening Standard* 14 Apr, *Birmingham Post* 14 Apr, *Tatler* 15 Apr, *Times* 16 Apr, *Country Life* 16 Apr, *Tribune* 17 Apr, *Scotsman* 18 Apr, *Financial Times* 21 Apr, *Time* 24 Apr, *Washington Post* 26 Apr, *Newsweek* 27 Apr, *New York Review of Books* 30 Apr, *Encounter* May, *TES* 20 May, *New Yorker* 13 Jun, *Harper's* Jul.

20 *The Hot Gates* and *The Pyramid*

Sources in the Faber and Faber archive: 1963: G to M 16 Oct, G to PS 6 Dec; 1964: M to Mark Kinkead-Weekes 4 Feb, M to G 4 Feb, M to G 6 Feb, G to M 6 Feb [wrongly dated 6 Jan], M to G 7 Feb, M to G 20 Feb, PS to G 23 Mar, G to M 2 Sep, G to M 3 Nov, M to G 5 Nov, M to G 15 Dec, PS to G 22 Dec; 1965: G to M 4 Jan, G to M 2 Feb, G to M 26 Mar, G to M 5 Apr [in Greek], PS to G 6 Apr, M to G 8 Apr [in Greek], Julian Muller to PS 31 Aug, G to PS 1 Sep, PS to G 9 Sep, G to PS 11 Sep; 1966: G to PS 13 Jan, G to M 13 Jan, G to M 10 Mar, M to G 28 Mar, G to M 30 Mar, M to G 31 Mar, M to G 19 Apr, G to M 25 Apr, M to G 29 Apr, G to M 3 May, G to M 17 Jun, M 24 Jun [internal memo], M to G 28 Jun, Julian Muller to PS 11 Jul, G to M 23 Aug, M to G 25 Aug, G to M 31 Aug, M to G 9 Sep, M 12 Sep [internal memo], G to M 17 Sep, M to G 20 Sep, G to PS 28 Sep, Julian Muller to M 9 Oct, Julian Muller to PS 16 Nov, M to Julian Muller 21 Nov, Julian Muller to M 2 Dec, G to M 6 Dec, PS to G 6 Dec, G to PS 7 Dec, M to G 8 Dec, G to M 29 Dec; 1967: M to G 10 Jan; 1971: G to M 28 Feb.

There is an undated, unsourced cutting of the Ruth Inglis interview in the Faber archive, and a transcript of the 28 Mar 1966 BBC *The Masters* broadcast.

Sources in the Golding archive: Golding's letter to Monteith in hospital, dated 14 Jun [1965]; *J* 1972: 3, 5 Aug; 1986: 28 Mar.

Sources for the Boscombe Down dig: E-mail, 9 Dec 2007, from Dr Andrew Fitzpatrick, Head of Communications, Wessex Archaeology; e-mail, 9 Dec 2007 from Judy Carver; *The Wiltshire Archaeological and Natural History Magazine*, Vol. 54, No. 195, Dec 1950, pp. 124–68.

Dates of *The Hot Gates* reviews: 1965: *Times* 28 Oct, *Observer* 31 Oct, *Yorkshire Post* 4 Nov, *TLS* 4 Nov, *Listener* 4 Nov, *New Statesman* 5 Nov, *Spectator* 5 Nov, *Irish Times* 20 Nov, *New Society* 2 Dec, *Sunday Times* 5 Dec, *Tribune* 31 Dec; 1966: *Tablet* 22 Jan, *Daily Telegraph* 3 Feb.

Other sources: Interview with David Golding 8 Aug 2007; phone conversation with Peter Green 23 Apr 2007 and e-mail from him 25 Apr 2007, and his essay in *Tribune*, pp. 45–56; Judy Carver e-mail, 14 Oct 2008; interviews with Frank Kermode, 8 Sep 2006, and James Lovelock, 23 Feb 2006; Robert Scoble's letter to me, 20 Feb 2006, enclosing a copy of Golding's letter to Scoble, 21 Oct 1968; Justine Hopkins, *Michael Ayrton: A Biography*, André Deutsch, 1994, pp. 217, 301, 319.

21 Disaster

Sources in the Faber and Faber archive: 1966: G to M 29 Dec; 1967: M to G 13 Feb, G to M 14 Feb, G to M 1 Mar, M to G 3 Mar, Rosemary Goad 13 Jun [internal memo], Ann Golding to the du Sautoys 20 Jul.

Sources in the Golding archive: *J* 1972: 26 Jan, 30 Jun; 1982: 22 Jun. Legal documents relating to the *Tenace* sinking: In the High Court of Justice, Probate, Divorce and Admiralty Division, 1967, Folio 295, Admiralty Action *in rem* against the ship HEIAN MARU. Golding to Judy, 6 Nov 1967.

Other sources: Peter Green, *Tribune*, pp. 35 and 49–50; copies of correspondence between VT and Golding supplied by Professor Tiger: 1967: VT to G 28 Mar, 10 Apr, 15 Apr; G to VT: 29 Mar, 12 Apr, 22 Apr, 2 May, 'Saturday' [probably 20 or 27 May], 31 Aug; G to Lionel Tiger 20 Jul; interviews with Professor Tiger 24 Apr and 9 Jul 2007, and her books, *William Golding: The Dark Fields of Discovery*, Calder and Boyars, 1974 and *William Golding: The Unmoved Target*, Marion Boyars, 2003; Stephen Medcalf letter of 15 May 2007 and *Tribune*, pp. 30–44; phone interviews with James Anderson 19 Apr 2006 and 17 Jan 2008, Paulette Anderson 19 Apr 2006 and 17 Jan 2008, and Wayland and Liz Kennet 23 Nov 2005; Judy Carver e-mails 10 Jul 2007, and 13 Jan and 14 Oct 2008; *Guardian* 15 Jul 1967.

Dates of *The Pyramid* reviews: 1967: *Times* 1 Jun, *Daily Telegraph* 1 Jun, *Financial Times* 1 Jun, *Oxford Mail* 1 Jun, *TLS* 1 Jun, *New Statesman* 2 Jun, *Guardian* 2 Jun, *Irish Times* 3 Jun, *Sunday Times* 4 Jun, *Observer* 4 Jun, *The Critics* 4 Jun BBC Home Service, 12.10 p.m., *Queen* 7 Jun, *Listener* 8 Jun, *Yorkshire Post* 8 Jun, *Evening Standard* 13 Jun, *Scotsman* 17 Jun, *Spectator* 30 Jun, *Tribune* 14 Jul, *New York Times Book Review* 15 Oct, CBC's *Critics on the Air* 22 Dec.

22 'The Jam' and a Breakdown

Sources in the Faber and Faber archive: 1968: M to G 5 Feb, Hilary Nash 15 Feb [internal memo], G to M 19 Feb, M to G 20 Feb, G to M 22 Feb, M to G 23 Feb, PS to G 28 Feb, G to M [undated postcard, acknowledged in next], M to G 7 Oct, G to

M 18 Oct, G to M 18 Dec, M to G 19 Dec; 1969: G to M 8 Mar, M to G 11 Mar, M to G 3 Apr, Rosemary Goad 8 Apr [internal memo], M to G 18 Apr, M to Graham Watson (Curtis Brown) 18 Apr, PS to G 23 Apr, G to PS 4 May, PS to G 6 May, Graham Watson to M 6 May, G to M 10 May, M to G 12 May, M to Graham Watson 14 May, Graham Watson to PS 16 May, PS to Graham Watson 5 Jun, Barbara Vagg (Curtis Brown) to PS 10 Jun, Rosemary Goad 4 Jul [internal memo], G to M [undated postcard]; G to PS 2 Oct; 1970: M to G 8 Jan, G to M 12 Jan, M to G 13 Jan, M to G 10 Jul, G to M 15 Jul, M to G 15 Jul, M to G 16 Jul, M to PS 16 Jul, PS to Julian Muller 6 Nov.

Sales figures for *Lord of the Flies* to Jul 1969 are given in an internal memo addressed to PS, dated 22 Feb 1969, and (with the addition of American sales figures) in a letter from PS to Michael Howard 25 Jul 1969.

Sources in the Golding archive: Manuscript and typescript of 'The Jam' (novel versions) and nine typescript synopses of the film version (of which, one has an italic typeface, and seems professionally typed, and all the others are in Golding's typescript, most with his manuscript annotations): none of these versions bears any shelfmark or identifying number. '*It was 1940*'. *J* 18 May 1972 and 18 Mar 1975. Eric Collieu's letter to Golding 29 Apr 1969.

Other sources: Letters from Golding to VT, supplied by Professor Tiger: 6 Nov [1968], 20 Mar [1969], 27 May [1969], 14 May [1970], undated [probably 25 May 1970]. Interview with Anthony Simmons, 23 Jan 2008. Judy Carver e-mail 15 Jan 2007.

23 *The Scorpion God* and 'History Of A Crisis'

Sources in the Faber and Faber archive: 1964: G to M 6 Feb [misdated 6 Jan], G to M 26 Apr; 1969: G to M 8 Mar, M to G 11 Mar; 1970: G to PS 12 May, M to G 10 Jul, G to M 15 Jul, M to PS 16 Jul [internal memo], M to G 13 Oct, M to G 29 Oct, G to M 29 Oct, G to M 3 Nov, M to G 6 Nov, M to G 13 Nov, G to M 15 Nov, M to G 20 Nov, G to M 5 Dec, M to G 11 Dec; 1971: M to G 25 Feb, M 22 Mar [internal memo], M to G 25 Mar, M to G 29 Mar, M to PS 29 Mar [internal memo], PS to Julian Muller 31 Mar, PS to G 7 Apr, G to M 10 Apr, M to G 3 May, G to M 4 May, Julian Muller to PS 6 May, PS to Julian Muller 13 May, PS to G 13 May, G to PS 18 May, PS to Julian Muller 24 May, G to PS 6 Jun, PS 24 Aug [internal memo], G to PS 30 Sep, G to M 8 Nov, G to M 16 Nov, M 21 Nov [internal memo], M to G 20 Dec.

Sources in the Golding archive: *J* 1971: 1 Mar, 19 Aug, 2, 7, 12 Nov; 1972: 7 Jan, 18 Feb, 1 Mar; 1974: 22 Oct, 1978: 4 Nov, 1981: 4 Feb.

Other sources: Interviews with Wayland and Liz Kennet, 23 Nov 2005; Andrew Sinclair, 28 Nov 2005 and Tim Brown, 2 Oct 2006. Judy Carver e-mail, 21 Jan 2008; Stephen Medcalf letter, 15 May 2007.

Dates of *The Scorpion God* reviews: 1971: *Sunday Times* 24 Oct, *Sunday Telegraph* 24 Oct, *Observer* 24 Oct, *Evening Standard* 26 Oct, *Daily Telegraph* 28 Oct, *Financial Times* 28 Oct, *Guardian* 28 Oct, *Listener* 28 Oct, *New Statesman* 29 Oct, *Spectator* 30 Oct, BBC *Now Read On* 8 Dec, BBC *Arts Commentary* 15 Dec.

24 Gap Years

Sources in the Golding archive: *J* 1972: 3, 19, 22, 23, 24, 26, 28 Jan, 4, 9, 22, 25 Feb, 7, 13, 16 Mar, 16, 19, 28, 29 Apr, 21, 24 May, 17, 21, 26 Jun, 28 Jul, 3, 5 Aug, 13 Aug–10 Oct, 18, 24 Nov, 13 Dec; 1973: 6–8 Feb, 24 Mar–12 Apr, 2 Jun, 4 Sep–29 Oct, 9 Dec; 1974: 3 Feb, 14, 29 Mar, 17, 24 Apr, 5, 9, 15, 20, 29, 31 May, 5 Jun, 29 Aug, 8, 24, 27, 28, 30 Sep, 3 Oct, 2, 3, 5, 6, 7, 10, 13, 24, 28, 29 Nov, 2, 9, 10, 11, 18, 24–5 Dec; 1975: 3 Jan, 1 Mar–10 Apr, 20 Apr, 17 May, 8, 18 Jun, 18 Jul, 23 Aug, 7, 26 Sep, 9 Oct; 1976: 27 Jan–3 Apr, 17, 18 Apr, 14–17 May, 4, 6, 7, 16, 29 Jun, 21 Jul; 1978: 22 Nov; 1979: 1 Sep; 1980: 10 Oct; 1982: 2 Mar; 1985: 2 Jul; 1986: 9 Aug, 26 Sep, 23 Nov; 1988: 5 Jan; 1989: 24 Jan.

The Richardson-pastiche letter to Judy [14 Nov 1974]; a set of MS notes about Middle-Eastern brothels; the MS of 'Niki'.

Sources in the Faber and Faber archive: 1972: G to M 9 Jan [wrongly dated 9 Dec], M to G 13 Jan, G to M 3 Mar; 1974: G to M 19 Apr, M to G 30 Apr; 1975: G to M 24 Mar [picture postcard from Gladstone], G to M 9 Apr [picture postcard from McLaren Vale, SA], M to G 28 Apr, M to G 3 Oct, G to M 13 and 14 Oct, M to G 16 Oct.

Other sources: Interviews with Andrew Sinclair, 28 Nov 2005; Harriet Harvey Wood, 6 Sep 2006; Stephen Medcalf, 12 and 13 Sep 2006; Mark and Joan Kinkead-Weekes, 14 Sep 2006; Tim Brown, 2 Oct 2006; Sally Brown, 4 Feb 2007. Ruth Padel e-mail 9 Nov 2007; Judy Carver e-mail 14 Oct 2008. *Listener* 3 Jan 1974; Jeanne Delbaere in F. Regard, ed., *Fingering Netsukes: Selected Papers from the First International William Golding Conference*, Publications de l'Université de Saint-Étienne, 1995, pp. 205–11.

25 *Darkness Visible*

Sources in the Golding archive: *J* 1972: 1, 4 Feb; 1973: 18 Dec; 1974: 17, 19 Jan, 6, 11 Jun, 8 Nov; 1975: 7, 17 Nov, 3, 11 Dec; 1976: 28 Apr, 3, 26, 27 May, 1 Sep; 1977: 11–13 Feb, 4, 5, 28 Apr, 5 Jun, 24 Jul, 20 Aug, 11 Oct–23 Nov, 4, 8–9, 17, 26 Dec; 1978: 4, 11, 18, 20, 23 Jan, 2, 25 Feb, 5, 6, 7 Mar, 12, 29 Apr, 4, 5, 6, 14–16, 20 May, 14 Jul, 2–4, 20, 21, 26, 29 Aug, 7 Sep–10 Oct, 16, 20, 25, 27, 28, 29 Oct; 1979: 20 Mar, 13, 21 Jul, 21, 22 Aug, 3 Sep–18 Oct, 25 Oct, 6, 10 Nov, 7 Dec.

Unfinished MS story and synopsis dated 10–15 Oct 1955 in exercise book labelled 'The Vertical'.

Golding's copy of A. C. Ainger's *Clivus*, and his MS notebook of completed exercises from it, are at Tullimaar.

Sources in the Faber and Faber archive: 1968: G to M 19 Feb; 1978: G to M 29 Jun, M to G 3 Jul [internal memo on phone conversation], M to G 4 Jul, M to Faber and

Faber Book Committee 24 Jul [internal memo], M to G 25 Jul, G to M 8 Aug, G to M 26 Oct, M to G 27 Oct [internal memo on telephone conversation], M to G 30 Oct, M to G 17 Nov, G to M 21 Nov, G to M 2 Dec, M to Book Committee 5 Dec [internal memo], G to M 20 Dec; 1979: M to G 10 Jan, G to M 13 Jan [enclosing blurb for *Darkness Visible*], RG to M 16 Jan, M to G 19 Jan, M to RG 24 Jan, G to M 29 Jan, ME to M 30 Jan, ME to G 30 Jan, M to G 5 Feb, G to M 9 Feb, M to G 13 Feb, G to M 17 Feb, M to G 21 Feb, Rosemary Goad to Rosalie Swedlin (Anthony Shiel Associates) 21 Mar, G to M 10 Jul, G to M 7 Aug, Rosalie Swedlin to M 5 Sep, G to M 22 Oct, M to G 5 Nov [telegram]; 1980: Peter McIntyre to M 23 Apr; 1985: G to M [undated, probably late April; replied to in next item], M to G 1 May.

Other sources: Judy Carver e-mail 3 Feb 2008 (on her research into the real-life Manderson); Golding's letter to VT 6 Nov 1968; interviews with Emily Young 22 Feb 2006, Mark Kinkead-Weekes 14 Sep 2006, Joanna Mackle 31 Aug 2006, Tim Brown 2 Oct 2006, and Matthew Evans 9 Apr 2008.

Dates of *Darkness Visible* reviews: 1979: *Now! Magazine* 28 Sep, *Observer* 30 Sep, *Times* 4 Oct, *Literary Review* 5 Oct, *London Review of Books* 25 Oct, *Quarto* Oct, *TLS* 23 Nov, *Books and Bookmen* Nov.

26 Rites of Passage

Sources in the Golding archive: *J* 1972: 6, 12 Jan, 17 Feb, 17 Mar, 31 May, 18 Nov; 1974: 4 Jan, 26 Feb, 20 Jul; 1976: 26 Apr, 17, 26 May, 12, 18 Jul, 6, 8, 11 Aug, 9, 15, 16, 19, 31 Oct, 5, 15, 31 Nov, 3, 17 Dec; 1977: 18 Jan, 11, 26 Mar, 14 Apr, 2, 17 Sep; 1978: 11, 30 Nov, 4 Dec; 1979: 12 Feb, 14 Mar, 13, 21, 27 Apr, 11 May, 6 Jun, 17, 27 Jul, 27 Sep, 12, 14, 25 Nov, 1, 12, 31 Dec; 1980: 8, 14, 21, 25, 28, 29 Jan, 30 Jan–6 Feb, 11, 17, 23, 29 Feb, 10 Mar, 9–14 Apr, 24 May, 3, 14, 19, 26 Jun, 2, 5, 7–17 Jul, 7 Aug–6 Sep, 15–19 Sep, 26 Sep, 1, 2, 4, 10, 21, 22 Oct, 1, 6–15 Nov; 1981: 18 Feb, 4, 26 Mar, 17 Sep, 2 Oct; 1982: 16, 29 May; 1986: 10 Jan; 1991: 22 Jul.

Sources in the Faber and Faber archive: 1979: M 17 Apr [internal memo about *South Bank Show*], M to Roger Straus 27 Jun, M to Book Committee 15 Aug [internal memo], G to M 22 Oct, M to G 24 Oct, G to M 31 Oct, M to G 2 Nov, G to M 14 Nov, M to G 29 Nov, G to M 10 Dec, M to G 19 Dec, M to RG 19 Dec; 1980: G to M 3 Jan, M to RG 17 Jan, RG to M 24 Jan, M to RG 5 Feb, G to M 13 Feb, RG to M 6 Mar, M to G 11 Mar, M to RG 13 Mar, David Blow to M 21 Feb [itinerary for Hamburg and Copenhagen trip], M to RG 13 Mar, G to M 15 Mar, M 26 Mar [internal circular about *South Bank Show*], G to M 30 Apr, M to RG 7 May, G to Heather Cooper 18 May [about cover-design for *Rites*], G to M 5 Jul, M to G 21 Aug, M to G 27 Aug, Giles de la Mare to ME 8 Sep, Roger Straus to G 29 Sep, M to Roger Straus 3 Oct, M to RG 8 Oct, M to G 31 Oct, G to M 2 Nov, RG to M 18 Nov, M to G 20 Nov, G to M 25 Nov, M to RG 28 Nov.

Other sources: Elizabeth Longford, *Wellington: The Years of the Sword*, Weidenfeld & Nicolson, 1969, p. 51; *Private Eye*, 11 May 1979 (on the Bryans case); Victoria

Glendinning, *Sunday Times* 19 Oct 1980; Bill Webb, *Guardian Weekend Arts* 11 Oct 1980; Ursula Buchan, *Spectator* 12 Mar 1994 (on J. L. Carr's thoughts about the Booker); Byron Roger, *The Last Englishman: The Life of J. L. Carr*, Aurum Press, 2003, p. 220.

Interviews with Matthew Evans 9 Apr 2008 and Melvyn Bragg 26 Sep 2008. John Fuller letter 17 Jan 2006; Claire Tomalin e-mail 18 Aug 2006.

Dates of *Rites* reviews: 1980: *Punch* 15 Oct, *Guardian* 16 Oct, *Times* 16 Oct, *New Statesman* 17 Oct, *TLS* 17 Oct, *Observer* 19 Oct.

27   *A Moving Target* and *The Paper Men*

Sources in the Golding archive: *J* 1975: 28 May; 1978: 5 Mar; 1979: 20 Jan, 15 Mar, 16 May, 5 Jun; 1980: 1 Mar, 6 Apr, 24 May; 1981: 9, 19, 21, 27, 30 Jan, 16, 22, 25, 28 Feb, 4, 6, 30 Apr, 5, 6, 7, 21, 22, 23 May, 2, 15 Jun, 3, 16 Jul, 1 Aug–3 Sep, 19, 29 Sep, 14 Nov, 1 Dec; 1982: 23 Jan, 2, 3, 21 Feb, 8, 18, 27, 30, 31 Mar, 14, 27 Apr, 9–16, 23, 27 May, 25 Jun, 16–18, 23 Jul, 5, 17, 25 Sep, 6–8 Oct, 8 Nov; 1983: 7–10 Jan, 27 Mar, 18–22 Apr, 2, 7, 13, 14, 21, 22, 25, 30 May, 2, 4, 13, 21–23, 28, 30 Jun, 8 Jul, 31 Jul–30 Aug, 2, 25, 26 Sep; 1986: 16 Jul, 10 Nov.

Typescript of the poem 'I read the book', headed, 'Τò Παιδίον' ('The Child'); the MS of Golding's speech given at the South East Asian Award ceremony, Oct 1984.

Letters to Golding from Rick Gekoski, 16 Sep [1982], Sylvère Monod, 17 Dec 1982, the president of La Sorbonne Nouvelle, Henri Behar, 15 Dec 1982, and Pam Schute (secretary of the Royal Society of Literature), 11 Apr 1983.

Sources in the Faber and Faber archive: 1981: G to Sarah Biggs 6 Feb [for attention of M], G to M 16 Feb, M to G 18 Feb [memo of telephone conversation], M to G 25 Feb, G to M 28 Feb, M to G 6 Mar [memo of telephone conversation], M to G 15 Jul, M to Roger Straus 15 Jul, G to M 18 Jul, M to G 22 Jul, G to M 23 Jul, G to M 26 Jul, M to G 3 Aug; 1982: Judith Fiennes to M 23 Feb, G to M 6 Apr, G to M 24 May, M to Book Committee 15 Jun [internal memo], G to M 4 Sep; 1983: M 26 Jan [internal memo], G to M 27 Mar, M 19 Apr [memo of phone conversation with G], G to M 7 May, M to G 25 May, M to G 8 Jun, G to M 1 Jul, Fiona McCrae (Faber and Faber) to G 5 Jul [and internal memo to M], G to M 'Thursday' [probably 14 Jul], M to G 21 Jul, M to Liz Bland (Faber copy-editor) 23 Aug, M to G 23 Aug, M to G 24 Aug, Rosemary Goad to G 31 Aug, M 13 Sep [internal memo], G to M 25 Sep, M to G 28 Sep, M to G 11 Oct.

Other sources: Biles, p. 18; Rick Gekoski, *Tolkien's Gown and Other Stories of Great Authors and Rare Books*, Constable, 1996, pp. 25–36. Judy Carver e-mail 14 Oct 2008; interviews with Rick Gekoski, 9 Sep 2008, and Terrell Carver, 7 Mar 2008, and phone interview with Christine Jordis, 7 Nov 2006.

Dates of *A Moving Target* reviews: 1982: *Critics' Forum*, 29 Mar, 5.45 p.m., BBC Radio 3, *Observer* 23 May, *Guardian* 27 May, *Sunday Telegraph* 6 Jun, *New Statesman* 11 Jun, *Sunday Times* 13 Jun, *London Review of Books* 17 Jun, *Listener* 24 Jun, *New York Times Book Review* 11 Jul, *Evening Standard* 14 Jul, *Scotsman* 24 Jul, *TES* 27 Aug.

28 The Nobel Prize and *An Egyptian Journal*

Sources in the Golding archive: *J* 1982: 12 Jun; 1983: 30 Sep, 6, 18, 20, 21, 26, 27 Oct, 3, 7, 10, 16–19, 30 Nov, 3 and 5–16 Dec; 1984: 3, 9, 19, 27, 30 Jan, 2 Feb, 5 Feb–6 Mar, 10, 11, 31 Mar, 15, 19 Apr, 19, 21 May, 7, 13, 15, 16, 25 Jul, 1–31 Aug, 17, 21 Sep, 4–16, 18, 24 Oct; 1992: 17 Jan.

Letters to Golding from Margaret Thatcher 7 Oct 1983, Knut Ahnlund 24 Oct 1983, Sven Broman of Bonnier Magazine Group 1 Aug 1984 and E. C. Wright (registrar of Bristol University) 30 Mar 1984.

A typewritten eyewitness account of the Nobel ceremony, dated 5 Jan 1984, by Edwin Reffell (an old boy of Bishop Wordsworth's School); an undated typewritten 'Memorandum on Certain Procedures at the Official Nobel Events', a printed *Guide to the Nobel Jubilee Events*, and a description of the Santa Lucia ceremony, included in an MS of Golding's speech at the Southeast Asian Awards ceremony (Oct 1984). A letter to the Goldings from Wylma Wayne 26 Oct 1983 and a letter to Ann Golding from Ahdaf Soueif, 9 Aug 1984.

Sources in the Faber and Faber archive: 1982: David Roberts to G 9 Jun, M to G 19 Aug, ME to G 13 Dec, G to ME 16 Dec; 1983: ME to G 10 Feb, Fiona McCrae to G 6 Oct, G to Fiona McCrae 9 Oct; 1984: M to G 9 Jan, M to G 22 Mar, G to M 16 Apr, Susannah Foreman (Faber and Faber) to G 24 Apr, G to M 26 Apr, M 13 Jun [memo of phone conversation with G 9 Jun], M to G 14 Jun, G to M 20 Jun, M to G 21 Jun, G to M 4 Jul, M 20 Jul [memo of phone conversation with G on 17 Jul], M 3 Aug [note for John Bodley], M to G 13 Sep, G to M 3 Oct [postcard], M to G 10 Oct, G to M [undated card, after 16 Oct], M to G 24 Oct, M to G 20 Nov.

Press articles on Lundkvist and the Nobel: 1983: *San Francisco Examiner* 6 Oct, *New York Times* 7 Oct, *Montreal Gazette* 7 Oct, *Evening Standard* 7 Oct, *Evening Gazette* (Colchester) 7 Oct, *Daily Telegraph* 8 Oct, *Guardian* 8 Oct, Chris Mosey and Peter Lennon, *Sunday Times* 9 Oct, *Greenville News* 9 Oct, Michael Davie, *Observer* 9 Oct, *Listener* 13 Oct, Paul Gray, *Time* 17 Oct, Auberon Waugh, *Spectator* 9 Dec.

Other sources: Interviews with David Roberts 7 Feb 2006, Patrick French 17 Aug 2006 and Terrell Carver 7 Mar 2008. Alan Franks in *The Times* 9 Jun 1984 (Oxford book signing); Ahdaf Soueif, *London Review of Books* 3 Oct 1985, p. 9.

Dates of *The Paper Men* reviews: 1984: *Financial Times* 4 Feb, *Observer* 5 Feb, *Sunday Express* 5 Feb, *Sunday Telegraph* 5 Feb, *Mail on Sunday* 5 Feb, *Standard* 8 Feb, *Guardian* 9 Feb, *Listener* 9 Feb, *Punch* 9 Feb, *Time Out* 9 Feb, *Times* 9 Feb, *Daily Telegraph* 10 Feb, *Sunday Times* 12 Feb, *Spectator* 18 Feb, *Vogue* Feb, *Books and Bookmen* Feb, *London Review of Books* 1 Mar.

29 A Move and *Close Quarters*

Sources in the Golding archive: *J* 1974: 14 Feb; 1981: 9, 14, 16, 28 Sep, 2, 10 Oct, 17, 21, 23 Nov, 1 Dec; 1984: 13 Dec; 1985: 14 Jan, 25, 26 Mar, 15 Apr, 13, 20 May, 2, 9 Jun, 16,

27 Jul, 1, 2, 15 Aug, 9, 27 Sep, 14 Oct–13 Dec, 28 Dec; 1986: 15 Mar, 4, 5, 18, 30 Apr, 1, 5, 13, 26 May, 2 Jun, 16 Jul, 1–31 Aug, 8, 14, 19, 22, 25 Sep, 7, 17, 24 Oct, 4, 5, 6, 12, 27 Nov; 1987: 6 Jan, 6 May, 8 Jun, 5 Sep, 5 Dec; 1992: 25 Jan, 24 Mar.

Sources in the Faber and Faber archive: 1984: G to M 11 Dec; 1985: M to G 18 Apr, G to M [undated, reply to previous item], M to G 1 May, M to G 15 May, M to G 30 May, G to M [undated, reply to previous item], M to Greg Gatenby (Harbourfront Festival) 10 Jul, Greg Gatenby to M 21 Jul, M to Greg Gatenby 8 Aug, M to Greg Gatenby 21 Nov; 1986: G to M [undated, Jan], M to G 15 Jan [reply to previous item], M to Sir Keith Joseph [about possible knighthood for G] 26 Feb, Sir Keith Joseph to M 14 Mar.

Other sources: E-mails from Tim Brown 27 May 2008 (on Michael Gilbert's novel), Pete Townshend 17 Jun 2008 and Antonia Fraser 11 Aug 2008. Interviews with Ken Mitchell and Jeanne Shami 28 Apr 2006, Matthew Evans 9 Apr 2008, Raleigh Trevelyan 9 Jul 2008 and Jessica Mann 18 Sep 2008. Letters from Golding 9 Oct 1986 and Stephen Medcalf 15 May 2007.

Printed sources: Ken Mitchell in *Brushes With Greatness*, ed. Russell Banks, Michael Ondaatje and David Young, Big Bang Books, Toronto, 1989; D. M. Thomas, *Guardian*, 10 Jun 2006; N. A. M. Rodger, *The Wooden World: An Anatomy of the Georgian Navy*, Collins, 1986, and Golding's review, *Guardian*, 12 Sep 1986; Blake Morrison interview, *Observer*, 31 May 1987.

Dates of *Close Quarters* reviews: 1987: *Mail on Sunday* 7 Jun, *Observer* 7 Jun, *Independent* 11 Jun, *Evening Standard* 11 Jun, *Guardian* 12 Jun, Hilary Spurling, *Daily Telegraph* 12 Jun, *Financial Times* 13 Jun, *Sunday Times* 14 Jun, *Sunday Mirror* 14 Jun, Barbara Hardy, *Times Educational Supplement* 19 Jun.

30 *Fire Down Below* and Globe-Trotting

Sources in the Golding archive: *J* 1980: 14 Jun; 1986: 5 May, 22 Jul, 17 Dec; 1987: 21 Jan–21 Mar, 17 Jun, 16, 19, 23 Jul, 1, 2 Aug, 2, 16, 19 Sep, 22 Nov; 1988: 3, 6, 17, 21, 22 Jan, 30 Jan–14 Feb, 1 Mar, 2, 14, 16, 22, 24–27, 29 Apr, 8, 18 May, 13 Jun, 5, 6, 19, 24, 27 Jul, 12, 16–31 Aug, 23 Sep–4 Oct, 15, 23 Oct, 4–15 Nov, 5 Dec; 1989: 16 Jan, 20, 31 Mar, 11, 25 May, 1, 23, 29 Jun, 19 Jul, 7, 8, 14 Aug, 12 Sep, 7–9 Oct, 20 Nov, 22 Nov–6 Dec; 1990: 14 Jan; a typescript of Golding's lecture for Japan headed, in his hand, 'Conservation'; letters to Golding from Peter Orr 15 Aug 1988, 20 Mar 1989, 9 May 1989, and a programme for the Stratford Poetry Festival, 1989.

Photocopies of the following letters are also in the Golding archive; they seem to be missing from the Faber and Faber archive: 1987: M to G and Ann 29 Jul, M to G 12 Oct, M to G 23 Oct; 1988: G to M 1 Jan, M to G 13 Jan, M to G 8, 29 Apr, M to G 26 Mar, G to M 4 May; 1989: G to M 1 Apr.

Other sources: Correspondence with Susheela Punitha Jul 2006; interviews with Clive Brasnett 22 Feb 2006, Robert Bellarmine 14 Jul 2006, Joanna Mackle 31 Aug

2006, Harriet Harvey Wood 6 Sep 2006, Mark Kinkead-Weekes 14 Sep 2006, Matthew Evans 9 Apr 2008 (and his e-mail of 28 Apr 2009), Jessica Mann 18 Sep 2008; phone interview with Christine Jordis 7 Nov 2006 (and her letter of 4 Jan 2007); letter from Stephen Medcalf 15 May 2007; e-mails from Judy Carver, 23 Jan 2007, Pete Townshend 17 Jun 2008 and Mohan Ramanan 19 Aug 2008.

Printed sources: Rick Gekoski, *Tolkien's Gown and Other Stories of Great Authors and Rare Books*, Constable, 1996, pp. 25–36; *New Straits Times*, 15 Feb 1988, p. 4; *Prize Writing: An Original Collection of Writings by Past Winners to Celebrate 21 Years of the Booker Prize*, edited and introduced by Martyn Goff, Sceptre, 1989, pp. 151–61; John Walsh interview, *Sunday Times*, 19 Mar 1989.

Dates of *Fire Down Below* reviews: 1989: *Guardian* 17 Mar, *Times Literary Supplement* 17 Mar, *Mail on Sunday* 19 Mar, *Sunday Telegraph* 19 Mar, *Sunday Times* 19 Mar, *Evening Standard* 23 Mar, *Times* 23 Mar, *New Statesman* 14 Apr, *London Review of Books* 20 Apr, *Gay Times* Jun.

31 *The Double Tongue*

Sources in the Golding archive: *J* 1973: 28 Jan; 1989: 13 Jan, 18 Feb, 24, 26, 28 Jun, 7 Jul, 6, 7 Aug; 1990: 6 Jan, 25, 27 Feb, 6–21, 23, 24 Mar, 7, 8 Apr, 17–21, 27 May, 3, 18 Sep, 14, 17, 23 Oct, 5 Dec; 1991: 30 Jan, 28 Feb, 3, 14 Mar, 22 May–2 Jun, 15 Jun, 26 Jul–1 Sep, 18, 24 Oct, 23–28 Nov, 3–20 Dec; 1992: 15 Jan, 19 Feb, 21 Mar, 28 Apr, 11, 24 May, 31 May–10 Jun, 11, 17, 20, 26, 30 Jun, 1, 10, 29 Jul, 4, 8, 17 Aug, 9 Sep, 3, 15–27 Oct, 3 Nov, 11–15, 26, 27, 29 Dec; 1993: 1–4, 7, 9, 13, 14 Jan, 1, 11, 12, 13, 16, 18, 25 Feb, 3, 8, 20 Mar, 10–13 Apr, 13, 21, 25 May, 6, 17 Jun.

Photocopies of the following letters are also in the Golding archive. They seem to be missing from the Faber and Faber archive: 1989: M to G 9 Aug, G to M 1 Nov; 1990: M to G and Ann 31 Jul, M to G 16 Aug; 1991: M to G and Ann 22 Feb.

The story of Herakles and his guardian angel is an untitled 29-page typescript, its pages numbered in Golding's hand in their top right-hand corners. The opening words are 'As the Ineffable conveyed'. Also in the archive are Golding's letter to Sir Andrew Huxley of 13 Jul 1990, and the brochure for *Sea Goddess II*.

Other sources: Letters from John Fuller 17 Jan 2006 and Dennis Burden 19 Nov 2006; Judy Carver interview 6–10 Aug 2007, and e-mails 14 and 24 Oct 2008; Andrew Motion's e-mail 9 Nov 2007 and John Monteith's 17 Nov 2008; interviews with Joanna Mackle 31 Aug 2006, Harriet Harvey Wood 6 Sep 2006, Terrell Carver 7 Mar 2008, Nigel Williams 11 Aug 2008, Jessica Mann 18 Sep 2008; phone conversations with Christine Jordis 7 Nov 2006 and Rosemary Goad 27 Oct 2008; Peter Green's reminiscences on the William Golding Ltd website (www.william-golding.co.uk).

Dennis Burden's letter to Golding, 13 Sep 1989, and his reply, 21 Sep, are in the Trinity College, Oxford archive.

Printed sources: 'The Life of Lord Riley', *Sunday Times* 6 May 1990; James Wood interview, *Guardian* 19 Sep 1991; D. M. Thomas, *Guardian* 10 Jun 2006.

Postscript

Sources in the Golding archive: *J* 1971: 9 Jan, 1 Mar; 1972: 27 Mar, 30 Sep; 1974: 18 Feb, 13 May; 1975: 25 Aug; 1976: 23 Mar, 28 Sep; 1977: 31 Jan; 1978: 10 Jan, 3 May; 1980: 10 Oct; 1982: 27 Apr; 1985: 15 Sep; 1989: 2 Nov; *Seahorse* MS.

Printed sources: Peter Green and Anthony Storr in *Tribute*, pp. 52, 114; 'William Golding – A Panel Discussion', compiled by Susheela Punitha, *Literature Alive*, Vol. 2 No. 1, Jun 1988; Lewis Wolpert, *Six Impossible Things Before Breakfast*, Faber and Faber, 2006.

Illustration Credits

Page 1: © Paul Joyce / National Portrait Gallery, London

Pages 2 and 3: Courtesy of the Golding Family Archive

Page 4: (top left and right) Courtesy of the Golding Family Archive; (bottom) courtesy of Professor James Lovelock

Page 5: (top) Courtesy of the Golding Family Archive; (bottom) courtesy of Salisbury Newspapers, www.journalphotos.co.uk

Page 6: (top left) Courtesy of Salisbury Newspapers, www.journalphotos.co.uk; (top and centre right, bottom) courtesy of the Golding Family Archive

Page 7: (top left) Courtesy Rosemary Goad / Faber Archive; (top right, bottom) Faber Archive

Page 8: (top left and right) Courtesy of the Golding Family Archive; (centre) courtesy of Glenn Collett; (bottom left) photo: John Milne; (bottom right) photo: The East Coast Yacht Agency Ltd

Page 9: (top) University Archives, Wyndham Robertson Library, Hollins University, Virginia; (centre) courtesy of the Golding Family Archive; (bottom) © Tom Hollyman

Page 10: (top left) Courtesy of the Golding Family Archive; (top right) Faber Archive; (bottom) © Rex Features Ltd

Page 11: (top) © Caroline Forbes; (bottom) Courtesy of the Golding Family Archive

Page 12: (top) Courtesy of Alaa Soueif; (centre left) courtesy of Glenn Collett; (centre right) courtesy of the Golding Family Archive; (bottom) courtesy of Ursula Straumann, D.Phil

Every effort has been made to trace or contact all copyright holders. The publishers would be pleased to rectify any omissions or errors brought to their notice at the earliest opportunity.

Appendix

Relative value of £1 sterling for the period covered in this biography, based on the retail price index:

1890   £1
1900   £1 0s 4d
1910   £1 1s 7d
1920   £2 14s 9d
1930   £1 14s 10d
1940   £2 0s 4d
1950   £3 3s 11d
1960   £4 15s 1d
1970   £7 1s 7d
1980   £23.34
1990   £44.03
2000   £59.46
2007   £72.13

Figures are from the economic history services website www.eh.net

Index

ff

Lord of the Flies

A plane crashes on a desert island and the only survivors, a group of schoolboys, assemble on the beach and wait to be rescued. By day they inhabit a land of bright fantastic birds and dark blue seas, but at night their dreams are haunted by the image of a terrifying beast. As the boys' delicate sense of order fades, so their childish dreams are transformed into something more primitive, and their behaviour starts to take on a murderous, savage significance. First published in 1954, *Lord of the Flies* is one of the most celebrated and widely read of modern classics.

The Inheritors

When the spring came the people – what was left of them – moved back by the old paths from the sea. But this year strange things were happening, terrifying things that had never happened before. Inexplicable sounds and smells; new, unimaginable creatures half-glimpsed through the leaves. What the people didn't, and perhaps never would, know, was that the day of their people was over. This is a startling recreation of the lost world of the Neanderthals, and a frightening vision of the beginning of a new age.

ff

Pincher Martin

Drowning in the freezing North Atlantic, Christopher Hadley Martin, temporary lieutenant, happens upon a grotesque rock, an island that appears only on weather charts. To drink there is a pool of rain water; to eat there are weeds and sea anemones. Through the long hours with only himself to talk to, Martin must try to assemble the truth of his fate, piece by terrible piece. *Pincher Martin* is a terrifying and unforgettable journey into one man's mind.

The Pyramid

Oliver is eighteen, and wants to enjoy himself before going to university. But this is the 1920s, and he lives in Stilbourne, a small English country town, where everyone knows what everyone else is getting up to, and where love, lust and rebellion are closely followed by revenge and embarrassment. Written with great perception and subtlety, *The Pyramid* is William Golding's funniest and most light-hearted novel, which probes the painful awkwardness of the late teens, the tragedy and farce of life in a small community and the consoling power of music.

ff

Free Fall

Somehow, somewhere, Sammy Mountjoy lost his freedom, the faculty of freewill 'that cannot be debated but only experienced, like a colour or the taste of potatoes'. As he retraces his life in an effort to discover why he no longer has the power to choose and decide for himself, the narrative moves between England and a prisoner-of-war camp in Germany. In *Free Fall*, his fourth novel, William Golding has created a poetic fiction, and an allegory, as moving as it is unforgettable.

The Spire

Dean Jocelin has a vision: that God has chosen him to erect a great spire on his cathedral. His mason anxiously advises against it, for the old cathedral was built without foundations. Nevertheless, the spire rises octagon upon octagon, pinnacle by pinnacle, until the stone pillars shriek and the ground beneath it swims. Its shadow falls ever darker on the world below, and on Dean Jocelin in particular.

ff

Darkness Visible

Darkness Visible opens at the height of the London Blitz, when a naked child steps out of an all-consuming fire. Miraculously saved but hideously scarred, soon tormented at school and at work, Matty becomes a wanderer, a seeker after some unknown redemption. Two more lost children await him, twins as exquisite as they are loveless. Toni dabbles in political violence, Sophy in sexual tyranny. As Golding weaves their destinies together, his book reveals both the inner and outer darkness of our world.

Rites of Passage

Sailing to Australia in the early years of the nineteenth century, Edmund Talbot keeps a journal to amuse his godfather back in England. Full of wit and disdain, he records the mounting tensions on the ancient, sinking warship where officers, sailors, soldiers and emigrants jostle in the cramped spaces below decks. Then a single passenger, the obsequious Reverend Colley, attracts the animosity of the sailors, and in the seclusion of the fo'castle something happens to bring him into a 'hell of degradation', where shame is a force deadlier than the sea itself.

ff

Close Quarters

In a wilderness of heat, stillness and sea mists, a ball is held on a ship becalmed halfway to Australia. In this surreal, fête-like atmosphere the passengers dance and flirt, while beneath them thickets of weed like green hair spread over the hull. The sequel to *Rites of Passage*, *Close Quarters*, the second volume in Golding's acclaimed *Sea Tilogy*, is imbued with his extraordinary sense of menace. Half-mad with fear, with drink, with love and opium, everyone on this leaky, unsound hulk is 'going to pieces'. And in a nightmarish climax the very planks seem to twist themselves alive as the ship begins to come apart at the seams.

Fire Down Below

The third volume of William Golding's acclaimed *Sea Trilogy*. A decrepit warship sails on the last stretch of its voyage to Sydney Cove. It has been blown off course and battered by wind, storm and ice. Nothing but rope holds the disintegrating hull together. And after a risky operation to reset its foremast with red-hot metal, an unseen fire begins to smoulder below decks.